Endorsed by
University of Cambridge International Examinations

Economics

A Complete Course for IGCSE

Dan Moynihan & Brian Titley

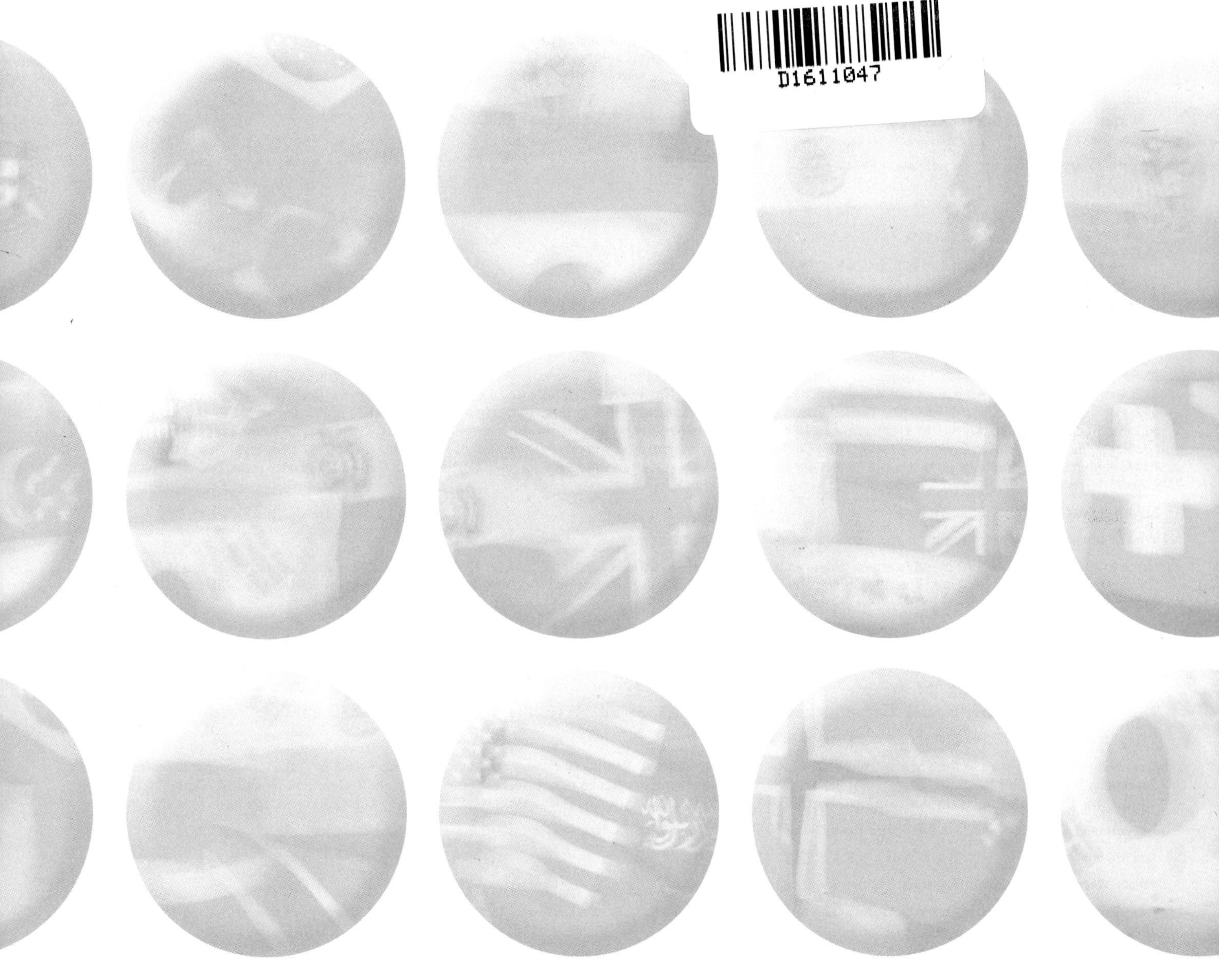

OXFORD
UNIVERSITY PRESS

Great Clarendon Street, Oxford OX2 6DP

Oxford University Press is a department of the University of Oxford. It furthers the University's objective of excellence in research, scholarship, and education by publishing worldwide in

Oxford New York

Auckland Cape Town Dar es Salaam Hong Kong Karachi Kuala Lumpur Madrid Melbourne Mexico City Nairobi New Delhi Shanghai Taipei Toronto

With offices in

Argentina Austria Brazil Chile Czech Republic France Greece Guatemala Hungary Italy Japan Poland Portugal Singapore South Korea Switzerland Thailand Turkey Ukraine Vietnam

Oxford is a registered trade mark of Oxford University Press in the UK and in certain other countries

First published 2007

British Library Cataloguing in Publication Data

Data available

ISBN-13: 978-0-19-915134-9
10 9 8 7 6 5 4 3 2 1

Printed in Great Britain by Bell and Bain Ltd, Glasgow

Acknowledgements

We are grateful for permission to reprint the following photographs:

P3: Oxford University Press; p4tl&r: Corbis; p5: Corbis; p7: Oxford University Press; p9l: Stockbyte/Superstock; p9r: Corbis; p11m&b: Oxford University Press; p15: Oxford University Press; p20b: Oxford University Press; p29: Oxford University Press; p37: Corbis; p51: Corbis; 056: p61: Corbis; p64: Oxford University Press; p67: Corbis; p70: Corbis; p74: Corbis; p75: Oxford University Press; p77: Format Photographers/Maggie Murray; p83: RHB; p137l: Corbis; p140: Corbis; p148: Corbis; p152 both: Corbis; p209: Oxford University Press; p210 both: Corbis; p76l: Volvo; p76r: Oxford University Press; p284: Corbis; p299: Getty Images/Hulto Archive; p325l: Corbis; p333l: Oxford University Press; p333: Corbis; p342: Oxford University Press; p361br: Oxford University Press; p361 tl&r, bl: Format Photographers; p373: Format Photoographers; p396: Oxford University Press; p398tc: Oxford University Press; p398b: Corbis; p400: Oxford University Press; p403: Corbis; p406bl&r: Oxford University Press; p416 all: Corbis.

All other photography by Brian Titley

We are grateful to the following for permission to reproduce copyright material:

Extracts and statistical data from publications produced by the UK Census, Office of National Statistics (ONS), National Savings & Investments and H M Treasury are Crown copyright material and are reproduced under the terms of the Click-Use Licence No. C2007001380 with the permission of the Controller of HMSO and the Queen's Printer for Scotland.

Tom Burgis for 'Global trade riots rock Hong Kong', *The Observer*, 18.12.05, copyright © Tom Burgis 2005.

Channel 4 Television for extracts from advertising case study on Cobra Beer at www.channel4sales.com http://www.channel4sales.com

Elizabeth C Economy, Director of Asia Studies, Council on Foreign Relations for extracts from E C Economy: 'Economic Boom, Environmental Bust', 2.10.04, www.cfr.org.

Ecumenical News International for extracts from 'Australians face Christmas personal debt crisis', *Ecumenical News International*, 5.12.06

ExxonMobil for extracts from press releases 26 and 27 July 2006.

Guardian News and Media Ltd for extracts from Polly Curtis: 'UK plans skills academies to close productivity gap', *The Guardian* 22.3.05, copyright © Guardian News and Media Ltd 2005; Larry Elliott: '[Chancellor] Brown calls for public sector pay freeze', *The Guardian* 6.6.06, copyright © Guardian News and Media Ltd 2006; and Mark Tran: 'Bank raises interest rates to 4.75%', *The Guardian Unlimited* 3.8.06, copyright © Guardian News and Media Ltd 2006.

International Labour Organization for figures from *Global Employment Trends 2006*, copyright © International Labour Organization, 2006.

The Manufacturer for extracts from 'March of the Robots', March 2005

Money Week for extract from 'UK trade deficit widens', *Money Week* 11.7.06

News International Syndication for extracts from 'The recipe for healthy profits?', *The Sunday Times*, 23.7.06; and 'Today is the day we start to eat Earth' by David Brown, *The London Paper*, 9.10.06.

OECD for extracts from 'Market reforms and structural change in the Russian Federation', from *The Russian Federation 1995: OECD Economic Surveys*, copyright © OECD 1995 and for tables, graphs and charts from *World Economic Outlook* and other OECD publications and data.

Solo Syndication for extracts from the *Daily Mail*: 'Heatwave means we are running out of veg', 29.7.06; 'Go ahead for GM crops threaten organic farms', 21.7.06; 'Families count cost of rush for a flat-screen TV', 18.7.06; 'UK fury at US steel tariffs', 13.3.02; and 'Defiant Iceland will hunt whales', 18.10.06.

Time Out Magazine Ltd for extract from 'New tax incentives finally approved', *Time Out* 23.11.06.

We have tried to trace and contact all copyright holders before publication. If notified, the publishers will be pleased to rectify any errors or omissions at the earliest opportunity.

Illustrations are by Barking Dog, Matt Buckly, Ian Heard and Thomson Digital.

Contents

Syllabus Coverage 2009

In 2009 the syllabus for IGCSE Economics published by the University of Cambridge International Examinations Board will undergo some revision. The table below shows show how the chapters and sections in this edition of *Economics: A Complete Course for IGCSE* map onto this new syllabus.

2009 Syllabus		Chapters	Sections
1	Basic Economic Problem:	1 The Economic Problem	All
	choice and the allocation of resources	2 Specialization and Exchange	1–4
2	The Allocation of Resources:	3 Economic Systems	All
	how the market works; market failure	7 How Prices are Determined	All
		21 Social Costs and Benefits	All
3	The Individual as Producer, Consumer and Borrower	2 Specialization and Exchange	5–11
		5 Trade Unions	All
		6 Financial Institutions	All
		10 Occupations and Wages	All
		11 Spending, Saving and Borrowing	All
4	The Private Firm as Producer and Employer	4 Types of Business Organization	All
		8 Market Structures	All
		12 Organizing Production	All
		13 Costs, Revenues and Profits	All
5	Role of Government in an Economy	14 Government Objectives and Policies	All
		15 Public Sector Finance	All
6	Economic Indicators	16 Prices and Employment	All
		17 Output and Growth	All
		19 Economic Development	2
7	Developed and Developing Economies:	19 Economic Development	1
	trends in production, population and living standards	20 Population	All
8	International Aspects	18 International Trade and Exchange Rates	All
		22 The Impact of Globalization	All

Preface

This new edition of our book *Economics: A Complete Course* has been completely updated and revised to meet the latest requirements for the International General Certificate of Secondary Education (IGCSE) and 'O' Level in economics. In addition, the text provides an excellent introduction to economics for first-year A level students.

The book now includes a wealth of international data and official statistics from around the world as available at the start of 2007. There are also many completely new sections, including development economics, the impact of globalization, environmental economics, world employment trends, international financial institutions, consumer spending and saving behaviour, and much more. In fact the book contains everything you will need to learn economics and fully meet the IGCSE and 'O' level assessment objectives.

There are a range of exercises to help you apply and revise your knowledge and understanding of economics throughout the book as well as assessment exercises to test your knowledge, judgement and skills of analysis and evaluation in economics. They include multiple choice and structured questions, many from past assessment papers for IGCSE economics, published by the University of Cambridge International Examinations Board. Marks for each structured question are shown in square brackets, and tips on how to answer particular questions are provided to help your exam preparation.

Some model answers to structured questions have also been prepared. However, you will not be required to write in so much depth or detail in the time available in your examinations to achieve a good pass. The model responses given are intended to show how you can apply and present economic arguments in full, and demonstrate excellence in achievement across the full range of assessment objectives.

Dan Moynihan
Brian Titley
March 2007

1 THE BASIC ECONOMIC PROBLEM: SCARCITY AND CHOICE

The resources available to produce goods and services are scarce compared to our limitless wants. Natural resources, labour and capital are scarce resources, or factors of production. Choosing between different uses for these resources involves a cost in terms of the other goods and services they may have produced instead. That is, choosing between different goods and services to produce always has an opportunity cost. This is the lost benefit from the next best alternative foregone.

Entrepreneurs organize resources into firms to make goods and services. Firms are organized so that the labour and other resources they employ specialize in the production of those goods and services they are best at. High levels of output achieved by specialization have helped satisfy more human needs and wants, but this could only be achieved because people developed money. A money is a commodity that everyone accepts in exchange for all other goods and services. Workers can earn money from the jobs they specialize in so that they can buy the different goods and services they want as produced by workers in other firms.

Scarcity of resources relative to human wants is the central problem in economics. Choosing what goods and services to produce, how to produce them and who to produce them for involves decisions about resource allocation. Economics is therefore about trying to find the best allocation of resources to maximize the welfare of people.

In a planned economic system, the allocation of resources is determined by the government. In a market economic system, consumers determine what, how and for whom to produce, simply by buying goods and services. Entrepreneurs who want to make a profit will allocate resources to making the goods and services consumers want and are willing to spend their money on. In a mixed economic system, both private sector firms and a public sector organized by the government allocate resources to the production of goods and services to satisfy people's needs and wants.

Chapter 1 The Economic Problem

Aims

At the end of this chapter you should be able to:

- define the nature of **the economic problem**
- realize that people's wants for **goods and services** are unlimited
- understand that **resources** used to make goods and services are **scarce**
- explain why **scarcity** of resources leads to **choice**
- define **opportunity cost** and describe examples to illustrate this concept
- evaluate the opportunity costs of making different choices
- understand how **economics** can be used to help increase choice

WORLD NEWS

TUESDAY 24th MAY 2127

OIL RUNS OUT

Today the world's oil suply has dried up. A crisis meeting of Premiers took place in Washington last night.

Yesterday the top oil producing companies of the world declared that the world's supply of oil was now exhausted. The last barrel of oil has been filled and the oil rigs will drill no more. The world now faces an energy crisis. No more oil will mean no more petrol for transport or machinery. There can be no more plastic for componnts in many household products like satellite television, digital recorders, cars and telephones.

Energy ministers from around the world are meeting today in Switzerland to discuss the crisis and try and find a solution. Coad deposits are low and nuclear power stations are already overworked to meet the demand for electricity. The world could face a black-out in the next ten years.

Section I What is the economic problem?

Resources

The newspaper article above paints a gloomy picture of what might happen in the future. It is hard to imagine a world without oil but even now there is only a limited amount of oil left in the ground. In other words it is **scarce** and as more and more is used up there will come a time when no oil remains. The world's oil took millions of years to form – we may use it all in little over a century!

However, it is not just oil that is scarce, but all natural materials, such as iron ore, coal, gold. Even the clean air that we breathe and the water we drink are limited in amount and may eventually run out.

If you imagine the world as a round ball then it is possible to see that only a limited amount of materials can be squeezed from it. All of these scarce materials are called **resources**.

Problem: resources are scarce

Resources include natural resources, machinery, people and land

Resources are important because they are used to make goods, like televisions, cars, houses, fruit and vegetables, and to provide **services**, like banking, insurance, transport, healthcare and cleaning.

Problem: scarce resources are used to make goods and services

Any resources that are not scarce are called **free goods**. The air that we breathe seems without limit and so is considered to be a free good. However, with increasing pollution in the world, fresh, clean air may become scarce!

At first sight it may seem that even though there is only a limited amount of resources in the world, the world is such a big place that these things might not be so scarce. Before you agree with this view look at the following exercise.

Exercise 1 Needs and wants

A

B

Look at the two photos A and B. Photo A represents modern city life; photo B represents a group of people living in a poor African village.

1. What needs have the two families in common?
2. Which family will not be able to satisfy all its needs?
3. What do you think are the wants of the family in picture A?
4. What do you think are the wants of the family in picture B?
5. Why can't the wants of either family be satisfied?
6. What do you think are the main differences between **needs** and **wants**?

Needs and wants

All people have the same basic needs. Whether rich or poor, we all need food, clothing, shelter and air to survive. However, people usually want more than they need. The human race is like an ever hungry beast – its wants are without limit. If we asked all of the people in the world to list what they wanted and then added these lists together we would find that not all of these things could be made. This is because the resources needed to make goods and services are scarce compared with people's wants. This is the central economic problem.

Problem: human wants are unlimited

Exercise 2 What do we need and what do we want?

Below is a jumbled collection of pictures of goods and services. Draw a table like the one below and sort them into needs and wants, giving reasons for your choice.

NEEDS	WANTS	REASON
EGGS	LCD-TV's	EGGS ARE FOOD TELEVISIONS BRING PLEASURE-BUT NOT ESSENTIAL FOR SURVIVAL

You should now understand the difference between needs and wants. Write a sentence to explain what these two words mean.

The creation of wants

The goods and services that we *need* are the things necessary for survival, for example, food and clothing. Whereas goods and services that we *want*, for example, televisions and DVD recorders, may bring pleasure, they are not necessary for us to survive. We have discovered that people have unlimited wants: we always want more. But why do we keep wanting more and more? This might be because some wants are created for us by others.

Exercise 3 Why do I want what I want?

Choose five of the wants that you listed in Exercise 2 and write down why you want them.

WANT	REASON
BICYCLE	MY FRIEND HAS ONE

Now compare your reasons with a friend and write down the most popular reasons for wanting goods and services.

Many wants are created by advertising. Advertisements use clever slogans and catch-phrases to try to persuade people to want particular goods and services (see Chapter 9).

Exercise 4 Catch-phrase

1 Try to write down four catch-phrases or slogans used by advertisers.

2 Now try these out on your friend to see if s/he can name the good or service that the advert is trying to create a want for.

Choosing what we want

We have learned that wants are unlimited but the resources used to produce the goods and services to satisfy these wants are limited. That is, there is **scarcity**. Nobody can have sufficient goods and services to satisfy all their needs and wants, so people must choose which wants they will satisfy. Choice is necessary because scarce resources can be used in lots of ways to make many different goods and services. Scarce resources have alternative uses.

Problem: scarce resources have alternative uses

For example, many soccer clubs have spare land next to their grounds. The problem facing these clubs is to choose what to do with this land. They could build a sports complex or leisure centre to serve the community, or a supermarket, or an apartment block or even an office complex. Whatever they do, they can only choose one of these options because land is a scarce resource.

For example, a piece of land can be used as:

motorway **farmland**

People, nations and the world must choose how scarce resources are to be used; must choose which goods and services to make because they cannot make everything that they want.

Exercise 5

Alternatives

Below is a list of resources. See how many alternative uses you can find for them, that is, see how many different goods and services they can help to produce.

1 An area of farmland.
2 A person who is good at maths.
3 A spade.
4 An egg.

Section 2 Opportunity cost: the cost of choice

Exercise 6

The next best thing

Choosing between goods and services involves a very special cost. Imagine that you have just bought the list of items below. Now imagine that you were unable to get any of these item and had to buy your second-best choice instead. Copy and complete the table.

What I have just bought	What could I have bought instead?
DVD recorder	
Four-bedroom house	
Box of chocolates	
A ticket to the World Cup Final	

In the second column you have listed your second-best choices, or your next best alternatives to the products in column one. For example, if you had bought a DVD recorder, you may be going without the benefit of a holiday. The benefit of the holiday given up is the real cost of owning the DVD recorder. The real cost of choosing one thing and not another is known as the **opportunity cost**. This measures the benefit you could have had from the next best alternative you have gone without.

Opportunity cost arises not only when we buy things, but also when we choose what goods and services to produce. For example, in deciding to use a piece of land to build a new sports complex, we may be going without the benefit of new houses, or farmland to grow food.

Exercise 7

The cost of making choices

A factory employs 10 people and has 2 machines able to produce and pack 300 glass bottles each day. The same employees and machines could instead be used in the same factory to make and pack 400 glass jars each day.

The same 10 employees used to work on a farm and were very skilled at growing and harvesting corn until the farm was sold and the factory was built on the farmland. Compared to the farm the factory is noisy and pollutes the air with smoke.

1 What is the opportunity cost to the factory owners of using the 10 employees and 2 machines to make 300 bottles each day?
2 What is the opportunity cost to the employees of working in the factory?
3 What is the opportunity cost to society of the factory?

Section 3 What is economics for?

We have now discovered the central problem in economics: resources are scarce and have alternative uses, but people's wants are unlimited. As raw materials, such as metals and chemicals, are extracted from the ground, less and less are left for the future, whilst people's wants are forever increasing. As the world develops and as its population grows, more and more wants are created, but not all of these wants can be satisfied. As a result scarcity on a worldwide basis is increasing all the time. The choice of alternative goods and services an individual country has depends upon its share of resources in the world.

Exercise 8 Free to choose?

Children in Bangladesh

Two Western boys

1 Look at the photographs above and copy the table below. Put a tick in the first column if you think the children in the left-hand photograph are free to choose. Tick the second column if the Western boys are free to choose.

Free to choose? ✗ or ✓	Children in Bangladesh	Western boys
Can go to a soccer match.		
Can eat in a restaurant.		
Can catch their own food.		
Can drive a car.		
Can visit foreign countries.		
Can own his or her own house.		
Can obtain medical help when needed.		
Can receive an Economics education.		
Can receive a daily paper.		
Can be independent.		
Can receive radio and TV.		

2 Which boy has more choice and why?

The boys in the second picture have a greater choice of goods and services to enjoy than the children in the first picture. This is because the boys in the second picture live in a country which has far more resources to produce more of the goods and services people want.

The children in Bangladesh have far less choice. There are fewer resources in their country that can be used to produce goods and services to satisfy their wants.

In some countries, many people may have very little choice. For example, in the poorest countries of Africa, not even basic needs for food can be satisfied with the available resources (see Chapter 19). This great difference in choice is caused by the relative lack of resources in the poorer countries. Yet in both rich and poor nations people want more resources than are available.

The purpose of Economics involves advising how best to use scarce resources in order to make goods and services to satisfy as many wants as possible. In other words, Economics attempts to increase people's choice and maximize their welfare. When people have more goods and services to choose from, they are better off. For example, the Western boys are better off than the Innuit boy simply because they have the ability to choose between more goods and services.

However, the satisfaction of wants by the making of goods and services has also brought with it the problems of pollution and the destruction of the environment. We will return to this in Chapters 21 and 22 when we investigate social and private costs and benefits.

Section 4 Choice: a conflict of interests

A motorway cutting through farmland

The example illustrates the choices that face people because of scarcity of resources with alternative uses. If resources are used in one way, for example, to build a motorway, they cannot be used in some other way, for example, as farmland. Whilst a motorway may satisfy the wants of motorists, it does not satisfy the wants of farmers, nature lovers and people who live near the motorway who must suffer the noise and pollution that it causes.

Clearly choice involves a conflict of interest. Not everyone can get what they want so some people will always be disappointed by the choices made by others.

Exercise 9 Anytown conflict: a case study

The local government of Anytown is under pressure from its local taxpayers. This is because the Anytown government has $10 million remaining of its budget to spend on resources.

The local housing development is in urgent need of repairs and the residents are angry.

'It is inhuman that we should have to live in such conditions; damp and dirt are everywhere. The local government should build some new properties.'

OR

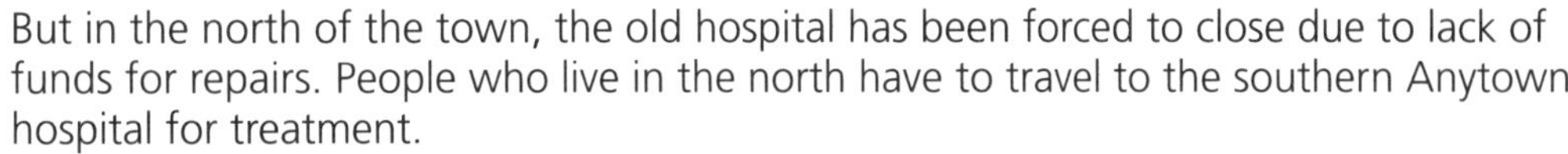

But in the north of the town, the old hospital has been forced to close due to lack of funds for repairs. People who live in the north have to travel to the southern Anytown hospital for treatment.

'It is intolerable that people like me have been forced to travel such a long way to receive health care. The local government should modernize and re-open the old hospital.'

The local government faces a choice. It can either build a new housing development or modernize the old hospital. Each scheme would cost an estimated $10 million but whatever choice the local government makes, only some of the local people's wants will be satisfied.

Your task

The people living in the north of Anytown and the people living on the housing development are locked in disagreement. They both want the local government to satisfy their wants, but only one of them can win.

Split up into an even number of groups of three or four students. Half of the groups are to represent the people in the north of Anytown and the other half are to represent the people from the housing development.

1. In your group write a speech to be read to the class outlining why your group's wants should be satisfied by the local government.
2. Choose one pair of opposing groups. These groups now read their speeches to the whole class and are then given five minutes to argue their case. The rest of the class will be the local government which then decides by majority vote how it will spend the $10 million.

Questions

1. Why is there disagreement or conflict in Anytown?
2. To avoid all conflict in Anytown, what is needed?
3. If there were enough resources to produce everything everybody wanted, would there be any opportunity costs? Explain your answer.

In your own words write down what you understand by the following:

Resources	**Wants**
Goods	**Scarcity**
Services	**Opportunity cost**
Free goods	**Needs**

Now go back through the chapter to check your understanding of the above terms.

These websites contain some helpful definitions and discussion of opportunity cost:

- *www.referenceforbusiness.com/encyclopedia/Oli-Per/Opportunity-Cost.htm*
- *en.wikipedia.org/wiki/opportunity_cost*

Chapter 2 Specialization and Exchange

FERTILIZER
I'LL NEVER GET THAT IN MY WALLET!...

Aims

At the end of this chapter you should be able to:

- understand what is meant by an **economy**
- define and classify factors of production into **land, labour, capital** and **enterprise**
- describe **specialization** and the need for **exchange**
- explain why the benefits of specialization could not be maximized without a generally acceptable medium of exchange called **money**
- list the main functions a money must perform and critically assess the suitability of different commodities for use as money
- describe the main forms of money in existence today

Section 1 What is an economy?

An **economy** is an area in which people make, or produce, goods and services. This area can be of any size, with any number of people involved. For example, we can talk of a local economy, such as a village, town or city. We can also talk of a national economy, such as the UK economy. In turn, the United Kingdom is part of the economy of Europe along with countries like France, Spain and Germany. Indeed, every country in the world can be considered an economy as long as it is involved in the production and exchange of goods and services. Similarly, all countries together make up the global economy.

As we shall see in Chapter 3, most economies are made up of two main economic sectors.

The private sector in an economy is made up of all the organizations and firms owned by members of the general public. It also consists of private individuals and voluntary organizations.

The public sector in an economy is owned and controlled by a government. It consists of government organizations, and goods and services provided by the government, such as the state education, roads, public parks, the armed forces and legal system (see Chapter 4).

Section 2 Production, consumption and exchange

Three key economic activities take place in all economies. These are production, consumption and exchange. All these activities take place within and between the private and public sectors of an economy (see Chapter 3).

The meaning of production

Production is any activity designed to satisfy people's wants. The things that satisfy people's wants are **goods**, like televisions, cars, furniture and food, and also **services** like teaching, window-cleaning, healthcare and retailing. Production, therefore, involves the making and selling of goods and services. However, if people do not want a certain good or service, like a plant that withers, a television without a picture, or a comedian who doesn't make people laugh, then the production of such goods and services would not be classed as production by an economist. The people who make and sell goods and services are known as **producers** (see also Chapter 12).

The meaning of consumption

The using up of goods and services to satisfy our wants is known as **consumption**. When we eat we are consuming food. When we watch television we are consuming electricity, the television set and the services of a television company. When we go to schools and colleges, we are consuming the services of teachers. We are consuming when we read books, sit on chairs, sleep on beds, put money into a bank account, ask a policeman the time, listen to the radio and use up any other goods and services in order to satisfy our wants.

The people who buy goods and services to satisfy their wants are known as **consumers** and their spending is called **consumption expenditure**.

The meaning of exchange

People can satisfy some of their wants by producing a number of goods and services for their own consumption. For example, keen gardeners may grow some vegetables to eat to satisfy part of their need or want for food. Others may make furniture from wood for their families to use. However, very few people can make all the things they want. In order to obtain the goods and services they cannot produce themselves they must engage in **trade** or **exchange**. In modern economies most people are able to do this by going to work to earn money. They then exchange this money for the goods and services they want that are produced by other workers.

Section 3 Resources: the factors of production

The scarce resources available for use in the production of goods and services to satisfy our wants are called **factors of production**. These are the **inputs** into a production process from which an **output** of goods and services emerges. They can be grouped under four main headings.

Land The fertile soil vital to the growth of plants, minerals such as coal and oil, and animals for their meat and skins, are known as **natural resources**, but to simplify economists call all of these **land**. Land therefore includes the seas and rivers of the world, forests and deserts, all manner of minerals from the ground, chemicals and gases from the air and earth's crust.

Labour Nothing can be produced without people. They provide the physical and mental effort to make goods and services. People who work with their hands and use their brains to help make goods and services provide **human resources**, or what is termed **labour**.

The size and ability of an economy's labour force are very important in determining the quantity and quality of the goods and services that can be produced. The greater the number of workers, and the better educated and skilled they are, the more an economy can produce.

Enterprise Whilst most people have the ability to contribute to the production of goods and services, not everyone could be a successful business person and be able to employ and organize resources in a **firm**. A firm is an organization that owns a factory or a number of factories, offices, or perhaps even shops, where goods and services are produced. Business know-how, or the ability to run a production process, is known as **enterprise**. The people who have enterprise and can control and manage firms are called **entrepreneurs**. They are the people who take the risks and decisions necessary to make a firm run successfully.

Capital To make the task of production easier, man has invented many tools: pens to write with, computers to calculate, screwdrivers, spanners, hammers, rulers, and many more. On a grander scale, turbines drive engines, tractors plough the land, ships transport goods, lathes shape and refine metals and wood, and factories and offices have been built to house many man-made tools and machines. These **man-made resources** which help to produce many other goods and services are known as **capital**.

Economists tend to talk of **units** of factors of production. For example, an economist might say that 'a firm has employed thirty more units of capital'. This simply means that it has bought thirty new machines. Similarly, if an economist talks of units of land, it could mean tonnes of coal, barrels of crude oil, or acres of land. Likewise working people are units of labour for the economist.

Exercise 1 Classifying resources

1 Below is a list of many of the scarce resources that are used to produce cartons of orange juice. Draw three columns and label them **natural resources**, **human resources** and **man-made resources**, and then in pairs decide in which column each item should go.

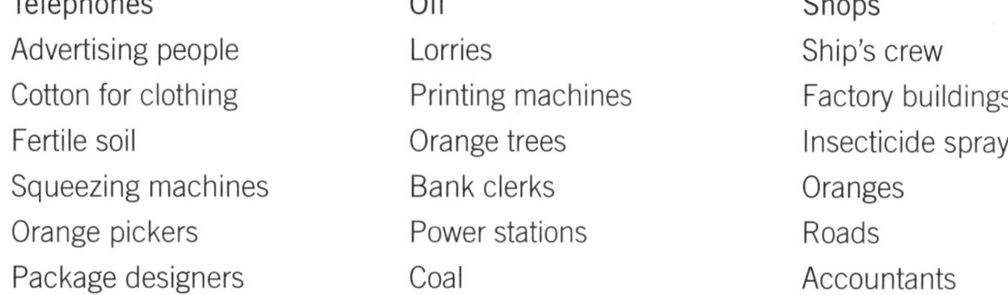

Telephones	Oil	Shops
Advertising people	Lorries	Ship's crew
Cotton for clothing	Printing machines	Factory buildings
Fertile soil	Orange trees	Insecticide sprays
Squeezing machines	Bank clerks	Oranges
Orange pickers	Power stations	Roads
Package designers	Coal	Accountants
Calculators	Warehouse workers	Shop assistants
Water	Lorry drivers	Wood

2 Now try to produce a list of resources you think help to produce cars. Compare your list with the rest of the class, and again sort them out into natural, human and man-made resources.

What do resources produce?

Consumer goods and services

A **consumer good** is any good that satisfies consumers' wants. Some of these consumer goods are called **consumer durable goods** because they last a long time, for example, cars, washing-machines, televisions, compact disc players, computers. **Non-durable goods** are those which have a short life, for example, food, drink, matches, petrol, washing powder.

Durable and non-durable goods

Sometimes our wants are satisfied by someone doing something for us. These are called **consumer services**. Examples would include the services of a doctor, banker, insurance agent, window-cleaner, teacher, policeman.

Capital goods

Man-made resources which help to produce other goods and services are known as **capital goods**. For example, screwdrivers, drills, ploughs, lorries, roads, power stations and factory buildings are capital goods because they are not wanted for themselves, but for what they can help to produce. Capital goods are bought by producers. The buying of capital goods is known as **investment**. Therefore, we can talk of a firm investing in new machinery and buildings to allow them to produce other goods and services. Investment in capital goods, like factories and machines, will increase production and help an economy grow (see Chapter 17).

Public goods

Imagine that someone came to your door and asked you to pay twenty euros towards the cost of powering the street lamp out in the street for another year. The collector argues that the street lamp provides you with light to help you see at night when you are driving or walking home. It also benefits your neighbours and the people across the street. You know that, if they all give twenty euros to the collector, this will keep the street lamp shining at night, whether you pay or not, and you can still enjoy the benefits of street-lighting even though you have not paid towards it. In this case consumption cannot be confined to those who have paid for it.

However, if all your neighbours thought in the same way as you, the collector would be unable to get twenty euros from anyone and the street light could not be kept running. The only way that street-lighting can be provided is if the government provides it and forces everyone to pay for it by collecting taxes.

Goods and services which are provided by a government because everyone benefits from them, even if they do not pay for them, are called **public goods**. A government provides these goods and services as no private firm would wish to produce them, because nobody would pay for their use. Examples of public goods include defence, the police, law and order, protection of the environment, lighthouses, and of course, street-lighting.

Merit goods

Sometimes a government provides goods and services because it thinks that people ought to benefit from them, even if they cannot afford to buy them, and to benefit the economy. Such goods and services are called **merit goods**. Examples of these goods are healthcare and education.

Section 5 Specialization

Exercise 2 The 'odds and ends' container game

You work in the manufacturing department of the 'Tidy Container Company', which supplies handy size containers for odds and ends, paper-clips, elastic bands and drawing pins all over the world. The aim of the exercise is for groups of four to five students to undertake a production process and organize the use of their time, labour and materials to produce containers of the highest quality with as little waste as possible.

Container design

The containers are made following the pattern below, starting with a sheet of plain A4 size paper or card.

Resources

Each group will be given the following:

Materials	Labour	Capital
20 sheets A4 paper or card	4–5 students for 1 hour	1 pair of scissors 2 sticks of paper glue 2 pencils 2 rulers

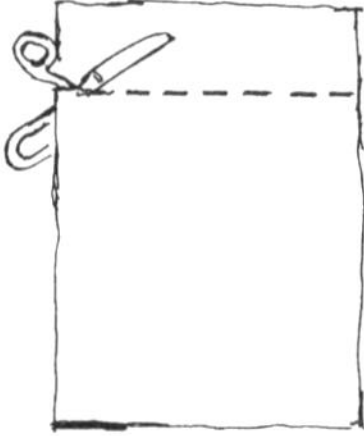

Stage 1
Cut a perfect square. Do not throw away end paper.

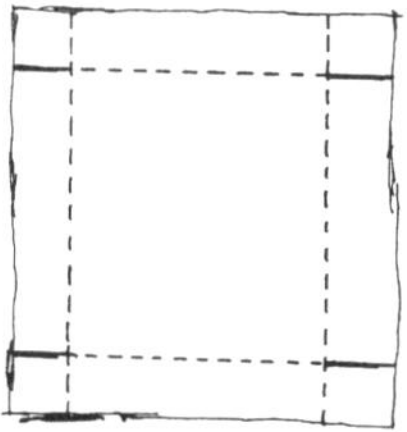

Stage 2
Draw markings as shown. Folds (---) and cuts (—). Now complete these.

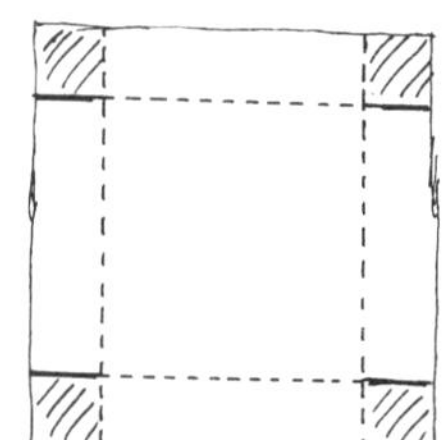

Stage 3
Apply glue to shaded area.

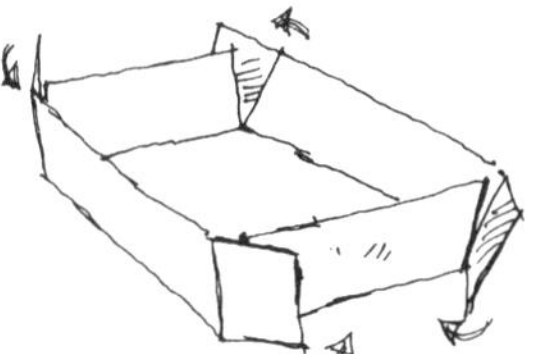

Stage 4
Secure sides of paper.

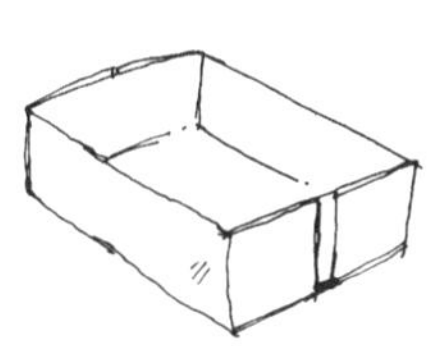

Stage 5
Check quality of container.

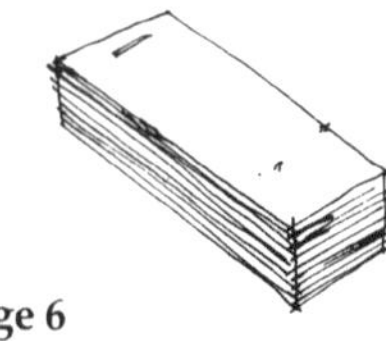

Stage 6
Collect up all end paper pieces for your group and hand them to your teacher at the end of the game. These can be stapled together to make rough note pads.

Advantages of the division of labour

In the early days of the motor-car industry one person would put together an entire engine. Then Henry Ford decided to separate the work involved into 84 varied operations. 84 people were needed to build a whole engine instead of just one person. This meant more engines could be built each day. In your own 'Odds and Ends' container game you may have found that the most successful group was the one that practised specialized production and divided labour into tasks.

The organization of labour into a number of divided and specialist tasks has brought a number of advantages to firms and to the economy.

1 More goods and services can be produced

When workers become specialists in the jobs they do, repetition of the same operation increases the skill and speed of the worker and as a result more is produced.

The Ford Model T

Work on the famous Model T began in 1907, and the production began two years later in 1910 at the company's new plant in Highland Park, Michigan.

As simple as the Model T was, there remained the problem of volume production. Each car was practically hand-built. To boost production Mr Ford and his associates began sub-dividing jobs, bringing parts to workers and scheduling parts to arrive at the right spot at the right time in the production process.

Finally, they devised the moving assembly line, which, with later refinements, pointed the way to mass production. In the beginning it took 12 hours and 28 minutes to assemble a Model T. The time was cut to 5 hours and 28 minutes, then to 93 minutes. Mr Ford set a goal of a car a minute, but eventually Model Ts were rolling off the assembly line at the rate of one every ten seconds of the working day. With increased production, the price came down and the pay of workers went up.

2 Full use is made of everyone's abilities

With the division of labour there is greater chance that people will be able to do those things at which they are best and which interest them the most.

3 Time is saved

If a person had to do many different tasks or operations then much time would be wasted switching from one task to another.

Time can also be saved when training people. It would take a great many years to train someone to be able to build a complete car, but a person can be trained quickly to fulfil one operation in the production process.

4 It allows the use of machinery

As labour is divided up into specialist tasks it becomes worthwhile to use machinery which allows a further saving in time and effort. For example, today cars are painted by robots instead of by hand. However, many workers are complaining that rather than helping them do their jobs, machines are actually taking them over and making people unemployed.

The disadvantages of the division of labour

1 Work may become boring

A worker who performs the same operation each and every day is likely to become very bored. To combat this some firms play music to their labour forces, or allow them to have a rest during part of each hour. Longer rest periods and annual holidays may also be introduced, while the number of hours in the working week may be reduced.

2 Workers may feel alienated

Workers may feel unimportant because they can no longer see the final result of their efforts.

Some firms, however, are trying to reverse this and generate more pride in their work among their workers. They are attempting this by allowing workers to do a greater variety of tasks. Boredom and alienation among workers is often thought to be one of the causes of labour going on strike in many countries (see Chapter 5).

3 People become too dependent upon each other

Specialization and the division of labour means that people come to rely on others for the provision of goods and services. For example, people who do not produce food rely on those who do, while the people who produce food rely on others for the provision of tractors, fertilizers and so on. This illustrates how dependent workers in one industry are upon those before them in the production process.

4 Products are all the same

The goods produced under a system of specialization are usually turned out in vast numbers and share the same design. They are **standardized**.

Whether this is a disadvantage is a matter of people's own opinion. For example, there is probably enough variation in the colour and design of cars and clothes to please most people. However, it is not possible to please everyone because in most factories it would be difficult and expensive to change the production process to suit one person's wishes. This is because most modern factories practise **mass production**. This term is used to describe a production process that aims to use the fewest workers to produce the greatest number of goods at the lowest cost possible (see also Chapter 13).

Worldwide specialization

Cuban cigars

Italian Shoes

Swiss watch

Chinese hi-fi

With the development of factories in many different economies in the eighteenth and nineteenth centuries different regions and their workforces in the same countries began to specialize in particular products and skills. For example, in England the Midlands area specialized in the production of bicycles and cars, while in the north coal mining, shipbuilding and textiles became major industries. The development of international trade has meant that whole countries also began to specialize in producing different commodities (see Chapter 22). For example, China is now a major producer of low-cost electronic equipment, Saudi Arabia is a major oil producer and Scotland is famed for its whisky production.

Section 7

Why do we need money?

Money is something we use to buy that new record or pair of jeans we always wanted, or even just to pay the gas bill. Money is in constant use, but we often take it for granted. Without it, life would become very difficult. Yet in the past, man existed for many thousands of years without the help of money.

Our primitive ancestors relied on the direct swapping of goods and services they produced. For example, if an early farmer had some spare corn and needed an axe he would travel to the local market with his corn. There he would try to find someone who would exchange an axe for the corn. This early form of exchange is known as **barter**.

Exercise 4

Imagine there is no money and we have to rely on swapping goods with each other. In groups of three, each member of the group acts out the role of either a ruler-maker, a pencil-maker or an eraser-maker.

1 Firstly, the pencil-maker wishes to exchange some pencils for some rulers. Try to arrange a swap on the best possible terms for yourself. What problems do you encounter?

2 Now the eraser-maker wants to exchange erasers for some pencils. But the pencil-maker is not interested in obtaining erasers. Your only hope is to involve the ruler-maker in the swap.

3 Imagine now that the goods being traded are eggs, milk and cheese. What problems would arise if you could not find anyone to swap your goods with? (Remember fridges have not been invented yet!)

You may have discovered that **bartering** is a most inconvenient way to carry out business. In fact three main problems arise:

1 Fixing a rate of exchange

How many pencils are worth one ruler? How many pencils are worth one apple? How many oranges are equivalent in value to one ruler? Indeed, how many rulers could Farmer Giles get for a cow? And so it goes on.

In a barter system the value of each and every good must be expressed in terms of every other good.

2 Finding someone to swap with

Miss Swap may want some apples from Mr Trade and in return may be prepared to offer him some cheese. If by chance Mr Trade would like some cheese they can barter. But, if Mr Trade does not like cheese no deal can take place. In this case an economist would say no **double coincidence of wants** exists. In other words, before two people can barter they must both want the good that the other person has.

3 Trying to save

A final problem is how to save under a barter system. A carpenter could store tables and chairs but would need a large room, but imagine trying to save some meat or cheese for a long period of time without the help of a refrigerator.

Section 8

The functions of money

By now you will be familiar with the problems involved in swapping goods and services in a barter system. It would be much easier if there was one commodity that everyone would be willing to accept in exchange for all other goods and services. This commodity is called money and overcomes the problems with barter by performing the following functions.

Money is a medium of exchange

Because money is a commodity that is generally acceptable in exchange for all other goods we do not have to search for a person who is willing to barter. That is, money overcomes the problem of needing a double coincidence of wants. Now, Miss Swap can sell her cheese to anyone who is prepared to buy it with money. In turn Miss Swap can use this money to buy the apples she wants from Mr Trade, or anyone who is willing to sell her some apples. Therefore, trade is brought about by two transactions with money being used in each.

Money is a measure of value

Just as a thermometer measures temperature and a ruler measures length, so money measures value. Using money helps traders to avoid the problems of fixing prices of goods and services in terms of all other goods and services.

Instead of arguing and attempting to remember how many pencils to one ruler, all goods have a price expressed in terms of one single commodity called money.

Money is a store of value

One of the problems with barter is that many commodities are difficult to save either because they use up too much space or they lose their value.

Money is usually a good store of value. Unless prices are rising rapidly, money tends to hold its value over time. In other words, it allows people to save in order to make purchases at a later date (see Chapter 11).

However, today some people save by storing valuable antiques and works of art, things that we do not regard as money but which can be exchanged for money in the future. People often save in this way because as prices of goods rise over time, the same amount of money will buy less and less. Therefore, the purchasing power of money, or what it will buy, is reduced. With a continued rise in prices, or **inflation**, money is unable to be such a good store of value (see Chapter 16).

Money is a means of deferred payment

When a person buys goods on credit the consumer has the use of the goods but does not have to pay for them immediately. The consumer can pay some time after he or she receives the goods. In the case of hire purchase, payment is made by instalments spread over a number of months or years.

Credit in a barter system would be very confusing and open to cheating. For example, imagine a person who trades a box of nails for a dozen apples to be paid one month later. Would the apples be fresh? Would they be large or small apples? Using money to pay later overcomes these problems and therefore encourages people to trade, reducing the worry of giving credit.

Exercise 5 

RAMPANT INFLATION HITS ISRAELI ECONOMY

One month ago this car cost . . .	One week ago it cost . . .	At 12.29 pm last Wednesday it cost . . .	At 12.31 pm last Wednesday it cost . . .	This week it will soar to over . . .
4,628,726 shekels	5,313,272 shekels	5,594,544 shekels	5,673,370 shekels	6,000,000 shekels

Israel is increasingly moving over to the US dollar as the only stable measure of value in an economy where rampant inflation slowly erodes the value of their currency (the Shekel). Most companies moved over to the dollar a long time ago. The president of one company said a year ago in 1983 that there was no point in asking him anything about the company's performance in Shekels.

'I simply can't understand anything in Shekels,' he said with a dismissive wave of his hand.

If you are paying for a babysitter or a cleaner on an hourly wage rate only dollars will do. Disbelievers need only look at any newspaper; the price of a new house or even a second-hand car are all listed in dollars. Many shop windows also only display dollar price tags.

1 For what reason did the Israeli economy move over to the US dollar as a measure of value in 1984?

2 Which of the following functions of money was the shekel failing to perform? **a** a medium of exchange, **b** a measure of value, **c** a store of value. Give reasons for your answers.

Section 9

The characteristics of a good money

In different countries around the world, and at different times, a vast range of objects have been used as a medium of exchange. These have ranged from beads used by the American Indians to large stone discs used by the inhabitants of Yap, a small island in the Pacific Ocean.

Money, as we know it today, is the product of a long period of development. Man has slowly discovered, by a process of trial and error, that some objects fulfil the functions of money better than others.

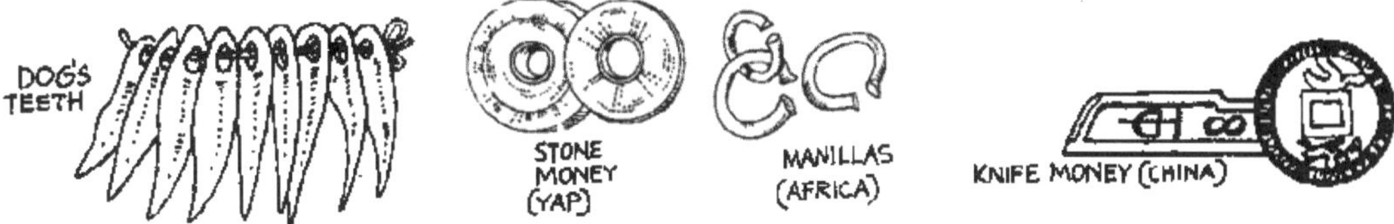

Exercise 6 **What is a 'good' money?**

In groups discuss which of the following items would make a good money. Appoint a spokesperson for your group to record your views and to present your arguments to the class.

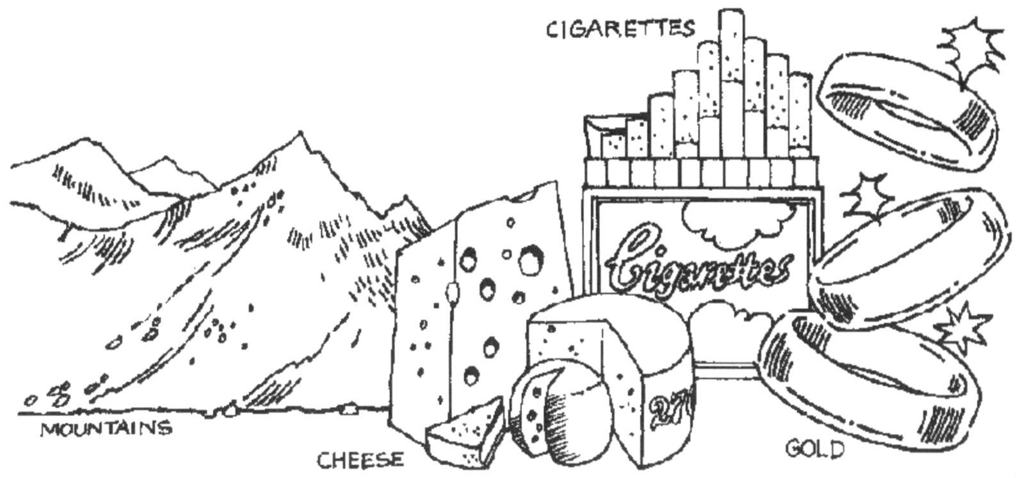

Your discussion may have led you to the conclusion that characteristics like the following are important for a good money to possess.

1 Acceptability

Anything can be used as money as long as it is generally acceptable. This is why a worthless piece of paper can be used as money, for example, a 10 dollar or a 50 euro note. It is only worth this amount in spending power because everyone accepts it as such. Thus our present money is a **token money** – as a piece of paper it is worth much less than the face value printed upon it.

2 Durability

Any commodity used as money must be hard-wearing. Money would be useless if it just melted away in your pocket. Coins and notes must be strong and durable so that they may act as a store of value.

3 Portability

Money should be easy to carry. A house would clearly be far too heavy to move. A cow would be reluctant to go shopping with you, and even more reluctant if you tried to squeeze it into your wallet or purse. Metal coins and paper notes are lightweight and fit easily into your pocket.

4 Divisibility

If cars were used as money a problem would arise if you tried to buy something priced at half your car. Sawing the vehicle into half would reduce its value. One whole working car is worth much more than two halves. Therefore it must be possible to divide money of a large value into smaller values to make small purchases or to give change, without it losing value.

5 Scarcity

Pebbles on a beach could not be used as money simply because anyone can pick them up. A shopkeeper would not exchange her goods for freely available pebbles that she could gather at any time, and in any quantity she wished. Only if money is scarce will people value it as a commodity that can be used in exchange.

So why is money important?

In section 5 we learnt how people living in a self-sufficient society began to specialize in the jobs they were most able to do. Specialization was the first step towards a wealthier society and a community which practised specialization was for the first time able to produce more than enough food, clothes, pots and other things that they needed. They had some left over – a surplus.

If people specialize they must trade. A man concentrating on making pins could not satisfy his need for food by eating them or his need for clothes by wearing them. Therefore trade is a necessity for the individual to obtain those things they cannot make on their own.

But in a barter system trade is difficult. There is no guarantee that an expert pin-maker will be able to find someone willing to swap their goods for his pins at a fair rate of exchange. The result is the pin-maker and others will be unable to specialize to their full potential. They would have to spend their time and effort producing a range of goods and services in order to increase their chances of trading successfully for the things they needed.

This would mean that much less would be produced by whole economies than if they had specialized in their production.

Money encourages specialization by making trade easier and so enables an economy to increase the level of national income and allow people to enjoy a much higher standard of living. In turn, the more an economy specializes the more money is needed to finance an increasing amount of trade.

Money is needed by consumers, firms and government to make payments to buy resources, and goods and services. The banking system can provide this money and make it easier to make payments. Therefore, as the output of an economy grows and more trade takes place, so the banking system must develop and create more money (see Chapter 6).

Section 10

There have been five main stages in the development of money. Each stage being the result of man's attempt to find objects that display the characteristics of a good money.

Stage 1

The earliest form of money was goods. Knives, beads and shoes among other objects were used as money because many people were willing to accept these in exchange for their produce. However, such **commodity money** was quickly abandoned because many of the goods did not possess the essential characteristics of a good money: divisibility, portability, durability, scarcity.

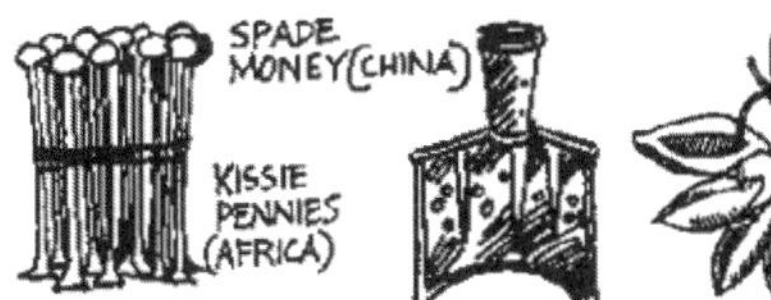

Stage 2

Precious metals, such as gold and silver, have always been scarce enough to make them a possible money. However, trading with metals involved carrying around a weighing scale and tools to cut the metals.

Stage 3

The problem of portability that cursed metals led to the natural development of **coinage.** Precious metals in predetermined weights were often stamped with the face of king or queen, and with another stamp to show their value.

But one problem remained. Throughout history the temptation to 'clip' coins, trimming a fine filing of the precious metal from the edges, has been greater than the fear of being caught.

Early coins of the United Kingdom

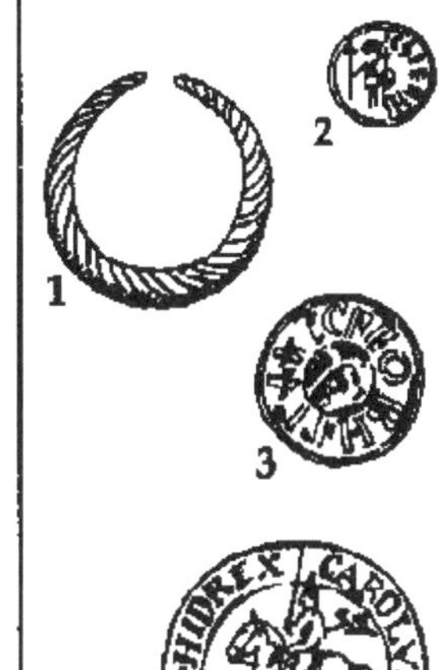

1 Ring money, Gold, 100–50 BC

2 Sceat, Silver, AD 734–766, Anglo-Saxon

3 Silver, AD 802–839, King Ecgberht, Anglo-Saxon

4 Halfcrown, Silver, AD 1644, Charles I

The invention of the ribbed edge on coins overcame the problem of 'clipping'. Another problem with early precious coins was that the rulers of countries often debased them. Coins would be called in for reminting on a special occasion. The rulers would then mix cheap metals with gold or silver, producing perhaps six coins for every four received, cleverly keeping two for themselves. The result of this today is that the metal content of coins is virtually worthless, yet people still accept such coins in exchange for goods because they know they are generally acceptable.

Stage 4

The first paper money was issued by early goldsmiths who accepted deposits of precious metals for keeping in their safes. In return they issued a paper receipt to the owner. It was quickly realized that these paper claims to gold were far easier to exchange for goods than spending time and effort withdrawing the gold only for it to be given to someone who would then re-deposit it with a goldsmith for safe keeping.

Stage 5

Goldsmiths' receipts for deposits of precious metals were to become the first paper money, and goldsmiths the first banks. In most countries today only the central bank has the right to issue notes and coins, but this money can no longer be converted into gold. Below is an example of an early paper note issued by the Bank of England in the United Kingdom.

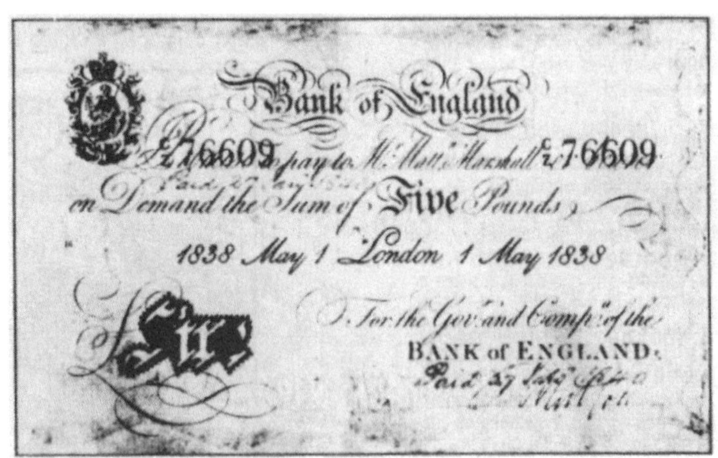

Section 11

What is money?

Money is a generally acceptable medium of exchange. However, we know that to be money a commodity must also act as store of value. Given this, our savings in banks and other financial institutions can be classified as money because one day we may withdraw these deposits so that they may be exchanged for the goods and services we want (see Chapter 6).

Notes and coins circulating in an economy and deposits with banks and other financial institutions make up the **money supply**.

Exercise 7

Mrs Mint's money

Mrs Mint is tempted by a luxury cruise advertised in the local travel agency. The only problem is the cost of $3 000. At home she tries to figure out just how much money she has.

Emptying the contents of her purse she finds that she has $50 in notes and coins. The jar on her sideboard contains $100 in crisp notes. But not nearly enough for that cruise!

Remembering that she has a savings account at the bank which allows her to withdraw any cash immediately, Mrs Mint calculates that another $300 can be added to her list. But still not enough to pay for that cruise!

After waiting seven days Mrs Mint can withdraw her savings from another account she also keeps at the bank. This account contains $400. It appears that she will have to withdraw her long-term savings. In 90 days she can obtain $600 from a government savings scheme. In 120 days $700 can be withdrawn from a credit union that she saves with each month. Mrs Mint also has $800 tied up for two years in a bond scheme. Finally, she considers selling some of the jewellery she has kept for several years to enable her to sail away on the luxury cruise liner for the holiday of a lifetime.

In the above passage Mrs Mint has a variety of ways by which she can raise the necessary money to pay for the luxury cruise.

1 If money is classed purely as a medium of exchange, list those items included in the passage that you consider would be money and give reasons for your choice.

2 If instead we focus upon money as a store of value, which would you class as money, giving reasons for your choice?

It is not an easy task to decide exactly what is money. For example, a 90-day savings account is a way of storing value but cannot become a medium of exchange or a measure of value until the end of that 90-day period. Savings tied up for two years will become a medium of exchange after two years has lapsed. So although such methods of savings, or **assets**, can possess all of the functions of money they do not possess them all at the same time or in equal amounts. Cash is a medium of exchange but loses its value due to inflation. Jewellery and other such physical assets may be a good store of value but are not generally acceptable in exchange for other goods.

A savings account in a bank may become a medium of exchange after seven days when it can be converted into cash. Assets that can be converted relatively quickly into cash are termed **near money** by economists. But jewellery and antiques act as a store of value for many years and may eventually become a medium of exchange given a long enough time to exchange them for notes and coins. However, if on converting such assets into cash the owner can only get less than they originally paid for them, that is, they have lost value, then these assets are **not** near money.

In summary, some assets are nearer money than others, for three main reasons.

1 Some assets fulfil the functions of money better than others. For example, cash is a good medium of exchange, but antiques are not.

2 Some assets can be converted to cash more quickly than others. For example, a bank deposit account can usually be withdrawn in 7 days, whereas some other saving schemes cannot be converted into cash for two years or more.

3 Some assets retain their value on conversion to cash better than others. For example, savings accounts hold their value because banks reward people who save with them with periodic payments or **interest**, whereas cars lose their value.

In a modern economy bank deposits have become the most important form of money. For example, look at the table below for the UK economy in 2006. Banks are able to create this deposit money by constantly re-lending any cash that returns to them in the form of bank deposits (see Chapter 8).

The supply of money in the UK, February 2006

	Amount (£ billion)	Percentage share of total
Notes and coins	45.23	3.36
Bank deposits	1229.20	96.64
Total	1344.43	100.00

Source: *Economic Trends*, May 2006 (UK Office for National Statistics *www.statistics.gov.uk*)

The national income is not the same as the supply of money. This is because notes and coins can be exchanged many times each year. For example, imagine you have just received one dollar in return for some work. You use the coin to buy a magazine. The shopkeeper then uses the dollar to buy some petrol. Already this one dollar has been used three times and created 3 dollars of income.

Two ways of creating money: printing notes and coins, and bank loans

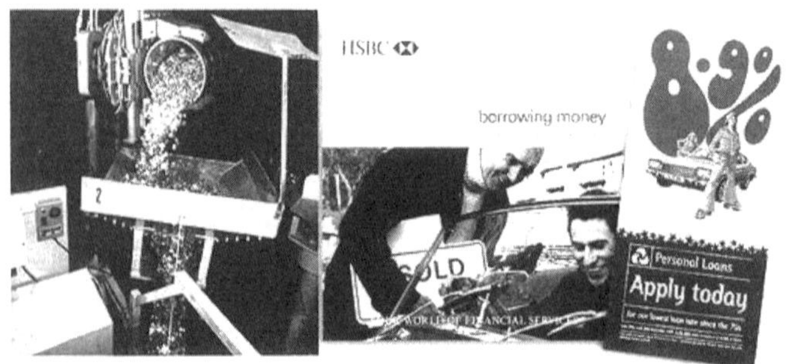

The number of times notes and coins are exchanged, or circulate in an economy, each year is called the **velocity of circulation**. This can vary over time but in the UK has been around 28 each year since 2000. This means, every note and coin in the UK has on average been exchanged 28 times each year. £45.23 billion of notes and coins in 2006 circulated 28 times equals £1266 billion – roughly equal to the gross national income in the UK that year.

Key crossword

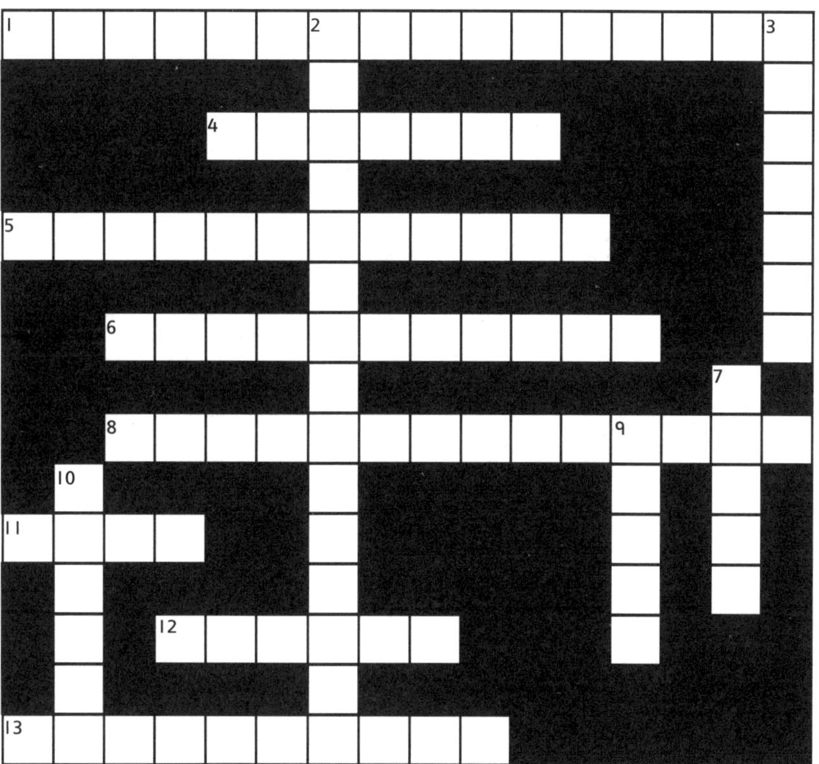

Clues across

1 A good money must fulfil this function (6,2,8)

4 Man made resources, such as factories and machinery (7)

5 A person with enterprise who organises production (12)

6 The using up of goods and services to satisfy wants (11)

8 The process by which factors of production concentrate on one or very few productive tasks they are best able to do (14)

11 Natural resources (4)

12 Human resources or another name for workers (6)

13 Making goods and services to satisfy wants (10)

Clues down

2 The benefit of the next best alternative foregone through making a choice how to use resources in a particular way (11,4)

3 Anywhere economic or productive activity takes place (7)

7 A commodity that is a generally accepted medium of exchange (5)

9 Another term used to describe the exchange of goods and services (5)

10 The swapping of goods and services without money (6)

Learn more about the functions of money at

- *www.bized.ac.uk/learn/economics/macro/notes/money.htm#Heading136*
- *www.economiceducation.us/fastfacts/FunctionsOfMoney.html*
- *en.wikipedia.org/wiki/money*

Chapter 3 Economic Systems

Aims

At the end of this chapter you should be able to:

- understand the problem of **resource allocation**
- describe different solutions to the problem of resource allocation in different types of economy
- explain the main differences between **market**, **planned** and **mixed economic systems**
- evaluate the advantages and disadvantages of these different economic systems
- understand why both the **public sector** and the **private sector** employ resources and produce goods and services in most modern economies

Section 1 Coping with scarcity

All countries suffer from scarcity of resources. Because of this, nations cannot satisfy all of their unlimited wants, so they must choose which wants to satisfy and how they will do this. For example, will they satisfy the want for power by producing electricity, and will this electricity be generated by a coal-fired power station or a nuclear power station?

There are a lot of different ways of choosing what to produce with scarce resources. Economists refer to this as the problem of **resource allocation**, that is, choosing what to produce and how much land, labour and capital is needed to produce these things. The allocation of resources therefore refers to the uses factors of production are put to.

Exercise 1 **Tropical trouble**

Divide into groups of three or four people. Now read on . . . you are part of the crew of a cargo vessel. After weeks at sea a violent storm lashes against your ship. It is forced on to rocks and a group of you are shipwrecked on a desert island. You salvage what little you can from the ship but most of your supplies are lost in the storm.

In the bright tropical sunlight of the next day you take stock of your available resources. You realize that the wreck of the ship provides metal and wood, and the natural vegetation of the uninhabited island provides a valuable source of food.

In your group discuss and provide answers to the following questions:

1 What is the central economic problem facing your group of survivors?

2 What is the best way of organizing and using the resources available to you?

Write down how your group has decided to overcome the problems facing it.

Section 2 What, how, and for whom to produce?

What to produce?

One problem facing people when there is scarcity is deciding exactly what goods and services to make. This involves choosing which wants to satisfy. Every society, no matter what its size, is faced with the same choice. In the case of the desert island the choice may be between food, clothing and shelter. In a more advanced country people may be forced to decide between more nuclear weapons or more hospitals.

How to produce?

Once it has been decided exactly what goods and services to produce there is the problem of deciding **how** to make them. What tools are needed? How many workers? How much land is needed? These questions have to be answered. In addition there are many different ways of making things. For example, when producing wheat a lot of machinery could be used to plough the land, plant seeds and eventually harvest the crop with relatively few workers. Alternatively, a lot of workers could be used to physically plough, plant and harvest, with very little machinery.

For whom do we produce?

When the questions of what to produce and how to produce have been answered a final problem remains. Because of scarcity not every person's wants can be satisfied so it must be decided whose wants to satisfy. In other words, it must be decided **who** gets the goods and services that have been made. Some people are stronger than others, whilst some people may work harder than others – perhaps they should obtain more goods and services? Others may be weak and be unable to work at all – should they get any goods and services? Or should everybody receive an equal share of all the goods and services produced, even if some people are in greater need than others? How did your group decide for whom to produce on the tropical island? The question of who should get the goods and services must be answered by society as a whole. Economists cannot tell us what is best simply because the answer depends on people's opinions. That is, it involves making a value judgement.

Section 3 Providing answers to what, how, and for whom

Exercise 2 Problem solving

Remember your solutions to the problems you faced as a group of survivors on a desert island.

1. Copy out the table below and write down your solutions to the problems posed in each column.
2. If you can think of any other ways to solve these problems include these in your table.
3. Compare your answers with another group in your class and make a note of any other ways they have thought of for providing answers to the three questions.

How to decide what to produce?	How to decide how to produce?	How to decide for whom to produce?
Build shelter	Everyone helps using large palm leaves	Everyone shares a shelter

There are many different answers to these three questions. Every society or country must choose and develop its own way of solving these problems. How a country decides what to produce, how to produce and for whom to produce is called its **economic system**. These systems are designed by people, just as you did on your imaginary island. Some people may be very caring and wish to share all their resources with others, whilst some people may want to be rich and powerful by owning all the resources themselves. They may even exploit other people. An economic system will develop from the way people think and behave, but without an economic system no decisions would be made and resources would be left idle.

Section 4 The market economic system

What is a market?

A market is a very important concept in economics as we will discover in Chapter 7. Very simply, a **market** consists of all those people or firms who wish to exchange a given good or service. Any market for a good or service is therefore made up of all the producers who make and sell that particular good or service and all those consumers willing and able to buy it.

We can say that the market for computers consist of all producers and all consumers of computers. Similarly there is a market for every different type of food, for clothes, televisions, cars, holidays, insurance and all other goods and services.

In economics a market does not refer to a particular location where goods and services might be traded, such as Billingsgate fish market in London, the famous Khan el-Khalili market in Cairo in Egypt, or the local market in a town or village where you live. For an economist, any organization or any person who wants to buy or sell a particular good or service, wherever they are in the world, is part of the market for that good or service. Markets can therefore be spread over a small area or a very large area. For example, the market for a local newspaper or the services of a particular hairdresser at a beauty salon will both tend to be very localized. The market for national daily newspapers such as *El País* in Spain, *The Times* in the UK, or *L'Express* in Mauritius will be national domestic markets. Some goods and services, however, are exchanged all over the world. For example, the markets for crude oil, aircraft and computers are **international** or **global markets**.

How a market economic system allocates resources

Now that we know what a market is in economics, we can now learn about the **market economic system** of resource allocation, often called the **free market system**. In a market economic system, producers and consumers decide what, how and for whom to produce through their exchange or trade in different goods and services. That is, markets determine what, how and for whom goods and services are produced.

Exercise 3

An introduction to the workings of a market system

Jennifer Johnson has thirty people working for her business. She owns a patch of land, a factory building and hires fifteen machines. Jennifer wants to make as much money or **profit** as possible for herself. This is the aim of her business. At present she uses her scarce resources to make pairs of bright multicoloured boots.

The latest fashion among young people is pastel-coloured shoes and Jennifer notices that sales of her boots are falling. That is, the market for boots is shrinking. Teenagers are no longer willing to use their money to buy brightly coloured boots, but will instead pay a high price for pastel-coloured shoes. In other words, the market for shoes is expanding.

As her profits begin to fall, Jennifer realizes there is more money to be made from the production of shoes and so switches her scarce resources away from making boots into the production of pairs of pastel shoes to satisfy the wants of teenagers.

Jennifer now faces a problem. There are two ways of making the shoes. The first method only requires twenty of her thirty workers and ten of her machines, and each pair of shoes will cost $6 to produce. The second method requires all thirty workers with only seven machines, and each pair of shoes will cost $10 to produce. Jennifer decides to use the first and cheapest method because she wishes to make as much profit from the sale of her shoes as possible.

After only a short time, Jennifer's profits have increased dramatically and are far greater than her profits when she made boots. Eager teenagers who can afford to pay for the pastel-coloured shoes can now satisfy their wants.

Questions

In a market economy there are many thousands of firms all behaving like Jennifer's.

1. What is the main aim of a business producing goods and services in a market economy?
2. How do firms in this type of economy decide **what** to produce? *Hint* Why did Jennifer decide to produce shoes instead of boots?
3. In a market system how do firms decide **how** to produce goods and services?
4. Once the goods and services have been produced **who** are they for? *Hint* Which teenagers could not satisfy their wants for shoes?
5. In deciding to produce shoes Jennifer chose the cheapest method which meant she needed only twenty of her thirty workers. What will happen to the ten workers who are not needed?

Deciding what, how and for whom to produce

All the resources in a market economy are privately owned by people and firms. Every business will aim to make as much **profit** as possible. Profit is the amount of money a business makes from selling goods and services less the money it costs to buy or hire resources (see Chapter 13). However, a business can only be profitable if it uses the scarce resources to make those goods and services that people will buy.

In a market economic system all firms aim to make a profit and they do this by moving scarce resources away from producing things people will not buy into the production of goods and services that they will buy. That is, firms will move out of markets that are shrinking as people are buying less, into markets which are expanding because people are buying more.

What is produced in a market economy depends therefore on what consumers want and are willing to pay for. Firms will produce what people want in the cheapest possible way so as to make the most profit. The people who are able to enjoy the goods and services produced, however, are only those with enough money to buy them.

How do firms know what is profitable?

If a firm finds that a particular good is selling very well, for example, Jennifer's pastel-coloured shoes, the firm can increase the price charged as they know that people will still purchase the goods and more profits can be made.

If the price of shoes rises it acts as a signal to other firms that there are more profits to be had from making and selling shoes. For example, the Clemence Clothing Company may decide it would be better off using their resources to produce shoes instead of clothing. The Clothing Company and other firms producing many different things will leave what they are currently producing and bring their resources into the production of shoes. That is, they will enter the market for shoes.

In a market economy high prices are the signal telling firms what people want, that is what will make the most profit. In the same manner, if the price of a product was to fall because people are simply not buying it any more, this will act as a signal to tell firms to move their resources into the production of something more profitable. This is known as the **price mechanism**. In this way **market forces** solve the problem of what, how and for whom to produce. In other words, the profit motive of firms and the changing preferences of consumers determine the allocation of resources, or how factors of production are used (see also Chapter 7).

How good is the market economic system?

Advantages of the market system

1 The market produces a wide variety of goods and services to meet consumers' wants

2 The free market responds quickly to people's wants

In the market system if people want a good or service and can afford to buy it, then it becomes profitable to make it and resources are quickly moved to the market to produce such goods and services. On the other hand, if the good is not wanted it becomes unprofitable and resources are directed away into more profitable uses.

3 The market system encourages the use of new and better methods and machines to produce goods and services

The aim of firms in a market economy is to make as much profit as possible. New methods and machines often reduce the costs of producing goods and services allowing firms to increase their profits. For example, the widespread use of computers in banks has enabled bank workers to make calculations much faster so that more work can be done each day.

What is wrong with the market system?

Disadvantages of the market system

1 Factors of production will be employed only if it is profitable to do so

If a profitable use cannot be found for some of the scarce resources then they will be unemployed. Labour is just another factor of production, and one reason why some people are unemployed today is that it is not profitable to employ them.

2 The free market can fail to provide certain goods and services

Some goods and services are consumed by everyone at the same time but some consumers may be unwilling to pay directly for them even though they may enjoy their use. For example, everyone enjoys the benefits of street-lighting at night but no private firm could provide this at a profit because it would be unable to force people to pay for it. Governments may therefore have to provide such goods and services for the general public. You may recall from Chapter 2 that such goods and services are known as Public Goods.

3 The free market may encourage the consumption of harmful goods

Some people may wish to buy dangerous drugs and if they can afford to buy them then the free market will find it profitable to provide these goods. However, such drugs are harmful and it may need a government to pass laws to stop people from selling them and others from using them.

4 The social effects of production may be ignored

Factories bellowing smoke into the air can affect us all. Pollution is causing damage to the natural environment and the destruction of plant and animal life around the world. Also the noise from factories, airports and roads affects people who live nearby. Private firms in a market economy may not consider the social effects of their actions.

5 The market system allocates more goods and services to those consumers who have more money than others

People with a lot of money have the freedom to choose and buy many different goods and services, but for those who have little money, like many unemployed and elderly people, there is much less freedom of choice.

Exercise 4 Freedom of choice in a market economy

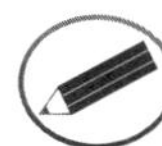

The two pictures below show two different groups of people who live in a market economy.

A casino

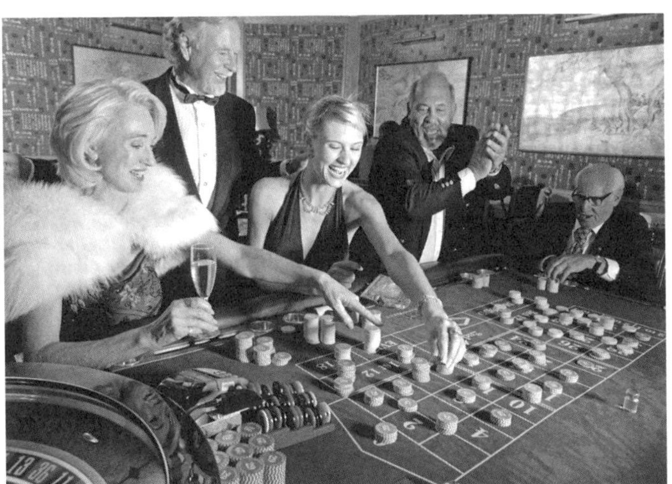

An unemployment queue

1. Which group of people has more freedom to choose to buy a foreign holiday, a new car and a new home?
2. Explain why this group of people has greater freedom of choice.

There are very few countries in the world today that rely purely on the market economic system. Most countries have a government that makes some of the decisions on what, how and for whom to produce.

Section 5 Planned economies

Because of the disadvantages of a market economic system, some economies in the world have tried to plan centrally what to produce, how to produce and for whom to produce rather than allow the actions of many different producers and consumers to determine the allocation of scarce resources through free market exchange. In the past, the governments of countries such as Poland, Romania, Hungary and Russia (as part of the former Soviet Union) have determined the allocation of resources. These countries had **planned economies** and such central government ownership and control of resources was often known as Communism.

In planned economies government planners decided how all scarce resources were to be used. This could involve the government providing millions of instructions to hundreds of thousands of firms on what exactly they should produce, and where people should work. In planned economies firms would not aim to produce what was profitable, instead they would aim to produce what the government wanted.

Exercise 5 Mustard

The following newspaper article illustrates how planning often went wrong and how waste occurred in the old planned economy of the Soviet Union.

Soviet mustard glut

Spicy scandal in giant jars

From Christopher Walker, Moscow

The recent acute shortage of mustard throughout the Soviet Union – it was classified as an unavailable product – has been rectified with a vengeance in the Ukrainian industrial region of Krasnadon, where shoppers are now able to buy it only in giant three litre jars

This latest example of the bizarre by-products of the Soviet system has been disclosed by the Moscow weekly *Literaturnaya Gazeta* (Literary Gazette), whose editors explained that they thought protest letters from readers in the Ukraine were a hoax.

As the complaints continued to pour in from many towns in Krasnadon – a region famed for the ferocity of its underground resistance to the Nazis during the Second World War – the magazine questioned Mr G. Stelyanko, the Ukrainian Minister of Trade, who admitted that the Krasnadon food factory had indeed taken to bottling mustard in such impractical jars.

The magazine, the official publication of the Soviet Writers' Union, decided to investigate whose idea it was to sell mustard in such enormous jars.

The results pointed to the very bureaucratic problems in the Soviet system that Mr Mikhail Gorbachov, the Kremlin leader, is struggling to eliminate as part of his campaign to streamline the country's ramshackle administration.

At first it appeared that the answer was simply that the factory had decided to make the change to cut its workload, by reducing from 10,000 to 333 the number of jars produced from each ton of pungent Soviet mustard.

Then the investigators discovered the irony went further. Mr Stelyanko, after further questioning, explained that the Krasnadon factory was suffering an acute shortage of small glass jars because state shops were refusing to refund money on empty jars.

The magazine concluded, with a note of despair, that as a result mustard in the giant jars would soon go off, forcing every family to throw it away. Then, once again, the Soviet Union will have another mustard deficit.

1. How were resources wasted in the economy of the former Soviet Union?
2. What is the aim of producing goods and services for firms in:

   a a market economy **b** a planned economy?
3. In a market economy why are mustard producers unlikely to make mustard in three-litre jars for the general public?

4 Apart from weight, what other instructions should the government planners in the former Soviet Union have given to the mustard producers for them to produce a suitable product for consumers?

5 What problem does the article illustrate about government planning of production in an economy? Explain your answer in full.

The main problem with planned economies was that the goods that were produced were what the government wanted, and not necessarily what the people wanted. In planned economies like the old Soviet Union, there were often shortages of consumer goods or the goods that were produced were of poor quality. The reason for this was that firms did not have an incentive to do a good job because they were not required to make a profit. Instead their job was to do as the government wanted, and there were just too many firms for governments to provide clear instructions to all of them. This led to the production of a limited range of poor-quality goods. This was one reason why the people in many countries controlled by communist governments wanted change.

Because there were so many disadvantages with planned economic systems, most planned economies have now changed their economic system to that of a mixed economy. Even countries still controlled by communist governments have moved away from fully planned systems – for example, China and Cuba. Firms once government-owned are now owned by the private sector. The advantage of a market system is that firms do not need to be given information by the government on what or how to produce. Consumer demand and spending soon tells firms whether they are producing the right goods in the right way by rewarding them with a profit or a loss.

Market reforms and structural change in the Russian Federation

Since the break-up of the Soviet Union, the Russian economy has been changing rapidly. The changes are primarily the result of the demise of central planning, which emphasised heavy industry, especially defence, over light industry, industry in general over services, and repressed the development of the consumer sector. Investment collapsed and crime has become commonplace. To this must be added the effects of the break-up of the Soviet Union itself, which severed links between parts of what was once a unified economy. Regional power struggles and military actions have resulted in some areas.

The intention of the Russian government to move towards a stable, market-based economic system has rarely been in doubt. However, the policies and ability of the Russian authorities to bring this about has not always been so clear. Fundamental disagreements over economic policy remain.

Significant moves towards market reform began in 1991 when the right to private property in productive assets was established – the first privatisation law – and in January 1992, when government price controls were removed and prices were able to find their own levels. Due to shortages of many, even basic, goods and services, prices leapt on average by 245% in the first month alone. Price inflation has since fallen but in 1995 was still above 5% per month. Some of the biggest price rises were for food items.

During 1992 the government of the Russian Federation cut defence spending by 68%. The size of this cut caused massive shifts in the economy. From 1991 to 1994 light industry and machine builders suffered the largest declines, while electric energy, fuel and metallurgy expanded as a share of industrial production. Given the inefficiency and poor product quality of many industries, their decline following market reforms was not surprising. Instead, there was a rapid increase in imported goods and a collapse in the value of the rouble on foreign exchange markets.

As a result of these and other changes the national income in Russia fell 50% between 1990 and 1995 according to official figures. Unemployment levels also increased steadily.

Over the same period Russia gradually moved towards a new system of social protection with a mixture of universal and means tested benefits. Some social benefits (maternity and child benefits, disability and old age pensions, and some health benefits) remain similar to their communist predecessors, some are new (unemployment and welfare benefits). Social security financing arrangements were changed; benefits are increasingly paid out of specialised insurance funds rather than from general tax revenues.

Adapted from 'The Russian Federation 1995', *OECD Economic Surveys*

The mixed economic system

Because of the disadvantages of both market and planned economic systems most countries in the world choose to use a **mixed economic system**.

The mixed economic system combines government planning with the use of the free market. In the mixed economy, just as in the market economy, people and firms in the **private sector** own scarce resources with the aim of making as much profit as possible. However, in mixed economies the government or **public sector** also owns some scarce resources to produce goods and services that they think their country, and its people, need and want.

Why have a mixed economic system?

1 Market economies experience high unemployment sometimes because it may not be profitable to employ people. In a mixed economy if there is unemployment the government may be able to create jobs for those people out of work by employing them in their own offices and factories, or by helping private firms to provide jobs.

2 Public goods, such as defence, law and order, and street-lighting, will not be provided by private firms in a market economy as it would be impossible to get people to pay for their use. In a mixed economy a government can provide these public goods and raise the money necessary to pay for them by taxing people's income and spending. In addition, the government may provide merit goods, such as education and health-care, which it feels people should have (see Chapter 14).

3 Because some people may want to buy dangerous goods like drugs, firms in a market economy may find it profitable to provide them. In a mixed economy a government may be able to stop people consuming harmful goods by making them illegal, for example, hard drugs, or by placing high taxes on them, for example, cigarettes.

4 Private firms only take into account their own costs and benefits when producing goods and services. For example, a private firm pouring waste into a river will not consider the cost to the environment. A government may use laws, or high taxes and fines on firms, to try and prevent them polluting the environment (see Chapter 21).

5 One of the main problems of a market economy is that poorer people with little money are unable to buy many of the goods and services that are available. Planning gives the government the power to give goods and services, or more money, to the people that it thinks needs them. For example, in the UK, the government provides unemployment benefits and free healthcare for those who cannot afford to pay.

A mixed economy attempts to overcome the disadvantages of a market economic system by using government intervention to control or regulate different markets. Government ownership of some of the scarce resources allows it to produce goods and services for those people it thinks needs them. However, if a government provides goods and services it must cover the cost of doing so by raising taxes from people and firms (see Chapter 15). High taxes may discourage people from working hard when some of the money they earn is simply taken away by the government.

Almost all countries today have a mixed economic system, but the amount of goods and services provided by the public sector relative to the private sector can vary greatly. For example, in 2003 the public sector in France accounted for over 48 per cent of all spending in the French economy, while in Bangladesh the public sector was responsible for just 9.1 per cent. In the US economy, the world's largest market-based economy, the public sector accounted for 21 per cent of total spending in 2003 (see also Chapter 15).

Public sector expenditure as a percentage of total spending, selected countries 2003

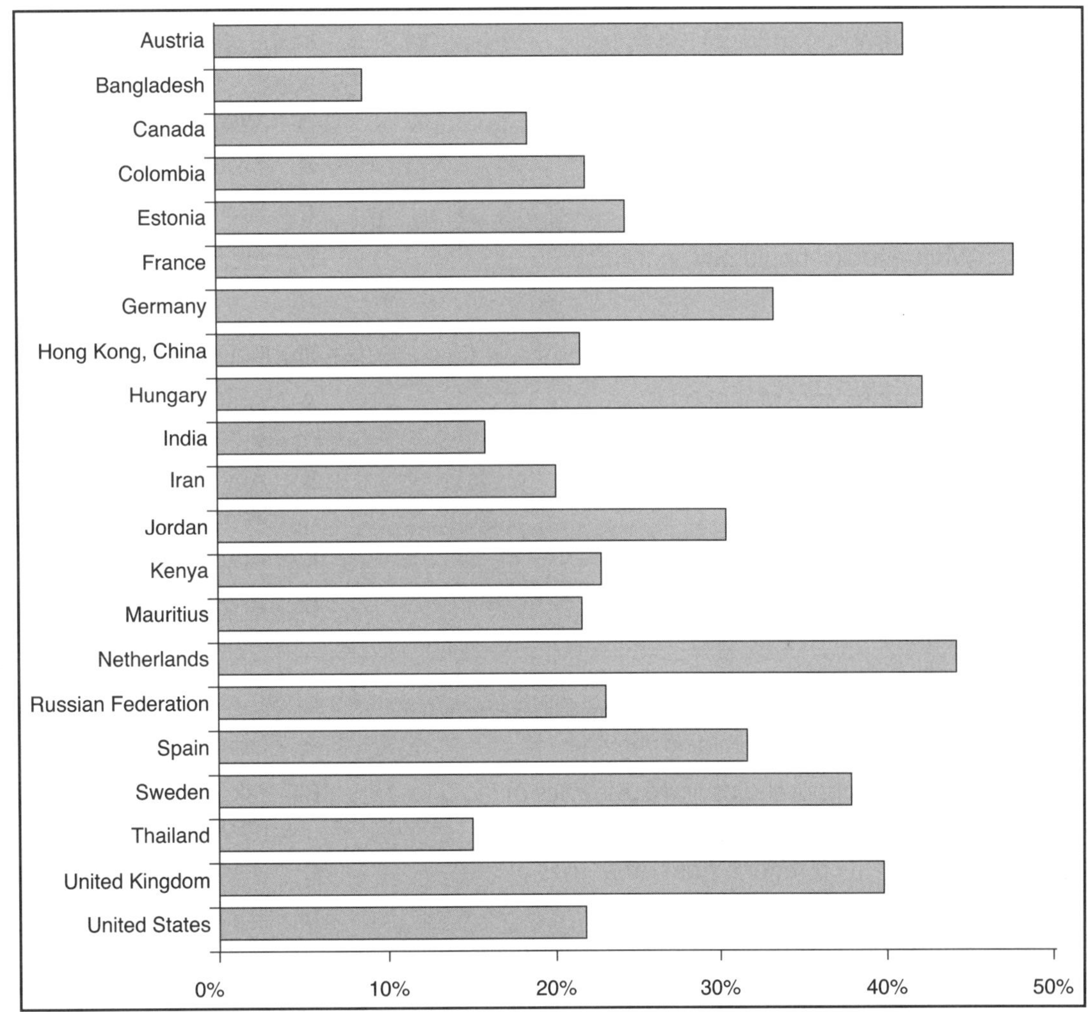

World Bank 2006, *www.worldbank.org*

Write definitions to explain the following terms:

Resource allocation	**Mixed economy**
Market	**Price mechanism**
Market economic system	**Planned economy**

Now go back through the chapter to check your understanding of these terms.

The following websites contain some helpful definitions and discussion of economic systems:

- *www.referenceforbusiness.com/encyclopedia/Ca-Clo/Centrally-Planned-Economy.html*
- *www.referenceforbusiness.com/encyclopedia/Man-Mix/Mixed-Economy.html*

Assessment exercises

Multiple choice

1 Which of the following is not included in the study of economics?

- **A** Scarce resources
- **B** Choice
- **C** What people should buy
- **D** Opportunity cost

2 The opportunity cost of a good is:

- **A** The total cost of the good.
- **B** What it can be sold for.
- **C** How much it is worth to its owner.
- **D** The benefit from the next best thing foregone.

3 A new dam is built in Turkey to provide hydroelectric power and a water supply. What is the opportunity cost to the economy of building the dam?

- **A** The cost to households and businesses of consuming the water supply.
- **B** The benefits foregone from other uses of the money used to pay for the dam.
- **C** The cost to consumers of using hydroelectric power.
- **D** The money used to pay for the construction and running of the dam.

4 A firm can produce a number of possible combinations of two goods. It can either produce 500 of good *x* and 300 of good *y*, or 600 *x* and 250 *y*. What is the opportunity cost of producing an extra 100 of good *x*?

- **A** 100 *y*
- **B** 250 *y*
- **C** 50 *y*
- **D** The extra wages paid to the workers.

5 In the study of economics, resources are also known as:

- **A** Workers and machines.
- **B** Raw materials.
- **C** Factors of production.
- **D** Profits.

6 Production can be defined as:

- **A** Any activity that turns raw materials into finished goods.
- **B** Any activity that makes and sells goods and services.
- **C** Any activity that is designed to satisfy wants.
- **D** Any activity that makes a profit.

7 An entrepreneur is someone who:

- **A** Owns a factory.
- **B** Takes the risks and decisions necessary to organize resources.
- **C** Is a supervisor in charge of workers.
- **D** Is a producer.

8 In which of the following situations would money cease to be a good store of value?

- **A** Prices of goods and services are falling slowly.
- **B** High unemployment.
- **C** Prices of goods and services are rising rapidly.
- **D** Prices of goods and services are rising slowly.

9 All the following are important characteristics of a good money *except:*

- **A** It is durable.
- **B** It is in unlimited supply.
- **C** It is generally accepted.
- **D** It is carried easily.

10 In general the supply of money in a modern economy is best defined as:

A Coins, notes and bank deposits.

B All items of legal tender.

C Coins, notes and bank loans.

D Notes and coins.

11 The basic economic problem faced by all economies is:

A Rising prices.

B Unemployment.

C Scarcity of resources.

D Low economic growth.

12 The problem of what to produce in a planned economy is solved mainly by:

A Consumers.

B The profit motive.

C Market forces.

D Government directives.

13 A mixed economy is one that has:

A Farms and factories.

B A public and a private sector.

C Capital and consumer goods.

D Goods and services.

14 In a free market economy the price mechanism:

A Helps the government to provide services.

B Measures the total value of wealth.

C Makes profits for firms.

D Determines the allocation of resources.

15 During the 1990s the economies of Eastern Europe changed from planned economies to market economic systems. Which of the following best describes the change that took place?

A More centralized government planning to allocate resources

B Fewer price controls

C Increased dependence on the price mechanism to allocate resources

D Increased resource unemployment

16 Which of the following is an advantage claimed for the market economic system?

A It responds quickly to consumer wants.

B It provides public goods.

C Unemployment can rise rapidly.

D It relies on traditional methods of production.

Structured questions

1

Alcohol and Government Policy

In the UK, the National Health Service often has to deal with the consequences of drinking alcohol. It is said that there is less trouble in other countries which have more relaxed licensing laws. In the UK, accidents caused by drinking alcohol result in 150 000 hospital admissions every year. Time taken dealing with these admissions prevents other treatment. There are about 22 000 deaths linked to alcohol-related illnesses every year.

There are also other consequences. Very many working days are lost each year because of alcohol abuse which it is estimated cost employers £6.4 million in lost production. There is also the cost of policing the city centres particularly at night and at weekends when excessive drinking causes riotous behaviour. It is argued that while police are controlling this behaviour it leaves property more vulnerable to burglary. Property owners, as a result, may have to pay extra insurance premiums and protect their property by paying for burglar alarms to be fitted. Then there are legal costs. If people are prosecuted for drink-related offences it involves court costs, lawyers' costs and costs for the witnesses to attend court.

There are also the costs of establishing centres that treat people who drink excessively and the costs of social workers who care for those who are victims of drink-related incidents.

One of the difficulties of trying to calculate the cost of alcohol use is how to estimate figures such as those above. How do we measure the cost of police time? How do we measure the costs of an emotional upset when someone is injured by a drink-related driving accident? How do we measure the effect of violence in the home caused by excessive drinking?

Yet there are benefits from alcohol. People gain pleasure from drinking: it is a social activity. Some alcohol is said to give health benefits.

The government places a tax on alcohol and gains a large amount of revenue as a result. Many people are employed in the manufacture and distribution of drinks. Others are employed in clubs and bars that serve alcohol.

a Define opportunity cost. [2]

b Identify and explain **one** example of opportunity cost from the above extract. [2]

c You are asked to investigate the economic arguments for and against a ban on the sale and consumption of alcohol. Discuss how helpful you would find the above extract and what further information you would seek. [10]

d The government decides not to introduce a ban on alcohol. Instead it considers either raising the existing indirect tax on alcohol or banning the advertising of alcohol. Discuss which of these two approaches you would favour and give reasons [9]

2 Some services, such as legal advice, are provided by private individuals while others, such as the police force, are provided by the public sector.

a Distinguish between the private sector and the public sector of an economy. [3]

b Discuss the advantages and disadvantages of allocating resources through the public sector. [10]

c In what ways may the provision of goods and services in the public sector be paid for? [6]

3 During the last decade of the 1990s many countries, including China and Russia, introduced policies that increased the role of the market system.

a Explain the most important features of 'the market system'. [4]

b Explain, with the use of a diagram, what will happen in a market system if a good becomes popular and there is a fall in the cost of production. [6]

c What are the advantages and disadvantages of relying more on the market system? [10]

4 The euro replaced the national currencies of many European countries in the European Union in 2002 to become the sole legal tender in the eurozone.

a List **four** functions euro notes and coins should perform. [4]

b Explain how consumer price inflation in Europe may affect these functions. [6]

How to answer question 1

a For two marks you need only give a short clear definition to demonstrate your knowledge and understanding of this key economic concept. Any of the following examples will earn you the maximum marks: the value of the next best alternative foregone when a choice is made; the benefit of an economic activity given up by the choice of another activity; the benefit foregone from not using a product or resource in its best alternative use.

b There are many examples of **opportunity cost** in the article to choose from. For example, at an individual level, a person who enjoys drinking a lot of alcohol may be doing so at the cost of his or her health and/or foregoing other goods and services they could have spent their money on instead. At the UK economy-wide level, **taxes** have to be raised to pay for hospitals and healthcare to treat alcohol-related diseases and injuries. This could mean people with other health problems may have to wait longer for their treatment, or the tax revenue could have instead been used to pay for other publicly provided goods and services, such as new schools and educational services. Taxes may have to be raised further to pay for more police to control people who get drunk and may be violent as a result. People who drink too much may also be enjoying this benefit at the expense of the owners of bars and public houses where alcohol is served who have to pay more for security measures and insurance which reduces their **profits**. Also, many working days are lost, resulting in higher costs to firms and lower **national output** and **income**, because people who had too much alcohol to drink the night before may be less productive at work or feel too unwell to go to work the next day.

c Part (b) requires you to pick just one example of an opportunity cost. However, this question is asking you to investigate and evaluate all the examples contained in the article and to consider any others you can think of to determine whether the **social costs** of the sale and consumption of alcohol exceed its **social benefits** (see also Chapter 21). If so, then a ban would be economically efficient. If, however, the social benefits of alcohol exceed its social costs (the sum of **private costs** and **external costs**) then a ban would not make sense economically. The private costs of alcohol can be measured by how much people spend on it but this data is not given in the article. This may also provide a measure of how much people enjoy alcohol and are prepared to pay for it. A good answer would however point out that the consumption of alcohol by one person can impose many negative externalities on others and the article is very helpful in providing many examples. So, for example, a loss of national output due to working days lost through alcohol abuse and healthcare costs imposed on others might suggest the sale and consumption of alcohol should be banned. However, drinking in moderation is enjoyable for many people and can lower stress and reduce stress-related health problems. The production and sale of alcohol also employs many people, and their incomes, the profits of alcohol producers and sellers, and excise duties on the sale of alcohol, all provide tax revenue for the government to spend on publicly provided goods and services that can benefit many more people and the economy. These economic arguments suggest a ban may not be economically beneficial.

If the article provided data on all these various costs and benefits then it would be possible to add them up to see if the sale and consumption of alcohol created more social costs in the UK economy than social benefits. If it did, then a ban may be economically advantageous. To make sure you get maximum marks, you should also consider what the further impacts of a ban might be, and whether there are any real-life examples we can study of where a ban has been introduced. For example, would it simply create an illegal market for alcohol imported from other countries? Perhaps people would go overseas more often to enjoy alcohol, thereby reducing **consumer expenditure** in the UK economy. Would people smoke more cigarettes instead?

d First of all you should define what is meant by an **indirect tax** and to do this you will need to read Chapter 15. Then you should use your judgement and analysis to describe clearly what could happen if indirect taxes on alcohol were raised in the UK. First, what will be the impact on the market prices and demand for alcoholic drinks? You will need to look at Chapter 7. If the demand for alcohol is relatively **price inelastic** then alcohol producers will be able to pass most of the tax increase on to consumers without having much impact on the level of demand. The government may enjoy more tax revenue but alcohol consumption may not reduce by very much.

You must then analyse possible wider effects of the indirect tax. For example, raising indirect taxes is **inflationary**. Higher indirect taxes on alcohol in the UK may simply encourage people to buy more alcohol from overseas where indirect taxes may be lower.

Now consider the impact of a ban on **advertising** alcohol, for example on television or in the cinema. This will only tend to reduce alcohol consumption if advertising helps create a want for alcohol (see Chapter 9). If not, a ban will only tend to harm advertising companies who will lose revenue. A ban would also be difficult to enforce in total across all forms of promotion, such as product placements in television programmes and films, or sponsorship of televised sporting events.

To maximize your marks you could draw a **market demand** and **supply** diagram like those in Chapter 7 to show the effect of increasing an indirect tax on the market supply of alcohol, and the effect an advertising ban may have on consumer demand.

It doesn't really matter which policy you favour so long as you have discussed the possible economic impacts of each one. On balance, however, raising tax on alcohol may be a better way of reducing consumption if demand is reasonably **price elastic**, but it may mean having to raise the tax significantly.

A model answer for question 3

Note that you will also need to study Chapter 7 in order to answer part (b).

a In a market economy, consumers buy goods and services to satisfy as many of their wants as they can, and private sector firms produce these goods and services to earn as much profit as they can. What is produced therefore depends on what consumers want and are willing to pay for. Firms will allocate the scarce resources of land, labour and capital, to produce the goods and services consumers want in the cheapest way possible so as to make as much profit as they can. The profit motive of firms and the preferences of consumers therefore determine how resources are allocated in a market economy.

Changes in the market prices of different goods and services act as signals to firms about how to use resources. For example, if the market price of a good is rising because consumers are buying more then this will provide a signal to producers to use more resources to produce more of that product. Being able to sell more to meet the increased demand and at a higher market price means a firm can earn more profit.

b We can use a diagram to show how changes in demand and supply can affect the market price and quantity traded of a particular good in a market economy. The diagram below plots the market price of a product against the quantity available to buy. The total market demand for the product by consumers at each and every possible price is plotted as a downward sloping line or curve because consumer demand tends to expand as price falls. Market supply is an upward sloping line because producers will tend to supply more, the higher the price they can sell their product for. The market equilibrium price (P) for the good and the quantity bought by consumers from producers (Q) occurs where the market demand curve (DD) crosses the market supply curve (SS).

If the good becomes more popular, more consumers will want it and be willing to buy more of it whatever its price. As a result the market demand curve shifts to the right, from D to D1. This has the effect of increasing the market price and quantity traded of the good, from P to P1 and from Q to Q1.

Suppose now the cost of wages or materials fall so producers can make the same good more cheaply than before. This means they could potentially earn more profit from its sale. Producers would therefore be willing to supply more of it than before at every possible price. New firms may also start producing the same good. The market supply curve will also shift to the right, from S to S1. As a result of this increase in supply the market price of the good falls from P1 to P2, and the total quantity bought by consumers from producers increases further from Q1 to Q2.

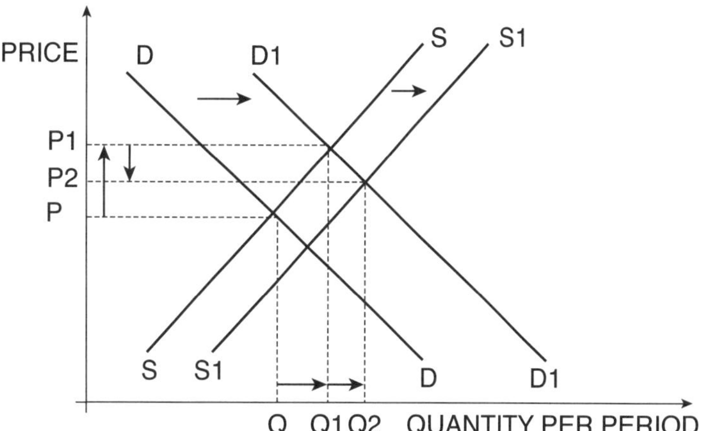

c Many countries, including old planned economies like China and Russia, are relying more on the market system to allocate scarce resources in their economies because of its advantages. For example, a market economy will tend to produce a wider variety of goods and services for consumers to choose from if it is profitable to do so. This of course depends on consumers being willing and able to buy them. As consumers' buying habits change then firms will quickly allocate resources to the production of those goods and services they want. In this way, consumers can quickly get what they want and can pay for in a market economy.

Private sector firms will compete for the custom of consumers to make profits. It is therefore in the interest of each firm to try to produce better-quality products at lower prices than their competitors in order to attract more consumer demand. New technology and methods of production can lower the cost of producing goods and services so that fewer resources can be used to make them. In this way more goods and services in total can be made, and more wants satisfied, from the scarce resources available in the economy.

Because a market system relies on the decisions of consumers and producers to determine the allocation of resources, there is little or no need for government intervention. As a result, government spending and levels of taxation can be much lower in economies that rely more on the market system.

However, there are some clear disadvantages with a market economic system. Clearly, those consumers with the most money will be able to buy the goods and services they want and need. Private firms may also produce goods and services these consumers want even if they are harmful to them, to other people, or the environment. For example, some consumers may want to buy dangerous drugs or guns. Firms may do little to reduce or clean up pollution from their productive activities because it may be expensive to do so and this would reduce their profits.

In contrast, consumers with little or no money, for example, because they are too old or disabled to work to earn money, may be unable to afford many basic goods and services. Firms will also fail to produce some of the goods and services they may need, such as healthcare or products that aid mobility, simply because it is not profitable to do so. Similarly, other goods or services like street lighting, a legal system and defence may not be provided in pure market economies because it will be difficult for private firms to identify and collect money from individual consumers who will benefit from them. This is because once provided it is difficult to exclude consumers from the benefit of, say, street lighting, whether they have paid for it or not.

High levels of unemployment among workers can also be a big problem in many market economies. Resources may become unemployed if the products they produce are no longer profitable.

2 THE NATURE AND FUNCTIONS OF ORGANIZATIONS AND INSTITUTIONS IN AN ECONOMY

An entrepreneur will organize scarce resources into a firm to produce goods and services. In a modern economy a firm may take a number of business forms.

A sole trader is a small, one-person business. In a partnership, ownership, control and finance of the business is shared between the partners. These small businesses tend to raise most of the finance they need from friends and family, and in loans or overdrafts from commercial banks. However, in order to finance significant business growth an entrepreneur will wish to consider forming a limited company.

Joint stock companies, also known as limited companies, can sell shares to investors. The shareholders of a company are its owners. A public limited company can raise a significant amount of finance by selling shares to the general public and other companies through stock exchanges. These are business organizations that specialize in providing facilities for the issuing, buying and selling of shares.

Most limited companies have a separate legal or corporate status from their owners. That is, a company will have a distinct name, can own property and shares in other companies, is liable to pay tax on its profits and can be taken to court.

Co-operatives are owned and run by a group of people for their mutual benefit. For example, a retail co-operative is owned by its customers, and a worker co-operative by its workers.

Public sector organizations are owned and controlled by local or central government. These provide goods and services on behalf of government. For example, public corporations run government-owned industries including postal services and railways in some countries. The central bank in an economy may also be run by a public corporation to provide banking facilities for the public sector and the commercial banking sector. For example, a central bank will hold tax, gold and foreign currency reserves for a government and help manage the government's monetary policy.

Labour employed in different private and public sector organizations can also organize into labour unions or trade unions to protect their rights as employees and to seek improvements in their pay and working conditions. Negotiations between trade unions and employers are known as collective bargaining. When negotiations fail, trade unions may take disruptive industrial action.

Chapter 4 Types of Business Organization

Aims

At the end of this chapter you should be able to:

- describe **types of business organization** in the private and public sectors
- define what is meant by **unlimited liability** and **limited liability**
- recognize different types of business organization according to how they are controlled, owned and financed
- distinguish between a **sole trader**, **partnership** and **joint stock company** and list their advantages and disadvantages
- describe and evaluate the effects of changes in the structure of business organizations
- explain what is meant by a **multinational** and evaluate the costs and benefits to an economy hosting a multinational
- describe the role of a **public corporation** and how public corporations are controlled

Section I Why are there different types of business organization?

To produce goods and services, the resources of land, labour and capital are needed. These resources on their own, however, will not satisfy our wants. For example, if we want football boots, it is no use just buying leather and hiring workers and land. Something else is needed before these resources can be used to produce boots. Resources need to be organized, and decisions need to be taken in order to manage or control the resources from day to day.

The person who makes these decisions and owns a business is called the **entrepreneur** (see Chapter 2).

It is the job of the entrepreneur to organize resources in a business organization or **firm**. In a modern economy an entrepreneur can choose many different types of business. Each type allows the entrepreneur to organize, manage, control the business and raise money in a different way. A small firm with just one owner will be different in the way it is controlled and financed than a large firm where there may be many thousands of owners.

Section 2 Types of firm

In a mixed economy, firms can be grouped into three main types of business organization according to how they are owned, controlled and financed. **Public corporations** run nationalized industries, are accountable to government and are therefore part of the public sector in an economy.

Private sector firms are owned by individuals and can range in size from small businesses known as **sole traders** owned and run by a single person, to very large **joint stock companies** owned by many thousands of people.

Co-operatives are owned and run by a group of people for their mutual benefit. For example, a retail co-operative is owned by its customers, and a worker co-operative by the people who work in the organization.

Starting a business

If we trace the growth of a business from a small one-person firm to a large company it will be possible to see the different types of business organization there are and the reasons for their existence.

Steve Oak is an unemployed school leaver in the UK. Stevey is good at carpentry and would like to set up a do-it-yourself (DIY) shop, selling materials and equipment for building and decorating, as well as doing carpentry jobs. Before starting up his business, Steve, like all entrepreneurs, must ask himself three questions. The answers to these questions will help to decide which type of business is best for him.

Question 1 Will I have enough money?

Starting a business can be very costly. The money put into a business is called **capital**, because it is often used to buy capital goods, such as machinery and buildings. Money spent on capital goods is known as **fixed capital**, while **working capital** is the money used to run a business from day to day, that is, money used to pay wages, electricity bills, telephone bills, heating and so on.

Fixed capital

Working capital

Some businesses need more capital than others. Steve Oak must ask himself if he has enough money to set up and run his business himself, in which case the type of business is called a **sole trader**.

If Steve Oak does not have enough money he may have to find other people who would like to share in the ownership of the business with him. These people have to pay money into the business in order to share in its ownership. This type of business is known as a **partnership**.

If still more money is needed, Steve Oak can turn his business into a **joint stock company** or **limited company**, with many tens or even thousands of owners, all paying in order to join.

Question 2 Can I manage the business alone?

If Steve is to start up his DIY business and undertake carpentry jobs he must ask himself if he can manage all of this alone, or will he need to take on partners? Steve is skilled in carpentry only, so this means there are many building jobs he might have to turn down because the work involves other things. However, if Steve was to take on partners with different skills, for example bricklayers, electricians and plasterers, then Steve's business would be able to do many more jobs than just carpentry work alone. All entrepreneurs, including Steve, must decide upon whether or not they can manage alone before choosing the sort of business they are going to start.

Question 3 Will I risk everything I own?

The owner of a business is entitled to a share of any profits made. However, the owner also has the responsibility of finding money to pay for the firm's debts if the business should fail. This financial responsibility is called the **owner's liability**.

Steve must decide before starting up his business if he is willing to risk all his savings and possessions on the venture. The answer to this question will influence the type of business chosen, because some businesses are more risky than others.

Some business owners have what is called **unlimited liability**. This means that if a business is not successful and goes bankrupt, the owner, or owners, will have to pay all the business debts and meet any other obligations to third parties, such as customers, employees, other firms or members of the public. The owners may have to sell all their possessions, like their houses, cars, furniture, and even clothing to pay off their business debts.

However, some business owners may have **limited liability**. This means that if a business goes bankrupt the owners would only lose the amount of money they have put into the business. They will not have to sell their own possessions to pay the company debts. Similarly, it will be the business organization and not the owners that will be liable for any injury caused to a third party as a result of the activities of the business, for example, if a customer or employee slips on a wet floor in the place of business and seeks compensation for their injury. In these ways, having limited liability reduces the risk of running a business and therefore helps to encourage entrepreneurship and new business start-ups in an economy.

Section 3 The sole trader

Ownership and control

Steve Oak decides he has enough money to start up on his own and he will be able to manage the DIY and carpentry business without help. He also decides that it is worth risking everything he has, because as his friends keep saying 'Nothing ventured means nothing gained'. Steve's DIY business, like many other small businesses such as newsagents and grocers, is a one-person business or sole trader. A sole trader may have more than one employee but it is always owned and controlled by only one person.

The sole trader is the oldest and most popular type of business in the world. There are many more sole traders than any other type of business . In fact, many very large and successful businesses started life as sole traders.

Exercise 1 The sole trader

Read the following article and list the advantages and disadvantages of being a one person business.

LOCAL TIMES

OAK DIY OPENS IN HIGH STREET

Steven Oak is now the proud owner of the Oak DIY shop in the High Street. We asked Steve why he decided to open his own shop.

'I was unemployed for a long time,' explained Steve. 'By running my own business I am ensured a job and I get any profits. But to do this I have to work every hour I can and run the business on my own.' Starting your own business is expensive as Steve soon discovered. 'I used most of my savings to get the company off the ground, and my bank manager supplied me with a loan. What with the rent of the shop space, hire of machinery, insurance payments, heating and lighting bills I have to make at least £600 a month from the shop before I can break even. And of course if I can't I am out of work again and left holding all the debts.'

With a prime location near to the car-park in the town centre, Steve may be able to look forward to a lot of customers and an expanding business. 'I hope so,' said Steve. 'I can even give other people jobs to do, but I will still be the boss. My own boss. I don't have to answer to anyone. Not bad is it?'

Oak DIY opens at 10 am next Monday with special first week price reductions on many of the tools, paints, wallpaper and other decorations the shop offers. If you cannot get what you want, Steve will be willing to order your requirements. Shoppers can look forward to a personal and friendly atmosphere in the shop. Most of the locals already know Steve and he promises that he will put the kettle on at regular intervals throughout the day for the benefit of callers.

Advantages of the sole trader

1 The sole trader business is a very personal one

The owner of the business will have personal contact with customers and staff. S/he will be able to find out quickly what people want and then change what the shop sells to suit what customers wish to buy. Furthermore, because anybody dealing with the firm deals with the owner personally this can encourage customers to be loyal to the business.

2 The sole trader is his/her own boss

Because s/he is the only owner of a business, the sole trader does not have to ask anyone's permission before making a decision. This means they can make decisions quickly. They can decide whether or not to expand the business, what jobs to do and when, who to employ, etc.

3 The sole trader receives all the profits

Being your own boss and not having to share the profits are important advantages to most people and this, in part, explains why the sole trader type of business is so popular.

4 It is easy to set up a sole trader business

Sole traders need very little capital to start up with, so it is fairly easy for one person to set up a business alone.

There are also very few legal formalities involved in starting up as a sole trader. Other larger types of business need a lot more capital and legal work before they can begin trading.

Disadvantages of the sole trader

1 The sole trader has unlimited liability

Unlimited liability means that the sole trader is liable to lose everything s/he has in order to pay off debts in the event of bankruptcy.

Unlimited liability exists because, in the eyes of the law, the sole trader business and its owner are seen as the same. So if the business owes money its owner must pay.

2 The sole trader has full responsibility

As the sole owner of a business, the sole trader must take all of the decisions. Most people, however, are not good at everything, but sole traders still need to be able to manage the business, do the book-keeping, advertising, buying and selling, and many other things. This means that often the sole trader may work long hours and if they are ill there is no one to take over the running of the business.

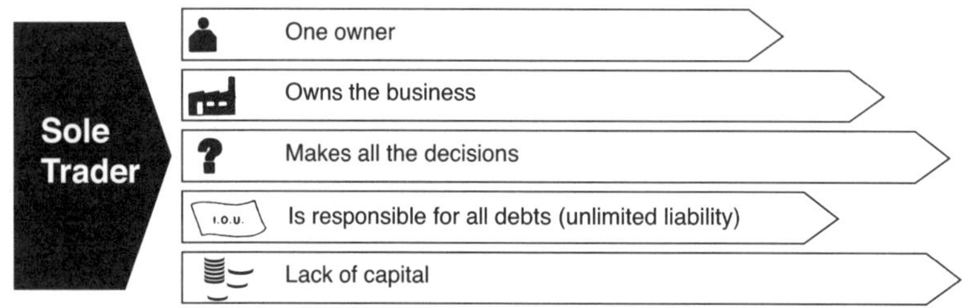

3 Sole traders lack capital

If Steve's DIY business is successful he may wish to make his business bigger and expand into a second shop. The problem is that enlarging a business requires more money and sole traders like Steve often do not have this extra money.

Steve could use some of his profits to help pay for a second shop but this would leave himself with very little. Bank loans are expensive and banks are reluctant to lend money to sole traders because they often cannot afford to repay the loan.

Section 4 Partnerships

Ownership and control

A sole trader may find that more money is needed to expand the business and that someone else is needed to help run the firm. Partnerships can be formed with little formality. Partnerships are common particularly amongst solicitors, doctors, veterinary surgeons and other professional occupations.

In law, a partnership is an agreement or declaration between individuals who agree to jointly own and run an enterprise, contribute to it by combining their money and knowledge, and share in its profits.

Let us assume that Steve's DIY and carpentry business is doing well and Steve decides to take on two partners Jan and Bill. Three people, Steve, Jan and Bill, now own the business, control it and share the profit together. The reasons why Steve decided to share his business are explained by the advantages of forming a partnership.

Exercise 2 **The partnership**

Read the article below and list the advantages and disadvantages of forming a partnership.

OAK STARTS TO GROW

Today Steve Oak of the Oak DIY shop celebrates over one year's successful trading with the opening of a new DIY store.

So what is Steve Oak's secret of success?

'Clearly there is a market for DIY products and home improvement centres,' he said. 'I offer a friendly and personal service that my larger competitors seem to lack. As a result people just come back again and again. I always help them out with their DIY problems if I can.'

Using his own money Steve Oak acquired the premises and equipped the existing store. Banks were unwilling to lend him money for the enterprise because of the obvious risks such an outlet faces from increasing competition from established DIY retailers. With giants such as Sainsburys and W.H. Smith also expanding into the home improvements market, the fear of competition became more acute. 'The banks are still unwilling to lend I'm afraid,' explained Mr Oak, 'but luckily I have made contacts in my business dealings and have two partners now to help run and finance the business. Not only have they put up a large amount of money but they will also be able to relieve me of some of the responsibilities I've carried for over a year now. For example, Jan is a qualified accountant and can do all the bookwork, and Bill is a trained electrician who will also be looking after the new shop.'

Jan Eversham and Bill Heston are the two new partners in the Oak enterprise. Running a business poses many risks and the collapse of the firm could mean all those personally involved losing their possessions to repay debts. So why did Jan take the risk? 'It's a challenge,' she said, 'I was an accountant, but now I'm a full-time housewife and I wanted something else to keep me occupied.'

What problems, if any, do the partners think may occur?

'Well,' they explained, 'finding the money to decorate and refit the shops is proving a problem, and we had initial disagreements about how to lay out the two stores. But we're all friends really!'

Advantages of partnerships

1 Partners bring new skills and ideas to a business

Steve has taken on Jan and Bill as partners because they have skills which the business needs.

2 More partners means more money for the business

If other people want to share in the ownership and control of a business then they must pay money to do so. This money can then be used to expand the business.

3 Partners can help in decision-making

A sole trader has full responsibility for making decisions in a business, whereas in a partnership all decisions are shared.

Disadvantages of partnerships

1 Partners can disagree

The more partners there are, the more likely are disagreements. If Steve, Jan and Bill find they cannot agree on important decisions affecting the company, the business may suffer.

2 Some partners may have joint unlimited liability

Like a sole trader, **general partners** stand to lose everything they have if the business goes bankrupt or is negligent and causes injury to a third party. Furthermore, each partner can be held responsible for the actions of other partners.

However, a partnership may also have a number of **limited partners** who have limited liability. A **silent partner**, also known as a **sleeping partner**, will provide money to the business in return for a share in the ownership and profits of the business, but will not be involved in its day-to-day management and running.

Since 2002 it has been possible to form a **limited liability partnership (LLP)** in the UK whereby all the partners have limited liability. It is very similar to a **limited liability company (LLC)** in the US. The business services firm PricewaterhouseCoopers (or PwC) is the world's largest LLP.

3 Partnerships lack capital

Because there are more people in a partnership the business will have more money than a sole trader, but it is still difficult for a partnership to have more than twenty partners (with exceptions for firms of solicitors, accountants and stockbrokers). This puts a limit on the amount of money that may be brought into a business.

Very few large businesses in the world are partnerships. This is simply because it is difficult for partnerships to raise the necessary capital to expand into a large enterprise.

Other types of business organization are needed to do this. These other forms of business enterprise are known as **joint stock companies**.

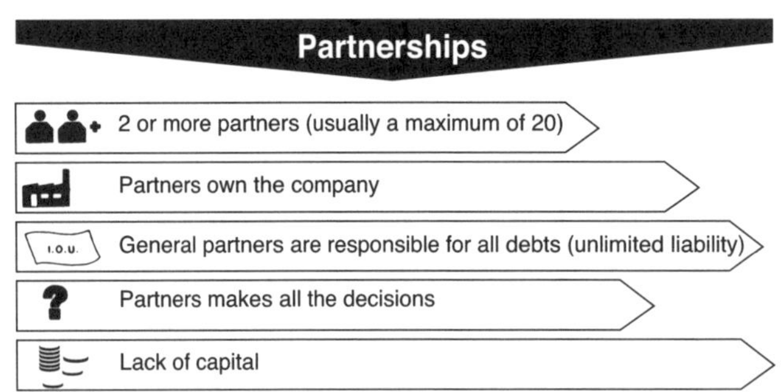

Partnerships
2 or more partners (usually a maximum of 20)
Partners own the company
I.O.U.
General partners are responsible for all debts (unlimited liability)
Partners makes all the decisions
Lack of capital

Exercise 3 Local businesses

Which of these shops are sole traders or partnerships?

Look around your local area and try to identify businesses that are:

a Sole traders

b Partnerships.

In each case try to explain why you think the type of business, and what it does, is suited to that particular form of business organization.

Section 5 Joint stock companies

Ownership and control

Joint stock companies are also known as **limited companies**. A limited company sells shares to investors in order to raise money for the business. Shareholders are the owners of the business but because in many cases there are so many of them, they will often appoint managers to run the business on their behalf.

"HE'S THE MAJORITY SHAREHOLDER!"

For example, imagine now that Oak DIY wants to raise £10 000 for expansion by selling 1000 shares at £10 each. The people who buy these shares are called **shareholders**. The more shares a person holds, the more of the company they will own and the bigger will be their share of any profits. Now suppose Oak DIY makes enough profit to pay £2 for every £10 share held. The profit paid out on each share is known as a **dividend**. A person who owns 10 shares in Oak DIY will therefore receive a total dividend of £20, while a person who owns 50 shares will receive a £100 dividend from profits.

Let's assume 250 different people have bought the shares issued by Oak DIY. All of these people are now owners of the business. However, they cannot all possibly manage the business from day to day. Such a large group of people would get in each other's way, may continually disagree on how best to run the business, and many would simply not have the expertise needed to run the business effectively.

To overcome this problem the shareholders are allowed to choose a **board of directors** to run the company on a daily basis. This is done by voting at shareholders' meetings. Each shareholder has one vote for each share they hold. The more shares a person holds, therefore, the more votes they can have. In our example, Steve, Jan and Bill, the original partners in Oak DIY, will wish to keep more shares than anyone else so that they will have more votes than any other shareholders.

This will enable them to vote for themselves to be directors if they wish, or at least give them greater power to choose the directors they want. Ideally, if Steve, Jan and Bill wanted to be directors and have control over the whole company they will need to hold over half of all the shares, leaving all the other shareholders with less than half the shares.

Any person, or group of people, who buys over 50 per cent of the shares in a company is said to have a **controlling interest** in that company. This is because they can outvote all other shareholders and therefore can control the business.

Legal status

There are two main types of limited company. A **private limited company** can only sell shares privately to people known to the existing shareholders, while a **public limited company** can sell shares publicly on the stock market. The stock market is made up of all buyers and sellers of shares (see Chapter 6). Share prices and the quantity of shares traded are determined by demand and supply like in any other free market (see Chapter 7).

In many countries, but not all, limited companies are business corporations. A **corporation** is a separate legal body from its owners. That is, a company with corporate status will have a distinct name, can own property and shares in other companies, enter into contracts, is liable to pay tax on its profits, can be sued by a third party and can in turn take third parties to court. Corporations also tend to be run and controlled day to day by managers who in most cases will not be the owners of the business.

Some abbreviations for corporations

Country	Public limited company	Private limited company or equivalent
France	S.A.	S.A.R.L.
Germany	A.G.	GmbH
Greece	A.E.	e.p.e.
Italy	S.p.A.	S.A.
India	LTD	Pvt Ltd.
Malaysia	Bhd	Sdn Bhd
Spain	S.A.	S.L.; S.L.N.E.; S.R.L.
UK	Plc	Ltd
US	Corp.; Inc.	LLC; LC; Ltd. Co.

Source: *en.wikipedia.org/wiki/Types_of_Companies*

The abbreviation S.A. after a company name normally means it is a corporation, for example, Telefónica S.A., and Air France-KLM S.A. It means anonymous company or share company in many languages. However, some countries use other abbreviations to denote corporate status, which can also have slightly different legal meanings in these countries. For example, in Greece the letters A.E. are often used, while Inc. is used in the US. You can therefore usually tell where a firm is registered as a company from the letters after its name.

Public limited companies are some of the largest and most successful firms in the world. In 2006 Exxon-Mobil Corp. was the world's largest oil company and corporation with revenues of over US $370 billion that year. In second place was Wal-Mart Stores, Inc., the largest retailer in the world. Other large corporations include Royal-Dutch Shell plc, DaimlerChrysler A.G., General Motors Corp. and Nestlé S.A.

There are more private limited companies in the world but they tend to be much smaller in size. Nevertheless, there are a number of very large privately held corporations, notably Koch Industries, Inc. and Cargill, Inc. Koch is involved in activities ranging from petroleum and chemicals, to ranching, securities and finance. Cargill's business activities include the purchase, processing and distribution of grain and other agricultural commodities.

Exercise 4 The private limited company

OAK DIY TO BECOME LIMITED COMPANY

Oak DIY, the chain of do-it-yourself stores, has just announced plans to become a Private Limited Company by selling shares in the company. This will raise capital to finance their new expansion programme. Mr Steve Oak, founder of the company, explained how allowing the company to be owned by more people can provide the money he needs to build more stores around the country.

'We simply invite people to buy share certificates in the company,' he said, 'and this allows them to become owners of the business and to share in its profits. These shareholders are also allowed to have a say in how the company should be run. Of course,' he continued, 'I would like to remain as a Director of Oak DIY, but if all the other shareholders decide they don't want me at the head of the company they can vote me out and elect other directors to run the business. Each year they can vote for directors at a special shareholders meeting.' The problem many small companies like Oak DIY face today is one of raising finance. If this is to be achieved through the sale of shares then the additional problem of finding people to buy them arises. Normally shares will be sold to family, friends and workers in the company.

We asked Steve Oak why people would wish to buy shares in his company. 'We are a growing and profitable company,' he replied, 'and the more profit we make the more shareholders receive.' This is called their dividend. Also as a Private Limited Company all shareholders would benefit from having limited liability, and so in the very unlikely event of Oak DIY closing down due to bad debts, shareholders would only lose, at the most, however much money they paid for their shares.

1 How do private limited companies like Oak DIY raise the money they need to expand their businesses?

2 What does the word 'limited' stand for in private limited company?

3 What is the name given to the people who are elected to run a private limited company?

4 Steve Oak suggests in the article that he would like to remain at the 'head of the company' to run the business from day to day. Who will decide if Steve can remain in this position, and how is this done?

5 What encourages people to buy shares in the ownership of a company?

How a private limited company raises money

Private limited companies can raise money for expansion by selling **shares** to people. A share is simply a piece of paper that states that the person who holds it has paid for part of the company and now has a share in its ownership. The value printed on the share, or its **face value**, is the price at which the company first sold the share (see Chapter 6).

Advantages of the private limited company

1 Shareholders have limited liability

This means a person who owns a company is only responsible for the repayment of any debts up to the amount of money they originally put into the company. Without limited liability people would be unwilling to buy shares because if the company went bankrupt they could end up losing a lot of money, and even their possessions, to repay large company debts.

2 Shareholders have no management worries

If shareholders in a company had to run the business, they would have to take on all the worries and responsibilities themselves. However, they can pass on this responsibility and elect directors to manage the business on their behalf. This is done by voting at an **Annual General Meeting (AGM)** of shareholders.

3 The company has a separate legal identity

In the eyes of the law a private limited company and its owners are seen as separate bodies. As a result if the company owes money, the company can be sued and taken to court, but the owners cannot. The company can be forced to pay its debts or pay compensation out of company funds, but the owners, because they have a separate legal identity, are not considered responsible.

Disadvantages of private limited companies

1 Limited companies must disclose information about themselves to the general public

In many countries limited companies are required by law to keep detailed records of their spending, revenues, profits, etc. and to publish this information so that their shareholders can read about what their company is doing.

This information is published by a company and sent to all its shareholders in the form of a set of annual accounts. These accounts give details of the profits made in the past year, total sales, the money the company owes and the people and institutions that they owe it to. Clearly it is an advantage for shareholders to have information about their company but the writing, printing and postage of such details can be very expensive. In addition, they allow competing companies to learn some of the company secrets.

2 Limited companies must hold an Annual General Meeting of shareholders each year

An AGM of shareholders must usually be held each year to allow these company owners to vote on such issues as how the company should be run, and who should run it. This is an advantage for shareholders as it allows them to give their views and reflect them in their votes. However, AGMs are not only expensive to set up but they can result in the original owners losing control over the company.

3 The original owners of the company may lose control

The vast majority of limited companies have a large number of owners, who can have a say in how the company is run and elect the directors who run it by voting at Annual General Meetings. In this way the original founders of the company may be voted out of their director positions and be replaced by newly elected directors.

4 Company profits are taxed twice

Companies will pay corporate taxes on their net income or profit because they are separate legal bodies. Profits remaining after corporate taxes have been paid are then distributed to shareholders as dividends. Shareholders will then have to pay income tax on their dividend income. However, corporate tax rates on profits and income tax rates on dividends are often lower than personal income tax rates on wages and other earnings.

5 Private limited companies cannot sell shares on the stock market

Private limited companies have to sell their shares privately to people they know, like family, friends and workers. This is a big disadvantage because it is possible to raise far more money by selling shares to the general public on the stock market (see Chapter 6). This means that these companies are often confined to being small to medium-sized firms, unable to raise vast amounts of money to expand.

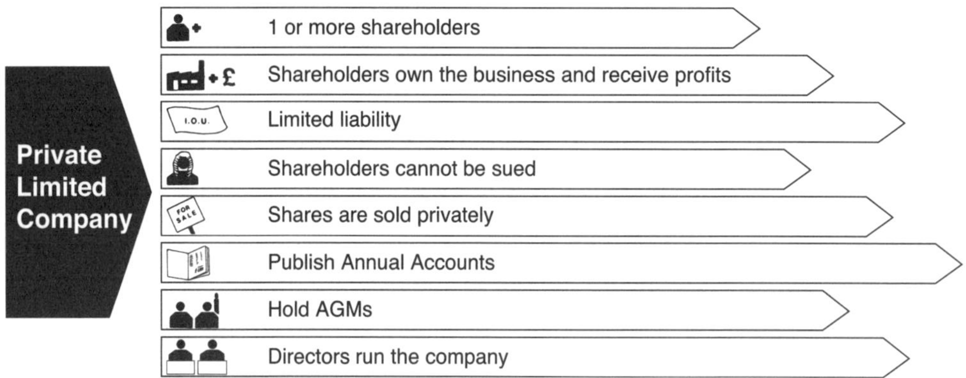

Exercise 5 The public limited company

Read the article on the next page about Oak DIY becoming a public limited company.

1. How do public limited companies like Oak plc raise finance for expansion?
2. How much money will the Oak share issue raise?
3. Why is it easier for a plc to sell shares than a private limited company?
4. What are meant by management diseconomies, and what other disadvantages can plague such a large company?
5. Why are the original owners of the plc more likely to lose their control of the company than if they were in a smaller company?

CITY TIMES

SEASONED OAK BLOSSOMS

Oak DIY, one of the country's leading do-it-yourself chain stores, has announced plans to sell shares on the Stock Exchange. The Council of the Stock Exchange revealed yesterday that the company has received a full listing which will allow it to float shares on the full stock market and become a Public Limited Company.

'Our plans are to open a chain of discount warehouse stores on a number of sites throughout the United Kingdom, and even one in France!' explained Jan Eversham, one of the original partners in Oak DIY. 'This, of course, requires a substantial injection of cash into the company, but we feel confident that sales and profits will be extremely good.'

Oak DIY, now Oak plc, was founded nine years ago by Mr Steve Oak, an unemployed carpenter from Leeds. The company first sold shares privately to friends and workers four years ago and has gone from strength to strength, with a sales turnover for last year tipping £10 million and a profit of £417,000.

The new issue of four million shares at 100 pence each will be available from next month and with dividend forecasts looking good it is likely that the shares will be snapped up quickly by many thousands of investors, hungry for gain. A major advertising campaign in national newspapers will prepare prospective shareholders for the launch of Oak plc on the full stock market. Clearly, going public by selling shares to the general public is an expensive business, but the financial rewards can be great.

The issue of who controls the large company will be discussed, and subject to vote, at the next AGM where the existing shareholders will be joined by many of the new shareholders. Mr Steve Oak, Mrs Jan Eversham and

Mr William Heston, the three original partners, are confident, however, that with their controlling interest in share ownership they can retain positions as Company Directors.

'My only fear,' explains Mrs Eversham, 'is that managerial diseconomies may arise if the company becomes too large. Good managers, who can run the various departments in the company and can work as a team, are hard to find.'

The application list for the purchase of shares will open on Thursday May 20th. Dealings in the shares are expected to start a week later.

Forming a public limited company

The UK Stock Exchange

A public limited company must have a minimum of two shareholders. Shares are normally issued for sale to the general public on the stock market. Hence the term **going public** is often used to describe a company that obtains a full or **public listing** to sell shares through a stock exchange or bourse (see Chapter 6). There are many stock exchanges throughout the world. Some notable examples include the New York Stock Exchange (NYSE) in the US, the London Stock Exchange in the UK, the Tokyo Stock Exchange in Japan and the Deutsche Börse in Frankfurt, Germany. Stock exchanges are simply other business organizations, usually public limited companies themselves, that provide facilities for the issuing, buying and selling of shares in public limited companies all over the world.

Before a limited company can offer its shares for sale through a stock exchange the governing body of the exchange will investigate the company to ensure that it is a trustworthy and well-run business, and meets agreed standards of practice and size. If a company meets these requirements then it will be allowed to sell its shares through the exchange. The public listing and sale of new shares in a company is sometimes called a **flotation**.

Advantages of the public limited company

The public limited company business structure has all the same advantages of the private limited company but some important additional features.

1 Public limited companies can sell shares publicly

A company that is able to sell its shares to members of the public and other companies through a stock exchange can potentially raise far more money to finance its business operations than any other type of business organization.

2 Public limited companies can publicly advertise their shares

A public limited company is able to advertise the sale of its shares in newspapers and magazines or even on television. This helps to create interest in the sale and can attract many more investors than might otherwise be the case.

Disadvantages of the public limited company

The public limited company business structure shares many of the same disadvantages as the private limited company but, because of their size and the way they raise finance through sales of shares to the public and other companies, they can suffer additional problems.

1 It can be expensive to form a public limited company

Many legal documents and checks are required before a firm can 'go public'. For example, a **prospectus** must be published either as a booklet or in a newspaper, informing would-be shareholders about the business, its activities and earnings, the current directors, and the number and price of the shares being issued.

2 The divorce of ownership from control

Shareholders have the right to attend Annual General Meetings to vote on company policy and to elect directors to manage the company from day to day. However, many public limited companies have many thousands of shareholders, many of whom will be unable or unwilling to attend such meetings. This may be especially true of individual shareholders who only hold a limited number of shares, and therefore have limited voting power. Only a handful of shareholders, often the largest ones, may actually use their votes and so directors, once elected, can often act very much on their own from day to day and may pursue business strategies that are in their interests far more than in the interests of their shareholders. For this reason the majority of shareholders tend to lose control of the companies they own. This is known as the divorce of ownership from control.

Another problem for the small shareholder is the fact that large financial institutions, including major banks, insurance companies and pension fund operators, have substantial shareholdings in many other companies and may often have controlling interests in some companies (see Chapter 6). As such they can easily outvote small shareholders on company policy and who should be on the board of directors.

3 Management diseconomies

Some companies may become so large that they become difficult to manage effectively. There may be communication problems between different parts of the business, and between different layers of management. Decision-making can be slow and disagreements between managers and owners can occur (see Chapter 12).

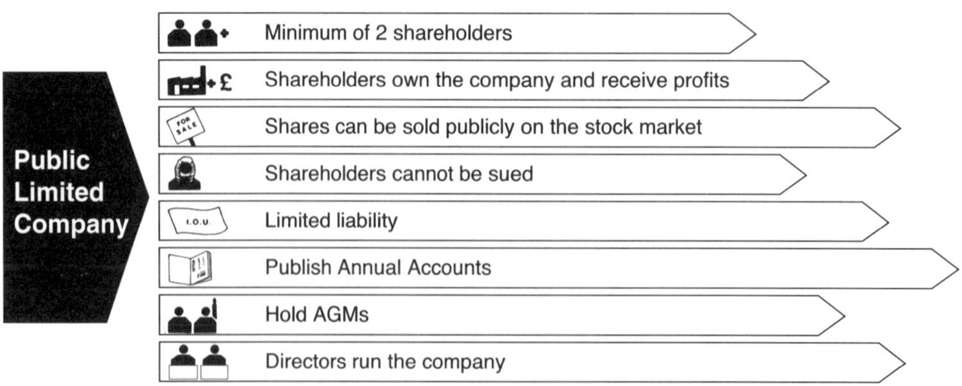

Exercise 6 Types of business organization

Below is a list of advantages and disadvantages of the sole trader enterprise.

Advantages for sole trader	Disadvantages for sole trader
1 Easy to set up the business 2 Freedom of being your own boss 3 Owner gets all profits	1 Unlimited liability 2 Owner has full responsibility 3 No one else to run the business if the owner is ill 4 Long hours of work 5 Lack of capital

Copy the above table and complete for the advantages and disadvantages of:

a partnerships **b** private limited companies **c** public limited companies

Section 6 Co-operatives

Types of co-operative

Co-operatives are business organizations that are owned and controlled by a group of people, to undertake an economic activity to their mutual benefit. That is, a co-operative provides benefits for its members. Anyone can usually become a member and, in turn, each member of a co-operative has an equal share in the ownership and control of the organization, regardless of how much money they may have invested in the business. That is, co-operatives operate a strict policy of one member, one vote.

There are two main types of co-operative. **Worker co-operatives** are owned and controlled by their workers. **Consumer co-operatives** are retail enterprises owned and controlled by their customers. They can aim to make a profit or be non-profit-making organizations (see Chapter 12). Co-operatives that aim to make a profit usually return any profit to their members either in the form of a dividend on their shareholdings, or as bonuses, or as lower prices in retail co-operatives.

Other common types of co-operative include:

- **Housing co-operatives** whereby residents share in the ownership or have occupancy rights in the property they live in together, such as an apartment block
- **Building co-operatives** in which people pool their resources, usually using their own labour, to build houses they can live in
- **Utility co-operatives** are a type of consumer co-operative set up by their customers to provide members usually in remote areas with utilities such as electric power
- **Farming co-operatives** are groups of farm owners who co-operate to grow, market and sell crops and farm animals. They are popular forms of business enterprise in many developing and less developed countries
- **Credit unions** and **co-operative savings banks** provide financial and banking services to their members. Many developed particularly in Europe to help lend money to farming co-operatives

It is estimated that over 800 million people worldwide are members of a co-operative and they provide some 100 million jobs.

Co-operatives run travel services and banks

Worker co-operatives

These are organizations owned by their workers, such as in a farming co-operative. They pool their money to buy equipment and share equally in decision-making and any business profits.

Worker co-operatives can employ people who are not members. Membership is not compulsory, but only employees can become members.

Worker co-operatives are relatively commonplace in Europe, especially in Italy, Spain and many Eastern European countries such as Poland. One of the largest and most successful is the Mondragón Co-operative Corporation in the Basque country of Spain. It consists of a group of manufacturing and retail companies across Spain and overseas.

Advantages of worker co-operatives

1. Worker co-operatives are popular with workers because they themselves are in charge and everyone has an equal say. They are also likely to work harder because they can take part in making decisions about how to run the business.
2. The workers receive the profits they make. Profits are paid out as dividends either on the basis of each worker getting an equal share, or according to how much money they put into the enterprise.

Disadvantages of worker co-operatives

1. One of the main reasons why worker co-operatives may not be successful is because they find it difficult to raise money. Worker co-operatives must rely on borrowing from banks, workers and local councils. This lack of capital means that worker co-operatives cannot expand easily and so tend to remain small businesses.
2. Worker co-operatives may be badly run simply because the workers making the decisions may have little business experience or entrepreneurial ability.

Consumer co-operatives

These are retailing businesses run for the benefit of their customers. The first retail co-operative society was formed in the UK in 1844 when a group of workers fed up with low pay and high food prices joined together to buy food direct from wholesalers. Because they were able to buy food in bulk, suppliers would often give them discounts. Today, any profits made in retail co-operatives are given back to their consumers as dividends or by keeping prices low.

The world's largest consumer co-operative is United Co-operatives in the UK, which has a variety of retail and financial services. It is owned in part by other co-operatives as well as by members. Japan also has well-developed consumer co-operatives with over 14 million members.

The principles of modern consumer co-operatives are unchanged since they were first formed:

- modern co-operatives are owned by their members
- any person can become a member by buying a share for as little as £1
- members elect a board of directors to run the co-operative
- each member is allowed one vote regardless of the number of shares they hold
- profits are shared between members

Today many of the smaller co-operative shops have closed because of competition with large supermarkets. To compete a number of co-operatives have formed into large superstores selling a wide variety of goods and services, normally located on large sites outside of town centres.

The co-operative movement has also successfully expanded into other retail activities such as banking, insurance, travel agents, funeral direction and bakeries.

Worker co-operatives	Retail co-operatives
Workers own all the shares Managed by its workers Workers have limited liability Workers share the profits	Owned by its members Managers run the organization Owners have limited liability Members receive profits

Exercise 7 Ownership, control and finance

Below is a table listing how different types of business are owned, controlled, raise finance and distribute their profits. Copy and complete the table by filling in the blank spaces. If you cannot remember all the details then read again sections 3 to 6.

	Types of business enterprise					
	Sole trader	Partnership	Private limited company	Public limited company	Worker co-op	Consumer co-op
Ownership						Owned by customers and shareholders
Control	Run by the owner					
Sources of finance	Own savings Bank loans			Sell shares		
Distribution of profits						Profits given to customers as stamps or lower prices

Section 7 Multinationals

A **multinational company** or **corporation** is a firm that operates in more than one country, although its headquarters may be in one particular country. These companies are some of the largest firms in the world, often selling billions of dollars worth of goods and services, and employing many thousands of workers around the globe.

The first multinational on the moon?

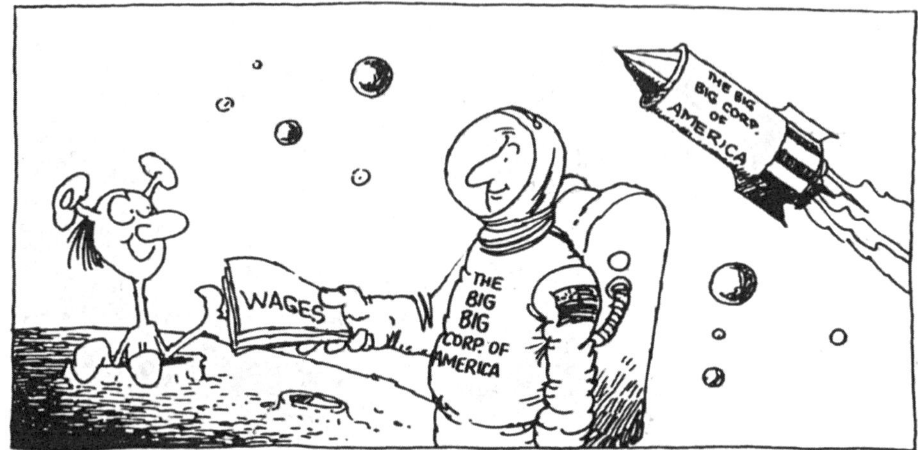

Many of the biggest multinationals in the world are US-owned corporations with interests in oil exploration and refining, and motor vehicle production. The largest by revenue in 2005/06 was ExxonMobil with business operations in almost 200 countries. The total market value of shares traded in the company was US$372 billion, the highest in the world, and it was also the most profitable company in the world, earning £36 billion.

World's ten largest multinationals by revenue, 2005/06

Company name	Principal activities	Total revenue (US$ billions)	Employees	Shares traded on the following stock exchanges
ExxonMobil Corp.	Oil and gas	$339.9	88,300	United States (NYSE)
Wal-Mart Stores, Inc.	Retailing	$315.6	1,500,000	United States (NYSE)
Royal Dutch Shell plc	Oil and gas	$306.7	112,000	Netherlands, UK, United States (NYSE)
BP	Oil and gas	$255.2	103,700	UK, United States (NYSE)
Chevron Corp.	Oil and gas	$198.2	61,533	United States (NYSE)
DaimlerChrysler AG	Motor vehicles	$193.0	362,063	Germany, United States, Singapore, Canada, Argentina, Netherlands, France, Austria, Switzerland, UK
General Motors Corp.	Motor vehicles	$192.6	323,000	United States (NYSE) and 32 other countries
Toyota Motor Corp.	Motor vehicles	$188.0	264,410	Japan, United States (NYSE)
ConocoPhillips	Oil and gas	$183.3	39,000	United States (NYSE)
Ford Motor Co.	Motor vehicles	$177.0	327,531	United States (NYSE

Of the world's largest 150 economic entities in 2005 in terms of annual income, 95 were corporations and just 55 were countries. Wal-Mart, BP, Exxon Mobil and Royal Dutch/Shell Group all ranked in the 25 largest entities in the world, above countries including Indonesia, Saudi Arabia, Norway, Denmark, Poland, South Africa and Greece. Multinationals are also responsible for around two thirds of total world trade and entire world industries can be dominated by a handful of these global giants (see also Chapter 8).

ExxonMobil and Wal-Mart – the largest publicity traded multinational companies in the world

Exercise 8 Multinationals

The following chart lists a number of multinational companies. Try to find out the country they originate from and what they produce to complete the table. The first one has been completed for you.

Company	Country of origin	Main activities/products
Sony	Japan	Electronics
Tesco		
Siemens		
BAE Systems		
Ferrovial		
Microsoft		
Total		
Procter & Gamble		
Matsushita		
Peugeot Citroën		
Nokia		

Governments will often compete against each other to try to get multinational companies to locate a plant in their countries because:

- They provide jobs.
- They bring business knowledge, skills and technology with them.
- They may pay taxes which boost government revenues.
- They bring money to the country by selling goods overseas.

Advantages of being a multinational

1 Multinational companies are able to sell far more than any other type of company

The ability to set up factories to produce goods in many different countries increases the number of potential consumers of the company's products.

2 Multinational companies can avoid transport costs

A company that sold goods all over the world would find that it had to pay many transport costs. By producing goods in different countries and selling them in those countries a multinational can reduce its transport costs. It can also locate its factories near to the raw materials it needs.

3 Multinationals can take advantage of different wage levels in different countries

By locating in less developed countries a multinational can often take advantage of lower wage costs than they would pay in developed countries where wages and living costs tend to be much higher.

4 Multinationals can achieve great economies of scale

By having massive production lines and producing millions of goods, multinationals are often able to lower the average cost of producing each good below the average costs faced by companies making fewer goods (see Chapter 13).

5 Multinationals have less chance of going bankrupt than smaller companies

Multinationals tend to produce a wide variety of goods so that if demand for one product falls they have other products they can fall back on. Similarly, selling to a large number of countries also reduces the risk of one particular country reducing its demand for the products of the multinational company. These are known as risk-bearing economies of scale (see Chapter 12).

6 Multinationals can carry out a lot of research and development

In order to improve old products and develop new ones to stay ahead of competing firms, multinationals may spend large amounts of money on research and development.

What price multinationals?

Multinationals are big powerful companies employing many people and earning a lot of money. Often their location is welcomed by governments around the world because of the benefits of employment, new technologies and wealth they bring to a country. However, there can be disadvantages for countries who play host to multinationals.

1 Multinationals move their factories to wherever it is profitable to produce

Multinational companies can move their factories from one country to another to maximize their profits. For example, if taxes on profits are higher in the UK than in Korea, a company might be able to make more profit by closing its UK factory, causing thousands to be unemployed, and opening a new plant in Korea. This means that workers in multinational companies may have little control over their jobs.

Because many countries have high unemployment, governments in these countries do not want multinationals to close their factories in their nations. These governments may offer incentives, such as help in the building of factories and lower taxes on profits to encourage multinationals to stay. In fact, different governments often compete with each other over multinationals and this allows such companies to force competing countries to give them more and more favourable treatment.

2 Multinationals may switch their profits between countries

Often multinationals can avoid paying any taxes to their host nation. This may happen in a less developed country because that country lacks the ability to collect taxes because of a poor tax service and legal framework. Multinationals may also transfer or switch their profits from countries with high taxes to countries with low taxes.

3 They may force competing firms out of business

The sheer size of multinationals and their great wealth may allow them to force smaller firms in their host country to go out of business. If they cause other companies to shut down, unemployment will rise.

4 Some multinationals may exploit workers

Many multinationals locate in countries where labour is cheap. By locating in less developed countries they are able to keep their wage costs low by paying workers far less for doing the same, or even more work, than a worker in a developed country. Health and safety standards may also be lower in less developed countries and employment laws weaker.

5 Some multinationals may interfere in the government of a country

Some commentators have suggested that some large powerful multinational companies have used subversive and illegal activities to try to influence a government of a country, to promote and protect their own interests.

Section 8 Public sector organizations

Public sector organizations are those owned or controlled by government. There are four main types of government organization.

Central government

Central government is responsible for making decisions on political, economic and other issues of national importance. For example, these can include matters of national security and defence, levels of interest rates and taxes, laws and regulations, education, and building hospitals and major roads. Responsibility for analysing these issues, making decisions and implementing actions is usually given to different government Departments or Ministries, or their agencies, for example, the Ministry of Defence, the Department of Social Security and the Ministry of Finance. Names and responsibilities will vary by country. Civil servants are employed in these bodies.

The main decision-making body in central government are government ministers. The Prime Minister or equivalent, as the head of government, appoints each minister to take responsibility for the activities of a particular department or ministry.

Local government

Local government organizations will often be given responsibilities by central government to implement its national policies at the regional, local or municipal level. However, they will also usually have the responsibility to make decisions on economic and other issues of local importance, such as the maintenance of local roads and parking enforcement, planning issues for new housing and retail developments, refuse collection and running parks and local leisure facilities such as libraries and swimming baths.

Government agencies

These are non-elected organizations given the responsibility for the oversight and administration of specific government functions, such as an intelligence agency or local health services. They are normally accountable to central government departments.

Public corporations

Public corporations include government-owned companies and trusts.

Postal services are provided by public corporations in a number of countries

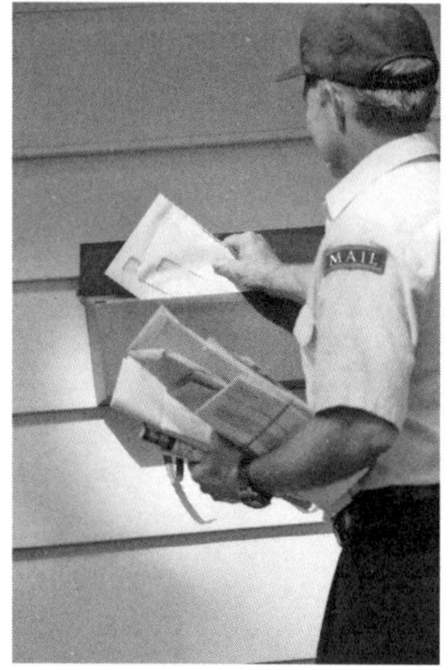

Most **public corporations** are responsible for the day-to-day running of businesses, owned and controlled by either central government or local government, to provide or sell goods and services to consumers. For example, the US government owns Amtrak, a train operator, and the United States Postal Service. The Post Office in the UK is also a public corporation and, until 1997, the UK government also controlled British Railways.

In many countries, public corporations have in the past, or still do, provide public utilities such as electricity and water supplies, bus and train services, and may run entire industries taken into government ownership because they were important for national security or could make many people unemployed if they were run by the private sector and went out of business. For example, in the past UK public corporations ran coal mines, the steel industry and even British Airways. Entire industries owned and controlled by government are called **nationalized industries** (see Chapter 14).

A public corporation may be run to make a profit, or it may resemble a not-for-profit organization as it has no need to pay dividends to shareholders. For example, the British Broadcasting Corporation (BBC) is a UK public corporation that does not aim to make a profit. It is a trust set up to provide television and radio broadcasting services. It is financed from an annual licence fee paid by all TV owners, and the money it makes from the sale of its programmes. The BBC has its own board of directors, but is answerable for its actions to the Minister for the Arts. Other examples include the British Waterways Board responsible for maintaining inland rivers and canals, and the Civil Aviation Authority.

Similarly, a number of local health trusts have been set up to run public hospitals and provide healthcare services locally in the UK. As trusts they do not seek to make a profit but aim to run local health services effectively on behalf of government, but free from its day-to-day control. However, they too are ultimately accountable to the Minister for Health.

A public corporation may also run the central bank in an economy. For example, the Bank of England in the UK is a public corporation (see Chapter 6).

Key features of public corporations

Ownership and control	• a Board of Directors runs a public corporation • Government establishes policy, and ensures they perform their funcv-tions properly • the relevant Government Minister can influence the choice of a corporation's Board and Chairperson. If serious problems arise, the Minister is questioned in Parliament, and is ultimately responsible • Parliamentary Select Committees and Consultative Committees may be set up to monitor and investigate any irregularities or complaints about public corporations
Legal status	• has a legal identity separate from its Board of Directors and from government
Finance	• much of their financing comes from central government, from taxes or grants • those that do make a profit may be self-financing and may be allowed by government to plough these profits back into improving services • alternatively, any profits may be used by central or local government to finance other public services or to reduce taxes

Public Corporations

- Government ownership
- Government receives any profits
- Government is responsible for debts
- Corporation can be sued. Government cannot be sued
- Corporation is accountable to a government minister
- Board of directors can be chosen by a government minister

Because of a number of problems associated with government ownership and control, some governments have privatized many of their business operations (see Chapter 14).

Write definitions for the following terms:

Fixed capital	**Face value**
Working capital	**Shareholders**
Unlimited liability	**Dividends**
Limited liability	**Board of Directors**
Sole trader	**Controlling interest**
Partnership	**AGM**
General partnership	**Flotation**
Limited partnership	**Public listing**
Sleeping partner	**Prospectus**
Joint stock company	**Consumer co-operative**
Private limited company	**Worker co-operative**
Corporation	**Multinational**
Shares	**Public corporation**

Now go back to the chapter and check your understanding of these terms.

Some useful web-based resources on types of business organizations:

- Fortune magazine on-line *money.cnn.com/magazines/fortune/global500*
- International Co-operative Alliance *www.coop.org/members/index.html*
- Resource list *students.shu.ac.uk/lits/guides/subjectguides/om/compinternet.html*
- UK Co-operative Enterprises *www.cooperatives-uk.coop/live/welcome.asp*
- *en.wikipedia.org/wiki/Corporation*

Chapter 5

Trade Unions

Aims

At the end of this chapter you should be able to:

- describe trade unions and their functions in an economy
- distinguish between different types of trade union
- describe how trade unions are organized
- understand the role of collective bargaining
- analyse why industrial disputes occur and how they are settled

Section I

What is a trade union?

Many workers belong to labour unions or **trade unions**. Trade unions exist primarily to promote and protect the interests of their members with the purpose of improving their wages and working conditions. In return, members will often pay a small fee to belong to a union.

Trade unions first developed in countries such as the UK during the industrial revolution in the eighteenth and nineteenth centuries with the development of factories and mass production using machinery. During this time the structure of the UK and other western economies changed rapidly from ones based on farming and craft industries, to industrialized economies in which manufacturing industries produced most of the total output and provided most of the jobs. Work in factories was often poorly paid and undertaken in appalling conditions. Workers began to organize themselves into unions to challenge the owners of factories to improve their conditions.

Exercise 1 Why I'm part of the Union!

The following articles were taken from the UK Transport and General Workers Union (T&G) website, *www.tgwu.org.uk*.

Pirelli Tyres workers vote to strike over pay

Workers at Pirelli Tyres have today voted overwhelmingly in favour of industrial action in a dispute over pay, the Transport and General Workers' Union said. More than 900 workers were balloted after rejecting the company's final pay offer of 2.2%, and union shop stewards will be meeting this week to decide what action to take.

1.9.2006

Pensions are under threat

All sectors are campaigning to protect final salary schemes which are being attacked by employers in many industries. Indeed, the TUC has described the current threat to pensions as the first serious attempt to cut wages and conditions since World War II. In addition the T&G is calling on the government to:

- Raise the basic state pension from £84.25 to at least £114 a week
- Restore the link between pensions and earnings
- Pay the full state pension equally to all men and women

Unions condemn lack of company consultation

Trade unions who met with TNT in The Hague yesterday condemned the company for refusing to begin proper negotiations on the future of the 36,000 workers of its soon to be sold logistics division.

26.7.2006

Training Courses

Through the T&G stewards, health and safety (H&S) representatives, branch officials and active members can benefit from an extensive range of training courses. These include

- Bargaining issues and negotiating skills
- Company information and accounts
- Human resource management
- New technology and change at work
- The law at work
- Communication and tutoring skills
- Trade unionists and the environment
- Organization and recruitment

The T&G Eastbourne Centre offers premium holiday accommodation to members looking for reduced rate holidays and short breaks. Convalescent patients can enjoy up to two weeks' free accommodation, subject to conditions. In addition, it boasts professional, state-of-the-art conferencing and seminar facilities.

1. From the above articles what do you think are the aims of trade unions?
2. What possible benefits or problems could arise in a firm where trade union membership among their workforce is high?
3. Would you join a trade union? What are the possible costs and benefits of membership?

The trade union movement worldwide has also helped fight and bring to an end child labour in many countries, improved worker safety, increased wages for both union and non-unionized workers, reduced hours of work, and improved education and other benefits to many poor and working families.

The functions of trade unions

Trade unions have a number of aims regarding the welfare of their members. These include:

- defending their employee rights and jobs
- securing improvements in their working conditions, including hours of work and health and safety at work
- improving their pay and other benefits, including holiday entitlements
- improving sick pay, pensions and industrial injury benefits
- encouraging firms to increase worker participation in business decision-making
- developing and protecting the skills of union members

Before trade unions existed, a worker had to negotiate on his or her own for increased pay and better working conditions with an employer. With few rights, a worker could face being sacked. Trade unions, however, can negotiate with, and put pressure on, employers on behalf of all their members to secure these aims. Trade unions helped redress the balance of power employers had over their workforces.

However, in some countries, unions may not have the legal right to represent workers, or this right may not be recognized by some employers and governments. In some countries, unions are even outlawed and union officials can be jailed.

In other countries unions are closely aligned with political parties and use their power to secure social policies and laws that are favourable to their members or to workers in general.

In addition, many trade unions offer their members education and training to improve their skills, and provide their members with recreational amenities including social clubs. Unions may also support the incomes of members who are on strike (see section 3).

Types of trade union

Trade unions are often grouped into four main types.

1. **General unions** represent workers from many different occupations and industries. For example, Amicus in the UK represents all sorts of clerical, manufacturing, transport and commercial workers in both the public and private sector.
2. **Industrial unions** represent workers in the same industry, e.g., the Turkish Union of Defence Workers (TÜRK HARB-İŞ), National Union of Mineworkers in South Africa (NUM) and the Overseas Telecommunications Services Employees Association of Mauritius (OTSEA).
3. **Craft unions** are often small and relatively few in number today. They usually represent workers with the same skills across several industries, such as the Union of Operators and Technicians in Cinema and Video Projection in Spain and the United Brotherhood of Carpenters and Joiners of America.
4. **Non-manual unions** and **professional associations**, sometimes called white-collar unions, represent workers in non-industrial and professional occupations, such as the Association of Iranian Journalists (AOIJ), All India Bank Officer Association (AIBOC), German Police Union (GDL) and the National Union of Teachers (NUT) in the UK.

Section 2 How trade unions are organized

The structure of a trade union

A union will consist of its members from different workplaces who belong to the union and full-time officials who are employed by the union at all levels in the organization to run and manage the union. Typically a union will be organized as follows:

General Secretary	The head of a union. The person who takes on this role will normally be elected by members
National Executive	This is the management tier of the union with executive members elected by union members to run the union nationally. It will decide union policy and strategy, consider and respond to government legislation that may affect members' interests, and be responsible for union finances
District committee	Branches can belong to a district or regional committee of elected union officials to run the union and look after union affairs in a region
Branch	All members in a local area will be part of a local branch and can attend branch meetings to discuss union business and issues that affect workers in different workplaces
Shop stewards	Employees who, in addition to their normal job, also represent union members in their workplace, help with any issues they have and carry out day-to-day tasks on behalf of the union
Members	Employees who belong to the union

Each year a union will usually hold an Annual General Meeting or Annual Congress where delegated members and shop stewards from different workplaces can attend to discuss common issues with the union **National Executive** and vote on union policies.

A meeting of the Trade Union Congress in the UK

Individual unions may also unite with, or affiliate to, a national union organization – a trade union congress or federation – which provides co-ordination and national representation for the union movement. These organizations can speak up on behalf of unions and their members to powerful employer associations, the media, and national and international governments to ensure union members' interests are taken into account. Examples include the Trades Union Congress in the UK (*www.tuc.org.uk*), the Malaysian Trade Union Congress (*www.mtuc.org.my*), the Indian National Trade Union Congress (*www.members.rediff.com/intuc*), and the Canadian Labour Congress (*canadianlabour.ca*).

International co-operation

National and regional trade unions representing workers in specific industries or occupations can also join global union federations, such as the International Transport Workers' Federation Union and the International Federation of Journalists. They can also join together to co-operate in pan-regional labour organizations such as the European Trade Union Confederation (ETUC), the International Confederation of Arab Trade Unions (ICATU) and the Organization of African Trade Union Unity (OATUU).

The largest organization of trade union members in the world is the International Confederation of Free Trade Unions (*www.ictfu.org*). In 2006 this had over 230 affiliated organizations in 150 countries and territories, with a combined membership of over 150 million. Other global trade union organizations are the World Confederation of Labour (*www.cmt-wcl.org*) and the World Federation of Trade Unions (*www.wftu.org*).

Union membership

Union membership in some countries has been rising while others have experienced falling membership. For example, between 1993 and 2003 union membership increased in Belgium, Ireland, Italy, Luxembourg, Malta, Spain, Norway and Cyprus. In contrast, union membership fell significantly in the US, Germany and the UK, and in a number of Eastern European countries including Bulgaria, Estonia and Latvia. In the US union membership fell from a peak of 22.5 million workers in 1975 to just under 16 million workers in 2005, around 12 per cent of the total US workforce.

The decline in the number and membership of unions in many western countries is often attributed to the decline in manufacturing industry and the growth of the service sector in these countries. For example, in the UK around 80 per cent of the total workforce is employed in service industries. Union membership in services tends to be lower than in manufacturing industries. Men are also more likely than women to be union members, but in some western countries the number of women union members is growing. Unions also tend to be much stronger in the public sector than the private sector. The decline in the size of the public sector in many former planned economies in Eastern Europe may help to explain falling union membership in some of these countries.

Section 3 Industrial disputes

Collective bargaining

The process of negotiating over pay and working conditions between trade unions and employers is known as **collective bargaining**. Depending on how collective bargaining is organized these negotiations can determine the pay and conditions for all workers in all firms in a particular industry in the economy, or they reach local area agreements between individual firms and their workforces.

Unions and employers will also negotiate about redundancies, pension rights, holiday entitlements, training and the introduction of new technology and working practices.

How collective bargaining is organized will largely depend on the relationship between a union and firms that employ unionized labour:

- In an **open shop** a firm can employ unionized and non-unionized labour.
- In a **closed shop** all workers in a place of work have to be union members. The closed shop is outlawed in some countries because it gave unions too much power to dictate who a firm could employ. A union could also call the entire workforce in a firm, or even an industry, out on strike. In these ways a union may act like a monopoly and restrict the supply of labour so as to force up the market wage for a job or occupation (see Chapter 8).
- Alternatively a firm may agree a **single union agreement**. This means one union can represent all the workers, whatever their occupation, in the same workplace. This is usually in return for certain commitments from the union on pay and productivity levels, and for agreeing not to take strike action. Negotiating with a single union rather than several at a time is much easier for a firm.

Why do industrial disputes occur?

Collective bargaining between trade unions and employers can sometimes fail to reach an agreement. For example, if a union demands a wage increase for its members not matched by higher productivity, then production costs will rise. Firms will either face trying to pass on higher wage costs to consumers in higher prices or the profits of the owners of the firm will be reduced. Demand for more holidays, better pensions and sick pay, and resistance to new working practices, will also tend to raise costs and could mean that a firm becomes uncompetitive. As a result a firm may try to reduce its costs by reducing its demand for labour and making some workers unemployed (see Chapter 10).

Disputes over demarcation can also arise. These occur when a union insists that its members can only carry out certain jobs and will not take on new tasks, or when a firm employs non-union members to carry out the same or similar tasks instead.

Industrial action

When negotiations fail, trade unions may take industrial action to put pressure on their employers. **Official action** means it has the backing of the union, and other unions may also take action in support. **Unofficial action** means that workers taking industrial action do not have the support of their union.

Ford car workers on strike over equal pay and skill recognition

1. **Overtime ban** – when workers refuse to work more than their normal hours
2. **Work-to-rule** – when workers comply with every rule and regulation at work in order to slow down production
3. **Go-slow** – working deliberately slowly
4. **Sit-in** – when workers refuse to leave their place of work, often in an attempt to stop a firm installing new machinery or closing down
5. **Strike** – when workers refuse to work and will often protest, or **picket**, outside their place of work to stop deliveries and non-unionized workers entering the firm

In some countries such as the UK, recent government legislation has severely weakened trade union power to take industrial action. For example, an employer can now sue a union for lost profits if industrial action is taken without a ballot of workers. Mass picketing is also unlawful. Only a handful of strikers are allowed to picket outside their workplace.

Arbitration may be necessary to settle some disputes if collective bargaining fails and industrial action is threatened or takes place. This involves employers and unions agreeing to let an independent referee help them reach an agreement. In the UK the independent Advisory Conciliation and Arbitration Service (ACAS) can help solve disputes.

Exercise 2 A tough negotiation

In groups of four, act out the following roles in an industrial dispute between an employer and a trade union. Your job is to try to find a settlement which both sides in the dispute are willing to accept. The roles in the dispute are:

Union representatives	**Employee representatives**
The shop steward	The managing director
A machine operator	The work study engineer

Union threatens action over new machinery

The Association of Metalworkers are today threatening to take industrial action if the decision to install new computer-assisted metal shaping and grinding machinery in PK Metals plc is taken without assurances on pay and redundancies. The local branch of the union has asked for a 5% wage increase for members to operate the new machinery.

'Any strike action could damage the company considerably,' explained Mr Graham Stone, managing director of PK Metals. A large overseas order has boosted the company's prospects recently and they are keen to fulfil it. Any disruption could threaten their international reputation. The management are also keen to avoid any increase in wage costs which may make them uncompetitive.

Workers are claiming that the new technology requires a higher level of skill and concentration and compensation is sought. They are also seeking management assurances that there will be no redundancies as a result of the new machines.

The two sides in the dispute have agreed to meet and negotiate today.

The Union Brief

The machine operators want a pay rise for operating more complex and demanding machinery. You also want to set an example for the future. You do not want your employer to think that every time it introduces new ways of working it can overlook its workforce. What you want is a share in the increased profits that can come from the increased output of the new machines.

You also fear that redundancies may follow as machines replace workers, and you want to limit the number of jobs lost.

You both know that the firm has recently received a large order from overseas, so you need to be careful that you do not cause the firm to lose the order. This could mean losing jobs.

Your tasks before negotiations

Before you enter negotiations write a brief report for all your union members to read, pointing out your demands and the management's position. This should include answers to questions like:

- What is your pay claim?
- Why have you made this pay claim?
- What has been the management response?
- What forms of action could the union take if necessary?
- Why are both you and the management keen to avoid a strike?

Your tasks after negotiations

Write a report highlighting the results of negotiations, that is, what agreements, if any, were reached.

If no firm agreement was reached, do you advise your members to accept or reject the management's offer? If no agreement was reached, what will the union do next?

The Employer's Brief

The work study engineer has concluded that the machines require no more effort to operate than the old ones. In fact, you feel that they ease pressure on the skilled operator. No pay rise is necessary to compensate.

As the managing director you fear that any cost reductions from the increased output from specialist machinery may be lost if workers push for higher wages. It may even allow lower-cost competitors to undercut your prices. If you are also unable to cut the number of jobs your plant will be overmanned and wage costs will be much higher than they need to be.

However, you do not want to lose the goodwill of the workforce at a critical time for the company with an overseas order to fulfil.

Your tasks before negotiation

Write an information sheet for the management team including answers to such questions as:

- What wage claim has the union asked for?
- What are the implications of accepting or rejecting this claim?
- Why you are keen to avoid a strike?
- What will be discussed with the union?

Task after negotiations

Prepare another management document to report on agreements reached and their effects on the company and the action that will be taken if negotiations break down and no firm agreement is reached.

The negotiations

The four people in the role-play should try to negotiate an agreement acceptable to both sides. If you cannot reach an agreement perhaps your tutor can join in to act as an independent commentator, or ask for the meeting to take a short break while you work out what to do next.

Write down your own descriptions of the following:

Trade union	**General unions**
Industrial unions	**Non-manual unions**
Shop steward	**National Executive**
Industrial action	**Collective bargaining**
Closed shop	**Work-to-rule**
Single union agreement	**Arbitration**

Now go back through the chapter to check your understanding of these terms.

Good sources of information to help you with your coursework are:

- the World Directory of Trade Unions *www.cf.ac.uk/socsi/union*
- the biz/ed education online service *www.bized.ac.uk/compfact/tuc/tuc11.htm*
- European Industrial Relations Observatory *www.eiro.eurofound.eu.int*

Chapter 6 Financial Institutions

CON, BADGER, STING
& SONS LOAN C°
£m
LOAN
AGREEMENT
I hate to hurry you along Mr Smythe
but the first payment is nearly due!

Aims

At the end of this chapter you should be able to:

- describe the functions of **commercial banks, stock exchanges** and **central banks**
- distinguish between different types of bank and the financial services they provide
- understand how companies raise finance from the sale of **shares**
- describe how a stock exchange works, and the role of **brokers** and **market makers**
- evaluate the role of a central bank in an economy, in managing the government's **monetary policy** and maintaining a stable currency

Section 1 The money market

We have learnt how scarce resources are organized into different types of firms to produce goods and services. Specialization in production has increased the quantity, quality and variety of goods and services available. However, in order to enjoy the full benefits of specialization a modern economy needs a commodity everyone will accept in exchange for goods and services. We know from Chapter 2 that such a commodity is called money.

In a modern economy, people, firms and government need somewhere they can keep their money safely and help them make payments to others. They may also want to borrow money, make investments and exchange the money used in their country for the currency used in another so they can make payments overseas. Business organizations that specialize in providing these services are called **financial institutions**. Without financial institutions, specialized production and trade on the scale enjoyed today would not be possible, costs of production would be much higher, economies would be less developed and economic growth would be much slower (see Chapter 17).

What is the money market?

The **money market** is really no different from any other market (see Chapter 7). It is made up of all those people and organizations that want money, and all the people and organizations willing and able to supply money, namely the banking system that creates deposit money, and a central bank that issues notes and coins.

What is a bank?

Banks are financial institutions in the money market. They are just like any other business except the product they supply is money, in the form of loans and other financial products.

Most but not all banks are large, profit-making public limited companies (see Chapter 4). In fact, banks are some of the biggest and most profitable corporations in the world. They can earn a profit for their shareholders in a number of ways:

- **Making loans**

Banks accept deposits of money and savings from their customers, and make loans from this money. They attract deposits and savings by paying customers interest on their money, or a share in their profits.

A bank will not keep all the customers' deposits and savings in its vaults. It will lend most of this money to other customers, including individuals and businesses, for example, to buy cars, overseas holidays and property. In turn, these people and firms pay others for goods and services, and these people and firms will then deposit or save the money they receive, with a bank. In this way, the banking system creates money in an economy.

As we known from Chapter 2, modern-day money consists of notes and coins and deposits in banks. Of course, if everyone wanted to withdraw their deposits and savings in the form of notes and coins at the same time all over the world there would not be enough notes and coins to go round, but this is never likely to happen on such a scale. However, it has happened from time to time in the past at an individual bank, causing it to run out of notes and coins and close down.

Banks are financial intermediaries between customers who want to deposit money and customers who want to borrow money

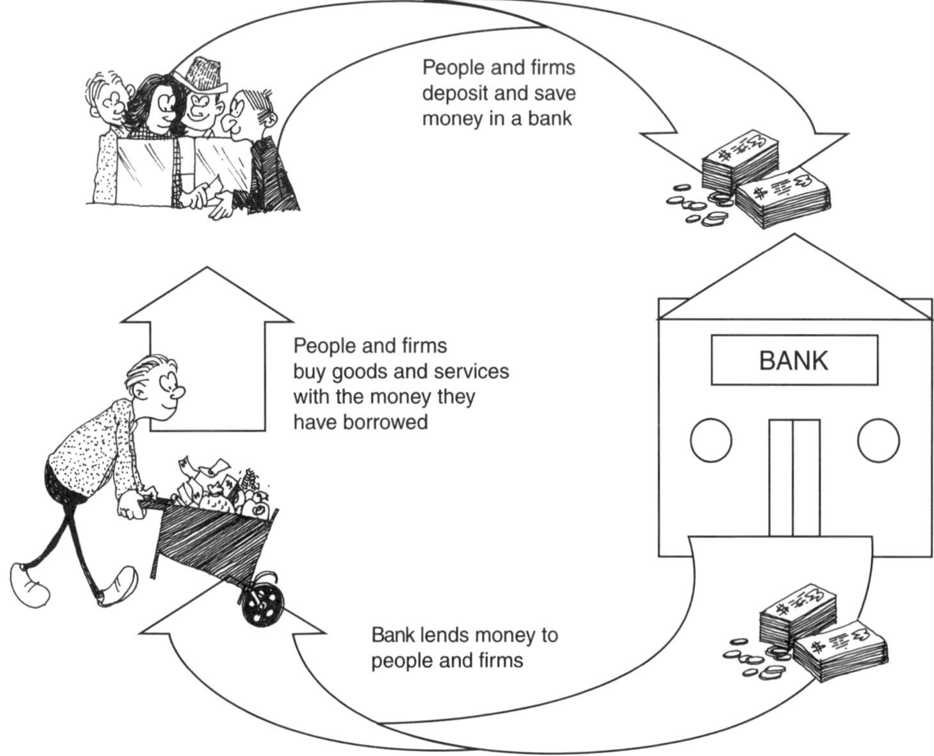
People and firms deposit and save money in a bank
People and firms buy goods and services with the money they have borrowed
BANK
Bank lends money to people and firms

- **Charging interest on loans**

The **interest rate** is the cost of borrowing money. For example, a bank that lends a customer $1000 and charges 5 per cent interest, all to be repaid in one year, will earn $50 in interest payments on that loan. Interest rates can vary over time and by different types of loan and customer.

For example, a big loan over 10 years to a new, small business may be charged a higher rate of interest than a smaller loan to be repaid over 2 years to a person in regular, paid employment. This is because the risk that the new business may run into trouble and not be able to repay the loan is greater than the risk of non-repayment by the individual customer. Making loans is inherently risky, so the higher the risk the more the interest a bank will charge. Further, over time, price inflation may rise and the value of the loan in terms of what the money can buy will be reduced (see Chapter 16). Interest charges will help offset any reduction in value of the money tied up in the loan due to rising price inflation.

As long as loans are repaid and interest charges on loans are higher than interest payments made on savings, a bank will make a profit from making loans.

- **Charging fees for their services**

For example, a bank may charge their customers fees to withdraw money using a cash machine (or **automated telling machine**; ATM), changing foreign currencies, making investments, arranging loans, issuing debit and credit cards, organizing automatic direct debit payments to other individuals and businesses from the customer's account, issuing and receiving cheques, telephone and internet banking services, etc.

- **Investing in shares in other companies**

Banks can use money deposited by customers to buy and sell shares in other public limited companies on behalf of its own shareholders. If it holds shares that go up in value the bank will make a gain from selling them. It can also earn dividends from profits made by these other companies (see Chapter 4).

The biggest banks in the world

Bank	Market capitalization as at 26 July 2006 US$ billion	Profit 2005 US$ billion
Citigroup	235	24.5
Bank of America	230	16.5
HSBC	200	15.9
JP Morgan Chase	150	8.4
Mitsubishi UFJ	145	6.8
Wells Fargo	120	7.8
UBS	110	11.2
Royal Bank of Scotland	100	10.0
China Construction Bank	100	5.7
Mizuho	95	5.8

Exercise 1 Why do we need banks?

Digital Dreams is a small but rapidly expanding company manufacturing video equipment. It has recently received a $200 000 loan repayable over 20 years to buy new business premises.

Digital Dreams sells much of its equipment online to customers who use credit and debit cards and so it accepts all these forms of payment. It also accepts cheques from customers.

The company keeps most of its sales revenues in a deposit account. The balance is kept in a current account to pay wages to employees and other costs, including electricity, gas and local taxes, by direct debit.

If there were no banks:

1 How would Digital Dreams have to make and receive payments?

2 Where would it have to store its sales revenues?

3 How would it have to pay for its new business premises?

4 What would be the likely impact on the costs of running Digital Dreams?

Types of bank

There are several different types of bank in a modern economy. They all offer very similar services, but tend to specialise in particular financial products and groups of consumers.

1 Commercial banks

HSBC is a global banking giant with branches all over the world

Commercial banks are also often called 'high-street banks' because they have so many branches located in cities and towns. However, many banks provide telephone and online banking facilities for their customers so there is no need to visit a branch.

Commercial banks were originally set up to provide financial services for small businesses but now they provide services for everyone from private individuals to both large and small businesses. These services will include:

- accepting deposits of money and savings
- helping customers make and receive payments
- making personal and commercial loans
- buying and selling shares for their customers
- providing insurance
- operating pension funds
- financial and tax planning advice
- storing valuables, and much more

RHB Bank Berhad is the third largest commercial bank in Malaysia with over 200 branches

Types of account

A **deposit account** is a convenient place to keep money and make payments from. You can arrange to have your wages, pension and other benefits paid transferred into your account electronically. You can also pay in cheques (checks) or cash, make withdrawals at ATMs with a cash card, and set up direct debits to pay regular bills automatically from your account.

A **current account** or **checking account** is a deposit account which offers the additional benefits of being able to write checks and use a debit card to make payments, and an overdraft facility.

A **savings account** is a safe place to store your savings. Interest will usually be added to your savings by a bank depending on how much you have saved and how often you can make withdrawals. The more you have saved, and the fewer times you are able to make a withdrawal, the better the rate of interest paid to you.

Types of loan

An **overdraft** allows a bank customer to overdraw their account by an agreed amount. It provides a convenient short-term loan, for example to pay unexpected bills. Interest is charged.

A **personal loan** is repaid with interest over a fixed period, usually for more than six months and up to 10 years.

A **commercial loan** is a loan to a business to pay for operating costs and the purchase of materials and machinery. The loan is repayable with interest over a fixed period of time.

A **mortgage** is a long-term loan, often up to 25 years, used by people and businesses to buy property. The loan is secured against the property, meaning that if the loan cannot be repaid the property has to be sold to repay the debt.

Methods of payment

Cash, or notes and coins, is the easiest way of paying for goods and services in person. Many banks allow account holders to withdraw cash from their accounts at any time of the day, from many different locations, using ATMs.

A **check** (or cheque) is a written promise to pay cash to, or transfer money into the account of, another person or organization. If you write a check it must show your name, your account number, the amount you are promising to pay, and to whom it is to be paid. The person or organization receiving your check will pay it into their bank account. Once received the amount written on the check will be transferred into their bank account from your bank account.

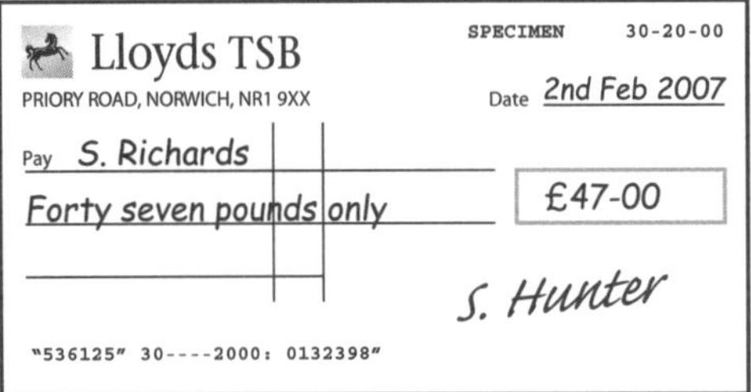

A **direct debit** is an easy way to make regular payments of varying amounts to the same organization from your account, for example, to pay monthly bills from an electricity or telephone supplier. Once set up, the supplier will simply provide your bank with their account details, the amount to be paid each month, and your bank will make these payments on your behalf.

A **debit card** is an electronic method of making payment to another business organization. It means you do not have to use cash or write a check. Once your card is 'swiped' through a payment machine, your bank details and the amount to be withdrawn from your account, and the details of the account to receive your payment, are transmitted electronically to your bank headquarters and the transfer is made instantaneously.

A **credit card** can make payments in much the same way as a debit card except it allows the card holder up to a month or longer to pay for the purchases made using their card. A credit card therefore provides a short-term loan. Interest is payable if the amount on the credit card is not repaid in full in the specified period.

2 Savings banks

These banks were originally set up to provide a safe and accessible place for people on low incomes to keep their savings. Many started as mutual savings banks, owned and run on behalf of their depositors, but many have since become limited companies owned by their shareholders. Many now offer similar services to individual customers as the commercial banks, and have branches in many towns and cities.

In some countries, national savings banks are government organizations set up to provide a secure place for ordinary people to keep money, and in so doing providing money which the government can borrow.

3 Savings and loans associations

These specialize in keeping savings deposits and lending money to people on low incomes to buy homes. These long-term loans are known as **mortgages**. Many began as non-profit-making mutual institutions owned and run by their members who held accounts. In the UK these are known as building societies. Today, SLAs can be owned by shareholders, aim to make a profit, and can offer a full range of financial services similar to commercial banks.

4 Credit unions

A credit union is a co-operative, not-for-profit organization, owned by its members. Credit unions were started by people who worked or lived together to provide low-cost loans to members who were on low incomes and unable to borrow money from other banks, for example, to help with home repairs, school fees and medical expenses. Credit unions are popular in the US, and many have now expanded the range of services they offer to include checks, credit cards and loans to small businesses.

5 Investment banks

These banks specialize in helping large business organizations raise finance to fund their operations and expansion, usually through helping them to issue and sell stocks and shares on the stock market (see section 2). They can also provide advice on company mergers and takeovers (see Chapter 12). Today, most large commercial banks also provide investment banking services.

Merchant banks are a type of investment bank. They were originally set up to help merchants finance the sale and transportation of goods overseas. Today, they provide finance for large companies through the purchase of their shares rather than providing loans.

6 Islamic banks

Islamic banking is based on principles of Islamic Sharia'a law, which forbids interest charges and payments. Instead, an Islamic bank can earn a profit from the fees it charges customers for banking services including making loans, and people who deposit their money will earn a share of the bank's profits rather than be paid interest.

Multinational banking organizations, like HSBC, also provide Sharia'a-compliant banking services in many countries.

Islamic banks do not charge or pay interest to customers

Other money market institutions

A number of other financial institutions operate in the global money market alongside banks. They specialize in particular types of financial products, although many large banks also compete to supply these products.

1 Finance houses

People and businesses can buy goods using money borrowed from finance houses who specialize in loans called hire purchase (HP). People and firms will select the good they want from a supplier and then pay a deposit, for example 10 per cent of the purchase price, to a finance house who will then lend them the rest of the money to make the purchase. HP is normally repaid each month with interest over an agreed period of time, usually between 6 months and 5 years. However, to encourage consumers to buy their goods and services some suppliers offer them interest-free credit deals by paying any interest to the finance house themselves.

2 Venture capitalists

These specialize in providing finance for new and risky business ventures, usually in return for some ownership and control of the new business. This type of finance is called **venture capital**.

3 Pension funds

People can save regularly for their old age in pension funds. Pension fund managers will then invest these savings to make a profit, part of which is added to people's pension savings and part of which pays the shareholders in the company managing the pension fund. Pension funds provide an important source of finance for companies and the government through the shares and government bonds they invest in.

4 Insurance companies

In the same way, people can save regularly with life insurance companies. Part of the money a person pays each month to a life insurance company will be for insurance premiums, and the rest will be added to their savings. An insurance company will then use these savings to invest in shares and bonds. Any profits they make from these investments will in part be used to pay bonuses to their savers and dividends to their own shareholders.

5 Investment and unit trusts

An **investment trust** is a company that buys shares in other companies it thinks will be profitable and will pay good dividends on their shares. In turn, the Trust uses the profits or dividends made on the shares it holds to pay their own shareholders who own the Trust.

Instead of buying shares in just one company, which can be risky if the company fails to make a profit, small savers often buy **unit trusts**.

Professional investors, who work for unit trust companies, use their savers' money to buy shares in a variety of companies they think will be profitable. The more profit they make, the more interest the unit trust company can pay to its savers. Unlike shares in investment trusts, units cannot be sold on the stock market and may only be sold back to the unit trust.

6 Building societies

Building societies are similar to banks but specialize in using their savers' money to help people buy houses, and other property (see also Chapter 19).

A loan given by a building society for the purpose of buying property is called a **mortgage**, and these are often repayable over a 20 to 30-year period. This money is also made available to industry for the purchase of commercial buildings.

Section 2 The stock market

What is the stock market?

Stock is the name used to describe money raised by a joint stock company or corporation through the issue and sale of shares. A **shareholder** is any person or organization that holds shares, as part owner of a corporation's stock. The total value of a corporation's issued shares is called its **market capitalization**.

Companies raise money from the sale of new shares. Unlike loans, a company will not have to repay the money it raises from the sale of its shares. The people and organizations that buy shares may, however, want to sell them in the future to get their money back. The **stock market** provides a global market for the buying and selling of new and second-hand shares. The stock market is one of the most important sources for companies to raise money. Governments can also issue loan stocks for sale to help finance pubic sector activities.

Functions of a stock exchange

A **stock exchange**, or bourse, is a business organization that helps companies and government authorities to sell their stocks and shares to people and other organizations that want to buy them. The interaction of the market demand for shares in a particular company and their market supply will determine the market price and quantity traded of those shares (see Chapter 7). People and other companies buy stocks and shares because they hope their price will rise so they can sell them at a profit, and also receive a dividend paid from the profits of the company that issued the shares.

The world's largest stock exchanges, February 2006

Stock exchange	Market capitalization US$ trillion
New York Stock Exchange	22.7
Tokyo Stock Exchange	4.65
NASDAQ	3.76
London Stock Exchange	3.25
Euronext	2.96
Toronto Stock Exchange	1.62
Frankfurt SE (Deutsche Börse)	1.38
Hong Kong Stock Exchange	1.30
Milan SE (Borsa Italiana)	0.89

World Federation of Exchanges

The largest stock exchange in the world is the New York Stock Exchange (NYSE). In February 2006 the total value, or market capitalization, of all stocks and shares traded through the NYSE was US$22.7 trillion.

Most trading in stocks and shares is now conducted electronically. The NASDAQ was the first fully electronic stock exchange, founded in 1971. NASDAQ stands for National Association of Securities Dealers Automated Quotations.

Without stock exchanges, companies would find it very difficult to raise the finance they need for their productive activities. Think of how difficult it and costly it would be for a new company to search for thousands, sometimes millions, of people and other companies to buy their shares. Even if it could, other people and companies might be reluctant to buy its shares because if they ever wanted to get their money back they would, in turn, have to search for other people and companies to sell them to.

A stock exchange brings buyers and sellers together, giving people and firms the confidence they can trade in both new and second-hand shares. It also gives investors confidence to buy shares in the following ways:

- It determines the structure of the markets for different types of shares.
- It makes rules and regulations for the way in which the markets work.
- It supervises the conduct of firms trading in shares.
- It provides up-to-the-minute information on share prices and trading.

There are two main types of company stock.

Types of stock

1 Preferred stocks or preference shares

A preference shareholder in a company will receive a share of any profits before the holders of other types of shares. That is, a **preferred stock** or **preference share** is given preference in the payment of dividends from profits. The dividend paid is usually a fixed percentage of the face value printed on the share. Dividend rights are often cumulative, so that if a dividend is not paid in one year it accumulates to be paid in future years.

Preference shareholders, however, are not usually allowed to vote on company policy or in the election of directors to run the company at Annual General Meetings.

2 Common stock or ordinary shares

Most shares held in limited companies are **common stock**, or **ordinary shares**. Ordinary shareholders receive a dividend from any profits remaining after preference shareholders have been paid. If no profits remain, ordinary shareholders will not receive a dividend. Holding ordinary shares can therefore be more risky than holding preference shares. However, ordinary shares carry one vote per share at Annual General Meetings. So, a person or organization that owns 10 000 ordinary shares in a company has 10 000 votes. The person or organization with the most ordinary shares in a company is the majority shareholder and can determine company policy and who sits on the board of directors (see Chapter 4).

An ordinary share certificate

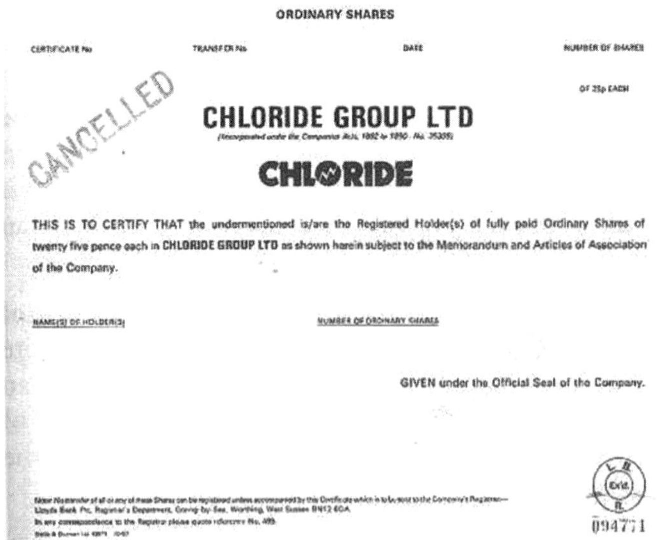

ORDINARY SHARES

CERTIFICATE No TRANSFER No DATE NUMBER OF SHARES

OF 25p EACH

CANCELLED

CHLORIDE GROUP LTD

CHLORIDE

THIS IS TO CERTIFY THAT the undermentioned is/are the Registered Holder(s) of fully paid Ordinary Shares of twenty five pence each in CHLORIDE GROUP LTD as shown herein subject to the Memorandum and Articles of Association of the Company.

NAME(S) OF HOLDER(S) NUMBER OF ORDINARY SHARES

GIVEN under the Official Seal of the Company.

094771

3 Government stock

Central and local government can also issues stocks for sale to raise additional finance for their activities. However, owners of government stocks are not shareholders in government.

Government stocks are loan stocks, which pay their holder a fixed rate of interest and are repaid after a fixed period of time. For example, UK government **gilt-edged securities** often mature – are repaid by the government – after 20 or 25 years. Within this time they can be bought and sold many times over by different investors. The final holder of the stock at maturity gets repaid its face value plus interest, but investors who buy and sell the stocks before maturity can make a profit from changes in their market price over time, which will usually be below the face value of the stock plus the interest that will eventually be paid on it.

Government stocks will normally be issued by the central bank in a country (see section 3).

How a stock exchange works

Stock exchanges are not open to the general public. This means that if a person or company wants to buy or sell some shares they must contact a share dealing firm (or **broker**) that is a member of a stock exchange.

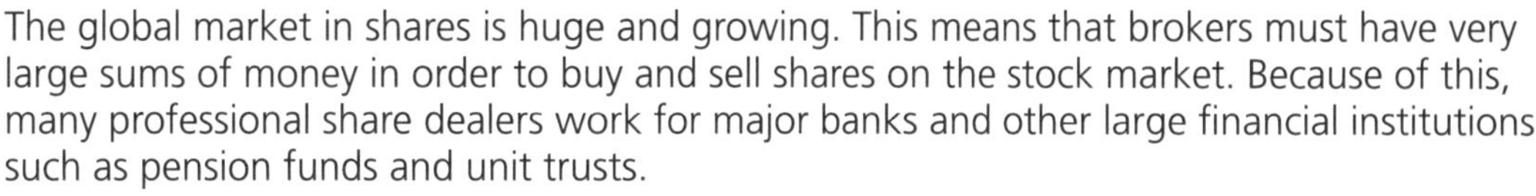

The global market in shares is huge and growing. This means that brokers must have very large sums of money in order to buy and sell shares on the stock market. Because of this, many professional share dealers work for major banks and other large financial institutions such as pension funds and unit trusts.

PSSST...
WANNA BUY SOME SHARES?

A member of the public or a company who wants to buy or sell shares can either contact a broker or simply go to their bank. It is very easy nowadays to simply buy and sell shares over the internet through online brokers and banks.

Brokers will buy and sell shares for a fee known as commission. For example, a customer might wish to buy 1000 shares in Google at no more than $10 a share. The broker and the customer will agree a commission to be paid to the broker for undertaking the work. For example, this might be a charge of 1 per cent of the total cost of the shares.

The broker will now attempt to buy shares in Google at the lowest possible price from other firms of brokers called **market makers**, usually by placing an order on a stock exchange computerized share dealing system. Market makers are special broker/dealers who create the market in shares. They do this by always being willing to buy and sell shares with other broker/dealers. These market makers make their profit by selling the shares they hold at a higher price than the price they paid for them.

Share price indices

Like the price of any other commodity, share prices reflect changes in market demand and supply (see Chapter 7). For example, if a company announces poor profits, shareholders may want to sell their shares because they will receive a poor dividend. However, a company that wins a significant customer order or announces a merger with another company to form a bigger, more profitable company may cause demand to rise for its shares. Movements in share prices can, therefore, reveal much about how well companies are performing.

Investors in shares can watch how share prices are changing over time either individually or by tracking a share price index. For example, the Dow Jones Industrial Average Index provides an up-to-date average market price on the NYSE of the shares in 30 of the largest and most widely held public companies in the United States. The most regularly quoted stock market indices also include the S&P 500 Index in the US, the French CAC 40, the German DAX and the Japanese Nikkei 225.

FTSE 100, year to 8 June 2007

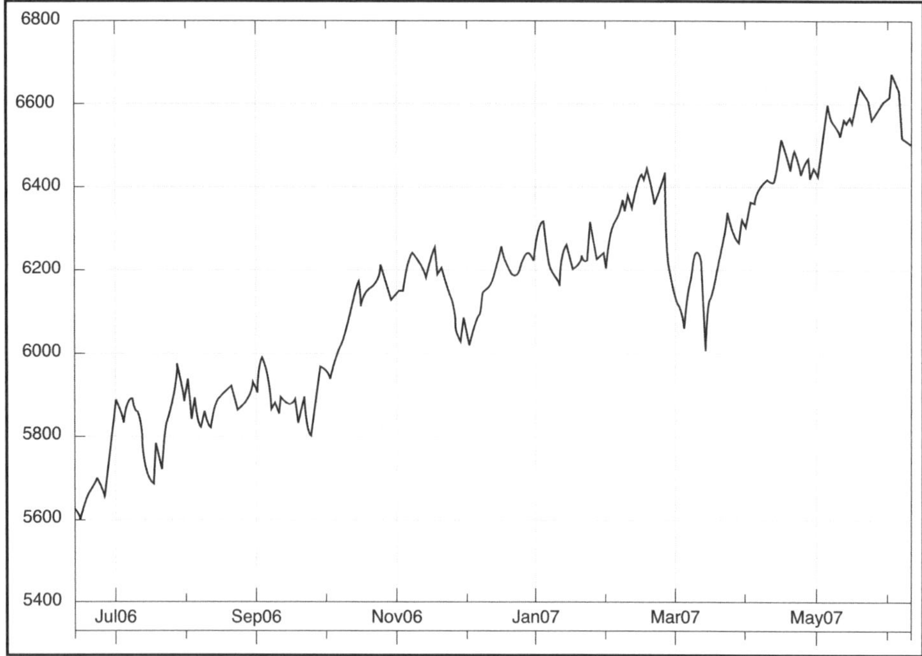

finance.yahoo.com/

The chart shows the movement in the FTSE 100 index (the 'footsie') over a 12-month period to 8 June 2007. It charts the movement in the average price of shares in the top 100 companies traded on the London Stock Exchange in the UK. The index is recalculated every minute relative to a base value of 1000 set in 1984. At the close of trading on 8 June 2007 the FTSE 100 index value was 6505.1 which means the average share price in the top 100 companies had increased by just over 650 per cent since 1984.

Speculating on share prices

The FTSE 100 chart shows how the market price of shares can change rapidly over time. It is possible for people and financial institutions to make money on the stock market by guessing which way shares prices are likely to move in the future. Attempting to make money from buying and selling shares in the hope their prices will change is called **speculation**.

Economist, 1.11.1997

People and firms who buy shares in the hope their price will rise so that they can sell them at a profit are called **bulls**. The stock market is called **bullish** if share prices are rising in general.

People and firms who sell shares in the hope their price will fall so that they can buy them back later at much lower prices are called **bears**. When share prices are falling the stock market is called **bearish**. 'Bears' buy the shares back despite their falling prices because they believe their prices will rise again in the long run and that dividend payments from company profits could be good.

People and firms who apply to buy up newly issued shares in the hope their price will rise quickly after dealing begins are called **stags**.

Exercise 2 Floating away

Saudi retailer initial public offering

Saudi retail franchiser Fawaz A Al Hokair Group will float 30% of its stock on the Saudi Stock Exchange between 7 – 16 October 2006, reported Arab News. The offer will be for 12 million shares at $2.66 each, with an allocation of 25 to 25 000 shares per bidder. HSBC and Saudi British Bank are the financial advisers, lead managers and underwriters.

Adapted from AME Info – Middle East Business Resource 2.8.2006, *ameinfo.com*

1. What is a stock market?
2. Explain how the Saudi Stock Exchange provides a stock market.
3. Why might the Saudi Arabian retail group in the article want to sell shares through the Saudi stock exchange?
4. How many shares will the business issue, and how much in total is it hoping to raise from their sale?
5. Why might the market price of shares traded in the Al Hokair Group exceed their face value of $2.66 per share?

Exercise 3 Share your success

Imagine you have $25 000 to invest in shares through a stock exchange. Use company news and financial pages of newspapers and websites to choose the shares of up to ten companies you want to buy, how many shares you will buy in each company and the market price you will have to pay.

Record this information in a table or on a spreadsheet. For example:

Name of company	Where are their shares listed?	Market prices per share ($)	Number of shares bought	Total value
Cadbury Schweppes plc	NYSE	$42.95	100	$4295
PT Indosat Tbk	NYSE	$24.74	50	$1237
Bancolombia S.A.	NYSE	$28.40	75	$2130
…				

Check and record the market prices of your shares at the end of every week over a 3 to 6-month period and calculate the gain or loss you have made in the value of your shares. Also add in and record any dividends you would be paid. As you do so, use the financial press to record reasons why the market prices of your shares have changed.

Section 3 The role of the central bank

What is a central bank?

The central bank sits at the centre of the banking system in an economy. It is the government's banker and the banker's bank. In most countries the central bank is owned by the government and run by a public corporation (see Chapter 4).

The main function of a **central bank** is to maintain the stability of the national currency and the money supply in its country or in its group of member states, such as the European Union.

The oldest central bank in the world is the Bank of Sweden, which was opened in 1668. This was followed in 1694 by the Bank of England in the UK.

The European Central Bank of the European Union was introduced in 1998 with the European single currency, the euro, to co-ordinate the European national banks, which continue to separately manage their own economies.

Functions of a central bank

1 It has sole right to issue notes and coins

The central bank in a country will normally have the exclusive right to print and issue notes and coins in that country.

2 It is the government's banker

A central bank will look after the tax revenues received by the government, and manage its payments, for example, spending on schools, roads and benefits.

3 It manages the nation's gold and foreign currency reserves

These reserves are used to make payments overseas and to stabilize the value of the national currency. For example, if the value of the currency is falling in terms of other world currencies the central bank can use these reserves to buy up their currency. As a result of this increase in demand for the national currency its value overseas will tend to rise (see Chapter 19).

4 It manages the national debt

A central bank can issue and repay loan stocks on behalf of the government (see Chapter 15).

5 It regulates and supervises the banking system

A central bank can set rules to determine how banks conduct their business and which organizations can become banks. It will also hold the deposits of commercial and other banks, and transfer funds between their accounts to settle the many millions of cheque, debit card and other payments made by their customers.

6 It is 'lender of the last resort'

A central bank will lend money to the banking system if one or more banking chains run into difficulties meeting payments, to prevent banks running out of money and going bankrupt.

7 It sets the official interest rate

The **monetary policy** of a government involves managing the supply of money in an economy to help control both price inflation and the country's exchange rate (see Chapter 14). The main instrument of monetary policy is the official interest rate.

It is usually the job of the government finance minister to decide what the interest rate should be, but some central banks are able to set interest rates without political interference from government ministers. For example, a government may lower interest rates for political reasons before an election simply to boost their popularity rather than for economic reasons to control inflation. Lowering interest rates too much may increase borrowing and as a result increase the problem of inflation in an economy. In contrast, a central bank can decide what the interest rate should be to control inflation over time by observing wage increases, raw material costs, house prices and other economic variables that provide an early warning of inflationary pressures in the economy.

Examples of 'independent central banks' include the US Federal Reserve, the Bank of England (since 1997), the Reserve Bank of India (1935), the Bank of Mexico (1993), the Bank of Japan, the Bank of Canada, the Reserve Bank of Australia and the European Central Bank.

Exercise 4 You can bank on it!

Compare and contrast the functions and activities of a commercial bank with the central bank in your country.

1. What are their main functions?
2. What services do they provide and to whom?
3. How are they organized, controlled and financed?
4. What are their relationships with other banks in your country and globally?
5. What role do they play in your economy?

There are a great many useful and interesting websites providing news and information on banking, financial products, stock markets and share prices. Here are just a few:

- Bloomberg markets magazine *www.bloomberg.com*
- Financial Times markets *www.ft.com/markets*
- Fortune business and financial news *money.cnn.com/magazines/fortune/*
- List of central banks *www.bis.org/cbanks.htm*
- Links to stock exchanges *www.tdd.lt/slnews/Stock_Exchanges/Stock.Exchanges.htm*
- List of websites on stock markets and prices *www.rba.co.uk/sources/stocks.htm*
- London Stock Exchange *www.londonstockexchange.com*
- NASDAQ stock market *www.nasdaq.com*
- New York Stock Exchange *www.nyse.com*
- *bized.ac.uk/learn/economics/markets/stockexchange/role.htm*

Key crossword

Clues across

3 Specialized finance for new and risky business ventures, usually in return for some ownership and control of the new business (7, 7)

5 The cost of borrowing money (8, 4)

7 The name given to a speculator who buys shares in the hope their price will rise quickly so they can sell them for a profit (4)

8 Short for a cash machine (1,1,1)

9 A share dealer, able to buy and sell shares on a stock exchange (6)

11 A type of major bank found in many towns and cities (10, 4)

12 An organization that brings together buyers and sellers of shares (5, 8)

Clues down

1 The main bank in an economy responsible for managing the stability of the national currency and the money supply (6, 4)

2 Another name for common company stock with voting rights (7, 5)

4 It consists of the banking system that supplies money and those people and organizations who demand money (5, 6)

6 A long-term loan for buying property (8)

10 Banks specialize in providing this type of finance. People and firms who borrow this money will have to repay it with interest over a fixed period of time (4)

Assessment exercises

Multiple choice

1 Which of the following is not a private sector business organization?

A Public Limited Company

B Partnership

C Public Corporation

D Consumer Co-operative

2 If a business owner has unlimited liability, this means that:

A The business cannot go bankrupt.

B The owner must meet all debts.

C The business has sold shares.

D The business is only small.

3 Which of the following is NOT a feature of the Private Limited Company?

A Shares cannot be sold on the Stock Exchange

B Shareholders have unlimited liability

C The company is managed by directors

D The company must hold an Annual General Meeting

4 Which of the following best describes a Public Limited Company?

A A company owned by the government

B A company that has factories and offices all over the world

C A company owned by its workers

D A company that is listed on a Stock Exchange

5 One of the main disadvantages of a large limited company is that:

A Owners of the company can lose control to the directors.

B Specialization is not possible.

C There are no organized markets where shares in the company can be purchased.

D There is a lack of capital.

6 The best description of a multinational company is:

A A company owned by governments in many different countries.

B A company that has its headquarters in one country but operates in many other countries.

C A company that is owned by shareholders all over the world.

D A company that enjoys large economies of scale.

7 Which of the following is an advantage to a country of hosting a multinational company?

A They may force other firms out of business.

B They may exploit cheap labour.

C They may switch profits between countries.

D They may have advanced technical knowledge.

8 A furniture-maker produces to order expensive, hand-made pieces of wooden furniture. In which type of business organization is the furniture-maker most likely to work?

A A private limited company

B A retail co-operative

C A sole trader

D A public limited company

9 A trade union may try to raise the wages of its members by all of the following except:

A Increasing their productivity.

B Threatening strike action.

C Increasing the supply of labour.

D Accepting revised working practices.

10 A single union agreement can have the following advantages for an employer except:

A It reduces time spent negotiating with unions.

B It can increase union bargaining power.

C It can protect the skills of the union workers.

D Union members may agree to increase their productivity.

11 Which type of union would best describe a union of musicians?

A Labour union.

B Craft union.

C Industrial union.

D General union.

12 Collective bargaining involves:

A Negotiations between employers and union representatives.

B Negotiations between individual workers and their employers.

C Negotiations between employers and government representatives.

D Negotiations between different employers.

13 Which of the following is NOT a function of a commercial bank?

A Making personal loans.

B Accepting deposits of money and savings.

C Providing financial advice.

D Issuing notes and coins.

Questions 14–16 refer to the following financial products:

A Ordinary shares.

B Loan stocks.

C Bank loans.

D Mortgages.

14 These can be issued by a government.

15 These shares have voting rights at annual general meetings.

16 Long-term finance used to buy property.

17 The stock market is a market for:

A New issues of shares.

B Stocks of goods and services.

C Financial products.

D New and second-hand shares.

18 Which of the following is NOT a function of a central bank?

A Making personal loans.

B Managing the national debt.

C Controlling the money supply.

D Supervising the banking system.

Structured questions

1

Exxon Mobil Corporation Announces Second Quarter 2006 Results

Exxon Mobil Corporation today reported a record second quarter 2006 result. Net income of $10,360 million, increased $2,720 million from the second quarter of 2005.

ExxonMobil is a global multinational with operations in over 200 countries and territories. Its shares are traded on the New York Stock Exchange. The Board of Directors declared a cash dividend of 32 cents per share will be paid to shareholders on September 11, 2006. This quarterly dividend is at the same level as the dividend paid in the previous quarter of 2006.

Liquids production of 2,701 thousands of barrels per day (kpd) was 233 kpd higher mainly due to higher production from projects in West Africa and increased volumes in Abu Dhabi.

Second quarter natural gas production was 8,769 millions of cubic feet per day (mcfd) compared with 8,709 mcfd last year. Higher volumes from projects in Qatar were partly offset by the impact of mature field decline and planned maintenance activity.

Adapted from ExxonMobil press releases 26-27.7.2006, *www.exxonmobil.com/corporate*

a What is a multinational? What evidence is there from the article that ExxonMobil is a multinational company? [4]

b Explain the likely advantages to ExxonMobil of its multinational structure. [4]

c How can a public limited company like ExxonMobil raise finance to fund its multinational expansion? [4]

d Explain **two** reasons why a government may encourage the location of a multinational in its country. What are the possible disadvantages? [6]

e Describe the main differences between a public limited company and a co-operative organization. [6]

2

UK interest rates raised to 4.75%

The Bank of England today delivered a blow to home-owners as it raised interest rates for the first time in two years in a pre-emptive strike against inflation.

In a precautionary move after inflation went up sharply in June, the Bank's monetary policy committee (MPC) lifted borrowing costs by a quarter of a percentage point to 4.75%. The increase is likely to be passed on to borrowers immediately by the main commercial banks and mortgage providers.

Interest rates also rose in the eurozone on Thursday. The European Central Bank announced a quarter-point increase – the fourth such hike in eight months – taking rates to 3%. Earlier in the week, the Australian Central Bank also raised its rates to 6%.

Adapted from *The Guardian*, 3.8.2006

a What is inflation? [2]

b How can an increase in interest rates help to 'keep inflation under control'? [2]

c Suggest two ways a commercial bank can lend money to individuals and businesses. [4]

d Describe two other functions of a commercial bank. [4]

e Why is a central bank described as the lender of the last resort to the banking sector in an economy? [4]

f Describe two other functions of a central bank. [4]

3

China's Progress

In 1992 China's per capita GDP was about the same as India's. In 2002 it was double India's. It outperformed India in almost every way, attracting ten times as much foreign capital and increasing its share of world markets. China kept its costs as low as possible, offered an even bigger domestic market than India and built better highways, power supplies, airfields and other infrastructure than India. Many Chinese people see foreign capital as an essential tool that brings not just money for production but also modern technology and management expertise, which increase efficiency.

The Chinese leadership sees economic growth as the key to retaining its hold on power and increasing its influence in the world. As part of that growth, they believe that foreign governments will be less hostile to China if they know there is much foreign capital invested in the country.

Some economists in India, by contrast, remain fiercely opposed to foreign investment, insisting that some multinational companies will have a bad effect on the Indian economy. In India, complicated administrative procedures, the poor infrastructure and the political system lead foreign investors to doubt whether they can make reasonable profits.

a What is meant by per capita GDP? [2]

b i What is meant by a multinational company? [2]

ii Explain why Indian economists think multinational companies have a bad effect on the Indian economy. [3]

c Explain why Chinese economists approve of foreign investment. [4]

d The article says that China's GDP per capita is now double that of India. Is this beneficial to the Chinese people? [8]

4 In 2006 the Slovakian Trade Union of Healthcare and Social Welfare threatened industrial action in Slovakian hospitals if they did not get higher wages.

a Suggest three forms of industrial action the union could take. [3]

b Describe the functions of trade unions and explain which function you consider to be the most important. [7]

5 British Gas is a large profit-making public company in the UK. A publicity leaflet from the company stated that the number of customers it served had increased. It also said that the company was more willing to pay compensation to customers for failure to meet required standards of service.

a Explain what is meant by the principle of profit maximization. [4]

b Discuss what might have happened to profits as a result of each of the changes mentioned in the leaflet. [6]

c Describe briefly the main types of business organization and consider which of them is likely to be the most significant in a developed economy. [10]

How to answer question 2

a This question simply requires you to writer a short definition of price inflation, and you should look at Chapter 16 for this. Simply describing **inflation** as rising prices might get you one mark whereas the following description or something very similar will get you the full two marks: Inflation is a sustained increase in the general level of prices in an economy.

b Again a short-answer question for just two marks, but make sure you get both by looking again at Chapter 16. This will tell you a government will often raise **interest rates** as part of their **monetary policy** in an attempt to reduce an excess of total demand in their economy that is pushing up **market prices**. Interest rates are the cost of **borrowing** money. Loans need to be repaid with interest. Individual consumers and firms borrow money to buy goods and services. The higher the rate of interest the more it will cost them to borrow money and this will tend to contract their demand for loans, which in turn should help reduce total or **aggregate demand** in the economy. You can explain this simply by saying higher interest rates will tend to reduce the demand for borrowed money and therefore help reduce a **demand-pull inflation**.

c Two short answers from this chapter will get you the full four marks. From section 1, you should recall that commercial or 'high street' banks can lend money in the form of personal and commercial bank **loans, overdrafts, mortgages** for property, and even debit and **credit cards**. You should of course provide a short description of the two you pick.

d Here again, two short but clear answers will be enough. Modern **commercial banks** perform many functions for their customers, from financial advice and tax planning to providing insurance. But don't forget one major function is providing customers with safe and secure savings accounts that usually pay interest.

e The role of a **central bank** in a national economy is described in Chapter 6, section 3. It can help boost your marks if you start with a short description of what is a central bank in an economy, and how it holds not only the tax revenues collected by the government and the national gold and foreign currency reserves, but also the deposits of commercial and other banks. If one or more of these banks runs short of money then a central bank can lend them money to prevent them going bankrupt, and potentially destabilizing the economy because people and firms who use the bank may no longer be able to access their money to make withdrawals and payments.

f If you have answered part (e) as suggested then you have already partially described at least three functions of a central bank. You could refer back to these here and add some further explanation to show off your knowledge. Alternatively you could explain that a central bank will have the sole right to issue notes and coins, manage the **national debt,** will regulate and supervise the banking system in the economy, and will often set the official interest rate.

A model answer for question 1

a A multinational organization has productive operations in more than one country. Multinationals are some of the largest firms in the world, often employing many millions of workers across many different countries. The article reports that ExxonMobil has operations in over 200 countries and territories.

b ExxonMobil benefits from its multinational structure by having access to oil and gas supplies and consumers in many different countries. This helps it lower its transport costs, increase its consumer base and make more profit. Its huge global scale also allows it to enjoy lower average production costs. These are called economies of scale. It can also take advantage of different wage levels in different countries and keep its overall wage costs low by employing more workers in low-wage economies.

c ExxonMobil is a public corporation listed on the New York Stock Exchange. This means it is able to sell shares to the general public to raise money to fund its expansion. It can also do this by reinvesting some of its huge profits, or by borrowing money from banks. Because of its scale, banks all over the world may be willing to lend it vast sums of money at relatively low interest rates because there is little risk of the company failing and being unable to repay these loans.

d The government of a country may encourage a multinational like ExxonMobil to locate a plant in its country because it can provide employment and incomes for many thousands of people. It can also teach the local workforce new skills and advanced methods of production that may benefit other firms in the economy.

However, in order to attract these types of firms a government may have to offer very attractive incentives to them, including subsidized land or factory buildings, and grants for machinery. These may be expensive and could divert government spending from the provision of other public services, or result in higher taxation. A multinational may also force any local competing firms out of business, thereby creating unemployment, and avoid paying taxes to the government on any profits earned in their country by transferring them to its plants or headquarters overseas.

e It is useful to look at the differences between public limited companies and co-operatives in terms of the way they are owned and controlled, how they are financed, and how they distribute their profits.

A public limited company is owned by its shareholders. The number of shareholders can range from just two or a handful of shareholders who own 100 per cent of the company, right up to many millions of shareholders who may be spread across many different countries. In these firms it is impossible for all the shareholders to manage and run the business from day to day so they usually appoint a board of directors to do this on their behalf. Owners of common stock or ordinary shareholders have voting rights to elect directors and to vote on company policies. The more ordinary shares a shareholder owns, the more votes they have.

In contrast, a co-operative is owned by its members. Any person can become a member by buying a share and each member is only allowed one vote regardless of the number of shares they hold. Members can vote on business policies and the election of a board of directors. In worker co-operatives, the workers in the business organization are its members or shareholders.

The sale of shares in the ownership of both public limited companies and co-operatives helps these businesses raise money to finance their activities. Co-operatives usually only sell shares to people who shop or work in their businesses. A public limited company, however, can advertise and sell shares to other companies and members of the general public through a stock exchange. As a result, it is often very expensive to set up a public limited company.

Any profits made by a public limited company are owned by its shareholders. Profits after tax and not reinvested in the business will be distributed to shareholders as dividends. Each share is paid a dividend from the profits, so the more shares a shareholder owns the greater the total dividend or share of profit they will receive. In the same way, the profits of a co-operative are distributed to its members. In retail co-operatives, profits may also be used to lower prices for members to enjoy.

3 HOW THE MARKET WORKS

In a free market the price of any good or service will be determined by the decisions of consumers and producers to buy and sell. Effective demand is the willingness and ability of consumers to buy goods and services. In general, as prices rise demand will tend to reduce. Supply refers to the willingness and ability of producers to provide goods and services. In general, as prices rise so producers would be willing to supply more.

The market price for a good or service will be determined when consumer demand for it matches supply. Demand may increase, thereby pushing up the market price, if consumers' incomes rise, the product becomes fashionable and tastes favour it, or if other similar products become more expensive. The supply of a good or service may increase, thereby pushing market price down, if the cost of producing it falls, for example, due to technological change.

Firms compete with others to supply consumers with the goods and services they want. They compete to increase their market share and profits. Advertising is often used to create a brand image for a product to grab the attention of consumers and tempt them away from rival products. Persuasive advertising can also be used to create demand for a new product. Price competition can involve undercutting rivals to force them out of the market. In some cases, this can lead to price wars between rival producers.

The amount of competition in a market can vary. In some markets one or a handful of dominant firms may have sufficient market power to restrict competition and influence the market price to their favour. A firm or group of firms acting in this way is a monopoly. This market structure can disadvantage consumers by restricting their choice of products to buy and, in the absence of competition, charging them a high price. However, some monopolies, because of their size and their ability to earn high profits, are able to spend a large amount of money on product improvements and more efficient production processes. They may also pass on some of their cost savings to their consumers in lower prices.

Chapter 7

How Prices are Determined

Aims

At the end of this chapter you should be able to:

- understand how the market forces of **consumer demand** and producer **supply** determine the price and quantity traded of a good or service
- derive a **market demand curve** and a **market supply curve**, and use them to demonstrate the principle of **equilibrium price**
- describe causes of changes in demand and supply conditions and analyse how such changes may affect price
- define **price elasticity of demand** and **price elasticity of supply**, perform simple calculations to find their values, and understand the usefulness of these measures to firms and the government
- discuss the effects of a **tax** or **subsidy** on the market supply and price of a commodity

Section 1

What is demand?

Consumers' demand for goods and services plays a large part in deciding how scarce resources are used. **Demand** is the want or willingness of consumers to buy goods and services. To be an **effective demand** consumers must have enough money to buy commodities given a number of possible prices. Producers in the private sector will only make those commodities if people have money to buy them.

Prices act as the signals for producers to show them how to use their scarce resources. If the price of a product is rising they may think they can earn more profits from its production and sale and therefore will use their resources to make this product. If the price of a product falls they may decide not to produce it any more as profits start to fall. This chapter looks at how this **price mechanism** works.

Exercise 1 Food for thought

The recipe for healthy profits?

There is a health revolution in the food industry. Over the past two years, according to Mintel market research, "the issue of health, diet and obesity has exploded… most major global food manufacturers are now involved in supplying and promoting healthy eating".

A senior analyst at TNS World Panel explained "there is a big pull from consumers and a big push due to messages we're getting from food standards authorities about health risks from obesity".

"Businesses are there to make money and they do that best when they follow consumer trends – they'd be stupid not to". The food firms themselves say that they are following their consumers.

Adapted from *The Sunday Times*, 23.7.2006

HEALTHY LABELS SELL

Food sales in the UK by £millions

	2002	2003	2004	2005
"Better for you" total market size	3,608	3,862	4,084	4,277
Reduced sugar	209.2	228.8	259.7	277.9
Reduced fat	3,336	3,550	3,714	3,880
Reduced carbohydrate	1.1	2.5	13.1	12.4
Reduced salt	31	48.1	62.5	70.7

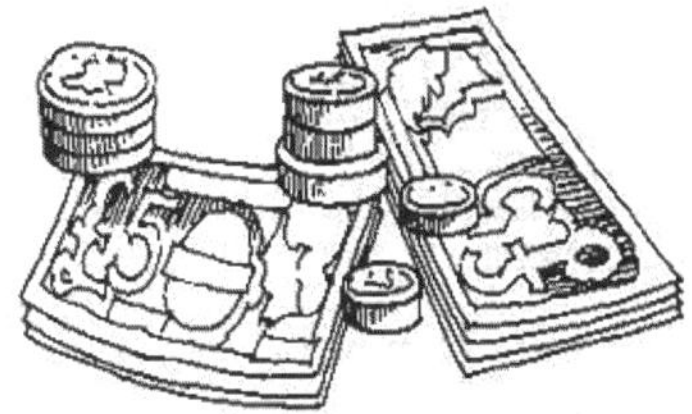

1. Who makes up the market for food products?
2. How are consumers' wants changing in the food industry?
3. What is likely impact on the allocation of resources in the food industry of the changing consumer demand?
4. Why do you think more consumers now want and are able to buy healthier food products?

The article above illustrates the changing pattern of consumer demand in the food industry. People are now spending more on healthier food products. Producers of food products have reacted by moving scarce resources of land, labour and capital, to the production of healthier food products, and are likely to continue to do so if this trend continues. In this way consumers get what they want in a market economy.

Demand curves

The amount of a good or service consumers are willing and able to buy is known as the **quantity demanded** of that product. Economists measure the quantity demanded of a particular good or service at a certain price over certain periods of time, say the number of oranges bought per week, litres of petrol per month, or the amount of DVDs per year.

Individual demand is the demand of just one consumer, while the **market demand** for a product is the total demand for that product from all its consumers.

Exercise 2 What is your individual demand?

1 Imagine your favourite chocolate bar was on offer at a number of possible prices. How many bars of chocolate would you be prepared to buy each month at each possible price?

Possible price of a chocolate bar (pence)	Your demand per month
200p	?
150p	
50p	
30p	
20p	
10p	
5p	
1p	

2 Copy and complete the table. You have now completed your **demand schedule** for your chocolate bar, that is, a table of figures relating quantity demanded to price.

Use this information to plot a line graph below to show your individual **demand curve** for the chocolate bar.

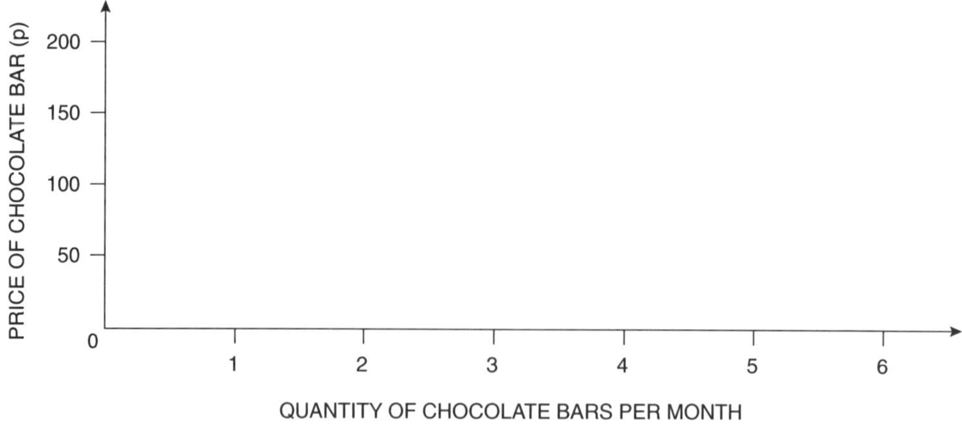

3 Which of the following statements applies to your demand curve?

- **a** It shows that as price rises, quantity demanded falls, and as price falls, quantity demanded rises.
- **b** It is roughly downward sloping.
- **c** Price and quantity demanded move in opposite directions.

Don't be surprised if all three statements apply to your demand curve. For the great majority of goods and services experience shows that quantities demanded will rise as their prices fall. In general, demand curves will be downward sloping when plotted against price.

A demand curve

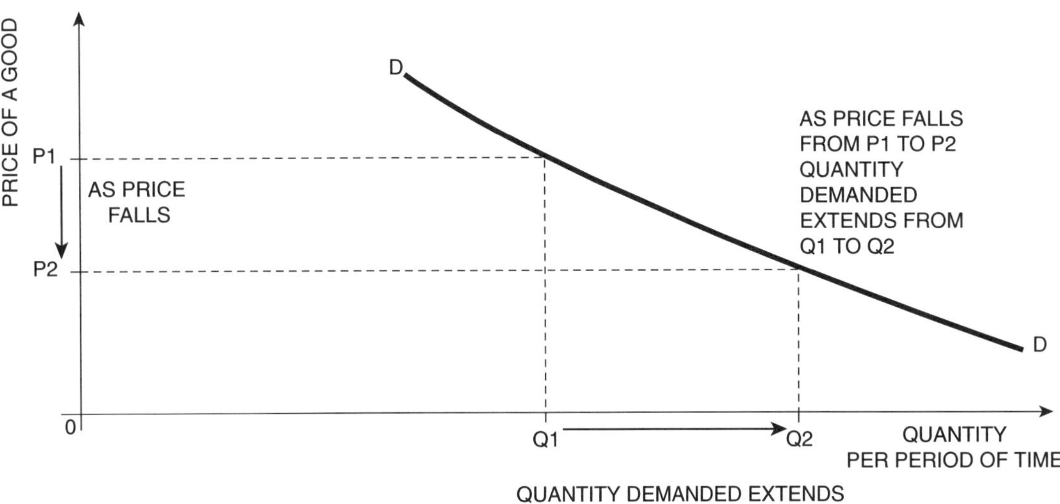

Thus, as the price of a product changes consumers *move along* their demand curve. That is, their demand extends as price falls, or contracts as price rises.

An extension of demand or increase in quantity demanded refers to the way in which demand changes with a fall in price, with no change in any other factor that could affect demand.

A contraction of demand or decrease in quantity demanded refers to the way in which demand changes when price rises, with no change in any other factor that may affect demand.

The market demand curve

The market demand curve for a particular good or service will display the demand of all the consumers of that commodity given a set of possible prices.

Exercise 3 Market demand curve

Producers of orange light bulbs have the following information about the amount of orange light bulbs consumers would buy each year given a number of possible prices. The market demand schedule is as follows.

Prices of orange light bulbs (pence)	Market demand per month
50	100 000
40	150 000
30	200 000
20	260 000
10	330 000
5	400 000

1 With price on the vertical axis, and quantity per year along the bottom axis, plot the market demand curve for orange light bulbs and label it DD.

2 Use the graph to work out how many orange light bulbs would be demanded at a price of:

a 35 pence

b 15 pence.

3 If orange light bulb producers together wished to sell the following amount of bulbs each year what price should they charge?

a 360 000

b 295 000

c 180 000

4 Explain why the market demand curve for orange light bulbs slopes downwards.

5 Explain the difference between individual demand and market demand.

In general the market demand curve for any good or service will be downward sloping showing the relationship between quantity demanded and price, assuming that nothing else changes that will affect how much consumers demand.

A market demand curve for a product

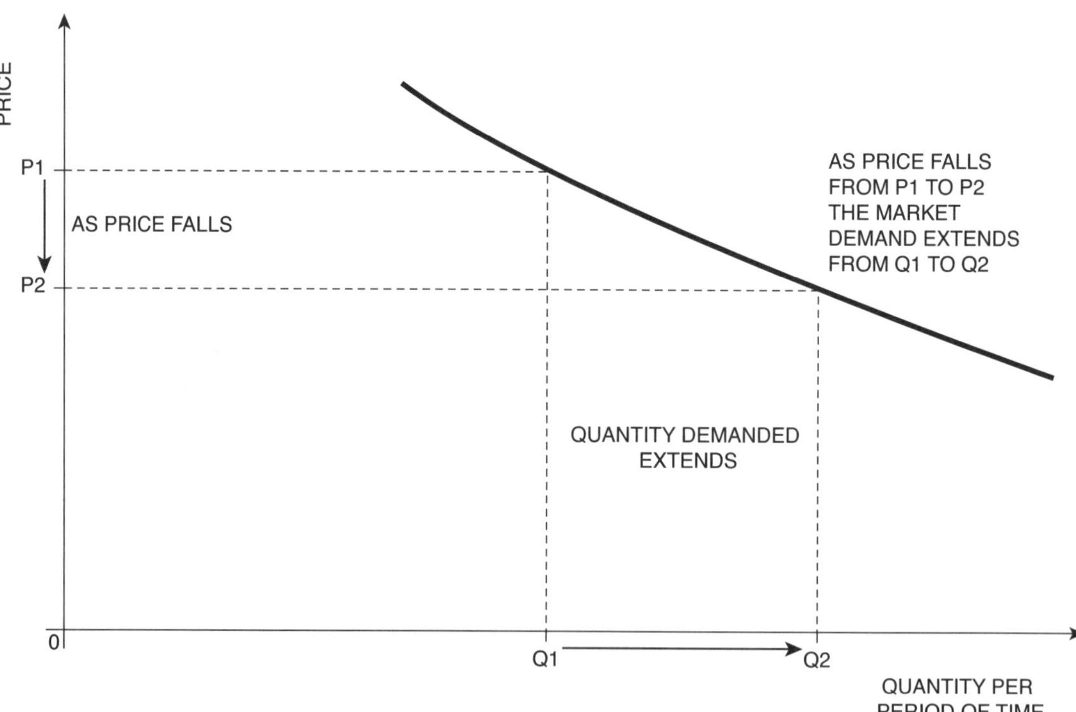

Shifts in demand

An increase in the price of a product will normally cause demand to contract. However, this assumes that no other factor that affects consumers' demand changes. Demand curves are drawn based on the assumption that nothing else changes other than price so only changes in the price of the product can be seen to affect demand. This is called the **ceteris paribus** assumption, meaning 'all other things remaining unchanged'.

However, what happens to the demand for particular goods and services when these things do change? For example, will a fall in people's income cause them to demand less of a product whatever its price? What effect will an advertising campaign for a product have on demand, regardless of the price of the product?

An increase in demand

For example, the market demand for chocolate bars:

Possible price (pence) of chocolate bars	Original demand per month	Increased demand per month
50	100 000	200 000
40	150 000	250 000
30	200 000	300 000
20	260 000	360 000
10	330 000	430 000
5	400 000	500 000

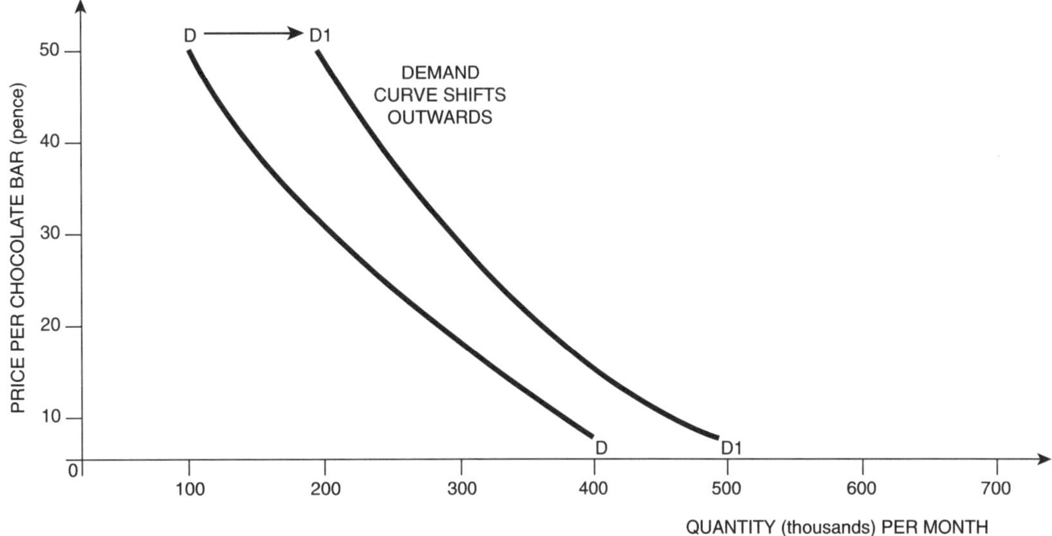

The diagram above shows an increase in demand for chocolate bars, but it could be any other good or service because the same rules apply. At each price consumers are now willing to buy more chocolate bars than they did before. The whole demand curve has shifted outwards from DD to D_1D_1.

An **increase in demand** means that consumers now demand more of a product at each and every price than they did before.

A fall in demand

For example, the market demand for DVD-R recordable discs.

Possible price per DVD-R disc (pence)	Original demand per week	Decreased demand per week
100	10000	5000
80	15000	10000
60	20000	15000
40	25000	20000
20	30000	25000

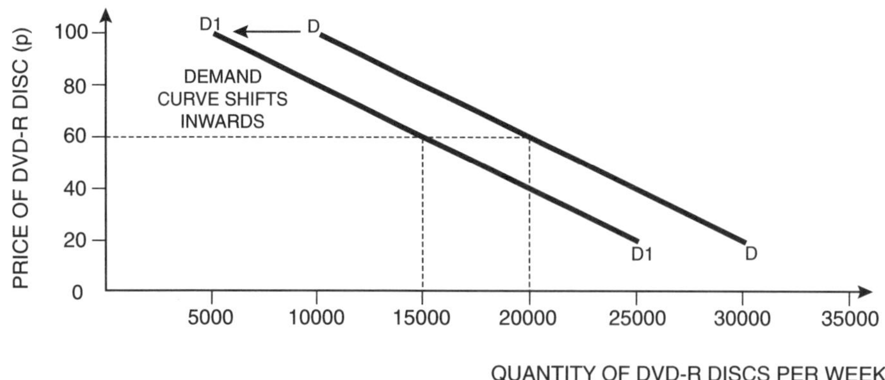

A fall in demand at all prices will cause the demand curve to shift to the left, or inwards, from DD to D_1D_1.

A **fall in demand** means that consumers now demand less of a product at each and every price than they did before.

Exercise 4 What causes a shift in demand?

Look at the following articles below and in each case say:

1. What factors have changed that will affect consumer demand?
2. Will demand increase, fall or remain unchanged given the changing factor?

Now draw a demand diagram to show the market demand curves for the products before and after the changes described in the articles.

Big Tax cuts in Australia

From 1 July 2006, all Australian taxpayers will share in tax cuts worth $36.7 billion over the next four years. The tax cuts will increase disposable incomes for all Australian taxpayers, provide further incentives for individuals to participate in the workforce and improve the international competitiveness of Australia's tax system.

From *Press Release, Treasurer of the Commonwealth of Australia,* 9.5.2006

Consumer confidence stays unchanged

Low levels of consumer confidence in the UK remained unchanged in June while confidence in the economy continued to fall, according to the latest Nationwide survey.

Last month's survey recorded a slump in spending maintaining this year's gloomy prospects for the retail sector, which has responded by continuing to keep prices at a low to encourage spending.

Adapted from Adfero Ltd news story, 7.7.2006

Heatwave means we are running out of veg

THE heatwave has brought a disastrous slump in vegetable crops, threatening shortages and higher prices.

The UK pea harvest is expected to be down by 20 per cent, while falls of up to 40 per cent are being forecast for other green vegetables.

The Daily Mail, 29.7.2006

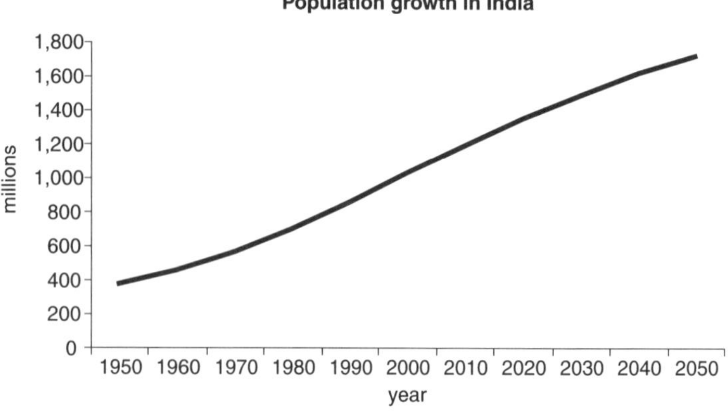

US Census Bureau, *www.census.gov/ipc/www/idbsum.html*

Go-ahead for GM crops threatens organic farms

Government ministers outlined the framework for the growing of GM crops on secret sites across the UK, which they said is likely to begin in 2009.

Organic farming will be threatened because buffer zones will not be large enough to prevent organic crops being contaminated by pollen spreading from genetically modified crops.

The Soil Association which sets organic farming standards said 'More and more scientific evidence of the risk to human health posed by genetic engineering has emerged.'

'It is outrageous that consumer demand for organic food – which is growing at 30 per cent a year – is being threatened by these proposals.'

Adapted from *The Daily Mail*, 21.7.2006

Eurozone interest rate rises

As expected, the European Central Bank raised interest rates on Thursday by 25 basis points to 2.75 percent.

Consumer price inflation was up 2.5 percent in May, above the ECB's target of below 2 percent.

However, some European politicians are worried that the rise in interest rates could choke off a potential European economic recovery after several years of weak growth and high unemployment.

Adapted from *worldeconomies.co.uk*, 6.8.2006

The following factors are likely to cause changes in demand and shifts in market demand curves:

1 Changes in consumers' incomes

Because effective demand is the willingness to buy a product backed by an ability to pay, it is clear that as incomes rise consumers will be able to buy more, while a fall in incomes will cause demand to fall. However, the precise nature of the relationship between income and demand will depend on the type of product considered and the level of consumers' income. For example, a rise in income is unlikely to make most consumers want to buy more salt or newspapers each day or week, but it might allow them to travel less by bus and take a taxi more often, or even buy a bigger car.

In general, if the demand for a product tends to rise as incomes rise the product is said to be a **normal good**. On the other hand, if demand tends to fall as incomes rise the product is said to be an **inferior good**. For example, as incomes rise people can afford to travel longer distances by plane rather than by train. Long-distance train journeys might therefore appear to behave like an inferior good as incomes rise.

2 Changes in taxes on incomes

Disposable income refers to the amount of income people have left to spend or save after taxes on their incomes have been deducted. Any change in the level of income tax rates and allowances are therefore likely to result in a change in the quantity of goods and services demanded.

3 The prices and availability of other goods and services

Complementary goods

Some of the goods and services we buy need other things, or accessories, to go with them. For example, cars need petrol, DVD discs need a DVD player, bread is consumed with butter or margarine. These **complementary goods** are said to be in **joint demand**.

If the prices of new cars rise consumer demand for them may contract and in turn reduce the demand for petrol. A fall in the price of DVD recorders may lead to a rise in the demand for recordable DVD discs and shift their market demand curve outwards as demand for the recorders expands.

Substitute goods

On the other hand, some goods and services are **substitutes**. A product is a substitute when its purchase can replace the want for another good or service. For example, margarine is considered a close substitute for butter. A rise in the price of one may therefore result in a rise in demand for the alternative. Different makes of car are also close substitutes: a fall in the price of Toyota cars may cause a rise in the demand for cars made by Ford.

A firm will find it useful to gather information on changes in the prices and quality of competing and complementary products from rival producers because any changes in them can affect the demand and, therefore, the sales revenues and profits of that firm.

Change in fashion can cause a shift in demand

4 Changes in tastes, habits and fashion

The demand for goods and services can change dramatically because of the changing tastes of consumers and fashion. For example, many consumers all over the world are now demanding goods that are kinder to the environment and animals, and foods that are healthier.

Carefully planned advertising campaigns based on market research information on consumers can also help to change tastes and shift demand curves for the advertised products out to the right (see Chapter 9).

5 Population change

An increase in population will tend to increase the demand for many goods and services in a country. For example, the population of India has expanded rapidly over time and is forecast to grow to around 1.7 billion people by 2050. In contrast, population growth in many western countries is now negligible. Birth and death rates have fallen and this has resulted in a rise in the average age of their populations and the growing number of middle-aged and elderly people has resulted in a changing pattern of demand (see Chapter 20).

6 Other factors

There are a great many other factors that can affect demand. The weather is one example. A hot summer can boost sales of cold drinks and ices. A cold winter will increase the demand for fuel for heating. Higher interest rates can increase the demand for savings schemes but reduce the amount of money people want to borrow, including mortgages for house purchases (see Chapter 11).

Changes in laws may also affect demand for some products. For example, it is illegal in many countries to ride a motorbike without a crash helmet, and an increasing number of countries are outlawing smoking in public places.

Exercise 5 Competing or complementary?

Below is a list of goods and services. Think of some possible complements and substitutes for each of them.

Goods and services	Possible substitutes	Goods and services	Possible complements
Electric oven Woollen jumpers Gas supplies iPods Passenger rail journeys	?	LCD TV displays Fountain pens Guitars Toothbrushes Computers	?

Section 2 What is supply?

Supply curves

Supply refers to the amount of a good or service firms or producers are willing to make and sell at a number of possible prices. The amount of a good or service producers are willing and able to make and sell to consumers in a market is known as the **quantity supplied** of that product, measured per period of time, say each week, month or year.

Clearly a firm interested in profit will only make and sell a product if it can do so at a price over and above what it cost the firm to make. The higher the price of the product, the more the firm will supply because the more profit it expects to make. This can be applied generally to the supply of all goods and services. As price rises, quantity supplied rises.

The **market supply** of a product will consist of the supply of all the individual producers competing to supply that product.

In general, the supply curve for any product will slope upwards, showing that as price rises, quantity supplied rises or extends.

As price falls, quantity supplied contracts. This is because as price falls firms will expect to earn less profits as revenue will exceed costs by a smaller amount.

A market supply curve for a product

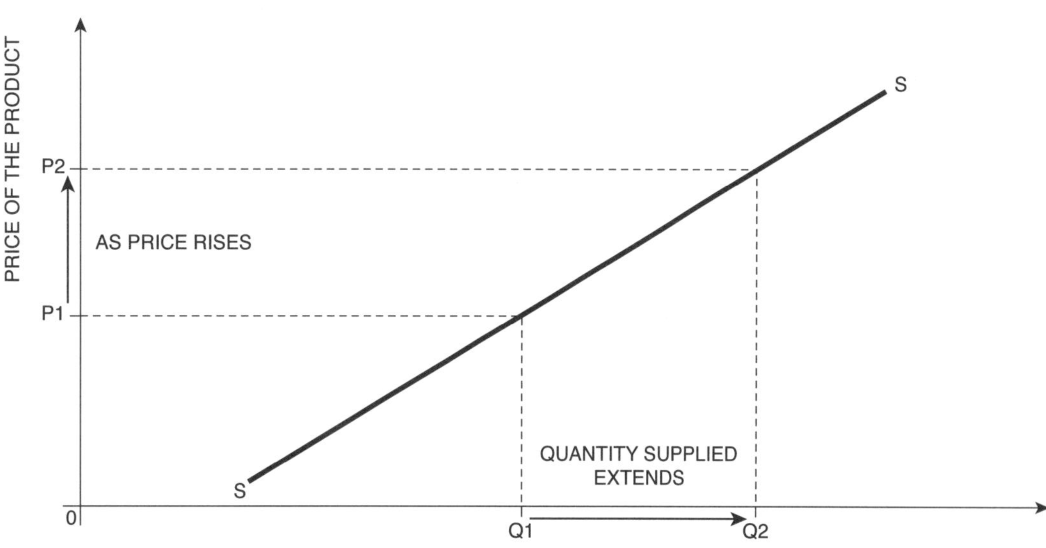

As price rises from P_1 to P_2 the market supply extends from Q_1 to Q_2. That is, a change in the price of the product causes a **movement along** the supply curve.

An **extension of supply** refers to how supply changes with a rise in the price of a product, given that no other factor affecting supply changes.

A **contraction of supply** refers to how supply changes with a fall in the price of a product, without a change in any other factor that may affect supply.

Exercise 6 The market supply curve

The following table represents the **market supply schedule** for silver-plated tankards. Copy the graph axis below, plot this information on the graph axis and label your curve the **market supply curve (SS)**.

Possible price of tankards $	Market supply per month
20	1600
16	1100
12	700
8	300
4	100

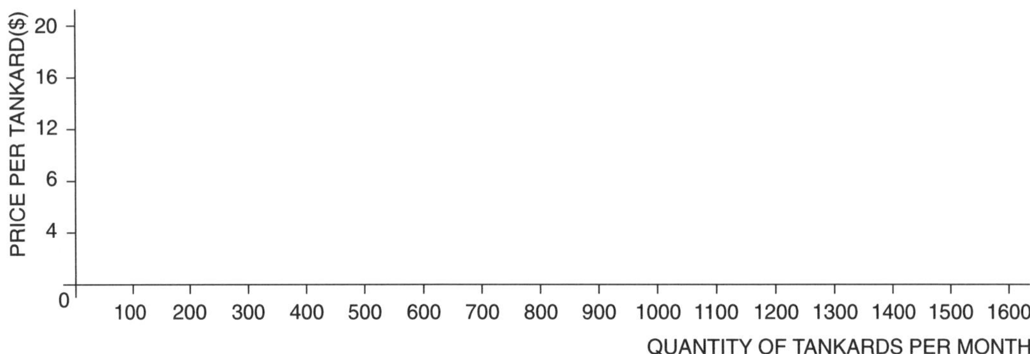

1 How does the quantity supplied change as price changes, making the assumption 'ceteris paribus', that is, that other factors that could affect supply do not change?

2 What will cause an extension in supply?

3 What will cause a contraction of supply?

4 Use your graph to work out how many tankards will be supplied at a price of:

   a 6 dollars

   b 10 dollars

5 a If consumers wished to be able to buy 700 tankards each month how much must they be prepared to pay for them?

   b What will be the tankard producers' total revenue?

6 The following table displays the costs and revenues involved in the production and sale of tankards by all the producers in the market. Using the market supply schedule complete the table and explain why the market supply curve for tankards slopes upwards from left to right.

Output of tankards per month	Total cost ($)	Total revenue ($) (price × output)	Profit ($)
100	100	400	300
300	280		
700	420		
1100	580		
1600	760		

Shifts in supply

A change in the price of a product will normally cause its supply to extend or contract. Changes in things other than the price of a good can cause its market supply curve to move. A movement of the supply curve for a good reflects either an increase or decrease in supply.

An increase in supply

For example, the market for disposable razors.

Possible price of razor (pence)	Original supply per month	Increased supply per month
50	10000	12000
40	8000	10000
30	6000	8000
20	4000	6000
10	2000	4000

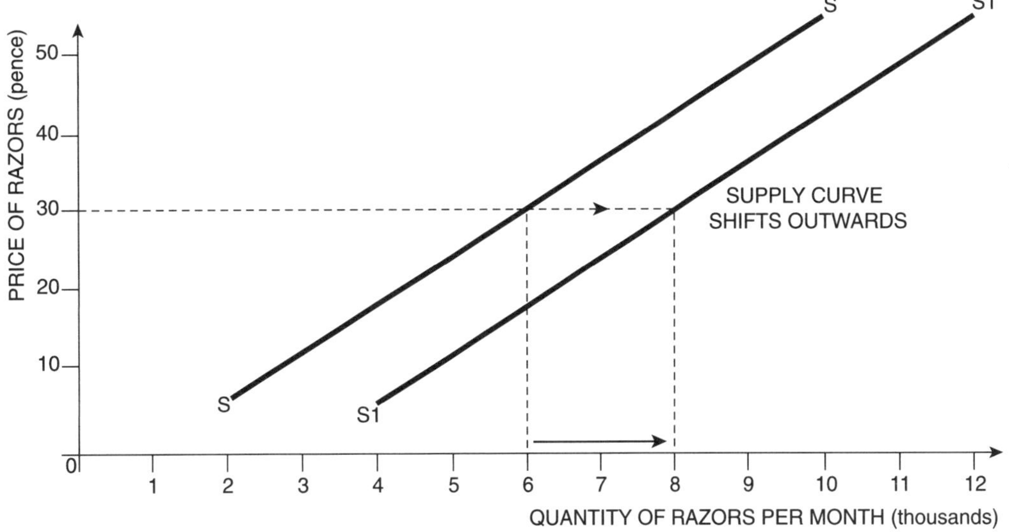

The diagram above shows an increase in the supply of disposable razors, but it could be any other good or service. At each and every price, razor producers are now willing to make and sell more razors than they did before. The whole supply curve has shifted outwards from SS to S_1S_1.

An increase in supply means that producers are now more willing and able to supply a product than they were before at all possible prices.

A fall in supply

For example, the market supply of potatoes.

Price per lb of potatoes (pence)	Original supply per month (kg)	Supply per month (kg)
100	50 000	40 000
80	40 000	30 000
60	30 000	20 000
40	20 000	10 000
20	10 000	0

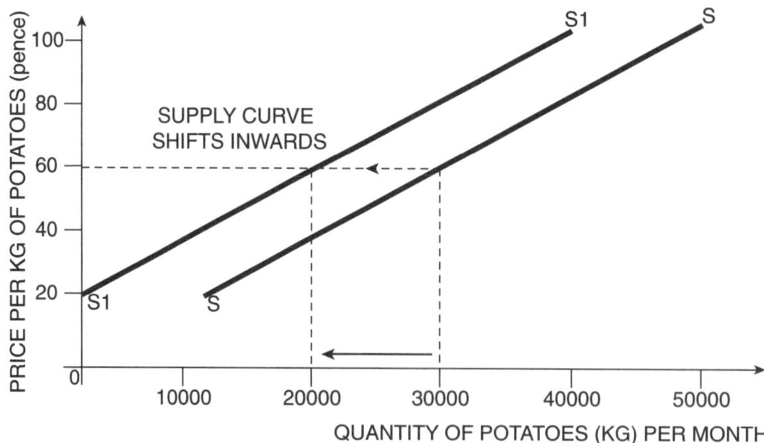

A fall in supply at all prices will cause the supply curve of a commodity to shift inwards from SS to S_1S_1.

A **fall in supply** means that producers are now less willing and able to supply a product at each and every price than they were before at all possible prices.

Exercise 7 What causes a shift in supply?

Read the following passage and try to pick out all the factors that have caused a change in the supply of potatoes and cabbages.

Farmer Bumpkin plans to plant five fields of potatoes and three fields of cabbages each year. The price he can usually get for a kilogram of potatoes is 30 pence, while the price of cabbages is 50 pence. Farmer Bumpkin has estimated that his time, effort, machinery and fertilizer costs add up to an average 12 pence per kg of potatoes and 20 pence per kg of cabbages.

Which crop is the more profitable one to grow?

However, in the following season the price of potatoes rises to 45 pence per kg.

What would you advise Farmer Bumpkin and farmers like him to do? Given your advice what will happen to the supply of cabbages?

In the very next growing season, Farmer Bumpkin discovers a new 'Speedo' cabbage harvester is available, and at a very reasonable price. He used to pay some boys and girls from the nearby village to help pick his crops each year, but now he can pick them all by himself using the machine. He estimates that this saving has reduced the average cost per cabbage grown to only 10 pence.

If the price of potatoes and cabbages have remained unchanged what would you now advise Farmer Bumpkin and farmers like him to do? How will this affect the supply of potatoes and cabbages?

In the very next season the landowner who rents her land to Farmer Bumpkin decides to cut the rent of land from £500 per year to £300. That is, from £100 per field to £60 per field. Farmer Bumpkin wonders if he should rent an additional field now that it costs much less to produce potatoes and cabbages. If he decided to do this what will be the likely effect on the supply of his potatoes and cabbages?

A farmer's year is not without its problems. Towards the end of the season an early but very hard frost damages Farmer Bumpkin's entire cabbage crop.

What will happen to the supply of cabbages now?

What factors have caused changes in the supply of potatoes and cabbages?

Changes in the following factors will cause changes in supply and shifts in the supply curve of a product.

1 Changes in the cost of factors of production

By far the largest determinant of supply is the cost of resources for production, i.e. payments made for raw materials and power supplies, wages for labour, and rents or leasing costs for buildings and machinery, etc.

A rise in the costs of production, for example, due to workers winning generous wage rises or a shortage of raw materials, will tend to reduce profits (see Chapter 13). Producers affected by these costs will tend to cut back their demand for labour and raw materials in an attempt to save money and will therefore be less willing and able to supply as much of their particular goods or services as they did before. An increase in the costs of land or payments for capital will also tend to have the same effect.

In contrast, a fall in the costs of land, labour and capital will tend to increase profits and market supply. This was the case in the last exercise as Farmer Bumpkin enjoyed a cut in the rent he paid for the land he uses to grow cabbages, encouraging him to increase production.

Governments may also try to influence the supply of goods and services by private sector firms through taxes and subsidies, as we will see in section 7. Taxes can be regarded as an additional cost of production while subsidies help offset costs.

2 Changes in the price of other goods and services

Price changes act as the signals to private sector firms to move their resources to and from the production of different goods and services. In a free market, resources are allocated to those goods and services that will yield the most profit.

In the Farmer Bumpkin exercise a rise in the price of potatoes will cause him to move his resources out of the production of cabbages into the production of potatoes. As a result the supply curve for cabbages will shift inwards at every possible price as farmers are now less willing to grow them.

The same will apply to almost all other goods and services. A fall in the price of one may cause producers to cut production and supply more of another, more profitable product.

3 Technological advance

Technical progress can mean improvements in the performance of machines, employees, production methods, management control, product quality, etc. This allows more to be produced, often at a lower cost, regardless of the price at which the product is sold. For example, advances in deep water mining technology and rig design have helped a number of countries to drill for oil in deep oceans once thought too costly to exploit.

In the case of Farmer Bumpkin his new 'Speedo' cabbage harvester will allow him to shift the supply curve of his cabbages outwards.

4 Business optimism and expectations

Fears of an economic downturn may cause some firms to move resources into the production of goods and services they feel will be less affected by a fall in consumer incomes and demand. For example, high-cost, luxury items such as cars and overseas holidays often fare badly during economic recessions (see Chapter 17). Conversely, expectations of an economic recovery may result in a reallocation of scarce resources into new markets, thereby shifting their supply curves out towards the right.

5 Global factors

The supply of goods and services can be affected by many factors that cannot be controlled by producers. For example, sudden climatic change, trade sanctions, wars, natural disasters and political factors can have a material impact on the supply of many goods and services.

On the Bumpkin farm the weather will be a major factor affecting the supply of the farmer's crops. A good summer growing season will help increase supply.

Market price

Reaching an equilibrium

We have now looked at the two market forces that determine price. For each good and service there is a market supply schedule and a market demand schedule. If the two are combined we will find that the quantity demanded and quantity supplied will be equal at one price. This is the **market price** at which the commodity will be sold in the market. The market price can also be found using the market demand and supply curve.

Exercise 8 Finding the market price

Consider the market demand and supply schedules for chocolate bars.

Possible price of chocolate bars (pence)	Quantity demanded per month	Quantity supplied per month
50	100 000	420 000
40	150 000	300 000
30	200 000	200 000
20	260 000	120 000
10	330 000	60 000
5	400 000	40 000

On graph paper plot the demand and supply curves for chocolate bars on one graph with 'Price per chocolate bar' on the vertical axis and 'Quantity per month' along the bottom axis.

1 Using the above table state at which price demand equals supply.

This will be the **market price** for chocolate bars because at that price producers are willing to make and sell just as many bars as consumers are willing to buy.

2 **a** Find the market price of chocolate bars using your demand and supply curves.

b What is the quantity of chocolate bars traded at this price in the market?

3 **a** When the quantity demanded is greater than the quantity supplied economists say there is an **excess demand**. At which prices in the table is there an excess demand for chocolate bars?

b Similarly when quantity supplied exceeds the quantity demanded there is said to be an **excess supply**. At which prices in the table is there an excess supply of chocolate bars?

4 **a** If there is excess demand what do you think will happen to the price of chocolate bars?

b If there is excess supply what do you think will happen to their price?

c At which price will there be no excess demand or supply?

In the above exercise it should be clear that a market price will be determined at 30 pence per chocolate bar. Only here will market demand equal market supply. Another name for market price is **equilibrium price** because it is the price at which the amount supplied equals or satisfies the amount demanded.

In a graph equilibrium is found where the demand and supply curves cross as in the diagram below. At this market price of 30 pence 200 000 chocolate bars will be traded each week.

Equilibrium in the market for chocolate bars

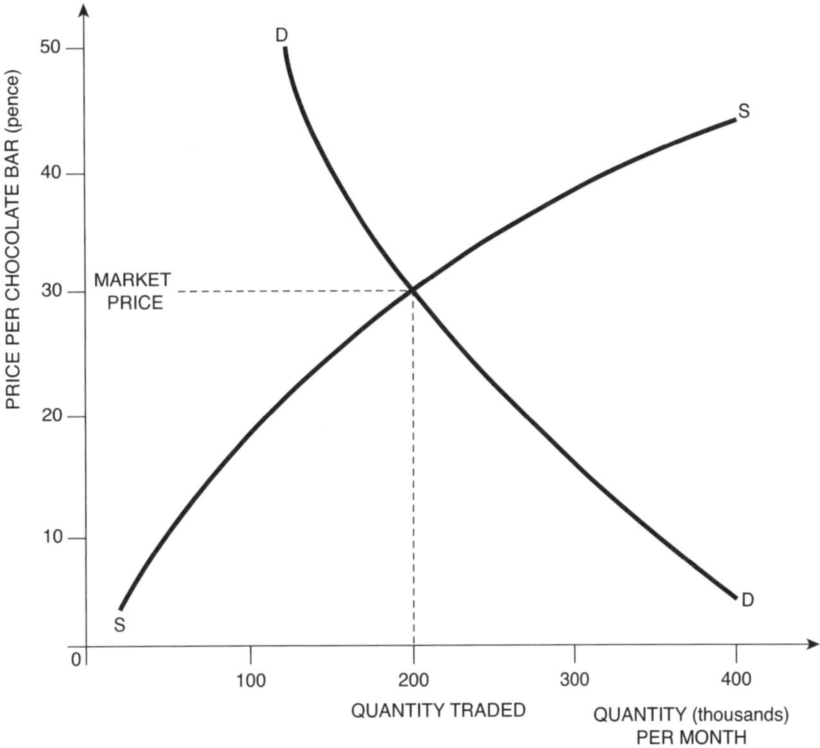

At prices higher than the market price (for example 40p) firms will supply more than consumers demand and so there will be an **excess supply**. In order to persuade consumers to buy up this excess supply the price will have to fall.

At prices lower than the market price (for example 20p) the quantity demanded by consumers exceeds what firms will supply. There will be an excess demand. As a result the price will rise.

When demand does not equal supply this is known as a **disequilibrium**.

Disequilibrium in the market for chocolate bars

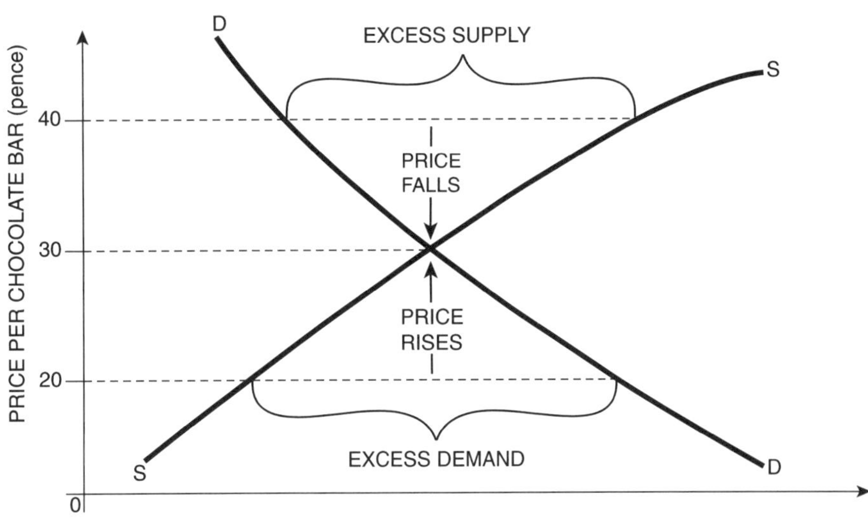

Only in equilibrium where demand equals supply will there be no forces trying to change price.

Changes in market prices

Changes in market prices will occur as a result of changes in demand and/ or supply.

1 A shift in demand

An increase in demand for a commodity, because people's incomes have risen, or the price of a substitute good has gone up, will cause the demand curve to shift outwards.

In the diagram below it shifts from DD to D_1D_1. As a result the market price rises from P to P_1.

Producers extend the supply of the product to meet the higher level of demand because they are willing to supply more at higher prices.

An increase in demand and market price

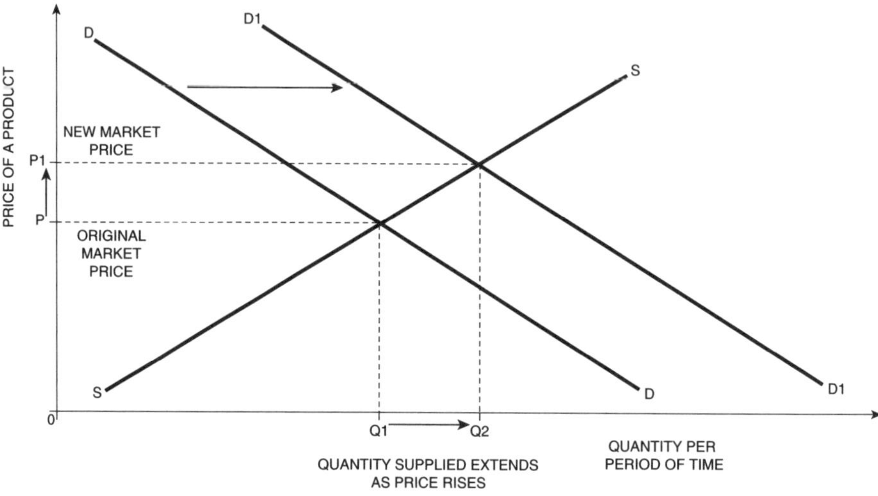

Exercise 9 A fall in demand and market price

Below is a market demand and supply schedule for ballpoint pens.

Price per pen (pence)	Original demand per week	Original supply per week
300	100	500
250	200	400
200	300	300
150	400	200
100	500	100

1 Plot and label the demand curve (DD) and supply curve (SS) for ballpoint pens.

2 Mark in the market price (P) and the quantity traded (Q) at this price.

3 Imagine now that demand falls by 200 units at each and every price. Draw and label the new demand curve (D_1D_1).

4 What is the new market price (P_1) and the new quantity traded (Q_1)? Show these on your graph.

5 What has happened to supply and why?

6 Suggest four reasons why demand for ballpoint pens might fall.

A shift in supply

An increase in supply of a product because workers have accepted lower wages, or technical progress has increased the performance of capital equipment, will be seen as a movement outwards in the supply curve from SS to S_1S_1. As a result market price will fall from P to P_1 as a greater supply is available. As the market price falls so consumers will extend their demand for the product from Q to Q_1.

An increase in supply and market price

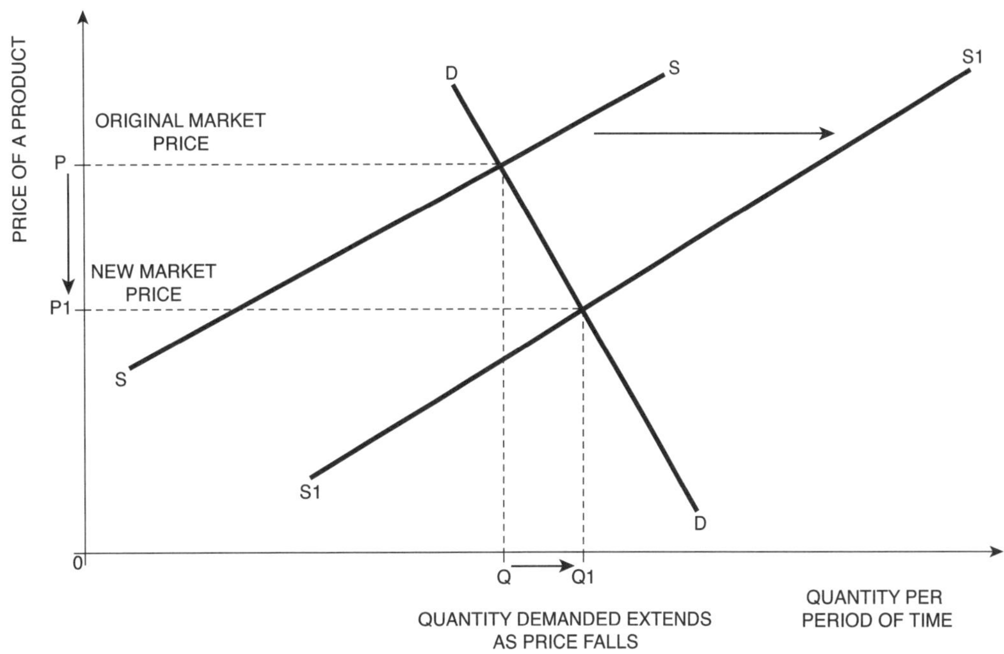

Exercise 10 A fall in supply and market price

Below is the market demand and supply schedule for wheat (tonnes per year).

Possible price per tonne (dollars)	Original demand per year	Original supply per year
500	100000	500000
400	200000	400000
300	300000	300000
200	400000	200000
100	500000	100000

1. Plot and label the demand curve (DD) for wheat and its supply curve (SS).
2. Mark in the market price (P) and the quantity traded (Q) at this price.
3. Imagine now that supply falls by 200000 tonnes at each and every price. Draw and label the new supply curve (S_1S_1).
4. What is the new market price (P_1) and the new quantity traded (Q_1)? Show these on your graph.
5. What has happened to demand and why?
6. Suggest four reasons why the supply of wheat may fall.

A fall in the supply of a product will cause its supply curve to shift inwards and market price will rise. Consumers' demand contracts along their demand curve as market price rises until demand equals supply once again.

The price mechanism

We have now seen how the price mechanism works in a free market. The forces of demand and supply establish the market price of a product. Changes in demand and supply will cause changes in price.

An increase in the demand for a good or service will raise market price. This will be the signal to producers to use more resources to supply more. This way consumers get what they want as firms compete for their custom. An increase in the supply of a product lowers market price and enables more people to share the increased supply.

Exercise 11 A flat-out market

Families count cost of rush for a flat-screen TV

FAMILIES who paid out for the latest in flat-screen TVs might be wishing now that they had waited a little longer.

Manufacturers have produced so many that there is a worldwide glut. Retailers are admitting that prices for state-of-the-art LCD and plasma sets, which originally cost in the thousands, are now 'dropping every day'.

Manufacturers and retailers launched a big push on the sets over the last six months, tied to the World Cup and the launch of high definition services promising much sharper pictures and sound.

During the build-up to the football World Cup, major retailers were selling a high value flat-screen television every 15 seconds. But even during the busiest periods retailers warned that there would be a lull in sales immediately after the tournament, which has now led to rival stores having to slash prices to clear stocks.

In the meantime, so many flat-screen TVs have been produced that the glut has forced manufacturers to slash their premium prices.

Adapted from *The Daily Mail,* 18.7.2006

1. What happened to the demand for large flat-screen televisions in the run-up to the World Cup?
2. What impact do you think the change in demand for flat-screen televisions has had on demand and supply in the market for ordinary (cathode ray tube) televisions?
3. What happened to the supply of large flat-screen televisions? What affect did this have on the prices of these products?
4. What is likely to happen to the quantity traded of flat-screen televisions following the increase in their supply?
5. Draw a diagram to illustrate the movements in demand and supply curves in the market for large flat-screen TVs.

Section 4 Price elasticity of demand

What is price elasticity of demand?

When prices rise we can assume that the quantity demanded will contract for most goods and services. However, firms and economists would like to know by how much demand will contract or expand as prices change.

For example, a train company would like to know what would happen to demand for its services, and therefore the revenue it earns from tickets, if it increased its fares. Increasing fares in peak periods when many people have to travel by train to and from work in busy cities may have very little impact on demand because many people have few or no alternatives. Journeys by road by car or bus may take too long, the traveller may not own a car, or car parking in the city is too expensive. However, raising train fares for journeys off-peak and at weekends may cause demand, and therefore revenue, to fall significantly because people may decide against travelling and spend their leisure time doing something else or travelling by car or bus because the roads are not so busy.

Similarly, a government would want to calculate how much tax revenue it could expect from a tax placed on a particular good or service. For example, many governments levy excise taxes on cigarettes to discourage people from smoking (see Chapter 15). However, despite the tax many people continue to smoke which in turn provides the government with a stream of tax revenue from the sale of cigarettes.

Consider the two diagrams below.

The demand curve is quite steep. As price rises by 25 per cent from 200p to 250p demand contracts very little from 1000 to 900 units per period, a fall of just 10 per cent. This might be very similar to the demand for train journeys during busy peak periods.

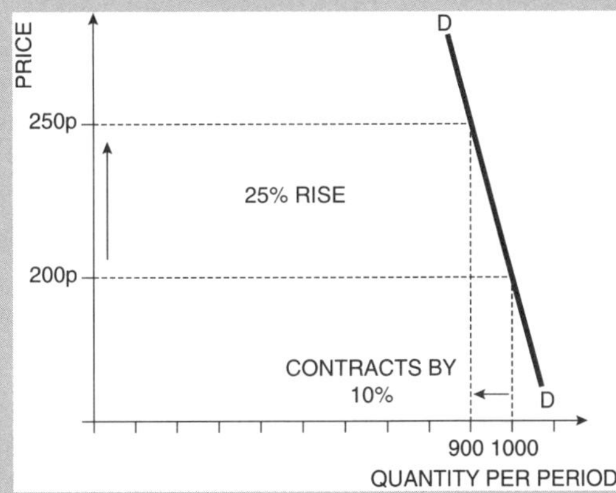

In this case **demand** is said to be **price inelastic** as the percentage change in price is much larger than the percentage change in demand.

The demand curve is quite flat. As price rises by 25 per cent from 200p to 250p demand contracts significantly, from 1000 to 500 units, a fall of 50 per cent. This could be what the demand curve for off-peak travel by train looks like.

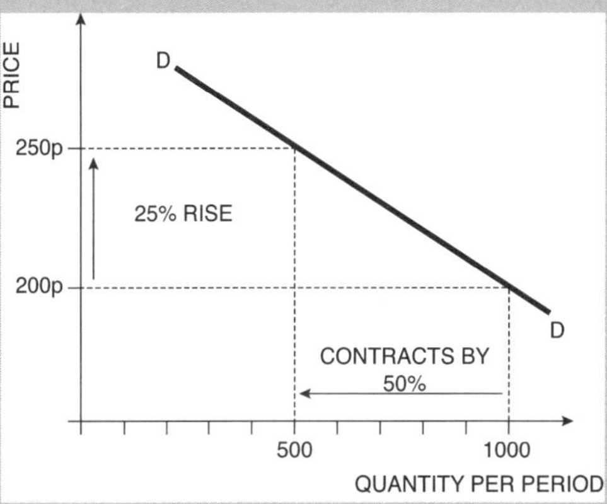

In this case **demand** is said to be **price elastic** as the percentage change in price is less than the percentage change in demand.

The responsiveness of quantity demanded to changes in the price of a good or service is known as the **price elasticity of demand (PEd)** of that product.

If a small change in the price of a product causes a big change in quantity demanded, the demand for that product is said to be price elastic. That is, quantity demanded *stretches* (expands or contracts) significantly when the price is changed.

On the other hand, if a small change in the price of a product causes only a very minor change in quantity demanded, the demand for that product is said to be price inelastic. That is, quantity demanded *stretches* very little when price changes.

Exercise 12 A problem to 'stretch' you

Assume there is a rise of about 10 per cent in the prices of the following goods. State whether there is likely to be large, small or no change in the quantity demanded. Then state whether you think demand is price elastic or inelastic, and why.

Product	Small or large change in quantity demanded	Price elastic or price inelastic	Why?
Oil			
DVD recorders			
Bread			
Cars			
Newspapers			

Products such as oil and bread are necessary items for many people. An increase in price may only have a very small impact on the quantity demanded. Demand for these goods therefore tends to be relatively price inelastic. Similarly, purchases of newspapers only account for a relatively small amount of many people's incomes and this tends to make demand for them price inelastic. In contrast, demand for more luxurious, high-value products such as DVD recorders and cars may contract significantly if their prices rise. Demand for these types of products tends to be price elastic.

How to measure price elasticity of demand

Price elasticity of demand compares the percentage change in quantity demanded with the percentage change in price that caused it. For example, imagine personal hi-fi producers raise their prices from \$20 to \$25, that is, by 25 per cent. If the quantity demanded contracted from 1 000 per week to 500 per week then this represents a 50 per cent reduction in quantity demanded, which is double the percentage change in price. As demand has changed by a greater percentage than price, demand is price elastic. That is, each 1 per cent change in price will cause a 2 per cent change in the quantity of personal hi-fis demanded.

If, on the other hand, the percentage change in price caused a much smaller percentage change in quantity demanded, demand would be price inelastic.

The price elasticity of demand for a product is calculated as follows:

$$\text{PEd} = \frac{\text{\% change in quantity demanded}}{\text{\% change in price}}$$

Percentage changes are worked out as follows:

$$\text{\% change in quantity demanded} = \frac{\text{change in quantity}}{\text{original quantity}} \times \frac{100}{1}$$

$$\text{\% change in price} = \frac{\text{change in price}}{\text{original price}} \times \frac{100}{1}$$

For example, look at the following demand schedule.

Price of the good	Quantity demanded per week
5 pence	100
4 pence	110

Taking 5 pence as the original price and 100 as the original quantity, the change in price is 1 pence and the change in quantity 10.

1 % change in quantity demand $= \frac{10}{100} \times \frac{100}{1} = \frac{1000}{100} = 10\%$

2 % change in price $= \frac{1p}{5p} \times \frac{100}{1} = \frac{100p}{5p} = 20\%$

3 $\text{PEd} = \frac{\%\text{ change in quantity demanded}}{\%\text{ change in price}} = \frac{10\%}{20\%} = \frac{1}{2} = 0.5$

Demand is price inelastic because the percentage change in price of 20 per cent is greater than the percentage change in quantity demanded of 10 per cent. The PEd is 0.5.

Exercise 13 Using the formula

Below is the demand schedule for tins of beans.

Price of beans per tin	Market demand per week
40 pence	1000
30 pence	1500

1 Calculate the price elasticity of demand. (*Hint* use 40 pence as your original price.)

2 Comment on its value.

3 What will the demand curve for beans look like? Draw a simple diagram to show this.

The demand for baked beans in the above example is price elastic because the per cent increase in quantity demanded of 50 per cent is greater than the 25 per cent fall in price that caused it (PEd = 2). The demand curve for beans will therefore be quite flat.

In general when PEd is **greater than 1**, demand is price **elastic**. If PEd is **less than 1**, demand is price **inelastic**.

Price elasticity and total revenue

A firm will wish to know if an increase in price will cause their total revenue to rise. However, if quantity demand contracts a lot, revenue is more likely to fall.

Exercise 14 What happens to total revenue?

Below are two demand schedules, one for bread and one for DVD recorders.

Price per loaf	Quantity demanded per month
*25 pence	10000
20 pence	10500

Price per DVD recorder	Quantity demanded per month
*$ 500	1 000
$ 400	1 800

* original price and quantity

1 In each case calculate the price elasticity of demand. Comment on their values.

2 Calculate the total revenue (price × quantity demanded) for bread and for DVD recorders, at each price.

3 **a** Would you advise bread-makers to cut the price of a loaf from 25 pence to 20 pence? Explain your answer.

b Would you advise manufacturers to cut the price of a DVD recorder from $500 to $400? Explain your answer.

4 Using the information above, decide which of the words in italics below does not apply in each case.

a Demand is price elastic when the percentage change in quantity demanded is *more/less* than the percentage change in price. A fall in price will cause a *large/small* extension in quantity demanded so that total sales revenue *falls/rises*. If price is increased, total revenue would *fall/rise.*

b Demand is price inelastic when quantity demanded changes by a *greater/smaller* percentage than price. A fall in price will cause a *small/large* extension in quantity demanded so that total sales revenue *fall/rises*. A rise in price therefore causes total revenue to *fall/rise.*

Price elasticity of demand and firms' revenues are closely linked.

In the case of bread, because demand is price inelastic (PEd = 0.4), when the price is lowered, there is only a very small extension in demand and so overall total revenue falls. An increase in price would therefore raise revenue. In the case of DVD recorders it is advisable for their producers to lower the price from $500 to $400. Because demand is price elastic (PEd = 4) sales expand greatly and revenue rises. An increase in price would therefore tend to reduce revenue.

Factors which affect price elasticity of demand

1 The number of substitutes

When consumers can choose between a large number of substitutes for a particular product, demand for any one of them is likely to be price elastic.

Demand will be price inelastic when there are few substitutes. For example, many foods like milk and medicines have few substitutes.

2 The period of time

If the price of a product rises consumers will search for cheaper substitutes. The longer they have, the more likely they are to find one. Demand will therefore be more price elastic in the long run.

3 The proportion of income spent on a commodity

Goods, like matches or newspapers, may be price inelastic in demand because they do not cost very much and any rise in their price will only take a little bit extra out of a person's income. If the price of cars was to rise by 10 per cent this could mean paying an extra $500 or more for a car. This is a considerable part of a person's income. Demand is more likely to be price elastic.

Some special demand curves

If a rise or fall in the price of a product causes no change in the quantity demanded of that product, demand is said to be **perfectly price inelastic**. That is, price elasticity of demand is 0.

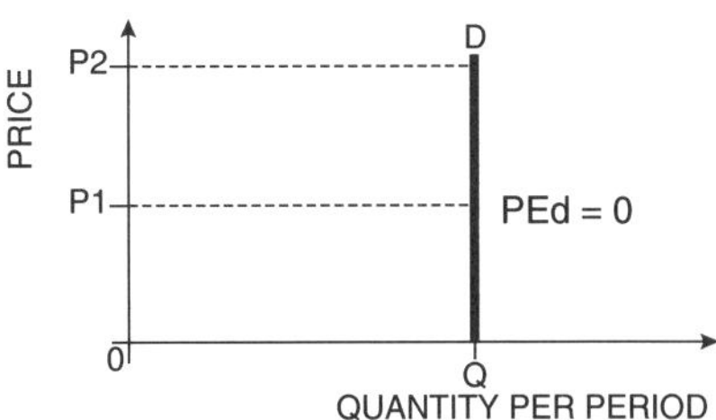

If a product is only demanded at one particular price, demand is said to be **infinitely price elastic**. That is, a small change in price will cause quantity demanded to fall to zero, that is, quantity demanded will change by an infinite amount.

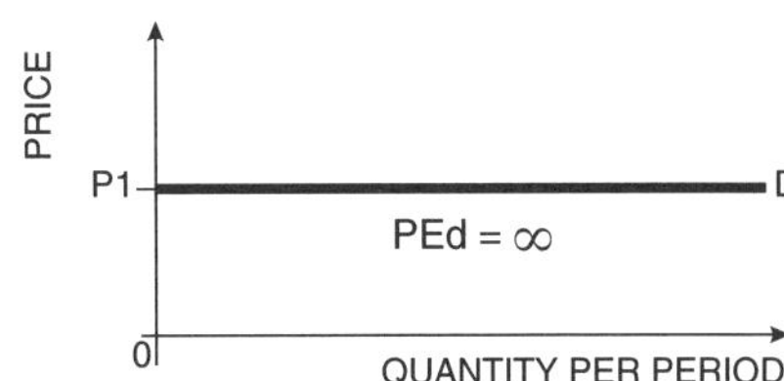

If the price elasticity of demand is 1 then demand is said to be of **unitary elasticity**. A percentage change in the price of a product will cause an equal percentage change in the quantity demanded. The result will be that the total amount spent on that product by consumers will remain the same whatever its price.

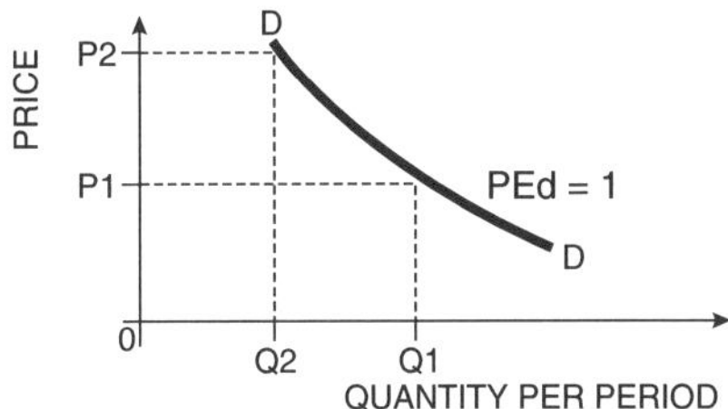

Exercise 15 Elastic brands

It may be hard to believe but the British high street is now probably the world's toughest battleground for consumer goods brands. For this blame a combination of powerful supermarket chains selling own label products and weak trademark legislation that allows the sales of lookalikes. With point-of-sale scanning enabling competitors to match each other's promotions instantly, costly advertising is now often the only way to keep weaker brands on supermarket shelves.

More than half of Britain's top 500 consumer-good brands (including supermarket own label products) have suffered falling sales over the past three years: only 184 saw sales growth. Price has increasingly become the key factor deciding a brand's fate: average prices for grocery items such as baked beans, kitchen towels and sliced bread have fallen by up to a fifth in real terms. But price cutting to gain a market share can often be a loser's game with no benefit to overall profit. So what should firms do?

A study by Will Hamilton of Kingston University Business School found the price elasticity of the top 500 brands averaged 1.85. In other words a 10 per cent cut in price should produce an 18.5 per cent increase in sales.

But the study also found wide variations across brands and categories. Thus with an elasticity of 1.01 household cleaning products are less price sensitive than dairy and bakery products (elasticity of 1.69). Unsurprisingly across all categories, market leading brands have lower price elasticities than their lesser rivals.

Mr Hamilton's study seems to prove what many marketers have long argued: that it makes sense to support brand leaders with advertising rather than price promotions because their lower elasticity means the increase in sales from price cuts may not add to profits.

1 Explain price elasticity of demand and what is meant by a 'price elasticity of 1.85'.

2 Why do you think that market leading brands might have a lower price elasticity than less well-known rivals?

3 Why might it 'make more sense' to improve profits through better advertising rather than price cutting for some brands?

Section 5 Price elasticity of supply

What is price elasticity of supply?

We have seen how the price mechanism works whereby an increase in demand will cause the market price of a product to rise. As a result, supply extends so that consumers get what they want. However, as economists we would wish to know by how much quantity supplied will change in response to the price change. **Price elasticity of supply (PEs)** is a measure of the responsiveness of quantity supplied to a change in price.

Price elasticity of supply

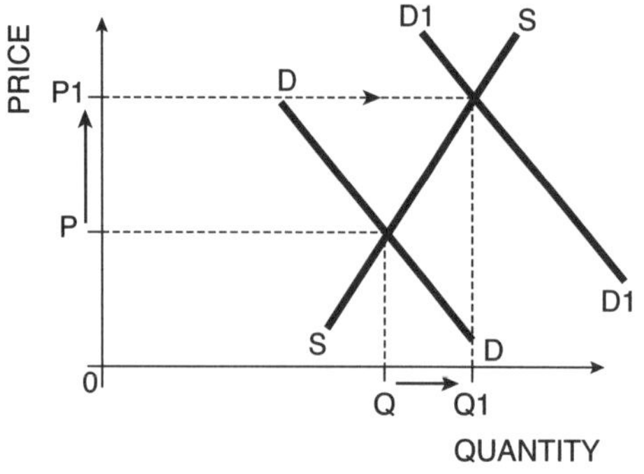

In the above diagram the increase in demand from DD to D1D1 has caused market price to rise from P to P1. However, despite this large rise in price the extension in supply is only small from Q to Q1. Supply is price **inelastic**.

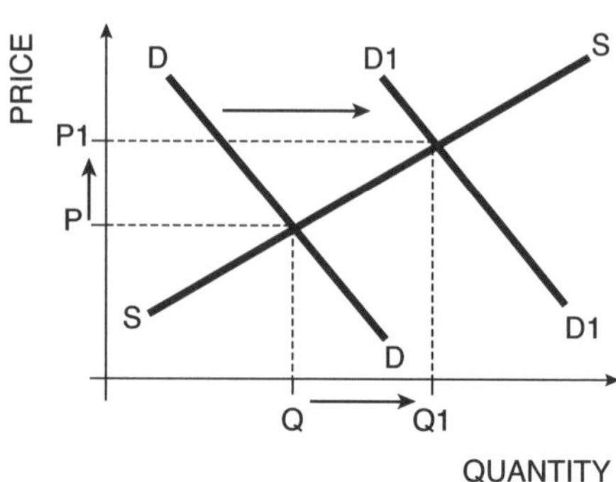

In this diagram the increase in demand from DD to D1D1 has caused only a small increase in price from P to P1 but a large extension in supply from Q to Q1. Supply is price **elastic**.

To measure price elasticity of supply we use the following formula:

$$\text{PEs} = \frac{\text{\% change in quantity supplied}}{\text{\% change in price}}$$

If the percentage change in price is greater than the percentage change in quantity supplied, supply is said to be price inelastic and the value of price elasticity of supply will be less than one.

If the percentage change in price causes a much larger percentage change in quantity supplied, supply is said to be price elastic. Price elasticity of supply will therefore be greater than one.

Below is the supply schedule for daffodils in the springtime.

Price per bunch of five daffodils	Quantity supplied per month
100 cents	10000
200 cents	12000

$$\text{\% change in quantity supplied} = \frac{\text{change in quantity}}{\text{original quantity}} \times \frac{100}{1} = \frac{2000}{10000} \times \frac{100}{1} = 20\%$$

$$\text{\% change in price} = \frac{\text{change in price}}{\text{original price}} \times \frac{100}{1} = \frac{100c}{100c} \times \frac{100}{1} = 100\%$$

$$\text{PEs} = \frac{\text{\% change in quantity supplied}}{\text{\% change in price}} = \frac{20}{100} = 0.2$$

The price elasticity of supply of daffodils is less than one, that is, supply is price inelastic. This is because even if there is a large rise in price more daffodils cannot be grown very quickly.

What affects the price elasticity of supply?

1 Time

The daffodil example illustrates how the price elasticity of supply can vary over time. Supply of most goods and services, including daffodils, will be fixed at any one moment in time. For example, a shop will only have a certain amount of newspapers, books, joints of beef. A market stall will only have a fixed amount of daffodils to sell. It will take time to get more of these things. In this special case the supply curve is a vertical line showing that whatever the price the quantity supplied will be the same.

Supply at any moment is fixed

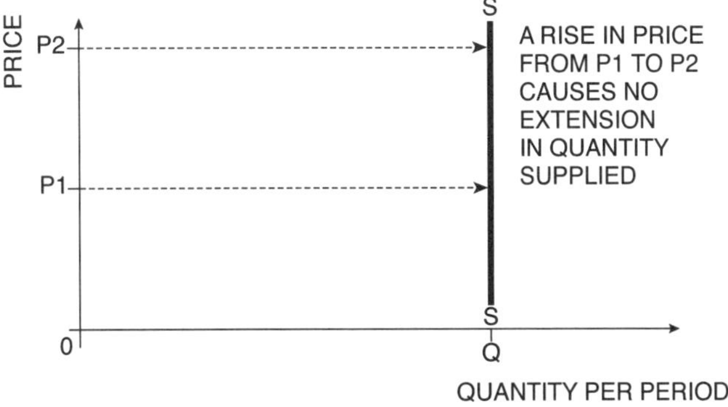

In the short run, firms can produce some more goods for sale, but only by using more labour, that is, by working overtime or employing more workers. More daffodils can be picked and sent to the market as price rises. However, supply can only rise a little because the amount of land, seeds and the season needed to grow the daffodils, will soon run out.

Supply is price inelastic in the short run

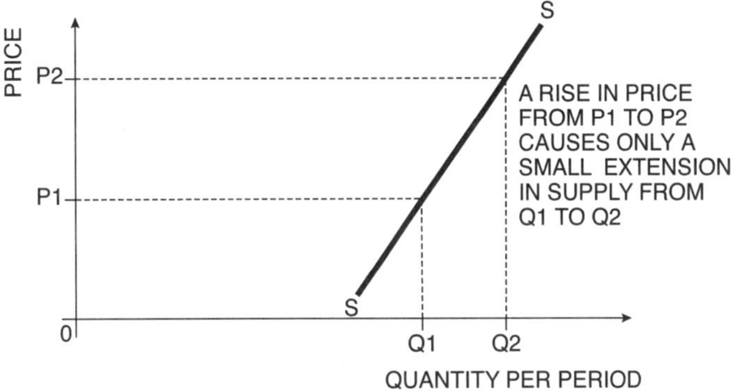

In the long run, firms can obtain more labour, land and capital to expand their scale of production, so in the long run the supply of most products becomes more price elastic.

Supply in the long run is price elastic

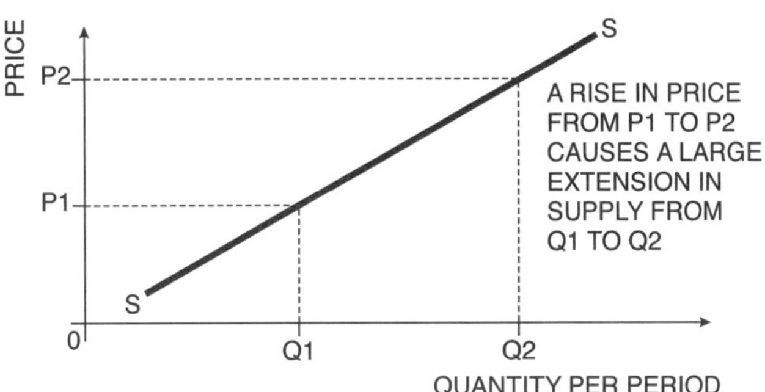

2 The availability of resources

If a firm wishes to expand production it will need more of the factors of production of land, labour and capital. If the economy is already using most of its scarce resources then firms will find it difficult to employ more and so output will not be able to rise. The supply of most goods and services will therefore be price inelastic.

If, however, there is much unemployment of resources, for example, labour, firms will be able to use them when they want to raise output and supply will be more price elastic.

Exercise 16 Stretching supply

Below are imaginary supply schedules for natural rubber and man-made rubber.

Price per kg	Quantity supplied of natural rubber per month
80 cents	1000
100 cents	1100
Price per kg	**Quantity supplied of man-made rubber per month**
80 cents	2000
100 cents	2800

1 Calculate the price elasticity of supply for natural rubber and man-made rubber.

2 Comment on their values and suggest reasons why they differ.

Some special supply curves

If the quantity supplied of a commodity remains the same whatever its price, supply is said to be **perfectly price inelastic**, that is, price elasticity of supply is 0.

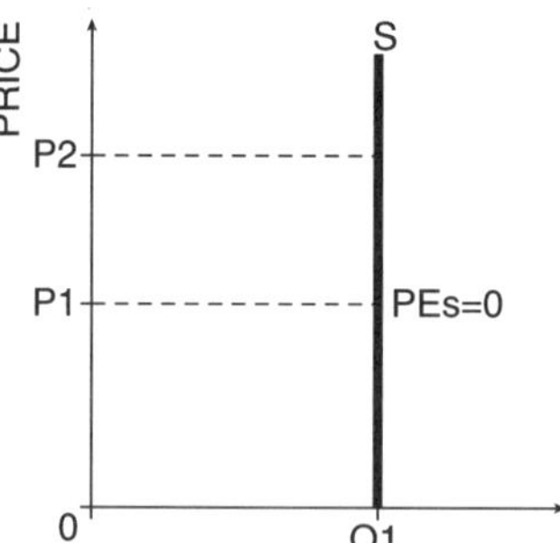

If producers are willing to supply as much as they can at one particular price and supply nothing at any other price then supply is said to be **infinitely price elastic**.

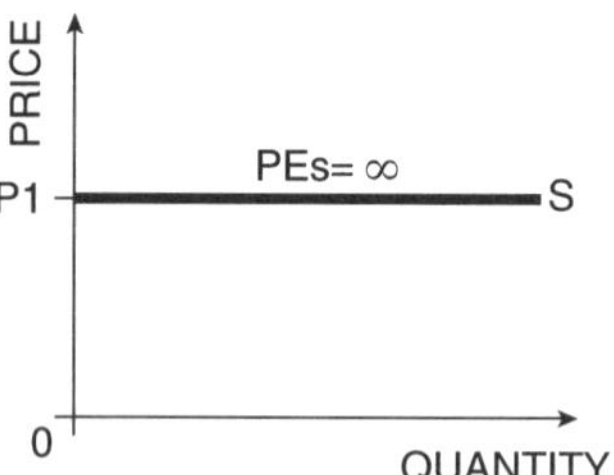

If the price elasticity of supply is 1 then supply is said to be of **unitary elasticity**. A percentage change in price will cause an equal percentage change in quantity supplied. This will be the case for any straight line supply curve that passes through the point of origin of its graph.

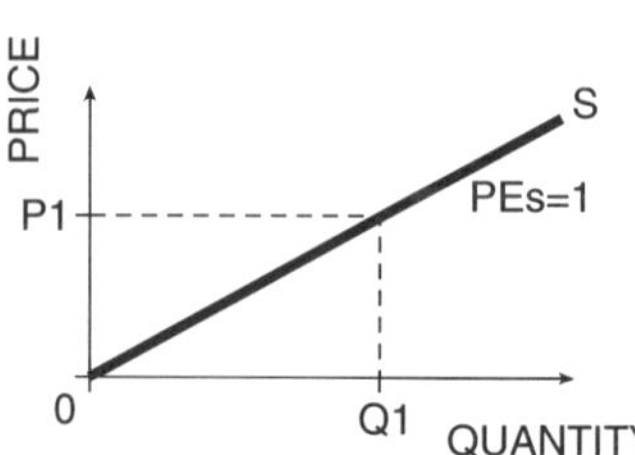

Section 6 Taxes and subsidies

The government may often intervene in free markets to influence the market price and quantity traded of certain goods and services (see Chapters 3 and 14). In general, a tax will raise the price of a product either directly and so tend to reduce the demand for that product, or the tax can be used to make production more expensive so reducing supply and forcing up market price. In contrast, a subsidy paid to a producer will help lower costs and increase market supply.

Tax and supply

Taxes placed on goods and services are called **indirect taxes** (see Chapter 15). Examples include *ad valorem* taxes such as Value Added Tax (VAT) and other sales taxes that are levied as a percentage of the selling price of a good or service, and specific **excise duties** such as those on petrol, alcohol and cigarettes, which are often a fixed tax mark-up on price. Such taxes have the effect of increasing market prices and thereby contracting consumer demand, especially if demand is price elastic.

These taxes can be regarded as an additional cost of production that has to be paid by the producer to the government. They have the effect of moving the market supply curve vertically upwards by the amount of the tax.

Tax and the brandy market

Price per bottle (dollars)	Quantity demanded per month	Quantity supplied per month	Quantity supplied after a 2 dollar tax
10	100	900	700
9	200	800	600
8	300	700	500
7	400	600	400
6	500	500	300
5	600	400	—
4	700	300	—

The imaginary schedule above shows how much producers of the alcoholic drink, brandy, are willing to supply and how many bottles consumers are willing to buy at each possible price before and after an excise duty of 2 dollars per bottle is applied. For example, before the tax producers were willing to supply 700 bottles per month at 8 dollars per bottle. At this price their revenue from monthly sales was 5600 dollars (i.e. 700 bottles × 8 dollars). However, if 2 dollars per bottle were then taken in tax from producers their revenue after tax would fall to 6 dollars per bottle or 4200 dollars in total. In order to continue to earn 5600 dollars per month after tax from the supply and sale of 700 bottles, producers would therefore want to achieve a price of 10 dollars per bottle. In fact at each possible level of supply producers would now want to obtain a higher price to offset the tax. As a result the market supply curve shifts up by the amount of the tax, that is, by 2 dollars at each level of supply against price.

The effect of a tax on market price

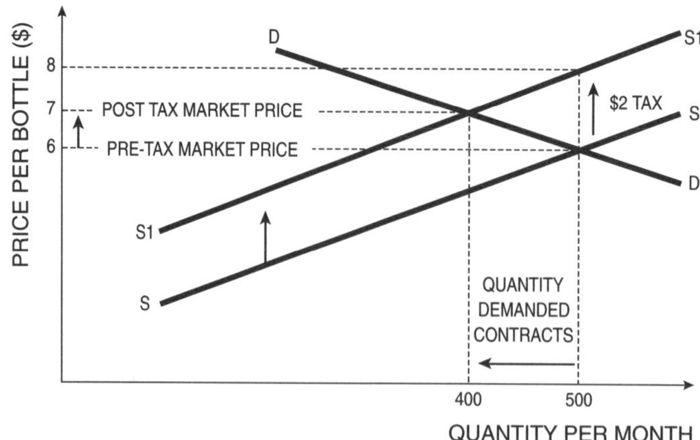

But look what happens to the market price. Before the tax of 2 dollars per bottle the market price for a bottle of brandy was 6 dollars. After the 2-dollar tax the market price has risen by only one dollar to 7 dollars. At first sight this may seem odd, but remember as price rises so consumer demand contracts because normal demand curves are downward sloping. So as producers of brandy try to pass on the full 2-dollar tax per bottle to their consumers, demand for brandy contracts and producers earn less revenue. As a result the 2-dollar tax ends up being shared between the producers of brandy who earn less revenue after tax and the consumers who must pay a higher price per bottle consumed. Only in the extreme case if demand is perfectly price inelastic will producers be able to pass on the full amount of tax to consumers because demand is unresponsive to price changes.

The effect of an ad valorem tax on supply

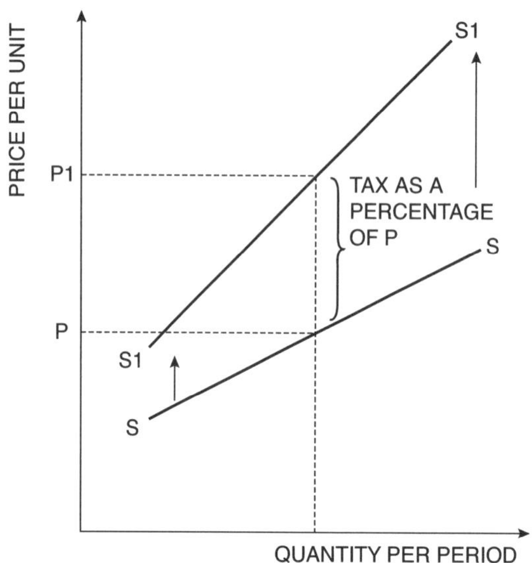

The effect of an ad valorem tax such as VAT is very similar. The supply curve will shift up by the amount of the tax as producers try to offset the tax by seeking to charge higher prices. The only difference is that the supply curve shifts up by more, the higher the price. This is because an ad valorem tax is levied as a percentage of the selling price. So, a tax of 15 per cent would add 1.5 dollars to the price of a good selling for 10 dollars and 3 dollars if the price was originally 20 dollars.

Subsidies and supply

A subsidy is a payment made to producers to help reduce their costs of production. As a result producers will tend to increase supply at every given price. As supply increases the market price will tend to fall, to the benefit of consumers.

Subsidies are often used in agriculture to support the incomes of farmers and encourage them to produce more essential foodstuffs. For example, in the diagram below a subsidy paid per tonne of maize produced has shifted the supply curve of maize down from SS to S_1S_1. The increase in supply at every possible price will result in a fall in the market price of maize so consumers can afford more and demand can expand.

The effect of a subsidy on market supply

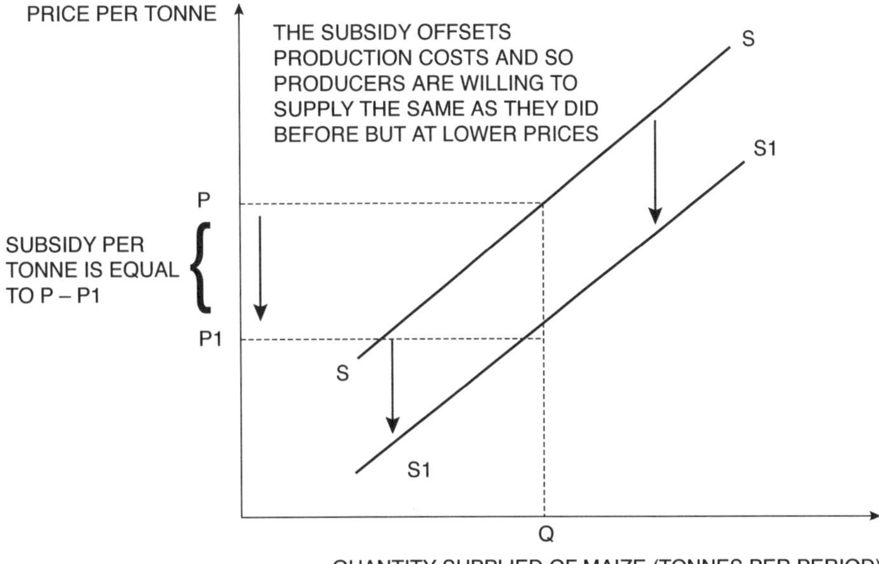

Subsidies are also used to encourage the production of new innovative goods and services, which private sector firms might otherwise find too costly and risky to produce initially.

Subsidies are also being used in countries such as the UK to help expand the production and lower the market price of solar panels and wind turbines. It is hoped this will encourage people to buy these products to generate their own renewable energy supplies and so reduce the need for oil, coal and gas-fired power stations which produce harmful greenhouse gases (see Chapter 22).

However, subsidies can often distort competition, for example, a country may subsidize its industry because it is inefficient and needs to lower its costs of production relative to countries with more efficient producers (see Chapters 18 and 22). As a result the more efficient producers may lose customers and be forced out of business. In 2005 the USA was accused by many other countries of subsidizing its inefficient steel industry at the expense of more efficient overseas producers.

Further, subsidies designed to encourage production can result in excess supply, causing market prices to collapse which in turn causes producers to move their resources out of that market and thereby defeat the aim of the subsidy. For example, generous subsidies to many European farmers in the past resulted in butter mountains and milk lakes which could not then be sold in Europe because market prices would have dropped and cut farmers' incomes significantly, forcing many of them to consider closing.

Write definitions for the following terms:

Market forces
Demand
Supply
Market price
Price mechanism
Effective demand
Excess demand
An extension of demand
A contraction of demand
An increase in demand
A fall in demand
An extension of supply
A contraction of supply
An increase in supply
A fall in supply
Ceteris paribus
Disposable income
Normal goods
Inferior goods
Complements
Substitutes
Excess supply
Price elasticity of demand
Price elastic
Price inelastic
Subsidy

Now return to the chapter to check understanding of these terms.

Learn more about market demand and supply at:

- *en.wikipedia.org/wiki/Supply_and_demand*
- *www.bized.ac.uk/learn/economics/markets/mechanism/notes.htm*
- *www.bized.ac.uk/educators/he/pearson/workshops/markets.htm*
- *www.investopedia.com/university/economics/economics3.asp*

Chapter 8 Market Structures

Aims

At the end of this chapter you should be able to:

- understand why markets can have different **market structures**
- distinguish between price competition and non-price competition
- explain how a **monopoly** may be able to dominate the market supply of a good or service and therefore determine its market price
- contrast how market prices and outputs may differ between a monopoly and a **competitive market**
- describe **barriers to entry** that may deter competition to supply a good or service

Section 1 Why do firms compete?

In a competitive market firms will compete with each other to produce and supply the market with their good or service to achieve a number of objectives. These are:

1 **To increase customer base:** firms will compete with each other on prices, product quality and through promotional strategies to increase the number of consumers buying their products.

2 **To increase sales:** firms will not only seek to increase the number of consumers buying their products but will also hope that existing customers will buy more. Cutting prices can increase sales revenues from products for which demand is price elastic. Advertising and other promotions, such as free gifts, can help to expand sales without the need for price cuts (see Chapter 9).

3 **To expand market share:** the market share of a firm can be calculated as its proportion of total volume sold or total sales revenues. For example, the global market for beer was worth US$331.8 billion in 2004. In terms of volume, Tsingtao Brewery Company was the leading supplier in the Asia-Pacific beer market in 2004, with a 10.5 per cent share, while the leading player in the US beer market is Anheuser-Busch with a 50.2 per cent market share.

   Many organizations will aim to increase their share of total sales in market. The larger an organization's market share, and the more widely established its product is, the more able it is to withstand new competition from new products and firms.

4 **To achieve product superiority:** this has two meanings. On one hand it refers to making a product that is clearly better than rival products for reasons of prestige and profit. A superior product will help a firm to achieve objectives of generating sales and expanding market share. However, product superiority also means the product dominates a market by outselling all others, which is not necessarily because it is the best product on the market.

5 **To enhance image:** firms will also compete on image. Consumers' perceptions of an organization will tend to be reflected in sales. A poor image will reduce sales; a good image will help to expand sales and market share.

6 **To maximize profits:** ultimately the achievement of the above objectives of competition should help increase total profits.

Types of competition

Firms can compete with each other in a number of ways.

Reducing the price at which a firm is willing to sell its product below the price of competing firms is one method that can help to boost sales. Competing on price is known as **price competition**. However, the ability of a firm to undercut rivals to increase sales will be constrained by market conditions and production costs. Cutting prices to expand sales will reduce the margin between revenues and costs. In the next section we will consider alternative **pricing strategies** that firms can pursue in competitive markets.

Firms can also compete on aspects other than price by differentiating features of their goods and services from rivals. When consumers buy a product they are not just looking for a low price but one that offers value for money in terms of the quality of the good or service, its size or shape, colour, smell or taste. Consumers are also looking for after-sales service should anything go wrong or if they want to exchange their product. Firms can compete on all these facets of a good and service to offer consumers what they want. This is known as **non-price competition**.

Promotion is also very important if consumers are to be tempted to buy one product over another. Free gifts, money-off coupons, attractive instore displays, publicity in magazines are all methods that can be used to persuade consumers to buy. Advertising, through media such as television or newspapers, is one of the main ways firms compete for sales (see Chapter 9).

Price and non-price competition

Is competition good or bad for the consumer?

Both price and non-price competition is good for consumers because it can reduce prices and increase the quality and availability of different products. However, advertising and excessive packaging are sometimes considered wasteful. Prices will tend to reflect the cost of these activities and will, therefore, tend to be higher than they could otherwise be so long as firms are able to pass on these costs to consumers as higher prices without a significant loss of sales.

Exercise 1

Competing for custom

Choose a firm you are familiar with, that sells a good or service. Gather information on how it competes with their rival firms. Try to find out:

- Why do they compete?
- What is their market share?
- Who are their main competitors?
- How do their prices compare?
- What forms of non-price competition do they use?
- How effective have their price and non-price competitive strategies been?

Section 2

Competitive pricing strategies

In a competitive market a firm might use a number of different short-term pricing strategies over time in an attempt to expand its sales and market share at the expense of rival producers. These are:

Penetration pricing involves setting product price low to encourage sales, especially important for a new or existing firm trying to establish a new product and stimulate consumer demand for it.

Expansion pricing is similar to penetration pricing. Product prices are set low to encourage consumers to buy. As demand increases the firm can raise output to meet demand and take advantage of economies of scale that will lower the average cost of producing each unit (see Chapter 13). Lower average production costs can either be passed on to consumers as lower prices, or if prices are held constant the lower costs will increase the firm's profits.

Market skimming, also known as **price creaming**, involves charging a high price for a new product to yield a high initial profit from consumers who are willing to pay extra because the product is new and unique. As competitors enter the market, supply increases and prices are reduced thereby expanding market demand.

Market skimming is a practice often observed in markets for new consumer technology such as audio and video products, mobile phones, personal computers, etc. This is because early adopters of the new technology are often willing to pay a premium price. For example, some of the first recordable DVD drives for personal computers made available in the late 1990s by manufacturers such as Pioneer and Philips were priced at around US$500 or more. By 2007 DVD+/−R drives could be bought for as little as US$30 each.

Price wars often occur in markets where the supply side is very competitive. Price wars are not popular among firms even though they frequently arise. This is because engaging in a price war is a very high-risk strategy. Gains tend to be short-lived as rival firms continually slash prices in an attempt to steal custom from each other. Only the consumer benefits as firms' profits are reduced by successive price cuts without a sustained increase in demand for their products. However, in the longer term the consumer may be worse off if some producers are forced out of business, leaving only one or a handful of powerful suppliers to dominate a market (see section 3).

Price leadership is often used to avoid destructive price wars between firms competing to dominate a market. The firms that dominate the market supply will tend to price their products in line with each other. In extreme cases they may even collude to 'fix' prices. However, sometimes agreements to fix prices or play 'follow my leader' break down and price wars can once again develop among rival firms.

Destruction pricing (also known as **predatory pricing**) is a more drastic version of penetration pricing usually practised by larger firms when threatened by new competition from smaller organizations. The objective is to destroy the sales of competitors by setting prices very low, even below costs, and sustaining a loss for a short period of time. Smaller firms, unable to suffer a loss, will be pushed out of the market.

Section 3 Market structure

Competitive markets

In the last chapter we learnt how the market demand and supply of a particular good or service will determine the price and quantity traded of that product. In highly competitive markets there will tend to be a large number of different firms producing it and an equally large number of consumers wanting to buy it. As such, all producers and consumers will trade at the equilibrium market price.

The world agricultural market is perhaps the closest example of what is known as a **perfectly competitive market**. Because there are so many producers of maize, barley and other crops of similar quality worldwide, individual producers must sell their produce at the prevailing market prices. That is, in a perfectly competitive market there are so many consumers and producers that no one alone can influence the market price. That is, they are all **price takers**. If a firm did try to raise its price above the market price it would lose custom to rival producers and soon go out of business. Similarly, a firm would be unable to lower its price below the market price without losing money unless it was able to produce so much more cheaply than others. Even if it did, it could not do so for long as other firms would soon find out how this was done and use the same methods to lower their production costs. Subsequently, market price would fall. As such it is hard to imagine why any firm in a perfectly competitive market, if they existed, would ever compete.

However, in reality most markets are not 'perfect'. Most markets involve competition between a small number of large firms who tend to dominate the market supply. For example, Boeing in the US and Airbus in Europe compete vigorously as the only suppliers of large passenger aircraft to airline operating companies in the world.

What is market structure?

In economics, **market structure** describes how a market is organized in terms of how much competition there is, usually on the supply side.

Competition between firms encourages them to make the best use of scarce resources, because in order to maximize profits they must produce outputs at the lowest possible cost that give consumers the best value for money to satisfy their wants. Any restriction on competition may therefore result in a suboptimal allocation of scarce resources with costs and prices higher than they would otherwise be and with fewer wants being satisfied. This is why economists will examine market structures and the degree of competition between firms. It is also a reason why governments often intervene in markets to ensure sufficient competition takes place.

We can examine the amount of competition in a market by looking at the following features:

- The amount of control a firm or group of firms has over market supply or output
- The amount of influence a firm or group of firms have over market price
- The freedom new suppliers have to enter a market
- Barriers to entry that restrict new competition

Exercise 2 Concentrating on market supply

The table below provides data on the share of total output of the five largest producers in a number of UK industries in 2003. For example, it shows that the five largest firms in the UK sugar industry accounted for 100 per cent of the total industry output by value.

UK industry concentrations, 2003 (% share of total output of 5 largest firms)

Industry	% share	Industry	% share
Cement, lime and plaster	69	Plastic products	4
Oils and fats	91	Construction	4
Sugar	100	Furniture	6
Confectionery	91	Metal forging, pressing, etc.	3
Soft drinks and mineral waters	73	Business services	6
Coal extraction	73	Advertising	8
Postal and courier services	68	Wood and wood products	10

From 'Input-Output: concentration ratios for businesses by industry in 2003'
UK Office of National Statistics 2005, *www.statistics.gov.uk*

1. Which UK industry was the most concentrated and which industry was the least concentrated in 2003?
2. What do the figures suggest about the market structure and degree of competition in these different industries?
3. What other information would you require to make a proper assessment of the degree of competition between producers in individual markets? For example: what about competition from foreign firms? Do market prices suggest there is a lack of price competition in these markets? Are the top five firms in each industry necessarily the same five each year? Investigate possible sources of data to provide answers to these and other questions about how to measure the degree of competition in markets.

Monopoly

In some markets one or a handful of dominant firms may have sufficient market power to restrict competition and influence the price and quantity traded to their favour. A firm or group of firms acting in this way is called a **monopoly**.

The opposite extreme in economics of a perfectly competitive market is a **pure monopoly**. A firm is a pure monopoly if it is the only supplier of a good or service wanted by consumers. For example, until 1998 British Gas supplied 100 per cent of households connected to the national gas supply network in the UK. In fact, many public utilities around the world supplying gas and electric power remain pure monopolies.

In a pure monopoly the single firm controls the total supply of the whole industry and is able to exert a significant degree of control over the price, by changing the quantity supplied. In this way, a monopoly is a **price maker** because it can restrict market supply to force up the market price. This helps a monopoly to maximize its profits. These are often called **excess profits** or **abnormal profits** because they will be higher than if the market was competitive. However, if the monopoly wants to protect its market power and profits it must prevent new firms from entering its market. Any increase in supply from new firms will force prices and profits down.

The impact of a monopoly on market supply and price

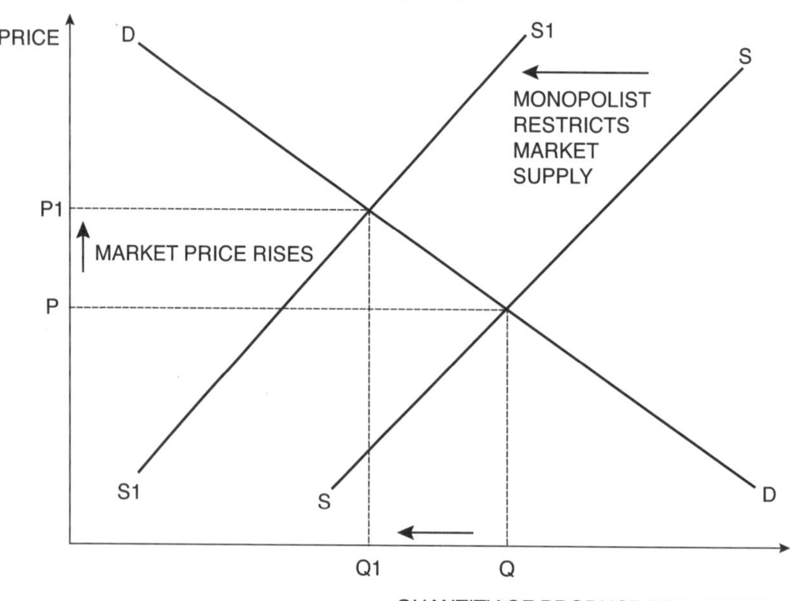

Oil extraction and petroleum refining is an example of an oligopoly

Today, most markets can be described as 'oligopolistic'. An **oligopoly** exists if a small number of firms dominate the supply of a particular good or service to a market. The oil extraction and petroleum market, commercial banking, the manufacture of soaps and detergents, and the manufacture of large passenger aircraft, are all example of oligopolies.

Sometimes firms in an oligopoly will collude to influence the market price by restricting supply and new competition, in effect forming a pure or near pure monopoly. As such, under the law of many countries oligopolies are deemed to be monopolies and are watched closely to ensure they do not abuse their dominant market power.

A **cartel** is a formal agreement between firms to regulate market supply and price. The best-known cartel is OPEC (Organization of Petroleum Exporting Countries) that attempts to manage the world supply of crude oil in order to determine its market price.

Cartels and **price collusion** between firms to fix prices at artificially high levels are outlawed in many countries because they are deemed to be against the public interest. Instead, **price leadership** and vigorous non-price competition are key features of many oligopolistic markets (see section 2). For example, despite the existence of numerous branded products the detergent market is supplied, primarily, by two very large producers (a **duopoly**) – Unilever and Procter & Gamble. Their competition concentrates on the creation of strong brand images and customer product loyalty through heavy advertising (see Chapter 9). Similarly, Boeing and Airbus are a duopoly in the manufacture and supply of large passenger aircraft.

How monopolies can restrict competition

A pure monopoly or group of firms acting together to dominate a market may try to prevent new firms from entering their market and reducing their markets share and profits by creating barriers to entry.

Natural barriers to entry

Some firms become monopolies simply because of their advantages.

1 Economies of scale

By increasing in size a firm may be able to reduce the average cost of producing each unit of output below the costs of smaller organizations (see Chapter 12). If one firm is able to produce the entire market supply at a lower average cost per unit than a number of smaller firms added together then it is known as a **natural monopoly**. Gas, electricity and water supply pipelines and grids are examples of natural monopolies. This is because it does not make economic sense to have more than one set of gas or water pipes or electricity cables supplying each house, office or factory in a country.

2 Capital size

The supply of a product may involve the input of such a vast amount of capital equipment that new competing firms will find it difficult to raise enough finance to buy or hire their own. For example, consider the amount of capital a firm would need to produce electricity from building a new nuclear power station.

3 Historical reasons

A business may have a monopoly because it was first to enter the market for a product and has built up an established customer base. For example, Lloyds of London dominates the world insurance market primarily because of its established expertise dating back to the eighteenth century.

4 Legal considerations

The development of new production methods and products can be expensive but can be encouraged by granting innovative producers **patents** or copyright to protect them from other firms copying their ideas and thereby reducing their potential profits. In this way a government can create a **legal monopoly** with the sole right to supply a new and innovative good or service.

Exercise 3 Creating a barrier

Divide into groups. Each group should consider one of the following cases based on imaginary firms. You play the role of company directors of different monopolies and your task is to find barriers to entry to stop competition from other firms.

Report your findings to your shareholders (the rest of the class) who will then vote on whether or not to allow the directors to continue to manage the company.

Big Sell Supermarkets plc

You are the board of directors of a large supermarket in a town. There are very few other food shops in the town apart from some very small stores. The supermarket is supplied by a nearby wholesaler and is its single most important customer.

Your monopoly position ensures that the supermarket earns high profits. However, other firms know this and now want to set up large shops in the neighbourhood. The owners of the supermarket are worried about losing trade and profits to these new stores. They have asked the board of directors to find barriers to prevent new shops from setting up nearby. They are not concerned about how you do this.

As directors you must report on what you plan to do before the next Annual General Meeting of shareholders, when they will decide whether or not to re-elect you as directors.

Flyhigh Airlines

You are the directors of a large airline flying to countries all over the world.

A new airline company, Cut Price Atlantic, is about to start up with two planes flying on your route between America and Britain. Cut Price Atlantic intends to undercut your $150 fare by $40 for a one-way flight between the two countries.

Shareholders in Flyhigh Airlines are very anxious. Because demand is price elastic they fear that the new company will make large sales on the route across the Atlantic and will be able to use their profits to buy more planes in order to start up cut-price flights on other routes as well.

Your task as directors is to stop the new airline from taking away custom from your company by devising barriers to entry. (*Hint*, your company operates many profitable routes throughout the world, so what can you afford to do to try and force Cut Price Airlines out of business? Remember, your failure to do so could mean your rejection as directors by shareholders at their next meeting.)

Spreadwell Limited

You are the board of directors of Spreadwell Limited. You hold a virtual monopoly in the market for margarine, producing nearly all of the well-known brands for sale in shops.

Spreadwell Limited relies heavily on television advertising to sell its products and will often help chains of supermarkets to publicize the sale of their margarines.

Because of your near monopoly position, Spreadwell earns high profits and shareholders are keen to protect them from new firms who wish to produce margarine.

As the board of directors you need to stop any new competition. Try to decide how you can set up barriers to entry. Your report must prove favourable to your shareholders.

Artificial barriers to entry

While some monopolies occur naturally, others may achieve and retain their powerful market position by creating their own artificial barriers to competition.

1 Restrictions on supplies

New firms will only enter an industry if they can obtain supplies of raw materials. Monopoly firms can threaten their suppliers that if they supply any new firms, the monopoly will take its custom to another supplier. This is likely to work if there are only a few suppliers and if these suppliers rely heavily on the monopolist for business. For example, in the case of the Big Sell Supermarket, the store could threaten their wholesaler that if they supply any new shops in the area they will lose their largest customer.

2 Predatory pricing

In the Flyhigh Airlines example, the large company had routes all over the world and made many millions of dollars in profits. A small competitor could not afford to operate so many routes. In fact, Cut Price Airlines could only afford to buy two planes to operate on just one route.

The new company offered fares for $110, being $40 cheaper than Flyhigh Airlines. To stop this competition Flyhigh could afford to cut their flight fares on the Atlantic route even more to force Cut Price out of business. Flyhigh will lose money on this route by offering low fares but can afford to cover these losses from profits on other routes. Once Cut Price has been forced to close, Flyhigh can again raise its prices.

This is an example of **predatory pricing**. It occurs when a large firm cuts its prices, even if this means losing money in the short run, in order to force new and smaller competing firms out of business. Once the new competitor has been removed, the dominant firm can raise its prices again.

3 Exclusive dealing

This involves a monopoly preventing retailers from stocking the products of competing firms. This method of restricting competition is particularly effective if the product supplied by the dominant firm is very popular and the retailer would lose too much trade if they did not sell it. In the example of Spreadwell Limited, the firm was the main supplier of popular margarines that retailers were able to use to attract consumers into their shops and sell at a good profit. Spreadwell can use this to threaten to stop supplying retailers who stocked competing margarines.

4 Full line forcing

This is similar to exclusive dealing. It means a large multi-product firm will only supply a retailer if they stock and sell their full range of products.

Disadvantages of monopoly

It is useful at this point to summarize and compare the key features of the different market structures ranging from a perfectly competitive market structure to pure monopoly. In this way the disadvantages of monopoly over more competitive market structures should become clear.

Market structure	No of suppliers	What pricing strategies do firms tend to use?	Do firms engage in non-price competition?	Can existing firms prevent new firms from entering the market?
Perfect competition	Many	All firms are price takers and trade at the market price	No	No
Competitive markets	Many	Expansion pricing Penetration pricing Price wars	Yes – producers differentiate their products from rivals in terms of quality, aftersales care, and through use of promotions	Not usually
Oligopoly	Few	Price wars Price leadership Price collusion Predatory pricing	Yes – fierce competition on product image, quality and promotions	Often
Pure monopoly	One (or a group of firms acting together in a cartel)	A monopoly can be a price maker and will restrict supply to force up market price	No competition so not necessary but may be used to expand demand	Very much so – there are significant barriers to entry

The following potential disadvantages of a pure monopoly, or group of firms acting together like a monopoly, are a source of concern for consumers and often governments.

1 Less consumer choice

By restricting competition from rival producers and products a monopoly offers the consumer less choice than would occur in a competitive market.

2 Higher prices

A monopoly can restrict market supply to set a higher market price than would otherwise occur in a competitive market. Consumers faced with few alternative choices may simply have to continue buying the product of the monopolist or go without. If consumer demand is relatively price inelastic, particularly if the product is a necessity, then demand will not contract by much and the monopolist will earn more revenue and profit.

3 Lower product quality

Faced with little or no competition, the monopolist has no great incentive to increase the quality of the good or service it supplies. On the contrary, a monopoly may reduce quality in order to reduce production costs so as to make more profit.

4 X inefficiency

Because a monopoly has little or no competition and earns high profits it may make less effort than a competitive firm to ensure its resources are used most efficiently. This means a monopoly may be inefficiently run and production costs may be higher than they would otherwise be in a competitive firm. This is called **X inefficiency**.

5 The need for regulation

Many governments around the world have introduced laws and regulations (collectively known as competition policy) to control monopolies that act against the public interest. Monopolies that are found to be anti-competitive and exploiting consumers by charging higher prices and providing lower product quality may even be forced to break up into smaller firms. Governments must therefore employ scarce resources paid for from tax revenues simply to examine and regulate monopoly behaviour. These scarce resources could have been put to other more productive uses instead.

Some monopolies, many being public utilities such as gas and electricity supply, are government owned in many countries and operate as part of the public sector (see Chapter 4). In this way a monopoly can be run in the public interest rather than solely in the interests of making a profit for its owners. However, many government-owned monopolies suffer the same disadvantages as private sector ones, with governments often abusing their market power to raise prices in order to increase government revenues.

Advantages of monopoly

It would be wrong to think all large firms try to exploit consumers by restricting competition. Many, because of their size and their ability to earn high profits, are able to spend a large amount of money on product improvements and more efficient production processes. Cost savings may be passed on to consumers as lower prices. Domestic monopolies and oligopolies may also face competition from close substitutes in other markets and from foreign competition.

If a market is a **contestable market**, that is, if barriers to entry are low and new competition can easily occur, a monopoly may behave competitively simply to ward off new competitors. So in a contestable monopoly the market price and quantity traded will tend to be the same as if there were a great many producers competing to supply that market.

This page is photocopyable

Key word search

Use the definitions below to find key words and terms in the word search below.

M	O	K	P	C	O	N	T	E	S	T	A	B	L	E	Y	V
O	L	F	I	K	W	S	G	T	O	D	E	T	O	C	M	B
J	M	O	N	O	P	O	L	Y	F	I	N	D	M	O	X	A
L	A	S	E	T	R	G	O	A	C	A	R	T	E	L	D	R
Q	R	L	E	S	E	R	T	H	A	N	G	O	F	L	T	R
X	K	C	U	F	D	S	I	N	E	P	A	X	I	U	Z	I
I	E	E	X	P	A	N	S	I	O	N	B	G	B	S	C	E
E	T	S	E	X	T	U	P	L	E	T	N	R	A	I	U	R
F	S	I	D	U	O	P	O	L	Y	X	O	U	C	O	T	S
F	H	T	P	Q	R	Z	S	I	B	C	R	N	D	N	U	T
I	A	O	U	L	Y	I	J	N	C	S	M	T	Y	U	P	O
C	R	P	R	I	C	E	W	A	R	W	A	W	O	T	F	E
I	E	M	E	C	D	E	S	T	R	A	L	O	R	J	O	N
E	K	Y	G	K	N	O	N	P	Y	M	P	A	T	E	N	T
N	C	F	U	U	L	E	G	A	L	W	R	T	O	T	D	R
C	I	A	V	P	O	L	I	G	O	P	O	L	Y	F	U	Y
Y	L	C	K	N	J	T	O	R	T	U	F	K	O	U	E	M
G	F	E	E	O	T	F	Y	P	O	L	I	L	U	J	S	U
M	A	R	K	E	T	S	T	R	U	C	T	U	R	E	T	P

Definitions

1 A firm or group of firms acting together to control the market supply of a good or service.

2 How a market for a product is organized in terms of the degree of competition there is between firms to supply that market.

3 The proportion of total sales revenue or volume sold in a particular market by an individual firm.

4 A formal agreement between firms to control market supply and determine price.

5 When firms act together to fix the market price.

6 A type of monopoly in which two firms control a market supply.

7 A type of monopoly when only one firm controls a market supply.

8 A firm may use this to protect a new product or innovation thereby forming a legal monopoly.

9 A type of market where supply is dominated by a handful of firms.

10 The name used to describe the profit of a monopoly when it is in excess of that level of profit that would otherwise have been earned in a competitive market.

11 Highly destructive pricing strategy fought between a handful of competing firms each trying to undercut their rivals to dominate market supply.

12 A pricing strategy used by a monopoly to deter new competition by setting price per unit sold below the production cost per unit of the new firm.

13 A pricing strategy used by firms aiming to grow consumer demand and expand the size of their market.

14 Obstructions, either occurring naturally or created artificially, by a dominant firm or group of firms acting together to restrict new competition.

15 Used to describe possible wastefulness and laziness resulting in higher costs in a monopoly caused by the absence of a competitive threat.

Some helpful websites on competition and market structure are:

- A 'blog' site that tries to make sense of the business pages in newspapers, particularly stories about large company formations *www.oligopolywatch.com*
- UK Competition Commission *www.competition-commission.org.uk*
- EU Competition Directorate-General *ec.europa.eu/comm/competition/index_en.html*
- biz/ed online service *www.bized.ac.uk/learn/economics/firms/structure/index.htm*
- *en.wikipedia.org/wiki/Competition_policy*
- *en.wikipedia.org/wiki/Competition_law*

Chapter 9 The Role of Advertising

Aims

At the end of this chapter you should be able to:

- describe the purpose and different methods of **advertising**
- analyse the use of advertising to create wants
- show the likely impact of advertising on market demand
- understand how **brands** can be used to create barriers to new competition

Section 1 Why do firms advertise?

Exercise 1 Cobra beer – advertising case study

Read the article on the next page about advertising a new beer and then answer the questions below.

1. What were the aims of the advertising campaign for Cobra beer?
2. What was the target audience for the advertising campaign?
3. How was the product advertised? What other methods could have been used?
4. What was impact of the advertising on consumer awareness and demand? Use a diagram to demonstrate this showing what might happen to market price and quantity traded as a result.
5. What is price elasticity of demand? What could be the impact of advertising Cobra beer on the price elasticity of demand for the product?

Fed up with the poor quality of much of the lager he was served whilst studying in the UK, Kiran Bilimoria, the man behind Cobra beer, set himself the task of developing an Indian lager with international appeal.

Today, Cobra is the UK's biggest selling bottled Indian beer and is one of the nation's fastest growing beer brands. As the brand strategy evolves and establishes Cobra beer as a premium beer with mainstream appeal, Cobra is focused on breaking into the global, mainstream market represented by restaurants, pubs, clubs and bars, and building market share.

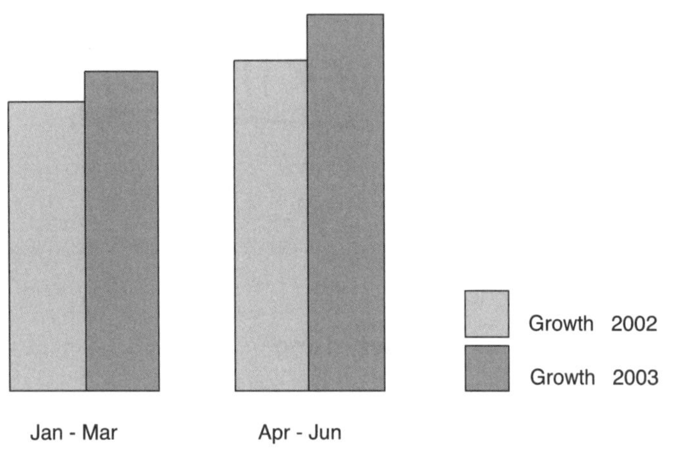

Given that Cobra's target audience is 18–35-year-old adults, Channel 4 and E4 were identified as the optimum television channels for effectively reaching this market. The campaign encompassed key programmes such as the new series of *Friends* and *ER*. Pre and post advertising research showed that total awareness of the brand had more than doubled amongst men aged 18–34 from socio-economic groups ABC1* and amongst bottled lager drinkers.

The campaign resulted in an increased growth rate of 10 per cent year on year and the product is now well positioned in the mainstream premium beer market and has established recognition among key potential consumers.

* A = Professional people and senior managers; B = middle management; C1 = junior management

Adapted from *www.channel4sales.com*

What is advertising?

Firms can communicate the prices, availability and key features of their goods and services to consumers using advertisements. **Advertising** is the commercial promotion of goods, services, companies and ideas, and some firms spend many millions of dollars each year designing and producing advertising campaigns. But why do they do this?

1 To create consumer wants

The main aim of most advertising is to create a consumer want for a new or existing product and thereby create sales. That is, firms will spend money on advertising because they hope it will create additional sales and revenue that exceeds the amount it spends on advertising so that profits will rise.

An advertisement that just creates interest in a product without converting that interest into increased demand is a failure. From Chapter 7 we learnt that an increase in demand for a product will tend to push up the market price and quantity traded. The increase in demand desired by a firm for its product may be achieved by advertisements that convince consumers that their product is new, or that it is somehow better than rival products, or that the consumer will benefit from buying the product, either through the features of the product or by 'buying into' the image created for that product.

The desired impact of an advertising campaign on demand

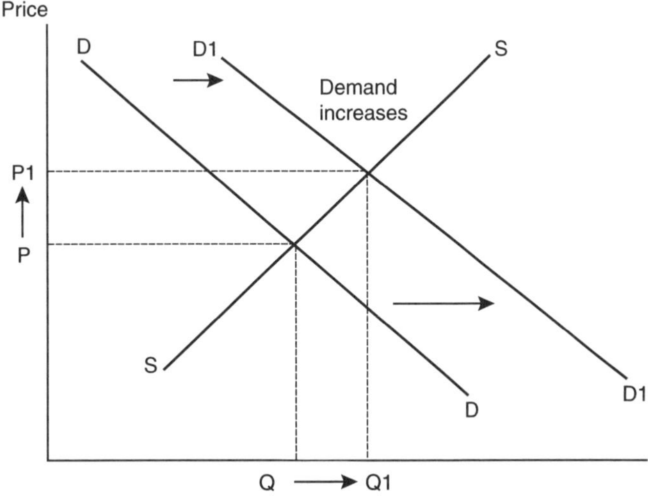

2 To create a brand image

Advertising can be designed to persuade consumers to buy a product they would not otherwise buy by changing their attitudes, opinions and perceptions of a product and the firms that make and sell it. In so doing firms that advertise their products can expand a market and capture a greater share of the market demand.

Consumers' perceptions of a product can be changed by creating a **brand image**. This can be done by using a distinctive name, logo, humorous catchphrase or visual treatment for a good or service to make it stand out from its close substitutes. That is, many firms differentiate their product from similar competing products to encourage consumers to buy it. This is called **product differentiation**.

Of course, it does not really matter whether the product really is very different: what matters is whether or not consumers think it is. For example, most washing detergents are very similar yet individual manufacturers of detergents often spend vast sums of money attempting to persuade consumers that their product is more powerful, smells better, leaves clothes softer or whiter, than other detergents. In this way they try to create **customer loyalty** to their product.

Customer loyalty benefits a firm in a number of ways:

- Repeat purchases from loyal customers provide a steady stream of income
- It protects the firm's market share of total sales revenue
- Loyal customers are more likely to continue to buy the product even if its price is raised slightly above competing products
- Loyal customers may continue to buy the product even if prices for rival products fall

In this way, product differentiation through the creation of a brand image to create customer loyalty makes consumer price elasticity of demand less elastic and relatively more price inelastic (see Chapter 7). Further, it provides the firm with a degree of monopoly control over consumer demand, allowing it to restrict supply and push up price (see Chapter 8).

Brand imaging is successful because firms have realized that consumers not only buy products but try to 'buy' into the images and lifestyles associated with them. For example, some television advertisements for products try to create the impression that they are bought by attractive people who subsequently enjoy a lavish lifestyle. Consumers buying the product may therefore believe they too will be viewed as attractive by others and able to enjoy the same lavish lifestyle.

Advertising can also be used to create a better image for a firm – for example, one that is more caring for the environment – or to make it more attractive to a particular group of consumers, for example, showing the firm as trendy to attract young people to its products, or reliable and good value to attract older people to buy its products.

Advertisements can influence consumers' perceptions of the lifestyle they can lead if they buy the product

3 To deter new competition

Creating a powerful brand image and spending a large amount of money on big advertising campaigns can create a barrier to the entry into that product market by new competing firms (see Chapter 8). A rival producer wanting to supply a similar product could be deterred by the need to spend equally large amounts of money on advertising campaigns, especially if it needs to reduce consumer loyalty to the existing product. This may be especially difficult for new, and therefore unknown, small firms attempting to enter the market.

4 To provide information

Another important aim of many advertisements is to provide factual information about goods and services, to let people know what is available, or to give instructions, for example, travel directions or the running times of buses and trains.

Governments and local authorities often use advertisements to provide information to people and firms about different laws and regulations, rights and responsibilities, and government schemes.

5 To maximize profits

It should be clear to you by now that the main aim of advertising for many private sector firms is to maximize their profits through the creation of consumer wants, brand loyalty and barriers to new competition (see Chapter 12).

However, designing and running advertising campaigns can be very expensive and these costs can reduce profits in the short run but hopefully, after sales have increased, profits will rise over the longer term.

Exercise 2 What's in a name?

Choosing a name or a logo for a product or a business is often as important as what is said about it in an advertisement.

1 What products or types of products do you associate with the product names below? What perception does the name in each case give you about these products? You can still try to answer this question even if the product is not known to you or sold under a different name in your own country.

Aquafresh	**Flora**	**PG Tips**	**Ambre Solaire**
Black Magic	**Radox**	**Imperial Leather**	**Allure**
Cif	**Gold Blend**	**Crunchie**	**Pampers**

2 Some products, groups of products and/or firms have such well-known logos or trademarks that consumers can instantly recognize them and remember the brand image they represent. How many of the following do you recognize? What products or firms do they advertise? What brand image do you have about them?

3 Can you think of some good brand names for the following products?

- A new chocolate bar
- A new perfume for young girls
- A new aftershave for men
- A new toothpaste
- A new car
- A new liquid washing detergent

Section 2 Types of advertisements

Targeting the right audience

If firms can identify the types of consumers who are most likely to buy their products they can design advertising messages and images that will appeal the most to them. That is, different advertisements can be targeted at different groups of consumers called **target**

audiences. For example, the target audience for advertisements for pop music magazines will be young people. The target audience for baby foods, clothes and buggies will be new parents and grandparents. Advertisements for sports cars tend to be targeted at affluent, young to middle-aged men, while advertisements for hatchbacks and so-called people carriers tend to be designed more for women and young mothers.

Persuasive or informative advertising

Analysing consumers for a particular good or service by their characteristics is called **market segmentation**. Each market segment will consist of a group of consumers with different characteristics, often segmented by their age, gender, income, marital status, lifestyle, religious beliefs, occupation, number of children, property ownership and buying habits or patterns. For example, the market for mobile telephone usage could be further segmented to the most frequent type and time of use, such as for business or pleasure, and at peak or off-peak times, and by how many texts different consumers tend to send and the downloads of ring-tones and music they make.The type of advertising messages communicated will depend on the particular good or service being promoted, the aims of the organization promoting it, and the target audience the advertising is aimed at. For example, government organizations will tend to provide public information; banks will inform you about their range of services, savings and borrowing schemes, but will also try to persuade you that they offer the best rates of interest, security and level of customer service over their rivals; manufacturers and retailers of beauty products such as face-creams try to convince consumers that their products give healthier, younger-looking skin.

The purpose of **informative advertising** is to provide the consumer with product information. Advertising messages that are designed only to inform are usually quite obvious – such as opening times, bus timetables, maps and directions, pop group tour dates, etc. In contrast, **persuasive advertising** is designed to encourage consumers to buy products, often using colourful and clever images, logos, catchphrases and music to create consumer wants. For example, one producer ran a very successful advertising campaign for soap powder for many years claiming it washed 'whiter than white' – clearly a meaningless phrase but one nonetheless that consumers remembered and therefore one that was influential in their buying decisions. Clearly, many advertisements are designed both to inform and to persuade.

An informative advertisement

A persuasive advertisement

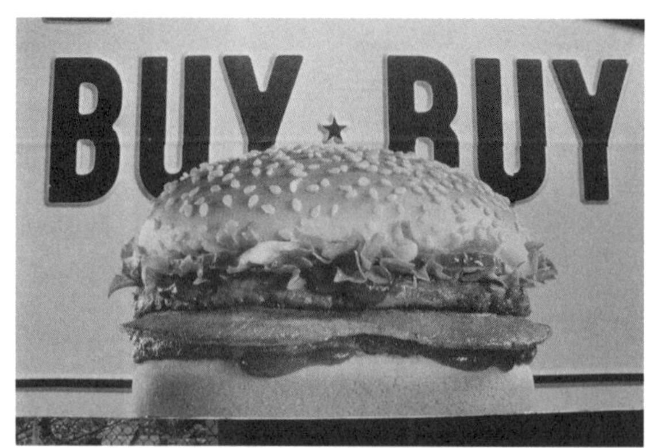

Section 3 Advertising standards and media

Advertising standards and codes of practice

Governments often intervene in advertising to ensure firms do not mislead or lie to consumers. For example, in the UK the Advertising Standards Authority (ASA) safeguards consumers by monitoring adverts to ensure rules contained in the British Code of Advertising Practice are adhered to. This states all advertisements should be:

- legal, decent, honest and truthful
- prepared with a sense of responsibility to the consumer and to safety
- in line with the principles of fair competition

The ASA acts to have advertisements changed or withdrawn if they do not comply with the code. Failure to comply can lead to adverse publicity for a product and producer (*www.asa.org.uk*).

Some industries have trade associations that also draw up voluntary codes of good practice which their member firms are encouraged to follow to protect the reputation of the industry as a whole with consumers.

Advertising media

Public and private sector organizations can choose from a wide variety of **advertising media** through which to promote their products and image, and to provide information. These include newspapers and magazines, television and radio, the cinema, leaflets and posters. Advertisements can even be placed on the packaging of other products, for example, on the back of matchboxes, on carrier bags and tee-shirts, even on hot-air balloons.

Most advertising is through newspapers, magazines and television. For example, in 2005 these media accounted for 70 per cent of the total advertising spend in the USA of US$143.3 billion.

Advertising on the internet is growing rapidly in importance as use of the internet grows, especially for online shopping, or **e-commerce**.

US advertising spend by medium, 2005

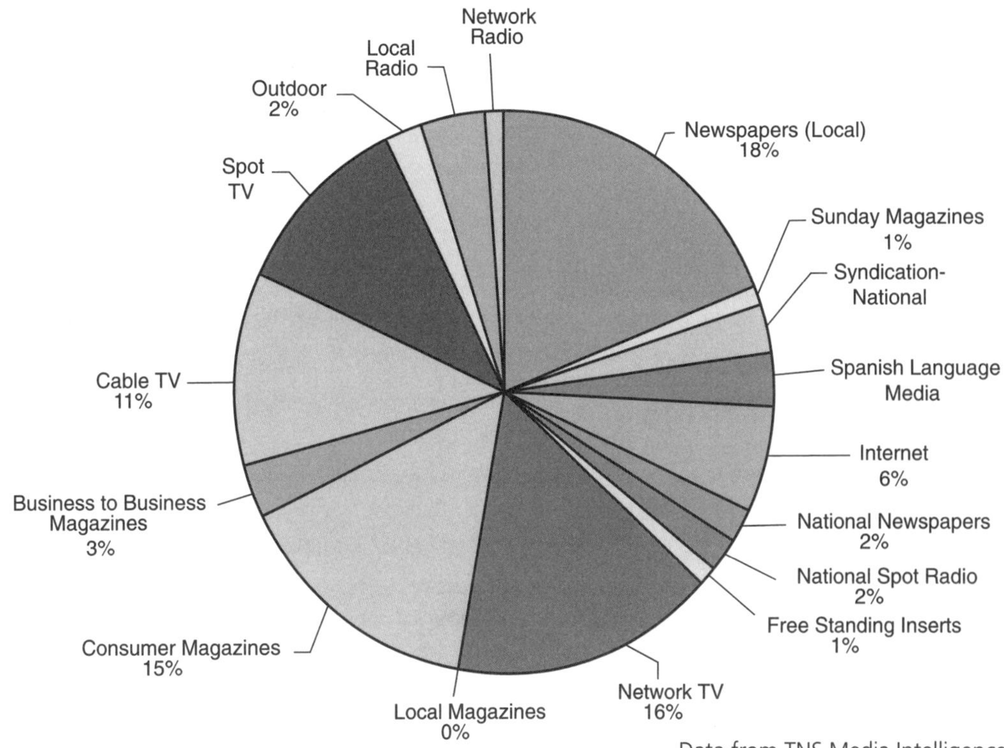

Data from TNS Media Intelligence, *www.tns-mi.com*

Choosing the right type of media

Firms will choose the most cost-effective ways of advertising to reach their target audience and to achieve their aim of increasing sales and market share, and maximizing profits.

Advertising media	Plus points	Minus points
National newspapers	Coverage is national Reader can refer back to advert Product information can be provided	Use of colour limited Smaller adverts tend to get 'lost' among others Readers often ignore adverts
Local newspapers	Adverts can be linked to local conditions Can be used for test-marketing before national launch	Reproduction and layout can be poor Average cost per reader relatively high due to more limited circulation
Magazines	Can use colour Adverts can be linked with feature articles Adverts can be targeted in specialist magazines	Adverts must be submitted a long time before publication Competitors' products often advertised alongside
Radio	Can use sound and music Relatively cheap to produce Growing number of stations Audiences can be targeted	Non-visual Message usually short-lived Listeners may switch off or ignore adverts
Television	Creative use of moving images, colour, and sound Can use visual endorsements by well-known personalities Repeats reinforce message Growing number of channels Adverts can be regional	High production costs Peak time can be expensive Message short-lived Viewers may ignore or switch over during adverts
Cinema	Creative use of images, colour and sound Adverts can be localized Adverts can be targeted at age groups at different films	Limited audiences compared with other media Audience restricted to mainly younger age groups Message may only be seen once due to infrequent visits to cinema
The Internet	Easy and relatively cheap to set up web pages Can present colourful moving images and sounds Adverts can be interactive Internet is worldwide and accessible 24 hours a day	Not everyone has access to a computer or the internet Web pages need to be updated regularly and quickly Increased risk of credit card fraud may put off people ordering goods over the net using their credit cards
Posters	Good cheap visual stimulus Can be placed near to points of sale National campaigns possible	Only limited information possible Susceptible to vandalism and adverse weather

Exercise 3 **Square eyes!**

Put your feet up in front of the television and watch some advertisements. Watch a sample of around 20 different advertisements at different times of the day and for each advertisement try to determine:

- The product, product range or company name being advertised.
- Who is the most likely intended target audience, and what are their key characteristics?
- Does it intend to inform consumers or persuade them to buy?
- Does it promote a brand image and lifestyle, and if so, how?
- Does it use meaningless statements, slogans or catchphrases?

To help you can draw and complete a table like the one started below.

Product/ Organization	Likely target audience	Informative?	Persuasive?	Brand image	Key statements/ Slogans
Washing powder	Housewives – middle income, young to middle age with children	No – but does say powder can be used at low temperatures and has not been tested on animals	Yes – use of bright images; emphasizes softness and smell of clothes after washing; argues powder is kind to environment	Yes – shows a well-off attractive family wearing bright coloured fashionable clothes	'The power to clean'
Income tax – Government tax authority	Taxpayers who need to complete self-assessment forms, self-employed, high income earners	Yes – when and how to complete form; who to call for advice	Partly – it tries to persuade people to complete their forms on time otherwise they will have to pay a fine	No, but it uses a 'friendly' cartoon character to give information	'Don't delay. Do it today'

Write definitions for the following terms:

Advertising | **Target audience**
Brand image | **Market segmentation**
Product differentiation | **Persuasive advertising**
Customer loyalty | **Informative advertising**
Advertising media | **e-commerce**

Now check your understanding of these terms by returning to the chapter.

There are many useful websites on advertising. Here are just a few:

- Advertising Age magazine online *www.adage.com*
- World Advertising Research Center *www.warc.com*
- UK Advertising Standards Authority *www.asa.org.uk/asa*
- Advertising links and articles *www.advertising.about.com*

Assessment exercises

Multiple choice

1 The diagram shows a shift in demand for product Z.

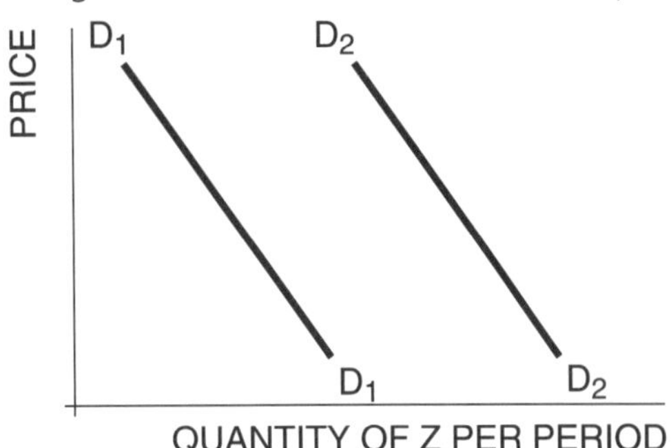

Which of the following may have caused the shift in demand curve D_1 to D_2?

A A fall in incomes.

B A rise in the price of a substitute.

C A rise in the price of a complement.

D A rise in the supply of Z.

2 Demand for a product is likely to be price-inelastic:

A The smaller the number of substitutes.

B The smaller the number of complements.

C The higher the price.

D The greater the fraction of income spent on it.

3 The best explanation of the shift in the supply curve from SS to S_1S_1 would be:

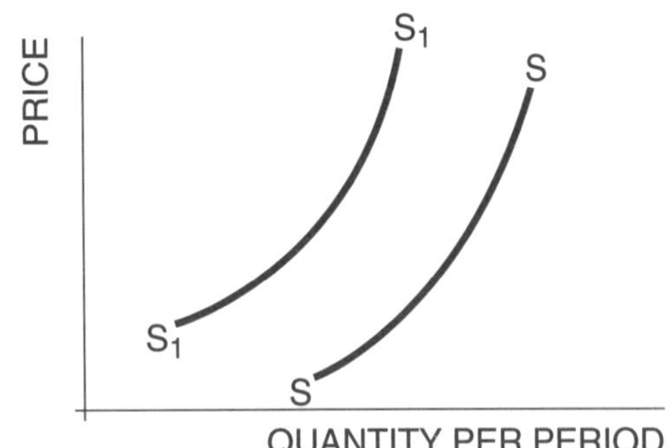

A A rise in the price of the product.

B A fall in the price of raw materials.

C Technical progress.

D A rise in wages paid to labour.

Questions 4–6 are based on the following diagram.

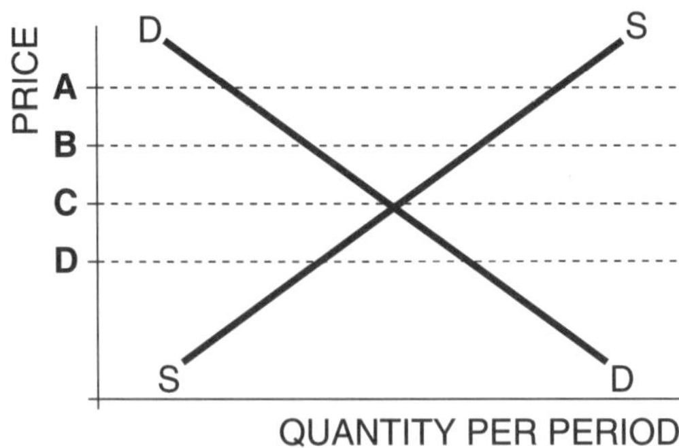

At which price will there be:

4 A market equilibrium?

5 The greatest excess demand?

6 The greatest excess supply?

7 If a rise in price from £1 to £1.10 caused supply to extend by 27%, price elasticity of supply would equal:

A 17

B 1.7

C 2.7

D 3.7

8 Which of the following pairs of commodities is an example of goods in complementary demand?

A Beef and lamb

B Coffee and tea

C Butter and margarine

D Quilts and quilt covers

9 Other things unchanged, an increase in demand for a product will cause:

A Market price to rise and supply to contract.

B Market price to fall and supply to extend.

C An increase in supply as market price rises.

D An increase in market price and an extension of supply.

4

THE INDIVIDUA PRODUCER, CON BORROWER

Individuals are both owners of factors
of goods and services. They earn mone
ices they want and need. Any income r
spend they can save. However, they ma
buy more goods and services than the
from their future income.

Most people earn money by supplying
labour to help them produce goods ar
wage rate and is determined in labour
industries. Equilibrium wage rates wil
falls or the demand for labour rises. W
skills in short supply relative to demar
wage rate relative to other groups of v
different jobs are called wage differen
differences in labour market conditio

People are attracted to different occup
monthly wages, or annual salaries, th
of hours they are required to work an
promotion prospects and how secure
other net advantages of jobs can there

The demand for labour will depend c
productive labour is, the less value it
revenue and profit, and so it may be r
equipment for labour.

Governments often intervene in labo
employment in the economy, to restr
powerful trade unions, to protect the
employees and employers, and to set

People with low incomes tend to spe
satisfying just their basic needs for fc
debt by borrowing money so they ca
to satisfy some of their wants. Unless
wealth will rise in future to cover th
borrowing might not be a wise deci
their incomes they may run into fina
discourage borrowing but encourag

Questions 10 and 11 are based on the following terms:

A A contraction of supply

B A contraction of demand

C A fall in demand

D A fall in supply

Which of the above best describes a situation where:

10 Crop disease leads to a poor harvest of corn?

11 An increase in air fares reduces the number of passenger flights?

12 Which of the following pricing strategies could best be pursued by a dominant firm trying to undercut new competition?

A Expansion pricing.

B Market pricing.

C Price creaming.

D Destruction pricing.

13 If a pure monopoly restricts market supply of a product, the most likely outcome will be:

A A fall in demand.

B A price war with rival producers.

C A fall in profit.

D A rise in market price.

14 A market dominated by just two suppliers is known as:

A A pure monopoly.

B A contestable market.

C A competitive market.

D A duopoly.

15 Which of the following is an artificial barrier to entry that may be used by a monopoly to restrict competition?

A Economies of scale in production.

B Predatory pricing strategy.

C Development of new products.

D Its significant capital size.

16 A market dominated by one or a handful of firms may be highly contestable if:

A Artificial barriers to entry are significant.

B There are no natural barriers to entry.

C Barriers to entry are low.

D Existing firms have legal monopolies.

17 Which of the following is most likely to be the subject of persuasive advertising?

A A bus timetable.

B A doctor's surgery times.

C A fizzy drink.

D Employment laws.

Chapter 10 Occupations and Wages

At the end of this chapter you should be able to:

- identify the factors affecting an individual's choice of **occupation**, including **wages** and non-wage factors
- distinguish between **labour markets** for different occupations and skills
- demonstrate how wages are determined by the **demand for labour** and the **supply of labour**
- examine reasons for changes in the demand for and supply of labour for different occupations
- describe differences in earnings between different occupational groups and different economic sectors, and analyse reasons for changes over time
- describe how and why governments intervene in labour markets

Section I What is the labour market?

Exercise 1 Just the job

Labourer Wanted
General labouring and odd jobs. Hours 8 am – 5pm. Monday to Friday. Must be willing to travel.

Restaurant and Bar Manager
To lead, manage and operate a restaurant and bar with cutting edge cocktails and global cuisine. 50 hours per week. Late evenings and shift-working required.

Economist
An international oil company is looking for an Economist to join their Business Environment Division, initially on a 2-year contract.
The successful candidate for this unusual opportunity to experience the oil industry at first hand is likely to have a degree and postgraduate degree in economics, a strong quantitative background including familiarity with PCs and a high level of analytical, written and oral communication skills. The post can be filled at various levels of previous experience, with a remuneration package to match, but preference will be given to those whose understanding of the UK economy within a global environment can be readily acknowledged.
The planning team is responsible for analysing the UK economic scene and for identifying economic trends and developments, in particular those relating to energy demand and supply.

PART-TIME SECURITY PERSON
We require a part-time security person for the reception area at our Group Head Office.
The hours of work involved are Monday to Friday 5pm to 7.30pm and duties include dealing with all visitors and deliveries to the building, whilst maintaining an effective security presence.
Applications are invited from mature persons who are confident and alert, and of a smart appearance.
We offer a good rate of pay for this responsible position.

WAREHOUSE STAFF
You could be earning instead of looking!
WAREHOUSE STAFF – We've found the way to make temporary assignments more interesting for YOU.
You'll have the opportunity to select from a variety of assignments locally or in London offering excellent rates of pay, holiday pay and other benefits.
If you're available for a week or more we can put you to work.

Book Shop Assistant
A great opportunity for a bright, enthusiastic person interested in literature, art, music and foreign languages to gain valuable experience in bookselling and publishing.
5 days per week. 10 am till 7 pm

Hair stylist
To wash and cut hair.
Part-time. Mornings only.

In groups, look at the job advertisements above.

1. For each job, discuss with your group what you think the monthly wage or annual salary for the job is likely to be.
2. Which job do you think offers the highest wage or salary, and which one offers the lowest? Why do you think this is the case?
3. Which job do you think is likely to get the most applicants and why? Try to think of reasons other than just the wage or salary.
4. Which of the jobs above would you most like to do and least like to do, and why? Again, try to think of reasons other than the amount of money the job might pay.
5. Which job would you most like to do when you leave school or college, and why? Try to find out what the job currently offers in terms of pay and other monetary and non-monetary benefits. Are you still attracted to this job?

Like the markets for all other goods and services, there are markets for the employment of labour. The market for labour in an economy will consist of all those people willing and able to supply themselves for work and all the people and organizations willing and able to employ them. We can therefore apply the same demand and supply analysis we used in Chapter 7 to examine the economics of labour markets, including what attracts people to different jobs, what determines the amount they earn, and why different people earn very different amounts of money.

There can be many different labour markets in an economy. Labour markets can be local, national or even international if people are willing and able to migrate overseas to work. There will also be a labour market for every occupation and type of skill. For example, there are labour markets for bricklayers, doctors, train drivers, accountants, soldiers, shop assistants, nurses and even economists. We can also distinguish between labour markets for young workers, who may have little work experience, and older workers, and between labour markets for temporary, part-time and full-time employees (see also Chapter 16).

The demand for labour

Firms and government organizations employ labour and other resources to produce goods and services. The demand for labour is therefore derived from the fact that people and other organizations want and need goods and services. It follows that the more goods and services demanded, and the higher their price and therefore the revenue from their sale, the more the demand for labour is likely to be.

However, private and public sector organizations are only likely to employ additional workers if they add more value than they cost to employ. In a private profit-making firm this value is measured by how much extra revenue and profit they create. So, for example, a worker will be worth employing if he or she generates an additional $5000 in revenue each month but only costs $3000 per month to employ. If, however, their employment would only generate extra output worth $2000 each month they would not be worth employing. The demand for labour is therefore closely related to the **wage rate** workers receive for their employment and how productive they are (see Chapter 12).

In general, therefore, the higher the wage rate in a particular labour market the more expensive it is to employ workers and the less will tend to be demanded. This is shown in the diagram below. We use the symbols n to denote labour and w to represent the wage rate. The demand curve for labour (D_nD_n) is downward sloping so that as the wage rate rises from w to w_1 the demand for labour contracts from n to n_1.

The demand for labour to an occupation

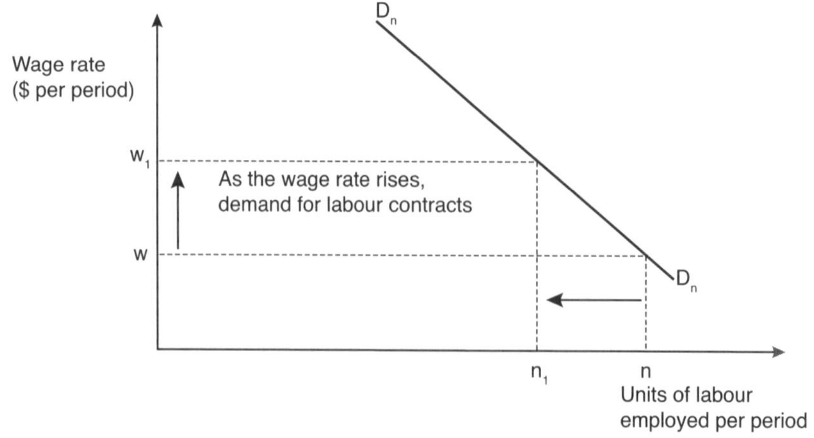

The wage rate paid for a particular job can be per hour, per week, per month or even a fixed amount per year known as a **salary**. Wages can be linked to labour productivity in a number of ways. Many workers receive a basic wage payment for a fixed number of hours of work each week, but may be able to increase their total wages by working extra hours. In contrast, piece rates link wages directly to productivity by paying each worker a fixed amount of money for each unit of output they produce, for example, for each article of clothing they make or kilogram of apples they pick. Some workers may also receive performance-related pay linked to higher profits or revenues in the firms they work in. The take-home pay or **earnings** of a worker may therefore be more than just his or her basic wage, and may include overtime and bonus payments.

The supply of labour

The total supply of labour in an economy is its labour force (see Chapter 16). The supply of labour to a particular labour market for an occupation will depend on how many people are willing and able to do the jobs on offer.

So, for example, the market supply of train drivers will consist of people currently employed as train drivers, people employed in other occupations who want to become train drivers, and people who are unemployed but are also willing and able to be train drivers.

It is likely that as the wages of train drivers rise, so more and more people will want to be train drivers. The market supply curve for train drivers will slope upwards. Indeed, this is generally the case. The higher the wage rate in a particular labour market the more labour will be supplied. This is shown in the next diagram. The supply curve for labour (S_nS_n) is upward sloping so that as the wage rate rises from w to w_1 the supply of labour extends from n to n_1.

The supply of labour to an occupation

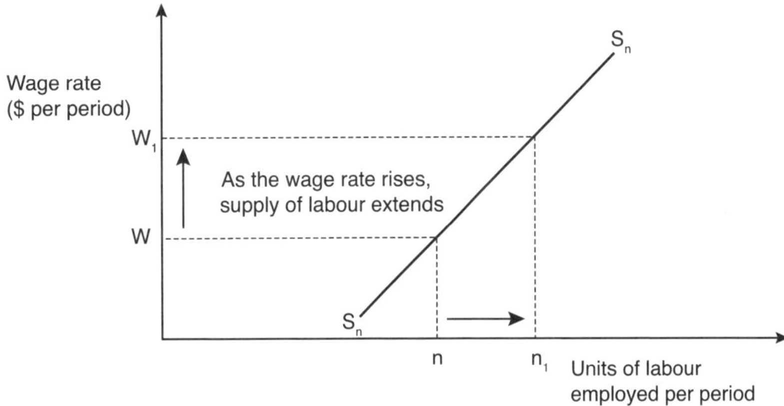

However, while the positive relationship between labour supply and wages holds in general, it may not always be the case that an individual will be willing to work more and more hours as wages rise. At some point a person might think they earn enough and would like more leisure time. As an example, consider a builder. At $7 per hour he might choose to work 35 hours each week and earn $245. At $10 per hour he may work 40 hours and earn $400. But at $15 per hour he may only work 32 hours and choose to spend more time relaxing because he is still better off earning $480 each week. As a result, the supply curve of our individual builder, and many other workers like him, will be **backward bending**. At very high wage rates it is possible to have both more wage income and more leisure.

The backward bending supply curve (S_nS_n) of our builder

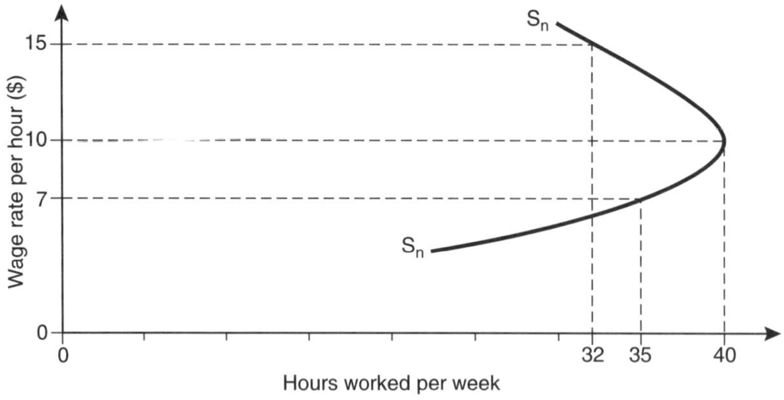

Even though most people do work a fixed number of hours per week, there is still evidence to suggest that the supply curve of labour is backward bending. This can be seen in trade union attempts to reduce working hours as living standards have improved, and in the reduction of the working week in many developed countries from 60 hours at the start of the century to an average of around 41 hours per week now.

Section 2 The market wage for a job

Equilibrium wage rates

Any labour market will consist of the demand for, and the supply of a particular group of workers. Just as in the markets for goods and services the equilibrium wage, or market price, of labour in a particular job will be determined by the forces of labour demand and labour supply. The equilibrium wage for a particular job can be illustrated graphically. At this wage we find how many workers will actually be employed.

The market for labour

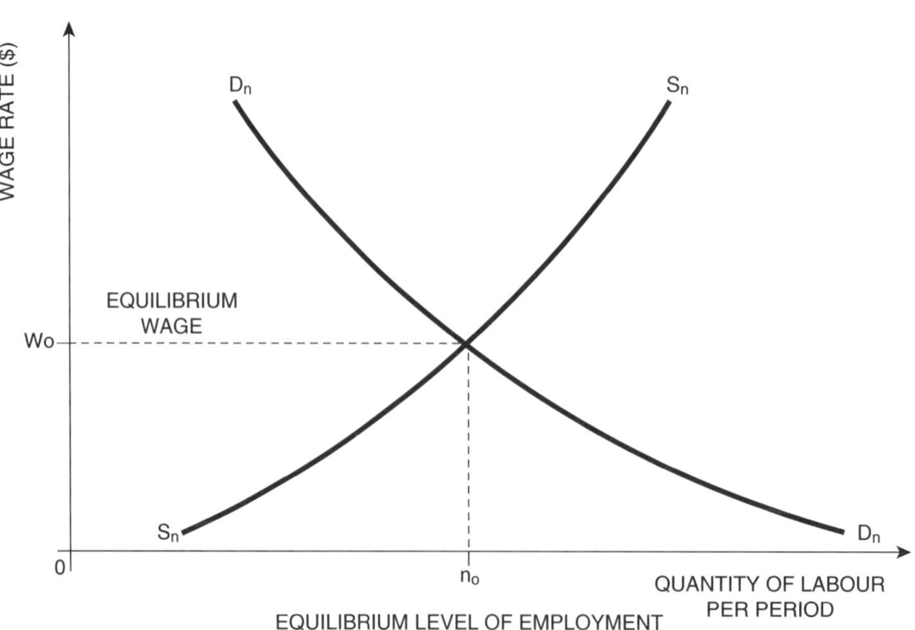

What can cause the demand for labour to shift?

The following factors may cause the demand for labour to change.

- **Consumer demand for goods and services**

If consumer demand rises, firms may expand output in response. To do so they will tend to increase their demand for labour. This may initially mean asking their existing workers to work overtime, but may also involve hiring more workers if the increase in consumer demand is permanent. Changes in the pattern of consumer demand over time, due to population changes and changing tastes, can therefore mean demand for some types of labour will be rising while demand for others is falling.

- **Increasing productivity**

If labour becomes more productive and adds more value to output over and above their wage costs, then firms may demand more labour. New technologies and working methods, and training programmes, can help increase the productivity of labour (see Chapter 12).

- **Changes in the price and productivity of capital**

If machinery and equipment becomes cheaper or more productive relative to labour, then a firm may replace labour with more capital-intensive production methods.

- **Changes in other employment costs**

Wages are not the only cost to an organization of employing people to work. For example, employers in many countries have to pay social security contributions for each worker they employ. If these are increased by the government then the demand for labour may fall. Regulations may also change over time, requiring employers to spend more on health and safety equipment in their workplaces in order to protect their workers.

What can cause the supply of labour to shift?

There are many things other than the wage rate or salary that might make a job attractive or unattractive to people. Changes in these factors can therefore cause shifts in the supply of labour to a particular occupation at any possible wage rate.

- **Changes in the net advantages of an occupation**

A person looking for paid employment is likely to compare the advantages and disadvantages of different jobs before reaching a decision. For example, in addition to wages they may consider the number of hours they are required to work and when, holiday entitlements, promotion prospects and how secure each job is. There may also be fringe benefits such as a company car, free medical insurance, increased pensions and a subsidized canteen. All the factors that affect the attractiveness of a job are called its **net advantages**.

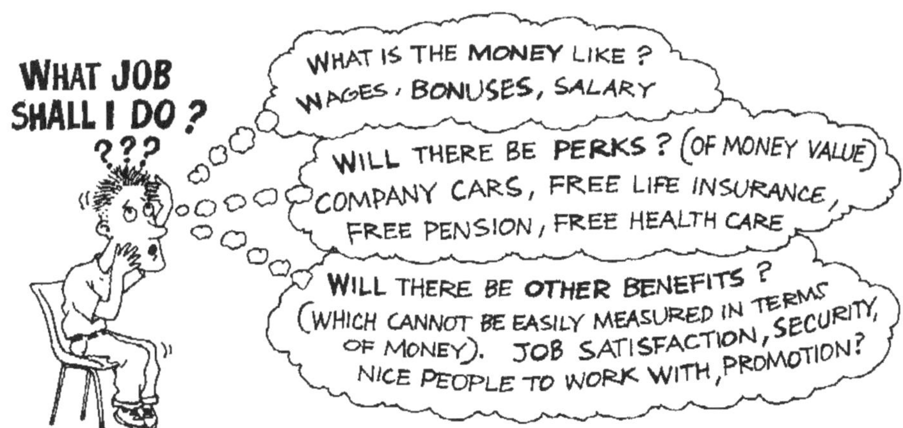

Changes in net advantages will therefore cause shifts in the amount of labour supplied to particular occupations. For example, a decline in the promotion prospects or holiday entitlement of school teachers relative to other occupations is likely to cause a fall in the supply of school teachers at every possible wage, from S_nS_n to $S_{n1}S_{n1}$ in the diagram below.

A fall in the supply of teachers results in their labour supply curve shifting inwards

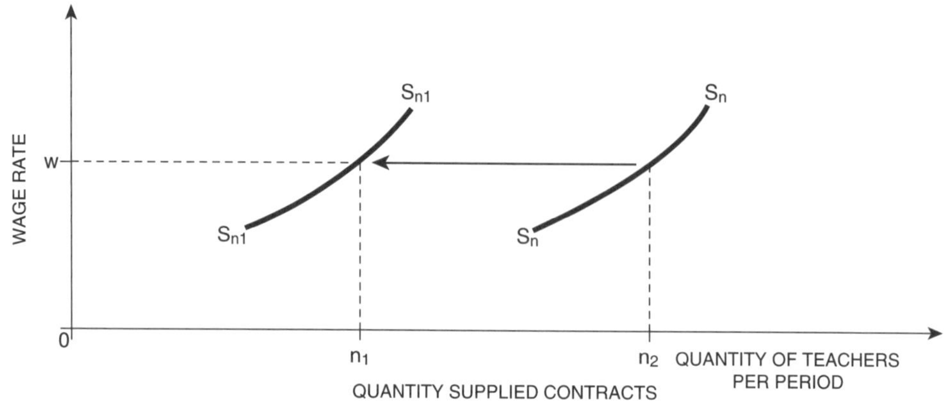

- **Demographic changes**

Changes in the size and age distribution of the population in a country will also cause changes in labour supply to different occupations (see Chapter 20). For example, inward migration to many developed economies has helped boost the supply of labour to many occupations. In contrast, the increasing average age of their populations as birth rates remain low means that more people are leaving the labour force due to old age, while others are moving from full-time employment in industry to part-time jobs in services as they get older and want to enjoy more leisure time.

- **Education and training**

Changes in the level and type of education and training courses offered can increase the supply of workers with different skills. For example, the introduction of courses in computer programming and cellular engineering has increased the number of people able to supply these skills to jobs that require them.

Will the equilibrium wage change?

Like any commodity, the wages of any group of workers will rise and fall given changes in the forces of demand and supply. A rise in the demand for labour, or a fall in its supply, will cause market wages to rise. A fall in the demand for labour, or a rise in its supply, will bring market wages down.

A rise in the demand for labour
Equilibrium wage rate rises from W to W1 and employment increases from n to n_1.

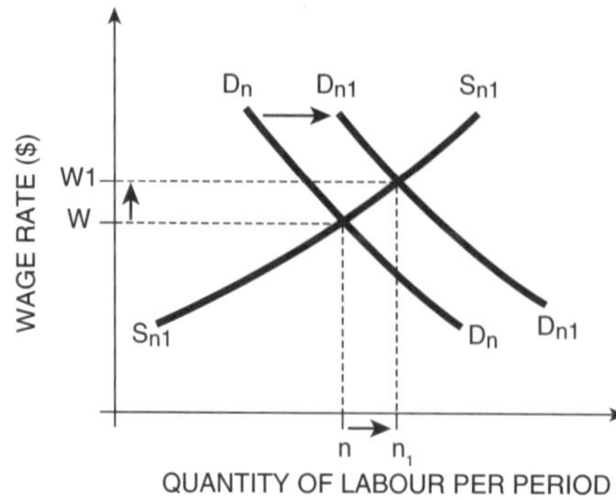

A fall in the supply of labour
Equilibrium wage rate rises from W to W1 and employment falls from n to n_1.

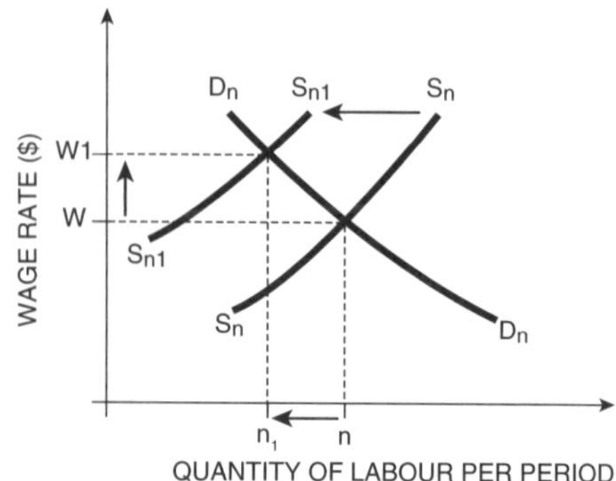

Exercise 2 The rise or fall in labour

Look at the list of changes below that might affect labour market outcomes. In each case indicate whether you think it will cause the demand for labour to rise or fall, or the supply of labour to rise or fall, and whether the market wage for each occupation will tend to rise or fall as a result.

What has changed?	Impact on labour demand?	Impact on labour supply?	Impact on market wage?
Nurses are offered new contracts with shorter working weeks			
Consumer spending on flat-screen televisions increases significantly			
Government raises retirement age of public sector workers			
Overtime payments for airline employees to be scrapped			
Computerized assembly lines boosts labour productivity in car plants			
Major retail chain announces it will remain open 24 hours each day			
Assaults on police increase			
Government announces it will tax tips received by restaurant and hotel staff from next April			
Survey finds more people are working part-time and flexible hours			
Statutory maternity leave and pay to be increased			
New technology means more office workers can now work from home			

Section 3 Why do people earn different amounts?

Wage differentials

Differences in wages between different jobs are called **wage differentials**. For example, a doctor may earn over $100 000 per year while a farm labourer in the same country may earn less than $10 000. Differences in the wages and earnings of workers are common in all countries. For example, the average earnings of full-time male employees in the UK were £487 per week in April 2006, and £387 for women. The top 10 per cent of the distribution of earnings in the UK earned more than £886 per week, while the bottom 10 per cent earned less than £244. Wages can also vary significantly between countries, even for the same job (see Chapter 19).

Why do people earn different amounts?

Clearly a person doing the same job for the same hourly wage rate as someone else but working fewer hours will take home less in earnings at the end of each week or month. But this is not our concern here. We want to examine how wage differentials occur because of differences in demand and supply in different labour markets. We already know from section 2 that the demand for labour in a particular market will be related to how productive labour is and the amount of demand for the goods or services it produces, while labour supply will depend on people having the right skills which business demands and also on the net advantages of different jobs. We can use our knowledge of these factors to explain wage differentials.

1 Different abilities and qualifications

Workers do not all have the same education, training and ability. For example, an accountant is a more skilled worker than a cashier. If both workers were paid the same amount, very few people would be willing to undertake the many years of study necessary to become an accountant.

Because the training period is so long for some jobs the supply of these particular workers may be very low and as a result their wages may be very high. For example, it takes doctors over six years to qualify to do their job.

People with skills that are in very short supply relative to the demand for those skills will tend to be offered very high wages. This explains why skilled footballers like David Beckham, and actresses like Julia Roberts, are able to command huge salaries.

2 'Dirty' jobs and unsociable hours

Some jobs are dirty or dangerous and so workers must be paid more in order attract a supply of labour. Some people have to work nights or other unsociable hours and may be paid more to compensate for this. These are called **compensating differentials**.

3 Satisfaction

Certain jobs, for example, nursing, are thought by some people to give a lot of job satisfaction and some people may be prepared to do them without very high pay.

4 Lack of information about jobs and wages

Sometimes workers work for less than they could earn simply because they do not know about better-paid jobs elsewhere. Lack of information about job availability is one reason for differences in earnings.

5 Immobility

People may earn different amounts because some workers may not wish to leave their families and friends in order to move to a better-paid job elsewhere. At the same time, other workers would like to be able to move to a better-paid job, but may not be able to do this because they cannot afford housing in the new area.

The ease with which workers can move between jobs and different parts of the country is known as **labour force mobility**. If workers are very mobile, they will move to the jobs that offer them the most pay, and they will also move from places with high unemployment to areas with job vacancies. High labour mobility or willingness to move can help reduce differences in unemployment and wage rates in different parts of a country.

6 Fringe benefits

Some jobs may offer lower wages than others because they offer more perks, such as company cars, free life insurance, cheap travel. However, it is usually the higher-paid jobs that also tend to offer the most perks.

Exercise 3 How different is your differential?

1 Look at the chart of average earnings by gender and broad occupational group in the UK. What economic factors could explain these differences in pay?

2 Find examples of jobs in each occupational group in your own country and compare their earnings. Do they follow the same pattern as in the UK?

UK Average weekly earnings before tax, winter 2005/6, full-time employees by main occupational group

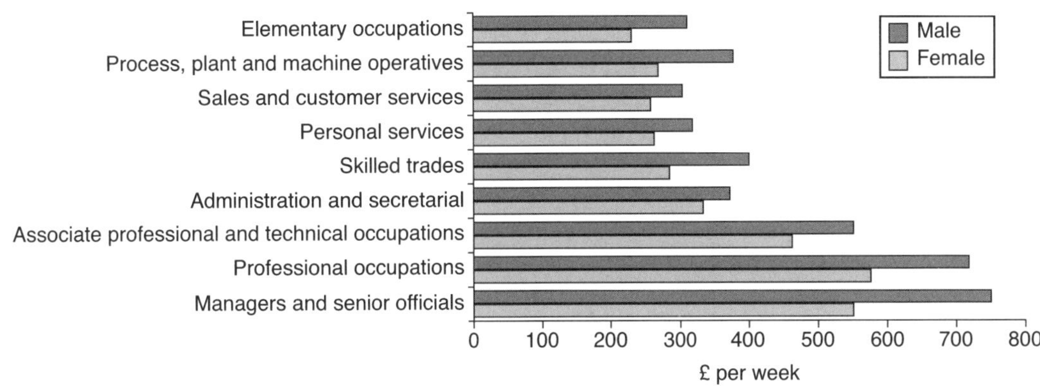

Elementary occupations include labourers, farm workers, cleaners, etc.

Labour Force Survey, UK Office for National Statistics

Why do people in a the same job earn different amounts?

People in different occupations can earn different amounts of money, but even people in the same jobs can earn very different amounts. This can happen because:

1 Regional differences in labour market conditions

For example, there may be shortages of workers with particular types of skills in some parts of the country. Firms in such areas needing these workers may offer higher wages to attract workers from rival firms or from elsewhere in the country.

2 Length of service

Many firms have pay scales that offer pay increases linked to the number of years a worker stays with the firm. This extra pay is both a bonus for loyalty and also a payment for having more experience and skill. Firms reward their more experienced and productive workers with higher pay because they want to keep them.

3 Local pay agreements

Some national trade unions may agree a national wage rate for their members through collective bargaining with employers (see Chapter 5). All workers belonging to the union with similar work experience and levels of skill will therefore receive the same wage wherever they work in a country. However, many workers and employers can often agree their pay locally, so regional differences in pay in the same occupation can occur.

4 Non-wage rewards

Some firms may offer their workers benefits other than higher pay, such as longer holidays, free healthcare and performance-related gifts. In some countries these non-pay rewards are not taxed so offer better value than paying higher wages from which income taxes and social security contributions will be deducted.

5 Discrimination

Workers doing the same job may be treated differently by employers simply because of their sex, age, race or religion. Such discrimination is outlawed in many countries.

Investigating wage differentials

Economists, social researchers, trade unions, employers' groups and governments often monitor the following key earnings differentials.

- **Public–private sector pay gap**

Governments are major employers in many countries. The public sector therefore competes with private sector firms to attract many of the same types of workers and so governments need to be aware what private sector firms are paying.

> **Chancellor calls for public sector pay freeze**
>
> The Chancellor of the Exchequer last night put the government on a collision course with millions of public sector workers when he called for a three-year pay freeze as part of the fight to control inflation and cut the budget deficit.
>
> A spokeswoman for Britain's biggest union, Unison, said: "Any attempt to artificially keep down pay in the public sector will only lead to bad feeling as workers see pay in the private sector overtaking them year on year."
>
> *The Guardian*, 14.7.2006

Yet some people argue governments have the power to hold down the wages of public sector workers relative to the private sector. However, lower public sector pay might be explained by many of its employees having more secure jobs and, in some cases, better pension rights. For example, civil servants, the police and teachers are not at risk of losing their jobs due to falling consumer demand like many private sector workers.

But data is mixed. While there are many relatively low-paid workers in public sector jobs, others appear to earn as much if not more than private sector workers in very similar jobs. For example, a recent study in Pakistan suggested its public sector workers earned on average 49 per cent more. This was explained by public sector workers generally having higher levels of education and productivity.

- **Skilled and unskilled workers**

Wage inequality has been increasing between skilled and unskilled workers in many developed and developing countries. This is partly explained by the increasing globalization of production. Less developed countries have many low-skilled workers who work for very low wages compared to other countries. It is therefore cheaper for many firms to produce goods and services in these countries. In addition, the demand for skills is rising and firms competing for skilled workers are offering higher wages to attract them. Trade union power has also decreased in many developed countries as manual labour-intensive industries have declined in importance (see Chapter 16).

- **Industrial wage differentials**

As we have learnt above, these usually reflect differences in labour market demand and supply conditions. Expanding industries will tend to offer higher wages to attract workers with the skills they need, especially if the supply of labour with these skills is relatively low. In contrast, the demand for labour in old, declining industries will be falling.

However, changes in some occupational and industrial wage differentials may be resisted by powerful trade unions that want to maintain the same differences in their members' pay relative to other groups of workers, regardless of changing labour market conditions (see Chapter 5). They are, therefore, concerned not only with wage differentials with other unions, but also unionized and non-unionized labour pay differences.

UK Average gross hourly earnings by industry, 2005/06

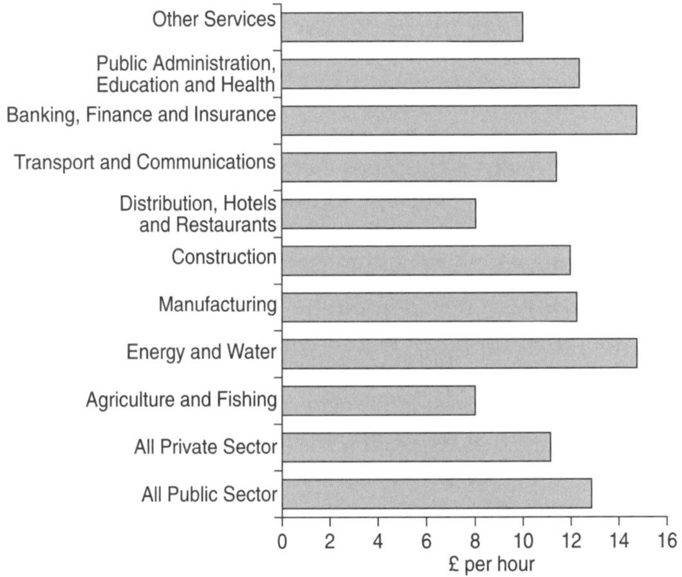

Labour Force Survey, UK Office for National Statistics, 2006

Gender pay gap, selected countries 2003: women's wages in manufacturing as a percentage of men's wages

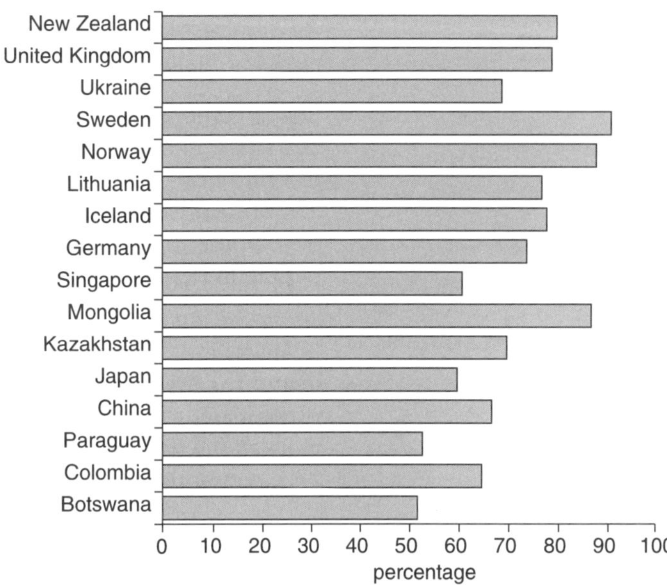

United Nations Survey, 2005

Hourly earnings in manufacturing, selected countries 2005 (US dollars, adjusted for differences in exchange rates)

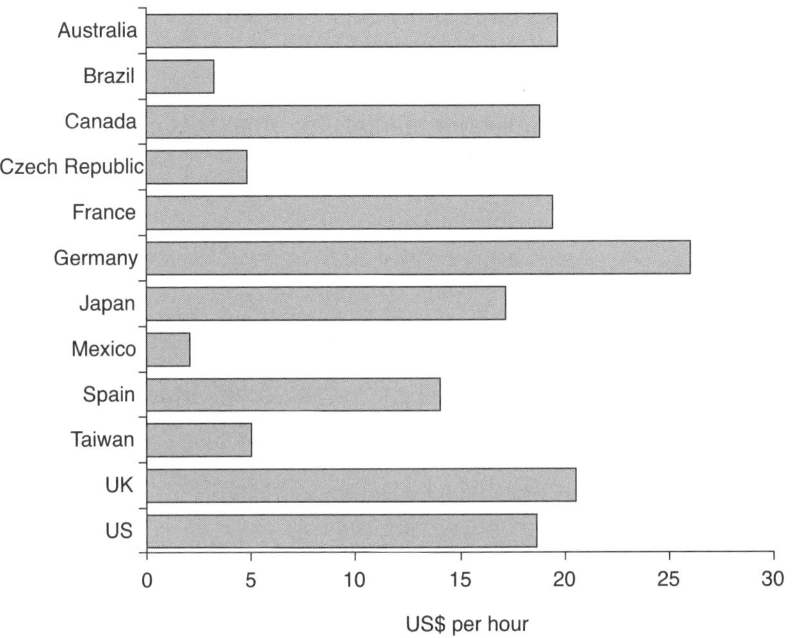

Adapted from US Bureau of Labor Statistics

- **Gender pay gap**

The average earnings of men usually exceed those of women the world over. For example, in the UK in 2006 women's hourly earnings were on average 12.6 per cent below those of men. Much of the difference in pay can be explained by the following factors:

- Differences in the occupational distribution of men and women. More women tend to work in occupations such as teaching, nursing and retailing than men. These occupations often receive relatively lower pay.
- Women often take career breaks to raise children, and therefore may build up less work experience than males and have less career progression.
- More women work part-time than full-time compared to men.

However, the pay gap between men and women has declined during the past two decades in most developed countries. This change reflects more women joining the labour force and going out to work, changes in attitudes in society towards women working and men sharing family responsibilities more, and the introduction of equal pay laws (see Chapter 16).

International pay differentials

Making international comparisons of wages and earnings is difficult. Data is not always available. However, it is clear that there are significant pay differentials between countries. Wages on average are higher in developed countries than in developing and less developed countries even after adjusting for prices and living costs which are often much higher in developed countries (see Chapter 19).

Real income and consumer spending on goods and services is far higher in developed countries. Remember that labour demand is related to the level of demand for, and revenue from, goods and services. In less developed countries incomes are generally low and consumer spending is, therefore, also low. Hence, countries with low economic development tend to have few industries and generally low demand for labour. Most people in less developed countries are employed in agriculture (see Chapter 20).

However, less developed countries have large potential labour forces but skill levels are relatively low. The combination of an abundant supply of labour with low demand for labour means wages will tend to remain low in many less developed countries. In contrast, wage levels are now starting to rise rapidly in fast developing economies such as China and India as the demand for goods and services, both at home and from overseas, grows rapidly and, consequently, the demand for labour from a growing number of industries increases.

Section 4 Government intervention in labour markets

The government is a major employer in many countries, often employing the labour of many thousands of teachers, doctors, civil servants, army personnel and other public sector workers. Because it is such a major source of demand for labour it is able to exert a big influence over the market wage rate for these public sector jobs.

However, governments also often intervene in labour markets for other reasons. For example:

Key legal responsibilities and rights (EU)

Employees	Employers
• to comply with the terms and conditions of their employment, for example, on hours of work, holidays, dress codes, maternity leave, disciplinary procedures, etc. • to comply with health and safety regulations, such as observing no-smoking signs and wearing protective clothing • to receive at least the legal minimum levels of sick and maternity pay, and redundancy compensation • to receive at least 4 weeks paid holiday per year and take minimum rest periods each day • not to have to work more than 48 hours each week, except for jobs involving the driving of goods and public service vehicles • protection from unfair dismissal and the right to defend their actions at an employment tribunal and the European Court of Justice	• to comply with the terms and conditions of their contract with an employee • not to discriminate against any worker because of their sex, marital status, race, religion, disability, union membership, or because they work part-time • to provide a healthy and safe working environment and any necessary equipment • to comply with the legal rights of employees to minimum daily rest periods, paid holiday entitlements, maximum weekly working hours, payments for sickness, maternity and redundancy • the right to legally terminate employment and to defend their actions at an employment tribunal and the European Court of Justice

1 To protect the rights of employees and employers

Employment laws and workplace health and safety regulations have been introduced in many countries not only to give employers and workers certain rights, but also to make them responsible for observing the rights and responsibilities of each other. In a totally free labour market for example, a powerful employer may not provide a safe working environment for employees or a powerful trade union may not deliver levels of labour productivity expected by employers. For example, the table above lists some of the key legal rights and responsibilities of employees and employers in the European Union.

2 To outlaw and regulate the restrictive practices of powerful trade unions and employers

In a free market wages will be set by the forces of supply and demand. However, a powerful employer may be able to pay wages that are too low while a trade union may seek wages that are too high and not matched by productivity.

Laws have been introduced in a number of countries to control the power of employers and unions over wages and working conditions (see Chapter 5). For example, in the UK employers must observe the legal rights of their employees, and trade unions no longer have the right to strike without first conducting a full ballot of their members. A trade union may also be liable for any damages or losses suffered by an employer from industrial action.

3 To raise the wages of very low-paid workers

Many countries have minimum wage laws designed to protect vulnerable and low-paid workers from exploitation by powerful employers. The first **national minimum wage law** was introduced in New Zealand in 1896, followed by Australia in 1899 and the United Kingdom in 1902, and again in 1999. In 2006 in the European Union, 18 out of 25 member states had national minimum wages. Apart from raising the pay of low-paid workers, it is argued that favourable minimum wages will make them work harder and achieve higher levels of productivity. However, some employers argue that minimum wages set above free market wage levels will simply raise production costs and reduce the demand for labour.

4 To reduce unemployment

Governments can often provide unemployed people with help re-training in new skills required to get a job and financial assistance to firms in areas of high unemployment. A government may also provide an employment service to help people look for jobs and prepare people for job interviews. In this way, a government can reduce the costs of searching for employment and increase the mobility of labour.

5 To stop discrimination

Some countries have laws which make it an offence to treat people looking for work or in work differently simply because of their sex, age, race or religion. For example, the Equal Pay Act in the UK makes it unlawful for employers to discriminate between men and women in terms of their pay and conditions where they are doing the same or similar work, or work of equal value.

Exercise 4 The minimum wage debate

Minimum wages do create some jobs – for economists. In America and the UK economists have been studying whether setting a floor under pay destroys jobs or reduces poverty.

A study by the OECD suggests the policy is ill suited to dealing with the problem of poverty. In most countries, many low earners have well-paid partners or affluent parents. Since most low-paid workers are not in poor households, most of the income gains that might come from a minimum wage would benefit families which are not poor.

Critics of minimum wages frequently argue that a government-mandated pay level reduces total employment because firms will scale back hiring rather than adding employees who must be paid more than they are worth. Those in favour argue an imposed wage minimum could have an opposite effect where the employer is large and powerful in relation to the pool of suitable workers. A powerful employer may be able to hold down wages by restricting its demand for labour. If a government sets a higher minimum wage, the employer no longer has this incentive. Because the employer must pay the higher wage there is no point any longer in restricting its demand for labour.

The OECD study – which considers data from nine countries, including America, Japan, France and Spain – finds that a 10 per cent rise in the minimum wage reduces teenage employment by around 3 per cent in both high and low minimum wage countries.

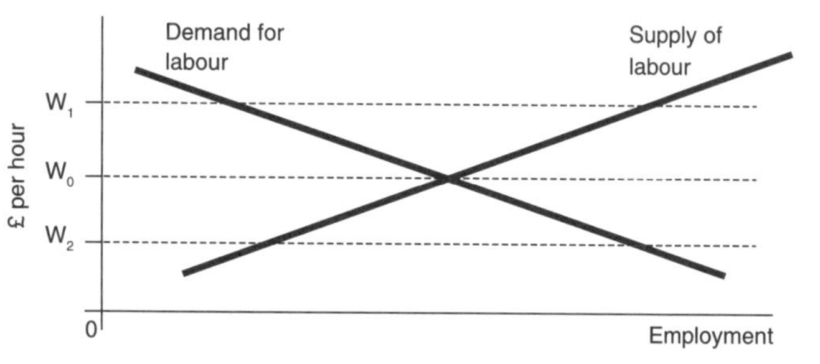

1 From the article, what are the arguments for and against a minimum wage? Does it matter what level the minimum wage is set at? Explain your answer using diagrams where possible.

2 How could you try to monitor the impact of a minimum wage over time?

3 In the diagram, what will be the impact of a minimum wage set at **a** W_1, **b** W_2?

4 Calculate the wage elasticity of demand for teenage labour suggested by the findings of the study.

Exercise 5 The best job you ever had?

Conduct a survey of friends and family members in paid employment. Find out as much as you can about their different jobs and their net advantages. For example, how much they earn per period, what makes up their earnings, what is their wage rate or annual salary, how long have they been in the same job, and what skills and qualifications does it require, etc. What other non-wage benefits do they receive in work, such as a subsidized canteen, free medical insurance, non-contributory pension, company car, etc.? What hours do they work and what is their annual holiday entitlement? Analyse the information you have collected and use it to try to explain the wage or earnings differentials between the different jobs your friends and family members have.

Write a few words to explain each of the following terms.

Labour market

Wage rate

Salary

Earnings

National minimum wage

Demand for labour

Supply of labour

Backward bending supply curve

Wage differentials

Compensating differentials

Now go back through the chapter to check your understanding.

Here are some websites to help you find out more about labour markets and wages:

- *www.bized.co.uk/learn/economics/wages/index.htm*
- *www.tutor2u.net/revision_notes_economics_gcse.asp* (select How we Work)
- International Labour Organization *laborsta.ilo.org*
- OECD (select Statistics then Labour) *www.oecd.org*
- UK Office for National Statistics (select Labour Market) *www.statistics.gov.uk*
- UK occupational classification *www.statistics.gov.uk/methods_quality/soc/structure.asp*
- US Department of Labor: Bureau of Labor Statistics *www.bls.gov*

Chapter 11 Spending, Saving and Borrowing

Aims

At the end of this chapter you should be able to:

- analyse the motives for **spending**, **saving** and **borrowing**
- describe how and why different income groups have different expenditure, saving and borrowing patterns
- analyse changes in patterns of expenditure between groups and over time

Section 1 Consumption

People hire out their services as labour in return for wages and other earnings. Some people also invest in companies and earn dividends from profits, while others invest in savings and other investment schemes and earn interest on their money. The same or other people may rent out land and buildings they own. But what do people do with all the income they earn?

People are both owners of factors of production and also consumers of goods and services. They earn money to buy the goods and services they want and need but do not produce themselves in their work (see Chapter 2). Any income they do not spend, and which is not taken in tax, can be saved.

Disposable income

Wages, dividends from profits, interest from savings and rents are taxable forms of income in most countries (see Chapter 15). The income a person has left after income-related taxes and any social security contributions have been deducted is called **disposable income**, because that person can dispose of it how he or she wants, i.e. they can choose to spend it or save it how they like.

The more disposable income person has, then the more their potential **consumer expenditure** on goods and services, and the more they will be able to save. But, how much a person can buy with their disposable income will also depend on prices. Increasing prices will reduce the real purchasing power of income (see Chapter 16). Therefore, the amount a person can choose to spend on goods and services depends on their **real disposable income**. Some people with very low real disposable incomes may only be able to afford to satisfy their basic needs for food and shelter, while other with high disposable incomes may chose to consume a vast array of different goods and services mainly for pleasure.

Economic growth has meant real income has been rising in many countries over time (see Chapter 17). At the same time consumer expenditure has been growing. For example, look at the charts below for China and the UK from 1985 to 2005.

The rise of income and spending in different countries, 1985–2005

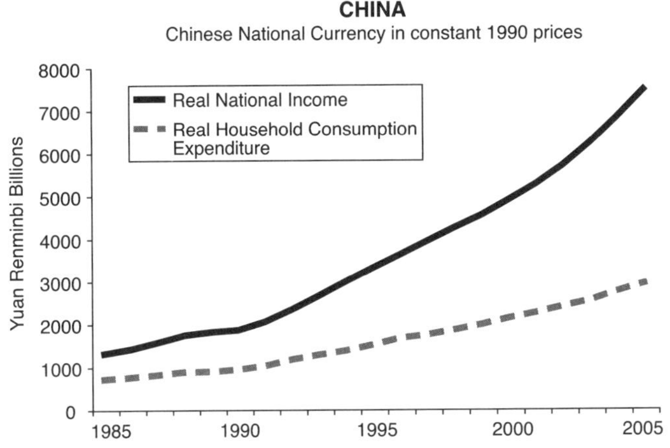

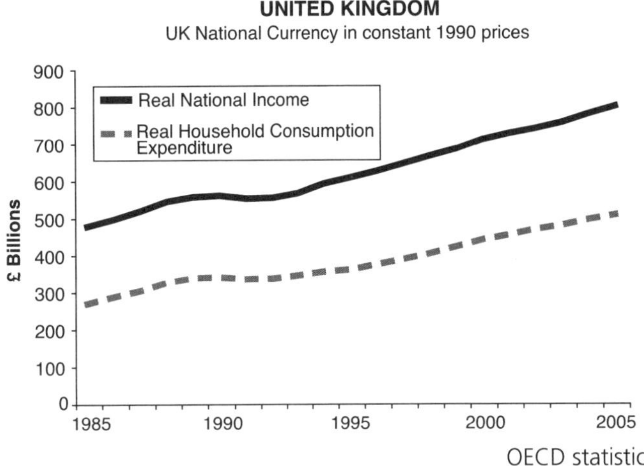

OECD statistics

Why do people consume goods and services?

People buy goods and services to satisfy their wants and needs. **Consumption** involves the using up of goods and services to satisfy wants.

In general, people will choose to spend their disposable incomes on consuming those goods and services that provide them with the most satisfaction, or **utility**. That is, a person with a given disposable income and faced with a set of prices and places to buy different goods and services will consume those goods and services that maximize his or her total utility.

Consider a simple example of a boy eating cakes. He likes cakes but if he buys too few to eat he will not maximize his utility. However, if he buys and eats too many at once he may start to feel sick, and his utility will start to fall. As such, he should have bought fewer cakes and instead spent that money on things that would have given him more pleasure than those extra cakes, such as a music CD or a visit to the cinema to watch a film. The same will apply to the consumption of shoes, holidays, cars and all other goods and services, hence the saying 'you can have too much of a good thing!'

Utility is rising

"Yum, Yum!"

Utility is maximized

"Oooh. Just right!"

Utility is falling

"Oh dear. I won't be doing that again!"

Patterns of consumer expenditure can vary greatly even between people with similar incomes simply because people have different tastes (see also Chapter 7). Tastes may vary between different groups of consumers according to their age, sex and family circumstances, for example, whether they are married and have children.

People's tastes can also change over time and may be influenced by the view of other consumers. For example, we might change our mind about going to the cinema to watch a particular film or visiting a local restaurant, because we have heard bad reports from other people who have seen the film or eaten at the restaurant. Similarly, we might use a car mechanic or hairdresser and really like their services, in which case we will tend to use them again and again. All these types of products are called **experience goods** and services, because it is hard to tell how much we might like them until we have consumed them, and because we can also tell other people about our experience of them.

What other factors affect total consumer expenditure?

After income the three most important factors that affect the level of consumer expenditure are:

- **Wealth**

The more wealthy people feel, the more likely they are to spend more on goods and services. Private **wealth** consists of a stock of goods that have a money value. It will include assets such as houses, jewellery and shares in companies, all of which can easily be sold for cash. Wealth also includes money saved in bank accounts and other investment schemes that can easily be withdrawn.

- **Consumer confidence**

If consumers are confident about their jobs and their incomes then this might encourage them to spend more now, perhaps even to borrow money to buy a house, a new car or other expensive items. However, income and employment can change over the economic cycle (see Chapter 17). If consumers think they may become unemployed or suffer falling income during an economic recession then this may persuade them to save more rather than spend.

- **Interest rates**

If interest rates are high people may save more of their disposable income because it pays them to do so. However, if interest rates are low people may spend more, and may even borrow more because loan repayments will be less (see Section 3).

Exercise 1 Spending patterns

Type of household expenditure as a percentage of total household expenditure, by lowest and highest gross income households, UK 2004–05

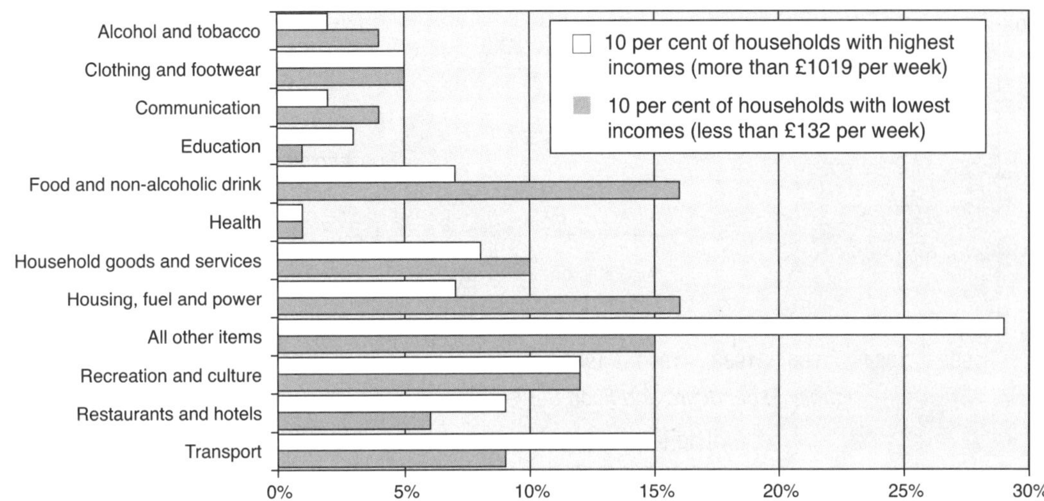

Family Expenditure and Food Survey, 2004–05, UK Office for National Statistics

Look at the chart comparing how the average low and high income households in the UK divide up their weekly spending between different goods and services.

1 Which type of household spent the highest proportion of their total spending on the following categories:

- food and non-alcoholic drinks
- housing, fuel and power
- communication
- alcohol and tobacco
- transport
- restaurants and hotels

2 What do you think can explain these different expenditure patterns?

Consumption patterns and trends

The proportion of disposable income a person spends, known as their propensity to consume, and what they spend it on, varies greatly across populations. We can examine consumption patterns by income group, gender and age, and also over time. Firms find this information useful because it allows them to target the goods and services they produce and advertise at particular groups of consumers they want to attract to buy them (see Chapter 9).

People on lower incomes tend to spend all of their money to meet basic needs for food, clothing, housing and heating, and if possible to satisfy a few wants from time to time. People on high incomes may spend far more, and on luxury items, leisure activities and other goods and services to satisfy their wants, but overall will tend to spend a lower proportion of their total disposable income.

What we buy tends to change as we get older. For example young people may spend more on fashionable clothes, going out to clubs and bars, and music CDs than older people, who will tend to spend more on household goods for their homes.

Trends in UK household expenditure, 1982–2004

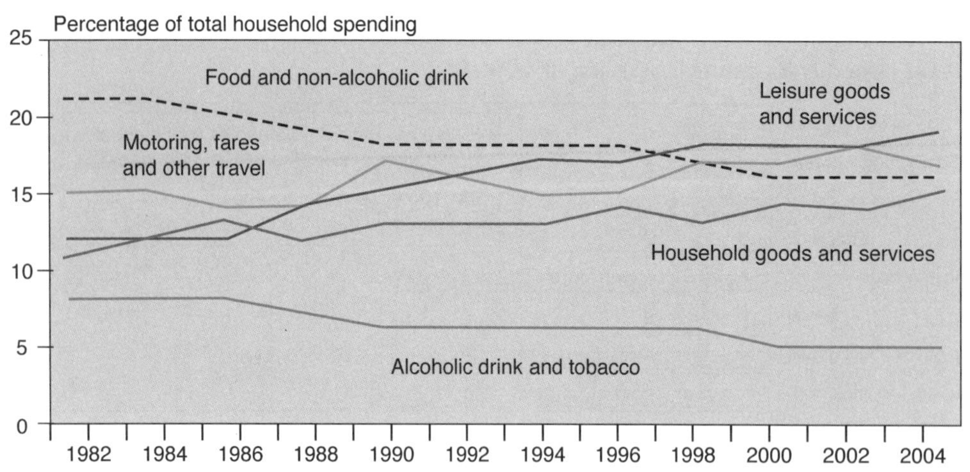

Family Expenditure and Food Survey, 2004–05, UK Office for National Statistics

The chart opposite shows how household spending patterns have changed over time in the UK. Spending on food, drink and tobacco as a proportion of their total spending has fallen and households are now devoting more of their expenditure to travel, leisure and household items. Over the same period the number of cars and owner-occupied dwellings in the UK has more than doubled. More people are now spending more repaying mortgages than paying rent for accommodation.

The same consumption trends have been observed in many developed countries, and also now in some developing countries, and are the result of a number of factors:

- **Real incomes have risen**

More people are now better off. Higher incomes enable people to spend more on satisfying their wants. The increased use of credit cards to boost spending also reflects a change in attitudes over time towards borrowing and debt.

- **People work fewer hours than many years ago**

This has given people more leisure time, and increased spending on holidays, sporting activities, garden plants and equipment, and eating out in restaurants.

- **Social attitudes have changed**

More women are going out to work in many countries. This means they have less time to look after their families and has increased the demand for time-saving appliances such as microwave ovens and dishwashers.

- **Couples are marrying later in life and having fewer children**

Consumption patterns for different goods and services, and also savings patterns, are therefore changing over time as the average age of populations rises in many developed and rapidly developing countries due to the fall in birth rates (see Chapter 20). It has also meant a growing number of single people and increase in the number of households, but a fall in their average size. This has helped to increase the amount spent on housing and household goods and furnishings over time. Single people tend to spend more on going out and travel.

- **People have become more health conscious**

Spending on sports activities, exercise equipment and gym membership has increased. Demand for healthier foods has also risen.

- **Concern for the environment is growing**

This has increased the demand for products which release fewer harmful pollutants into the atmosphere when they are produced or consumed, can be recycled, and are not tested on animals.

- **Technology has advanced rapidly**

New products have become available and created new consumer wants. Spending on DVDs, computers, mobile phones, big screen televisions, internet services, games consoles and other advanced consumer products has increased.

Exercise 2 Shop 'til they drop

1 Look at the graphs below for the UK. What past trends in consumer spending patterns can you identify?

2 Suggest possible reasons for these trends in consumption patterns in the UK.

3 How might private firms and the UK government use this information and why?

4 Choose one particular product from those shown, and suggest whether you think the trend will continue or change in the future, and why.

5 How do these trends compare to consumption patterns in your own country? Explain reasons for any similarities or differences.

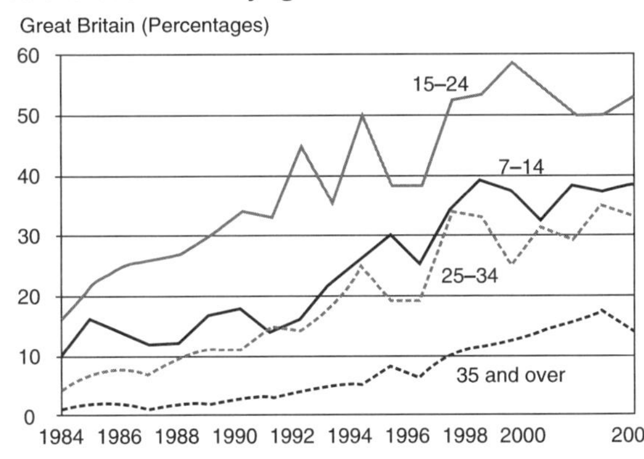

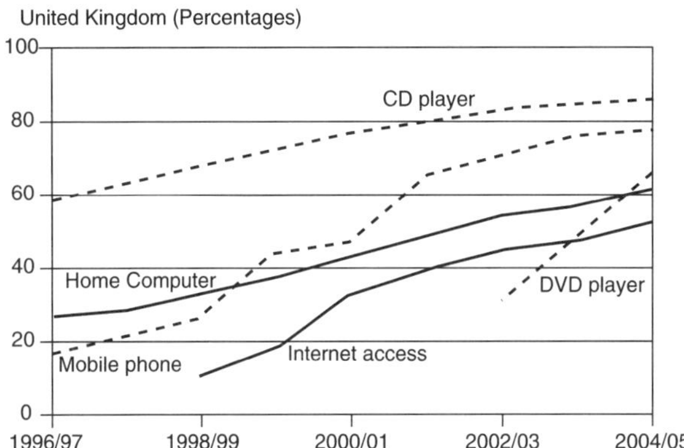

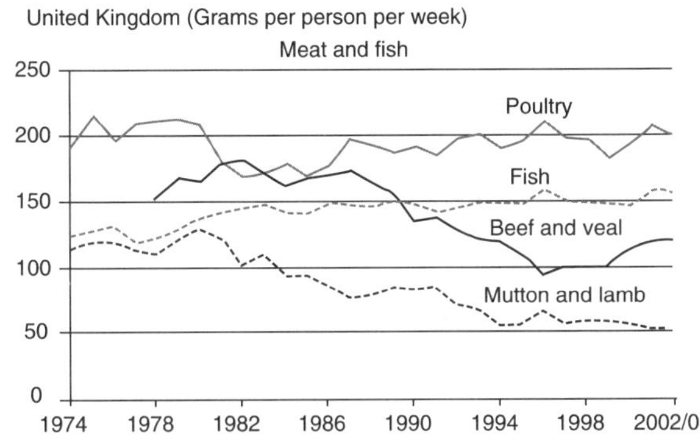

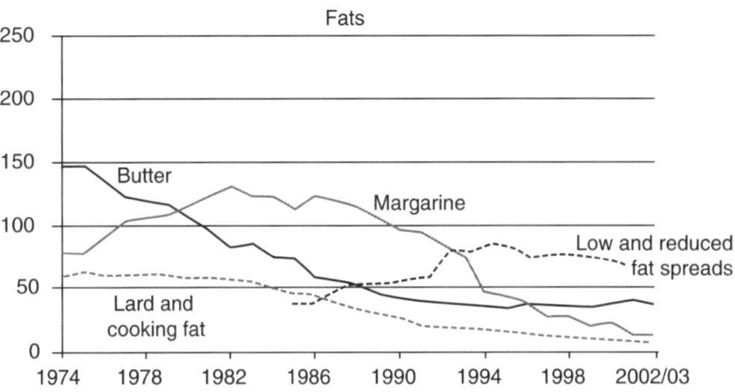

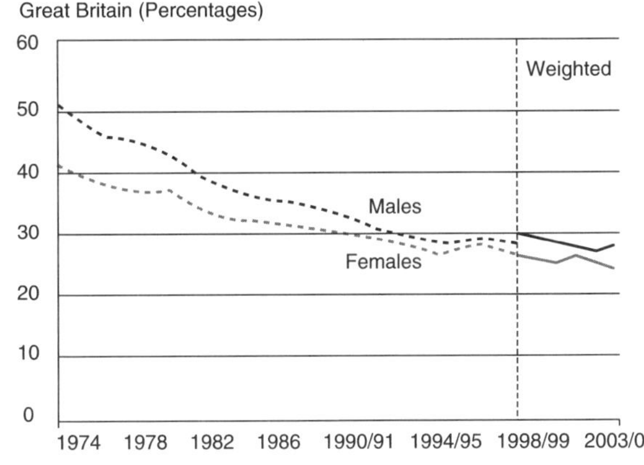

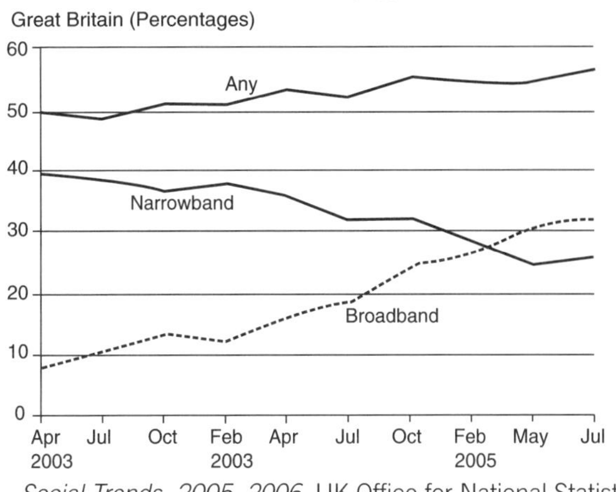

Social Trends, 2005, 2006, UK Office for National Statistics

Saving

What determines savings?

Saving involves a person delaying consumption until some later time when they withdraw and spend their savings plus any interest. Just like consumer spending, the more disposable income a person has the more they will be able to save. So, as income rises, total savings tend to rise. But the relationship is not so straightforward.

The **savings ratio** measures the proportion of the total disposable income saved in an economy. The chart below shows the savings ratio for the UK economy between 1985 and 2005. It has varied a lot, from a peak of 11.7 per cent in 1992 to a low point of 3.7 per cent in 2004. This is despite rising real income over time.

UK Savings ratio: savings as a percentage of disposable income

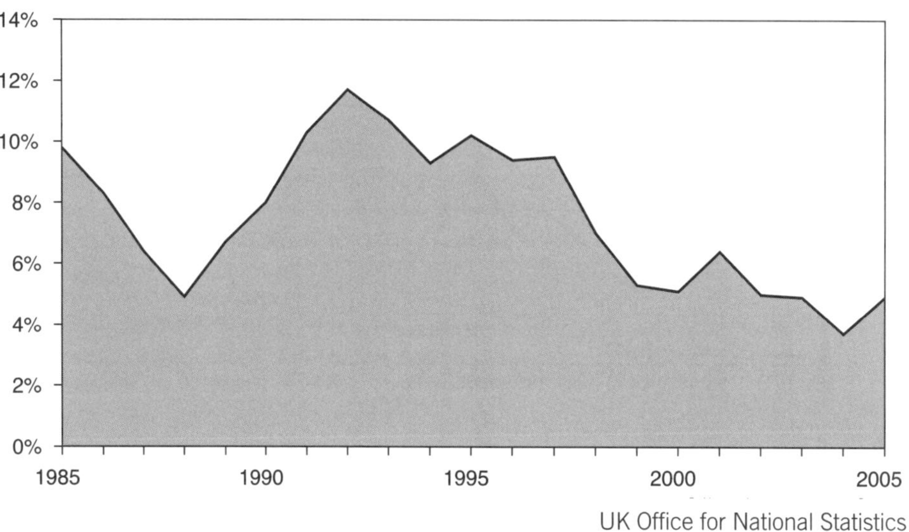

UK Office for National Statistics

The **savings ratios** in many other countries also tend to vary widely as a proportion of their income over time. This suggests the amount of savings in an economy depends on many other factors.

Why do people save?

Just like the consumption of goods and services, saving money and feeling wealthier also gives people utility. But the amount people choose to spend will depend on a number of factors.

- **For consumption**

This might seem odd at first but people often save money in order to make bigger purchases later on, for example, the purchase of a new car, or for a deposit on an apartment or house. They may also save money to spend on goods and services when they get older and only have a pension to live on. Many people save money in pension schemes.

- **Interest rates**

Interest is the return to saving, or the opportunity cost of consuming what could have been saved instead (see Chapter 1). The higher the rate of interest the more return a person could earn by saving their income, or the more they will forego if they spend it on goods and services. If interest rates are low, and especially if price inflation is higher, people may choose to save less and consume more. This is because the value of any savings in terms of their purchasing power, or real value, will be eroded by price inflation (see Chapter 16).

- **Consumer confidence**

How confident people feel about their financial situation now and in the future can affect consumption and savings behaviour. Many people save as a precaution in case their circumstances change. If people think they could be made unemployed in the future then they may start saving more so they can draw on their savings when they lose their jobs and have little or no income. Similarly, if people think inflation will rise in future they may save more now so that they can afford to pay the higher prices of goods and services later on. They may also increase their savings during periods of rising price inflation in order to protect the overall value of their wealth.

- **Availability of saving schemes**

The more ways people can save, the more they might be tempted to do so. Banks and other financial institutions now offer a wide variety of savings schemes with different terms and conditions to suit different people (see Chapter 6). The more a person is willing to save, and the longer they are willing to save without withdrawing their money, the higher the rate of interest they can normally get. Similarly, there are schemes that offer returns that are tax-free, linked to stock market performance, or a mark-up over the rate of price inflation (see Chapter 16). Some governments even offer national savings schemes that do not pay interest but enter people's savings certificates into a draw each month to win prize money. A national savings scheme is a way of borrowing money from savers by a government (see Chapter 15).

Saving patterns

Not everyone saves money, even if they could. Our desire and ability to save tends to vary according to our income, age and family circumstances.

In general, the higher a person's income the more they tend to save. Young people also tend to save less of their incomes than middle-aged people, and people with children tend to save more to help pay for their children's education later in life. However, people on low incomes with children, especially single-parent families, often find it very difficult to save. Similarly, older people also tend to save less in general because they face greater financial hardships and lower incomes from pensions in their old age.

Saving patterns by age group, UK 2005

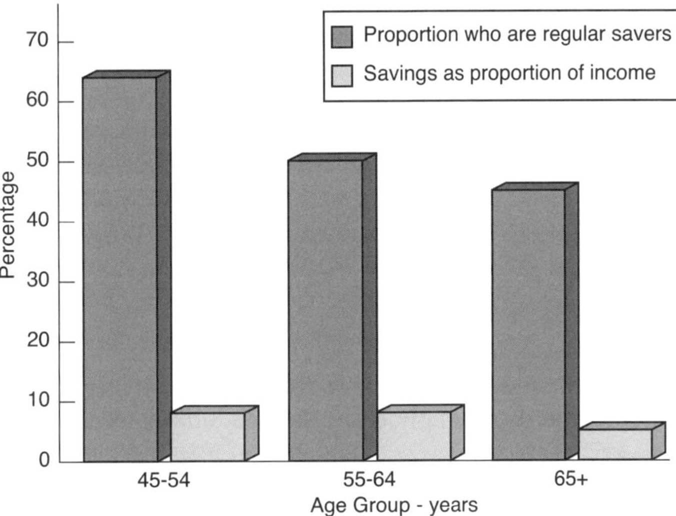

UK National Savings and Investments, *www.nsandi.com*

Savings behaviour can also vary due to differences in culture. For example, people in China tend to save a far higher proportion of their incomes than people in many other countries. A recent study found that the average person in China saves around 25 per cent of their disposable income despite returns on savings being relatively low. The household saving rate in Japan is also relatively high. Similarly, another study found savings rates in Germany were relatively high and stable over time compared to many other countries, with saving for old age being a big motive.

Section 3 Borrowing money

Why do people borrow money?

A consumer may borrow money to increase their expenditure on goods and services, usually for a particular good or service they want, such as a new car or overseas holiday, that is expensive relative to their weekly or monthly earnings. They can then make loan repayments over time from their future earnings. However, some people on very low incomes may borrow simply to pay everyday bills like electricity and phone charges.

One of the biggest purchases a person or family can make is to buy a house or apartment to live in. Loans to buy property are called **mortgages** and may take many years to pay off (see Chapter 6). However, property is an asset and will add to the stock of wealth a person has. It can therefore be considered to be a form of saving. For most people their home is their biggest asset. Some people may also borrow money to buy other assets such as shares in companies, hoping the share dividends and appreciation in the value of shares will be more than enough to repay the loan and leave them with a nice profit.

A small business owner may also borrow money to help set up their business and will repay their loan from future revenues (see Chapter 4). Similarly, a self-employed worker may borrow money to buy tools that will help him or her do their job. For example, a builder may need to buy a van and power tools.

A person may also borrow money to finance a training or education course that will help improve his or her skills and qualifications so that they can get a better-paid job in the future. For example, low-interest government loans to students are common in many countries to help them finance studies at university. They are then able to repay their loans from their future earnings, with the amount repaid per month often depending on how much they earn. So, if their earnings are low they may not be required to make any repayments.

Personal debt

The total stock of accumulated borrowing by a person is called their personal **debt**. So, for example, if a person borrows $100 000 to buy a house, another $15 000 to buy a car, and $5 000 to go on a luxury holiday their personal debt will be $120 000. If the interest rate is 10 per cent per year on all these loans then they will have to pay $1 200 in interest in the first year even before they are able to pay off some of their debt.

What determines the level of borrowing?

You will not be surprised to learn that the main reasons are very much the same as those that determine consumption and savings, but by far the most important is the interest rate.

- **Interest rates**

Interest is the cost of borrowing money. Often the larger the amount a person borrows, the longer the loan takes to repay, and the more risk it involves then the higher the interest rate that will be charged by the financial institutions granting the loan (see Chapter 6).

The base rate of interest in an economy is determined by the central bank and this is the rate at which it will lend money to the entire banking system. Commercial banks and other financial institutions will therefore charge their customers interest rates at or above the base rate. A rise in the base rate of interest in an economy will therefore mean all other interest rates rise, and rising interest rates make borrowing more expensive so demand for loans is likely to fall. Low interest rates, however, will tend to increase the demand for loans.

- **Wealth**

A wealthy person may be more willing to take out a loan because he or she will be confident they can repay it by selling off some of their assets if need be. Further, a bank or other lender may be more willing to lend money to a wealthy person, and at lower interest rate, because there is less risk that person will default on the loan. To default means failing to repay. In some cases a loan may be taken out against an asset, for example a mortgage against a house. Then if the person defaults the house has to be sold to repay the loan. In this way, a house or other valuable assets will offer the lender security, or **collateral**, against their loan. Rising house prices in the UK and some other countries have been blamed in part for a big increase in mortgage borrowing by house-owners who feel wealthier as a result, but also by people trying to buy a house for the first time who have to borrow more to pay the higher prices.

- **Consumer confidence**

How confident people feel about their financial situation in the future may affect their decision to borrow money. If a person thinks they could be made unemployed then they may decide against taking out a loan because they may not be able to repay it should they lose their jobs. Similarly, if people think inflation will rise rapidly in future they may borrow now to make their purchases before prices rise.

- **Ways of borrowing and the availability of credit**

The easier it is to borrow money, that is the greater the availability of credit, the more inclined people may be to borrow. These days it is possible for many more people to arrange credit and in so many different ways than ever before. People can arrange overdrafts, loans and mortgages with banks, simply over the Internet. They can use credit and charge cards issued by banks, credit card companies or even retail shopping chains. They can also buy goods on hire purchase through specialist finance houses (see Chapter 6).

Non-cash transactions: by method of payment

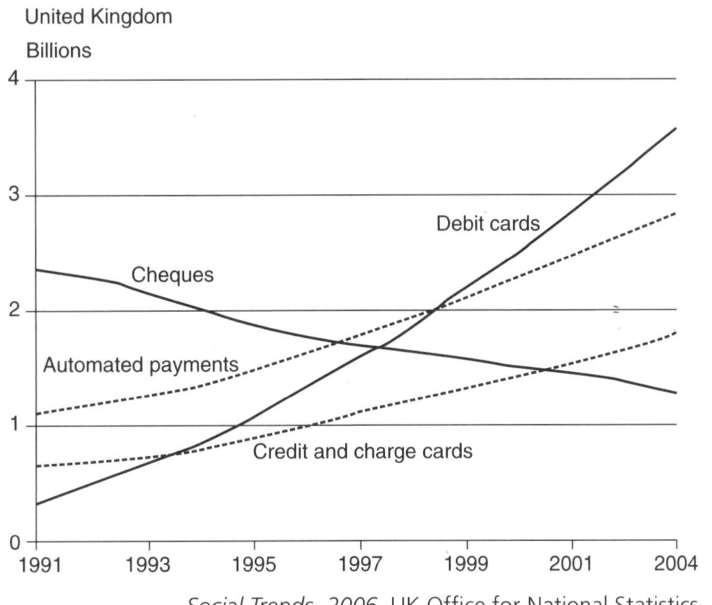

Social Trends, 2006, UK Office for National Statistics

The chart opposite shows how use of plastic cards as a method of payment has increased rapidly over time in the UK. The same is true in many countries. However, using credit cards and Internet banking can involve risks. Card and Internet fraud is on the increase. It involves criminals hacking into personal bank accounts and stealing credit card details. These criminals can then use this information to make fraudulent purchases and to take out loans.

Problems with borrowing

Borrowing money is not a problem as long as you can afford to repay the loan with interest. If your income rises each year then loan and interest repayments become easier. However, a person will quickly run into problems if they keep on borrowing so that repayments rise more quickly than their income, or if their income falls and they cannot continue to make repayments perhaps because they have become unemployed or their business has been forced to close down.

Personal borrowing and debt levels have increased significantly in a number of developed countries. This is causing concern that borrowing money has become too easy and some people may not realize just how much they will have to repay, especially if interest rates rise in future. Much of this borrowing has been in the form of large mortgages to buy houses. Even a small rise in interest rates can therefore mean monthly repayments go up significantly. For example, if a person has borrowed $100 000 a rise in interest rates from 5 per cent to 6 per cent will increase their annual interest payment, on top of any loan repayment, from $5 000 to $6 000. Further, a big fall in house prices due to a downturn in the economy may mean they end up owing more money than the value of their house.

People who cannot afford to repay their personal debts may be declared bankrupt or insolvent by a law court. They may even have property and other goods they have bought with loans, credit cards or on hire purchase repossessed by the lender, or creditor. Or they may be forced to sell their assets to repay the money they owe.

Total lending to individuals has increased significantly in the UK...

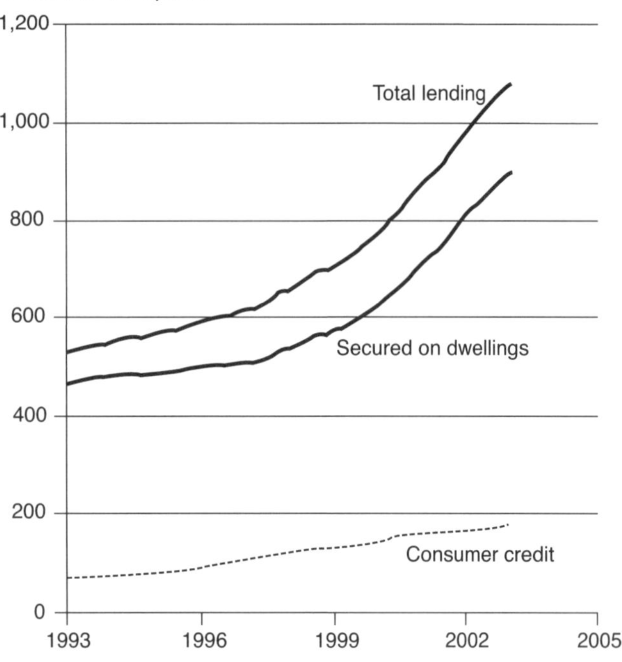

...but so too have individual insolvencies and bankruptcies

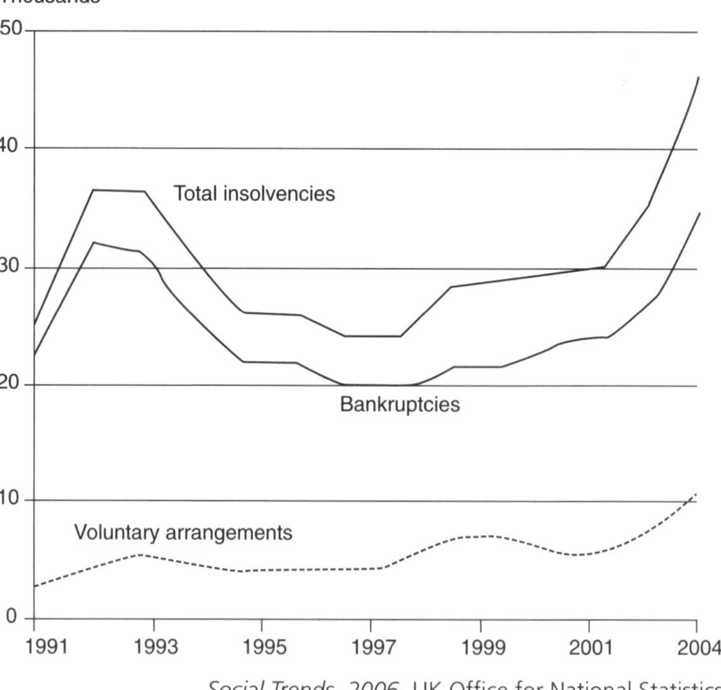

Social Trends, 2006, UK Office for National Statistics

Exercise 3 Lend us a fiver! 

Australians face Christmas personal debt crisis

As Christmas approaches, Australian families are turning to church financial counsellors in increasing numbers. "It's a consumer driven thing" says Barbara Jones, manager of financial counselling for Mission Australia. "Many households have the latest electrical appliances, but need food assistance parcels or money to pay phone bills."

Consumers are being drawn further into debt by increased opportunities for borrowing. Some use one credit card to make repayments on other cards. Rising credit limits and high interest 'buy now, pay later' plans are an attractive short-term solution to financial difficulties. Christmas is often the catalyst for further borrowing, say counsellors.

Welfare organisations say that poor budgeting skills are partly responsible for household debt. "Often people take out a mortgage on their home which they can only just pay on their current salary and they don't allow for anything else to happen in life."

Adapted from *Ecumenical News International*, 5.12.2006

British personal debt nears 'Time Bomb' levels

Higher property prices have helped pushed consumer debt to £1.3 trillion ($2.6 trillion) – more than the entire UK GDP – making it harder for shoppers to spend more in stores. UK stores attracted fewer shoppers last week compared with a year earlier as consumers delayed holiday spending. Unemployment has reached a five-year high in October and wage growth has slowed.

The number of UK personal bankruptcies will exceed 100,000 for the first time this year. New laws have made it easier to recover from bankruptcy by shortening the insolvency period from three years to one. There is also concern that some debt advisers are pushing borrowers too readily into Individual Voluntary Arrangements which let people reduce their debts by about 65% and clear the remainder over a period of years without the stigma of bankruptcy. "There has been a societal shift in attitude toward consumer debt in the UK," reported one financial consultant, adding that young people are told by some debt advisers that defaulting on loans is a smart strategy.

Banks and other lenders are also attracting criticism. In the last 12 months almost eight out of ten borrowers were issued loans without the lender carrying out any checks that the borrower could afford to repay the debt and almost 1.6 million loans were approved without properly verifying people's incomes. A recent report reveals that the UK is responsible for a third of all unsecured debt in Western Europe and that the average UK consumer owes over twice as much as the average western European owes.

Adapted from *Times News Network* 5.12.2006

1. Describe two factors that, according to the articles, have increased consumer borrowing.
2. What problems are highlighted in the articles concerning high levels of consumer borrowing?
3. Suggest two ways governments could try to reduce borrowing.
4. Describe how and why consumer spending and savings patterns may differ between the following types of household in a developed economy: young, unmarried university graduate; married couple with young children; retired couple on a low old-age pension.
5. What impact could a significant reduction in consumer borrowing and borrowing by firms for new investment have on an economy?

Key words

Match the key words and terms with possible definitions in the jumble below.

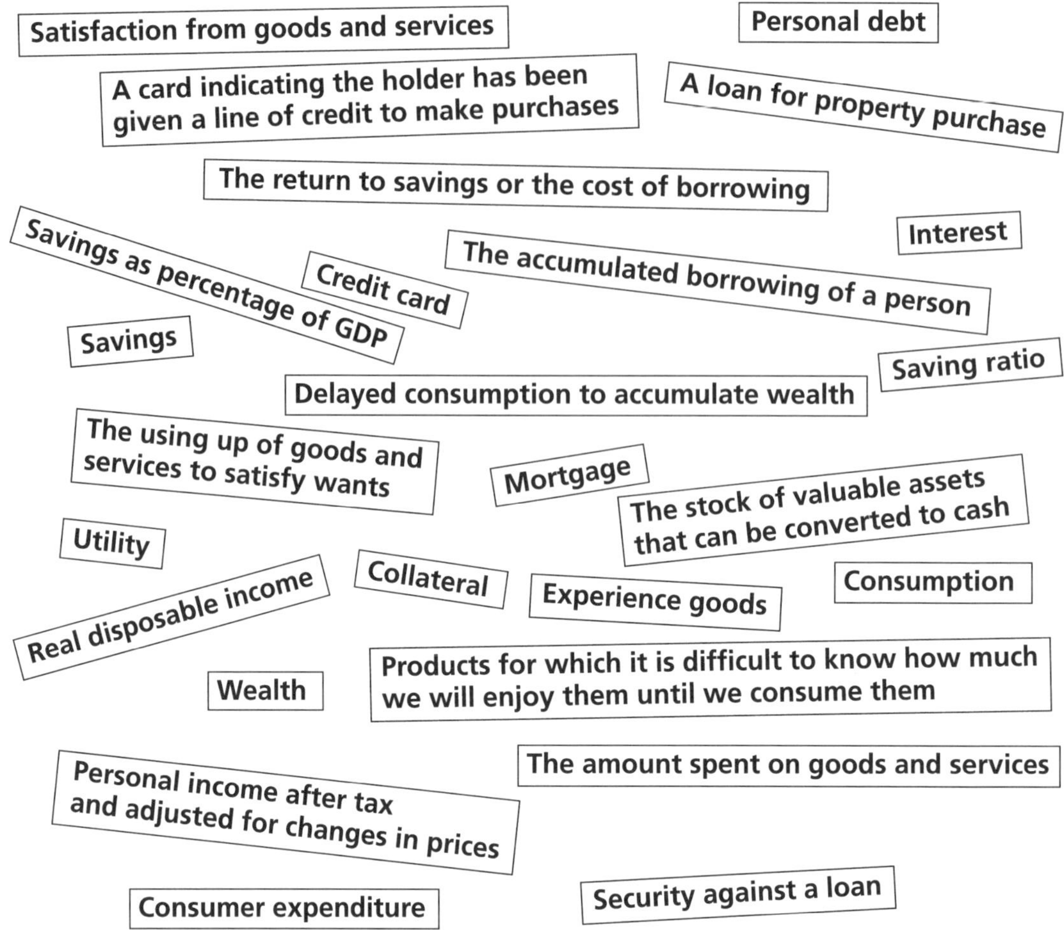
Satisfaction from goods and services
Personal debt
A card indicating the holder has been given a line of credit to make purchases
A loan for property purchase
The return to savings or the cost of borrowing
Interest
Savings as percentage of GDP
Credit card
The accumulated borrowing of a person
Savings
Saving ratio
Delayed consumption to accumulate wealth
The using up of goods and services to satisfy wants
Mortgage
The stock of valuable assets that can be converted to cash
Utility
Collateral
Experience goods
Consumption
Real disposable income
Wealth
Products for which it is difficult to know how much we will enjoy them until we consume them
The amount spent on goods and services
Personal income after tax and adjusted for changes in prices
Consumer expenditure
Security against a loan

www

Take a look at the following websites to learn more about consumption, savings and borrowing:

- *www.economicswebinstitute.org/glossary/con*
- *www.tutor2u.net/economics/content/topics/consumption/savings_ratio.htm*
- *www.tutor2u.net/economics/gcse/revision_notes/money_interest_rates.htm*

Assessment exercises

Multiple choice

1 The wages of carpenters will tend to rise if:

A The supply of carpenters falls.

B Their productivity rises.

C The price of wooden products falls.

D Demand for plastic products rises.

2 The best explanation for the rise in demand for labour from D_n to D_{n1} is:

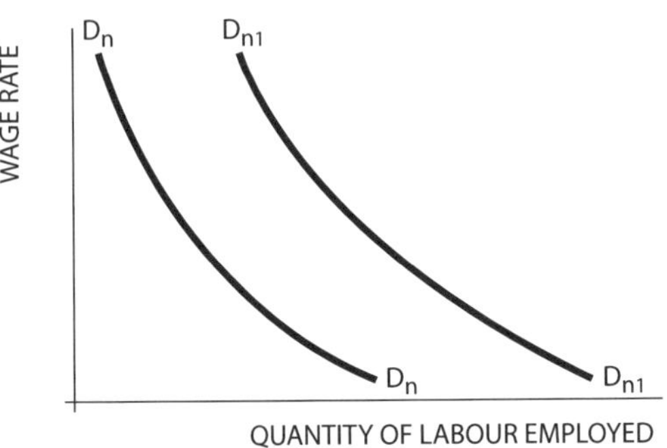

A A fall in wages.

B A fall in the price of the product they produce.

C An increase in unemployment.

D Increasing productivity of labour.

3 Disposable income is:

A Gross income before tax.

B Personal income.

C Taxable income.

D Personal income after taxes on income are deducted.

4 Which of the following factors is most likely to lead to a fall in the savings ratio?

A An increase in taxes.

B A cut in interest rates.

C A cut in borrowing.

D A fall in people's propensity to consume.

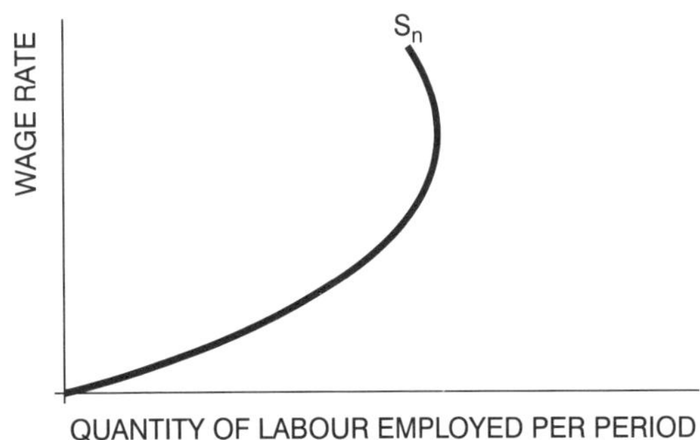

5 The supply curve above shows that:

A Wages fall as the amount of labour increases.

B A rise in wages reduces the size of the working population.

C After a certain level of wages labour chooses more leisure than work.

D Supply rises as wages fall.

6 The supply of labour to an occupation will tend to rise when:

A Promotion prospects improve.

B There are fewer perks.

C Holiday entitlement is cut.

D Unemployment benefit rises.

7 Which one of the following is the least likely explanation for the observed increase in consumer spending on leisure goods and services over time in many countries?

A Increasing real disposable income per head.

B Consumers want healthier lifestyles.

C Increasing levels of personal debt.

D Increased wealth.

8 Which one of the following types of household is most likely to spend the highest proportion of its disposable income?

A High income, middle aged with no children.

B Low income, young single parent with young children.

C Middle income, young single person, no children.

D High income, middle-aged couple with two grown-up children.

9 Which of the following is a non-economic reason why women may earn less than male employees?

A They may be discriminated against.

B They undertake more part-time work.

C Married women may be less mobile than men.

D They take more career breaks to raise children.

10 What has happened in the diagram to the equilibrium wage and employment?

A Wages and employment have risen.

B Wages and employment have fallen.

C Wages have risen; employment has fallen.

D Wages have fallen; employment has risen.

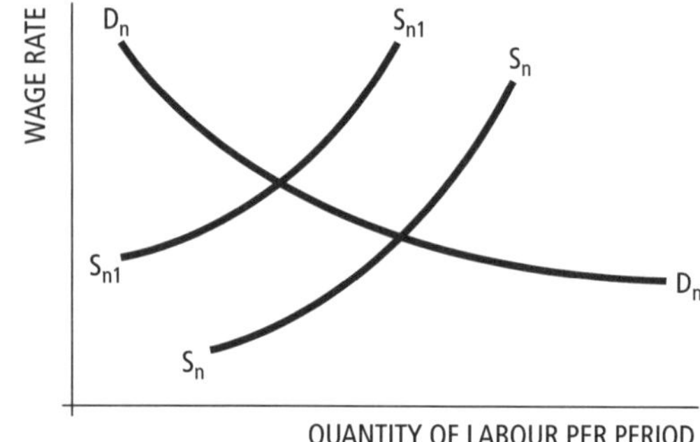

11 Personal borrowing has increased in many countries. Which one of the following factors is the most likely explanation?

A Higher real interest rates.

B Reduced personal wealth.

C Increased availability of credit.

D Increased public sector borrowing.

12 The savings ratio in an economy measures:

A Deposits in banks as proportion of total savings.

B Total savings as proportion of gross household income.

C Long-term savings relative to total savings.

D Total savings as proportion of total disposable income.

13 Disposable income will tend to rise if:

A Indirect taxes are reduced.

B Interest rates are cut.

C Price inflation falls.

D Direct taxes are reduced.

14 Which of the following changes is most likely to attract an increase in the supply of labour to engineering professions?

A An increase in training requirements.

B An increase in holiday entitlements.

C An increase in contracted hours of work.

D A cut in income taxes.

Structured questions

1

SAVING IN SOUTH AFRICA

In South Africa, between 1995 and 1998, savers were able to benefit from higher interest rates and reduced inflation. Moreover, they did not have to pay income tax on some of their income from savings. However, between 1990 and 1998 the amount of income from savings that was exempt from income tax (the 'tax allowance') remained unchanged.

The level of personal savings in South Africa in 1998 was thought to be low and meant that less than 10% of the people were able to retire financially independent. An economist at the Industrial Development Corporation (IDC) in South Africa suggested that an increase in the level that was exempt from tax would encourage people to save. In 2002 this level was raised from R4000 to R6000. (R = rand, the currency of South Africa.)

Changes in taxes can, however, have other effects. There is no guarantee that an increase in the amount of income exempt from tax will result in increased savings. Lower taxes do increase disposable income but this might result in extra spending rather than extra savings.

a Explain how savers can benefit from **i** high interest rates; **ii** reduced inflation. [1, 3]

b Using information in the article, comment on the effect that changes in tax allowances might have on total savings in an economy. [5]

c The article says that not many people will be financially independent when they retire. Why might this be a concern for the government? [5]

d **i** What is meant by the expression 'disposable income'? [2]

ii You are asked to investigate the differences in the spending and savings patterns of people with low disposable income and those with high disposable income. What do you think you would discover? [9]

2

Private home ownership is increasing in China. For years the urban Chinese relied on overcrowded housing rented from the state and often waited a long time to have their own apartment. Now, with the increase in the market economy, the government is encouraging city dwellers to buy their own homes by giving cheap loans and tax relief. Home buying will help China's economy. New home-owners need to spend money on furniture, appliances and decorating. GDP grew by 8% in 2005, of which the housing industry contributed about a fifth. The housing changes will affect social and political issues as well as the economy. In the old system people had to live close to their work, and it was difficult to change jobs because no other housing was available. Single people had no hope of being allocated an apartment. Now anyone with money can buy a home and choose where they wish to live.

a Explain what is meant by the market economy. [4]

b Explain the meaning of complements and substitutes, giving an example of each from the passage. [4]

c Identify four factors that might influence a worker's choice of occupation. [4]

d How far do you think the change in the provision of housing is likely to affect a worker's choice of occupation? [3]

e Discuss whether the change in the provision of housing is likely to benefit everybody. [5]

3 It was reported that in a country the poorest households spent 30% of their income on food while the richest households spent 13% on food.

a Do these figures mean that the actual amount that the richest households spent on food is lower than that spent by the poorest households? Explain your answer. [4]

b Ali has started his first job. Faizal is now in a senior position in her company. Describe how the expenditure pattern of these two people might be different. [4]

c Analyse the motives that might cause a person to save rather than to spend. [6]

d What might be the result of a general increase in the level of consumers' spending in an economy? [6]

4 Some workers work long hours but earn little because the rate they receive for each hour worked is very low.

a Why do you think a worker would be prepared to work for very low wages? [5]

b What reasons might make a worker decide to move to another job at the same rate of pay? [5]

c Some workers belong to a trade union. Explain how membership of a trade union might be beneficial to a worker. [5]

d An older skilled worker's pattern of spending and saving is likely to be different from that of a younger unskilled worker. Discuss why. [5]

5 a Explain the terms scarcity and opportunity cost. [4]

b Describe the factors that affect an individual's choice of occupation and show how the idea of opportunity cost might be relevant to that choice. [6]

c Analyse how a person's earnings are likely to change during their working life. [4]

d Discuss why different occupations have different rates of pay. [6]

How to answer question 1

a First, you should note the distribution of marks for this question. Part (i) about interest rates has only one mark and therefore requires only a very short answer. In contrast, part (ii) has three marks and so a more detailed response will be required to demonstrate your understanding and analysis. For maximum marks, your response on the impact of reduced **inflation** on savers should include a definition of what price inflation is and also consider briefly how it may not benefit savers. Remember that inflation erodes the purchasing power of money, while interest payments on savings will help to offset this. If however the **interest rate** is below the inflation rate, the real value of savings will still be eroded over time.

b This question requires you to analyse the impact an increase in income tax allowances could have on the amount people save from their incomes. There is no single answer so you must explore the possibilities. First, you should note how raising the income tax allowance will lower the amount of tax paid by individuals and therefore increase their **disposable income**, or after-tax income. This is equivalent to a cut in their average tax rate. An individual can then decide whether to spend all or just some of this increase, or save all or part of it, depending on which use will give them the most additional **utility** or satisfaction.

Question (a) also provides you with some clues that the answer to (b) is not straightforward because people's **saving** and **consumption** choices will be affected by many other factors in addition to changes in tax rates and allowances. Whether or not people choose to save an increase in their after-tax income will in part depend on the interest rate they could receive and what is happening to inflation, their job prospects and overall level of wealth.

c In many countries, income support, healthcare, low-cost housing and other benefits are provided to people on low incomes by their governments from tax revenues. State pensions may also be paid to people who have retired from full-time work. If more people retire in a country with few savings and little other income of their own, then the government may have spend more tax revenues providing them with pensions or income support, more public healthcare and other welfare benefits. This means public spending on other goods and services, for example, investments in education and infrastructure, will have to be cut or taxes on people in work will have to rise. These changes could have important macro-economic impacts the government would also be concerned about. You will need to discuss these (see Chapter 15). Many developed countries are also experiencing ageing populations with increasing numbers of elderly retired people, thereby potentially placing an even greater strain on public services (see Chapter 20).

d **i** If you have answered question (b) in full you will already have explained what disposable income is. This part simply requires you to write a short definition. For example, it is the amount of income remaining that an individual is able to consume or save following the deduction of income-related taxes and social security contributions.

ii This part of the question carries a mammoth nine marks. To earn all these you will need to demonstrate the full application of your economic knowledge to analyse how consumer spending and saving patterns may differ with disposable income.

You should first explain the key economic relationships that can usually be observed between spending, saving and income. They will generally be positively related so the more income a person earns the more they are able to spend and save in total. However, while the total amount spent may rise with income, the proportion of income spent may fall as the proportion devoted to savings rises. In contrast, a person on a low income may have little choice but to spend all of it on the goods and services they need to live.

You should then explore other economic and non-economic factors that may explain differences in spending and savings patterns, and how these may in turn be related to income. For example, spending and savings **preferences** tend to differ with age. Older people tend to save more, for example in pension schemes, but they may also tend to earn more than younger people doing the same or similar jobs because they have more work experience and skills.

To complete your answer you should now consider under what circumstances the relationships you have described between income, spending and saving may not hold. For example, could two people with exactly the same income have very different spending and savings patterns? The answer is of course yes. One may choose to spend a far greater proportion of their income than the other because it gives them more utility. Factors such as interest rates, the availability of credit, consumer confidence and cultural factors can also affect people's preferences for spending and saving, regardless of the amount of income they earn.

In preparing your answer it might be useful to think about how spending and savings patterns could differ between the following groups of consumers and why:

- same age, sex, cultural background, but different incomes;
- different age, sex, cultural background, but same income;
- same age, sex, cultural background, same income but different countries with different economic, financial and political systems.

Giving a few examples of types of goods and services different groups of consumers may buy is also a good idea.

A model answer for question 4

a Workers supply their labour to firms to undertake productive activities in return for wages, usually paid per period of time or in some cases per unit of output produced. In general, the higher the wage rate for a job the more labour workers will be willing to supply, in the form of increased hours and/or because more workers overall are attracted to the occupation.

If the supply of labour to an occupation greatly exceeds the demand for that labour, then the market wage rate is likely to be quite low. However, even at a relatively low wage some workers would fill the available jobs. This is likely to be because they are relatively low-skilled with low levels of productivity and would be unable to command higher wages in alternative occupations.

However, in choosing between occupations workers will also consider their net advantages in addition to any differences in wage rates. For example, they will compare such factors as when and how long they are required to work each day or week, holiday entitlements, promotion prospects, job security, and any non-wage benefits such as free medical insurance, subsidized canteens, or the provision of a company car or free travel. So, for example, a worker may choose a job that offers a relatively low wage over another job with a higher wage because it offers more holidays, greater job security, and other benefits which more than offset the wage differential in their preferences.

Some people also work for relatively low wages in charities that help people and animals in need because of the job satisfaction it gives them.

b A worker may choose to move between different jobs for reasons other than pay. Some may want to move geographically, because they are moving house or want to spend less time commuting to and from their current address to their place of work, as well as moving to a different occupation.

A worker will compare the advantages and disadvantages of different jobs and will tend to choose that job which offers the greatest net overall advantage to them. For example, in addition to pay, a worker will compare such factors as hours of work, holiday entitlements, and journey times and costs to and from work and whether travel is subsidized for example by the offer of a company car. Different employers may also compete to attract workers with free pension, life insurance or medical care provision. Some jobs also offer better longer-term promotion prospects and job security than others. It follows that changes in the net advantages of different occupations other than pay can result in changes in the supply of labour to them. So, for example, a person serving in a supermarket for $10 per hour may choose to change their job to work in a factory as a machine operator because it offers more sociable hours of work, a subsidized canteen, and free healthcare compared to the supermarket, even if the wage rate paid is exactly the same at $10 per hour.

c A trade union is an organization of workers formed to promote and protect the rights and interests of its members concerning wages and working conditions, including reduced hours of work, increased holiday entitlements and improved health and safety at work. For example, the trade union movement worldwide has helped fight and bring an end to child labour in many countries and helped to increase the earnings and standard of living of both unionized and non-unionized labour.

Trade unions also aim to agree improved sick pay, pensions and other benefits for their members, and often encourage employers to increase worker participation in business decision-making.

Trade unions can often secure these improvements because they have significant bargaining power in negotiations with employers because they represent many workers. For example, a union may threaten to instruct its membership to take industrial action if an employer or group of employers is unwilling to negotiate. This ultimately may include strike action, and although striking workers may suffer lost wages some unions will provide them with strike pay. Unions can also use their collective bargaining strength to resist or negotiate job cuts that would make their members unemployed.

In addition, trade unions will often provide training and education courses to their members to develop the skills they need to do their jobs. This of course can also benefit the employers they work for because better-skilled workers will be more productive. Unions may also provide free or low-cost social and sporting facilities for their members to use.

d Workers supply their labour in return for wage income they can use to spend on goods and services, and possibly also to save, to satisfy their needs and wants and thereby maximize their overall level of utility. The ability to spend and save rises with income. An older skilled worker may earn more income than a younger unskilled worker because he or she has more experience and his or her skills may be in greater demand. As a result the market wage a skilled worker can earn may be much higher than someone who is unskilled.

However, patterns of spending and savings can vary significantly between people with very similar incomes because people have different tastes or preferences. Consumer preferences can vary with age, sex, family circumstances, cultural background and a host of other factors. For example, someone who is concerned about the impact their consumption has on the environment may prefer to buy organic food products and other goods that come in packaging that can be recycled, and which use ingredients that have not been tested on animals. To explain likely differences in spending and savings patterns between an older skilled worker and a younger unskilled worker we should therefore consider all of the above factors.

For example, people may become more health conscious as they get older, and may increase their spending on healthcare products and exercising. An older worker may also be more likely to have a family than a younger person and will tend to spend money on goods and services their children will need and want, such as clothes, toys and their schooling. They may also set up savings schemes for their children's future and also for themselves, for example, to save for a pension for when they retire from work. In contrast, a younger person may spend most, if not all, of their income on renting accommodation, fashionable clothes, music, travel and enjoying their leisure time.

Older people with higher incomes, more secure jobs and who are also home-owners may also be able to borrow more money from banks to enable them to buy luxury items like overseas holidays, a new car and furnishings for their homes. Older people may therefore spend more on loan repayments. In contrast, loan repayments may be at greater risk from younger people who have only recently started in work, earn relatively low incomes and have no property to offer as collateral or security against loans. Consequently, banks may be less inclined to offer younger people loans.

5 THE PRIVATE FIRM AS PRODUCER AND EMPLOYER

Land, labour and capital are organized into firms by entrepreneurs to produce goods and services to satisfy consumers' wants. Production involves a chain of activity, from primary production of natural resources, right through to the sale of finished goods and services to consumers. Secondary production involves processing natural resources to produce machinery and components for other manufacturers, as well as finished goods for consumers. Tertiary industries provide services such as banking, insurance and retailing services for other firms and individual consumers.

The owners of factors of production receive payments, such as wages for labour, and the owners of firms receive profits if they are successful. But not all productive organizations aim to make a profit. For example, charities aim to cover the costs of their activities from grants and donations.

An increase in consumer demand for goods and services will tend to increase the demand for labour and capital by firms. An increase in the productivity of labour and capital will also tend to increase demand for these factors of production. This is because an increase in productivity means more output can be produced from the same input of labour and capital. A firm can lower its costs and increase profits by increasing the productivity of its resources. Technological advance has greatly increased the productivity, and lowered the cost, of machinery and other equipment. As a result, many firms have substituted labour with automated production.

The difference between total revenue from the sale of goods and services and their total cost of production is profit. Total costs include variable costs such as wages and materials, that vary with the amount of output, and fixed costs such as rents, loan repayments and machinery hire charges. By increasing their scale of production, large firms can enjoy cost advantages over smaller firms. These are known as economies of scale. However, a firm that grows too big may experience diseconomies of scale, or rising costs, often due to management and coordination problems. Firms may increase their scale of output through internal growth or by merging with other firms.

Despite the advantages of large-scale production there are still a great many small firms throughout the world economy. Many firms remain small either through personal choice or mainly because they serve small, localized markets. However, many small firms may also lack the finance needed to expand.

Chapter 12 Organizing Production

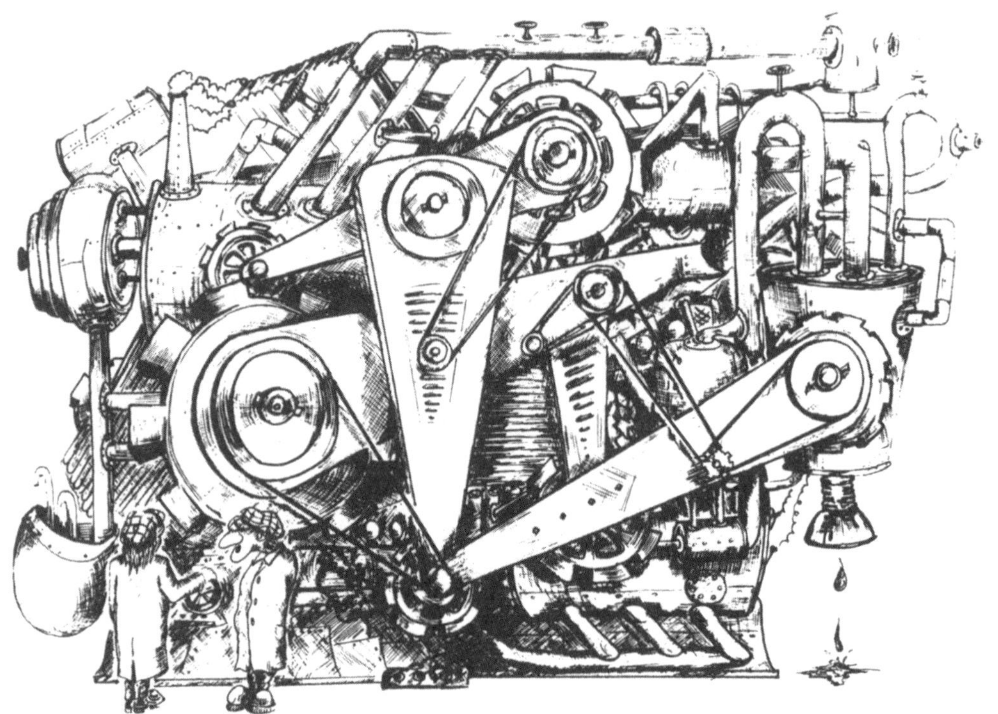

And where do I switch it on?

Aims

At the end of this chapter you should be able to:

- identify **production** as any activity that satisfies consumer wants
- describe the principle of **profit maximization** as a goal
- account for why some firms may have other objectives
- identify the stages involved in a **chain of production**
- describe what determines the demand for **factor of productions**
- understand **factor substitution**, and analyse why firms may substitute one factor of production for another
- distinguish between **large-scale production** and **small-scale production**, and describe the main reasons for the different sizes of firms
- define **integration**, and explain how and why firms can integrate to form larger enterprises

Section I

What is production?

Production and the creation of wealth

Goods and services, are produced in order to satisfy people's wants. **Production** refers to the making of these goods and the production of services. Firms or businesses are producers. They are responsible for producing goods and services. The firm uses the resources of land, labour and capital (**input**) to make goods and services (**output**).

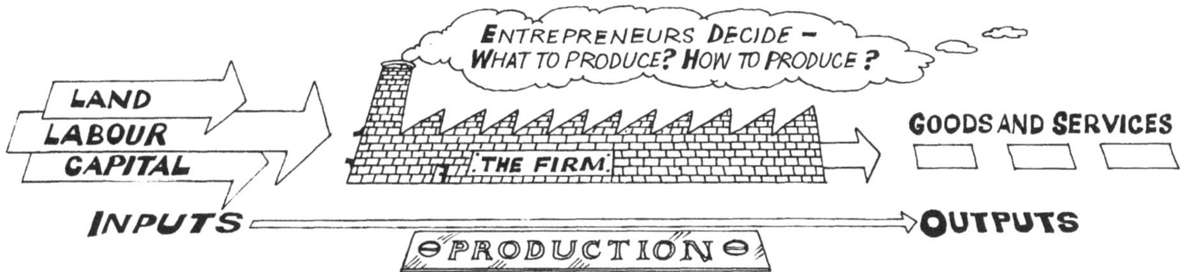

Given the aim of production is to satisfy the wants of people, the process is not complete until the goods and services actually reach the people who want them. Warehouses and shops that sell goods and services to consumers, as well as all those people and machines involved in transportation, insurance and many other tasks, are all part of the production process.

By combining resource inputs to produce outputs consumers want and are willing and able to buy, productive activity **adds value** to resources. For example, a firm that produces 1 million chocolate bars which are sold for $1 each but cost only $600 000 to produce has added $400 000 to the value of the resources used in their production – labour, cocoa powder, milk, paper, machinery, vehicles, power, etc.

Productivity

Productivity refers to the amount of output that can be produced from a given input of resources. For example, a firm that uses 10 units of labour, land and capital to produce 40 units of output is twice as productive as a firm that uses 10 units of these resources to produce 20 units of output.

The aim of any business will be to combine its resources in the most efficient way. That is, it will attempt to maximize the productivity of its resources in order to produce as much as it can at the lowest cost possible. For example, a construction firm that employs ten carpenters and yet supplies only one hammer, drill and chisel between them has clearly not combined labour and capital in the most efficient way. By increasing the input of capital – i.e. some more hammers and drills, etc. – the firm will increase productivity.

In general, productivity in a firm will increase if more output can be produced with the same input of resources, or if fewer resources can be used to produce the same amount of output.

Productive

More productive

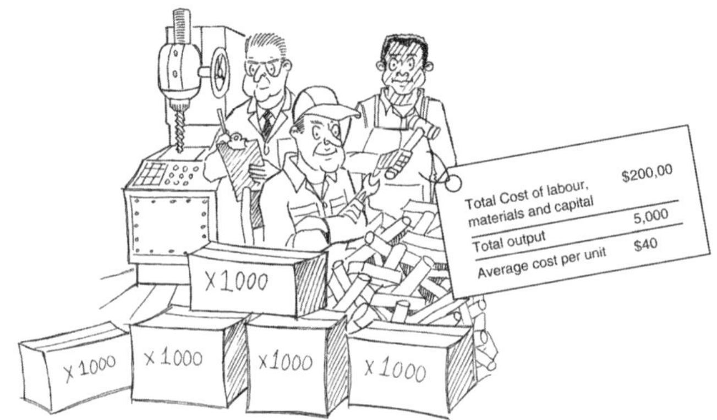

If the same amount of labour, land and capital employed can produce more output for the same total cost, then the cost of each unit of output will have fallen. Increasing productivity can therefore lower business costs and increase profits.

A firm that fails to increase productivity at the same or a faster pace than its competitors will face higher costs and lower profits. It will be unable to cut prices to compete for consumer demand without reducing profits or even making a loss. If a firm is unable to offer quality products at competitive prices, then demand for its products will fall. In the long run the firm will face closure and workers will be made redundant.

Where does production take place?

Entrepreneurs organize factors of production into firms. In economics a firm turns these inputs into outputs of goods and services. A **firm** may be owned and managed by one person, a group of people or even by a government (see Chapter 4). Some firms can be very large companies with many thousands of owners, others may be one-person businesses. Some firms even exist to own and manage other firms making different types of goods and services.

A firm may own one or more plants where factors of production are employed to produce and supply goods or services. A **plant** is simply a workplace, usually at one location, such as a factory, shop, warehouse, hotel, restaurant or office. Some may be very large, occupying large premises, and employing many thousands of workers and different machinery. Other plants may be very small, perhaps no bigger than a shed where a single entrepreneur runs an Internet business.

An **industry** consists of all the firms in an economy producing very similar goods or services for a particular market. For example, the car manufacturing industry consists of all those firms engaged in making cars. Some industries may be dominated by one or a handful of very large firms (see Chapter 8).

The stages of production

Production is a chain of economic activity linking many different firms together, from those that produce natural materials such as coal, wheat and oil, to those who use these materials to make components and finished goods and services, and finally to those who operate warehouses and shops to sell the finished products to the consumers who want them. Helping this chain of activity along will be firms that distribute goods and services between different locations and producers who provide banking, insurance and advertising services. For the economist, it is useful to group firms and industries according their position in these chains of production and by the type of goods or services they supply.

Exercise 1 Making music

A Below is a jumble of pictures and descriptions explaining how music compact discs are produced. Match each picture to a description. Write down the descriptions to form a chain of the productive activities involved in producing CDs, from their initial stages right through to their final sale to consumers. Some descriptions may be used more than once.

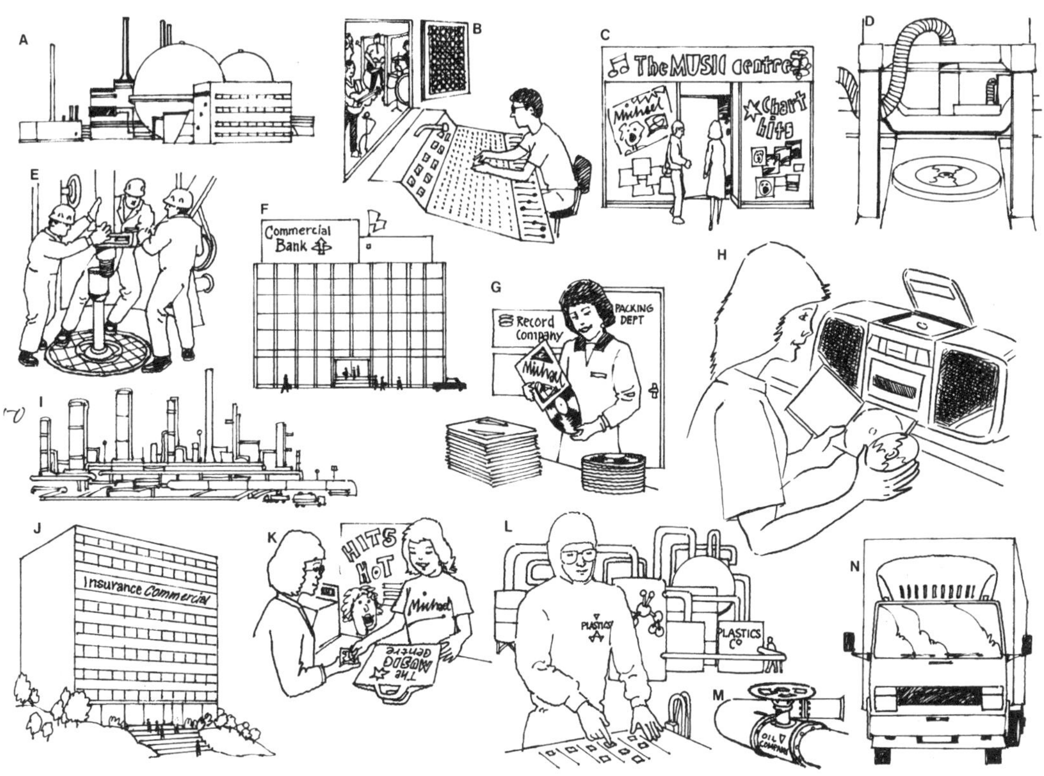

Descriptions

1 Recording engineers record pop group in a studio.

2 Coal and oil are used to power electricity stations for use by firms and households.

3 Crude oil is refined.

4 Shops and online retailers sell CDs.

5 Road hauliers transport goods and people.

6 Consumers buy CDs.

7 Coal and oil are dug and drilled from the ground.

8 Chemical firms use oil to produce plastic.

9 Insurance firms provide insurance to protect firms from risk of damage or theft.

10 CDs are mastered and pressed.

11 Pipeline carries oil to oil refinery.

12 Consumers play CDs on their hi-fis.

13 CDs are packed in plastic cases with paper inserts.

14 Banks provide finance for firms.

B Investigate and list the chain of productive activities involved in the production and sale of the following products:

- A new computer game
- Fresh orange juice
- Chocolate bars
- Washing powders
- Hairdressing
- A good or service of your choice

Producing CDs for sale to consumers is a long and complicated business. In the earliest stages, natural resources, such as coal and oil, need to be extracted from the ground to fire electricity stations. Oil, in turn, is the raw material used to produce plastic for records, which are pressed and shaped by a great many machines. Tape recorders and sound engineers are needed to record the music of a pop group for the CD. The shop is the final destination of the disc before it is sold. Throughout the process a great many banks have probably loaned a lot of money to many firms. Insurance companies have been involved in case of damage or theft, and transport companies ferry raw materials and finished goods to and fro. We can classify all the firms who perform these tasks according to what they do.

Primary industry

Those firms which produce natural resources by growing plants, like wheat and barley, digging for minerals, such as coal and copper, or breeding animals, are called **primary firms** and belong to the primary section or **primary industry** in an economy. Primary means it is the first stage of production, as many of the raw materials grown or dug out of the ground are used to produce something else. **Primary industries** are also called **extractive industries**.

Secondary industry

Using natural resources to make other goods is a process called **manufacturing** and firms that engage in this activity belong to the manufacturing or **secondary industry**. For example, compact discs are made from plastics made from oil. Cars and vans, and many of their component parts, are made from metals and plastics, and glass is made from sand. Paper and cardboard products are made from pulped wood. Construction firms using materials to build homes, offices, roads and other infrastructure are also part of the secondary sector in an economy.

Tertiary industry

A great many firms do not produce any goods at all. Many sell goods, transport them, or provide financial services, like the banks and insurance companies. Your school provides an education service, your local hospital a health service. There are also many more personal services, like hairdressers, window-cleaners, tailors, gardeners. All these firms provide a service and belong to the service sector in the economy.

Collectively they are also known as the **tertiary industry**, or service sector, because many of these firms provide the final link in the chain of production by selling goods to the consumer. However, it is clear that without services, like transport, insurance and many others, primary and secondary firms would find it hard to produce anything.

Examples of primary, secondary and tertiary industries

Exercise 2 Which stage of production?

1. Go back to exercise 1 on compact discs; look again at the activities being carried out in each picture and state which are primary, secondary or tertiary.
2. Under three column headings sort out the following list of industries into primary, secondary and tertiary industries.

Television broadcasting	Health service	Advertising
Film-making	Farming	Shipbuilding
Shipping	Banking	Universities
Decorating	Hotels	Motor cars
Construction	Furniture	Mining
Fishing	Retailing (shops)	Chemicals
Forestry	Engineering	Restaurants

Section 2 The aims of production

Maximizing profits

Most private sector firms produce and sell goods and services to make as much **profit** as they can. Profit is a reward to successful business owners, or entrepreneurs, for taking the risk of setting up a firm. They will not know in advance how much of a particular product consumers will buy and how much they will be willing and able to pay for it. Even so, entrepreneurs must pay in advance for the services of land, labour and capital in order to make their chosen good or service. In some cases, there may be a very long time between first designing and making a product and selling that product. For example, designing, making and testing a new aircraft takes many years and costs many billions of pounds before the manufacturer is ready to start making them for sale to airlines.

Selling goods and services earns revenue for a firm. Profit is what is left from revenue after all costs have been deducted. A firm that is unable to cover its costs with enough sales revenue will make a **loss** and could be forced to close down if losses continue. A firm may make a loss if it fails to make a product consumers want, at the price or quality they want, or provides a poor customer service. A firm may also make a loss if it is unable to produce products at the same or a cheaper cost than rival firms. It is therefore important for firms to be efficient and continually try to reduce their costs of production (see Chapter 13).

Other objectives

Not all firms or organizations in mixed or market economies want to make a profit. Some provide a public service or a charity.

1 **Providing a public service.** Many organizations owned or funded by government use resources to provide services people need and might not be able to afford to buy if they were produced for a profit. For example, education and healthcare are often provided by government (see Chapter 14).

2 **Providing a charity.** Charitable organizations rely on donations and endowments of money to provide help and care for people and animals in need. Organizations such as OXFAM and the WSPA do not aim to make a profit. All the money they receive is used to cover the costs of providing their services.

3 **Non-profit-making organizations.** Some not-for-profit organizations are not charities. For example, credit unions do not aim to make a profit. Any revenue they make in excess of their costs is used to offer their savers better rates of interest or is used to update and expand their operations. Similarly, local clubs may be run as non-profit-making organizations.

Charities do not aim to make profits

Section 3 Productivity and factor demand

Combining factors of production

When a firm combines factors of production to produce a good or service it can decide to use **labour-intensive** techniques involving a larger proportion of labour than capital, or **capital-intensive** techniques using more plant and machinery relative to labour.

Capital intensive production

Labour intensive production

The demand for labour and capital by a firm will depend on a number of factors.

1 The amount of goods and services consumers demand

The more goods and services consumers want and are willing and able to buy, the more factors of production firms will tend to employ. That is, demand for factors of production is a **derived demand**. The demand for labour and capital in a firm depends on there being demand for the goods and services they produce.

2 The price of labour and capital

Just like the demand for other goods and services, the demand for factors of production by firms is related to their price (see Chapter 7). For example, as wages rise, the demand for labour by firms will tend to contract. Similarly, if the cost of buying or hiring capital increases then demand for capital will also tend to contract. It follows that if wages rise while the cost of capital equipment falls, then a firm might consider reducing the number of workers it employs and using more machinery instead. But this will also depend on the productivity of capital relative to labour.

3 The productivity of labour and capital

In general, a profit-maximizing firm will only employ an extra amount of labour or capital if the value of output added by doing so is greater than or at least equal to the cost of their employment. For example, if the cost of employing an extra worker is $100 in wages per week, but that extra worker could only produce an extra $90 worth of output each week, then he or she would not be worth employing.

Imagine a firm producing table lamps. Each lamp sells for $10. At present, four workers, or units of labour, are employed producing a total output of 300 lamps each week. The firm wants to increase output but doesn't know how many extra workers to employ. To help the firm decide, it estimates how much more output each additional worker is likely to produce.

Table lamp production

Number of workers	Total output per week	Extra output per worker per week	Value of extra output (quantity x price)
4	300	-	-
5	350	50	$500
6	390	40	$400
7	420	30	$300
8	440	20	$200
9	450	10	$100

The firm has estimated that adding a fifth worker would raise total output by 50 lamps each week. When these extra lamps are sold, the firm's revenue will increase by $500. If the wage rate is $300 per week, it is worth employing that worker as well as a sixth worker. A seventh worker will add $300 to the value of total output each week, and costs $300 in wages to employ. In a profit-maximizing firm this worker is worth employing because each one of the extra lamps produced will be adding to profit. However, if the firm attempted to employ an eighth worker it would gain only $200 in extra output but lose $300 in extra wage costs. Profits would fall by $100. The only way the firm would extend its demand for labour to eight workers would be if wages fell to $200 each week. The firm's demand curve for labour slopes downwards (see Chapter 10).

Alternatively, our table lamp firm could attempt to increase the productivity of its workers. It estimates that if it trains new and existing employees in more productive techniques each worker could produce a further 10 lamps worth an additional $100 each week. So now, a fifth worker would raise output by 60 lamps each week, worth $600 in extra revenue. A sixth worker would increase output by another 50 lamps, worth $500 in revenue, and so on. This has the impact of shifting the demand curve for labour to the right at every possible wage rate (from D_nD_n to $D_{n1}D_{n1}$ in the diagram on the next page). If the weekly wage rate remains at $300 per worker, then clearly it is now worth employing up to eight workers, since the eighth worker will now add as much to revenue as he or she will cost to employ.

Demand for table lamp makers

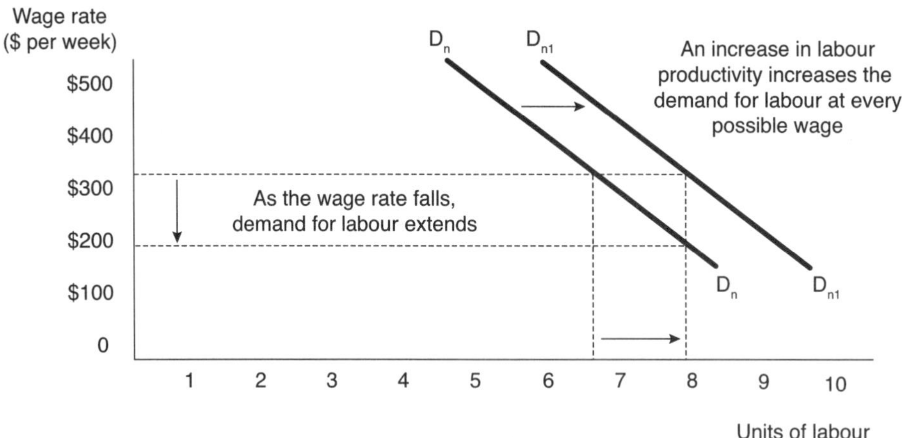

Exactly the same will apply to a decision to increase the amount of capital employed in the table lamp firm if it could employ computerized machinery to make the lamps instead of extra workers. If the productivity of capital rises, and/or the cost of capital falls, firms will tend to expand their demand for capital.

A firm will want to combine its resources in the most efficient way to maximize their overall productivity for the minimum of costs. It will therefore compare the costs and productivity of labour with capital and will tend to employ more of the most productive factor. It follows, that if wages rise or the productivity of capital rises, a firm will tend to replace labour with more capital. This is known as **factor substitution**.

Factor substitution

The substitution of capital for labour has occurred in many modern industries where much of the work is now carried out by computer-operated machinery. This can be contrasted with many less developed countries, where wages are relatively low and production in many industries remains labour intensive (see Chapter 19).

However, labour and capital are not perfect substitutes. The ability of a firm to substitute capital for labour will very much depend on the type of product and the production process used. For example, automated mass production processes are used to produce many thousands or millions of very similar products, such as newspapers, discs and cars, to supply markets all over the world. But in some cases the substitution of capital will not be possible. As of yet machines cannot undertake the work of a hairdresser, a window cleaner, an economist or a nurse, although clearly many of these workers will use capital equipment, from hairdryers to computers, to help them do their jobs. Similarly, some consumers want personalized jewellery or furniture made for them. Their production is usually by hand, and involves many hours of labour.

The costs of installing and maintaining new machinery and other equipment can also be very expensive and will affect the decision by a firm to employ more capital at the expense of labour, even if the new capital is more productive. Short-term production costs may also rise, as workers need to be retrained to use new machinery and equipment.

Substituting capital for labour may also cause bitter labour disputes between trade unions and their employers over possible job losses (see Chapter 5). Strikes by workers and redundancy payments for those forced to leave can be very expensive for a firm.

The impact of technology

Technological advance has greatly increased the productivity and lowered the cost of new capital equipment resulting in a fall in demand for labour in many firms. For example, the work of once skilled typesetters and compositors in the printing industry has now been replaced by desk-top publishing software on computers operated by writers and journalists. Intelligent robots controlled by computer are increasingly overtaking human tasks in manufacturing processes such as car assembly and food packaging. This is known as **computer aided manufacture (CAM)**.

However, technological advance has also brought about the following changes:

- New products and services such as DVD recorders, satellite communications, automated banking, solar panels to generate electricity from the sun
- New materials, such as polythene, nylon, silicon chips for computer motherboards
- New and more efficient methods of production, such as robotic assembly and welding, genetic engineering to produce hardy vegetable crops, recycling and waste management, laser precision measurements and cutting, 'keyhole' surgery in hospitals

All of these changes have greatly increased the demand for labour in firms supplying advanced goods and services, and employing new technology in production. For example, there has been an increase in demand for computer technicians and operators, electronic engineers, technology and management consultants, software designers, and many more advanced skills.

Measuring the productivity of labour

Labour productivity in an organization can be calculated by dividing total output in a given period of time (for example, each day, week or month) by the number of workers employed.

$$\text{Average product of labour per period} = \frac{\text{Total output per period}}{\text{Number of employees}}$$

The **average product** of labour is a useful measure of how efficient workers are. For example, if a company employs 10 workers to produce 200 DVD players per day, the average product per employee per day is 20 players. If output rises to 220 DVD players per day without the company employing any more workers, then productivity will have increased to 22 players per worker per day.

Productivity in firms providing services can be more difficult to measure. For example, in a hair salon we might use a measure of the number of haircuts per hour per employee, but not all employees in the hair salon will be hairdressers. Some may be office staff and cleaners. How will we measure their productivity? In this case we might employ a better measure of productivity by calculating the total revenue per worker per period:

$$\text{Average revenue per worker per period} = \frac{\text{Total revenue per period}}{\text{Number of employees}}$$

Similarly, it is difficult to measure productivity in organizations where there is no physical output or sales revenues, for example, in free hospitals and schools, or in government departments. Other measures, such as time spent waiting for an operation, or meeting deadlines, or numbers of students obtaining qualifications, will have to be used.

Another problem with measures of productivity is that they tell us very little about the quality of work. Productivity is also about increasing the quality of work and outputs – because consumers demand, and are willing to pay for, better quality goods and services.

How can firms raise the productivity of labour?

A firm can attempt to raise the productivity of its workers through a combination of the following:

- Training workers to improve their existing skills and learn new skills.
- Rewarding increased productivity with performance-related pay and bonus payments.
- Encouraging employees to buy shares in their organization. Improved productivity will help to raise profits and pay higher dividends on shares.
- Improving job satisfaction – for example, by improving the working environment, making jobs more interesting, teamworking, involving workers in business decision making and giving regular feedback on performance.
- Replacing old plant and machinery with new, more efficient machines and tools for workers.
- Introducing new production processes and working practices designed to continually reduce waste, increase speed, improve quality and raise output in all areas of a firm. This is often known as **lean manufacturing** but its principles can equally apply to the production of services.

Many of the above will tend to raise the cost of employing labour in the short run. However, if productivity improves, average costs will fall and profits will tend to rise. Lower costs can be passed on to consumers as lower prices in an attempt to increase consumer demand and generate more sales revenues. If consumer demand expands, then the demand for labour may also increase.

Exercise 3 March of the Robots

What operator will work 24/7 for 365 days of the year, to a consistent standard and quality, without ever complaining about the working conditions? Obviously, only a robot. And, outside the automotive industry, the UK is making less use of them than virtually any other industrialised nation. At the end of 2002, about 770,000 industrial robots were in operation worldwide, of which 350,000 were in Japan, 233,000 in the EU and about 104,000 in North America. In Europe, Germany was in the lead with just under 105,000 units, followed by Italy with 47,000, France with 24,000 and Spain with 18,000. And the UK? We barely scraped 14,000.

Non-UK companies are using robots to make themselves more productive and more profitable. Take just a couple of examples. A pet food factory in Bremen, North Germany, has installed three Toshiba Machine ceiling-mounted robots, supplied by TM Robotics. They package birdseed sticks at ninety per minute. Where once seven people worked on this line across three shifts, three robots now achieve the same results. The people have been re-deployed. Ceiling mounting is also saving space where it is at a premium. Similarly, two robots are helping to cut manpower requirements by two thirds in a Danish shellfish processing plant. Initial trials suggest that the new factory will produce the same annual output as the company's previous facility with only six operators handling the entire process instead of 18.

However, there are a number of British companies reporting remarkable gains through this kind of automation. Prompted by the need to reduce man-hours on the shop floor while increasing production, C&C Marshall installed two robots at one of its UK plastics moulding plants. They position components within dry lining box moulds, shifting 10,000 dry lining boxes a day. Three people now operate the entire system instead of eight. Payback was achieved in just six months.

Adapted from 'The Manufacturer', March 2005, *www.themanufacturer.com*

1. What are the advantages of employing robots for the firms in the article?
2. Why are industrial robots often described as labour-saving technology?
3. What are the possible implications for employees, consumers and the economy from the increased use of robots in firms?
4. What do you think might be the main obstacles to employing more robots in more firms in the UK and other countries?

Section 4

The scale of production

What determines firm size?

Firm size can be measured in a number of ways – by the amount of output they produce or the revenue they earn, by the number of people they employ, or by the amount they have invested in capital. Usually, the larger the firm the more capital and labour they employ and the more output they produce. That is, as the productive capacity or scale of a firm increases, the more labour and/or capital they tend to employ and the more output they tend to produce. So firm size and productive scale are usually very closely related.

Firms can range in size, from very small firms employing one or just a few workers and very little capital equipment, to huge multinational enterprises employing many thousands of employees and billions of dollars worth of plant and machinery all over the world (see Chapter 4). In addition, some firms produce one particular type of good or service, while others produce many different products. Some firms even own and run other firms.

But what factors determine firm size? Let's first consider why some firms remain small, especially when they face often very fierce competition from much larger firms.

Exercise 4 Why are there small firms?

Read the following passages and try to list all those factors you think are helping these *small firms* to survive in the economy today.

Mr Granger runs a local newsagent in a small town. It is the only newsagent for some miles around and he stocks a variety of goods ranging from general household items, such as washing-up liquid, to foodstuffs. Mrs Scuttle is a regular customer and she comes for the variety of goods the newsagent is able to supply.

'Well,' she said, 'you can pick up most of the things you need here, so why go elsewhere. Old Bill, that's Mr Granger, goes out of his way to provide a good stock of goods and he's only too happy to help you out any time. Me and the other locals get on with Bill like old school pals …'

Bahir Engineering is a small manufacturing firm run by Osman Bahir making fuseboxes for a hugely successful, international motor-car manufacturer. Osman started his own business when his previous company collapsed in the winter of 2005. Using a bank loan underwritten by the government he obtained small premises and some equipment. 'Our initial success was due to the fact that the new type of fusebox I designed was protected by a patent so that only I could produce them,' Osman explained. 'It was then that the car giant got interested.'

Adil and Delisha Mallam decided to start up their own business shortly after leaving Art College. Adil had been unemployed for some time but was entitled to financial help from the government for his first 6 months in business.

'The money came in very handy,' Delisha explained. 'We had a cash flow problem to start with. We make "exclusive" pattern jumpers that sell for around \$100 to \$250 each. Our market is limited, our trade coming from the "well to do" 18 to 30-year-old age group … I suppose it's the very specialized and luxury nature of our sweaters that has kept us going.'

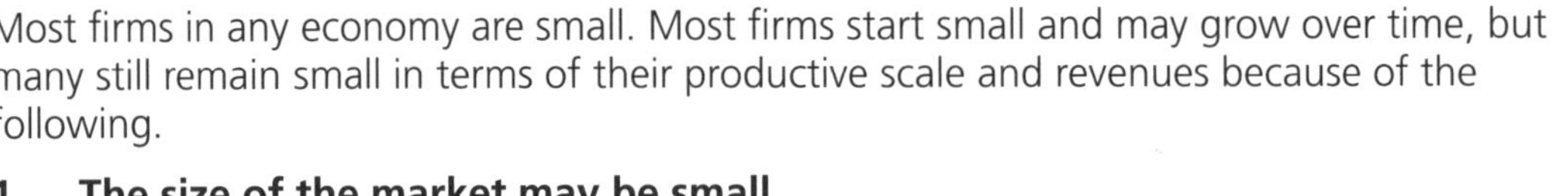

Most firms in any economy are small. Most firms start small and may grow over time, but many still remain small in terms of their productive scale and revenues because of the following.

1 The size of the market may be small

When there is only a small number of consumers willing to buy a product there is no point in a firm growing to a large size. It is better to remain small, producing just enough for the relatively small number of people to buy. The size of the market will therefore determine the size of the firm. There may be a number of reasons why the market for a particular good or service is small:

a The market is local

Mr Granger's newsagent was the only one for miles around and so people would regularly visit to buy the products he sold. Local bakeries, butchers, farms and local newspapers can also enjoy the advantages of regular custom and profits. Where only one small firm is able to supply a good or service to the people of a particular area we call it a **local monopoly** (see Chapter 8).

b A wide variety of goods and services are wanted

Some firms face the problem that consumers want a wide choice of products in different colours, styles and designs. Large firms that mass produce goods cannot afford to keep changing the colours and design. Smaller firms, however, can often cater for a variety of tastes. Tailors can make suits to measure, carpenters can make furniture to order.

c Luxury items are highly priced

The market may be limited by price. That is, high prices mean that only a handful of rich people can afford to buy a product. For example, Adil and Delisha Mallam's 'exclusive' jumpers of between $100 and $250. Expensive jewellery, luxury cars and yachts will tend to be produced by small firms for a relatively small market.

d People like personal service

Industries which provide personal services rather than goods usually consist of a large number of small firms. Mr Granger the newsagent was able to chat and be friendly to customers. In large supermarkets or department stores it is often difficult to get personal attention. In other areas where personal attention is required we find many small businesses. For example, lawyers, accountants, doctors, dentists, hairdressers and many more.

e A large firm requires component parts

Osman Bahir's small firm was able to survive because the large car firm required the components he made on a regular basis. Osman also had the advantages of having his fuseboxes protected by a **patent** which disallows by law any other firm from copying his idea. Many small firms can survive by producing parts for large manufacturers.

2 Capital is limited

Small firms may not be able to raise enough money to buy bigger premises and the equipment they need to increase their scale of production. Investments in new technologies can also be expensive. Owners of small firms often have to invest their own savings or borrow from banks to raise finance. Loan repayments can be very costly.

3 Government assistance

Many governments encourage the start-up of new small firms by providing them with grants to cover the costs of premises and equipment, or by subsidizing wages. They may also benefit from lower rates of tax on their profits, and can often seek help and advice on business issues from specialist advisers employed by government agencies. Governments do this because small firms are often very innovative, and invent new products that boost trade, and new processes that other firms can eventually use to increase their productivity. Some small firms will eventually grow into much larger firms that help create wealth in an economy by providing employment to many people and earning big profits.

4 Personal choice

Some entrepreneurs may simply decide they do not want their firm to grow in size, so long as they continue to earn reasonable profits. Running a bigger firm can take up many more hours, and also may mean they have to share ownership and control of the business with others (see Chapter 4). Growth in firm size usually involves a change in the structure and control of the organization. Also, some entrepreneurs may simply lack the skills they need to manage and run bigger firms employing many more people and much more capital.

There are two main determinants of firm size therefore. First, the size of the market for the good or service produced by a firm, and second, the amount of capital required and the ability of the firm to raise the money needed to finance it.

Market size

The average size of firms in an industry will be closely related to the size of their markets. If the market is small a firm is likely to remain small, even if is able to dominate the market supply. The markets for cars and computers are global and they are relatively expensive to produce. Firms will need factories, specialist engineers and machinery. These are expensive and so a firm must be sufficiently large enough to generate enough revenue to afford to buy or hire them. In contrast, the markets for a local newspaper, restaurant or cinema will be relatively limited and this will limit the size to which it is sensible for a firm to grow. However, clearly a large firm may own and control more than one local newspaper or own a chain of restaurants or cinemas.

Capital

Larger firms often benefit from access to more and cheaper sources of finance. For example, joint stock companies can raise money from the sale of shares on a stock exchange. So-called share capital never has to be repaid (see Chapter 6). They can also borrow more from banks at lower rates of interest because they are large, well-established firms and therefore pose less risk than smaller firms that might go out of business. Large firms can also afford to employ highly skilled and productive labour, and can also save costs by buying the materials they need in bulk. These are called **economies of scale** (see Chapter 13). However, a firm must be careful not to expand too much. Sometimes, very large firms can suffer from management and communication problems, especially if the firm has plants or shops or offices spread over many different locations, and if it has many different shareholders with different ideas on how to run the business. In Chapter 13 we will learn that the optimum size for a firm is one where the average cost per unit of its output is at a minimum.

Section 5 How firms can grow in size

Internal growth

Firms can grow in size and scale in a number of ways. The first is by internal growth, also often called organic growth because it involves a firm increasing its own scale of production 'from within'. However, to finance this growth a firm will have to reinvest its profits, borrow significantly from banks and other lenders, or become a joint stock company and raise finance through the sale of shares in its ownership (see Chapter 4).

Take-overs and mergers

The second, and more common method today, is by external growth or **amalgamation** (or **integration**). This occurs where one or more firms join together to form a larger enterprise.

Firms can amalgamate or integrate in one of these two ways.

1 Take-over

A take-over or **acquisition** occurs when one company buys all, or a controlling interest, of the shares in the ownership of another company.

In this way, the firm being taken over by another company often loses its own identity and becomes part of the other company.

Alternatively an entirely new company may be formed for the sole purpose of buying up shares in the ownership of a number of other companies. This is known as a **holding company**. The companies acquired in this way may keep their own names and management but their overall policies are decided by their holding company. For example, HSBC Holdings plc is one of the biggest UK companies and owns many other companies around the world in the banking industry.

2 Merger

A merger occurs when two or more firms agree to join to form a new enterprise. This is usually done by shareholders of the two or more companies exchanging their shares for new shares in the new company.

Types of integration

There are three main forms of integration or amalgamation between firms.

1 Horizontal integration

This occurs when firms engaged in the production of the same type of good or service combine. Most amalgamations are of this type, for example the joining of British Petroleum with Amoco in the oil and gas industry.

This type of integration may provide a number of economies of scale. For example, the employment of more specialized machines and labour, the spreading of administration costs and bulk buying.

The major criticism of firms linking horizontally is that very large firms are formed which are able to dominate the market. They may be able to raise prices and reduce competition by creating entry barriers for new firms (see Chapter 8).

2 Vertical integration

This occurs when firms engaged in different stages of production combine. This would be the case if an oil refinery combined with a chain of petrol stations. This is called **forward integration**. In this way, the oil refinery is assured places to sell its petrol. Firms can also undertake **backward integration**, for example, a bread manufacturer combining with a wheat producers' association. In this way the firm can ensure a supply of materials.

3 Lateral integration

This happens when firms in the same stage of production, for example, primary or secondary production, but producing different products combine. This is often termed a **conglomerate merger** to form conglomerates which are firms which produce a wide range of products. This may be to reduce the risk of a fall in demand for one of their products or to seek out the profitmaking potential of selling other products in other markets. For example, Unilever is a firm famous for its detergents but with interests in food, chemicals, paper, plastics, animal feeds, transport and tropical plantations.

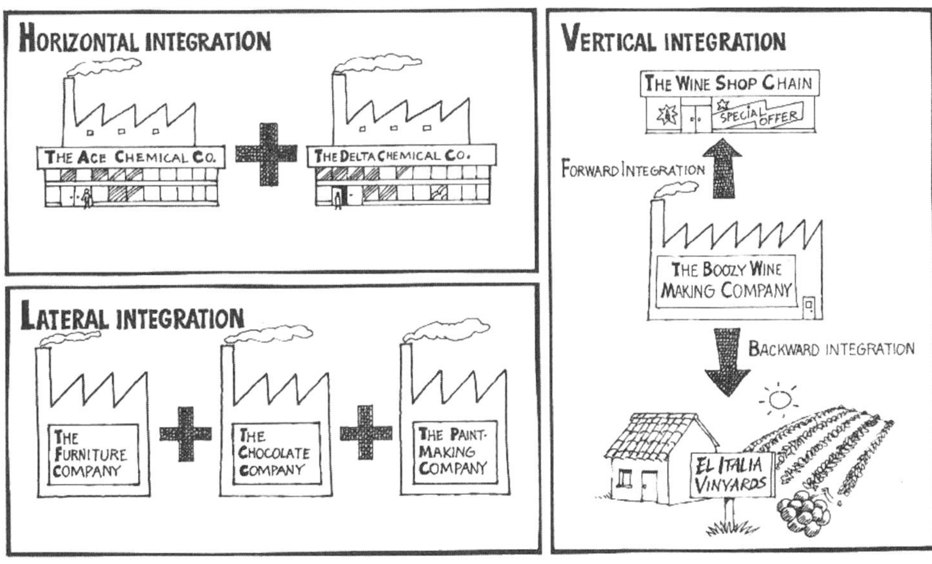

Exercise 5 What type of integration?

From the following amalgamations of firms state which form of integration applies: horizontal, vertical or lateral?

1. A firm producing cars takes over a steel manufacturer.
2. A bank merges with a travel agent.
3. A menswear shop chain merges with a women's fashion store chain.
4. A bus manufacturer merges with a car-maker.
5. A sand quarry merges with a gravel quarry company.
6. A brewery takes over a chain of pubs.
7. A chain of clothes shops takes over a clothing manufacturer.
8. A shoe-maker is taken over by a cigarette manufacturer.

Learn more about organizing production, productivity and firm growth at:

- *www.answers.com/topic/productivity-economics*
- *www.bized.ac.uk/educators/level2/busactivity/lesson/production1.htm*
- *www.economicswebinstitute.org/glossary/prdctvt.htm*
- *www.themanufacturer.com*
- *en.wikipedia.org/wiki/Category:Economics_of_production*
- *en.wikipedia.org/wiki/Productivity*

Key word search

In the jumble of letters below, find and circle or highlight key words and terms from this chapter that fit the definitions below.

C	O	L	A	B	O	U	R	I	N	T	E	N	S	I	V	E	K	F
X	P	R	D	O	Z	L	A	N	D	G	R	A	B	I	T	W	M	A
P	R	I	M	A	R	Y	I	N	D	U	S	T	R	Y	X	P	I	C
G	O	R	O	M	I	T	A	N	D	W	E	A	L	L	A	R	E	T
U	F	U	R	A	O	R	G	A	N	I	C	O	N	T	A	O	L	O
S	I	O	N	F	O	U	R	L	E	G	O	S	A	R	S	D	E	R
F	T	U	K	E	R	C	O	P	L	A	N	T	I	N	G	U	D	S
L	M	E	R	G	E	R	I	C	K	M	D	Y	T	P	E	C	T	U
E	A	N	I	S	B	V	T	C	H	D	A	P	A	R	L	T	H	B
O	X	Y	G	E	N	E	I	N	T	E	R	N	K	B	A	I	E	S
P	I	M	X	T	E	R	T	I	A	R	Y	S	E	C	T	O	R	T
E	M	R	T	E	R	T	I	M	T	Y	I	N	O	O	E	N	O	I
F	I	R	M	S	L	I	U	M	P	X	N	O	V	N	R	V	A	T
R	Z	T	I	R	O	C	M	A	I	E	D	B	E	T	A	A	D	U
A	A	V	X	S	L	A	D	E	O	P	U	I	R	I	L	S	A	T
O	T	O	M	A	N	L	I	M	C	D	S	N	C	N	L	O	H	I
E	I	X	F	A	P	R	O	D	U	C	T	I	V	I	T	Y	E	O
H	O	R	I	Z	O	N	T	A	L	P	R	M	B	U	N	P	A	N
D	N	U	P	Y	E	R	B	M	P	V	Y	C	X	E	A	N	D	O

Definitions

1. The aim of production for most private sector firms
2. Economic activity designed to satisfy consumer wants
3. An organization of factors of production for the purpose of productive activity
4. The term used for any workplace where productive activity takes place
5. Another name given to internal growth in the size of a firm
6. Replacing one factor of production with another, more productive, factor
7. Type of production that employs much more labour relative to capital
8. All firms engaged in farming, mining and other extractive production
9. Collective name given to all firms engaged in manufacturing and construction
10. That sector of an economy consisting of all service industries
11. When two or more firms agree to integrate
12. When one firm buys a controlling share in another
13. Integration between firms involved in the same productive activity
14. Integration between firms involved in different stages of production
15. Integration between firms producing different products at the same stage of production
16. Measurement of output per unit of a factor of production

Chapter 13 Costs, Revenues and Profits

Aims

At the end of this chapter you should be able to:

- define **fixed cost** and **variable cost**
- define **total cost** and **average cost**
- analyse how changes in output affect total and average costs
- define **total revenue** and **average revenue**
- calculate **profit** or **loss** as the difference between total revenue and total cost
- define and give examples of **economies of scale** and **diseconomies of scale**

Making a profit

Exercise 1 The Bear Necessities

Sue Brennan used to make toys when she was a young girl at school. Her friends and relatives thought that they were so good that they asked her to make some for them to give as presents to others. This gave Sue an idea for the future.

When she left school she went to work in a local furniture-making factory for two years where she gained experience of using cloth to make seat covers. She saved some money and asked her bank to lend her some more so that she could start up her own firm under the name of 'Bear Necessities'.

Sue rented a small factory unit on a new industrial estate. The cost of the building including fittings is $100 per week. She also hired some machinery at a cost of $45 per week. Sue employs her two brothers to help her to make toy bears. Sue pays herself and her brothers $1 for each bear they complete.

Since she started, Sue's toy bears have become very popular and she has many orders for them. She must, however, rely on regular custom from other firms and shops for her bears and so she must try and keep quality high and prices low. The average price she charges for her bears is $10 each.

The costs of Bear Necessities

In running her toy-making business Sue has a number of things she has to pay for. These are her costs. Some things have to be paid for each and every week no matter how many bears Sue makes and sells. These are her **fixed costs** which do not vary with the number of bears she produces. On the other hand **variable costs** change with the number of bears produced. The more Sue produces the more materials and foam she needs. Wages to herself and her brothers also rise.

Fixed costs per week ($)		Variable costs per bear ($)	
Rent and rates of factory	100.00	Materials	6.00
Hire and machines	45.00	Foam	1.00
Heating and lighting	5.00	Wages	1.00
Repayment of bank loan	50.00		
	200.00		8.00

Sue keeps any profit that is left after she has taken away her costs from the money or **revenue** she earns from selling bears.

Answer the following questions.

1 Write down a definition of fixed costs and give two examples.

2 If Sue produced 100 bears in a week, how much would her fixed costs be that week?

3 If Sue produced 1000 bears in a week, how much would her fixed costs be that week?

4 Write down a definition of variable costs and give two examples.

5 If Sue produced 100 bears, how much would her variable costs be?

6 If Sue produced 1000 bears, how much would her variable costs be?

7 The **total cost** of producing bears is found by adding together the fixed costs (FC) and variable costs (VC).

Total cost (TC) = FC + VC

a If Sue produced 100 bears in a week, what would her total cost be?

b If Sue produced 1000 bears in a week, what would her total cost be?

8 Copy the table below and work out the fixed, variable and total costs of producing different numbers of toy bears in a week. The costs of producing 400 bears and 500 bears have already been done for you. We will then plot all this information on a graph.

Bears produced in a week	Fixed costs $	Variable costs $	Total costs $	Average costs $
0				
50				
100				
200				
300				
400	200	3 200	3 400	8.5
500	200	4 000	4 200	8.4
600				
700				
800				
900				
1000				

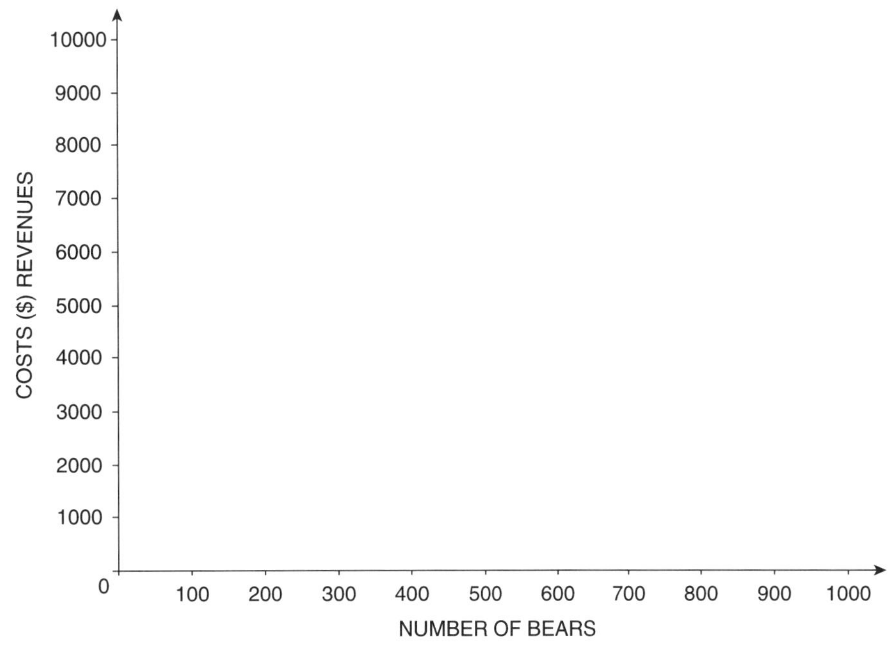

9 Now draw a pair of axes for a graph like the one above on a large piece of graph paper. Use your calculations to plot the fixed cost curve, variable cost curve and total cost curve which show how costs change with the number of bears produced. Do not forget to label each line you plot with its correct name.

10 What is the price charged for each bear?

11 How much money or revenue does Sue receive from the sale of each bear?

You will notice that your answers to questions 10 and 11 are the same.

Clearly if Sue sold five bears for $10 each, the revenue per bear is $10, while her **total revenue** is $50. Total sales revenue is also known as **turnover**.

Total revenue (TR) = Price per bear × number of bears sold

If the total revenue from the sale of five bears is $50, then the **average revenue** for each of those bears is $10, which is the same as the price of each bear.

$$\textbf{Average revenue (AR)} = \frac{\text{Total revenue}}{\text{Number of bears sold}}$$

12 If Sue sold 100 bears what would her total revenue be?

13 If Sue sold 1000 bears what would her total revenue be?

14 Draw the following table in your books and calculate the total revenue from the number of bears sold. Again, this has already been done for 400 and 500 bears sold.

15 Now look back at the graph you drew earlier and on it plot your figures for total revenue in a different colour and label this line **total revenue**.

Number of bears sold in a week	Total revenue $	Total costs $	Profit/loss $
0			
50			
100			
200			
300			
400	4000	3400	600
500	5000	4200	800
600			
700			
800			
900			
1000			

16 To calculate the **profit** or **loss** Sue makes from producing and selling bears we take away her total cost (TC) from her total revenue (TR). If her total costs are greater than her total revenue, Sue will make a loss. If she is successful, her total revenue will exceed her total costs and she will make a profit.

Profit (or loss) = TR − TC

On the table you copied in question 14 write in the total costs of producing the different number of bears and calculate the profit or loss. We assume Sue sells all the bears she makes.

On your graph the area between the total revenue and the total cost curve represents the profit or loss. Where the total cost curve is above the total revenue curve the area in between them represents loss. Label this area and shade in one colour. Where the total cost curve lies below the total revenue curve the area in between represents profit. Label this area and shade in another colour.

Where the two curves cross, no profit or loss is made. This level of output and sales is known as the **break-even point of production**. This means that if Sue manages to sell all the bears she makes at this point, she will just cover her costs and be able to remain in business. You should find from your tables and graphs that to do this Sue must make and sell at least 100 bears.

Break-even point of production is where TR = TC

17 Now look again at the total costs of producing a different amount of bears each week. We now wish to calculate for Sue just how much it costs on average to make one bear. This is known as the **average cost** or **unit cost** of production.

We found in question 8 that when Sue produced 400 bears per week her total costs were $3400. Clearly then if 400 bears cost $3400 to make then one bear costs $8.50 to make (i.e. $3400/400).

$$\textbf{Average cost (AC)} = \frac{\text{Total cost}}{\text{Number of bears produced}}$$

Go back to the table you drew in question 8 and calculate the average cost of producing each bear if 50, 100, 200 and so on bears were made.

18 We will now plot the average cost curve on another graph with the number of bears produced along the bottom axis and cost ($) on the horizontal axis. You will need to go up to $12 for your costs axis. When you have done this write down what you notice about the slope of the curve, that is, what happens to the average costs of production as more and more bears are produced? Can you suggest reasons for this? (*Hint:* Even if no bears or 1000 bears are produced what costs does Sue have to pay?)

Well done. By completing this exercise about Bear Necessities you have learnt all about costs and revenues associated with production in a firm, how to calculate them and what they mean for profit. The rest of this chapter will now help you to fully understand these important business and economic concepts, and to apply your knowledge to other examples.

Section 2 Identifying costs

Just like the Bear Necessities toy-making business in section 1, most private firms aim to make as much profit as possible (see Chapter 12). Profit is calculated as the difference between what it costs a firm to produce its goods or services and the revenue it earns from their sale. That is,

Profit = total revenue − total cost

Therefore, in order to maximize profit a firm will not only aim to raise as much revenue as it can using various advertising and pricing strategies (see Chapters 8 and 9), but will also aim to minimize costs. Controlling costs is also very important in non-profit making-organizations such as charities, who will need to cover their business costs. However, in order to control costs a firm must be able to identify and measure the cost of all the factors of production it employs or uses up in production. These are the cost of wages for labour, payments for capital goods, components and materials, and the costs of many other goods and services produced by other firms, such as electric power providers, insurance companies and postal services.

Fixed costs

Factors of production are organized into firms to produce goods and services. But even before production can begin a firm will need to hire or buy premises, for example, a factory, shop or an office. It will also need to hire or buy machinery, tools and many other fixtures and fittings, such as office furniture and filing cabinets. **Fixed costs**, such as mortgage payments or rents on premises, interest charges on bank loans, leasing charges for machinery, telephone bills, cleaning costs and insurance charges, will continue to be paid once production has started no matter how much a firm produces and sells. That is, fixed costs do not vary with the level of output.

We can plot the total of fixed costs for a firm on a graph just like the one you drew for Bear Necessities in exercise 1. You will have noticed from your graph that the fixed cost curve is flat because fixed costs do not vary with the level of output. However, this is only true up to the point at which a firm is operating at full capacity, that is, when a firm has no more space or equipment to raise output further and so needs to hire or buy more.

A fixed cost curve for cars

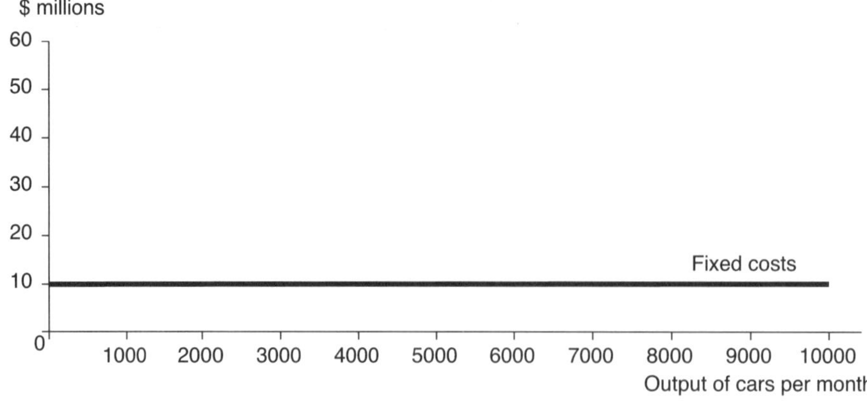

For example, in the graph above, a large firm manufacturing cars can produce up to 10 000 cars each month and has fixed costs of $10 million each month whether it produces 10 000 cars or not. If it wants to increase its scale of production up to say 20 000 cars each month it will need to hire or buy a new, bigger factory and more equipment.

Variable costs

To increase output a firm will need more materials or component parts. Similarly, more electricity may be needed to power machines and computers, and to heat and light premises, for longer periods of time. The firm may also need to employ more workers or pay its existing workers overtime to work more hours.

If we plot these variable costs for a firm on a graph the variable cost curve will slope upwards. This is because **variable costs** vary directly with the level of output. For example, our car manufacturing firm can produce up to 10 000 cars per month with its existing factory and equipment. The cost of materials and other variable items per car is $2 000. So, if the variable cost of producing one car is $2 000, then the total variable cost of producing 10 000 cars will be $20 million.

A variable cost curve for cars

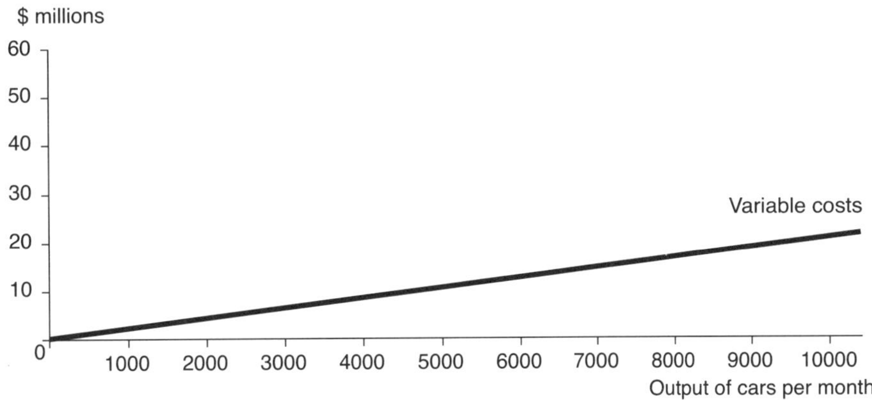

In general, therefore, the total variable cost of a given level of output is therefore calculated as follows:

Total variable cost = variable cost per unit × quantity produced

Total costs

If we add together all the fixed and variable costs of production in a firm we can calculate the total cost of production of each level of output a firm can produce.

Total cost = total fixed cost + total variable cost

If a firm produces no goods or services its total costs will be equal to its fixed costs. Adding variable costs to fixed costs means total costs will also increase as output rises, so the total cost curve will be upwards sloping.

In our car firm the total cost of producing no cars will therefore be the fixed costs it will have to continue paying for at $10 million per month, while the total cost of producing 10 000 cars each month will be $30 million of fixed plus variable costs.

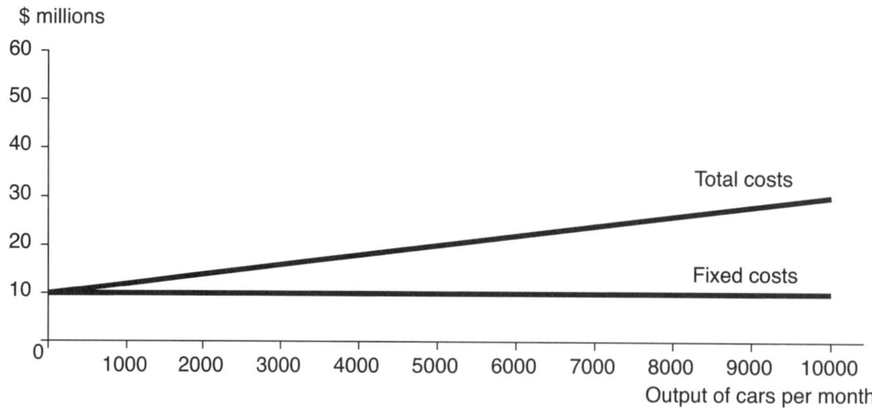

Average cost

If the total cost of producing 10 000 cars each month is $30 million, then the average cost of producing each car is $3 000. We can calculate the average cost per unit of output using the following equation:

$$\textbf{Average cost per unit} = \frac{\textbf{Total cost}}{\textbf{Total output}}$$

In order to make a profit the car company must therefore sell each car for more than $3 000 to make enough revenue to cover its costs and leave a surplus. But the car company must be careful not to charge too high a price for each car, otherwise consumers may not buy them especially if demand for cars is very price elastic (see Chapter 7).

A firm can calculate the average cost per unit of providing a service in exactly the same way. For example, the average cost of one hour of labour from a car mechanic, the average cost of one mile of journey on a train, or the average cost of treating one patient at a hospital. All a firm needs to know are the fixed and variable costs of providing its service. So, if it costs a passenger rail company a total of $20 000 each day to run a train service over 1 000 kilometres then the average cost per kilometre travelled is $20.

From exercise 1 you will have discovered how the average cost of producing a toy bear fell as the number of bears produced by Bear Necessities increased. Each bear cost on average $8.50 to produce when they produced 400 bears each week, and only $8.20 each if output increased to 1 000 bears each week. Similarly, if our car firm produced only 500 cars each month the average cost would be a massive $22 000 per car, which is unlikely to be a profitable level of production.

In general, therefore, the average cost of each unit of a good or service will tend to fall with the amount produced simply because fixed costs remain the same but their burden is spread over a much larger output. But, after a point, average costs may start to rise again because it can sometimes prove difficult to increase output. For example, in the Bear Necessities firm from exercise 1, its owner Sue Brennan may find that if they attempt to produce 1100 bears each week the shop where they buy the fur material and foam may not be able to supply any more. Sue may then have to buy the extra she wants from another shop where prices are higher. More importantly Sue may have to employ more people to work for her and may have to pay them more money. For example, imagine now that Sue pays herself and her two brothers $100 each week regardless of how many bears they produce. Her total wage bill per week is now $300. If she employs another three workers to help produce bears, wage costs will double to $600 or may more than double if she has to pay them more for them to agree to work for her. However, as more labour is added, output will rise but may only do so at a diminishing rate. Thus, while wage costs double, the output of bears may not double. Therefore, the average cost of producing each bear will begin to rise. If we plot the average cost of production on a graph it will appear as a flat bowl or 'U' shape curve for many firms, showing that as output rises, average costs fall up to a point and may then begin to increase slowly.

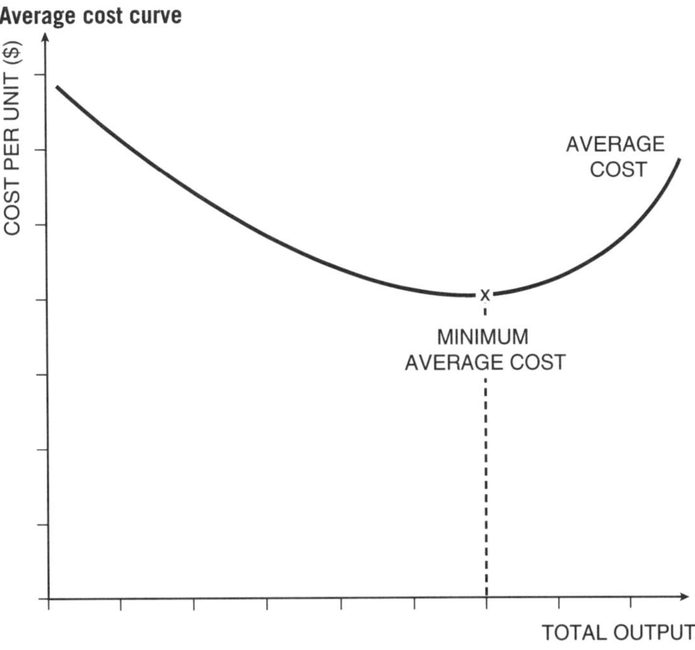

Similarly, our car manufacturer may find that there is a shortage of the skilled manufacturing workers it needs to increase output from say 8 000 cars per month up to full capacity of 10 000 cars per month. It may have to hire unskilled workers and spend more money training them, or it will have to increase wages to attract skilled workers away from other manufacturing firms. It too will find, therefore, that its average cost curve is U shaped, with the average cost of producing each car falling at first but then tending to rise after output reaches 8 000 cars per month.

In section 4 we will learn more about the relationship between average costs and the level of output in a firm.

Section 3 Calculating revenue, profit and break-even

Revenue

Firms earn **revenue** from the sale of their goods and services to consumers. Total revenue is therefore the total amount sold multiplied by the price per unit sold.

Total revenue = price per unit × quantity sold

Revenue from sales is also known as **turnover**. But, what if a firm sells its goods or services for different prices? For example, in exercise 1 Bear Necessities charged a price of $10 per bear. Now imagine that the firm wants to expand into overseas markets, but to do so the bears will have be sold at a lower price than $10 each in order to attract consumers in other countries to buy them. For example, if the firm sells 1 000 bears at $10 each and another 500 overseas at $7 each then total revenue will be $13 500, and the average revenue per bear sold will be $9 as follows:

Total revenue = ($10 × 1 000 bears) + ($7 × 500 bears) = $13 500

$$\textbf{Average revenue per bear sold} = \frac{\$13\,500}{1\,500} = \$9$$

A firm can calculate the average revenue or average price per unit of output sold using the following equation:

$$\textbf{Average revenue per unit} = \frac{\textbf{Total revenue}}{\textbf{Total units sold}}$$

Because demand tends to expand as price falls it is often the case that firms need to lower prices to expand their sales. A firm entering a new market may also price low to attract demand. This pricing strategy is known as penetration pricing (see Chapter 8). As such, average revenue can often fall as output and sales rise.

Profit or loss

Any firm will want to keep a close eye on its total revenue and average revenue so that it can calculate whether it is making a profit or a loss. Profit or loss is calculated as the difference between total revenue and total cost at each level of output. If total revenue exceeds total cost a firm will make a profit. But, if total revenue does not cover total costs, a firm will make a loss. If this continues the firm will go out of business and its resources will move to more profitable uses.

Profit (or loss) = total revenue − total cost

We can identify profit and loss from a graph of total revenue and total cost just like you did in exercise 1 for the Bear Necessities firm. Returning now to our other example of a car manufacturer, let us assume each car sells for $6 000. Total revenue therefore appears as an upward sloping curve, from zero when no cars are sold to $60 million when 10 000 are sold, and so on. The car firm makes a loss from sales up to 2 500 cars per month, and a profit from any sales over and above this level of output.

Total revenue, total cost, profit and loss for cars

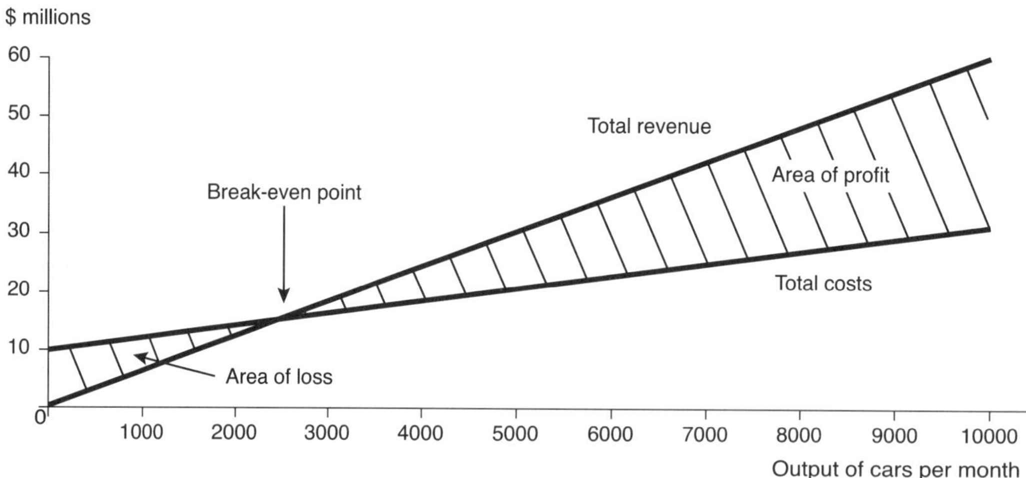

It is useful to know how much profit or loss is made for every unit of a good or service produced and sold by calculating the difference between average revenue and average cost:

Profit (or loss) per unit = average revenue − average cost

This is particularly informative for a firm to know when planning to expand production. We already know that average cost per unit may start to rise after a certain level of output is reached because extra wages may have to be paid to attract more workers or there may be supply problems with component parts and other materials. We also know that average revenue may start to fall after a certain level of sales is reached as prices need to be lowered to attract additional demand or to enter new markets. It follows that a firm may find it unprofitable to expand output too much if its average revenue falls below its average costs.

Break-even level of output

A firm will **break even** when the level of output it produces and sells costs as much to produce as it earns in revenue so that profit or loss is zero. That is,

Total revenue − total cost = 0 = break even

For example, Bear Necessities broke even when output and sales reached 100 bears per month. Sales below this level of output made a loss, while sales above it earned a profit. Similarly, our car firm has a break-even level of output of 2 500 cars per month.

On a graph, the break-even level of output can be found where the total revenue line crosses the total cost curve. At break-even a firm is able to cover all its costs and so can remain in business, although clearly if it wants to make a profit it must either raise revenues and/or lower costs otherwise it might as well stop production and move its resources to more profitable uses.

How to calculate the break-even level of output for a firm without using a graph

If you want to it is easy to calculate the level of output a firm needs to sell to break even using the equation below. All you need to know is the price at which the good or service is to be sold and its fixed and variable costs:

$$\textbf{Break-even level of output} = \frac{\textbf{total fixed costs}}{\textbf{price per unit – variable cost per unit}}$$

Let's quickly calculate break-even this way for Bear Necessities and our car firm example.

From exercise 1 we know the fixed costs of bear production were $200 per month, variable costs were $8 per bear and the final price per bear sold was $10. So, the break-even point is:

$200/($10 − $8) = $200/$2 = 100 bears per month

Our car firm has fixed costs of $10 million per month, variable costs of $2 000 per car, and sells its cars for $6 000 each. So, the level of output and sales needed to break even is:

$10 000 000/($6 000 − $2 000) = $10 000 000/$4 000 = 2 500 cars per month

Exercise 2 A calculated issue

1 Below are different levels of output of a new rock and pop magazine. The producer of the magazine intends to price each copy for sale at $5 each. The cost of hiring printing machinery is $2 400 per month and the print factory costs $1 600 per month to rent. The cost of materials and wages per magazine is $3. There are no other costs in this simple example. Use a calculator or a spreadsheet to complete the table with costs, revenues and profits.

Magazines per month	Fixed cost	Variable cost	Total cost	Average cost	Total revenue	Profit or loss
0	$4 000	0	$4 000	—	0	−$4 000
1000						
2000						
3000						
4000						
5000	$4 000	$15 000	$19 000	$3.80	$25 000	$6 000
6000						
7000						
8000						

2 At what level of output will the magazine publisher break even?

3 Plot and label the following curves on a graph with 'magazines per month' along the bottom axis and costs and revenues ($) in $1 000 intervals along the side axis. This needs to extend up to $40 000.

- **a** Fixed costs.
- **b** Variable costs.
- **c** Total costs.
- **d** Total revenue.

4 Label those areas that represent profit and loss on your graph.

5 Investigate productive activities in a local small business. How is production organized?

Identify different costs incurred running the business as fixed and variable costs. How do costs vary with the scale of production or level of service provided (for example, if a shop opened longer hours or a hairdresser's booked more appointments)? At what level of output per period does the business break even at current prices and costs? Suggest potential advantages and disadvantages to the business from expanding its current level of output or service.

Section 4 The relationship between costs and the scale of production

Increasing output in the short run and the long run

A firm can consider increasing its output in a number of ways. If it needs to increase output quickly or just temporarily to meet an increase in demand, then it can:

- Reorganize its existing production processes to make them more efficient
- Pay its existing labour to work overtime
- Motivate its existing workforce to increase its productivity, for example, by paying wage bonuses linked to increased output
- Hire some more labour on short-term contracts

Reorganizing and employing more labour will help increase output in the **short run**, but a firm will only be able to increase production significantly by expanding its premises and hiring or buying new capital equipment, including tools, machinery or computers. Economists say this can only occur in the **long run**. For some firms, this may take more time than others. For example, a retail chain may be able to buy and decorate a new retail outlet in a matter of months while an electricity supply company may take years to build new power stations. But it is clearly useful for all firms to distinguish between the short run when they can increase or decrease the amount of labour they employ relatively easily, and the long run when they can increase or decrease the **scale of production** by changing the amount of capital they employ. In the short run, capital is a fixed factor of production (see Chapter 2).

But what exactly will happen to output in a firm that expands its scale of production in the long run by employing more factors of production? Output should rise, but by how much? Let us consider the example of three different firms all making chocolates.

Exercise 3 Chewing over a problem?

The following three chocolate manufacturing firms have expanded the scale of their production in two years. All three firms have doubled their inputs or the factors of production they use. But what has happened to their output of chocolate boxes? The figures are given below.

The ACE Company		The BOOM Company		The CRIKEY Company	
Year 1					
Labour units	50	Labour units	40	Labour units	60
Number of machines	10	Number of machines	15	Number of machines	5
Number of factories	1	Number of factories	1	Number of factories	1
Total output	10 000	Total output	12 000	Total output	9 000
Year 2					
Labour units	100	Labour units	80	Labour units	120
Number of machines	20	Number of machines	30	Number of machines	10
Number of factories	2	Number of factories	2	Number of factories	2
Total output	25 000	Total output	20 000	Total output	18 000

A firm that doubles all its inputs and more than doubles its output of goods or services as a result is said to be experiencing **increasing returns to scale**. This is what happened in the Ace Chocolate Company above. The Boom Company, however, doubled its input but did not manage to double its output of chocolate boxes. Firms like this are said to be experiencing **decreasing** or **diminishing returns to scale**. On the other hand, the Crikey Chocolate Company experienced **constant returns to scale** because as it doubled its inputs it also doubled its output.

Exercise 4 Chewing it over again

Our three chocolate companies have doubled all their inputs and have therefore doubled their total costs. One firm managed to more than double its output, one firm doubled its output while the other did not manage to do this at all. Calculate what has happened to the average cost of producing boxes of chocolates in each company as they moved from year one to year two.

The ACE Company		The BOOM Company		The CRIKEY Company	
Year 1					
Total cost of all inputs:	$10 000	Total cost of all inputs:	$12 000	Total cost of all inputs:	$9 000
Total output	10 000	Total output	12 000	Total output	9 000
Average cost	**$1**	**Average cost**	**$1**	**Average cost**	**$1**
Year 2					
Total cost of all inputs:	$20 000	Total cost of all inputs:	$24 000	Total cost of all inputs:	$18 000
Total output	25 000	Total output	20 000	Total output	18 000
Average cost	**?**	**Average cost**	**?**	**Average cost**	**?**

Which of the firms above has doubled all its inputs in the long run and experienced:

1 Falling average costs?

2 Rising average costs?

3 No change to their average costs?

So what happens to average costs in the long run?

Falling average costs are an important benefit to a firm. We say that a firm experiences **economies of scale** if it makes cost savings from increasing the scale of production, that is, by raising output. This was certainly the case for the Ace Chocolate Company whose average costs per box of chocolates fell from $1 to 80 cents as it doubled all its inputs and total costs; it experienced increasing returns to scale and more than doubled output. If the average costs of production rise as more is produced then a firm is experiencing **diseconomies of scale**, because a firm is producing too much and has become inefficient. This happened to the Boom Company as it doubled its inputs but failed to double its outputs. Diminishing returns to scale here meant that the firm's average costs increased from $1.00 to $1.20 per box. The Boom Company, like any firm in this situation, would regret taking the decision to expand its scale of production.

So how big should a firm be?

Deciding how large a firm should be is not easy for an entrepreneur. If a firm expands its scale of production it may be lucky and experience falling average costs or economies of scale. If a firm expands too much and watches its average costs rise, like the Boom Company did, it has experienced diseconomies of scale. Clearly then the best size or **optimum size** for a firm is where it can reduce average costs to their lowest point in the long run, that is, at that level of output that corresponds with the lowest point on a U-shaped average cost curve. Here a firm can benefit fully from economies of scale. With average costs low, profits will be bigger. The firm could use these profits to improve their factory and their products, and may even lower prices to attract consumers away from competing firms.

Section 5 The advantages of large-scale production

Economies of scale

When a firm expands the scale of production it has a chance to become more efficient and lower its average costs. This is because it gives the management or owners a chance to re-organize the way the firm is run and financed. Such decisions are taken within the firm and so the advantages or economies they bring are known as internal economies of scale. These are the cost savings that result from a firm being large. We shall now look at these in detail.

Exercise 5 Big is beautiful?

Case 1: Cleaning up their act

A famous detergent manufacturer has recently decided to expand its production plant and install the latest equipment. Studies have shown that they would produce a maximum output more efficiently if they employed several of the new machines. This, the study said, would lower their unit costs compared with their smaller competitors, who could not afford to employ as many machines.

To meet the costs of this expansion the company decided to raise the funds from banks. Banks were only too willing to lend on very reasonable terms, because the firm had offered to put up its premises as security. The banks also noticed that, because of the number of different products the firm had produced for the home and international market, any demand fluctuations would not seriously affect the firm's ability to repay the loan. Its smaller competitors, however, found it hard to raise money for their modernization, and even when funds were secured, the interest rate they were charged was much higher and consequently this meant their average costs were higher.

The large firm has a new soap coming on to the market next week, and they are planning a massive advertising campaign to launch it. The cost of the campaign is around $1 million, but with an output of 10 million, this clearly only adds 10 cents to the cost of producing each unit of soap. Smaller firms could not possibly advertise on such a scale, because with outputs of around 3 million, it would add 33 cents to the cost of producing each unit.

Case 2: Blasting off!

The large iron smelting company in Northern Ecoland has recently announced how pleased it is at having achieved a big overseas order, as a result of it being able to offer a lower price than its foreign counterparts in Nomicia.

'Our specialist sales staff were a great help in winning the order,' enthused Mr Justin Time, the Company Director. 'The Nomicians could not afford to employ such specialists.'

He went on to say how his company had managed to offer a lower price than the Nomicians. He explained that their unit costs were much lower because their plant had managed to employ a large blast furnace, while the smaller Nomician plants had to band together in certain areas to be able to afford such furnaces. Mr Time also added that some Nomician firms incurred higher transport costs as a result of their scale of operations being smaller. The Ecoland Company, however, has been able to purchase large juggernauts which can carry far more tons of iron than could their smaller lorries, but clearly do not require any more drivers and only use fractionally more petrol per journey.

He also told us how his firm's average costs were lower than that of the Nomicians, as a result of their purchase of vast quantities of iron ore. 'You see because we buy 40 million tons of the stuff every year, our suppliers are willing to sell it for $50 per ton,' he said, 'whereas the average Nomician firm only buys 10 million tons a year, but at $60 per ton.'

1 Read the two case studies above and with your partner list all the ways that large firms are able to enjoy cost advantages which smaller firms can not.

2 Compare your list with another group's list.

3 Now use your list to try to decide which of the internal economies of scale could be called:

   a **Financial economies:** cost savings that arise from the way in which large firms raise money.

   b **Marketing economies:** cost savings resulting from the way in which firms sell their products.

   c **Technical economies:** cost savings caused by the methods of production used.

   d **Risk-bearing economies:** cost savings that result from the way in which firms try to reduce the risk of a fall in demand for some of their products.

Let us now consider the four main types of internal economies of scale.

1 Financial economies

A large firm has several financial advantages because it is large, well known and becomes a more credit-worthy borrower than a smaller firm. This means:

- A large firm can borrow money from a number of different sources, to buy new machines, etc. Large firms may also be able to raise money from the general public by selling them shares through a stock exchange (see Chapter 6)
- Large firms may own more assets than a small firm, like machinery, factories and offices, that they can offer to the lenders in case of the unlikely event that they cannot repay the loan. Because this event is so unlikely financial institutions are very willing to lend money to large firms
- Because large firms represent such low risk borrowers, financial institutions may not charge them so much interest on their loans

2 Marketing economies

The way large firms buy materials, transport and sell their products can also bring them advantages.

- A large firm is able to buy in bulk large quantities of the materials they need and may also be able to store them. Because of this, suppliers will often sell things in bulk at discount prices. They may also offer to deliver the goods to the firm at special low rates to secure their regular custom
- A large firm may be able to afford to employ specialist buyers who have the knowledge and the skills necessary to buy the best quality materials at the best possible prices
- In large shops specialist sales staff can help customers to buy the things they want, while large manufacturing firms can employ specially-trained staff to visit shops and warehouses to promote the products they make
- Although large firms spend huge amounts of money on advertising their products to create a want for them, their advertising costs are spread over a very large output

3 Technical economies

The larger firm can afford to use different methods of production.

- Large firms can afford to employ specialist workers and machines. They can divide up the production process into specialized tasks so that production becomes faster as each worker becomes an expert in their particular job. In small firms there are simply not enough workers or specialized machinery to make this profitable.
- Large firms can also afford to research and develop new faster methods of production and new products. The cost may be high but it is spread out over a very large output.
- The larger the firm the more transport it needs to carry materials and products to and fro. As a firm grows in size it can afford to use large types of transport, like juggernauts, or, in the case of oil companies, supertankers.

4 Risk-bearing economies

Running a firm is a risky business and clearly the bigger the firm the more things can go wrong. Therefore larger firms try to overcome this risk in a number of ways.

- A small firm is likely to need only small amounts of raw materials or components to produce goods or services and so it would probably only obtain these from one supplier. A large firm will, however, need to buy materials in bulk and if they cannot obtain these for some reason, for example, a strike at their suppliers or some transport problems, then their whole operation will grind to a halt. Large firms will try to reduce the risk of this happening by using many different suppliers, buying some of the materials they need from each.
- A small firm is only likely to produce one particular good or service and they could find themselves in trouble if consumers suddenly decided not to buy that product. If a large firm did the same, a fall in consumers' demand for their product could have devastating effects. In order to reduce the risk of a fall in consumer demand damaging the firm, large enterprises often produce a variety of goods or services, so that if demand for one falls they still have others they can make and sell. This is known as **diversification**. For example, Unilever is famous for its soap and detergent products but it also has interests in the production of food, paper, plastics, animal feeds, transport and tropical plantations.

Technical economies

Marketing economies

Diseconomies of scale

It seems very beneficial for a firm to grow to a large size so that it may enjoy economies of scale. However, some firms become too large and this can cause inefficiency: production slows down and costs rise. This is caused by **diseconomies of scale**.

1 Management diseconomies

Large firms have to be divided up into many specialist departments, for example, the planning department, human resources, accounts, production, design, sales, etc. Each department will have a manager responsible for running it. For the firm to run successfully all the departments must work together, but with so many departmental managers decisions could take a long time and there may be disagreements.

2 Labour diseconomies

Large firms use very specialized mass-production techniques. Labour is divided up into many specialized tasks but workers may become very bored with their repetitive and often monotonous jobs. The workforce may then become less co-operative or less attentive to their work, so that the quality of the products they produce suffers. Strikes and disruptions may also occur if the workers feel they are poorly treated (see Chapter 5).

In your own words write down what you understand by the following:

Fixed costs	**Break even**
Variable costs	**Scale of production**
Total costs	**Increasing returns to scale**
Average cost	**Decreasing returns to scale**
Total revenue	**Constant returns to scale**
Average revenue	**Economies of scale**
Turnover	**Diseconomies of scale**
Profit/Loss	**Diversification**

Check your understanding of these terms by working through the chapter again.

The following websites contain additional examples and explanations to help you learn more about costs and revenues in economics:

- *www.bized.ac.uk/learn/economics/firms/costrevenue/index.htm*
- *en.wikipedia.org/wiki/Break_even_analysis*

Assessment exercises

Multiple choice

1 Which of the following can be defined as a secondary industry?

- **A** Insurance services.
- **B** Coal mining.
- **C** Paper making.
- **D** Banking.

2 Which one of the following reasons will not help explain why small firms exist and survive?

- **A** Lack of finance.
- **B** Consumers like personalized service.
- **C** Government financial help.
- **D** Low start-up costs.

3 Which of the following is unlikely to raise productivity in a firm?

- **A** Training workers in new skills.
- **B** Performance-related pay.
- **C** Investing in new equipment.
- **D** Reducing overtime working.

4 A firm employs 25 full-time employees. They produce 500 tee-shirts each week. What is their average labour productivity?

- **A** 25
- **B** 500
- **C** 20
- **D** 12 500

5 Which of the following reasons can explain why a firm may substitute capital for labour in production?

- **A** Wages fall.
- **B** The cost of borrowing rises.
- **C** Consumer demand rises.
- **D** The productivity of labour falls.

6 Which of the following mergers between two firms is an example of vertical integration?

- **A** A bank and an insurance company.
- **B** A car rental firm and a car maker.
- **C** A tin mine and a coal mine.
- **D** A restaurant and a hot food take-away.

Questions 7–9 are based on the following table of costs and revenues for a firm making digital alarm clocks.

	Output per week	Total cost ($)	Total revenue ($)
A	1000	10000	13000
B	2000	16000	30000
C	3000	18000	42000
D	4000	28000	56000

7 At what level of output is average cost at a minimum?

8 At what level of output is average revenue at a maximum?

9 At what level of output is profit maximized?

10 Which of the following is a variable cost of production?

- **A** Purchases of component parts.
- **B** Insurance premiums.
- **C** Loan repayments.
- **D** Computer repair costs.

11 A firm expands its scale of production by investing in additional factory space and machinery. What is the most likely impact of this decision on costs?

- **A** Variable costs will fall.
- **B** Fixed costs will rise.
- **C** Total costs will be unchanged.
- **D** Average costs will rise.

12 On the graph, what level of output represents the break-even point of production?

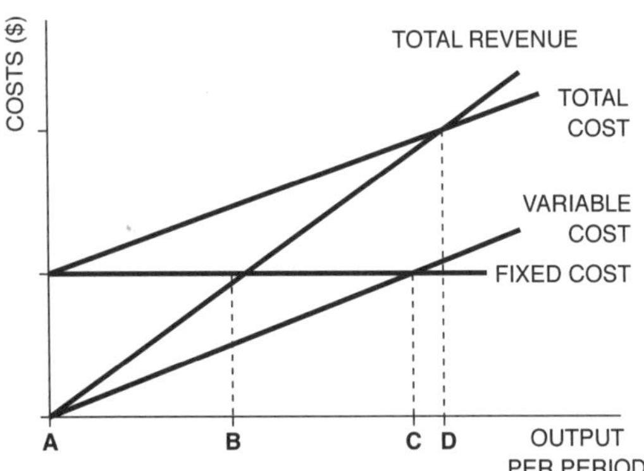

Questions 13–16 relate to the following table of costs:

Total output of compact discs	Total costs
0	$ 100
100	$ 800
200	$ 1500
300	$ 2200
400	$ 2900
500	$ 2600
600	$ 4300

13 The average cost of producing 200 compact discs is:

A $7

B $70

C $7.50

D $1500

14 The fixed costs of production are:

A $1

B $10

C $100

D $800

15 The variable cost of producing a compact disc is:

A $7

B $8

C $7.50

D $5

16 If the company produces 500 compact discs and wanted to make a $1400 profit from their sale, the price of each disc must be:

A $5

B $10

C $2.80

D $7.20

17 If a firm doubles all its factor inputs of land, labour and capital, and output more than doubles, we can say the firm has experienced:

A Constant returns to scale.

B Diminishing returns to labour.

C Decreasing returns to scale.

D Increasing returns to scale.

Structured questions

1

GERMAN TELEVISION ADVERTISING

In 2003 a German TV broadcasting company reduced its costs by 13%. The measures that it took included spending less on TV programmes, merging departments within its organization and decreasing its workforce by 4%. These measures helped the company compensate for a decrease in advertising revenue, which generated approximately 90% of the company's total revenue. The company had lost nearly 20% of its advertising revenue in the previous two years.

a Identify the reason why the television company needed to cut costs. [1]

b Costs can be classed as fixed costs or variable costs. Explain which of the company's costs mentioned are fixed and which are variable. [6]

c Calculate the percentage of total revenue that the company lost. [1]

d Describe the possible benefits of advertising to producers and consumers. [5]

e The Directors of the company wish to know how the company could improve its profit levels. If you had to report to the Directors what would you need to investigate? [7]

2

In the UK the computer games industry is bigger than the film and music industry and twice the size of the home video market. The industry employed over 22 000 people in the UK in 2004, and it helps support the employment of many more people in games retailing and other computer-related industries. Around 6000 people in the UK work directly in games development. The global market for games software in 2003 was worth $20 billion with UK exports accounting for over 35%. About 70% of the games made by Japanese-owned companies are designed within 30 miles of one city in the UK.

a Identify **three** ways of measuring whether an industry in a country is large or small. [3]

b Discuss whether you would classify the size of the UK computer games industry as large or small. [4]

c Explain what is meant by specialization. [3]

d Explain whether there is any example of specialization in the article. [2]

e Are specialization and large company size advantageous for a producer? [8]

3 Some car manufacturers are multinational companies with plants in several countries. These plants produce thousands of cars a year and are capital-intensive.

a Define the term 'capital-intensive'. [3]

b Why are some organizations capital-intensive and others labour-intensive? [7]

c Identify **three** possible advantages for the car manufacturer of establishing production in another country. [3]

d Discuss how an increase in car production through the establishment of a new plant might affect a country's Gross National Product. [7]

4 A major electronics company announced in 2005 that its profits had fallen.

a Explain what might cause profits to fall. [5]

b There are some very large electronics companies. How might a firm become large? [5]

c Some companies are often said to benefit from economies of scale. Briefly describe **three** types of economies of scale that an electronics company might experience. [6]

d Discuss why a company might change its use of different factors of production. [4]

5 **a** What is meant by fixed cost, variable cost and average total cost? [4]

b Discuss what might happen to these costs if a firm replaces labour with machines. [6]

c Some firms integrate with others. Explain the different forms of integration, and suggest why integration happens. [10]

In the UK four large supermarket companies dominate the sale of food but there are also many small food shops.

a Define a fixed cost and a variable cost, and identify one fixed cost and one variable cost that the supermarket might have. [4]

b Discuss why a small food shop might survive when there are very large supermarkets. [6]

c How do some firms become large? [4]

d Discuss how a supermarket might benefit from economies of scale. [6]

How to answer question 4

a Remember first to define what profits are before you explain what might cause them to fall. You will recall that most **private sector** organizations aim to make a profit from their productive activities. That is, **profit** is one of the main motives for production in a **market economy**. Profit is calculated as the difference between revenue and costs, thus any factor that causes **revenues** to fall or **costs** to rise will reduce profit. However, to demonstrate your ability to apply economic analysis to this problem you should give some examples. For example, what factors may have caused a fall in the **market demand** for electronics products? Or perhaps the fall in demand and revenues is just for the electronic products of this company relative to its business competitors? Similarly, what factors could have caused production costs, either **fixed or variable costs**, for electronic goods to rise?

b It is always useful to pause before you launch into answering a question to think carefully about exactly what it is asking. Most questions that carry more than one or two marks want you to use your analysis and judgement, and in this case the question is really about two things. What is a large firm, and what are the constraints to growth?

We can measure the size of a **firm** by the total value or volume of output it produces, and further by its share of the total market it supplies. We can also measure size by the amount of **capital** and/or **labour** a firm employs.

So what is the main factor that will determine whether a firm can grow in size or not? If you haven't immediately written down the size of the market then you should re-read Chapters 7 and 12. Clearly, if the size of the market a firm supplies is small then this ultimately will place a limit on the size it can grow to. A firm will only be able to grow if the market it supplies is increasing in size, and/or if it increases its share of total sales at the expense of rival firms.

Now let us consider the resources firms will need to grow. A firm that wants to grow in size will need money to finance its expansion. Its ability to raise finance for new capital may ultimately constrain its ability to grow. Ways in which firms can raise finance are discussed in Chapter 6. Some of the largest firms raise the money they need to become large organizations by selling shares as public limited companies on the **stock market**.

Growing firms will also need skilled labour and managers. The availability and cost of skilled workers and managers will also determine how large a firm can grow. Recall also from Chapter 13 that the optimum or most efficient size for a firm measured by output is where average production costs are minimized.

c As always, start with a short definition of the main economic concept in the question to show your knowledge and understanding. In this case, the concept is **economies of scale**, or falling **average costs** associated with an increased scale of output, but if you really want to stand out you can point out these can be internal economies resulting from a firm being large, or external economies resulting from an entire industry being large.

Remember that **internal economies of scale** can be financial, technical, related to marketing and spreading the risk of a downturn in demand over a diversified range of products or markets. **External economies of scale** can be enjoyed by firms locating together so that they can benefit from shared services or joint access to skilled labour.

You only need to select three examples but apply these to a large electronics company. Examples related to finance, technical economies and access to highly skilled labour may be particularly relevant in this case.

d Although the name of the economic concept in this question is not given, show off your knowledge and start by defining the concept of factor substitution. You could also provide an example, for example, the use of robots replacing labour in many assembly line manufacturing processes.

Now think what additional concepts **factor substitution** involves. This will help you answer the question in full. Remember that firms will want to combine their factors of production in the most efficient way to maximize their overall productivity for the minimum of costs. A firm will therefore compare the costs and **productivity** of labour with capital and will tend to employ more of the cheapest and most productive factor. A firm that does not do so will face higher costs, lower sales and lower profits than rival firms.

Having explained all this you are now in a position to answer the question by describing how changes in the relative cost or productivity of capital and labour will cause firms to substitute one for another. For example, describe what is likely to happen if new technology lowers the costs and increases the productivity of new machinery. Or what if workers push for wage rises that are not matched by an increase in their own productivity?

Although the question simply asks why firms may substitute one factor of production for another, a clear related question is how easy is it for firms to do so? Therefore, to fully demonstrate your analytical skills in economics you could round off your answer if you have time, by explaining why labour and capital are not always perfect substitutes, and how cutting labour can sometimes result in costly industrial disputes in firms.

A model answer for question 5

a Firms employ resources to produce goods and services. Payments made by a firm for resources are its costs of production. In economics we distinguish between fixed costs and variable costs.

Fixed costs do not vary with the level of output. For example, fixed costs of production may include interest charges on loans and mortgages, cleaning and telephone bills, rents of premises and insurance charges. These will need to be paid whether a firm produces ten or ten thousand units of output.

Variable costs are those costs that do vary with output. For example, the total variable costs of materials, component parts and packaging will tend to rise the more output is produced.

If we add together the total of fixed costs and total of variable costs in a firm we can calculate the total cost of production of each level of output it could produce. For example, consider a firm with fixed costs of $1000 per month and a variable cost per unit of output of $2. If the firm produces no output one month then its total costs that month will be equal to its fixed costs of $1000. If in the following month it produced 500 units of output, then its total costs will be $1000 of fixed costs plus 500 × $2 of variable costs: $2000 in total.

The average total cost per unit is calculated as the total cost of a given level of output divided by that level of output. It follows that if the total cost of producing 500 units of output each month is $2000, then the average total cost per unit of output will be $4, or $2000 divided by 500 units.

b A firm may substitute labour for capital in the form of new machinery, if capital has become more productive and cheaper to employ than labour. Higher levels of output and/or lower costs may be achieved for the same or a lower overall level of resource input than before.

If we assume the new machinery is paid for outright, is hired or leased for a fixed payment per period, or purchased with a bank loan which will need to be repaid in instalments each month with interest, then the employment of new machinery will tend to increase fixed costs. If the machinery can produce more output per period than labour, then total variable costs will also rise.

Whether overall fixed costs rise or fall following the introduction of the new machines depends on whether wages are a fixed or a variable cost of production. If the total wage bill does not vary from month to month regardless of the level of output produced then wages can be viewed as a fixed cost, and cutting the labour force will reduce fixed costs. However, if wage costs vary with output, for example, because labour is paid piece rates related to the amount produced, then wages will be a variable cost and any reduction in the labour force will cut variable costs of production. Similarly, variable wage costs may be cut if the firm no longer has to employ workers on overtime to produce higher levels of output because it can now employ machines to do so.

Overall, if we assume the new machines are more productive than labour then the average cost of production will tend to fall following the factor substitution. This is because total fixed costs will be spread over a far greater output than before. For example, imagine fixed costs in the firm in question (a) above rise to $1200 per month following the introduction of the new machines, and output rises to 800 units. Total production costs are now $1200 of fixed costs plus total variable costs of $1600, or $2 × 800 units. The average cost of producing each unit of output has therefore fallen to $3.5, or $2800 divided by 800 units.

However, a firm's costs may rise in the short run and output fall if the workforce tries to resist the introduction of the new machines and a loss of jobs by taking industrial action that disrupts production.

c External growth in the size and scale of firms occurs when one or more firms join together, or integrate, to form a much larger enterprise. This can occur due to a takeover or merger. A takeover occurs when one company acquires a controlling interest in the ownership of another company through the purchase of its shares. A merger occurs when two or more companies agree to join together, and usually involves new shares being issued to existing and new shareholders.

If a takeover or merger occurs between two firms engaged in the production of the same type of good or service, for example two oil producers or two retail chains, it is known as horizontal integration. Firms that combine horizontally can increase their share and dominance of their market at the expense of rival firms, and also may benefit from economies of scale, for example, by spreading their running costs over their larger combined output, gaining access to lower cost sources of finance, and through employing more specialized labour and machinery.

Firms involved in different stages of productive activity may integrate vertically. For example, a clothing manufacturer that acquires a clothing retailer through forward vertical integration will be assured access to the highly competitive clothing market by having places to sell its clothes. In contrast, a power supplier may undertake backward integration with a mining company to ensure it has a steady supply of low-cost coal or oil to use in its power stations.

Lateral integration can occur between firms involved in the production of very different goods and services in the same stage of production. This is often called conglomerate merger. Conglomerates often combine with other profitable firms to increase overall profits. Conglomerates can also enjoy significant financial economies of scale, and can often spread fixed administration and day-to-day running costs across their various firms. By producing a wide range of different products the conglomerate is also protected from a downturn in consumer demand for any one of these. For example, General Electric of the US is one of the world's largest multinational conglomerates, with business interests as diverse as finance and insurance, aviation, advanced materials, energy, water and healthcare.

6 THE ROLE OF GOVERNMENT IN AN ECONOMY

Government economic policy in most countries has four main macroeconomic objectives: low and stable inflation in the general level of prices; high and stable employment, and therefore a low level of unemployment; economic growth in the national output and income; a favourable balance of international transactions. There may also be additional objectives aimed at improving economic welfare through poverty reduction and environmental protection.

To achieve its objectives a government will attempt to influence total demand and supply in the national economy (macroeconomy). For example, rising total demand may result in rising price inflation especially if the total output of goods and services is unable to expand at the same rate. Demand-side policies will aim to reduce growth in total demand and, therefore, inflation. A government may contract its own public expenditure or raise taxes to reduce people's disposable incomes to reduce total demand. This is known as contractionary fiscal policy. It may also raise interest rates in the economy using monetary policy to encourage more saving and less borrowing. Higher interest rates will also tend to increase the value of the national currency on the foreign exchange market and will help reduce the price of imported goods and services. However, this may stimulate demand for imports and make the balance of trade less favourable.

An expansionary fiscal policy involves raising public expenditure and/or lowering taxes to boost total demand with the aim of stimulating higher output and employment. However, this may also cause inflationary pressure.

A government may also use supply-side policies to stimulate an increase in total supply in the economy to meet rising total demand. This will help reduce pressure on prices while at the same time boosting output and employment. Supply-side policies aim to remove any barriers to growth in total supply, for example, by reducing the burden of tax on incentives to work and start businesses, using competition policy to control the ability of monopoly firms to restrict market supply, removing burdensome and costly regulations on businesses, tax breaks and subsidies to invest in new research and development, and allowing private sector firms with a profit motive to provide public services more efficiently than the public sector could. This last policy is known as privatization and can involve the sale and break-up of government-owned nationalized industries to private firms.

Taxes are the main way of financing public sector expenditure as well as being a key policy tool for managing the macroeconomy. Direct taxes are levied directly on incomes and wealth. They include income taxes, corporation taxes on company profits, taxes on property and capital gains. Indirect taxes are taxes on goods and services. They include ad valorem taxes, such as VAT, and excise duties, such as those levied on fuel, tobacco and alcohol in many countries. Ad valorem taxes are charged as a percentage of the selling price while excise duties are fixed amounts of tax levied on the amount rather than the value of goods purchased. Most taxes are national but local taxes may also be levied to help finance local government spending.

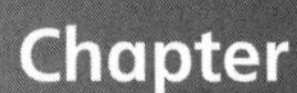

Chapter 14 Government Objectives and Policies

Aims

At the end of this chapter you should be able to:

- describe government as both a producer and consumer of goods and services, and an employer
- describe the aims of **government policy** and assess possible conflicts between government aims
- distinguish between **demand-side policies** that attempt to influence total demand in an economy and **supply-side policies** that try to expand the productive capability of an economy
- describe the instruments of **fiscal policy** and **monetary policy** and analyse the possible impact of changes in these policies on an economy
- describe different supply-side policies, including **tax policy**, **competition policy**, **privatization** and **deregulation**, and explain how changes in these policies can affect output and employment in an economy
- discuss and reach reasoned conclusions on a government's influence on private producers

Section I Macroeconomic objectives

Exercise 1 Economic management

Below are two letters from opposing political party members expressing their concern over the state of the economy. The letters are addressed to their economic advisers asking them to write a report outlining a number of policies each party should pursue to manage the economy.

In groups of three or four pick one of these letters and write a report outlining the economic policies you propose given the view of the economy expressed by your party leader.

When you have finished your report compare your policies to those of the opposition party. Do you agree or disagree?

Government Chambers

Dear Economic Advisers,

As you are aware, we are approaching an election and wish to tell the public about our policies to put the economy right. Please prepare a report on your policy recommendations to combat the following disturbing trends in our economy.

Unemployment is rising due to the low level of spending of consumers and firms. We must try to encourage them to spend more and give them the ability to do so. Without a boost to demand the rate of growth in the economy will be badly affected.

Inflation is also on the up as workers wage demands and import prices continue to rise. Yet there are an increasing number of imports entering our country and this again is putting our workers out of a job. In addition, the high value of our currency is making foreigners less willing to buy our exports. Action must be taken to stop this rot.

I look forward to seeing your report on your policy recommendations.

Your sincerely,

B. Keen

The Right Hon. B. Keen
(Leader of the Intervention Party)

Government Chambers

Dear Economic Advisers,

As the election nears we seek your recommendation for effective policy measures to combat the following disturbing trends in our economy.

Trade unions have managed to price their members out of jobs and unemployment has risen due to their ability to increase their members' wages. This has made the price of our goods appear uncompetative.

Our citizens are now buying more imports and foreigners are reluctant to buy our goods. In addition, the productivity of our workers is low compared to our foreign counterparts who are given tax incentives to make them want to work harder and earn more without their tax burden increasing. However, we feel unemployment in our country is high because it is too easy to live on unemployment benefit.

Economic growth will only take place if the economy becomes more competitive. Lower prices and better levels of quality and service are needed. Trade unions and monopolies, like the nationalized industries, are uncompetitive and hold up wages and prices.

In addition, with a lack of growth in output the fast-increasing supply of money in the economy is simply feeding into prices as banks step up their lending and people are spending borrowed funds. However, we must help firms invest in new technology and reduce their cost of doing so.

I await your report on policy recommendations.

Yours sincerely,

B. Free

The Right Hon. B. Free
(Leader of the Market Party)

Government objectives

Most national governments have four main economic objectives for their national economies. These are:

- to achieve a low and stable rate of inflation in the general level of prices
- to achieve a high and stable level of employment, and therefore a low level of unemployment
- to encourage economic growth in the national output and income
- to encourage trade and secure a favourable balance of international transactions.

A government may also have additional objectives which aim to improve the economic welfare of people in the economy, including:

- to reduce poverty and reduce inequalities in income and wealth
- to reduce pollution and waste, and therefore encourage more sustainable economic growth.

If a government can achieve these aims it will create a favourable economic climate for business and improve people's living standards. For example, when prices are rising rapidly, consumers may not be able to keep up and may have to cut their demand for goods and services. As a result firms may cut back production and their demand for labour. Unemployment and the loss of wage income may cause hardship for many families. In addition, exports from the economy will become less competitive because of their high prices and the balance of trade may become unfavourable and cause the exchange rate to fall.

The causes of and problems associated with price inflation, unemployment, low economic growth and international trade imbalances are discussed in detail in Chapters 16 to 18. However, if governments are to achieve their economic aims they must examine how their economies work and how their policies may affect the behaviour of consumers and firms. This requires the study of macroeconomics and microeconomics.

What is the macroeconomy?

Macroeconomics is the study of how a national economy works with a view to understanding the interaction between growth in national income, employment and price inflation. In contrast, **microeconomics** examines the economic behaviour of individual consumers, households and businesses and how individual markets work.

Clearly, macroeconomics and microeconomics are very closely related. The national or macroeconomy of a country is made up of many different markets for goods and services, and therefore changes in the behaviour of consumers and businesses will affect the overall level of economic growth, employment and price inflation in the macroeconomy.

In a similar way to, say, the market for oil, or the market for insurance services, we can think of a macroeconomy as one big market consisting of the total demand for all goods and services available in the economy, and the total supply of all those goods and services (see Chapter 7). It follows that rising total demand or falling total supply will tend to cause inflation by pushing up market prices in the economy. However, falling total supply will tend to reduce economic growth as less output is produced. Similarly, falling total demand will help lower price inflation but could result in higher unemployment as firms cut back production in response to lower demand for their goods and services.

Total demand and supply in a simple macroeconomy

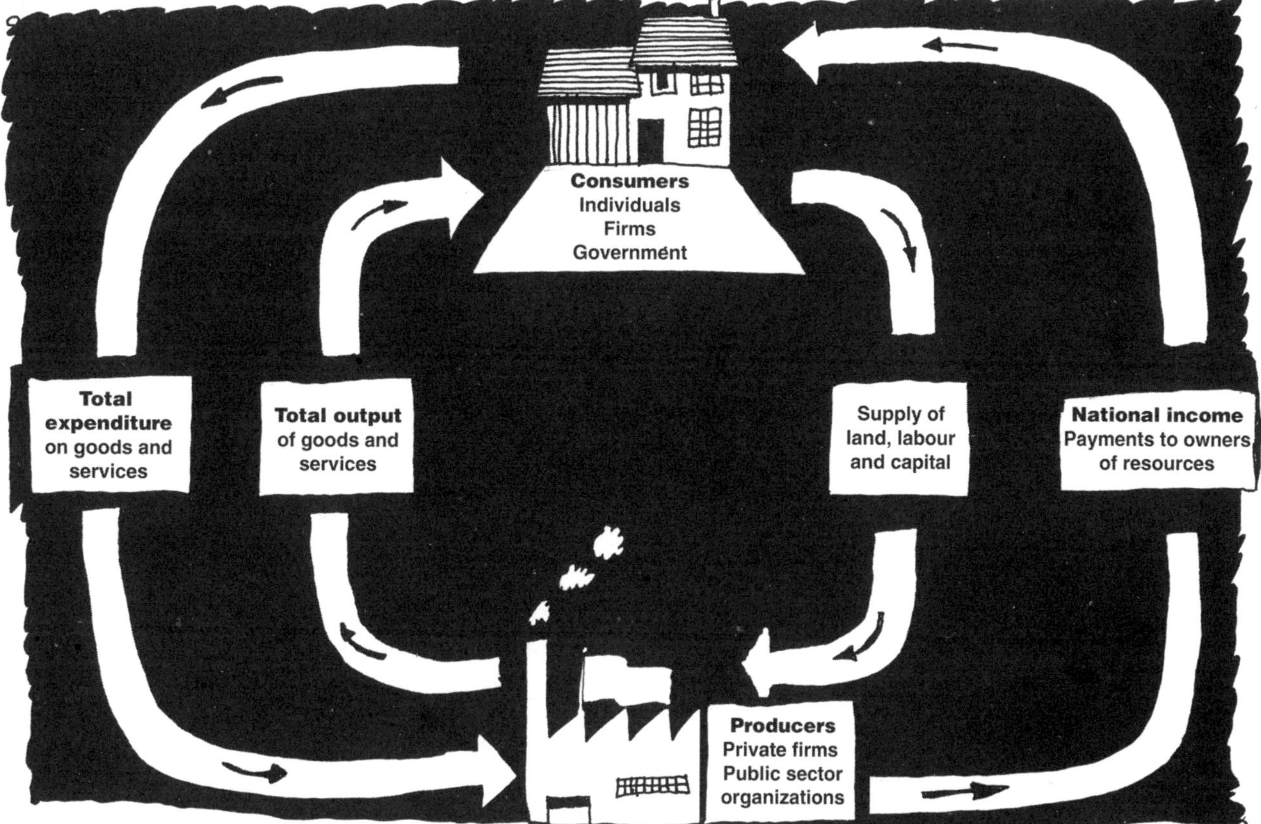

The very simple diagram above represents a macroeconomy. The total output of goods and services is paid for by the total expenditure of consumers, firms and government. Workers and owners of land and capital supply their resources to private firms and public sector organizations to produce those goods and services. In return they are paid income; their total income is therefore the national income (see also Chapter 17).

Total expenditure or **aggregate demand** in a macroeconomy is therefore the sum of:

- consumers' expenditure on goods and services
- investment expenditure by firms on new plant and machinery
- government expenditure on goods and services
- spending from overseas on exports of goods and services from the economy

Total expenditure in an economy is therefore spent on the total or **aggregate supply** of all goods and services in that economy. This is the sum of all goods and services provided by private firms and public sector organizations in the economy (see Chapter 4).

You will note that in a macroeconomy, government is both a producer, organizing land, labour and capital to provide goods and services such as healthcare, defence, roads and street lighting, and also a consumer of goods and services produced by private firms, including computers, paper and furniture for government offices.

Government policy instruments

We now know that a macroeconomy has a demand side and a supply side. A government can therefore design different policies that attempt to control aggregate demand or aggregate supply in order to influence price inflation, employment, economic growth or trade imbalances in the macroeconomy.

Demand-side policies try to influence the level of aggregate demand in an economy using a number of policy instruments. These are:

- the overall level of taxation
- the total amount of government expenditure
- the rate of interest

These demand-side policy instruments can be effective because:

- The amount consumers have to spend on goods and services depends on their level of **disposable income** after income taxes have been deducted.
- Taxes on profits affect the amount of money firms have to spend.
- The interest rate is the cost of borrowing money (see Chapter 6). As interest rates rise consumers may save more and/or borrow less to spend on consumer goods and services. Similarly, firms may cut their borrowing for new investment.
- A rising interest rate may attract more investment to the economy from overseas. This will increase demand for the national currency and push up its exchange rate. A higher exchange rate will reduce the price at which exports are sold overseas and help to boost international demand for them.
- Governments often spend a significant amount of money each year on goods and services. This can include current expenditure on public sector wages and social security benefits, and capital expenditures on investments in new infrastructure such as roads, sea defences and public hospitals (see Chapter 15). Increasing these government expenditures can boost total demand and, therefore, stimulate higher output and employment in an economy.

ECONOMIC GROWTH IS STIMULATED BY COMPETITION - LOWER TAXES, REDUCING THE POWER OF THE UNIONS AND MONOPOLIES, HELPING BUSINESS.
OUTPUT
TIME
ROUND 1
ROUND 2
ROUND 3

Supply-side policies are aimed at increasing economic growth by raising the productive potential of an economy. An increase in the aggregate supply of goods and services will require more labour and other resources to be employed, help reduce pressure on prices, and provide more goods and services available for export.

Supply-side policy instruments are aimed at reducing barriers to increased employment and higher productivity in domestic and international markets, and at creating the right incentives for firms and workers to increase their output. Policy instruments can include:

- **Tax and subsidy incentives:** for example, reducing taxes on wages and profits to increase the reward from work and enterprise, and using subsidies to help firms fund research and development into new, more efficient production processes and products.
- **Educational and training reforms:** to teach existing and future workers new skills to make them more productive at work.
- **Labour market reforms:** such as minimum wage laws to incentivize people into work, and legislation to curb the restrictive practices of some powerful trade unions.
- **Competition policy:** legislation to outlaw unfair and anti-competitive trading by large powerful firms.
- **Removing international trade barriers:** to encourage more free trade between countries.
- **Deregulation:** removing old and unnecessary rules and regulations on business.
- **Privatization:** the transfer of public sector activities to private sector firms.

Section 2 Demand-side policies

What is fiscal policy?

Fiscal policy involves changing the level of public spending and/or taxation to affect the level of aggregate demand.

During an economic downturn or recession increasing the aggregate demand for goods and services can help boost output and reduce unemployment. If private sector spending is too low, then a government can increase its own spending. This can be combined with cuts in taxes on people's incomes and firms' profits. This will give them more money to spend. However, there is a risk they will simply save this extra money or spend it on imported goods and services.

Fiscal policy can be used to influence prices, output and employment if . . .

INFLATION IS CAUSED BY TOO MUCH AGGREGATE DEMAND *Some agree it is also due to increasing costs*

UNEMPLOYMENT IS CAUSED BY LACK OF DEMAND.

Fiscal policy may also be used to redistribute incomes between rich and poor people in an economy. For example, taxes may be raised on people with high incomes and the money used to fund benefits and public services for people on low incomes, or those unable to work because they are old, sick or unemployed (see also Chapter 15).

Increasing government spending and/or cutting taxes to boost aggregate demand, output and employment in an economy is known as **expansionary fiscal policy**. An expansionary fiscal policy usually means running or increasing a **budget deficit**. The budget refers to the amount a government has to spend each year relative to the amount of revenue it raises from taxation. If government spending exceeds tax revenues in any year the budget will be in deficit. An expansionary fiscal policy that increases public expenditure and/or lowers taxes will therefore increase the budget deficit. To pay for the deficit a government will have to borrow money (see Chapter 15).

In contrast, a **contractionary fiscal policy** aims to reduce pressure on prices in the economy by cutting aggregate demand through reductions in government spending and/or by raising taxes. As a result the budget deficit will be cut or may even go into surplus if tax revenues exceed public sector spending.

However, a contractionary or deflationary fiscal policy may reduce employment and growth in real output.

Exercise 2 Can increased public expenditure create jobs?

The diagram below shows how the building of new hospitals by a government can help create jobs and incomes. In your own words explain what is happening in the diagram, and how an expansionary fiscal policy can boost demand, output and jobs in an economy. How might the impact of the policy on the economy and your explanation change if the increase in public expenditure is paid for by **a** raising taxes, or **b** raising interest rates to encourage people and firms to lend the money to the government?

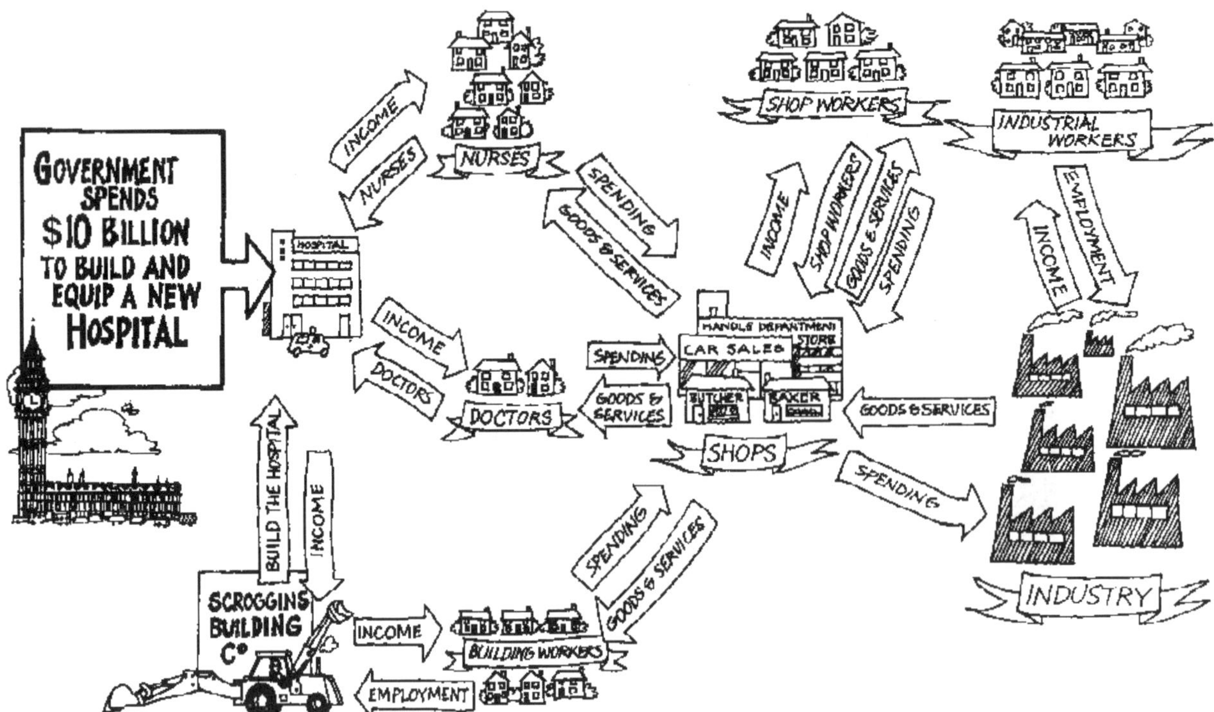

Problems with fiscal policy

The use of fiscal policy to influence the level of demand in an economy has been criticized by many economists. They argue fiscal policy has not worked in the past. Instead inflation and unemployment got much worse in many countries, for example, in the UK during the 1970s and 1980s when the rate of price inflation climbed as high as 25% over a 12-month period and more than 3 million people became unemployed (see Chapter 16).

1 Fiscal policy is cumbersome to use

It is difficult for a government to know precisely when and by how much to expand public spending or cut taxes in a recession, or cut spending and raise taxes during a boom.

Boosting aggregate demand by increasing public spending and/or cutting taxes may cause an economy to 'overheat'. That is, demand may rise too much and too quickly. If the supply of goods and services to buy does not rise as quickly as demand there will be demand-pull inflation. On the other hand, a government may cut spending and raise taxes by too much following a period of high inflation and cause unemployment to rise.

2 Public spending crowds out private spending

To finance an increase in public spending and/or cut in taxation a government may borrow the money from the private sector. The more money the private sector lends to a government the less it has available to spend itself. This is called **crowding out**.

To encourage people, firms and the banking system to lend money to the government it may raise interest rates. However, higher interest rates may discourage other people and firms from borrowing money to spend on consumption and investment. Reducing investment in modern and more productive equipment can reduce economic growth (see Chapter 17).

3 Raising taxes on incomes and profits reduces work incentives, employment and economic growth

If taxes are too high, people and firms may not work as hard. This reduces productivity, output and profits. As productivity falls firms' costs increase and they are less able to compete on product price and quality against more efficient firms overseas. As a result demand for their goods and services may fall and unemployment may rise.

4 Expansionary fiscal policy increases expectations of inflation

As a result, people will push for higher wages to protect them from higher prices in the future. Rising wages increases production costs and reduces the demand for labour (see Chapter 2). This in turn causes cost-push inflation and rising unemployment.

Fiscal rules

In recent years, many national governments have accepted these arguments and no longer use fiscal policy to try to boost aggregate demand in recessions and cut demand in booms. Instead, they have adopted a number of fiscal rules which govern public spending and borrowing. These may include:

- Current and capital expenditures are managed and controlled separately. This is so that the costs and benefits of long-term capital investments (e.g. in new roads, hospitals and school buildings) can be easily identified.
- Government should only borrow money to pay for public investment and not to fund current spending on public sector wages and consumables, such as stationery.
- Public sector debt as a proportion of GDP should be kept at a low and stable level, so that debt interest payments do not become a burden.

Fiscal rules help to keep public spending and borrowing under control so that interest rates and taxes can be kept reasonably low.

What is monetary policy?

Monetary policy refers to actions taken by a government to try to control either the supply of money in the economy or the price of money. Interest rates are the price of borrowing money, or the reward for lending money.

Why use monetary policy?

EXCESSIVE GROWTH IN THE MONEY SUPPLY CAUSES INFLATION.

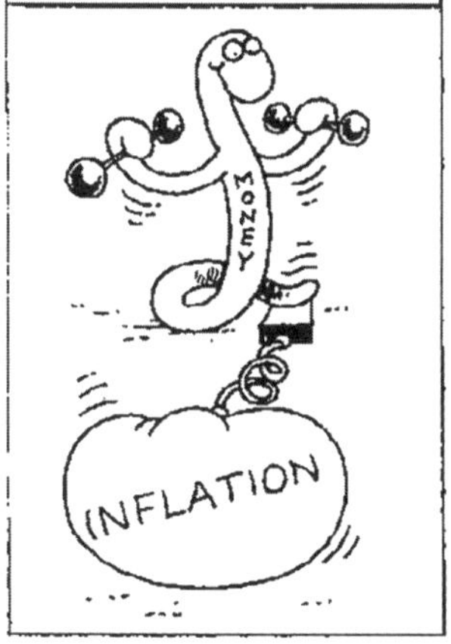

1 Growth in the money supply can cause inflation

If the supply of money increases people will have more to spend on goods and services. If the output of goods and services available to buy does not rise as fast as the money supply, the increase in demand will cause demand-pull inflation (see Chapter 16).

2 Changes in interest rates cause changes in aggregate demand

Interest rates are the price of money. If interest rates fall, people and firms will find it cheaper to borrow, while others will be less willing to save money and will spend it instead. That is, as interest rates fall more people will want to spend more money.

Consumer expenditure and firms' investment in new machines and buildings will rise. Increased aggregate demand helps to create jobs and reduces unemployment. Increased investment helps to create economic growth as firms will be able to produce more output in total.

However, it might be difficult to encourage consumers and firms to spend more by lowering interest rates if there is a deep economic recession when unemployment is rising and incomes are falling. People may not want to get into debt in case they too lose their jobs, and firms may not want to invest in new productive capacity if there is falling demand.

3 Interest rates can be used to affect the exchange rate

Interest rates can be raised to help increase the value of the national currency compared to other countries' currencies (see Chapter 18).

For example, if interest rates are higher in the UK than in other countries, wealthy foreigners will prefer to keep their savings in the UK and so earn high rates of interest on their money. However, to put their money in the UK, overseas residents must buy the UK currency, sterling, with their currencies. This increase in demand for sterling will cause its price, or value, to rise in terms of other currencies.

This can help to reduce imported inflation but will also increase the foreign currency prices of UK exports. As a result, consumer demand overseas for exports of goods and services from the UK may fall.

Monetary policy therefore involves influencing the supply of money and interest rates to control the level of inflation, unemployment, economic growth and the exchange rate.

What to control? Money supply or interest rates?

Control of the money supply can influence the aggregate demand for goods and services and the rate of inflation, while control of interest rates can also influence aggregate demand and the exchange rate for a currency.

It would be very convenient if a government could control both the price of money and the supply of money at the same time. However, it can only control one at a time.

Exercise 3 The market for money

The price of money, or interest rate, like the price of any good is determined by the forces of demand and supply. The equilibrium rate of interest in the economy is where the demand for money and the supply of money are equal.

Note: The demand for money (D_M) shows that as interest rates fall people and firms want more money to spend. As interest rates rise people prefer to save and borrow less, rather than hold money.

Equilibrium in the money market

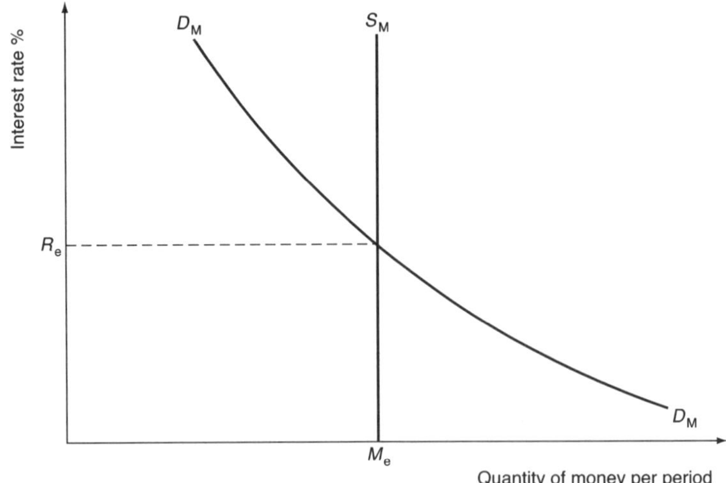

The supply of money (S_M) is assumed to be fixed. That is, the stock or quantity of money cannot change in the time period under consideration. If the interest rate is too high and above its equilibrium rate (R_e) there will be an excess supply of money. Banks and other financial institutions will have a lot of money to lend but not many people will want to borrow it. To encourage them to do so they will lower their interest rates.

1 Explain what will happen if the rate of interest is too low and below its equilibrium (R_e).

2 a Copy the diagram showing the market for money and show the effect of a reduction in the quantity, or supply, of money available in the economy.

b What will happen to the interest rate and why?

3 a Now show on the diagram the effect of an increase in the supply of money.

b What will happen to the interest rate and why?

4 Assume that the government now wishes to reduce the money supply to lower inflation and also wishes to reduce the interest rate to encourage firms to borrow money to invest. Will it be able to do both? Use supply and demand analysis to explain your answer.

If a government wishes to reduce the supply of money it must let interest rates find their own level. If the supply of money falls, banks and other financial institutions find they have less money to lend to people and firms. To try to obtain more money they will increase their interest rates to attract savers to put their money in deposit accounts. On the other hand, if the supply of money rises banks will lower their interest rates to try to encourage people and firms to borrow all this money. That is, a government cannot choose to keep interest rates stable or the same if they want to change the money supply.

If a government wishes to increase interest rates, for example, to protect the value of the pound, then clearly it cannot leave the money supply alone. To engineer a rise in interest rates they must reduce the amount of money banks have to lend.

Therefore, a government must choose which to control: the money supply or interest rates. It cannot control both at the same time. It is usually the job of the central bank in a country to control interest rates on behalf of the national government (see Chapter 6).

A central bank is able to change interest rates in an economy by changing the interest rate it charges on the loans it makes to the banking system when it is short of money. The rate of interest charged on loans from the central bank to other banks is called the **base rate** of interest in the economy. If the central bank wants interest rates to rise it will raise the base rate. If it costs financial institutions more to borrow money, then to cover this cost they will tend to raise the interest rates they charge their customers for loans. In this way an increase in base rate causes a general rise in interest rates throughout the economy.

If a central bank wants to reduce interest rates it will lower the base rate on loans to the banking system. As the cost of borrowing from the central bank falls, financial institutions can lower their interest rates.

Controlling the money supply

In most countries deposits of money in banks and other financial institutions make up the bulk of the money supply. For example, in the UK in 2006 only 3.4% of the money supply was notes and coins (see Chapter 2). Therefore, when a government attempts to control the supply of money it will concentrate on the creation of bank deposits rather than on the amount of notes and coins in circulation.

1 Open market operations

These refer to the borrowing and repayment of short-term public sector debt by private sector firms and individuals.

For example, in the UK the Bank of England can borrow money for short periods of time from the private sector by selling them 'promises to pay' called Treasury Bills. These are normally repaid after 3 months with a rate of interest.

For example, Mrs Save buys a £100 000 treasury bill from the Bank of England. It allows her to pay £95 000 for the bill with the promise to repay her the full £100 000 (that is, the £95 000 loan plus £5 000 interest) after 3 months. Mrs Save pays for the bill with a £95 000 cheque drawn on her personal account. Her bank must now pay the government this sum of money. As a result, government borrowing has reduced banks' deposits of money. With less money available banks cannot lend out as much money as before.

Selling short-term debt to the private sector, therefore, reduces the supply of money. Selling more short-term debt than a government needs to cover a budget deficit is called overfunding and can help reduce bank deposits and the supply of money even further. To make short-term debt attractive to buy, a government will often raise the interest rate they pay.

2 Special deposits

A central bank can reduce the money supply by calling for special deposits. The central bank can order commercial banks to deposit money with it for a certain period of time. Calling in special deposits automatically reduces the amount of money that the banks have available to lend to their customers.

3 Funding

From the above we know that a government can borrow money from the private sector to reduce the supply of money by selling short-term debt. However, in the same way a government can also sell long-term debt that it does not have to repay so soon (see Chapter 6). Long-term government securities or bonds may only mature with interest after as much as 25 years or more. In this way, the government can fund its expenditure and help keep down growth in the money supply over a longer period of time.

Exercise 4 A walk on the supply side

The articles below refer to some different supply-side policies. What are they and how are they intended to boost output and employment?

Milk market deregulation benefits Australian consumer

Six months after the deregulation of Australia's dairy industry, milk prices have fallen by as much as 40 cents a litre with the likelihood of further drops, said the Australian Competition and Consumer Commission (ACCC) this week.

Adapted from *foodnavigator.com* 11.4.2001

New tax incentives finally approved

After months of back and forth, The European Commission has finally approved the UK's new film industry tax incentives.

The new tax credit is expected to take effect from January 1st, and will benefit film-makers investing at least 25% of their budget in the UK.

Adapted from *Time out* 23.11.2006

The Pakistan Telecommunications Authority today found Mobilink, the country's leading cellular company, guilty of anti-competitive practices by overcharging its 'valued subscribers' for making calls to other cellular operators. The PTA has ordered Mobilink to make revisions to its tariffs.

From *www.thenews.com.pk*, 12.6.2006

UK plans skills academies to close productivity gap

Workers are to be offered free vocational training as part of a huge government drive to tackle the chronic lack of basic skills among millions of adults, ministers are set to announce today.

The Guardian, 22.3.2005

Romania claims privatization in the energy sector was a step forward towards a healthy economy. New investors entering the energy market will bring substantial benefits to companies and the competition environment.

Trade unions protest against anti-strike laws

Boosting the supply side of a macroeconomy can help raise output, employment and growth, reduce inflationary pressures and stimulate the supply of exports, thereby helping a government to move closer to achieving its macroeconomic objectives.

Supply-side policy instruments aim to stimulate incentives to work and increase output, and remove barriers that may restrict competition, innovation and higher levels of productivity.

Tax incentives

High rates of tax on incomes may reduce incentives to work hard or even seek paid employment. Similarly, high rates of tax on profits can reduce entrepreneurs' incentives to start new businesses, and invest in new products and production methods if additional profits are highly taxed. Cutting taxes on incomes and profits can therefore have a direct impact on the productive efforts of workers and firms. Tax relief may also be given to firms investing significantly in building new plants and equipment, and in new technologies.

Selective subsidies

Subsidies are grants of money provided by a government often to selected business organizations to stimulate or protect productive activity (see Chapter 7). They can be used to help new businesses that might otherwise lack the finance they need to start up, and to reduce the cost of investing in research and development by existing firms in new production methods, machines, materials and products. Technological advance can increase the efficiency of production, lower costs and create new markets for new products.

Improving education and training

In order for firms to be successful when competing in international markets it is essential they have access to a highly trained and skilled workforce. Skill needs in industry are rising as the pace of change in competition and technology increases. A well-educated and trained workforce can raise labour productivity and will be better able to adapt to new production methods and technologies. A government can assist firms by helping them design and finance training programmes, funding universities and providing access for more people to attend colleges and higher education.

Labour market reforms

Legislation can be used to curb the power of trade unions to call strikes and other disruptive industrial actions (see Chapter 5). Some powerful unions may also use their power to force up the wages of members, which may simply reduce the demand for labour and raise unemployment. They may also resist attempts to introduce new, more efficient production and working methods. Reforms have often brought protest from trade unions.

A number of governments have also introduced minimum wage laws to protect low-paid workers from being exploited by some employers, and also to encourage more people into work (see Chapter 12). In contrast, employers often argue that raising minimum wages will reduce the demand for labour.

High social security benefits may also discourage some people from seeking paid employment. In some countries, benefits paid to the unemployed have therefore been lowered, are time limited and/or linked to evidence a person is actively seeking work in order to encourage them back into paid employment and not to rely on benefit payments. This, however, may conflict with a government's aims to reduce hardship and poverty which may often be the result of long periods of unemployment.

Competition policy

Some firms may be large enough to exercise control over the supply of a particular good or service to a market. They may use this power to restrict competition, charge consumers high prices and reduce the quality of products. Competition policy concerns the removal of such barriers to help stimulate competition, expand output and lower prices.

Many governments around the world have introduced laws and regulations to control monopolies that act against the public interest (see Chapter 8). Monopolies that are found to be anti-competitive and exploiting consumers may be fined or even forced to break up into smaller firms.

Removing international trade barriers

In much the same way as a monopoly, a national government may seek to protect its domestic firms and employment from competition from overseas by using barriers against free trade (see Chapter 22). Some goods and services may be produced much more efficiently and at a far lower cost by firms overseas. However, a government may tax imports or simply restrict their entry into a country to protect their national firms producing the same goods and services even if they do so at a higher cost. By removing these barriers to trade, firms in other countries can expand by selling to many more consumers all over the world, and similarly those countries which restricted free trade can then enjoy lower-priced goods and services, and use their own resources more efficiently to produce others.

Deregulation

Deregulation involves removing or simplifying old, unnecessary or over-complex rules and regulations on what businesses can or cannot do. For example, reforms might include removing restrictions on opening hours and Sunday shopping, reducing product information and labelling requirements, reducing the burden of health and safety inspections and much more. The removal of such restrictions should help cut business costs, increase competition and help firms increase output and lower prices.

Privatization

Privatization involves the transfer or sale of public sector activities to the private sector. It is argued that private sector firms will run these activities more efficiently because they have a profit motive to do so, and therefore both consumers and the taxpayer will benefit. We will consider privatization in more detail in the next section because it has become an important supply-side policy in many developed and developing countries, especially as many former planned economies such as China and Russia transform their economies into market economies (see Chapter 3).

Section 4 Privatization

Public ownership

In many countries, entire industries are owned and controlled by the government. They may include public utilities such as electricity and water supplies, bus and train services, the heath service, postal services, or even the national airline. Industries owned and controlled by government are called **nationalized industries** (see Chapter 4).

Why were industries nationalized?

Governments have in the past taken into public sector ownership entire industries for the following reasons:

- **To control natural monopolies**

In some industries firms need to grow very large in order to take full advantage of the cost savings large-scale production can bring (see Chapter 13). However, this can result in one very large firm becoming the only supplier of a product to a market and, if unchecked, it could take advantage of this market power to charge high prices to consumers. To prevent this, natural monopoly providers of gas, water, electricity and railway supply networks are in some countries controlled by government.

- **For safety**

Some industries, such as nuclear energy, are thought to be too dangerous to be controlled by private entrepreneurs.

- **To protect employment**

Some firms were nationalized because they faced closure as private sector loss-making organizations. For example, in 1975 the UK government rescued British Leyland to protect the jobs of car workers.

- **To maintain a public service**

Nationalized industries can provide services even if they make a loss, such as postal deliveries and rail services in rural areas. Private firms seeking to make profit would not operate these services.

What is privatization?

Privatization involves private sector firms taking over public sector activities in the following ways:

- **The sale of public sector assets**

This involves a government selling shares in the ownership of government-owned industries to private firms and individuals. For example, in 1986 the UK government sold British Gas for £6 billion. The gas network and all gas suppliers in the UK are now all private firms.

- **Joint ventures with private with firms**

This can involve public sector organizations and private firms working together to supply a public service. For example, in the UK the London underground train service is still government-owned but services are operated in 'public-private partnership' with private train operators.

- **Contracting out**

This involves a government awarding contracts to private firms to provide services it formerly provided. For example, this may include a private firm collecting household refuse, road sweeping, the management and upkeep of public parks, catering services in public schools and hospitals, parking enforcement and even running prisons.

- **Removing barriers to competition**

By allowing private firms to compete with public sector organizations, for example, in the provision of postal services and bus services.

Exercise 5 Sold down the river?

Read the article about the privatization of water and sewer systems on the next page.

1. What is privatization?
2. How is the town of Lee planning to privatize its water and sewer systems?
3. What economic arguments could you use for and against the privatization of Lee's water and sewer systems?
4. What are the potential implications and conflicts arising from the privatization policy for the employees, local residents and local taxpayers?
5. Investigate examples of privatization in your own country. What arguments have different groups of people used for and against these privatizations? What impact, if any, has privatization had on you and your family?

Lee plans meeting on water-sewer privatization

There is to be a special informational meeting on the potential privatization of the town's sewer and water systems. Privatization means that the town would hire an independent company to take over the operation of its sewer and water systems.

The company would be under contract to the town of Lee, and would run the two systems under one company umbrella. The principal reason for such a move would be to save money. At this point, most town officials concede that it is unclear whether privatizing the sewer and water operation would be a money-saver. A consulting engineer would, in theory, be able to make that assessment.

Many residents fear the principal task of the private sector firm would be making money for itself and have asked town officials how they would be able to ensure consistent quality service from a profit-making entity.

But perhaps the most controversial aspect of the plan is that the present workforce would all have to reapply for their jobs. Many workers have argued that there was no way to ensure they would get the same health and retirement benefits they currently do as public employees of Lee. In addition, the for-profit entity would not be bound to retain the work force presently under contract to the town.

Adapted from the *Berkshire Eagle*,6.3.2004

The main economic arguments used in favour of privatization concern efficiency and competition. Unlike the public sector, private firms aim to make profits and they do this by using resources more efficiently and reducing costs. Secondly, nationalized industries are large monopolies which means there is no competition to supply consumers. Privatization opens up the market to new competition and consumers will benefit from firms competing with each other to supply them with new and better quality products at lower prices. However, others argue that because privatized firms want to make profits the prices they charge will be higher and their quality of service lower. They will also cut their costs by laying off workers, which conflicts with aims to reduce unemployment.

Those in support of privatization argue:

- If these industries are forced to compete for profit they will become more competitive, improve their product quality, and lower prices.
- Whereas there used to be only one nationalized supplier, consumers will be able to choose from a wide variety of goods and services from different producers. For example, there are now many rival suppliers of communication services to British Telecom.
- The sale of shares in these industries raises revenue for a government which can be used to lower taxes.
- Private individuals can own shares in these organizations and vote on how they should be run.

Those against privatization argue:

- Many privatized industries still dominate the markets they supply and have been able to raise their prices and cut services. For example, private rail and water companies are local monopoly suppliers.
- Private sector organizations will not protect public services. For example, many fear private sector firms providing railway services will cut services and raise fares in the long run. Complaints about rail services are rising all the time.
- Most of the shares in privatized organizations have been bought by large financial organizations such as banks and insurance companies who are interested only in making big profits.

Policy conflicts

The various aims of governments might be difficult to achieve all at once. In some cases policy aims might conflict. For example, boosting aggregate demand during an economic recession might help raise output and employment in an economy but may also increase demand for imports and make the trade balance less favourable. Increasing demand may also increase pressure on prices to rise while higher levels of output may create more pollution and waste (see also Chapters 17 and 22).

Similarly, raising taxes or interest rates, and cutting public expenditure to reduce price inflation by lowering total demand, may result in lower output and more unemployment. The impact of higher taxes and lower government spending may also fall heavily on people on lower incomes in an economy, especially if social security benefits from government are cut back.

In the same way, policies that directly aim to redistribute income may also conflict between different groups in society. For example, taxes on high-income households may be raised and the tax revenues used to pay for increased benefits to very low-income families. Alternatively, taxes on business profits could be raised but this may conflict with an aim of encouraging more people to start their own business and the aim of attracting overseas firms to locate in the economy.

However, not all economists accept there will always be trade-offs between government objectives. That is, they see no reason why low taxes, low rates of unemployment and high economic growth can only be achieved at the expense of achieving low price inflation, a favourable international trade balance and reduced poverty in society. Government policy, they argue, can and should be designed to achieve all these aims at the same time.

Their argument runs as follows. If price inflation can be reduced to a low and stable rate then low unemployment, faster economic growth and a favourable balance of payments will follow. Rising national income and employment also means people will become better off thereby helping to reduce poverty. Rising incomes will also mean tax revenues collected by the government from wages and profits will be increasing and can be used to fund higher social security payments, investments in new infrastructure such as roads and schools, and other public expenditures that benefit the economy.

Reducing inflation will help make domestically produced goods and services more competitive. Demand for them will tend to rise at home and overseas. This will help to improve the balance of trade. Firms will respond by increasing output and their demand for labour. Firms will also want to invest in new machinery and production facilities as the economy expands. This is because they will be more confident that their investments will make a good return, and any money they may have borrowed to fund them can be repaid from increased revenues. Further, if people expect price inflation to remain low and stable then they will not push for such high wage rises in future that would otherwise increase production costs and reduce profits.

Exercise 6 Conflicts

Look at the graphs on the next page of the US macroeconomy between 1985 and 2005.

1 How successful do you think US governments have been over time in achieving the four main macroeconomic aims?

2 What evidence is there, if any, from the US economic experience to support the view that economic policy aims may conflict?

3 Compare and contrast the US economic experience with that of your own country over the same period. How successful do you think the national government in your country has been in achieving its macroeconomic aims, and why?

US Economic growth (% annual change in read GDP)

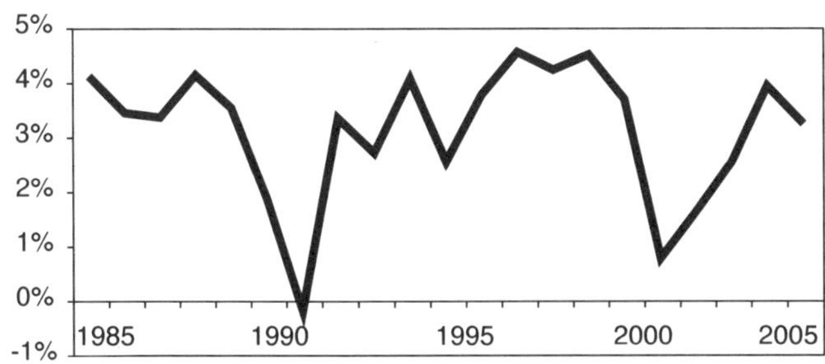

US Inflation (% annual change in CPI)

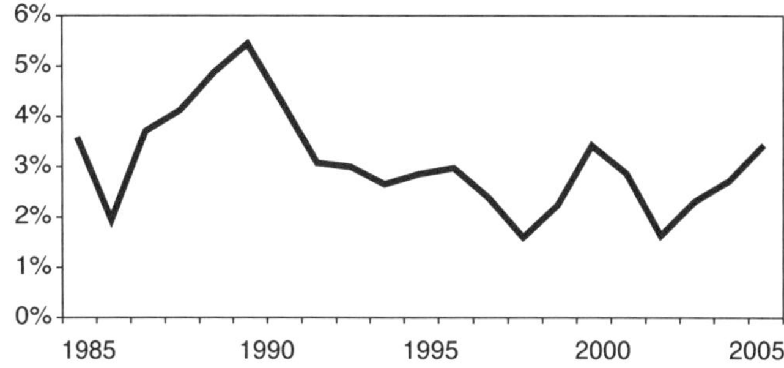

US Balance of trade ($ billion)

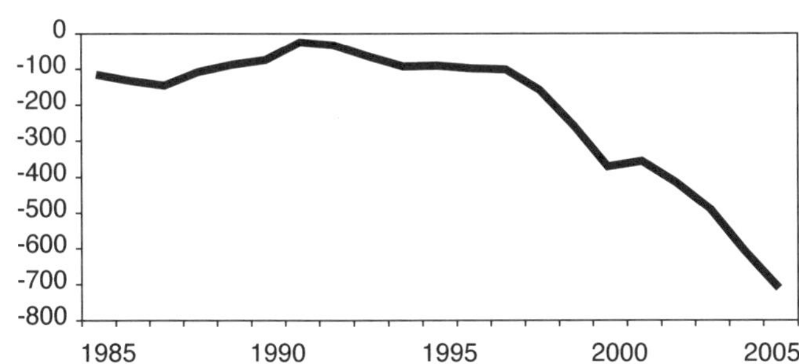

US Unemployment rate, %

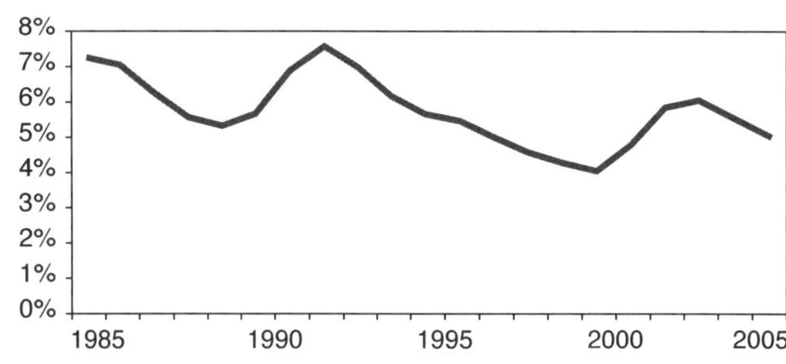

Key words

In your own words write down what you understand by the following key words and terms in this chapter.

Macroeconomics	**Disposable income**	**Budget deficit**
Microeconomics	**Fiscal policy**	**Crowding out**
Aggregate demand	**Monetary policy**	**Base rate of interest**
Aggregate supply	**Deregulation**	**Nationalized industries**
Demand-side policies	**Competition policy**	**Privatization**
Supply-side policies		

Learn more about government economic policies at the following websites:

- *www.answers.com/topic/fiscal-policy*
- *www.answers.com/topic/monetary-policy*
- *www.bized.co.uk/learn/economics/govpol/macrotargets/index.htm*
- *www.bized.co.uk/virtual/economy/policy/advisors/fiscal.htm*
- *www.bized.co.uk/virtual/economy/policy/advisors/monetary.htm*
- *www.tutor2u.net/economics/content/topics/macroeconomy/macroeconomics.htm*
- *www.tutor2u.net/economics/content/topics/supplyside/labour_policies.htm*
- *www.tutor2u.net/economics/content/topics/supplyside/product_markets.htm*
- *www.tutor2u.net/economics/flashdecks/europe/competition_policy/competition_policy.swf*
- *en.wikipedia.org/wiki/Monetary_policy*
- *rru.worldbank.org/privatization/*
- *www.privatizationlink.com/topic/factsheet.cfm*

Chapter 15 Public Sector Finance

Aims

At the end of this chapter you should be able to:

- describe types of national and local **taxation**
- assess the impact and **incidence** of taxation
- understand the purposes of taxation
- identify **direct taxes** and **indirect taxes**
- distinguish between **progressive** and **regressive** forms of taxation
- analyse the meaning and importance of **public sector borrowing** and **national debt**

Section I

Public expenditure

The public sector in an economy delivers goods and services provided by government, whether by the national or central government, or regional or local/municipal government. It consists of the offices, departments and agencies of the national, regional and/or local governments, and public corporations that run nationalized industries (see Chapter 4).

Some examples of Central Government services	Some examples of Local Government services
Major road building and maintenance	Street lighting
Tax assessment and collection	Parking enforcement
Armed services	Refuse collection
Social security system	Parks
Collection of economic and social statistics	Schools
Consumer protection	Local road building and maintenance
Immigration services	Social housing
Law and order	Town planning
Nationalized industries	Fire services

The public sector in many countries is responsible for the employment of often many thousands of people and spending large amounts of money on the provision of goods and services, and on capital investments. To finance all this, the public sector in an economy raises revenues from taxes and other sources.

Current and capital expenditures

Public sector spending, or **public expenditure**, can be divided up into a number of different categories.

One method is to distinguish between **current expenditure** and **capital expenditure**. Current expenditure covers public sector workers' wages and salaries, social security benefits paid to the unemployed and those on low incomes, and spending on consumable goods such as medicines for public healthcare services, and paper, pens and electric power supplies for government offices. That is, current expenditure tends to cover the day-to-day running expenses of the public sector. In contrast, capital expenditures involve government investments in new roads, school buildings, sea defences and military defence equipment.

Transfer payments

Another way is to distinguish between public expenditure to purchase goods and services that contribute to the productivity of the public sector and the economy, and **transfer payments** to other people.

A large amount of public expenditure in many countries is not spent by government, but is given to people in the form of cash benefits such as pensions, unemployment insurance and other social security payments. The people who receive these benefits can use the money to buy the goods and services they need and want. They are called transfer payments because a government is simply transferring money collected through taxes from people in work to those who are not able to be productive.

Reasons for public spending

There are a number of reasons why governments spend money.

1 To provide public goods

You may remember from Chapter 2 that some goods, known as public goods, cannot be provided profitably by private firms. For example, private firms would find it difficult to collect revenue from people in payments for street lighting, a police force or national defence system. This is because once they have been provided it is difficult to exclude people from benefiting from these public goods simply because they haven't paid directly for the amount they have used. These public goods are nevertheless of great value to people and an economy, and so the public sector provides them.

2 To provide merit goods

Governments also spend money on the provision of merit goods. These are goods or services a government thinks everyone should benefit from, whether they can afford to pay for them or not. Such merit goods can include state schools and a public healthcare service. An economy will benefit from an educated and healthy workforce. If people did have to pay for them directly then they might not consume as much as they should.

3 To reduce inequalities and help vulnerable people

People on very low incomes, including elderly and disabled people, the unemployed and homeless, single-parent families and the long-term sick, often need help with living expenses, or finding and affording accommodation. The public sector can provide a safety net for poor and vulnerable people through the provision of social security benefits, low-cost social housing, free healthcare, free bus passes and other welfare benefits.

4 To invest in the economic infrastructure

A modern economy needs a modern infrastructure such as roads and railways, public buildings, parks, waterways, and much more. The investment required to provide these can cost many billions of dollars, but they benefit both individuals and firms and help economic growth (see Chapter 17).

5 To support agriculture and industry

Grants and subsidies are often paid to farmers and owners of firms to help them increase production and employment, invest in new plant and machinery, and pay for new research and development. This can help to boost output and economic growth in an economy (see Chapter 17). However, other countries might argue that such subsidies are unfair and that they protect inefficient domestic firms from products imported from more efficient producers overseas (see Chapter 22).

6 To control the macroeconomy

The public sector in many countries is a very big spender, raising large amounts of money through taxation to pay for it all. A change in the amount of public expenditure or taxation can therefore have a big effect on the total level of demand in an economy and therefore on the level of output, employment, prices and national income. A government can therefore use its spending and taxation policies to help it achieve its macroeconomic objectives. This is called **fiscal policy** (see Chapter 14).

7 To give overseas aid

Some public spending may be paid overseas to help countries in need because they have suffered wars or natural disasters such as droughts, earthquakes and tsunamis. Overseas aid can help provide food and medicine and pay for new roads and schools (see Chapter 22).

Exercise 1 Current or capital?

Look at the jumble of goods and services provided or paid for by public expenditure. They relate to the provision of a public health service and public, or state, education.

Nurses' wages	Laboratories	Swimming pool
Uniforms	Beds	Sports equipment
X-ray equipment	Pens	Photocopy paper
Medicines	Computers	Teachers' salaries
Heating	Exercise books	Knives
Electric power	New school buildings	Ambulances
Heart monitors	Kidney machines	Pens
Breathing equipment	Bandages	New hospital wing

1. Rearrange the jumble into two lists: (a) those goods and services you think would be needed to provide a public health service and (b) those you would expect are required to run a school and teach students. Some items may appear in both your lists.
2. Now for each list identify those items or services that will be paid for by current expenditure and those that will be classified as capital expenditure.

Some trends in public expenditure

Public expenditure has increased in many countries over time, both in total and as a proportion of total spending in those economies as they have grown over time and become more complex economic and trading systems.

For example, the graph below shows that public expenditure increased in the UK from around 18 per cent of total expenditure in 1900 as measured by GDP, to over 40 per cent in 2005. That is, the UK public sector spent around 40 pence in every £1 in the UK that year. Of this, 92 per cent was for current expenditures on goods and services, social security payments and other transfer payments. The remaining 8 per cent was capital expenditure. The graph clearly shows UK public spending has remained near to or above 40 per cent of GDP since 1970.

Public expenditure as percentage of GDP, UK 1990–2005

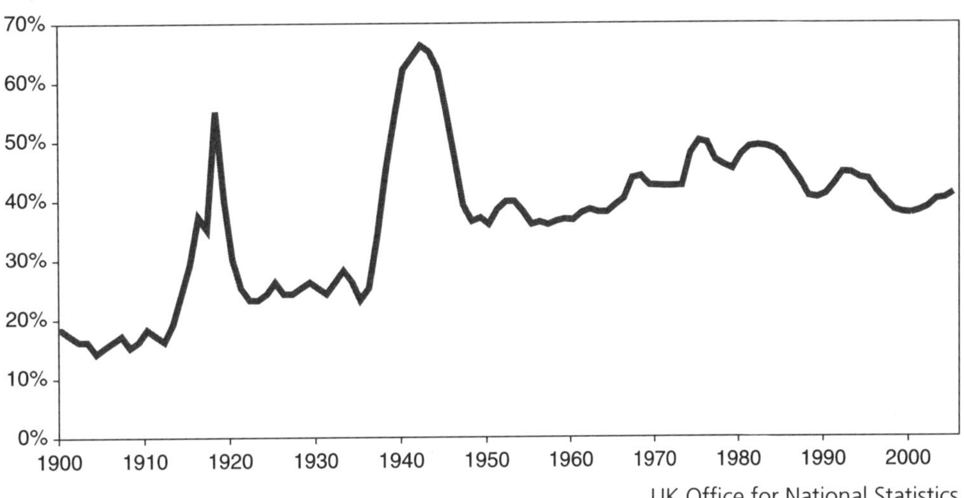

UK Office for National Statistics

Public expenditure of over 40 per cent of GDP may seem on high side but this is about average for the 30 major economies that are members of the Organization for Economic Cooperation and Development (OECD). However, this is relatively low when compared to Belgium, Denmark, Finland, France and Sweden where public sector spending accounted for over 50 per cent of their GDPs in 2006.

Public expenditure as percentage of GDP, OECD average 1988–2006

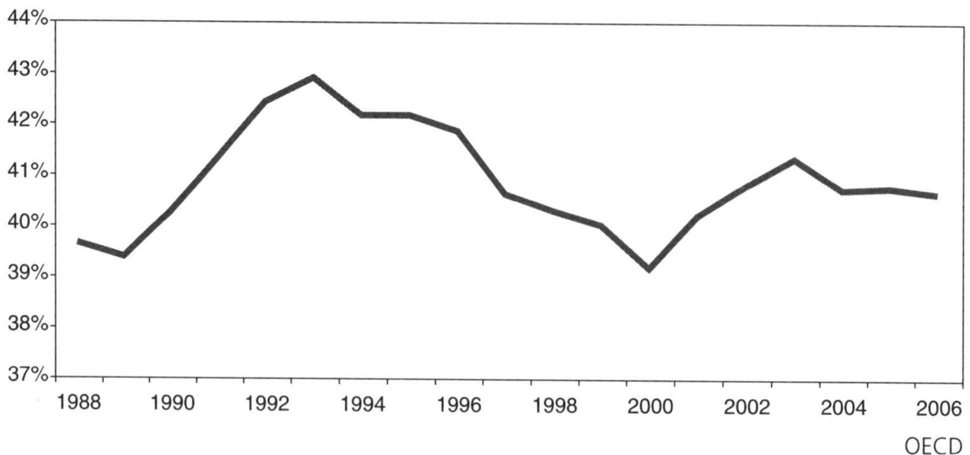

OECD

Section 2 Financing public expenditure

Sources of revenue

The public sector in an economy raises revenue to pay for its public expenditure in a number of ways:

- Borrowing money from the general public.
- Interest payments on loans of money made to individuals and private sector firms, and overseas governments.
- Rent from publicly owned buildings and land, and any admission charges, for example, from museums and national monuments.
- Revenues from government agencies and public corporations that sell goods or services (see Chapter 4).
- Proceeds from the sale (or privatization) of government-owned industries and other publicly owned assets, such as land and public buildings (see Chapter 14).
- Taxes on incomes, wealth and expenditures.

Tax burden

By far the most revenue is raised from taxation. In some countries governments tax as much as half of all their national income or GDP. For example, in 2005 Sweden taxed over 51 per cent of its national income. In contrast, the total tax take from GDP in Mexico in the same year was just 19 per cent.

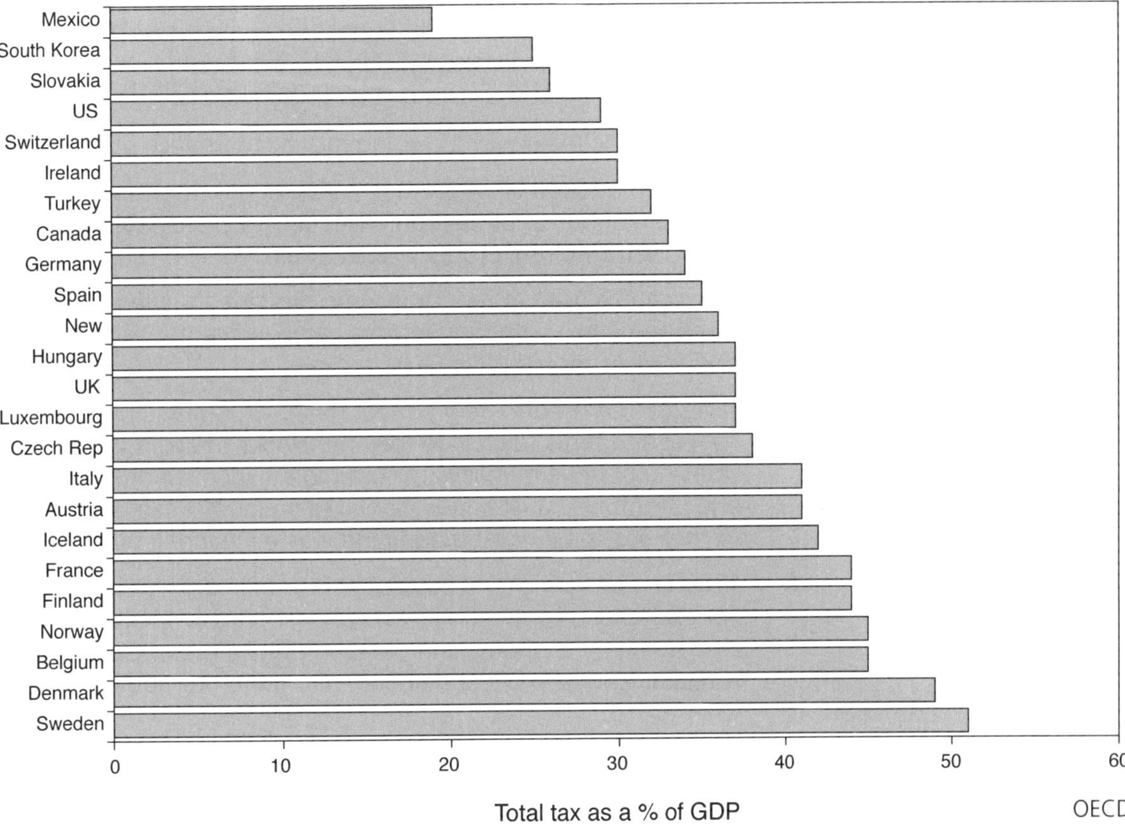

The proportion of tax taken from national income in a country measures the total **tax burden** in that national economy. Individuals and firms also have personal or corporate tax burdens measured by the amount of tax they each have to pay as a proportion of their incomes. Tax burdens can vary greatly between different individuals and firms depending on the design of the tax system in a country (see section 3).

Tax evasion and avoidance

Taxes are compulsory payments backed by laws. Non-payment of tax or tax evasion is a punishable offence.

Some taxes can, however, be avoided legally. For example, taxes on cars or petroleum can be avoided by not owning or driving a car. Wealthy people, pop stars, and so on, can also avoid tax in one country by moving their wealth to a country with low tax rates.

Exercise 2 Why have taxes?

In pairs, read the statements below and then write down as many reasons as you can think of for government taxes.

'British Government needs to raise £2 billion for new motorway.'

'Smoking and alcoholism cause record number of deaths.'

'The rich are getting richer and the poor are getting poorer.'

'Imports of foreign electrical goods are causing rising unemployment among workers in domestic electrical industries.'

'Record spending boom causes prices to rise.'

'Car users do not realise the external costs of their actions. Increased car use is causing congestion and air pollution.'

What are taxes for?

Many taxes were first introduced many hundreds of years ago by kings or governments to pay for wars. For example, the US federal government in 1862 introduced an income tax for the first time to pay for the Civil War. It was 3 per cent of incomes above $600, rising to 5% for incomes above $10 000. Today, the reasons for taxes are far more complex:

1. Taxes are the main way of raising money to finance public sector spending.
2. Taxes can be used to discourage consumption, for example by imposing tariffs on imported goods to protect domestic firms from overseas competition, or by raising the price of harmful products such as alcohol and tobacco.
3. Taxes can be used to reduce incomes and wealth inequalities. Revenues from high taxes on people with high incomes or significant wealth can be used to fund benefits and services for people on low incomes.
4. Taxes can be used to help protect the environment. They are used to encourage people and firms to change their behaviour to avoid the tax. For example, raising taxes on petroleum makes car use more expensive and so may help to cut car use and harmful exhaust emissions. Taxes on landfill can encourage firms to recycle more of their waste by making dumping waste in landfill sites more expensive.
5. Taxes can be varied by a government to help achieve its macroeconomic objectives. For example, a contractionary fiscal policy involves raising taxes to reduce total demand in an economy and demand-pull inflation. Cutting taxes during an economic recession can help boost demand, and therefore output and employment (see Chapter 14).

Exercise 3

When is a tax a good tax?

Look at the proposed imaginary tax changes below. Do you think they are good or bad changes from the point of view of:

- **a** The tax-payer
- **b** The government
- **c** The whole economy?

Height tax to be introduced on all people under 5 feet and over 6 feet tall, says Minister of Finance, who is 5 feet 6 inches, in his Budget speech.

Overtime to be taxed at 95 per cent of earnings.

Pay-as-you-earn income tax to be abolished. Tax-payers will receive bills every two years.

New tax office set up at an annual cost of $15 million to administer tax on pet cats. The government expects its cat tax to raise $7 million in revenue each year.

Tax system to be simplified! All taxes to be abolished and to be replaced by equal tax payment of $2 000 per person per year over the age of 18 years.

What is a good tax?

A good tax must possess the following qualities:

1 **Fairness** Taxes must be fair. If most people think that a tax is unfair, they are unlikely to pay it. For example a tax based on height would be very unfair.

2 **Must not discourage people from working** A tax should not discourage people from working. If taxes are too high, then people may decide that it is not worth trying to earn more.

3 **Cheap to collect** There is little point introducing a tax if it costs more money to collect than it earns in revenue for a government. For example, a tax costing $10 million to collect but only bringing in $3 million in revenue would be pointless and a waste of public money.

4 **Convenience** Imagine how inconvenient it would be if tax-payers were expected to work out their own tax bills and then had to keep enough money back to pay them once every two years. People who are not very good at managing their own money would find themselves in trouble when called to pay their taxes. For this reason it is important that taxes are easy to pay and easy to understand. A goverment will also need to raise tax revenues regularly to pay for its expenditures.

Exercise 4 Window tax: Good or bad?

Government proposes new tax

Only a month after the last budget, the Government last night announced plans to once again broaden the existing tax base in the economy. Such plans include imposing a flat rate tax on the number and size of windows in a property.

Speaking at a meeting of industrialists, the Finance Minister told delegates that the issue of reducing the amount of Government borrowing must not be 'glazed over' and that if the public wished for public sector provision to remain at a high level then they must be prepared to provide the necessary funds.

Raising taxes on income and expenditure would only further reduce demand and output in the economy as work incentives and consumption plans would be damaged.

Businessmen speculating that double glazed windows may be subject to a higher rate of tax argued that such a move may seriously damage this particular growth area. The Government was, however, quick to reject such fears.

A Green paper looking into the feasibility of the tax should be ready in time for next year's budget which already promises to provide the economy with a major tax shake up.

Divide into groups of three or four. Imagine you have been appointed to research the feasibility of the proposed window tax for the Green Report. You are to write a report assessing the tax on the following grounds:

a Fairness.

b The effect on consumption expenditure, output and employment.

c The cost of collection.

d The ease with which the tax payable can be calculated.

Your completed reports can form the basis of a class discussion. (You may be surprised to know that a window tax did exist in the UK many years ago but has long since been abolished).

Section 3 Tax systems

Progressive, regressive or proportional?

All of the taxes in a country are together called the **tax system**. Governments must decide whether they want a **progressive, regressive** or **proportional** tax system. Each type of system will affect people differently.

A progressive tax system is one where the proportion of income taken in taxation rises as incomes rise. This means better-off people pay a higher proportion of their incomes in taxes than poorer people. Governments use progressive taxation because they feel that people on higher incomes can afford to pay a larger proportion of their incomes in tax.

An example of a progressive tax system

Annual income	% tax paid	$ tax paid
$20 000	20	4 000
$50 000	40	20 000
$80 000	60	48 000

A regressive tax system takes a smaller proportion of income in tax as income rises. It may be considered unfair to people on low incomes because a much larger fraction of their income is taken as tax.

An example of a regressive tax system

Annual income	% tax paid	$ tax paid
$20 000	50	10 000
$50 000	40	20 000
$80 000	30	24 000

A proportional tax is one where the proportion of income taken in tax is the same whatever the level of income. For example, a tax of 20% on all incomes of all tax-payers is an example of a proportional tax.

Exercise 5 Tax systems

Look at the following graph.

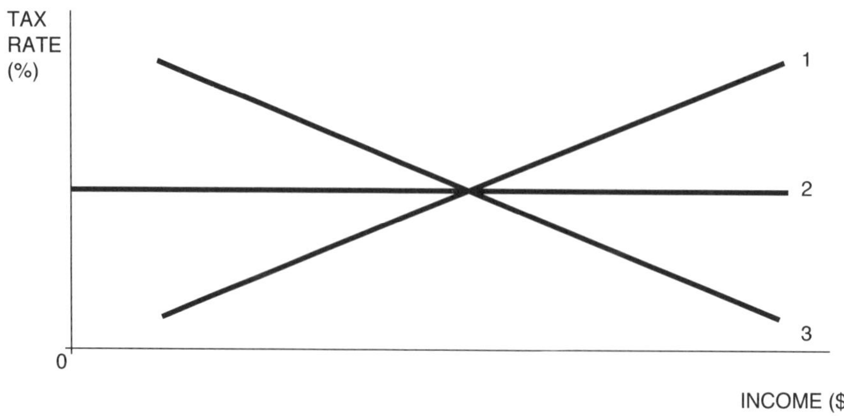

1 Which of the lines, 1, 2, or 3 represents a tax which is: **a** progressive **b** regressive **c** proportional? Explain your answers.

2 Now look at the three tax systems below. Calculate the percentage of tax paid on each income and state whether the systems are progressive, regressive or proportional.

Tax system 1		Tax system 2		Tax system 3	
Annual income	£ tax paid	Annual income	£ tax paid	Annual income	£ tax paid
£5 000	1 500	£10 000	1 000	£8 000	3 200
£15 000	4 500	£16 000	2 400	£12 000	3 600
£25 000	7 500	£30 000	6 600	£20 000	4 000

Direct and indirect taxation

In economics there are two main types of taxes: **direct taxes** and **indirect taxes**. Their meaning in law in different countries can differ from how we define these taxes in economics.

Direct taxes are taken directly from a person or firm and their incomes or wealth. They include income taxes, corporation taxes on company profits, capital gains taxes on property and other valuable assets, and inheritance taxes.

Indirect taxes are taxes taken only indirectly from incomes when they are spent on goods and services, and they are normally collected from those people or firms selling them. Indirect taxes include sales taxes, ad valorem taxes, tariffs and excise duties, which are all added to the price of goods and services.

The next figure shows how much revenue was raised by different direct and indirect taxes in the UK in the financial year from April 2006 to the end of March 2007, and how the money was spent. By far the most revenue was raised from direct taxes on incomes, wealth and profits. This is true of many countries. But you will also notice that the UK government spent more than it received. This means there was a public sector deficit (see section 6).

UK government receipts and spending, 2006–2007

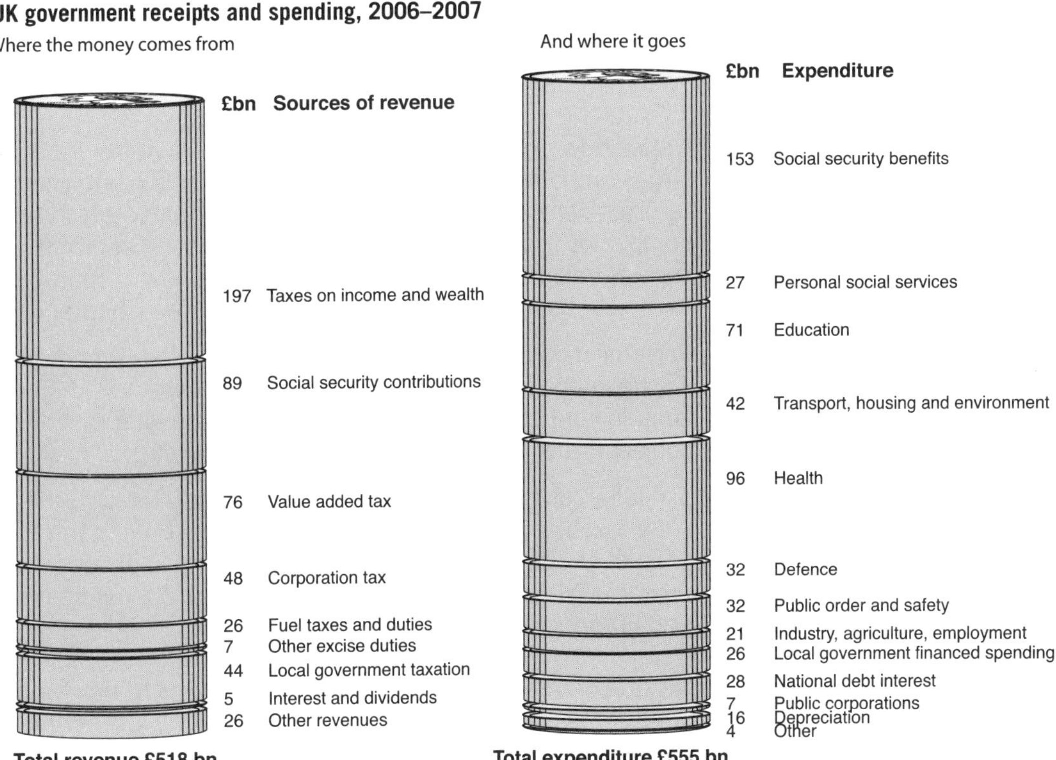

H M Treasury *Pre–Budget Report*, 12.2006

Most taxes are set, or levied, as a percentage (the **tax rate**) of a certain value (the **tax base**). Tax rates can vary significantly from country to country. The table below compares rates of income tax on people's earnings, corporation tax on large company profits and value added tax on the prices of many goods and services in some different countries.

Corporate, income and value added tax rates, selected countries, 2005–06

Country	Corporation tax %	Personal income tax %	VAT (or sales tax) %
Australia	30	15–45	10
Bulgaria	15	10–24	20
China	33	5–45	17
Colombia	35	0–35	16
Egypt	40	20–40	—
France	33.33	10–48.09	19.6
India	30–40	10–30	12.5
Ireland	12.50	20–42	21
Japan	30	10–37	5
Mexico	29	3–29	15
Norway	28	28–51.3	25
Pakistan	35	7.5–35	15
Spain	35	15–45	16
Turkey	20	15–35	18
United Arab Emirates	0	0	0
UK	30	10–40	17.5
US	35	0–35	State & local sales tax, up to 14.5
Zambia	35	10–30	17.5

OECD statistics

Notice how similar corporation tax rates are in different countries. This is largely because large companies today are internationally mobile and can relocate their production facilities quite easily around the world. A country which taxes profits highly risks losing companies to countries that offer low tax rates on profits. However, some countries such as Ireland and Bulgaria clearly do offer low corporation taxes to attract foreign multinational companies to locate in them (see Chapter 4).

Personal income tax rates vary rather more, and often rise with income. So, for example, Australia taxes low incomes at 15 per cent but much higher incomes at up to 45 per cent. In contrast, personal incomes, including all forms of salary and capital gains, are not subject to tax in any of the United Arab Emirates.

Similarly, corporation taxes on profits are zero rated in the UAE except foreign banks that were taxed at 20 per cent of their taxable income in the Emirates of Abu-Dhabi, Dubai and Sharjah in 2007. The tax is restricted to the taxable income that is earned in that particular emirate. Oil companies also pay a flat rate of 55 per cent on their taxable income in Dubai and 50 per cent in the other Emirates.

National and local taxation

Most taxes are levied by national governments to pay for public expenditures and to help control the macroeconomy. However, regional, local or municipal government authorities also spend money to provide local public services. Many receive the bulk of their money in grants from their national governments, but some countries also allow local governments to levy their own taxes to raise revenue from local residents and businesses.

There are many examples of local tax systems in the world. For example, in Sweden municipal and county governments can raise money from local income taxes. These can vary by area and are paid in addition to the national income tax. Together these make the overall rate of income tax in Sweden very high.

Similarly, in the US each state has its own tax system in addition to national taxes. Local taxes usually include taxes on property, income taxes and sales taxes on the prices of goods and services. Some states, including Alaska, Florida and Washington, do not levy an individual income tax. US cities and counties may also levy additional taxes, for instance to pay directly for the upkeep of parks or schools, or for a police and fire service, local roads and other services. Local taxes on hotel rooms are also common.

Local governments in China can also impose local taxes, including taxes on property, taxes on business turnover and even a slaughter tax on value of meat from slaughtered animals.

Section 4 Types of direct tax

Income tax

Income tax is a tax levied on an individual's earnings. Most countries allow people to earn a certain amount of income tax free, usually known as a personal allowance. For example, in the UK in 2007/8 a single person could earn up to £5 225 each year, or up to £7 550 if aged between 65 and 74, or £7 690 if over 75, before becoming liable to pay income tax.

Exactly how much tax a person pays in income tax will depend on how much they earn and in some cases their personal circumstances, for example, whether they are single, married, with or without children, old and retired. Income tax in most countries is a progressive tax. That is, higher **marginal tax rates** are usually applied to progressively higher parts of a person's income. They may also differ for different groups of people. Allowances and marginal rates of tax tend to be more generous for old people and for people with children so that they pay less tax overall than a person who earns the same amount but is single and has no children.

US Income tax structure, 2006

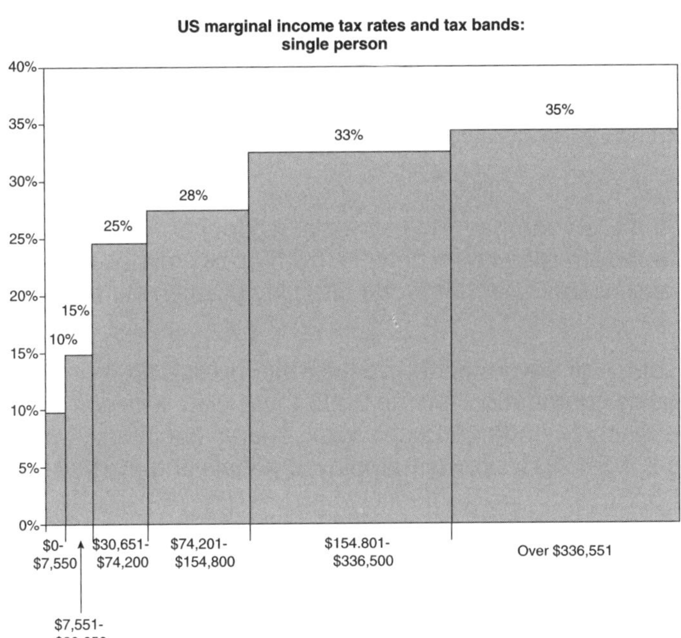

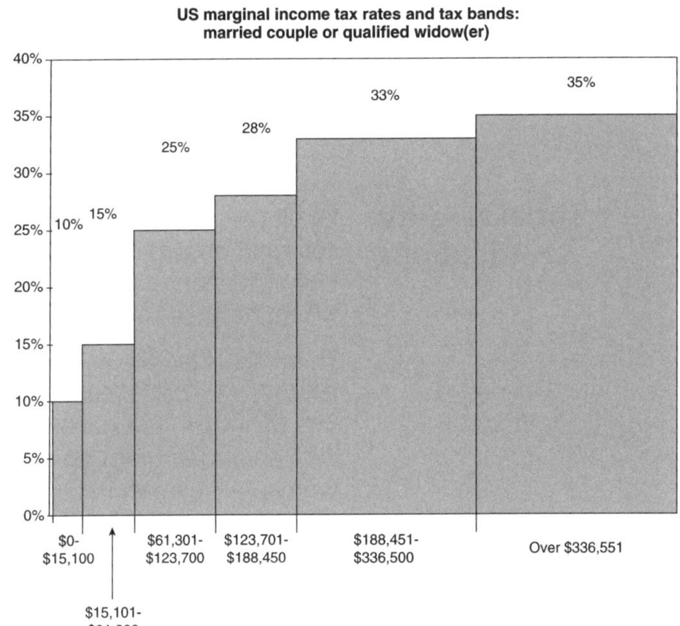

It is useful to distinguish between the average tax rate a person pays and their marginal tax rate. The **average tax** rate is the total amount of tax paid by a person divided by their total amount of earnings. The marginal rate is the rate of tax paid on a particular slice of a person's income. For example, the diagram shows the US income tax system in 2006. It has six marginal tax rates rising from 10 per cent to 35 per cent applied to six different income tax bands. The highest marginal tax rate of 35 per cent applied only to that part of a single person's or married couple's annual income over and above $336 551.

So, a single person living in the US earning $100 000 a year will pay a marginal rate of tax of 28 per cent on that top part of their income over $74 200, but overall will pay an average rate of tax of 22.3 per cent. This is calculated as follows.

US marginal and average income tax rates for a single person earning $100 000

Slices of income up to $100,000 per year	Marginal tax rate % (A)	Amount of income marginal tax rate is applied to (B)	Amount of tax paid $ (A x B)
$0 – $7 550	10	$7 500	755.00
$7 551 – $30 650	15	$23 100	3 465.00
$30 651 – $74 200	25	$43 550	10 887.50
$74 201 – $100 000	28	$25 800	7 224.00
Average tax rate % $= \frac{\$22\,331.50}{\$100\,000.00} = 22.3\%$		Total Income: $100 000	Total Tax: $22 331.50

Income tax is normally collected each month from employees by their employers. Workers will receive their wages or salaries net of tax. This means, after tax has already been deducted. An employer will then pay the income tax collected to the government tax authority. In the US this is called the Inland Revenue Service. People who are self-employed must provide evidence of their annual earnings and will pay their income tax direct to the government usually only once or twice each year.

The US is unlike most other countries because it taxes US citizens on their worldwide income no matter where in the world they live. US citizens therefore cannot avoid paying US taxes either by emigrating or by transferring their wealth overseas.

In the UK benefits in kind given to employees by their employer instead of additional wages or salaries are also subject to income tax. For example, free gifts such as free holidays or cars are taxed on their cash equivalent value.

Social security contributions

Employees, and their employers, in many countries also pay social security or welfare contributions from their earnings in return for welfare benefits from government such as unemployment benefits, old age and widow's pensions, and disability payments if and when they need such help.

These are often the next biggest source of government revenue after income taxes. In the UK these are called national insurance contributions and in 2006 these were levied at a rate of 11 per cent of earnings between £97 and £645 per week, and an additional 1 per cent on any earnings over £645 per week. Rates for self-employed people and married women were lower.

In the US both employees and employers pay FICA (Federal Insurance and Contributions Act). In 2006 it was 6.2 per cent of an employee's income paid by the employer, and 6.2 per cent paid by the employee on annual income up to $94 200. The US also has a payroll tax to support unemployment insurance and a Medicare tax to fund a health insurance program.

Some employers argue that the social security contributions they must pay for the workers they employ increases the cost of employment and therefore reduces their demand for labour (see Chapter 10). Some employers will simply pass on this extra cost to their workers in reduced wages. In this way the cost of paying the tax, or its incidence, may fall not on the employer but on the employee.

International comparisons of personal tax burdens

The OECD adds income taxes and social security contributions together each year to make international comparisons of individuals' tax burdens on their incomes. The charts below show that average tax rates paid by people with children are generally lower worldwide than average tax rates paid by single people on the same level of income. However, average tax rates vary widely. The average tax rate for single people in Belgium in 2005 was over 55 per cent of their average earnings, while a single person in Korea paid just over 17 per cent. A married person with children on average earnings in Ireland paid just over 8 per cent on average in income tax and social security contributions compared to over 42 per cent in Sweden.

International comparison of average tax rates (income tax and social security contributions), selected countries 2005

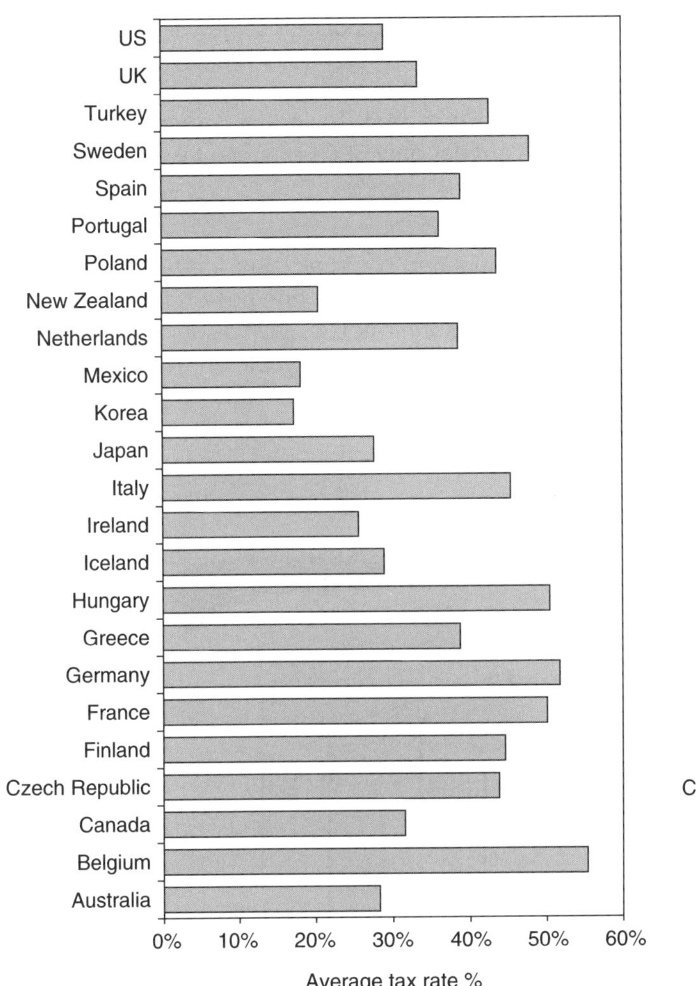

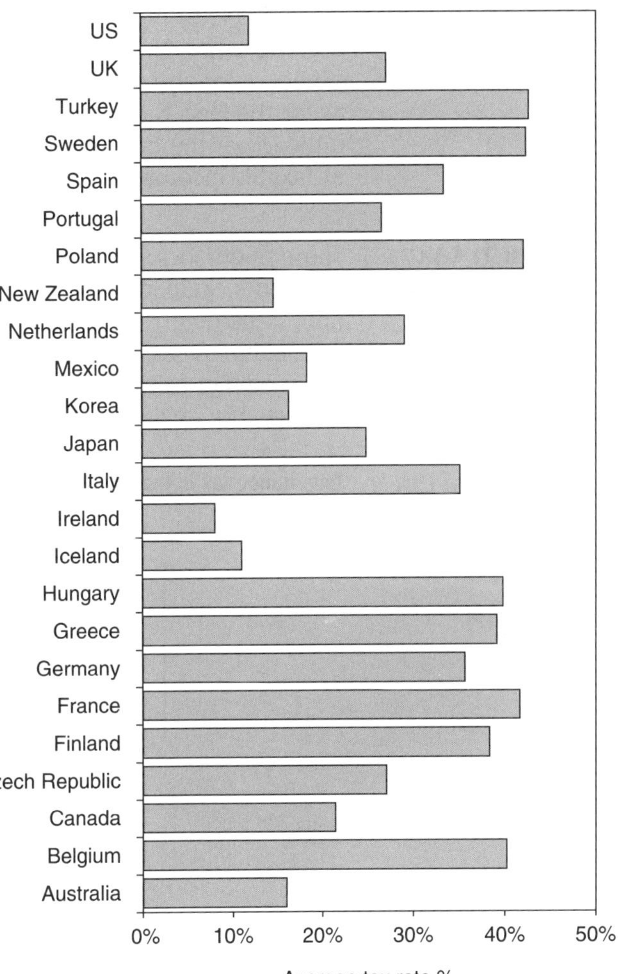

Exercise 6 Taxing US

1. Use the information on page 277 on marginal income tax rates in the US in 2006. For each of the following people determine what the highest marginal tax rate they each pay on their incomes and their average income tax rates:
   - Single person with annual income **a** \$20 000 **b** \$500 000.
   - Married person with annual income **c** \$150 000 **d** \$800 000.
2. How progressive do you think the US income tax system is? For example, how do average tax rates compare for people on middle to high incomes? Explain your answer.

Corporation tax

This is a tax on company profits, and may also be called a profits tax. Sometimes a government may also impose a one-off windfall tax on the profits of a company either thought to be a monopoly and making very significant profits, or benefiting from world events that boosted their profits. For example, the UK has from time to time imposed a windfall tax on the often huge profits of oil companies that have benefited simply as a result of a rise in world oil prices over which they have no direct control.

To encourage new businesses to start up, corporate tax rates on relatively small profits of smaller companies are less, even zero, in some countries, than tax rates on larger companies. Corporation tax rates often rise with the scale of profits.

Capital gains tax

It is possible to make profits from the sale of shares, famous paintings, jewellery and other valuable assets that have increased in value over time. Profits made in this way are called capital gains and may be taxed by a government. Sometimes allowances are made, such as for the length of time someone has held an asset so that the longer someone has held it the lower the tax they pay. For example, in Canada, only 50% of a capital gain is classed as taxable income.

Wealth taxes

These might include taxes on the value of residential and commercial property. Wealth taxes can also include inheritance taxes on the transfer of wealth from one person to another upon their death. When an individual dies and leaves their house, savings and/or other valuable possessions to someone else, inheritance tax might be payable on the total value inherited. For example, in the UK in 2007/8 inherited wealth up to a value of £300 000 was tax free, but any wealth inherited over and above this sum was taxed at 40 per cent.

Inheritance tax in the UK, 2007/8

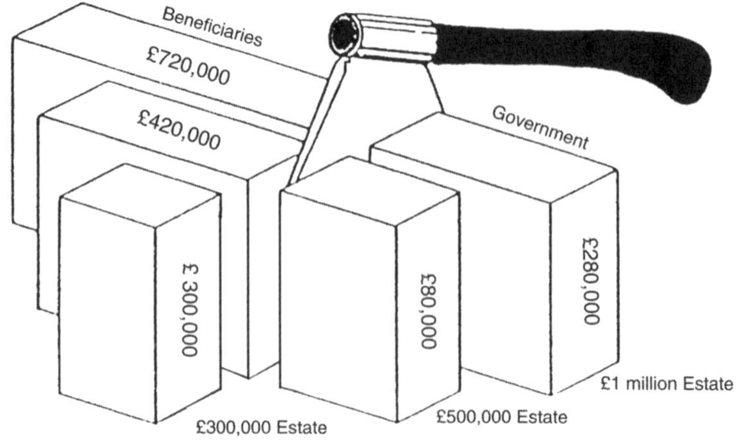

Advantages of direct taxes

1 Revenue

The chief advantages of direct taxes, like income tax and corporation tax, are that they have a high yield of revenue compared with their cost of collection. The total amount of money collected can be estimated with reasonable accuracy in advance, which is of great help to a government when planning how much it can spend.

2 Redistribution

The progressive nature of many direct taxes means that wealthier members of society are taxed more heavily than poorer groups to help reduce income inequalities.

3 Ability to pay

Direct taxes are constructed so that they take account of firms' and people's ability to pay tax. Family commitments, dependants, etc., are taken into consideration and a system of tax allowances can be used to reflect these responsibilities.

Disadvantages of direct tax

1 Work incentives

A high rate of tax on income may cause people to work less hard because they know that the more they earn the greater the proportion of their income they will have to pay in tax.

2 Enterprise

Corporation tax on a firm's profits reduces the incentive for entrepreneurs to start up firms to earn a profit. It also means that a firm will have less profits to re-invest in their business.

3 Tax evasion

High tax rates increase the advantages of evading taxes and finding loopholes in tax laws. As a result, revenues are lower and the trouble of trying to catch up with tax evaders increases a government's costs.

Section 5 Types of indirect tax

Value added tax

An ad valorem tax or value added tax (VAT) is a tax on goods and services levied as a percentage of their selling price (see also Chapter 7). It is normally a fixed rate but some goods and services may be taxed at a lower rate, or even zero-rated if their consumption is encouraged or because they are things which people on low incomes often buy. For example, many foods, medicines, books and public transport fares are zero rated, or exempt from VAT, in the UK.

VAT is a regressive tax because it is a fixed percentage rate and because people on low incomes tend to spend all or most of their incomes on goods and services. For example, if an unemployed man receiving $50 per week in benefits buys a pair of jeans for $20 and pays 20 per cent or $4 in VAT on top, then this tax will represent 8 per cent of his income. If a lawyer earning $500 a week buys the same pair of jeans, the VAT she pays will take only 0.8 per cent of her income.

VAT is levied not just on finished goods and services but also on semi-finished components and natural materials bought by producers. VAT is therefore added at every stage of production. However, a producer can recover the VAT he or she had to pay on inputs of materials and components from the VAT they collect when they sell their output of goods and services.

Similar ad valorem taxes around the world that are levied on prices, spending or sales revenues are sales tax, business tax and turnover tax.

Tariffs

A tariff, also called a customs duty or an impost, is a tax levied on the price of goods imported from overseas as they enter a country. Tariffs are used to discourage people from buying imports in an attempt to protect domestic industries (see Chapter 22). High tariffs can encourage illegal smuggling and so governments that impose tariffs may use part of the revenue they raise to pay for police and navy border patrols.

Excise duties

Excise duties are taxes placed on certain goods based on the quantity, not the value, of product purchased. Examples include duties on fuel, vehicles, tobacco and alcohol. They are used not only to raise revenue but also to discourage the consumption of certain products such as cigarettes and alcohol that can be damaging to health.

Excise duties are also increasingly being used to discourage activities that harm the environment and to encourage the consumption of those that do not. These are becoming known as 'green taxes'. Examples of such taxes in the UK include fuel duties and vehicle excise duties which are in part designed to stop people buying and driving big cars which produce more emissions than smaller vehicles or to travel on buses or trains instead. Similarly, the air passenger duty is a type of poll tax (a fixed charge per person, and in this case also per flight) designed to raise the price of air travel and so discourage flying which also causes harmful air pollution.

User taxes or charges

These are just another type of excise duty linked to specific goods or activities. For example, they include toll charges to use major bridges or roads and pay for their upkeep. London and other major cities around the world have also introduced congestion charges that charge vehicle drivers a fixed amount to enter these cities. Some of the revenue raised from these charges is used to pay for better public transport.

A tax on a specific good or activity used to raise revenue for a specific purpose, such as paying for road or public transport improvements rather than simply adding to total tax revenue, is called a **hypothecated tax**.

Advantages of indirect taxes

1 Cost of collection

Indirect taxes are cheap to collect. The burden of collecting taxes in this way lies mainly with the manufacturers, wholesalers and retailers collecting VAT, and importers paying custom and excise duties.

2 Wider tax base

Indirect taxes are paid by young, old, employed and unemployed alike when they buy goods and services, not just by people with earned incomes. As a result, the effects of indirect taxes are spread more widely throughout the community.

3 Selective aims

Indirect taxes can be used to achieve specific aims. Taxes on cigarettes and alcohol can discourage harmful consumption. Taxes on oil can reduce the demand for a valuable resource which will one day run out and help reduce air pollution.

4 Tax alterations

It is often quicker and easier for a government to alter tax rates for VAT and excise duties than to make changes to income tax and other direct taxes. As such the effect of these changes on consumption patterns and the macroeconomy is quicker.

Disadvantages of indirect taxes

1 Uncertainty

A government can only guess how much people will spend on taxed goods and services and so will be uncertain as to how much revenue indirect taxes will raise. This makes planning future public expenditure based on likely tax revenues difficult. If actual tax revenues are below forecast then a government can end up with a budget deficit and a borrowing requirement it did not plan for.

2 Regressive

Indirect taxes are regressive in nature. That is, their burden is greater on poorer people as a proportion of their incomes than it is on people with high incomes.

3 Inflation

Indirect taxes add to the prices of goods and services and can therefore increase price inflation. However, firms that sell goods and services may not be able to pass on all the VAT or excise duties levied on them to consumers (see Chapter 7). If demand for them is very price elastic, consumer demand for the taxed goods and services will fall significantly and sellers will earn far less revenue and profit. As a result, producers may only pass on part of the tax to consumers and pay the rest themselves in order to keep price increases as low as possible. Unsurprisingly many producers do not like indirect taxes as they argue it increases their costs and lowers consumer demand.

Exercise 7 A taxing problem

What is the name of the tax that would normally be paid on each of the following?

- **a** A footballer's weekly wages.
- **b** A gift of $1 million.
- **c** Imports of machinery from the another county.
- **d** Profits made on the buying and selling of shares.
- **e** The purchase of a meal from a restaurant.
- **f** A company's profits.

Balancing the budget

What is the budget?

In any organization a budget is simply a forecast of spending and revenues over the next 12 months or so, and will be used to monitor actual expenditures and revenues as they occur to look at how similar or how different they are from forecast and why.

The UK Chancellor of the Exchequer (1997–2007) prepares to give budget details to the UK parliament

In exactly the same way a government will set out in its budget its plans for spending and raising tax revenues in the financial year ahead. In most countries it is so important it is simply called **'the budget'**.

In the budget a government sometimes announces new taxes, abolishes old taxes or just alters existing tax rates. The budget is also used to announce ambitious spending plans, and in this way many governments hope to win votes. However, sometimes governments must announce spending cuts that may be unpopular, although high tax burdens to pay for high public spending can be equally unpopular and can also damage economic growth.

Because government spending and taxation are so great, changes in them can have important effects on the economy and a government can use this fact to influence inflation, employment and output. For example, if a government budgets for a deficit it will pump more money into the economy. A **budget deficit** means government is spending more than it receives in tax revenue. More money in the economy is likely to cause increased spending on goods and services and so increase employment.

If government reduces its deficit by raising taxes and spending less, the amount of money flowing around the economy is reduced. Less money in the economy is likely to cause spending on output to fall and may lead to lower price rises, possibly at the cost of higher unemployment.

If a government raises more in tax revenue than it spends, it is said to be budgeting for a surplus.

If a government spends as much as it raises in tax revenue exactly, the budget is said to be balanced.

Using public spending and taxation to influence the level of demand or spending in the economy is known as fiscal policy (see Chapter 14).

Public sector borrowing

Very often governments spend more than they raise in tax and any other revenues. To make up the difference a government will have to borrow money from the private sector and/or from overseas. The amount of borrowed money the public sector needs in order to balance its spending is usually called the **public sector borrowing requirement** or very similar. In the UK it is called the net cash requirement and the table below shows how much it was each year between 1995–96 and 2005–06.

UK public sector borrowing, 1995–96 to 2005–06

Financial year	Net cash requirement £ billion	Net cash requirement as a % of GDP
1995–96	40.2	5.6%
1996–97	33.8	4.4%
1997–98	17.3	2.1%
1998–99	−0.5	−0.1%
1999–00	−10.4	−1.1%
2000–01	−16.1	−1.7%
2001–02	−9.8	−1.0%
2002–03	17.2	1.6%
2003–04	36.2	3.5%
2004–05	37.7	3.2%
2005–06	36.8	3.2%

For example, in the financial year 1995–96 the UK government had to borrow £40.2 billion to pay for spending more than it received in revenue. During times of economic recession, as the UK experienced in the early to mid 1990s, tax revenues tend to fall as profits tend to fall and unemployment rises, but expenditure on social security benefits tends to rise.

However, during periods of surplus revenue the borrowing requirement turns negative. That is, there is no need to borrow money and the surplus of public sector tax and other revenues over and above public spending can be used to pay off some previous borrowing. This happened in the UK during the economic boom period between 1998 and 2002. Over this period the UK government was able to pay off almost £37 billion of national debt.

UK public sector borrowing has since increased again and had reached £36.8 billion by 2005–06 as the government increased spending significantly on public services such as schools and healthcare.

Governments usually borrow by selling loan stocks, or securities, such as government bonds (see Chapter 6). Short-term debt is generally repaid with interest within one year or less. Long-term debt usually lasts for ten years or more. Medium-term debt reaches **maturity**, i.e. is repaid by government, somewhere in between these periods.

Government debt can be internal debt, owed to private individuals, firms and the banking system within the same country, and external debt owed to foreign lenders.

National debt

Each year a government must sell enough debt or secure loans to finance its borrowing requirement. However, every year a government borrows more money it will add to its total stock of debt. All the money borrowed by the public sector over time that has yet to be repaid is called the public sector debt or **national debt**.

The national debt is money owed by all levels of government: central, regional, local or municipal government. As the government of a country represents its people and borrows money to finance public spending on their behalf, the national debt is indirectly the debt of taxpayers.

The US national debt was a staggering $8.5 trillion in 2006, equivalent to 67.5 per cent of the US national income that year. It has risen significantly over time. In 1960 it was $290 billion or 56 per cent of national income.

US national debt, 1960–2006

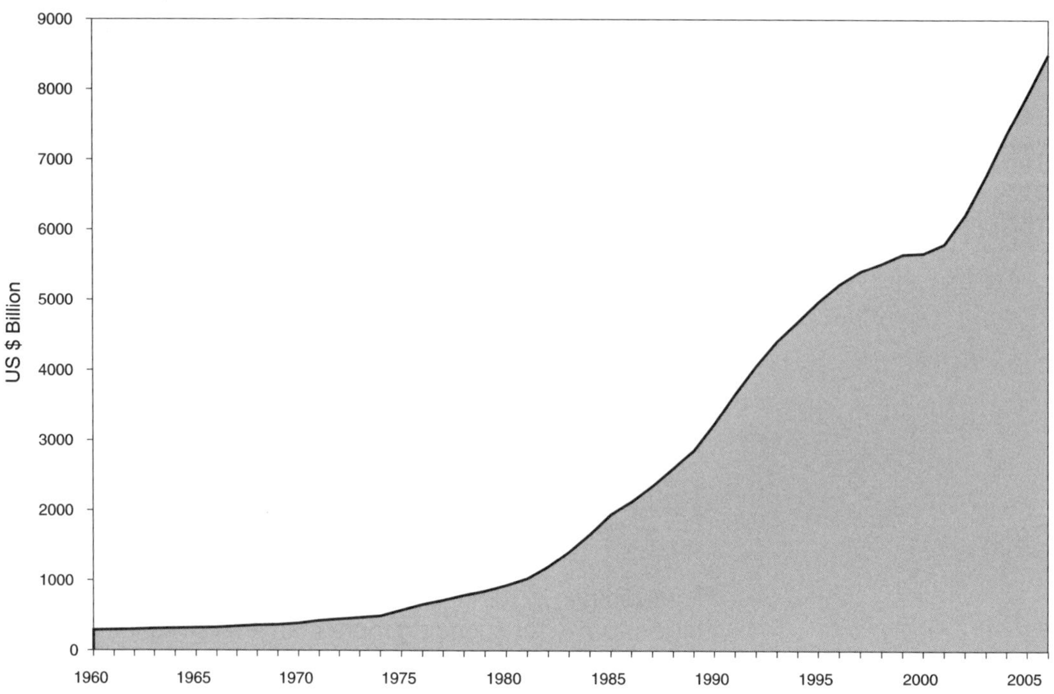

... and as a proportion of US GDP

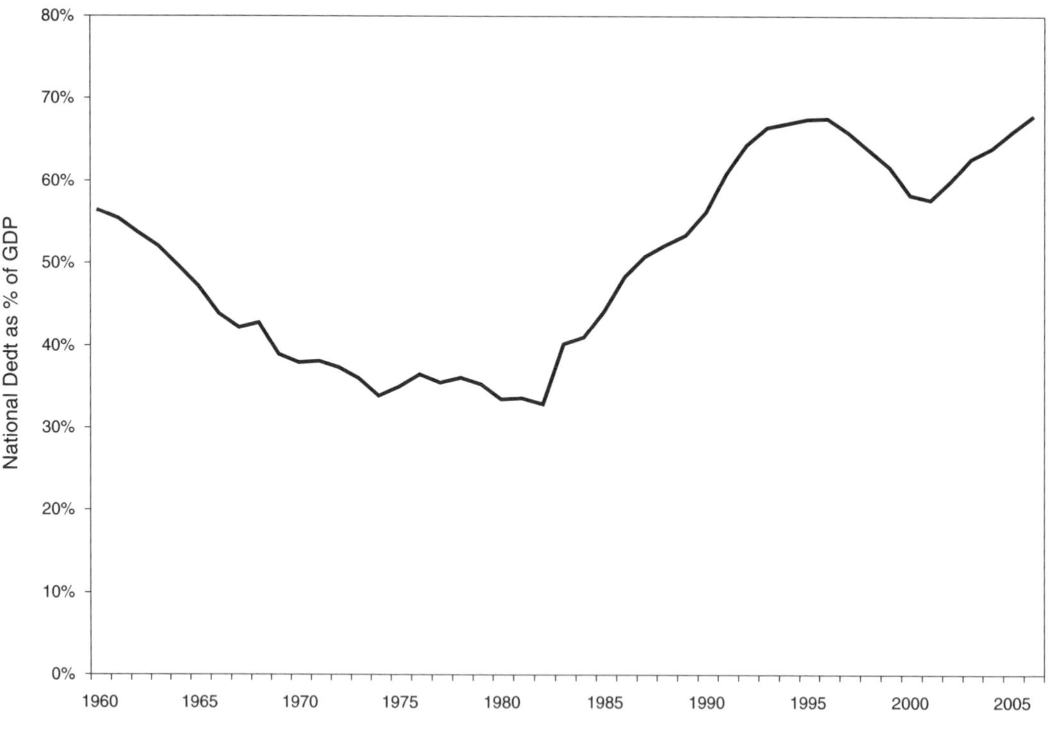

US Office of Management and Budget, *www.whitehouse.gov/omb/*

It is useful to compare the national debt of a country with its national income or GDP because it tells us about the ability of a country to manage and repay its debts. The table below lists the ten countries with highest national debt to GDP ratios, and the ten countries with the lowest. You will note that Malawi in Africa had a national debt in 2005 almost twice its entire national income while countries such as Libya, Chile and Estonia have relatively little debt compared to their national incomes.

Countries with the highest and lowest ratios of national debt to GDP, 2005

Country	National debt (% of GDP)	Country	National debt (% of GDP)
Malawi	195.9%	Nigeria	11.0%
Lebanon	180.5%	Latvia	10.9%
Seychelles	167.0%	Kazakhstan	10.5%
Japan	158.0%	Libya	8.2%
Jamaica	128.7%	Oman	8.1%
Zimbabwe	109.8%	Chile	7.5%
Italy	108.8%	Botswana	6.2%
Sudan	107.0%	Wallis and Futuna	5.6%
Greece	106.8%	Estonia	4.8%
Egypt	104.7%	Hong Kong	1.8%

CIA World Factbook

As the national debt of a country rises, both in terms of money and especially as a proportion of its national income, so the burden of paying interest to the people and firms that hold the debt rises.

Rising public sector debt and rising interest payments need not be a bad thing as long as the national income or GDP of a country rises quicker than the total debt. If this happens the burden of debt as a proportion of GDP will fall. This is just the same for individuals who borrow money from a bank. The burden of their debt and interest payments will fall as their income and ability to pay back their loan rises.

Some politicians and people still claim the national debt is a burden on a country. This is because a government must raise extra money in tax from people and companies to pay interest payments. However, if the extra taxes pay for interest on internal debt held by people and firms in the same country then all the government will be doing is raising taxes from some to pay interest to others. That is, interest payments made to people and firms in the same country are simply a transfer from one group of taxpayers to another, and overall that country is no worse off. Yet, clearly, if taxes have to be very high to repay huge interest payments then people and firms may not have the incentive to work so hard and this may damage economic growth (see Chapters 14 and 17).

Interest payments on external debt held overseas are, however, a drain on an economy. This is because extra tax revenue will have to be raised simply to pay interest payments to lenders overseas, and the country will be worse off as a result.

Some useful websites on public finance, taxation and related statistics include:

- *en.wikipedia.org/wiki/Tax*
- *en.wikipedia.org/wiki/National_debt*
- *www.tutor2u.net/economics/gcse/revision_notes/tools_taxation.htm*
- *www.taxworld.org/History/TaxHistory.htm*
- *US National Debt Clock www.brillig.com/debt_clock/*
- *French National Debt clock cluaran.free.fr/dette.html*
- *US Office of Management and Budget, www.whitehouse.gov/omb/*
- *UK HM Treasury www.hm-treasury.gov.uk/*
- *US Inland Revenue Service www.irs.gov/index.html*

Key word search

Search the jumble of letters to find the key words and terms for the definitions below.

B	U	D	G	E	T	A	X	D	E	B	P	T	C	A	P	R
S	U	I	F	O	R	G	C	E	T	O	L	K	D	F	E	I
A	S	R	U	M	P	A	U	Z	U	I	P	H	E	L	E	P
L	L	E	X	A	F	U	R	C	K	V	R	T	A	S	E	U
A	I	C	O	R	G	O	R	A	T	I	O	N	T	A	X	T
N	P	T	S	G	R	H	E	N	A	M	G	R	U	R	C	H
C	K	B	M	I	O	L	N	A	X	O	R	T	A	S	I	Y
E	N	O	A	N	U	O	T	M	J	N	E	A	D	T	S	P
R	L	N	C	A	R	E	G	R	E	S	S	I	V	E	E	O
U	M	J	K	L	P	O	J	I	C	E	S	T	A	X	D	T
T	E	O	M	T	W	P	E	P	A	X	I	R	L	C	U	H
A	T	V	Y	A	I	E	D	C	P	D	V	U	O	S	T	E
R	A	A	B	X	Z	N	Q	U	I	Y	E	S	R	L	Y	C
I	N	D	I	R	E	C	T	G	T	I	N	T	E	A	S	A
F	L	G	R	A	V	I	R	V	A	S	U	C	M	D	L	T
F	I	N	A	T	I	O	N	A	L	D	E	B	T	E	I	E
Q	U	I	F	E	C	U	S	T	T	R	A	N	S	F	E	D
W	A	X	A	V	E	R	A	G	E	T	A	X	R	A	T	E

Definitions

- These types of taxes are levied on incomes and wealth
- These types of taxes can be avoided if you don't buy anything!
- The stock of public sector borrowing
- A tax on company profits
- A tax added as a percentage to the prices of goods and services
- A tax applied to certain goods and services based on quantity and not value
- Duties sometimes imposed on certain imported goods
- Name given to a tax on a specific good or activity used to raise revenue for a specific purpose, such as paying for road or public transport improvements
- An annual estimate and plan for public sector spending and taxation
- A tax system designed to tax a greater proportion of a high income than a low income
- A tax system designed to fall as proportion of income as income rises
- Name given to public expenditure for investment
- Name given to public expenditure on consumable goods and services, transfer payments, public sector wages and day-to-day running costs
- That rate of tax paid on the next slice or taxable band of income
- The proportion of total income paid in tax

Assessment exercises

Multiple choice

1 Expansionary fiscal policy to increase aggregate demand involves:

A Increasing public spending and taxes.

B Reducing public spending and taxes.

C Reducing interest rates and the money supply.

D Increasing public spending and reducing taxes.

2 Monetary policy involves control of:

A Interest rates.

B Notes and coins.

C Exchange rates.

D Tax revenues.

3 An increase in the money supply will:

A Lower interest rates.

B Reduce consumer borrowing.

C Reduce inflation.

D Reduce the national debt.

4 To increase demand in a developed economy a government could try to:

A Cut subsidies to industry.

B Encourage savings.

C Budget for a surplus.

D Cut taxes.

5 A government wishes to reduce total consumer spending in an economy. What should it increase?

A Government expenditure

B Unemployment benefits

C Interest rates

D Public sector pay

Questions 6–9 refer to the following instruments of economic policy:

A Reducing taxes on company profits

B Increasing the interest rate

C Raising welfare benefits

D Increasing income taxes

Which of the above instruments best describes the following government actions:

6 A fiscal measure to reduce growth in consumer spending?

7 Tightening monetary policy to reduce consumer demand?

8 A supply-side measure to encourage businesses to invest and expand output?

9 A fiscal policy expansion to encourage economic growth?

10 Which of the following is an indirect tax?

A A tax on inherited wealth

B A tax on consumer goods and services

C A tax on company profits

D A tax on interest earned in savings

11 Mehdi Hussein earns $12 000 per year and pays $3 000 in income tax. Mary Brown earns $18 000 per year and pays $6 000 in income tax. This income tax is:

A Proportional

B Regressive

C Progressive

D A poll tax

12 The following are a government's receipts from taxation.

	$ million
VAT	400
Corporation tax	200
Excise duties	100
Income tax	750
Capital gains tax	250

What is the total amount of indirect tax revenue?

A $950m **C** $500m

B $400m **D** $700m

13 In which of the following situations will there be a budget deficit?

A Government revenue exceeds government spending.

B Government spending exceeds total tax revenue.

C Government spending exceeds direct tax revenues.

D Government spending exceeds indirect tax revenues.

14 The use of taxation and government spending to influence the economy is known as:

A Tax policy.

B Monetary policy.

C Competition policy.

D Fiscal policy.

15 The national debt of a country is

A The budget deficit.

B The annual public sector borrowing requirement.

C The total stock of public and private sector borrowing.

D The total accumulated stock of public sector borrowing.

16 Which of the following is not included in public expenditure?

A Capital investments by public limited companies

B Wages paid to public sector employees

C Interest payments on local authority borrowing

D Investments in roads by central government

Questions 17–19 are based on the following table of information on taxes paid on different levels of income under different tax systems (A–D).

Weekly income $	Tax paid from income ($)			
	A	B	C	D
150	30	15	45	30
200	40	20	50	60
400	50	40	55	150

Which of the tax systems in the table is

17 the most progressive?

18 the most regressive?

19 proportional?

20 Which of the following is a direct tax?

A VAT

B Fuel duties

C Tariffs on imports

D Inheritance tax

Structured questions

1

EUROPEAN RECESSION

In 2003 Germany, Italy and the Netherlands were in a period of recession. GDP in Germany fell by 0.2% between January and April, and by 0.1% between April and June. The recession spread to Italy, which is dependent on Germany as a market for its exports. The weakest of the three was the Netherlands, where output fell by 0.5% between April and June following a fall for the previous eight months. The German government planned to encourage consumer spending by introducing cuts in both indirect and direct taxation. It also approved measures to increase employment opportunities.

a Why does the article refer to the Netherlands as the weakest economy? [2]

b Explain what is meant by GDP. [3]

c Using examples, describe the difference between direct and indirect taxes. [4]

d How might a reduction in taxation help any **two** macro-economic aims of a government? [6]

e Why might a government wish to increase employment opportunities? [5]

2

CHANGES IN AUSTRALIA'S TAX SYSTEM

From July 2000 Australia had a new tax structure as part of its economic reform programme. Before the changes were introduced, consumer groups expressed concern about their likely effects. The new system involved a redistribution from direct to indirect taxes through a new tax on goods and services charged at 10%. However, to compensate for this, income tax was cut and social security benefits were increased. Those in favour of the change insisted that the new system would improve economic efficiency. The new tax covered services, by far the most important sector of the economy, which had previously escaped the tax. As compensation for companies, there were reductions in company tax. Those against the new tax feared that it would cause a sharp increase in inflation, which was already beginning to increase as a result of strong domestic demand and a rise in the price of imported oil.

a Explain the difference between a direct and an indirect tax and give **two** examples of a direct tax from the above information. [3]

b If you had to decide whether consumers were disadvantaged by the changes in the tax system, what evidence would you need to investigate? [10]

3 Expenditure in an economy may be either private expenditure or public expenditure.

a Explain the difference between these types of expenditure, giving one example of each. [3]

b Why might public expenditure fall if an economy comes to rely more on the market system? [3]

c Explain how public expenditure can be paid for. [8]

d Discuss, with examples, how decisions on public expenditure might illustrate the idea of opportunity cost. [6]

4 **a** Distinguish with the use of examples between

i direct and indirect taxes, [3]

ii progressive and regressive taxes. [3]

b Explain why governments impose taxes. [6]

c Discuss what might happen in an economy if a government increases income tax rates. [8]

5 In 2000 the Singapore government revenue from income tax, motor vehicle tax, betting tax and the tax on goods and services all increased. However, the revenue from the tax on goods and services doubled while that from income tax rose 7%. Singapore depends on its tourist trade for part of its wealth.

a Explain the difference between direct and indirect tax and identify **one** direct and **one** indirect tax in the above statement. [4]

b Discuss why governments impose taxes. [6]

c An increase in revenue from taxes is mentioned in the extract. Discuss whether you can draw conclusions about what might have happened in Singapore to

i the numbers of tourists, [4]

ii the level of unemployment. [6]

How to answer question 3

a This question is a nice easy introduction but remember to write clearly and concisely, and to demonstrate your understanding of these terms in full. For example, **private expenditures** will include spending by individual consumers and **private sector** organizations, including **profit** and **non-profit making enterprises**. It will therefore include **consumer expenditure** on **consumer services** and **durable and non-durable goods**, and **investment** by firms in new plant and machinery.

Don't forget that **public expenditure** is spending undertaken by the **public sector** in a country, and so will include spending by **central, regional and local government** authorities as well as spending by **public corporations** that run **nationalized industries**. Public expenditure can be **current expenditure** on public sector workers' wages and government office running costs, or **capital expenditure** on new roads, hospitals and military equipment.

b Another short-answer question. You should describe the key characteristics of a **market economic system** in terms of how **scarce resources** are allocated. If you do this correctly you will be able to explain clearly why there may be less need for a government to determine how resources are allocated. Public sector spending and **taxation** can therefore be lower if more resources in their economy are allocated through the **price mechanism** according to the preferences and spending decisions of **consumers**, and the production decisions of **firms**.

c This question carries eight marks. This suggests it is looking for you to list at least four main ways a government can fund its public expenditure. However, you will need to explain these in full, and briefly cover any additional sources of public sector finance, if you are to maximize your marks.

Before you write down your answer, start by making a list of sources of government revenue, and try to put these in order of how big or important they are. In most countries **tax revenues** should be your first choice. **Public sector borrowing** will probably be next, although proceeds from the sale of government-owned industries and assets, known as **privatization**, may be a close second in some countries. For governments that still own and run **nationalized industries** that sell goods or services to consumers, sales revenues will also be an important source of revenue. Refresh your knowledge of these by looking back at Chapter 4.

Other, usually more minor sources of revenue may include rents on government-owned buildings, admission charges to publicly owned museums and national monuments, and interest payments on loans made by government authorities.

Now for the more difficult bit. It is clearly not enough to simply answer that taxes provide a major source of revenue for government. To demonstrate your understanding of **tax systems** you should explain that taxes can be levied on individuals and firms, on wealth, incomes and expenditures, **direct or indirect, progressive, proportional or regressive, national or local**, and provide definitions and examples wherever possible.

Similarly, demonstrate your understanding of how and why governments borrow money and the impact increased public sector borrowing will have on the **national debt** of a country. Also describe clearly and concisely, again giving examples, what is meant by a public corporation and nationalized industry, and by privatization.

d If you cannot define **opportunity cost** and explain why it is so important in economics then you really should go back to read Chapter 1 again. Remember it concerns the allocation and use of scarce resources, and how these decisions involve **choice**. Therefore every decision by government on public expenditure involves choice and will have an opportunity cost in terms of the next best alternative foregone. So, for example, spending more on military equipment will have a cost in terms of foregone schools, roads or any other items the government could have spent this money on instead. As always, remember to give some examples.

However, there are many other important choices you will need to explain to provide evidence of your analytical skills and broad understanding of economics. Your answers to questions (a) to (c) should provide clues.

In question (a) you have distinguished between private sector spending and public expenditure, while in (b) you have described how the size and role of government may diminish in an economy which makes greater use of the market economic system to allocate scarce resources. In question (c) you have described how in most countries public spending is financed mainly from taxes. It follows that increased public expenditure has an opportunity cost in terms of higher levels of taxation and reduced private sector expenditure.

A government also faces a choice between financing public spending from more direct taxes on income and wealth, or more direct taxes on expenditures. This may also involve a choice between a more progressive or more regressive tax structure. If a government decides against raising taxes to pay for more spending, then it may have to borrow more which will involve raising interest rates and increasing the national debt. This in turn increases the amount of public expenditure in future years that must be used to repay the national debt and interest payments, leaving less to spend on other publicly provided goods and services.

To complete your answer you should go back to consider why governments intervene in market economies and raise taxes to finance their spending. What are some of the disadvantages of the market economic system? For example, the government of a market-based economy may face a choice between having a high level of unemployment and poverty or intervening through tax and spending measures to create jobs, boost incomes and provide welfare payments. Now would be a good time to revise your understanding of the market economic system and reasons for government intervention in Chapter 3.

A market system may also allocate resources to uses which are not the most efficient because firms' decisions will often overlook the **external costs** of their production, for example, in terms of their damage to the environment. A government may use its tax and spending decisions to redirect resources to more efficient uses that maximize **economic welfare**. This too is a choice a government and a society have to make.

A model answer for question 4

a **i** Direct taxes are levied directly on an individual person's or company's income and wealth. They include income tax, corporation tax on profits, taxes on interest paid on savings, and capital gains taxes on the appreciation in value of various assets.

In contrast, indirect taxes are those that are paid from incomes only when they are spent on the purchase or use of various goods and services. Indirect taxes are added to the price of goods and services, either as a percentage of the selling price (otherwise known as ad valorem taxes) or as a fixed tax sum. For example, excise duties include duties on alcohol and tobacco, motor vehicles, petroleum and air travel. These can vary by country.

Value Added Tax (VAT) is an ad valorem tax. Rates of VAT vary by country. For example, it is currently levied at 17.5 per cent of the price of many goods and services in the UK.

ii A progressive tax takes proportionally more tax from higher levels of income than from lower incomes. For example, a tax that is levied at 0 per cent on any income up to $5 000 per year, 10 per cent on each dollar of income thereafter from $5 001 to $40 000 per year, and 20 per cent on each dollar of income thereafter from $40 001 upwards, is an example of a progressive tax. Many income tax systems are progressive in nature and can be used to reduce inequalities in income.

A regressive tax, however, takes proportionally less from a higher income than a lower income. Many indirect taxes tend to be regressive in nature. For example, consider an excise duty of $5 on the price of a good. If a person earning $100 per week buys this good then the excise duty will take 5 per cent of his or her income while the same duty will take only 0.5 per cent from the income of a person earning $1 000 per week. Because of this many people argue that regressive taxes are unfair.

b A government imposes direct and indirect taxes for many reasons. A primary reason is to raise revenue to pay for government spending including wages of public sector workers and investments in infrastructure including new schools and roads. In this way a government can direct spending at goods and services that can help increase economic growth and economic welfare. For example, tax revenues can finance welfare benefits paid to the old, sick and unemployed. In this way, taxes, particularly those levied on incomes and wealth, can be used to help alleviate poverty and reduce inequalities in wealth and incomes between people.

Government fiscal policy involves changing the overall level of tax collected and public expenditure to vary the total level of demand in an economy. Raising taxes and lower spending can help reduce a demand-pull inflation caused by an excess of aggregate demand for goods and services in an economy. In contrast, lowering taxes and increasing public expenditure can help boost total demand during an economic recession when unemployment may be high and rising due to low demand for goods and services. Taxes can therefore be used to influence the level of economic activity in an economy and help a government to achieve its overall macroeconomic aims.

Individual taxes on specific goods or services can also be used to influence the level of consumer demand for these products. For example, indirect taxes on tobacco products, such as cigarettes, can help to discourage their consumption and therefore reduce the incidence of health problems, lung cancers and deaths that may be caused by smoking. Similarly, by helping to reduce demand for car use, excise duties on petroleum can help conserve oil and reduce harmful exhaust emissions which can pollute the natural environment and contribute to harmful climate change.

c Raising income tax rates may have a number of different economic impacts. Disposable income will fall and will tend to reduce consumer expenditure as a result unless consumers instead run down their savings. Falling demand in the economy may help to reduce any demand-pull inflationary pressure on prices, however it may also result in higher levels of unemployment if firms cut back production as demand for their products falls. Further, firms may reduce their investments in new plant and machinery. This will reduce the productive potential of the economy in the future and will tend therefore to slow down economic growth. However, the overall impact on aggregate demand and growth in the economy will depend on how the additional tax revenue is used and/or whether other taxes have at the same time been lowered to offset the impact of the increased income tax rates. For example, the government may use the additional tax revenue to increase spending on employment and training programmes, grants to firms' new research and development, or an expanded road network, all of which will help create jobs and stimulate economic growth.

However, increased taxes on income may reduce people's incentives to work. This may reduce their productivity and slow down economic growth. Workers may demand higher wages from their employers to help compensate the income tax increase. Higher wages will tend to reduce firms' demand for labour and may contribute to a cost-push inflation as firms attempt to pass on their higher wage costs to their consumers.

Finally, higher income tax rates may increase tax avoidance. For example, instead of receiving higher wages workers may ask to be paid in other ways instead, such as receiving more non-taxable gifts or holiday entitlement. Some workers may even illegally evade income tax altogether by working for unreported cash payments only. Tax avoidance and evasion will tend to reduce tax revenues which the government may have hoped for following their policy to increase income tax rates.

7

ECONOMIC INDICATORS: RECENT CHANGES AND CURRENT TRENDS IN AN ECONOMY AND THEIR CONSEQUENCES

Government macroeconomic objectives seek low and stable price inflation, low unemployment, economic growth in output and incomes, and a favourable balance of international transactions. To measure progress towards its macroeconomic objectives a government will collect and analyse data on these variables.

High and rising inflation, caused either by an excess demand for goods and services or rising production costs, is a concern because it erodes the value of money which may cause particular hardship for people on low and fixed incomes. It can also make export prices uncompetitive overseas and lead to a fall in business confidence. The rate of inflation is normally measured by changes in a consumer price index calculated from the average prices of a basket of commonly consumed goods and services in an economy.

High unemployment can also cause hardship for those without paid employment, but importantly is a waste of resources that could otherwise be used to produce goods and services. Some unemployment in an economy for short periods of time may be inevitable as people move between jobs, and some people may of course choose to remain unemployed perhaps because unemployment benefits paid to them by government are more generous compared to wages they could expect to earn. However, changes in the industrial structure of an economy can result in high unemployment over long periods of time, as redundant workers need to retrain in new skills required by new and growing industries. Globally, employment has been rising, especially in services, while the share of employment accounted for by agriculture and industry has been falling.

Rates of inflation and unemployment also tend to vary with the economic cycle in activity in an economy. During an economic recession falling incomes and demand can lead to higher unemployment and lower prices. During a boom, rising demand for goods and services can boost output and employment, but may also boost price inflation and suck in more imports from overseas, causing an unfavourable balance of trade with the rest of the world.

Government policies not only try to reduce cyclical variations in economic activity but also try to raise the overall rate of growth in national income and output in their economies. However, faster economic growth in output may also mean scarce resources are used up more quickly, and can result in higher levels of pollution and waste. This may not be sustainable in the long term.

Chapter 16 Prices and Employment

Aims

At the end of this chapter you should be able to:

- define **consumer price index** and its simple calculation
- discuss the causes and consequences of **inflation**
- describe changing patterns and levels of employment
- discuss the causes and consequences of **unemployment**

Section 1 What is inflation?

Many of the news headlines on the next page express concern over how the prices of many goods and services are rising, or inflating, over time. However, not all prices rise at the same rate. The prices of some goods and services may even fall over time, perhaps because consumer demand has dropped or because there has been technical progress that has reduced production costs. So what exactly is inflation, and why is it a cause for concern, for consumers, workers, businesses and governments?

13% rise in house prices
ROW OVER FARES RISE
Cheap food era 'over' as prices rise 10pc in supermarkets
Finance Minister concerned about inflation
Price of petrol soars
Industry demands inquiry into surging gas bills
LCD prices fall; on weak PC sales

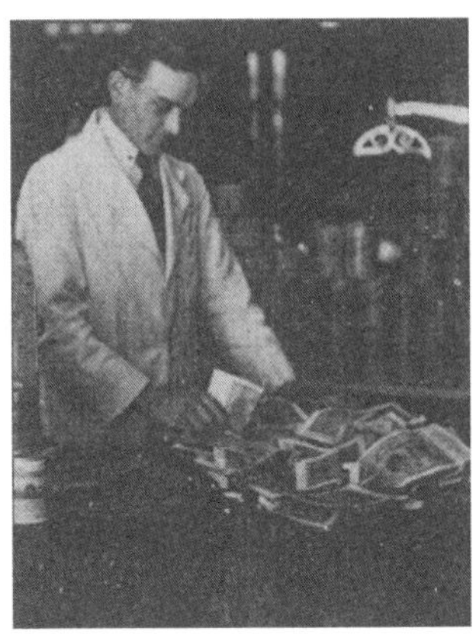

Inflation refers to a general and sustained rise in the level of prices of goods and services. That is, prices of the vast majority of goods and services on sale to consumers just keep on rising and rising. Prices change over time so inflation is always given per period of time – per month or per year. For example, in 2006 the inflation rate in the UK was 2.5 percent. That is, on average the prices of all goods and services rose by 2.9 pence in every pound over that year. However, compared to 1975 this increase in prices appears quite low. In 1975 the inflation rate in the UK was at approximately 25 percent: a good that cost £100 at the start of 1975 would have cost £125 by the start of 1976. But even this inflation rate is low in comparison to the increase in prices some countries have faced at different times in history. In the mid-1990s Brazil experienced a rise in prices by an average of 2 300% in one year while Bolivia faced an inflation rate of 20 000% during the 1980s! This type of runaway inflation during which prices rise at phenomenal rates and money becomes almost worthless has been named **hyperinflation**.

Living with 24,000% Inflation

Germany in the 1920s is often cited as the best example of so-callled "hyperinflation". The Berlin government printed huge quantities of worthless paper money to pay off its debts after World War I. People needed a wheelbarrow full of money to buy one loaf of bread; the joke was that thieves would steal the wheelbarrow – and leave the pile of worthless money behind.

Deflation

Strange as it might seem, a sustained fall in the general level of prices in an economy, or **deflation**, is also a cause for concern. This is because deflation will usually occur when demand for goods and services is falling. Firms are able to sell fewer goods and services and so cut their prices and lose profits. Because they do not need to produce so much, and as they try to cut their costs, firms will reduce the size of their workforces and may even require their remaining workers to take a cut in wages. Household incomes fall as unemployment rises, further reducing demand for goods and services. The value of debts held by people and firms will also rise in real terms as prices fall and the burden of making loan repayments will increase. Eventually the economy goes into a deep recession as demand, output, the demand for labour, and incomes continue to fall (see Chapter 17). Many firms may go out of business because demand continues to fall and they are unable to make any profit no matter how much they cut their prices.

There have been two significant periods of deflation in the world, between 1873 and 1896 following the American Civil War when prices fell in the US on average by 1.7% a year, and in Britain by 0.8% a year, and during the Great Depression in the early 1930s when the rate of deflation in the US was around 10 per cent each year and unemployment reached 25 per cent of the workforce. More recently the worst case of deflation was experienced by Japan, starting in the early 1990s and lasting through to 2006.

Exercise 1 Price inflation in the UK

The graph below shows how the rate of price inflation in the UK varied between 1960 and 2006. A similar historical pattern has been experienced in many other developed countries.

UK Price inflation 1960-2006

% annual change in all items (excluding housing) retail prices index

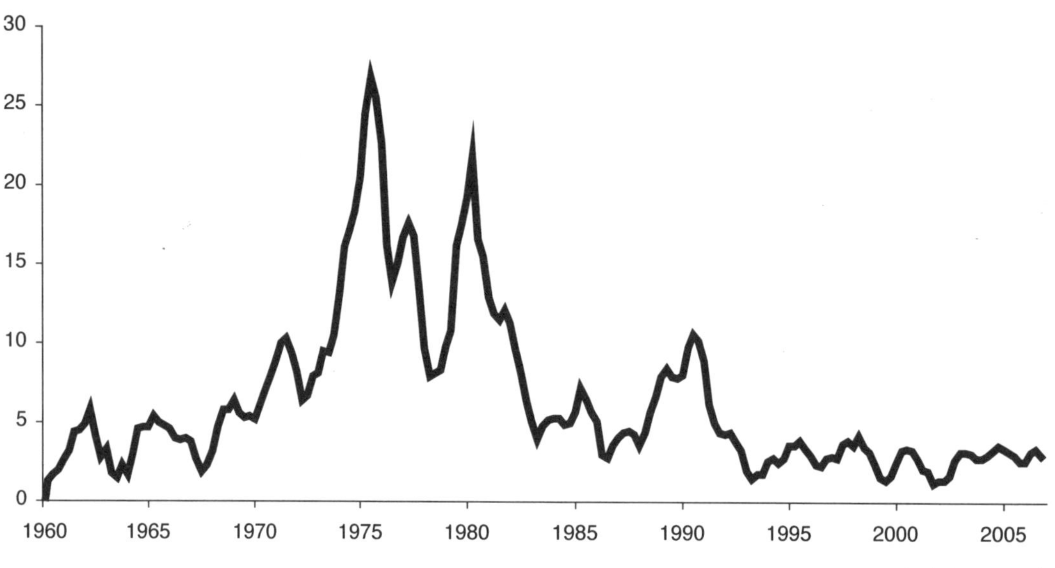

www.statistics.gov.uk

The UK inflation experience can be divided into three broad phases. During the 1960s the rate of price inflation was relatively low and stable, averaging just 3.5 per cent each year. Over the next 15 years from 1970 annual recorded price inflation increased significantly and became much more volatile, averaging 11.6 per cent per year and peaking at nearly 25 per cent in 1975 following a dramatic increase in world oil prices in 1974. This means that between 1970 and the start of 1985 the general level of prices increased almost fivefold, reducing the purchasing power of £1 in 1970 to the equivalent of just 21 pence by 1985. The rapid rise in inflation during the 1970s was accompanied by rising unemployment. The term **stagflation** is used to describe the economic situation when prices and unemployment rise together.

Despite rising back to almost 10 per cent per year in 1990, UK price inflation since then has been relatively low and stable again. From 1991 to 2006 it has averaged just 2.8 per cent per year, falling as low as just 1 per cent in early 2001 and only rising as high as 4.3 per cent in 1991and again in 1998.

1. From the graph, in which year was UK price inflation at its **a** highest **b** lowest?
2. Over which ten-year period was UK price inflation at its **a** highest **b** lowest?
3. Explain the statement 'between 1970 and the start of 1985 the general level of prices increased almost fivefold, reducing the purchasing power of £1 in 1970 to the equivalent of just 21 pence by 1985'. If UK prices rose on average by another 200 per cent between 1985 and 2006 how much would that same £1 be worth in 2006?

Section 2 How to measure inflation

Consumer price indices

The rate of price inflation in an economy is measured by calculating the average percentage change in the prices of all goods and services, from one point in time to another, usually each month and year on year.

However, it is often difficult to obtain up-to-date price information on all the millions of different goods and services in an economy, so most countries track the prices of a selection of goods and services. The goods and services chosen will normally be those purchased by a 'typical' family or household. The prices of this typical 'basket' of goods and services will then be monitored at a selection of different retail outlets across the economy, nowadays also including online retailers. This price information will then be used to compile a **consumer price index (CPI)**. A CPI is used as the main measure of price inflation affecting consumers in an economy, and is often considered to provide a cost-of-living index.

A CPI will usually include any sales taxes and excise taxes paid by consumers on their purchases of goods and services, but exclude changes in income taxes and the prices of assets such as stocks and shares, life insurance and homes. The prices of oil, electricity, gas and food are also often excluded from the calculation of a CPI because their prices can be highly volatile, both up and then down again, due to relatively short-lived shortages caused by the weather, such as droughts or severe winters, or OPEC-led cutbacks in oil production (see Chapter 8). These products are therefore excluded on the grounds they can distort measures of more 'usual' price inflation.

Calculating a price index

Index number series, or indices, are simply a way of expressing the change in the prices of a number of different products as a movement in just one single number. The average price of the 'basket' of products in the first year of calculation, or **base year**, is given the number 100. Then, if on average the prices of all the goods and services in the same 'basket' rise by 25 per cent over the following year, the price index at the end of the second year will be 125. If, in the next year, prices rise on average by a further 10 per cent, the price index will rise to 137.5 (that is, 125 + (125 × 10%) = 137.5). This tells us consumer prices have risen on average by 37.5 per cent over a two-year period.

Consider the following simple example to construct a consumer price index. Imagine there are 100 households in our simple economy. The weekly spending patterns of these households have been observed over a 12-month period: the base year. The table below shows what they spend their total income on, less their spending on food and fuel. The average prices of the goods and services they buy have been calculated for each category of their spending from a sample of different shops.

How to calculate a simple CPI: spending profile of households in base year

Types of goods and services	Proportion of weekly household income spent on each category	Average price ($) of goods and services purchased in each category	Weighted average price ($)
Travel and leisure	15%	$20.00	0.15 × $20.00 = $3.00
Household goods and services	25%	$40.00	0.25 × $40.00 = $10.00
Clothing and footwear	40%	$30.00	0.40 × $30.00 = $12.00
Transport	20%	$25.00	0.20 × $25.00 = $5.00
	Total = 100%		*Price of basket = $30.00*

The proportion of total household income spent on each category is used to weight the average prices of each type of good and service to find their weighted average prices. These tell us how big an impact a change in the price of one particular type of good or service will have on the cost of living of our households. For example, from the table it should be clear that a 10 per cent increase in the average price of household goods and services, from $40 to $44 per item, will matter less than a 10 per cent increase in clothing and footwear prices, from $30 to $33 per item, because our households spend proportionately more on clothes and shoes. The weighted average price per item of clothing and footwear purchased is higher than the weighted average price of household items purchased.

Adding up the weighted average prices for the basket of goods and services in the table above equals $30. We set this overall weighted average price in our base year equal to 100 to begin our consumer price index.

We now observe how prices and the weekly spending patterns of the same households change over time over the following year in order to recalculate weighted average prices and the consumer price index. Notice how both prices and the proportion of household income spent on each category of goods and services have changed in the table below. The biggest increases in prices have been in clothing and footwear, followed by household goods and services, up by almost 27 per cent and 15 per cent respectively. As a result households are now spending proportionately less of their income on these items. In contrast, spending on travel and leisure has increased while the proportion of income spent on transport has fallen as transport prices have fallen. This suggests household demand for transport in our simple economy is price inelastic (see Chapter 7).

How to calculate a simple CPI: spending profile of households in year 1

Types of goods and services	Proportion of weekly household income spent on each category	Average price ($) of goods and services purchased in each category	Weighted average price ($)
Travel and leisure	25%	$22.00	0.25 × $22.00 = $5.50
Household goods and services	25%	$46.00	0.25 × $46.00 = $11.50
Clothing and footwear	35%	$38.00	0.35 × $38.00 = $13.30
Transport	15%	$20.00	0.15 × $20.00 = $3.00
	Total = 100%		*Price of basket = $33.30*

The overall weighted average price of the basket of goods and services at the end of year 1 is now $33.30. This represents an 11 per cent increase in the price of the basket since the base year. That is, consumer price inflation has been 11 per cent over the year since the base year. The consumer price index at the end of year 1 is therefore 111, i.e.

$$\text{CPI in year 1} = \frac{\text{Weighted average price year 1}}{\text{Weighted average price base year}} = \frac{\$33.30}{\$30.00} \times 100 = 111$$

Imagine now we repeat the entire exercise for a further year and calculate a weighted average price for the basket of goods and services of $36.00. The consumer price index at the end of year 2 will then be 120.

$$\text{CPI in year 2} = \frac{\text{Weighted average price year 2}}{\text{Weighted average price base year}} = \frac{\$36.30}{\$30.00} \times 100 = 120$$

This tells us that average consumer prices have risen by 20 per cent since the base year.

Exercise 2 A calculated problem

1. Continuing the same example above, use the information on average prices and household spending patterns in the table below to calculate the weighted price of the basket of goods and services at the end of years 3 and 4.
2. Use the weighted average price of the basket at the end of each year to calculate the consumer price index.
3. Overall, by how much has the weighted average price of the basket of consumer goods and services risen by since the base year?
4. In which year was price inflation at its **a** highest **b** lowest?

Types of goods and services	Proportion of weekly household income spent on each category		Average price ($) of goods and services purchased in each category	
	Year 3	Year 4	Year 3	Year 4
Travel and leisure	25%	28%	30	40
Household goods and services	24%	20%	55	60
Clothing and footwear	35%	35%	46	50
Transport	16%	16%	22	25

5. Suggest why and how you might account for the following changes in the calculation of your consumer price index over time:
   - Changes in the number, structure and composition of households, for example, due to inward migration and an ageing population.
   - Changes in retailing, for example, online retailing over the Internet.
   - Changes in the quality of goods and services, for example, the increased performance and efficiency of cars and household goods such as microwaves and ovens.
   - New goods and services not previously available, such as LCD televisions and iPODs.

Uses of CPI data

There are three main uses of a consumer price index in most modern economies:

1 As an economic indicator

The CPI is a widely used measure of price inflation, and therefore as a measure of changes in the cost of living. Governments try to control price inflation using their macroeconomic policies (see Chapter 14). The CPI in an economy will also be used by workers to seek increases in their wages that match or exceed the increase in their cost of living, and by entrepreneurs in making many business decisions concerning their purchases, and the setting of wages and prices.

2 As a price deflator

Rising prices reduce the purchasing power, or real value, of money. Rising prices will therefore affect the real value of wages, profits, pensions, savings, interest payments on loans, tax revenues and a host of other economic variables of importance to different groups of people and decision makers. A CPI is therefore used to deflate other economic series to calculate their real or inflation-free values. For example, if wages have risen by 10 per cent, but price inflation has risen by 15 per cent, then the real value of wages will actually have fallen by 5 per cent because the purchasing power of those wages has been reduced by inflation.

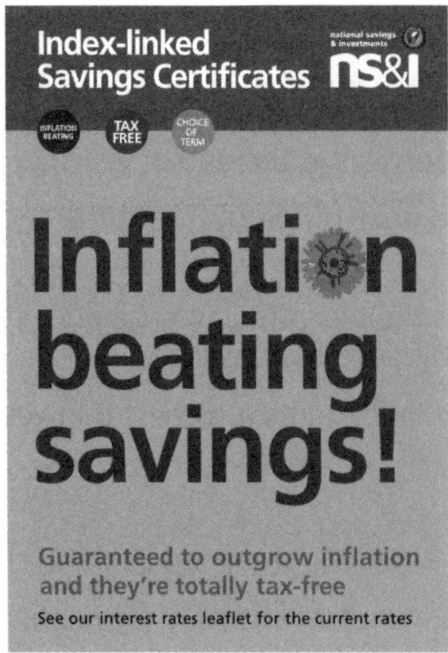

3 Indexation

Indexation involves tying certain payments to the rate of increase in the CPI. For example, pensions paid to retired people by a government may be indexed so that they increase by the rate of inflation each year. Similarly, savings may be index-linked, meaning that the interest rate is set equal to the CPI thereby protecting the real value of people's savings. Many workers may also be covered by collective bargaining agreements that tie their wage increases to changes in the CPI (see Chapter 5). A government may also index the threshold at which people start to pay tax or higher rates of tax on their incomes, otherwise people would end up paying more income tax simply due to price inflation even if their real incomes were unchanged each year (see Chapter 15).

Some problems with price indices

Over time the 'typical' household and basket of goods and services will tend to change. A CPI will need to take account of these changes but deciding how and when to make them can be difficult. For example, household spending patterns will tend to change over time due to:

- changes in tastes and fashion
- the introduction of new goods and services, such as mobile phones, LCD televisions and iPODs
- the changing composition of the population and households, due to migration, changes in birth and death rates, later marriages (see Chapter 20).

Similarly, a CPI will also need to take account of changes in the quality of goods and services over time, and how and where households buy goods and services, including the introduction of new shops, TV shopping channels and the increasing use of online shopping using the Internet.

International comparisons of consumer price inflation are difficult to make because household composition and spending patterns can differ widely between countries.

It is also argued that the exclusion of such items as food, energy and house prices, and income taxes, means that a CPI may not provide an accurate measure of changes in the cost of living of many households if, for example, income taxes, house prices and energy prices are all rising rapidly.

Section 3 What causes inflation?

Inflation and the supply of money

Economists today tend to agree that the main cause of inflation is 'too much money chasing too few goods'. This means people are able to increase their spending on goods and services faster than producers can supply the goods and services they want to buy. The rise in spending causes an excess of aggregate demand for goods and services and their prices are forced upwards.

A government can allow the supply of money to rise in an economy by issuing more notes and coins or allowing the banking system to create more credit, that is, lending more to people and firms to spend (see Chapter 6). A government may expand the money supply:

- to increase total demand in the economy in an attempt to reduce unemployment
- in response to an increase in demand for goods and services from consumers and firms
- in response to workers demands for higher wages, or a rise in the other costs of production

Exercise 3 The money supply and prices

The graph below shows the rate of inflation in the UK as measured by the consumer price index, and the rate of growth in the money supply from 1970 to 2005. (The money supply here is defined as all notes and coins in circulation plus money held by private sector individuals and firms in deposit accounts with banks and building societies; see Chapter 2.)

UK Money supply and price inflation 1970-2005
% annual change

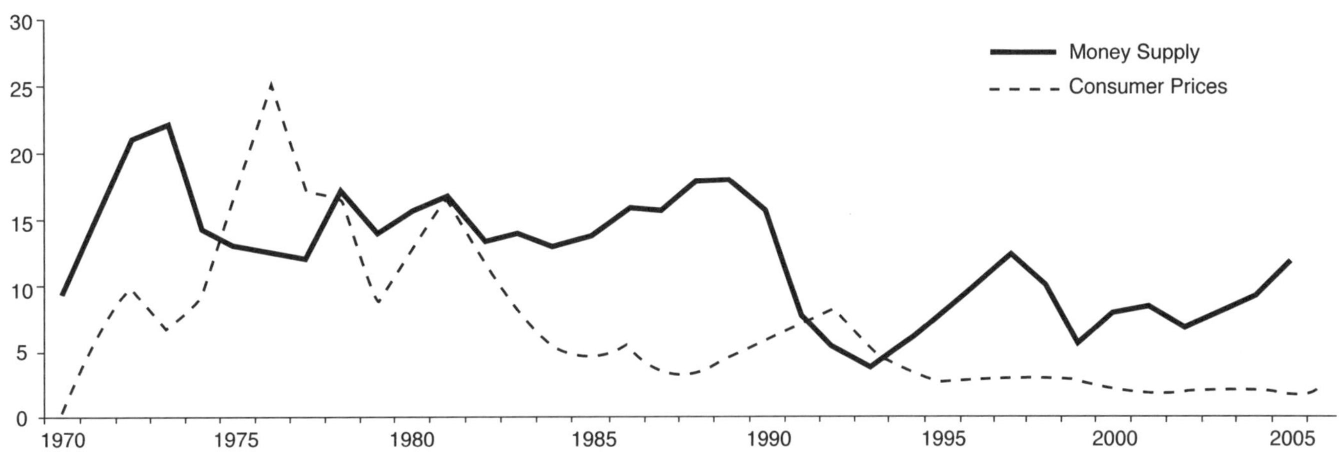

1. If the supply of money rises, how will this affect the amount of spending on goods and services?
2. Given what is likely to happen to spending, what effect will this change in demand have on the prices of goods and services?
3. If people try to spend more on goods and services but there are no more available, suggest what will happen to their prices and why.
4. Does the graph suggest that an increase in the rate of growth in the money supply causes higher inflation one year or so later? Give examples from the graph to support your view.

If the money supply expands people will have more money to spend. As they spend this money the increase in demand forces up the prices of the goods and services they buy. To understand why increases in the rate of growth in the money supply cause inflation let us consider a very simple example.

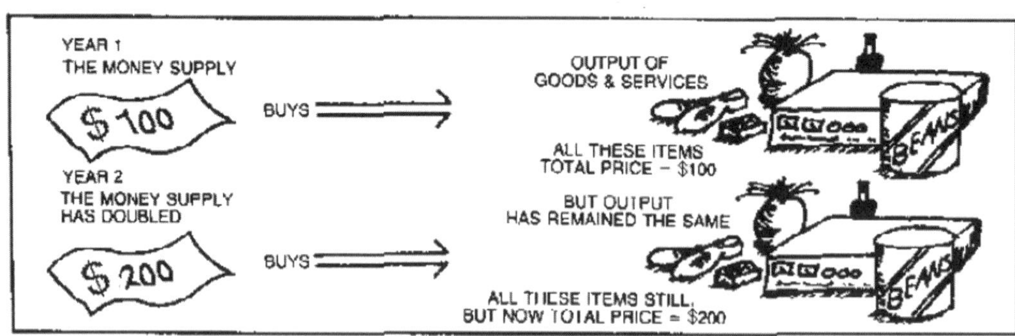

In year 1 the money supply stood at $100 and bought six items for a total cost of $100. In the second year output has remained the same. The simple economy can only produce six items. There are no more resources available to make any more each year. Now suppose the growth in the money supply is 100 per cent. That is it doubles to $200. As consumers try to spend this money they find there are no extra goods and services to buy. With a fixed supply prices must rise. Indeed, they double. Inflation is 100 per cent! Clearly, if output could have risen prices need not have gone up by so much, if at all.

A monetary rule

Economists argue that what is true in the simple example above is true for a highly complex economy. Any increase in the supply of money will cause inflation to accelerate if there is no growth in real output. Only if the output of goods and services rises should the money supply rise, so that people have enough money to buy up these extra products.

This means there is a **monetary rule** a government can follow if it wants to keep inflation low and stable in the economy: it should only allow the supply of money to expand at the same rate as the increase in real output or real GDP over time. Increases in the money supply over and above increases in output simply cause inflation to rise. However, this can take time. It may take a year or more before prices increase faster after a rise in the money supply. It takes time for consumers' spending to rise, firms to realize demand has increased, and for firms to raise their prices.

Government policy and inflation

Some economists argue that different governments over time only have themselves to blame for the high inflation rates many countries experienced during the 1970s and 1980s. This is because they tried to boost demand to reduce unemployment in their economies in periods when labour unemployment was high and rising. They did this by allowing the money supply to expand faster than output was growing. For a time the increase in demand would reduce unemployment as firms took on more resources to produce more goods and services. However, inflation soon began to rise as aggregate demand increased faster than output. Eventually the high inflation would reduce the purchasing power of people's incomes and demand for goods and services would begin to fall. Workers would demand higher wages to keep pace with the rising cost of living and so unemployment would rise again as firms reduced their demand for labour. As a result, government policy was responsible for **stagflation** – a situation when inflation and unemployment were high and/or rising together.

Demand-pull inflation

Inflation caused by an increase in total demand is called **demand-pull inflation**. Total or aggregate demand in an economy will rise if spending by governments, consumers and/or firms increases. Consumers will be able to spend more of their incomes if they reduce savings or if a government cuts income taxes.

An increase in aggregate demand will cause prices to increase and inflation to rise if firms are unable to increase the supply of goods and services at the same rate as demand.

To finance an increase in aggregate demand consumers and firms may borrow more from the banking system and/or the government can issue more notes and coins. Both these ways of financing an increase in demand involve increasing the supply of money in an economy.

Cost-push inflation

Inflation caused by higher costs feeding into higher prices is called **cost-push inflation**. The cost of producing goods and services can rise because workers demand increases in wages not matched by increased productivity (see Chapter 12). Firms may pass these higher costs on to consumers as higher prices so that they do not have to suffer a cut in their profits. However, as wages rise the demand for labour will tend to fall and workers could be made unemployed. To prevent a rise in unemployment the government may expand the supply of money to boost aggregate demand.

Continual increases in prices may take place if workers demand more and more wages time and time again. This will cause a **wage–price spiral**. As prices rise, workers will want more wages so they can buy the more expensive products. However, these higher wages simply add to firms' costs and so prices rise even further prompting even higher wage demands. And so it goes on.

Increases in the cost of materials, transport, power and other costs of production can also cause inflation if the higher costs are passed on to consumers as higher prices. Inflation rose rapidly in many economics in 1974 and 1979 following significant increases in the world price of oil.

Imported inflation

Rising prices in one country may be 'exported' to other countries through international trade in many different goods and services (see Chapter 18). Rising import prices can cause **imported inflation**. Similarly, a fall in the value of the currency of one country against the currencies of other countries will mean imports become more expensive in that country. For example, if value of the euro against the Indian rupee falls from €1 = 60 rupees to €1 = 30 rupees, then a product imported to Europe from India costing 600 rupees will rise from €10 to €20 (see also Chapter 18).

It has been argued that one of the reasons many developed economies have enjoyed relatively low and stable price inflation since around 2000 has been the expansion of the Chinese economy and increasing trade with China. Low wages in China and the increase in the global supply of many of the goods and services now exported from China have kept prices low. However, this may change as China develops further and there is pressure to increase wages in the country.

Section 4 The costs of inflation

People are always moaning about rising prices. But why is inflation thought to be so bad?

Exercise 4 How inflation can affect different households

The diagram below shows how different income groups in a developed economy might allocate their spending among different goods and services.

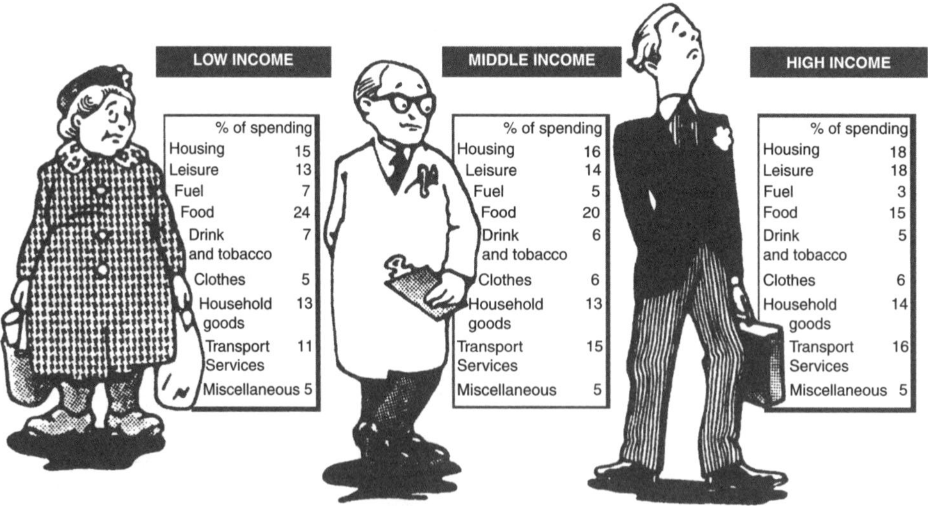

1. How does inflation affect the amount of goods and services money can buy?
2. Which income group displayed above will be the most affected by a rise in the price of:
   a. food, heating fuel and housing costs?
   b. household goods and transport?
3. Are people always worse off if prices rise? Explain your answer.
4. Which income groups above are probably the:
   a. most able
   b. least able to increase their incomes?

The personal costs of inflation

Rising prices reduce the **purchasing power** of people's incomes. That is, their **real income**, in terms of what it can buy, falls. For example, if a person's income in terms of money, or their **money income** (also called **nominal income**), was $100 it could buy ten goods at $10 each. If each one of those goods goes up in price to $20 their money income of $100 will now only buy five of those goods. That is, real income has fallen. Clearly, if that person could increase their money income to $200 they will be no worse off. However, many people will face hardship if they are unable to increase their money incomes.

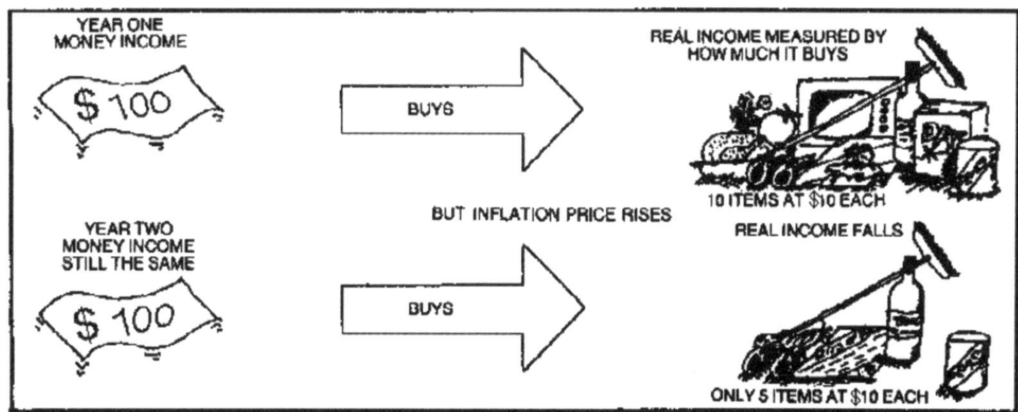

People like pensioners and students are often on fixed incomes decided by their government. If the prices of the goods and services they buy rise they may not be able to afford as much food and heating as before. Their real incomes and therefore their living standards will fall. For example, if the general level of prices rises by 10% in one year real incomes will have fallen by 10 per cent.

Professional people and workers in strong trade unions may be able to ask for wage or salary increases that match price rises to protect their real wages or incomes. Indeed, they may be able to secure a rise in their money incomes that exceeds the rate of inflation. For example, if inflation is 10 per cent in one year and money incomes rise by 15 per cent, then in real terms they will be 5 per cent better off. However, many workers, especially the low paid and nonunionized workers, may not be able to do this. As prices rise they become worse off.

People who save or lend money may also be hurt by inflation. If they find the interest rate received on money they have saved or loaned is lower than the inflation rate the real value of their money will fall. They will be worse off. On the other hand, people who borrow money will benefit by repaying less in real terms than they borrowed.

Old age pensioners and other people on fixed incomes, are particularly vulnerable to high and rising inflation. Their incomes may not rise as fast as prices and will therefore buy them less and less over time. Raising pensions and other fixed incomes in line with inflation, known as indexation or index-linking, can help overcome this problem.

In demand-pull inflation increased spending tends to boost company profits. However, in cost-push inflation their profits are squeezed. Rising prices may also yield the government more tax revenue as the tax paid, as a percentage of the price of goods and services, rises as their prices rise. However, the government will also have to pay more for the goods and services it buys.

The costs of inflation to the economy

Some economists argue that inflation causes unemployment. As prices rise, people cannot afford to buy so many goods and services and so demand falls. In addition, some people save more in times of high inflation to protect the real value of their savings. This again means less spending on goods and services. As a result firms may cut their output and make resources, including labour, unemployed.

Many economies suffered both high rates of unemployment and price inflation in the 1970s and 1980s at the same time.

If the rate of inflation in, for example, Germany is higher than the rate of price inflation in other countries then it becomes more and more difficult for German firms to sell their increasingly expensive goods and services overseas. In addition, German consumers may increase their spending on cheaper imports and buy fewer domestic products.

The argument continues as follows. If Germany can reduce its inflation rate it will become more competitive and be able to sell more goods and services. If this is so, more workers will be needed and unemployment will fall. The same will be true in other countries suffering from relatively high rates of inflation and unemployment.

Section 5 Employment trends

Most governments have an objective to maintain a high and stable level of employment in their economies, and a low level of unemployment. Employment provides people with incomes and wealth. In contrast, unemployment wastes productive resources.

Because of these objectives, governments and economists will be interested in keeping a close eye on the following employment trends.

Key employment indicators

Labour force	The total number of people of working age in work or actively seeking work
Labour force participation rate	The labour force as a proportion of the total working age population
Employment by industrial sector	How many people work in agriculture and manufacturing industries, relative to services
Employment status	The number of people employed full-time, part-time or in temporary work
Unemployment	The number of people registered as being without work, and as a proportion of the total labour force (the unemployment rate)

Global employment and unemployment, 1995–2005

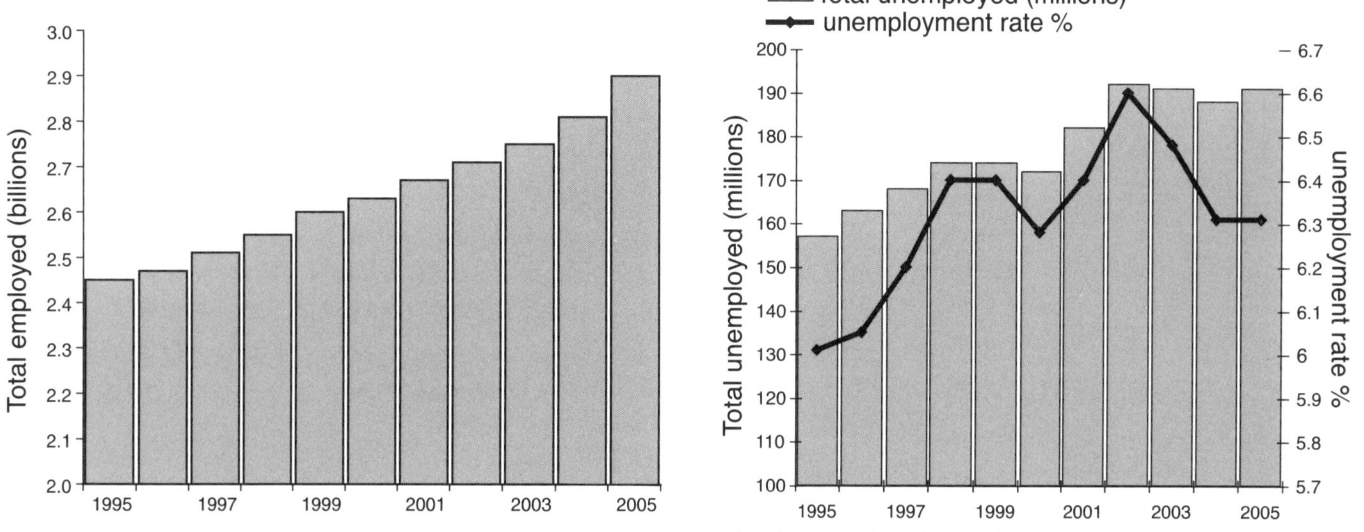

International Labour Organization (ILO) *Global Employment Trends*, 2006

Labour force participation

Between 1995 and 2005 the global labour force grew by 438 million workers, to just over 3 billion. The **labour force** or **working population** of a country represents all those people of working age who are both able and willing to work. That is, it will represent the total supply of labour in a country and usually includes people who are employed by private sector firms and public sector organizations, the self-employed, the armed forces, those on work-related government training programmes and even people who are unemployed but looking for work. People not counted as part of the labour force include students in education, retired people, stay-at-home parents, people in prisons or similar institutions, as well as people who simply do not want to work.

The working population

The **labour force participation rate** is a measure of the proportion of working-age population that is either working or looking for work and therefore able to produce goods and services. Globally the labour force participation rate has fallen slightly, from 66.9 per cent in 1995 to 65.7 per cent over the 10-year period to 2005. Part of this decline is explained by the increasing number of younger people in education worldwide and the growing number of old and retired people in many developed countries (see Chapter 20).

Labour force participation rates (%), world and selected countries 1995–2005

	1995			2000			2005		
	Total	Male	Female	**Total**	Male	Female	**Total**	Male	Female
World	66.9	*80.6*	*53.1*	66.2	*79.9*	*52.6*	65.7	*79.0*	*52.5*
Germany	58.5	*69.7*	*48.2*	57.1	*66.6*	*48.2*	58.0	*65.9*	*50.5*
Indonesia	67.8	*84.8*	*51.3*	67.9	*84.6*	*51.5*	68.0	*85.6*	*50.6*
Pakistan	48.4	*82.3*	*12.7*	50.4	*83.2*	*16.3*	50.7	*82.7*	*18.0*
Morocco	48.1	*75.1*	*22.3*	51.3	*77.9*	*25.5*	52.6	*77.5*	*28.4*
UK	62.4	*71.9*	*53.4*	63.1	*71.7*	*54.9*	62.6	*69.8*	*55.9*
US	66.6	*78.9*	*58.9*	67.1	*74.7*	*60.2*	66.0	*73.3*	*64.9*

International Labour Organization (ILO) labour statistics

In contrast, participation in the labour force has been rising over time in many countries, and especially among females. There are a number of reasons for this. In less developed countries, poverty has forced many people to seek paid employment rather than work on the land to grow the food they need and hopefully to make a surplus to sell. However, a great many workers in less developed countries earn only very low wages (see Chapter 19).

Increasing real wages in many developed and developing countries have also attracted more people into work (see Chapter 10). The rising cost of living in many of these same countries has also meant more people going into work or working longer hours to earn the money they need to continue to satisfy their needs and wants for goods and services. This in part can help explain mothers returning to work after raising children, or younger women going out to work rather than starting a family. Social attitudes have also changed towards wives and mothers working and many more part-time jobs have become available to them.

However, male participation rates have generally been falling. This has been linked to the changing industrial structure in many developed countries, with traditionally male-dominated jobs in mining and manufacturing disappearing over time.

Employment by industrial sector

In 2005, agriculture accounted for 40 per cent of total world employment, or around 1.1 billion workers. This compared to 21 per cent employed in mining, construction and manufacturing industries, and 38.9 per cent in services.

There are big regional differences. In developed economies such as the US and Europe, agriculture employed just 3.7 per cent of their employees in 2005. The service sector dominates these economies accounting for over 71 per cent of their total employment. In stark contrast, agriculture dominates employment in countries in South Asia and sub-Saharan Africa, employing over 60 per cent of all employees in these countries (see also Chapter 20).

However, all countries are experiencing the same broad trends. The share of employment accounted for by jobs in agriculture and industry has been falling as the share of total employment accounted for by services has risen. Globally, services employed almost 39 per cent of the world's employees in 2005 compared to 34.5 per cent in 1995.

Changes in the industrial structure of economies have been a cause for some concern. The loss of jobs from mining and manufacturing industries has resulted in high unemployment in some cases, especially in areas where these industries dominated. The decline of employment in agriculture and the expansion of jobs in industry and services has also meant that many people have moved from rural areas into urban areas in many countries. The rapid growth of densely populated urban areas, increasing demands for energy, rising car use and overcrowding are causing many problems (see Chapters 20 and 22).

Employment share (%) by industrial sector, 1995 and 2005

	Agriculture		Industry		Services	
Region	1995	2005	1995	2005	1995	2005
World	44.4	40.1	21.1	21.0	34.5	38.9
Developed Economies and European Union	5.1	3.7	28.7	24.8	66.1	71.4
Central and Eastern Europe (Non-EU), CIS*	27.9	22.7	27.5	27.4	44.6	49.9
East Asia	54.4	49.5	25.9	26.1	19.7	24.4
South East Asia and the Pacific	55.3	43.3	15.4	20.7	29.3	36.0
South Asia	64.1	61.2	13.4	14.1	22.5	24.6
Latin America and the Caribbean	23.4	17.1	20.2	20.3	56.4	62.5
Middle East and North Africa	30.8	26.3	20.3	25.0	48.9	48.7
Sub-Saharan Africa	70.1	63.6	8.2	8.9	21.7	27.5

* Commonwealth of Independent States of former Soviet Republics *ILO Global Employment Trends*, 2006

Employment status

Most workers, especially males, work full-time which for many means working Monday to Friday each week, for around 7 to 8 hours each day. However, hours of work vary greatly in different countries. For example, the average US worker worked 43.6 hours each week in 2005, up from 41 hours in 2000. This compared to an average in 2005 of 47.5 hours per worker per week in China, 34.8 hours in Spain, 51.4 hours in Turkey and around 56 hours in Egypt.

In many countries, average hours worked per week have fallen slightly over time as working conditions have improved, and as a result of more part-time working. For example, average hours worked in France fell from 40 in 1995 to just over 37 hours per week by 2005.

There has been rapid growth in part-time work in the past few decades and in Sunday working in many developed economies. These trends are related to the increase in the female participation rate, but also linked to growth in the services sector, and particularly in retailing. Hiring part-time workers allows firms greater flexibility to remain operational for more hours each day and to use more staff during busy periods.

Unemployment

People without work but who are actively looking for work are considered to be unemployed. In 2005, nearly 192 million people were unemployed, an increase of 34.4 million since 1995. Almost half of the unemployed are young people. Young workers often lack the skills and experience they need in work and are often the first to be laid off when firms are cutting back staff to reduce costs or during an economic recession when demand is falling (see Chapter 17).

Unemployment is usually measured by the number of people claiming unemployment benefits. However, in many countries benefits may only be paid for a short period of time, and some people who want to work may not receive unemployment benefits. This group might include people who are old or disabled, mothers looking after children at home, students who want to work but instead continue with their education, and people who may only work a few hours each week but would like to work longer. In practice, therefore, measuring the number of unemployed workers actually seeking work is very difficult and can vary by country. Some countries do not pay benefits to unemployed people and may not even count the number of people without paid work, so numbers are estimated where possible.

Unemployment rate (%), 1995–2005

Region	1995	2005
World	6.0	6.3
Developed economies and European Union	7.8	6.7
Central and Eastern Europe (Non-EU) & CIS	9.4	9.7
East Asia	3.7	3.8
South East Asia and the Pacific	3.9	6.1
South Asia	4.0	4.7
Latin America and the Caribbean	7.6	7.7
Middle East and North Africa	14.3	13.2
Sub-Saharan Africa	9.2	9.7

ILO *Global Employment Trends*, 2006

Countries with the highest unemployment rates (%)

Country	Unemployment rate (%) est.
Nauru	90
Liberia	85
Zimbabwe	80
Turkmenistan	60
Cocos (Keeling) Islands	60
Zambia	50
East Timor	50
Djibouti	50
Senegal	48
Bosnia and Herzegovina	46

CIA World Factbook, 2006

The **unemployment rate** in a country is the number of unemployed workers divided by its total labour force. Unemployment rates across the world changed very little between 2000 and 2005. In 2005, the Middle East and North Africa region had the highest unemployment rate in the world at 13.2 per cent, although it was down from 14.3 per cent in 1995. Over the same period the unemployment rate in South East Asia and the Pacific increased significantly from 3.9 per cent to 6.1 per cent of the region's labour force.

Exercise 5 Calculating unemployment rates

The table below presents date on the labour force and number of people unemployed in selected countries in 2000 and 2005. From these, calculate the unemployment rate in each country for each year using the following formula.

$$\text{Unemployment rate (\%)} = \frac{\text{Number unemployed}}{\text{Labour force}} \times \frac{100}{1}$$

Country	Labour force ('000s)		Unemployment ('000s)	
	2000	2005	2000	2005
Croatia	1945	1802	297	229
France	26226	27447	2590	2727
Japan	67680	66500	3190	2940
Philippines	47742	53252	2689	3258
South Africa	16000	16485	4208	4385
UK	29412	29517	1619	1352
USA	140863	149320	5655	7591

International Labour Organization (ILO) Labour statistics

Many developed economies have successfully reduced the high rates of unemployment suffered particularly in the 1980s, largely as a result of rapid decline in manufacturing jobs. For example, unemployment peaked at nearly 12 per cent of the labour force or 3.3 million people in UK during the early to mid 1980s. Nearly 11 million people were unemployed in the US in the early 1980s, around 9.5 per cent of the labour force. However, in France unemployment has remained high at over 2.5 million people, while in Japan it has increased markedly from just over 1.1 million in the early 1980s to a peak of nearly 3.6 million people in 2002. However, in contrast to developed economies such as these, many countries in Africa continue to suffer the very highest rates of unemployment among their populations.

Section 6 Unemployment

Exercise 6 What causes unemployment?

Look at the extracts below. What do they suggest causes unemployment? In groups, write a report for your government expressing a summary of your thoughts on the possible causes of unemployment and what action you would take to reduce it.

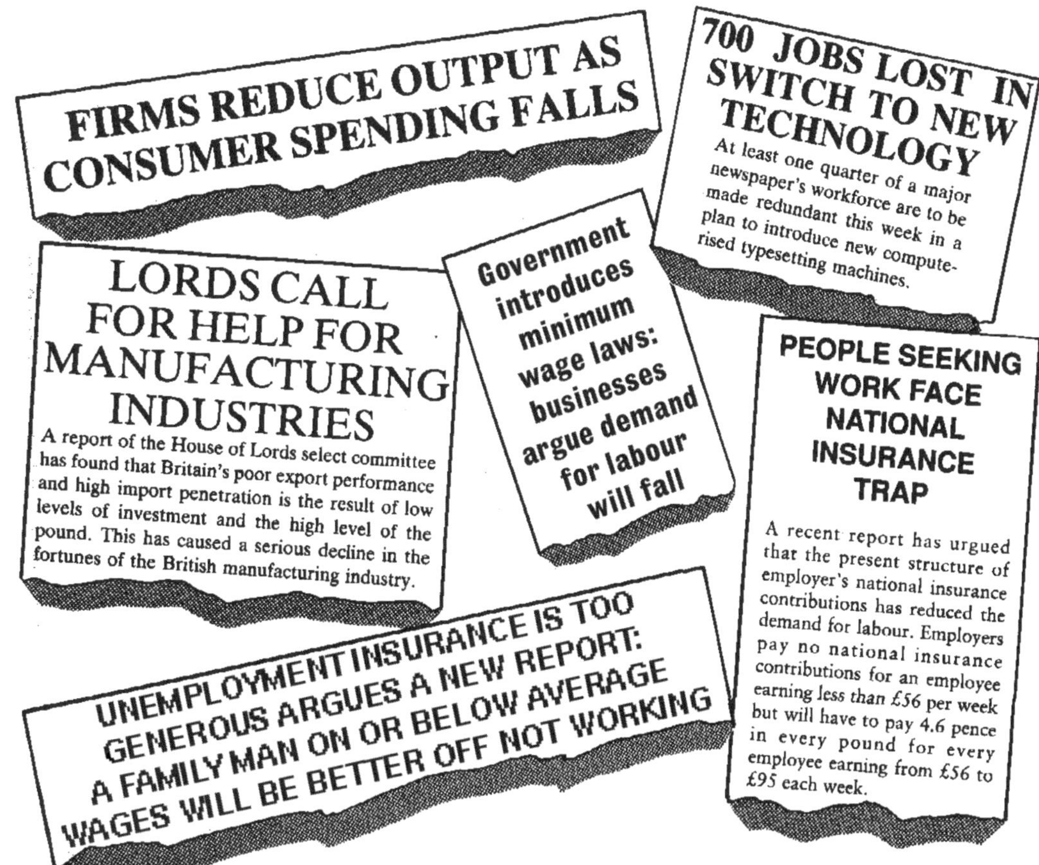

FIRMS REDUCE OUTPUT AS CONSUMER SPENDING FALLS

700 JOBS LOST IN SWITCH TO NEW TECHNOLOGY

At least one quarter of a major newspaper's workforce are to be made redundant this week in a plan to introduce new computerised typesetting machines.

LORDS CALL FOR HELP FOR MANUFACTURING INDUSTRIES

A report of the House of Lords select committee has found that Britain's poor export performance and high import penetration is the result of low levels of investment and the high level of the pound. This has caused a serious decline in the fortunes of the British manufacturing industry.

Government introduces minimum wage laws: businesses argue demand for labour will fall

PEOPLE SEEKING WORK FACE NATIONAL INSURANCE TRAP

A recent report has urged that the present structure of employer's national insurance contributions has reduced the demand for labour. Employers pay no national insurance contributions for an employee earning less than £56 per week but will have to pay 4.6 pence in every pound for every employee earning from £56 to £95 each week.

UNEMPLOYMENT INSURANCE IS TOO GENEROUS ARGUES A NEW REPORT: A FAMILY MAN ON OR BELOW AVERAGE WAGES WILL BE BETTER OFF NOT WORKING

There will always be some unemployment in an economy. **Frictional unemployment** occurs as workers change jobs and spend some time looking for a new one. Workers may become unemployed for relatively short periods as they leave jobs they dislike, move to higher paid jobs, move their homes, are made redundant or are sacked. People who are 'in-between jobs' do not tend to remain unemployed for long.

Seasonal unemployment occurs because consumer demand for some goods and services is seasonal. For example, the number of jobs in the tourist industry tends to expand during the summer because that is when most people want to take holidays. However, are during winter months many workers in hotels and holiday resorts are not required. The building industry also tends to be very seasonal.

Frictional and seasonal unemployment are not a big problem. Most governments, however, are concerned with unemployment that is long-lived and due to more serious problems in their economies.

Falling demand

Falling demand for goods and services can have a downward multiplier effect on output, employment and incomes.

Cyclical unemployment occurs when there is too little demand for goods and services in the economy during an economic recession (see Chapter 16). Falling demand during a slump in an economic cycle will mean falling spending on goods and services. In response firms will reduce production and workers may become unemployed. The mass unemployment experienced in many countries during the 1930s was the result of a deep world recession.

A change in aggregate demand whatever its source, be it consumption expenditure, investment by firms, government spending and/or spending on exports by foreign countries, can have widespread effects in the economy. Once started, a change in expenditure will tend to carry on. Why is this so?

Exercise 7 The rise and rise of unemployment

A small fall in demand in an economy can have widespread effects. This is known as the multiplier effect.

Here is an example of how unemployment can spread. Suppose the demand for motor cars falls.

Imagine there is a car manufacturer called Fast Cars UK. It has a plant in the south-east of England that assembles cars from parts made all over the UK at different sites.
As people buy fewer cars Fast Cars UK has no need to make so many. Thus, 400 people are made redundant (i.e. lose their jobs). Now see how this spreads.

1 How many jobs are lost immediately as a result of the fall in demand for cars?

2 How many jobs are lost in Fast Cars UK in total?

3 All the factories use electricity. As they now produce fewer cars they do not need as much electricity. What will happen to workers at power stations?

4 Power stations run on coal and oil. What will happen to the demand for coal and oil? What will happen to coal-miners and oil-drillers?

5 All the people who have lost their jobs now have less money to spend on clothes, records, entertainment, food and many other things. What will happen to the level of demand for all other goods?

In the example the fall in demand for cars caused Fast Cars UK to reduce production and employment in many of its factories. Fast Cars UK buys materials and uses power produced by other industries which reduce their output as demand for their commodity falls. The workers who find themselves out of work have less money to spend. Shops suffer and have to reduce their orders from wholesalers and manufacturers. The fall in demand for goods and services is general now and causes many more firms to reduce their output and employment. As unemployment rises so aggregate demand falls. Firms reduce output and employment further. This is known as the **multiplier effect** whereby a small change in spending can cause large changes in income, output and employment.

Structural change

If the fall in demand for some goods and services is permanent because of a change in people's tastes, for example, in favour of new goods and services or cheaper sources of supply from overseas firms, the change in demand is called structural.

Structural unemployment arises from long-term changes in the structure of the economy as entire industries close down because of a lack of demand for the goods or services they produce. As a result, many workers are made unemployed and have skills which are no longer wanted. That is, they are occupationally immobile. Re-training in new skills may help them become more mobile and find new jobs.

Structural change is evident in many developed and developing economies. Many years ago far more people were employed in agriculture than in manufacturing industries. Manufacturing has also changed over time in many countries from labour-intensive production in industries such as shipbuilding, coal mining and textiles, to high-tech capital-intensive production of computers, pharmaceuticals and audio-visual equipment. Nowadays most workers in developed countries are employed in services.

Technological advance

Technological progress has meant machines have become smaller but are able to undertake much more work. Computers and microchip technology have revolutionized the production of many goods and services, and in some cases labour has been replaced by machines giving rise to what some people term technological unemployment. However, as economists we should recognize the potential benefits of being able to reallocate these unemployed resources to other uses. For example, there has been a rapid growth in employment in technologically advanced industries such as electronics, computers and communications.

Imperfections in the labour market

In a free labour market the forces of demand and supply will determine the wages workers are paid for different jobs and how many workers are employed (see Chapter 10). However, it is often argued that labour markets in many countries have imperfections. That is, there are factors that interfere with the way markets work and reduce the number of workers employed.

1 Powerful trade unions demand wages that are too high

Trade unions may attempt to increase the wages of their members which are not matched by improvements in productivity – for example, by threatening to take industrial action (see Chapter 5). As wages rise, employers may not be able to afford as many workers and so reduce their demand for labour. Reducing the power of trade unions, it is argued, may allow wages to fall and employment to rise.

2 Benefits paid to the unemployed can reduce the incentive to work

Some countries provide cash and social security benefits to people who become unemployed. However, some people argue this can reduce the incentive to seek work, especially if these benefits are too generous.

People who decide not to work (**voluntary unemployment**) may be forced back to work by cutting the benefits they receive. However, this may be unfair to those people who are out of work through no fault of their own because of a fall in the demand for the good or service they produce (**involuntary unemployment**).

3 Other employment costs are too high

Firms that employ workers may have to pay more than just their wages to do so. As well as wages and salaries, total labour costs may include taxes and social contributions paid by an employer on behalf of each employee, and other non-wage costs including sickness, maternity and paternity costs, recruitment and training costs. If any of these additional costs increase, the demand for labour by firms may fall and unemployment will tend to rise.

4 A lack of job information prevents people from finding jobs

Workers who leave their jobs to search for better ones are probably never fully aware of all the available jobs, and the wages, conditions and other factors involved in these jobs. As a result, it is unlikely that a worker will take the first job offered to him or her and will therefore be unemployed for some time as he/she searches for work. Improving information on jobs available is one way of increasing workers' knowledge of jobs and reducing the likelihood of them spending a lot of time searching for jobs. To this end, governments often provide people with help to search for jobs through government-funded employment offices and agencies.

5 Minimum wage laws have increased wages and increased unemployment

Many countries have introduced laws that make it an offence for a firm to pay its workers less than a certain hourly, daily or monthly wage. The first national minimum wage laws were introduced by New Zealand in 1896. Minimum wages are designed to raise the wages of the poorest workers. However, some employers argue they have been set too high in some countries and reduced their demand for labour, especially for low skilled workers with low levels of productivity (see Chapter 12).

6 The immobility of labour prevents workers from finding new jobs

When economists talk of labour **immobility** they refer to the inability of workers to move to other jobs.

If workers are unable to move to a different job requiring different skills they may be unable to do so because they are not qualified. This is known as **occupational immobility**. In some cases re-training in the skills required will allow them to take on different jobs. However, in some cases a trade union closed shop may prevent non-union members taking on a particular job (see Chapter 5). Professional associations of solicitors or architects, for example, may act in the same way and prevent people entering their occupation unless they have taken certain examinations.

Some employers may even refuse to employ some people because of their sex or colour, although this is illegal if it can be proved.

Other workers are immobile if they are unable or unwilling to move to another area to take up a job. In this case a worker is said to be **geographically immobile**. Regional differences in house prices, ties with family and friends, children's schooling and many other factors may prevent people from moving in search of work.

When workers are immobile they will tend to stay unemployed for longer periods of time.

Section 7 The costs of unemployment

Labour unemployment has been described as a 'drain on a nation' and 'a waste of resources'. In this section we will try to discover the consequences of labour unemployment.

Exercise 8 A sorry tale to tell 

Unemployed drown their sorrows

Beneath the national aggregates for disposable income and consumer durables, modern Britain is fostering an under-class of unemployed and unskilled workers, afflicted by family breakdown and also alcoholism. David Walker, Social Policy Correspondent, describes the two nations disclosed by the new edition of Social Tends.

In recent years a network of advisory and counselling services has grown up, among them Alcoholics Anonymous. In the 6 years before 1983, AA's clients increased from 13,4000 to 30,000 and the organization expanded from 895 to 1880 branches, a reflection of growing alcohol abuse and Social Trends shows how for men of all ages serious alcohol problems are much more prevalent in Ulster and Scotland and among the unemployed. In spite of the fact that the unemployed usually have less to spend on drink and everything else there is a considerably higher proportion of heavy drinkers among unemployed men.

About 43% of unemployed men aged 25 to 46 are counted as heavy drinkers, compared with 28% of men of the same age in work.

Unemployment's effects are more evident than in previous editions of Social Trends. Divorce rates among couples where the man is jobless are noticeably high. There is a link with chronic illness.

1 How does the article suggest unemployment can affect family life?

2 What other personal costs can an unemployed person face?

3 Ronald Reagan, the 40th president of the USA, once famously described the payment of unemployment benefits as 'a pre-paid vacation for freeloaders'. Using information from the article and drawing on your own experience of people who have been or are unemployed, write a series of three short letters of complaint to a national newspaper to express how you might feel about being out of work if you were:

- **a** a teenager living with parents who are unemployed
- **b** an unemployed person in their early thirties with children to support
- **c** a person in their late fifties who until recently has been in work all their life

Compare your views on how these people might feel with the views of others in your class.

The personal costs of unemployment

Unemployment can have both economic and emotional costs. People who lose their jobs will lose their income and may have to rely on charity or government benefits to live. Unemployed people can also lose their working skills if they are unemployed for a long period of time and, without retraining, they may find it even harder to find work. They may become depressed, possibly even ill, and it may also put a strain on other family members and health services.

The cost to people in work

Governments in many countries pay benefits to people who are unemployed, usually as part of the national social security or welfare system. In many cases the benefits paid may only be enough to pay for food and other necessities. Unemployment benefits, in some countries also called unemployment insurance, are generally given only to those who register as unemployed, and on condition that they are actively seeking work and do not currently have a job. For example, in the UK the main payment made to unemployed people is called the Jobseekers Allowance.

Unemployment benefits are paid from taxes on the incomes and expenditures of people in work. However, as unemployment increases so tax revenues will tend to fall. This may mean that people remaining in work may have to pay higher taxes to support those not in work. As the cost of unemployment benefits rise and tax revenues fall, a government may also be forced to cut back public spending in other areas, such as on schools, healthcare and roads. The standard of living of many more people may fall as a result while cuts in public spending may mean fewer jobs and even more unemployment in the long run.

The cost for the whole economy

As economists we should realize that leaving labour unemployed is a waste of resources. With unemployment rising total output falls and people have fewer goods and services to share. That is, the opportunity cost of having so many workers unemployed is the goods and services they could have produced. In addition, there is the opportunity cost to tax-payers. The tax revenue used to pay for any unemployment benefits could have been used to fund other projects in the economy, like roads and new hospitals.

What key words in this chapter fit the following definitions?

- A sustained increase in the general price level.
- Runaway inflation at very high rates.
- When inflation and unemployment occur together.
- A measure of price inflation based on the change in the average price of a basket of different goods and services.
- A sustained decrease in the general level of prices.
- The type of inflation caused by rising demand.
- The type of inflation caused by rising costs.
- Inflation from overseas or caused by a falling exchange rate.
- The number of people unemployed as a percentage of the labour force in an economy.
- A situation when workers find it difficult to change jobs.
- The type of unemployment that occurs in a recession.
- Usually short-lived unemployment as people move between jobs.
- Unemployment that occurs due to changes in the industrial structure of an economy.
- A measure of the proportion of a country's working-age population that is either working or looking for work.

The following websites can help you learn more about the topics in this chapter and provide you with access to really useful statistics about inflation and employment.

Inflation

- *www.bized.co.uk/virtual/economy/policy/outcomes/inflation/inflth.htm*
- *en.wikipedia.org/wiki/Inflation*
- *en.wikipedia.org/wiki/Consumer_price_index*
- *www.cia.gov/cia/publications/factbook/fields/2092.html*

Employment and unemployment

- International Labour Organization statistical databases *laborsta.ilo.org/*
- CIA World Factbook *cia.gov/cia/publications/factbook/rankorder/2129rank.html*
- *www.bized.co.uk/virtual/economy/policy/outcomes/unemployment/unempth.htm*
- *en.wikipedia.org/wiki/Unemployment*

Chapter 

Output and Growth

Aims

At the end of this chapter you should be able to:

- define **gross domestic product** as a measure of **economic growth**
- distinguish between **real GDP** and nominal GDP
- evaluate policies designed to increase **economic growth**
- analyse the costs and benefits of economic growth
- define and describe **the economic cycle**

Section 1 Measuring output

As economists we would like to measure the total or national output of a country, and track how it changes over time. In a macroeconomy, the total value of output of goods and services produced is known as the **national output**. Factors of production – land, labour and capital – are used to produce the national output (see Chapter 1). Firms pay workers, and the owners of natural resources and capital, for their use in production. These payments are a cost to firms but an income for the owners of factors of production. Similarly, owners of firms will receive income in the form of profits if their businesses are successful (see Chapter 13). The total amount of income earned in a macroeconomy is therefore its **national income**.

The value of total output can be measured by how much people and organizations pay for all the goods and services it comprises. It follows that the total or national output should also be the same as the total or national expenditure in a macroeconomy. What people and organizations spend on goods and services provides an income to those people and firms that make and supply goods and services.

It should by now be clear that all three measures of the total output of a macroeconomy should be the same, i.e.

National output = National income = National expenditure

Government experts and economists in many countries collect statistics on all three of these measures. In practice, however, their values do not always add up exactly to the same amount. This is because economic activity is complex. Flows of incomes and expenditures occur between many millions of different people, firms and governments, all over the world.

From GDP to GNP

The total value of output produced by all domestic firms in your country is known as the **gross domestic product (GDP)**. The same is true in all countries. GDP is the most quoted measure of the national income of a country. However, your GDP will not give us the final total of goods and services available to people and firms in your country. This is because some of their income will also be earned from interest on loans they make overseas, rent from property they own overseas, profits from companies they own overseas, and dividends from shares they hold in foreign companies. We must add any incomes from overseas to our calculation of GDP.

On the other hand, resources owned by people and firms who live in other countries make some of the total output produced in your country. This means some income will flow out of your country to people and firms overseas. As this does not represent work carried out in your country it should be deducted from our measure of GDP.

The difference between the flows of income coming into your country and those being paid overseas is usually known as **net property income from abroad**. The diagram below illustrates these income flows between the UK and other countries.

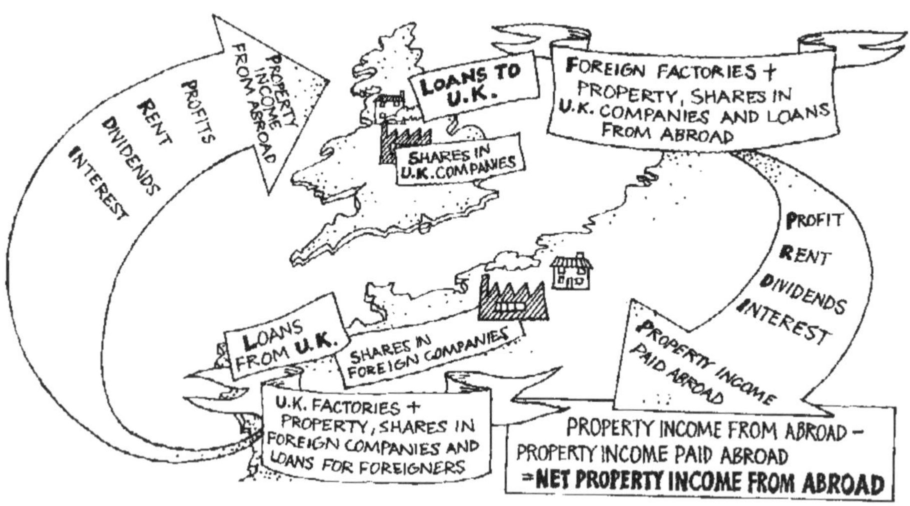

If we add net property income from abroad to gross domestic product we obtain a figure for **gross national product (GNP)**.

Gross national product (GNP) = Gross domestic product (GDP) + Net property income from abroad

GNP is therefore the total value of output from resources owned by people who live in a country, wherever these resources are located.

From GNP to NNP

Machines, cars, trains, boats, cranes, typewriters, screwdrivers and hammers become worn out as they are used, or rust over a number of years. Buildings too can become old and in need of repair. Many of these capital goods will therefore need repair or even replacing. The amount spent on the repair or replacement of old, worn-out capital is known as **depreciation**. It is also known as **capital consumption** which tells us that capital is being used up. However, a country will never be able to enjoy more goods and services if its resources are used just to repair or replace old, worn-out capital goods.

If the total output of resources owned by a country was ten computers each year, this would be its gross national product. If the computers never wear out, GNP after two years will be the value of twenty computers. If, however, each computer only lasts one year, then the GNP every year will only be the value of ten computers. If computers are produced solely to replace old ones, the economy has gained no extra capital goods.

If, on the other hand, only four computers need replacing after one year, the economy will gain six new computers.

This gain in the number of computers available for use is called the country's **net national product (NNP)**. It is calculated by deducting the value of capital goods replaced, that is, depreciation, from the total output of the economy, that is, GNP.

Net National Product (NNP) = Gross National Product (GNP) − Depreciation

The net national product of an economy consists of all the goods and services becoming available plus any additions to the total amount of capital goods in existence. This is the total generally known as **national income** that is, the money value of the total new output of an economy in a period of time.

Exercise 1 Calculating national income

The figures below set out the value of output in different industries in the imaginary economy of Zetaland for the years 2000 and 2005.

Zetaland Output by industry ($ billions)	2000	2005
Agriculture, forestry and fishing	10	12
Mining and quarrying	15	12
Manufacturing	57	65
Construction	20	30
Transport	13	18
Insurance, banking and finance	18	25
Distributive trades	25	40
Other services	22	32
Gross domestic product (GDP) =	—	—
***Net property income from abroad**	**5**	**10**
Gross national product (GNP) =	—	—
***Depreciation**	**20**	**28**
Net national product (NNP) =	—	—

*Be careful – do you add or take away?

1 Calculate GDP, GNP and NNP in Zetaland for 2000 and 2005.

2 Define GDP, GNP and NNP and explain why these figures differ.

3 a What has happened to national income in Zetaland between 2000 and 2005?

  b Assuming all prices have not changed since 2000 explain what may have caused this change in national income.

  c Still assuming prices have not changed in Zetaland, what possible advantages may the change in national income bring its people?

Real national income and money national income

The measurement of national income is carried out in terms of money values. Output values are measured in terms of what is paid for them in terms of money. But using money as a measure can give rise to problems when prices rise and, as a result, the value of output, spending and incomes change. Just because the value of output, spending and incomes has risen in terms of money, due to higher prices, people may be no better off. Indeed, they may even be worse off, because what matters is how much, in terms of the amount of goods and services, incomes can buy. The amount of goods and services the national income can buy is known as the **real value of output** or **real national income**.

As economists, therefore, it is important to know, when measuring national income from year to year, how much of its increase is due simply to rising prices and how much is due to an increase in the number of goods and services available for the people in a country to enjoy (see Chapter 16).

Using national income figures

In early times no one was very interested in national income and output figures. However, in the Second World War many governments realized there was a need to know how much food and ammunition their nations could produce because it was difficult for many to import goods and services during the war. Since then, governments all over the world collect and publish figures on their national output, incomes and expenditures.

These figures can help a government and economists in a number of ways.

1. If a government knows how resources are being used, and what they are making, it is more able to try and change the allocation of resources. For example, if a government finds the economy is producing too many consumer goods, it may try to encourage the production of capital goods instead.
2. It allows comparison to be made of the standard of living in one year compared to the next. If the amount of goods and services produced in an economy has increased over time, and therefore national income is higher, we can assume most people are better off.
3. The figures allow us to compare the standard of living in different countries. Dividing national income by the population in a country gives an indication of how much each person on average earns in a country.

Section 2 Measuring growth

An increase in real output

People's demands for higher living standards have made governments try to achieve faster rates of **economic growth**. When economists and politicians talk of economic growth they refer to the increase in the amount of goods and services the whole economy can produce over and above what it produced in the last year. That is, there has been economic growth if there is an increase in the **real output** of the economy over time.

How can we measure growth?

The production and sale of goods and services generates incomes for people: wages, rents, interest and profits. Economists therefore measure the rate of economic growth by how much national income, or **gross domestic product (GDP)**, has increased each year in a country.

However, as prices rise, the sale of goods and services raises firms' revenues, and therefore people's incomes, without any more goods and services being produced. When prices rise there may be no real growth in output or incomes. Economists say this represents a rise in **nominal** or **money GDP** but without growth in real GDP. To find out by how much real output has changed, if at all, the effects of inflation must be taken into account.

✓Let us consider an example. In 2005 the small island of Costas produced 1000 tonnes of oranges. This is the real output of that country. If each tonne of oranges sells for $50, the value of this output is $50000, and therefore the country's income will be $50000. In the following year inflation increases the price of one tonne of oranges to $60. Their real output remains the same at 1000 tonnes, but the money value of this output has been inflated to $60000. It appears as if there has been growth, but this growth is only in money terms and not in real terms. This is because $60000 in 2006 can buy no more oranges than $50000 did in 2005. There has been no increase in real output or GDP.

If, however, Costas can produce more than 1000 tonnes of oranges, say 1020 tonnes in 2007, then there will have been economic growth.

For economists people are only better off if **real GDP per capita**, that is, real income per head, increases. This is calculated by dividing the real GDP of an economy by the size of its population.

Does economic growth really make us 'better off'?

If there is an increase in real output, there has been economic growth. However, whether people have higher living standards really depends on which goods and services have increased in supply. If, for example, a government builds more nuclear weapons, total output would have increased but most people would not view themselves as being better off.

Incomes and wealth in many economies are very unequal. If an increase in real output is simply shared out among a few rich people, the vast majority of the people in an economy will be no better off.

People might even become worse off if the population of the economy increases and goods and services become shared among more and more people. In this case real GDP per capita will fall. There will have been negative growth.

International growth comparisons

The table below shows annual average growth rates in the value of real total output, or real GDP, in a number of countries. For example, the UAE economy grew by an average of 5.4 per cent each year between 1995 and 2004. That is, the UAE economy produced 5.4 per cent more real output each year over this period. In contrast, some economies are 'shrinking' due to negative economic growth. For example, between 1995 and 2004 the total real output of Zimbabwe shrunk by 3.3 per cent each year on average. This means that by the end of 2004 Zimbabwe was generating almost 40 per cent less real GDP than it did in 1995.

Growth in real output, 1995–2004, % annual average selected countries

Country	% Growth	Country	% Growth
China	8.2%	Pakistan	3.3%
Kazakhstan	6.3%	United Kingdom	2.8%
India	5.7%	South Africa	2.8%
Belarus	5.7%	France	2.3%
United Arab Emirates	5.4%	Lebanon	2.1%
Mauritius	5.3%	Brazil	1.9%
Iran	4.7%	Italy	1.6%
Egypt	4.3%	Germany	1.4%
Hungary	4.0%	Colombia	1.4%
Greece	3.9%	Japan	1.0%
Malaysia	3.9%	Argentina	0.1%
Poland	3.8%	Serbia and Montenegro	−0.2%
Spain	3.7%	Solomon Islands	−3.1%
United States	3.3%	Zimbabwe	−3.3%

United Nations Conference on Trade and Development, Handbook of Statistics online, *www.unctad.org*

Section 3

How to achieve growth

As economists we want scarce resources to be used as fully as possible, in the best possible way, to produce as many goods and services as possible. This will satisfy the most wants.

If resources are unemployed, that is, if labour is out of work, land disused or capital lying idle, then an increase in the amount of goods and services can be achieved simply by using these available resources more fully. The problem of economic growth, however, is how to increase output when all resources are fully employed. Clearly economic growth can only be achieved if these resources can be used more efficiently to produce more or if there is an increase in the resources of land, labour and capital available.

The following are ways in which economic growth can be achieved:

1 The discovery of more natural resources

The discovery of gas and oil has given a number of countries the ability to increase their total output. Indeed, the discovery of more natural resources, like coal, gold or even new varieties of fruit or cereals, would help any economy to increase output. Searching for new natural resources, however, costs a lot of money. Some countries, particularly those in the less-developed world, often do not have enough money to do this.

2 Investment in capital

Investment, or the production of new capital equipment, that is, tools, machinery and factories, is often said to be the key to growth. People can produce much more if they have the tools and machines to help them, and buildings to make things in. Investment can come from private sector firms and the government.

By lowering interest rates, a government can make it less costly for private sector firms to borrow money to buy new machines.

3 Technical progress

New inventions, better production techniques that produce more efficiently, better organization and management of firms, better training, better transport and communications all come under the banner of technical progress.

All these things allow a country to increase output. Progress and investment often go together when old machines are replaced by new, more sophisticated machines that can work faster.

The development of robotics and ICT has helped stimulate economic growth

A government may help firms to research and develop new machines and techniques by giving them cash grants or tax allowances.

4 Increasing the amount and quality of human resources

Education and training are often called 'investments in 'human capital'. A more skilled and knowledgeable workforce, able to produce more and better goods and services, will result from better education and training.

Improving healthcare and medicines can improve the health of the workforce in a country and help them to have fewer days off sick. As a result, a healthier workforce is a more productive workforce able to raise output.

While the quality of human resources can be improved with education and healthcare, the actual amount of human resources or labour can also be increased in a number of ways. Longer hours and fewer holidays is one way, but would probably prove unpopular with the vast majority of workers. Income tax cuts may encourage more people into work and to work harder.

In many countries, more women are now going to work to help produce more. This has the effect of increasing the working population which could only be further increased by reducing the school-leaving age, which can harm growth, raising the retirement age, inward migration, or waiting for a natural increase in the population and waiting for the newly born to grow up (see Chapter 20). As long as real output rises faster than the population, real GDP per capita will rise.

5 A reallocation of resources

As a country develops, resources tend to move out of primary production and into manufacturing and services where large increases in output have occurred. This has led to economic growth.

Section 4 The benefits and costs of economic growth

The benefits of growth

The benefits of economic growth and increased output can be enjoyed in a number of ways.

1. Higher levels of consumption for all to enjoy, providing they have the money to buy these goods.
2. Higher levels of output can probably be achieved using fewer labour. People may benefit from shorter working weeks and longer holidays.
3. Rising incomes means more tax revenue for a government. It can use this money to spend on schools and colleges, hospitals, roads and many other services that may benefit us all.

The costs of growth

Despite the benefits growth can bring, there are always costs to be considered.

1. There is an opportunity cost of growth. Economic growth may be achieved by producing more capital goods but at the expense of fewer consumer goods, like televisions, fashionable clothes and compact discs.
2. Economic growth may mean we use up scarce resources more quickly. Oil, coal, metals and other natural resources are limited and may soon run out. When they do, there can be no more capital goods, food supplies may diminish and the population of the world may suffer.
3. An increase in the number of factories producing goods and services will mean less land available for parks and other recreational activities. Noise, fumes, river and scenic pollution may increase as economies strive to produce more. These too can destroy plants and animals.
4. Technical progress may replace workers with machines so that many people find themselves without work and unemployed for long periods of time.

Because economic growth has costs as well as benefits, many governments are now concerned with using their policies to achieve **sustainable growth**. This means using policy to minimize the costs and any harmful effects of economic growth – for example, by placing restrictions on emissions of harmful pollutants from power stations and vehicle exhausts, raising taxes on petrol to reduce car use, limiting developments of large superstores in out-of-town locations (see also Chapter 22).

Exercise 2 Economic boom, environmental bust

China's spectacular economic growth – averaging 8% or more annually over the past two decades – has produced an impressive increase in the standard of living for hundreds of millions of Chinese citizens. At the same time, this economic development has had severe ramifications for the natural environment. There has been a dramatic increase in the demand for natural resources of all kinds, including water, land and energy. Forest resources have been depleted, triggering a range of devastating secondary impacts such as desertification, flooding and species loss. Moreover, poorly regulated industrial and household emissions and waste have caused levels of water and air pollution to skyrocket. China's development and environment practices have also made the country one of the world's leading contributors to regional and global environmental problems, including acid rain, ozone depletion, global climate change and biodiversity loss.

China's environmental crisis is evident everywhere. The country's air quality is among the worst in the world: According to the World Bank, 16 of the world's 20 most polluted cities are on the mainland, and acid rain affects one-third of China's agricultural land. The country is already one-quarter desert, and that desert is advancing at a rate of 1 300 square miles per year.

It is the dramatic effect the country's environmental problems are having on Chinese economic productivity, however, that is finally making Beijing take notice. All told, according to the World Bank, environmental degradation and pollution cost the Chinese economy the equivalent of 8% to 12% of GDP annually due to crop and fishery losses, factory closings and increased medical care.

The Chinese government could make real headway by taking three steps. First, increase its investment in environmental protection from 1.2% of GDP to at least 2.2%, the amount that experts have said is necessary just to keep the situation from deteriorating further.

Second, raise the price of scarce natural resources such as water, now grossly undervalued in many regions of the country. This would alleviate some of the scarcity and pollution issues by promoting conservation and encouraging waste-water treatment.

Third, enforcement of existing policies must be strengthened. Often, environmental-protection officials are overruled by powerful local interests who have a political or financial stake in the operation of a polluting activity, no matter what the long-term costs are.

Adapted from Elizabeth C Economy, Council of Foreign Relations, 22.10.2004, *www.cfr.or*

1. What is economic growth?
2. By how much has the Chinese economy grown on average each year?
3. What have been the likely benefits of this growth to Chinese people?
4. According to the article, is the fast pace of economic growth in China sustainable?
5. From the article identify social and environmental costs of economic growth in China.
6. In groups discuss the possible impacts the policy measures suggested in the article could have on firms, consumers, employees and the economy in China, and globally.

Section 5 Growth cycles

What is economic growth?

Many governments around the world are not only interested in achieving long-term sustainable growth in their real national output and income, but also stable economic growth.

If the total amount of goods and services, or **real output**, an economy can produce increases over time there has been economic growth. As a result, the national income will grow in real terms (that is, incomes can buy more goods and services). Plotted against time it should look like a steadily rising line. However, even if there is a tendency for growth in the long run, national output and income can display many ups and downs in the short run.

The ups and downs of national income

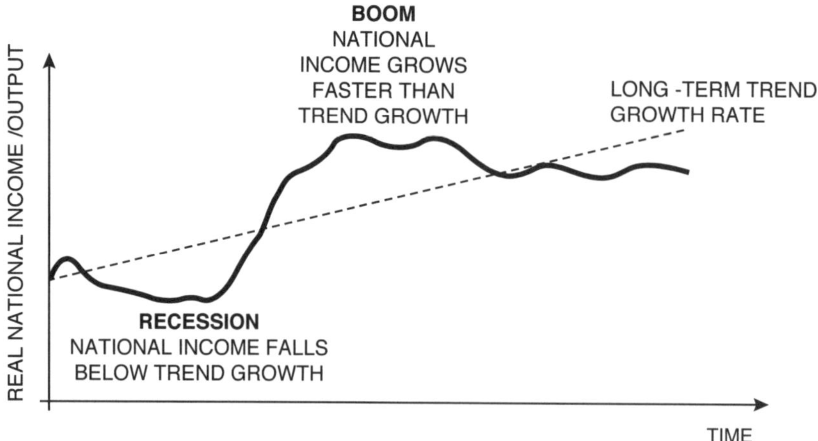

These continuous ups and downs in national income are displayed in many economies and have been labelled the **economic cycle**. When an economy experiences a **boom**, real output and national income appear to grow faster than normal, while in **recessions** or **slumps** they tend to fall. That is, real output and national income may grow more slowly than usual and may even shrink or experience negative growth. The economic cycle therefore involves cyclical fluctuations, or ups and downs, in the rate of growth in real GDP around its more normal, or long-term trend, growth rate.

In periods of boom there is a high level of spending. Investment in new machines by firms also tends to be high as they try to increase output. That is, aggregate demand is high and exceeds national output. Firms try to increase output by employing more factors of production but they eventually reach a position when all the available scarce resources in their economy are fully employed. No more suitable land, labour, capital or even entrepreneurs are available. As a result, the prices of goods and services will tend to rise. There will be an increase in the general level of prices, or **inflation**, as firms cannot meet demand (see Chapter 16). Therefore, booms tend to be associated with a high level of spending, low unemployment, rising prices and profits, and a high level of output.

As people in the economy cannot buy domestic goods and services they will tend to buy more imports. In turn, rising prices make our exports expensive and overseas demand for them will start to fall. Rising prices at home will also serve to reduce consumers' expenditure after a while, as they become unable to afford to buy so much. As aggregate demand starts to fall so the boom breaks.

Falling total demand can eventually result in a recession. Firms no longer wish to invest and this causes a further fall in spending. They try to cut back output and therefore employment falls as demand falls. Unemployment rises and national income falls. The rate at which prices rise will slow down, and there may even be deflation.

Prices may fall as firms try to increase the demand for their products. Profits fall and many firms may even go out of business. However, falling prices may cause an increase in demand for exports. Firms producing exports will start to increase output and employment. Slowly incomes start to rise and this causes a rise in spending. Eventually the economy is lifted out of recession and on to the road of recovery. And so the cycle goes on, powered by changes in the level of demand in the economy.

Exercise 3 Boom or bust?

The charts below show cyclical changes in real GDP growth in the Japanese and German economies between 1992 and 2006. Economic growth in both these economies during this period has been relatively slow historically, at just 1.3 per cent and 1.4 per cent per year on average respectively, and compared to many other countries.

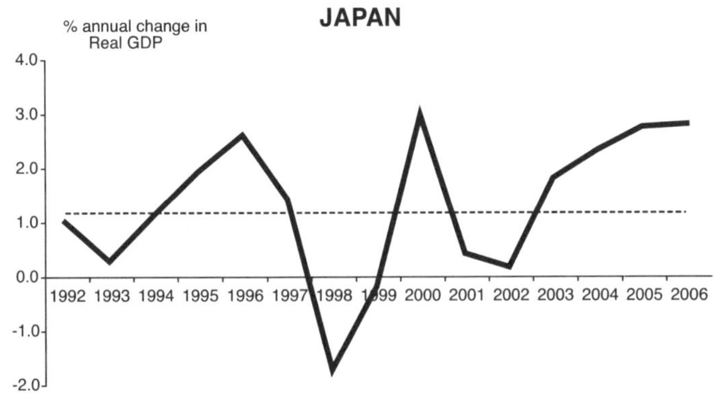

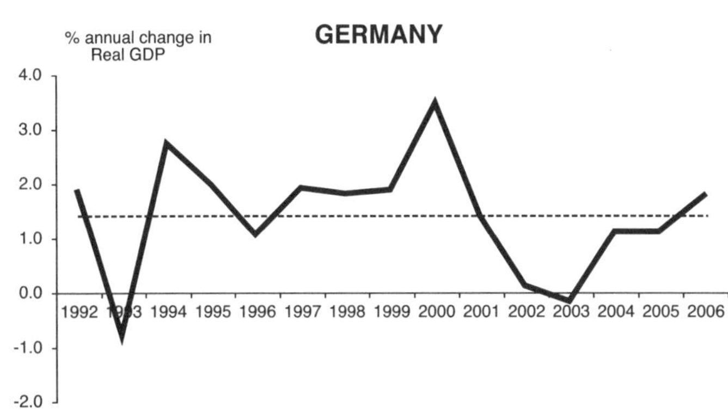

1. What is the economic cycle?
2. In which years did Japan and Germany experience economic booms?
3. In which years did Japan and Germany experience economic recessions or slumps?
4. Describe what is likely to be happening to the growth in output, price inflation, consumer expenditure, business investment, employment and tax revenues during a boom and a recession.

Key words

Write definitions for the following terms in this chapter:

Gross domestic product	**Real GDP**
Gross national product	**Money GDP**
Net national product	**Real GDP per capita**
National income	**Sustainable growth**
Capital consumption	**Economic cycle**
Economic growth	**Boom**
Sustainable growth	**Recession**

Learn more about economic growth and find GDP statistics at:

- *en.wikipedia.org/wiki/Economic_growth*
- *www.bized.ac.uk/learn/economics/growth/gdp/notes.htm*
- *www.oecd.org* (go to statistics then select national accounts)
- *www.unctad.org* (go to Handbook of Statistics On-line and select Indicators of Development)
- *econ.worldbank.org* (select World Development Indicators then select WDI data)

Chapter 18

International Trade and Exchange Rates

EXPORTS
IMPORTS
AND NOW FOR MY FAMOUS BALANCING TRICK...

Aims

At the end of this chapter you should be able to:

- describe the structure of the **balance of payments**
- describe the changing patterns of **imports** and **exports** and their effects on the balance of payments
- distinguish between trade in **visible** and **invisible imports** and **exports**
- define **exchange rates**
- give reasons why exchange rates fluctuate
- describe the differences between **fixed** and **floating exchange rates**

Section 1

Exports and imports

No country is self-sufficient and able to produce all the goods and services it needs and wants (see Chapter 2). All countries therefore need to trade internationally in order to survive.

International trade provides access to goods and services a country may not be able to produce, or is only able to produce at a higher cost or lower quality than other countries. In this way, consumers, firms and governments in different countries can benefit from the biggest and cheapest workforces, raw materials and technology anywhere in the world. Without international trade, consumers in many countries would have fewer goods and services to choose from, workers would find it harder to get jobs, and many producers would go out of business (see Chapter 22).

Each year countries such as the US, Japan and India sell many billions of dollars worth of goods and services to each other and to many other countries. Goods and services sold to other countries are known as **exports**. An export from a country is represented by a flow of money back into that country as revenue from the sale of the export.

At the same time, these same countries buy many billions of dollars worth of goods and services from each other and many other countries. Goods and services bought from overseas are known as **imports**. An import into a country is represented by a flow of money leaving that country and going overseas in payment for the import.

Exercise 1 Where in the world?

Look at the different products you have in your home. Visit local shops and look at the different products they sell. Examine the product labels and make a list of the countries where they have been produced. How many have been imported from overseas? Compare your list with students in your class. What other goods and services do you buy that are produced overseas? What are your country's biggest exports and which countries overseas are their biggest customers?

Visible trade

Visible trade involves trade in natural resources such as crude oil and timbers, parts and components to be used in the making of other goods, and finished products such as machinery, clothes, cars and equipment. Trade in goods, or merchandise, is called **visible trade** simply because visible exports and imports can be seen, touched and weighed as they pass through ports and across borders.

Visible exports

Oil

Machinery

The trade balance

When a country such as Japan sells visible exports, such as machinery and other manufactured goods to other countries, it earns money. When Japan buys visible imports it pays out money overseas.

If Japan pays out more for imported goods than it earns from the sale of its exports then its trade balance is said to be in **deficit**. If, however, the value of Japan's exported goods is greater than the value of the goods it imports, then the Japanese trade balance will be in **surplus**.

The **balance of trade** measures the flows of money into and out of a country for visible exports and imports.

Balance of trade = value of visible exports − value of visible imports

The balance of trade in Japan is calculated in terms of its currency, the yen (symbol ¥). For example, in 2005 Japan sold ¥62 631 billion worth of visible exports and bought ¥52 297 billion worth of visible imports. It therefore had a trade surplus of ¥10 335 billion. A country is said to have a **favourable trade balance** if it is in surplus, or an **unfavourable trade balance** if it is in deficit.

The balance of trade of many countries has changed over time as other countries have developed their manufacturing industries and have become more efficient at producing goods for export. For example, in 1980 the UK had a small visible trade surplus due largely to the export of crude oil from the North Sea and because the UK was a major exporter of manufactured goods, particularly in industrial machinery. However, since 1983 the UK has had a growing trade deficit as imports of manufactured goods have increased at a faster rate than UK exports, and as North Sea oil production has fallen. In 2005 the UK trade deficit was an unfavourable £68.7 billion.

UK balance of trade, 1980–2005

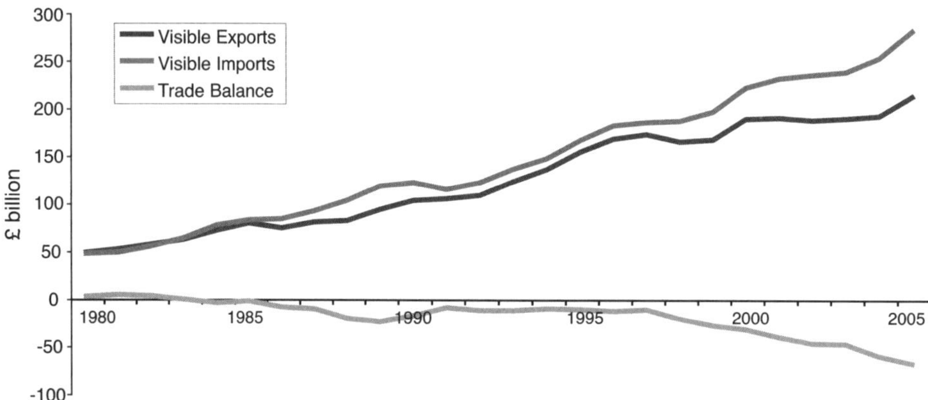

UK Office for National Statistics, *www.statistics.gov.uk*

Invisible trade

Invisible trade involves trade in services. Exports and imports of services, such as insurance, banking and tourism, cannot be seen or touched at ports or border crossings, hence the name invisibles.

If a Japanese resident goes on holiday to Europe, he or she is paying for overseas services such as staying in hotels, tickets for public transport and eating in European restaurants. This debit of money from the Japanese economy represents an **invisible import** to Japan.

If, on the other hand, a Canadian resident buys insurance from a Japanese insurance company, he or she is buying a Japanese service so the insurance premiums bring money into Japan. This credit to the Japanese economy represents an **invisible export**.

If Japan pays out more for imported services than it earns from invisible exports then its balance on invisibles will be in deficit. If, however, the flow of money into Japan for invisible exports is greater than the value of invisible imports, then the Japanese balance on invisibles will be in surplus.

The **balance on invisibles** measures the flows of money into and out of a country for invisible exports and imports.

Balance of invisible trade = value of invisible exports − value of invisible imports

In 2005 invisible exports credited to Japan were ¥12 081 billion while invisible imports debited from Japan were ¥14 723 billion. Japan therefore had an invisible trade deficit of – ¥2 642 billion.

Exercise 2 Now you see them, now you don't!

The following diagrams and descriptions show international transactions between the UK and other countries.

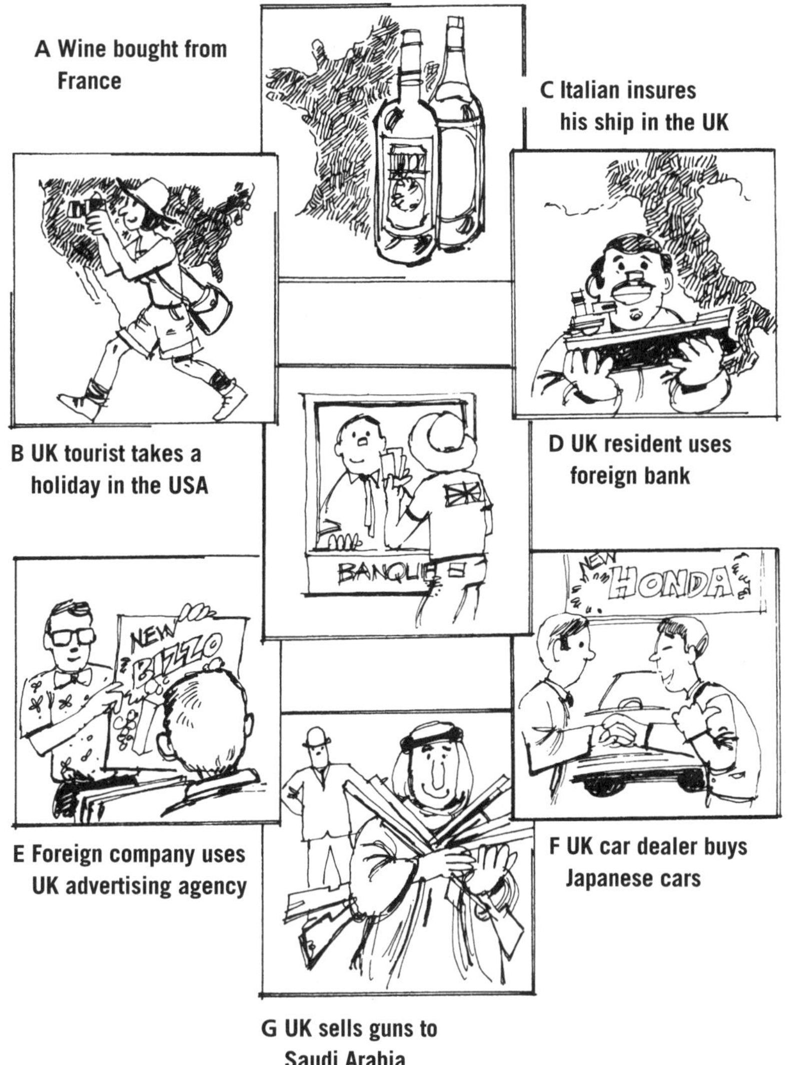

1 Which of these transactions represent visible and invisible exports from the UK, and visible and invisible imports to the UK?

2 Calculate the balance of trade and the invisible balance from the following figures:

	$ million
Invisible imports	10000
Visible exports	15000
Invisible exports	20000
Visible imports	17000

3 Taking visible and invisible trade together state whether the country in the table above is gaining or losing money. What effect will this have on output, employment and national income in its economy?

World trade patterns

For many years international trade flows were dominated by raw materials such as iron ore, oil and wheat. Much of this trade was from less developed countries in the southern hemisphere to the more developed, industrialized nations in the north (see Chapter 19). However, global trade patterns have since changed significantly.

Global trade in visible exports, 1960–2005

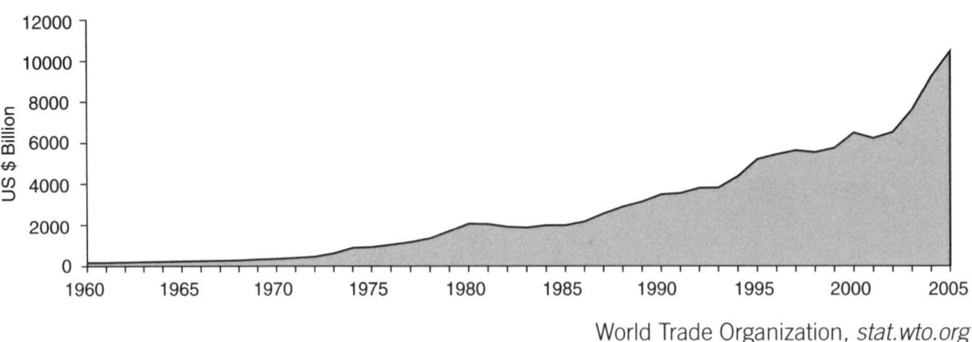

World Trade Organization, *stat.wto.org*

- Total world trade volumes and values have increased significantly. In 1960 the global trade in merchandise was worth US$130 billion. By 2005 this had increased to over $10 trillion.
- Trade in manufactured goods has grown significantly. They accounted for 53 per cent of world exports in 1963. By 2005 this share had climbed to around 74 per cent. The globalization of production has increased trade in manufactured goods while technological advances in transport, particularly containerization, have meant faster and more efficient handling of goods in bulk at ports.
- In contrast, the share of agricultural products in world trade has fallen, from around 28 per cent in the early 1960s to just 7 per cent in 2005. Processed food products have increased and now account for nearly half of agricultural trade.
- Trade in goods and services have grown at broadly similar rates. Between 1990 and 2005, trade in commercial services and goods both grew by about 6 per cent per year on average, and services' share of world trade has therefore remained around 20% over the entire period.
- Services such as computer and information services, financial services, insurance, telecommunications, and personal, cultural and recreational services have increased their share of world exports from just over 6 per cent in 1985 to almost 10 per cent in 2005.
- Developed countries still accounted for three quarters of the global trade in 2000, but developing countries have seen their share climb to one third by 2005 and it continues to rise. Many industrial processes which initially took place in developed countries have relocated to countries offering lower production costs, namely in lower wages. As a result, global trade flows are now characterized by significant flows of goods from developing to developed countries.

Visible exports, % global share by major category

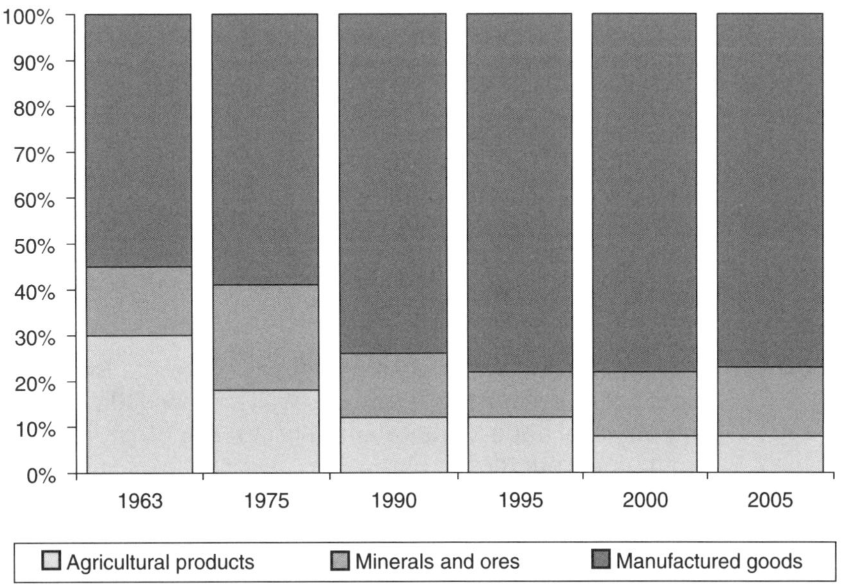

World Trade Organization, 2006

- World trade remains dominated by a small number of countries, mainly in North America and Europe. The US, Germany and Japan alone account for around a third of all global trade. The US is the world's single largest importer. But a growing share is now accounted for by the developing countries of Asia, especially China and India. For example, bilateral trade between these countries alone grew from just $2 billion in 1999 to $17 billion. China was the 7th largest exporter in the world in 2000 and the 3rd largest by 2005.

Top ten exporters in world merchandise trade, 2005

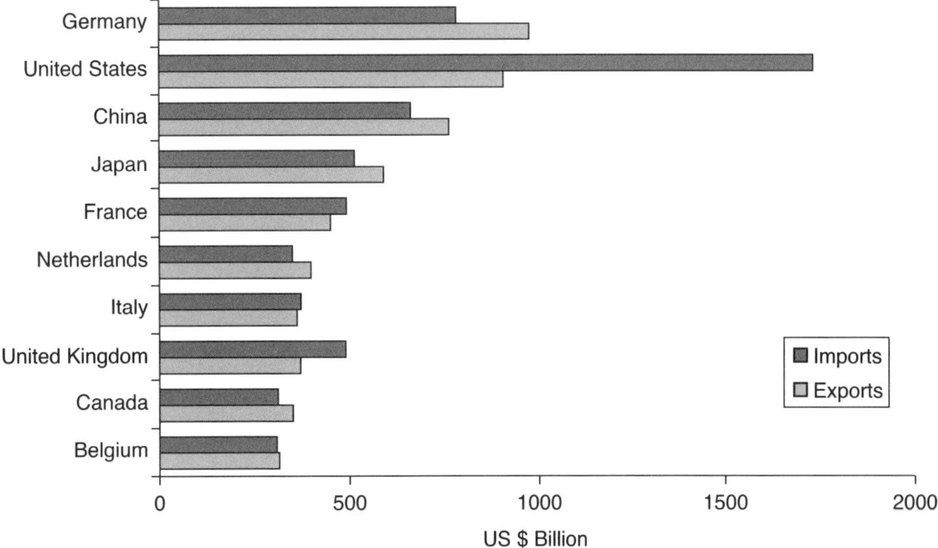

World Trade Organization, 2006

The balance of payments

Visible and invisible exports and imports are accounted for by flows of money into and out of a national economy. However, there are also other flows of money into and out of an economy, including investments, loans, profits and dividends on shares. The balance of payments of a country records all inward and outward transactions with the other countries it trades with. It is usually split into three main accounts: the current account, the capital account and the financial account.

We will look at the structure of the balance of payments of a country using the UK as an example.

The current account

Each month and year a government will collect statistics of the **balance of payments on current account** to show how well or how badly the national economy is doing in international trade in goods and services, and other flows of incomes and transfers to and from other countries.

The current account for the UK economy therefore includes:

- UK visible trade in exports and imports.
- UK invisible trade in services.
- Balance of income flows to and from the UK in payment for the use of factors of production:
  - income debits include wages paid to foreign workers temporarily working in the UK, and any **interest, profits and dividends (IPD)** paid out to overseas residents and firms investing in the UK
  - income credits include wages paid to UK workers temporarily working overseas, and interest and dividends earned by UK residents and firms on investments they have in other countries.
- Balance of current transfers to and from the UK:
  - debits from the UK will include taxes and excise duties payable to the European Union and contributions to the European Union budget
  - credits to the UK include subsidies received from the European Union.

To illustrate, the UK balance of payments on current account between 1995 and 2005 are summarized below.

UK balance of payments on current account

£ billion, current prices	1995	2005
Visible exports	*153.6*	*212.8*
Visible imports	*165.6*	*280.1*
Balance of trade (A)	**−12.0**	**−67.3**
Invisible exports	*50.6*	*111.3*
Invisible imports	*41.6*	*88.3*
Balance on services (B)	**9.0**	**23.0**
Income balance (C)	**2.2**	**29.9**
Current transfers balance (D)	**−7.6**	**−12.2**
Current balance (A + B + C + D)	**−8.5**	**−26.6**

UK balance of payments on current account, 1995–2005

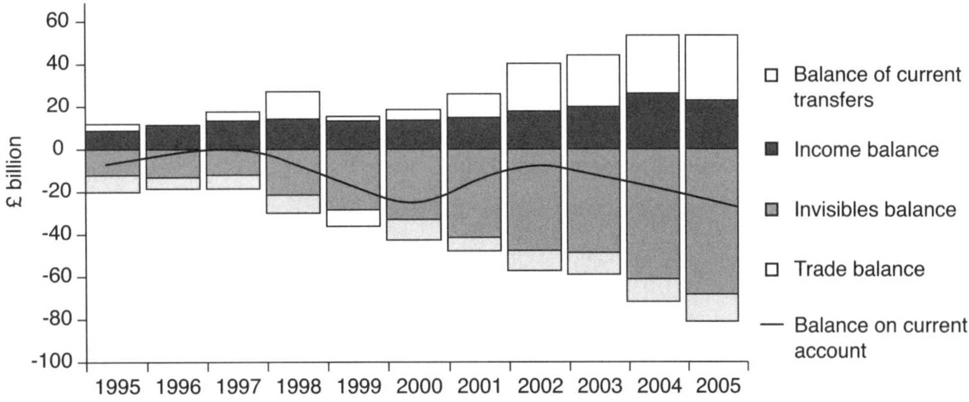

UK Office for National Statistics, *www.statistics.gov.uk*

The capital account

Flows of money into and out of a national economy to pay for the change in ownership of fixed assets, such as houses, machinery and factory buildings, the sale of fixed assets, or the cancellation of debts, appear in the capital account of the balance of payments. In most countries, the size of capital account transactions is normally small compared to the current and financial accounts of the balance of payments.

Fixed assets will be transferred between countries as firms and workers relocate overseas. For example, money brought into the UK by overseas migrants are credits to the UK capital account, while money taken overseas by UK residents leaving the UK to live abroad are recorded as debits.

The financial account

The financial account records flows of money into and out of a national economy for investments in capital, company shares and as loans. Any interest, profits and dividends (IPD) resulting from these investments are recorded as factor incomes in the current account.

A country receives **direct inward investment** whenever a foreign-owned firm sets up a factory, office or retail outlet in it. For example, the location of Japanese car manufacturers such as Nissan and Toyota in the UK are examples of direct inward investments to the UK economy. Any profits reinvested in their UK operations, rather than paid out to shareholders, will also score as direct investment credits.

Inward **portfolio investments** into an economy involve the purchase of shares (equity) in companies by overseas investors and loans of money from overseas (debt). So when overseas firms and residents buy shares in, or lend money to, UK companies these portfolio investments are recorded as credits to the UK economy.

These inward investments will create **external liabilities** for the country receiving them because it will eventually have to repay them or pay interest on loans and dividends on shares held by the overseas investors. In contrast, outward investments debited overseas by a country will create **external assets** because someday they will be repaid and provide a stream of interest or dividend income into the future from overseas. The UK financial account for 2005, tabulated on the next page, illustrates these transactions.

If an economy invests more overseas than it receives in inward investments from other countries its balance of payments on financial account will be in deficit. This is often the case when the balance of payments on current account is in surplus because the extra money the economy is earning from trade can then be invested overseas. When the current account is in deficit, however, an economy will have less money to invest elsewhere. It may also try to attract more inward loans and investments from overseas to help balance the current account deficit.

Movements in 'hot money' can often cause large changes in the financial account balance of a country. Hot money refers to short-term investments of large sums of money that are moved by investors from country to country in search of the best short-term interest rates and returns. For example, high interest rates in the UK relative to other countries will tend to attract an inward flow of hot money from overseas investors.

UK financial account, 2005

UK investments abroad (UK assets = net debits)	£ million	Inward investments in the UK (UK liabilities = net credits)	£ million
Direct investment abroad	**56 539**	**Direct investment abroad**	**87 725**
Equity capital	16 672	Equity capital	76 531
Reinvested earnings	40 597	Reinvested earnings	11 095
Other capital transactions	−730	Other capital transactions	99
Portfolio investments abroad	**160 710**	**Portfolio investments abroad**	**127 021**
Equity	64 766	Equity	2 670
Debt	95 944	Debt	124 351
Other investments abroad	497 712	Other investments in the UK	518 347
Reserve assets (net debits) (drawings +/additions to −)	−656		
Total	**715 615**	**Total**	**733 093**
Financial account net transactions (net credits *less* net debits) = £17.476 billion			

UK Office for National Statistics, *www.statistics.gov.uk*

Balancing items

When the total amount of money flowing out of a national economy e.g. the UK exceeds the amount flowing in from sales of exports, and from transfers and investments, there will be an overall deficit that must be paid for somehow. A government can do this by drawing on its **reserve assets**, namely its reserves of gold and foreign currencies. If these are insufficient then, as a last resort, it could borrow from the International Monetary Fund or from the central banks of other countries. If, however, there is an overall surplus, the economy can use it to repay foreign loans or boost its gold and foreign currency reserves.

Changes in reserve assets are usually recorded in the financial account as a net debit and should balance the overall balance of payments. However, inflows and outflows of money to a national economy may not always match precisely because overseas trade and financial transactions figures are compiled from a great many sources by a large number of people over long periods of time and things may be left out or recorded with error. **Net errors and omissions** are therefore included to balance the accounts. The table below shows these adjustments to the UK balance of payments in 1995 and 2005.

UK balance of payments, 1995 and 2005

£ billion	1995	2005
Current account (A)	−8.5	−26.6
Capital account balance (B)	0.5	2.4
Financial account net transactions (C)	2.6	17.5
(A + B + C)	−5.4	−6.7
Net errors and omissions	5.4	6.7

Exercise 3 Balancing the books

1 Look at the charts below for Japanese exports and imports over time. What trends can you see in Japan's balance of trade with her major trading partners?

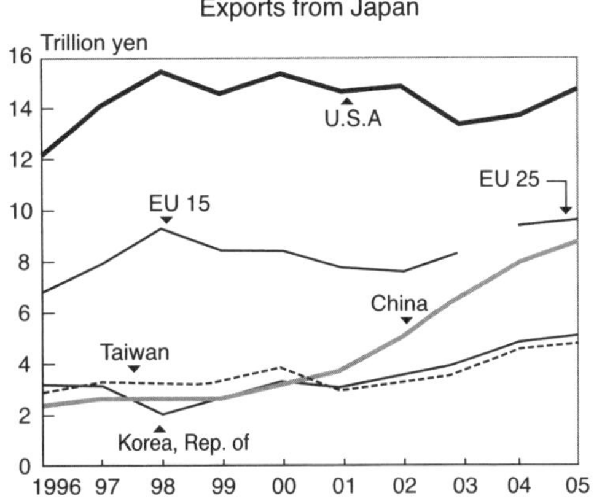

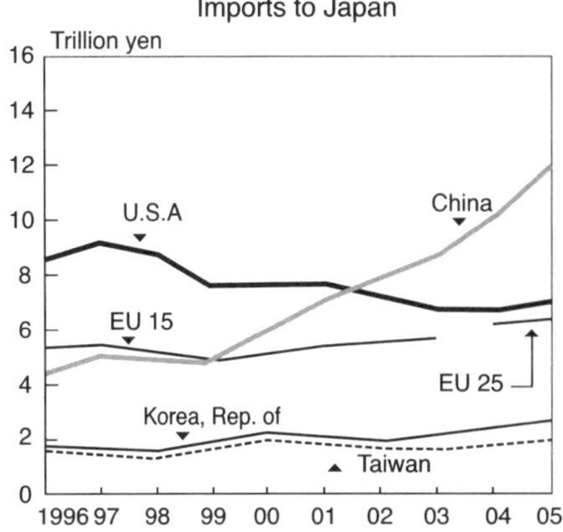

2 The table gives figures from the Japanese balance of payments in 2005. Complete the table by calculating the balance on current account and the balancing item of net errors and omissions needed to balance the accounts.

Balance of payments, Japan 2005	Yen (billion)	
Current account	______	
Trade balance		*10334.8*
Services		*−2641.8*
Net income		*11381.7*
Net current transfers		*−815.7*
Capital account	− 549.0	
Financial account	−13457.9	
Change in reserves	−2546.2	
Net errors and omissions	______	

Ministry of Finance, Japan

Section 3 Exchange rates

The foreign exchange market

When individual consumers, firms or governments buy imports of goods and services from overseas they must pay the country they bought them from in their own currency. International trade, therefore, not only involves the exchange of goods, services, investments and incomes but also the exchange of currencies.

The currency of one country can be exchanged for the currency of another through the **foreign exchange market**. Foreign currencies can be bought and sold all ove r the world just like most other products. The market for foreign currencies consists of all those consumers, firms and governments willing and able to buy foreign currency and all those willing and able to supply foreign currency.

When a product is bought and sold it is done so at a price. The price of a foreign currency is known as its **exchange rate** in terms of another currency. So, for example, the value of the Japanese currency, the yen, will have an exchange rate with the US dollar, another with the euro, another in terms of how many Indian rupees it will buy, etc.

Tables of currency exchange rates like the one below are a common feature in daily national newspapers. The table shows the foreign exchange rates for a number of major currencies used in international trade on 24 November 2006. You can find the exchange rate at which one currency can be bought by other currencies by looking across each row, or down each column. So for example, on the global currency market on 24 November 2006 one UK pound exchanged for 223.915 Japanese yen or, looking at it the other way round, one yen exchanged for just 0.4 UK pence.

International currency exchange rates, selected currencies 24.11.2006

	Australian Dollar AU$1	Swiss Franc CHF1	Euro Zone Euro $1	Japanese Yen ¥1	UK Sterling £1	US Dollar $1
Australian Dollar AU$1	1.000	0.943	0.595	90.211	0.403	0.778
Swiss Franc CHF1	1.061	1.000	0.631	95.686	0.427	0.825
Euro Zone Euro € 1	1.681	1.585	1.000	151.637	0.677	1.308
Japan Yen ¥1	0.011	0.010	0.006	1.000	0.004	0.008
UK Sterling £1	2.482	2.340	1.476	223.915	1.000	1.931
US Dollar $1	1.285	1.211	0.764	115.935	0.518	1.000

What determines the exchange rate of a currency?

The foreign exchange rate of a currency is simply its price in terms of other currencies. Like any other commodity, the price of a currency will be determined by its market demand and supply, and therefore by any factors both at home and overseas that affect these (see Chapter 4). To illustrate how this works for all currencies traded internationally let's consider the market for the UK currency sterling against the US dollar.

1 **Why is UK sterling demanded?**

Consumers, firms and governments in other countries buy UK pounds to pay for their imports of goods and services from the UK. They may also want UK pounds to save money in UK financial institutions and to invest in UK companies.

2 **Why is UK sterling supplied?**

UK consumers, firms and government use their holdings of UK pounds to buy foreign currencies so they too can buy imports of goods or services from other countries or to make investments overseas.

The diagram below shows the demand for UK pounds (D£D£) and their supply (S£S£) on the foreign exchange market. The price of the pound is expressed in terms of US dollars for simplification, but it could be in terms of any other foreign currency you care to think of.

The higher the price of pounds, the more are supplied but the fewer are demanded. The market price or equilibrium price of a pound is determined where demand equals supply in the diagram at an exchange rate of $2 = £1. Given this, a car sold for £10 000 in the UK, when exported to the USA, will sell for $20 000.

The value of the pound can be expressed in the terms of any currency, for example £1 = $2 or £1 = ¥200. However, the value of currencies can change. For example, the price of the pound may fall to £1 = $1.5. At the same time the price of the pound may go up in terms of yen to £1 = ¥240. Because the value of a currency can move in different directions against different currencies reflecting their particular trading and economic conditions, it is difficult to judge overall whether the pound is increasing in value or not on the global market for foreign exchange.

Equilibrium in the foreign exchange market

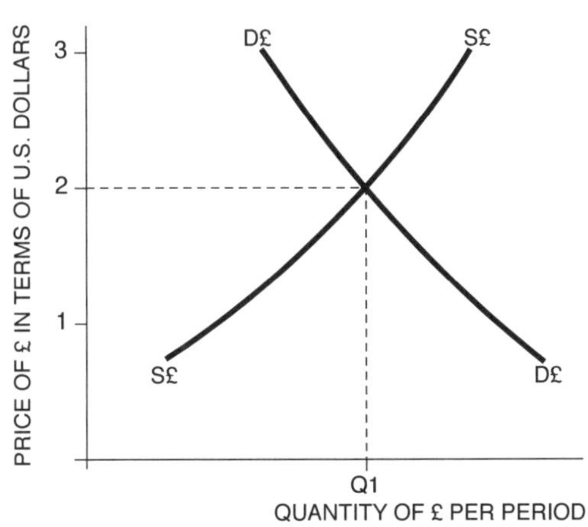

The demand and supply for UK sterling

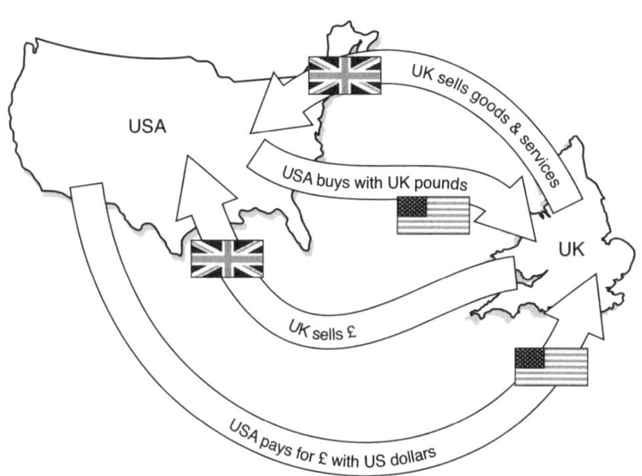

To overcome this problem, the UK government calculates the average value of the pound against the currencies of those countries that are the UK's major international trading partners. This average value of £1 is calculated as an index number in a similar way to the consumer prices index (see Chapter 16). It is known as the sterling **exchange rate index** and its fluctuating value between 1980 and 2005 can be seen in the chart below. Clearly, in 2005 the value of the UK pound on the global currency market was still below its average value in 1980 but had improved since a low in the mid 1990s.

Similarly, other governments also calculate indices for the value of their currencies against other major currencies over time.

UK sterling exchange rate index, 1980–2005 (1980=100)

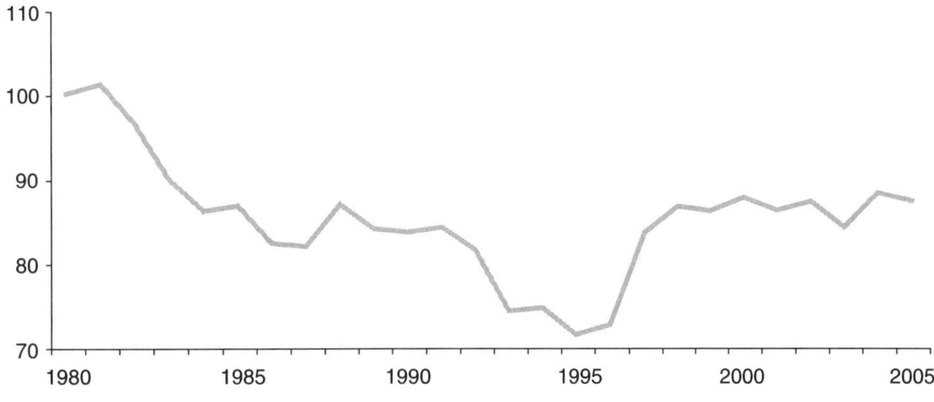

UK Office for National Statistics, *www.statistics.gov.uk*

Section 4 Floating and fixed exchange rates

Floating exchange rates

If an exchange rate, the price of a currency, is allowed to *float* it means that it will be determined freely by the forces of demand and supply without interference by governments. Changes in the forces of demand and supply will therefore cause changes in the value of a currency.

When the value of one currency falls against other currencies it is known as a **depreciation** in its value. On the other hand, if the value of a currency rises against one or more other currencies there will have been an **appreciation** in its value. We will examine what may cause the value of a currency to depreciate or appreciate against other currencies on the foreign exchange market by considering, as our example, the value of UK pounds in terms of US dollars.

Exercise 4 Floating around

Look at the cases below. For each case:

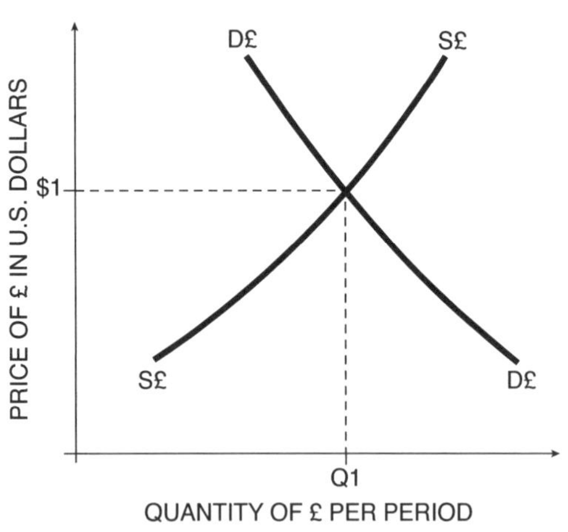

Case 1

UK Trade Deficit Widens

Britain's trade deficit widened well ahead of expectations in May, to its second highest level on record, as the country was forced to import more oil.

The Office for National Statistics said the UK's goods trade gap widened to £6.7bn in May from a downwardly revised £5.5bn a month earlier. Estimates had put the figure in the region of £5.7bn.

Money Week, 11.7.2006
www.moneyweek.com

Case 2

British pound weakens as dollar rises on lower oil prices

The British pound fell to a seven-week low against the dollar. The US greenback strengthened as oil prices came down and increased speculation about economic growth and higher US interest rates. The damage caused by Hurricane Rita was much lower than expected. Last week the Fed hiked interest rates by a quarter of a percentage point.

Adapted from Forex Reader 26.9.2005,
www.forexreader.com

Case 3

Pound falls on inflation news

Sterling has lost ground to its major rivals following a statement from the Bank of England that British 12-month inflation was likely to move further above its 2.0-percent target in the months ahead. "It is likely that inflation will rise further above the target in the near term, but then fall back as energy and import price inflation abate," the central bank said.

At 1337 GMT, the pound was trading at 1.8990 against the dollar, down from 1.9067 just before the rate announcement at 1200 GMT, while the euro rose to a 20-day high against the British currency of 1.4859 from 1.4914.

Adapted from Yahoo news 9.11.2006, *uk.news.yahoo.com*

1 State what factor has changed that may affect the value of the UK pound.

2 State whether you think the pound will depreciate or appreciate against the dollar.

3 State the effect of the changing factor on the demand and/or supply of the UK pound.

4 Copy the diagram of the foreign exchange market between the UK pound and US dollars on the previous page. Use your diagram to show the shift in the demand and/or supply curves of £s which best illustrates what is likely to happen (or has happened).

There are a number of reasons why the value of a currency changes or fluctuates. Using the value of the UK pound as our example, the main factors are:

1 Changes in the balance of trade in goods and services

If the UK imports a greater value of goods and services than it exports there is said to be a current account deficit. If the deficit increases further it means the UK is buying more imports, or losing its export trade. As a result, more pounds must be supplied to pay for the imports, while less pounds are demanded by overseas residents because they are buying less of UK exports. As a result, the price of the pound will depreciate.

If, on the other hand, the UK earns more from its exports than it pays for its imports its current account will be in surplus. More pounds will be demanded to pay for UK exports while the UK will not supply so many pounds as it buys less imports. The value of the pound will appreciate.

2 Inflation

If the UK's inflation rate is higher than that of other countries the price of UK goods and services will be rising faster than foreign prices. As a result UK goods will become uncompetitive. Demand for UK exports, and therefore for pounds, will fall. On the other hand, imports become more competitive and more will be demanded in return for more pounds being supplied to pay for them. High UK inflation will tend to reduce the value of the pound.

3 Changes in interest rates

When UK interest rates are high or rising, overseas residents may be keen to save or invest money in UK banks and other financial institutions. The demand for pounds rises, increasing the value of the pound. The UK government can use interest rates to affect the value of the pound and the price of imported goods and services (see Chapter 14). A rise in other countries' interest rates may lead to the withdrawal of foreign investment from the UK with a depressing effect on the value of the pound.

4 Speculation

A **foreign currency speculator** is a person or firm, for example, a bank, that tries to make money by buying and selling foreign currencies to try to make speculative gains.

For example, if speculators think the value of the pound is going to fall, because, for example, UK interest rates may go down, they may sell pounds and buy other currencies. This increase in the supply of pounds reduces their value. The speculators can then buy back pounds at a cheaper price. The difference between the price they sold pounds for and the price they buy them back for is their profit. The following diagram illustrates how this is done.

If speculators believe the value of the pound will rise, as a result of a balance of payments surplus for example, they will buy pounds now and try to make a profit out of a rising pound. Of course, their increased demand for pounds helps its price to rise.

Managing floating exchange rates

It is often the case that governments manage their floating exchange rates to stop them from fluctuating too much and causing economic uncertainty. This is known as **managed flexibility**.

A steep rise in the value of a currency internationally will mean exports will become more expensive to buy overseas and this may reduce overseas demand for them. Export producers may experience a fall in sales and cut back output and employment. In order to stop their currency value rising too far a government may supply more on the global exchange market from its reserves. The increase in the supply will lower the exchange rate. Alternatively, a government may lower interest rates to reduce the flow of hot money and other investments into their economy from overseas and so reduce demand for its currency.

In contrast, a sharp fall in the value of the currency makes buying imports more expensive because currency values overseas will have risen. To try to prevent imported inflation a government may use its gold and foreign currency reserves to buy their own currency. This increase in the demand for their currency on the global currency market will help push up its market exchange rate. Alternatively, interest rates could be raised to curb domestic demand for imports and to stimulate demand for the currency from overseas investments looking for a high return.

Fixed exchange rates

In the same way as managed flexibility, a government can use its reserves of gold and foreign currency to buy or sell its currency on the global foreign exchange market to stabilize or fix its exchange rate against another currency or basket of currencies, buying up its currency when its value is too low or selling it when its value is too high.

In fact, until relatively recently most countries had a system of fixed exchange rates with each other. For example, until 1918 the value of the UK pound was fixed at $3.70. Then, following the Second World War the value of the UK pound was fixed once more but at $4.02, then at $2.80 following a devaluation in 1949, and again at $2.40 from 1967 until 1972. Since then the UK exchange rate has been allowed to float freely, except for a brief period between 1990 and 1992 when the UK was a member of the European Exchange Rate Mechanism (ERM) that fixed the currency values of the European Union member countries prior to the creation of the single European currency, the euro, in 2000.

The diagrams below show how the movements of a fixed exchange rate will differ from those of a freely floating exchange rate over time.

Fixed exchange rate

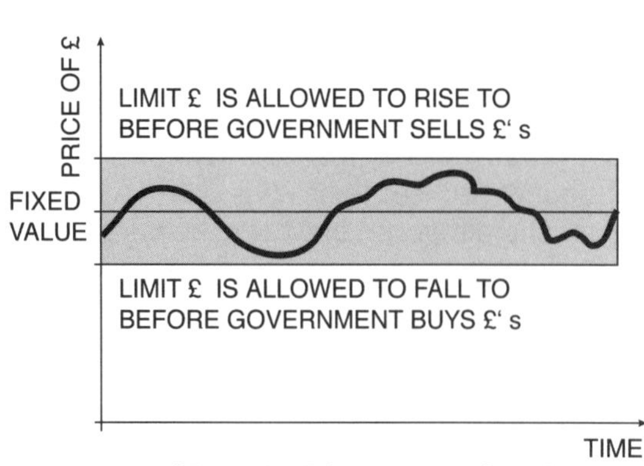

Floating exchange rate

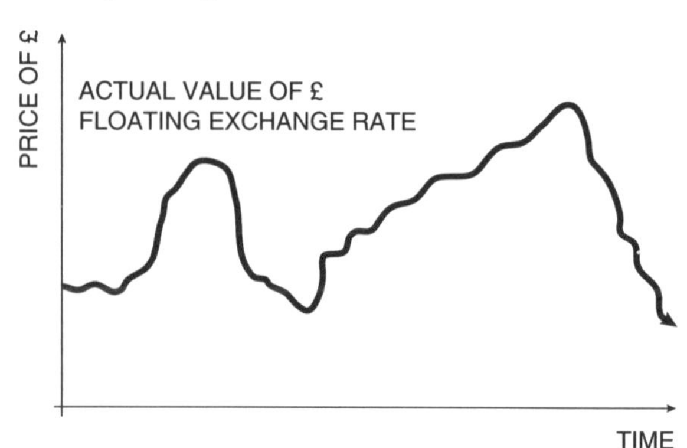

Correcting trade imbalances

Large trade imbalances, whether a big deficit or a big surplus, can cause problems for a national economy. Consider a very simple example where there are just two countries in the world engaged in international trade with each other. Let's call these countries Surpland and Dearth. Surpland exports far more to Dearth than she imports and has a trade surplus. Dearth buys more imports from Surpland than she sells in exports and therefore has a trade deficit. Clearly, because Surpland has a trade surplus, it follows that Dearth must have a trade deficit. In fact, this will also be true in the real world. If one or more countries have a trade surplus, then one or more other countries must have a trade deficit equal in value to the surplus of other countries.

Problems with a trade surplus

It is not immediately obvious why having a trade surplus should be a problem. However, having a big persistent trade surplus can cause the following problems for an economy:

- There may be political and economic pressure on the government from other countries to reduce its trade surplus so they can reduce their trade deficits.
- Exporting firms will enjoy significant overseas revenues – profits and wages may rise – but the increase in demand may cause demand-push inflation.
- But eventually, because a surplus causes the value of the currency to stay high, may reduce demand for exports and cause a loss of jobs.

Problems with a trade deficit

In contrast, a sustained and significant trade deficit could have the following problems:

- If more money is paid out for imports than is earned from exports then this loss of money from an economy may mean less can be spent on domestic goods and services. Domestic firms facing a fall in demand for their products may cut back production and their demand for labour resulting in higher unemployment.
- The value of the exchange rate will fall, causing imports to become more expensive and resulting in imported inflation. If demand for imports is generally price inelastic then more money will be paid out for imports and demand for domestically produced goods and services may fall further.
- The trade deficit may itself be a symptom of a declining industrial base, with fewer firms in the economy over time producing goods and services for export.

A government may decide to try to correct a trade imbalance in a number of ways:

How to correct a trade imbalance

1 Do nothing, because a floating exchange rate will correct it

Trade deficits and surpluses can be self-correcting if the exchange rate is allowed to adjust freely. For example, a trade deficit in the UK economy will mean more pounds must be used to buy up foreign currencies to pay for imports. The subsequent fall in the sterling exchange rate will cause a rise in the price of imports. For example, if the exchange rate is £1 = €2 then a bottle of French wine priced at €4 would cost £2 to buy when imported to the UK. A fall in the value of sterling to say £1 = €1.6 would cause the price of the same bottle of wine to rise to £2.50. The rise in prices should help reduce demand for imports but rising import prices also means rising inflation (see Chapter 16).

The fall in the value of the pound should, however, boost the demand for UK exports abroad. A falling pound means falling prices for UK goods in foreign countries. For example, at an exchange rate of £1 = €2 a UK computer costing £500 will sell for €1 000 in Germany. If the exchange rate then falls to say £1 = €1.8 the price of the computer in Germany will fall to €900. A boost in demand for UK exports will mean more money flowing into the UK. Exporting firms will raise their output and jobs may be created.

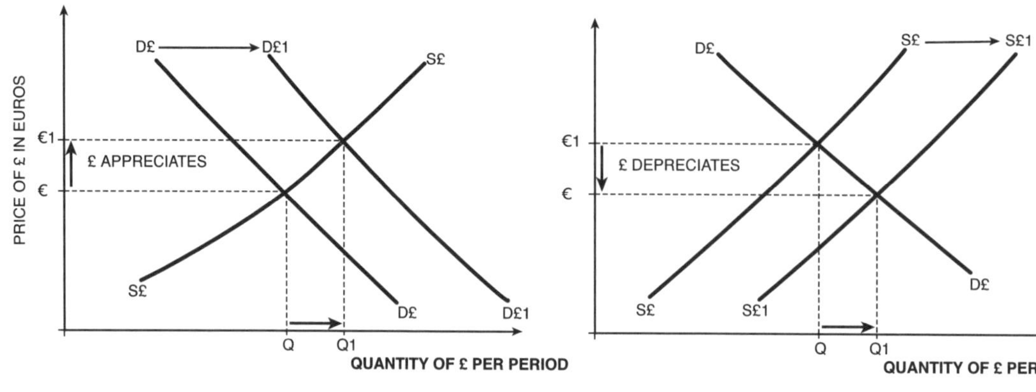

A rise in demand for sterling causes its value to appreciate

So, a fall in demand for pounds causes their value to depreciate.

A rise in the supply of sterling causes its value to depreciate

So, a fall in the supply of pounds causes their value to appreciate.

2 Fiscal policy

A government may cut public expenditure and raise taxes to reduce total demand in their economy so people have less to spend on imports (see Chapter 14). This will help to reduce a trade deficit. However, the fall in demand may also affect domestic firms, who may cut output and employment in response to a fall in demand.

In contrast, an expansionary fiscal policy involving lower taxes and higher public expenditure may boost spending on imports and help to correct a trade surplus. However, it may also help domestic firms if demand for their goods and services also rises, and may help to halt any decline in the industrial base.

3 Adjust interest rates

A government may attempt to attract more inward investments to their economy to help offset a trade deficit by raising interest rates. Higher interest rates will also make borrowing more expensive and reduce the demand for loans by consumers and firms that may be used to pay for goods and services supplied from overseas.

In contrast, lowering interest rates will help correct for a trade surplus by lowering the cost of borrowing by firms and consumers, and will lower the return overseas investors can expect on their inward investments in the economy so that they invest elsewhere instead.

4 Protectionism

A country may use trade barriers to make imports more expensive to buy or simply to limit the amount of imports in order to correct a trade deficit (see Chapter 22). For example, a tariff is a tax on the price of imports. If demand for the imports is price elastic, an increase in price due to a tariff will cause the demand for them to fall significantly. A country may also subsidize the production of goods and services for export so they can be sold more cheaply overseas. However, trade barriers restrict free trade and consumer choice, and often lead to other countries retaliating with trade barriers of their own.

Useful websites for data and more information include:

International trade and balance of payments

- *www.oecd.org* (go to statistics then International Trade and Balance of Payments)
- World Trade Organization *www.wto.org*
- WTO statistical database *stat.wto.org*
- *en.wikipedia.org/wiki/Balance_of_payments*
- *en.wikipedia.org/wiki/International_trade*

Exchange rates

- *www.exchangerate.com/*
- *finance.yahoo.com/currency?u*
- *www.x-rates.com/*
- en.wikipedia.org/wiki/Exchange_rate

Key crossword

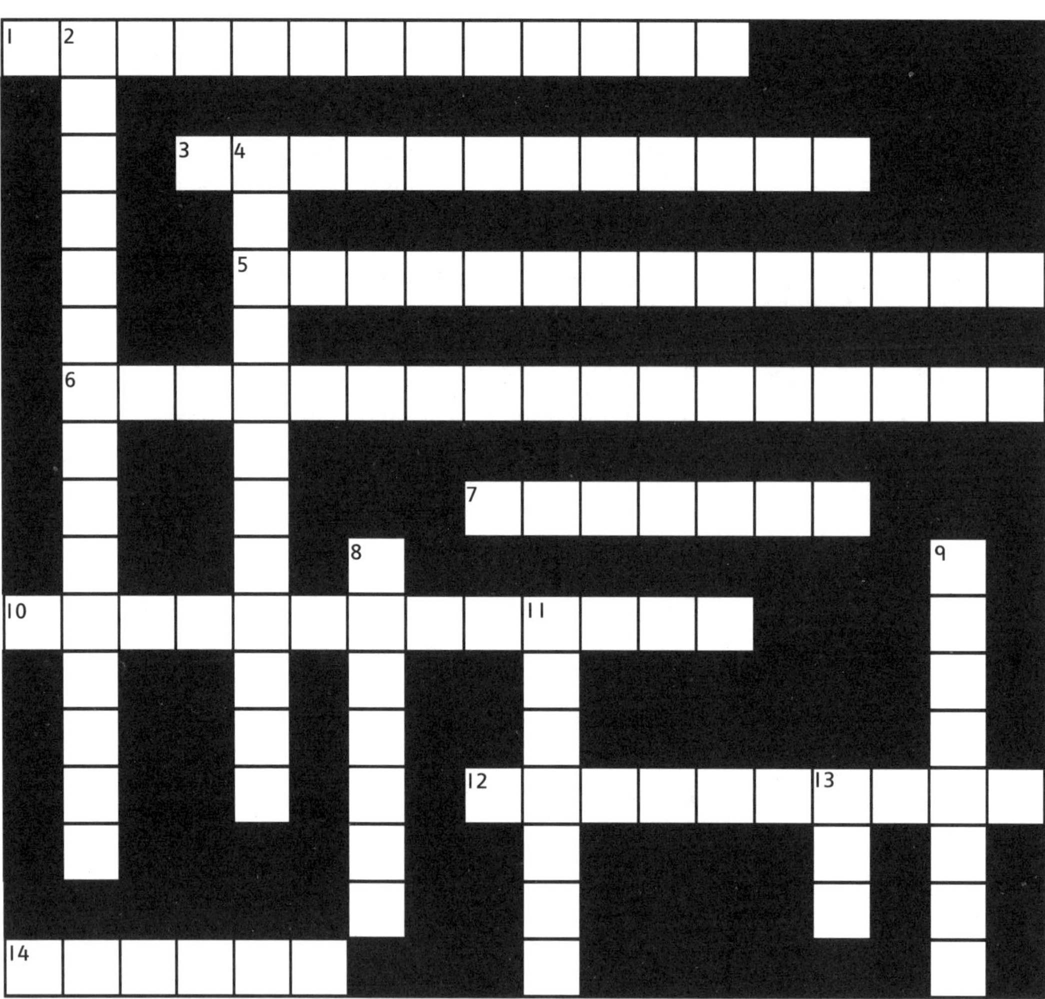

Clues across

1 A physical product bought from overseas (7, 6)

3 Term used to describe a rise in the exchange rate of a currency (12)

5 This records international trade in goods and services, income flows and transfers (7, 7)

6 A record of all international transactions to and from a national economy (7, 2, 8)

7 The balance of trade if imports exceed exports (7)

10 An investment overseas will create this (7, 5)

12 The exchange rate of a currency will do this when it rises in value (10)

14 Along with any omissions, these must be added to the balance of payments to make sure it balances (6)

Clues down

2 A credit received from a service purchased by an overseas resident (9, 6)

4 The price of a currency in terms of another (8, 4)

8 This balance of payments account records flows of money into and out of an economy to pay for the change in ownership of fixed assets (7)

9 Term used to describe the free market determination of exchange rates (8)

11 The balance of trade if exports exceed imports (7)

13 Short-hand for income credits and debits in the balance of payments current account resulting from international investments (1,1,1)

Assessment exercises

Multiple choice

1 Which of the following are most likely to benefit when there is rapid inflation?

A Pensioners

B Borrowers

C Savers

D Consumers

2 Which type of unemployment occurs when demand in an economy falls during an economic recession?

B Seasonal

C Voluntary

D Structural

E Cyclical

3 Study the following table.

Year	Inflation	Increase in wages (average)
1	7%	12%
2	10%	13.2%
3	16.4%	10.1%
4	12%	13%

In which year was there the largest increase in real wages?

A Year 1

B Year 2

C Year 3

D Year 4

4 All of the following may cause cost-push inflation *except:*

A An increase in wages.

B An increase in rent.

C An increase in oil prices.

D An increase in consumer expenditure.

5

Item	Price index	Weight
Food	120	50
Housing	130	40
Services	110	10
	All items =	100

What is the weighted price index for all items?

A 360

B 123

C 120

D 100

6 Which of the following is least likely to contribute to economic growth?

A An increase in technical progress.

B An increase in training.

C An increase in investment.

D An increase in tax rates.

7 Which of the following provides the best measure of economic growth over time?

A The increase in national income.

B The increase in total expenditure.

C The increase in nominal GDP.

D The increase in real GDP per head.

8 Which of the following would be classified as an invisible import to the UK?

A A German car.

B A loan of money to Spain.

C A bottle of wine from Chile.

D A Japanese tourist's spending.

Questions 9 and 10 are based on the following table of data on selected economies in 2005.

Country	% Growth in nominal GDP	% Change in consumer price index
Brazil	9.4%	6.9%
India	12.1%	4.2%
Seychelles	−1.5%	1.6%

9 Which of the following statements does the table support about Brazil?

A Real GDP increased.

B Inflation fell.

C Real GDP per head increased.

D Economic growth was negative.

10 Which of the following statements does the table support?

A Real GDP per head fell in India.

B The Brazilian economy expanded faster than India.

C There was a recession in India.

D Real GDP fell in the Seychelles.

11 Which of the following best describes the economic cycle in an economy?

A Successive booms and busts in consumer spending.

B Cyclical changes in the growth of real GDP around its trend growth rate.

C Cyclical changes in price inflation.

D Seasonal fluctuations in total national expenditure.

12 The value of the Egyptian pound appreciates in value against the Turkish lira. What is the most likely reason for this?

A Speculative buying of Turkish lira.

B Rising inflation in Egypt.

C Higher interest rates in Egypt.

D A fall in demand for Egyptian exports.

13 A country has a visible trade deficit of $5bn and a surplus of invisible trade of $12bn. This means the country has

A A balance of payments surplus.

B A surplus on capital account.

C A current account surplus.

D A deficit on the financial account.

14 Which of the following is an invisible export of Mauritius?

A A resident of Mauritius visiting Europe

B Dividends paid by a company in Mauritius to overseas shareholders

C A loan to Mauritius from France

D Loan interest payments to France

15 Which of the following transactions will be recorded in the financial account of the balance of payments of Jamaica?

A The purchase of a Jamaican company by a Japanese company

B Spending by US tourists visiting Jamaica

C Spending by Jamaican tourists in the USA

D Dividends paid to Japanese shareholders in a Jamaican company

Structured questions

1

Economic Growth in Africa

The tables show figures for Gross Domestic Product in some African countries.

Table 1 Gross Domestic Product Million US$, current prices			Table 2 % annual change in real GDP
Country	**2001**	**2005**	**Average 2001–2005**
Angola	8 936	32 811	9.9
Botswana	6 033	10 317	5.9
Chad	1 702	5 469	14.5
Ghana	5 313	10 720	5.1
Malawi	1 717	2 072	3.4
Rwanda	1 703	2 153	5.1
South Africa	118 479	239 543	3.7
Zimbabwe	10 256	3 372	-5.9

World Bank Data and Research, *www world bank.org.*

a What is meant by economic growth? [3]

b What is meant by the use of the word 'real' in Table 2? [2]

c What has happened to economic growth in Zimbabwe? [2]

d You have been told that economic growth brings great benefits and you decide that you would like to live in a country that had the biggest economic growth between 1995 and 2005.

i Of the countries shown which one would this be? [1]

ii What other information would you need in order to decide whether you would in fact be much better off in this country than any of the others shown? [8]

2 In 2004, economists were concerned about the inflationary impact of unusually high oil prices, which were caused by political uncertainty in the Middle East.

a Explain how inflation is measured. [6]

b Low inflation is one of the aims of government policy. Choose **two** other macro-economic aims of the government and explain what they mean. [4]

c Explain how high oil prices may cause inflation. [4]

d Discuss the actions that a government might take to control inflation. [6]

3 Unemployment in Eurozone countries fell to a record low towards the end of 2006. As a result there was concern that inflation could increase.

a Identify **two** possible advantages for an economy if unemployment falls. [2]

b Define inflation and briefly describe how it is calculated. [8]

c Identify **three** types of unemployment and explain how they are caused. [6]

d Discuss whether a reduction in unemployment should be the main aim of government policy. [5]

e Explain why a reduction in unemployment might increase inflation. [5]

4 A government minister of a developing country has stated that exports must be increased if Gross Domestic Product is to rise and standards of living are to be improved.

a Define Gross Domestic Product. [3]

b How would an increase in its exports affect the balance of payments of a developing country? [4]

c Why might an increase in Gross Domestic Product improve the standards of living in the country? [6]

d Discuss how a developing country might differ from a developed country in the types of industries and services that are most likely to contribute to Gross Domestic Product. [7]

5 Namibia's inflation rate in 2005, measured as an annual percentage change in the Consumer Price Index, was estimated at just under 3%, down from 4.3% in 2004. Examples of some of the annual increases in prices of the major components that make up the weighted price index were household goods (3.8%), food (3.3%), housing, fuel and power (2.4%), transport and communications (8.4%). Examples of increases in prices of some of the minor items in the index were alcohol and tobacco (7.2%), recreation and entertainment (0.9%), education (3.9%) and medical care (-0.1%).

a What is meant by inflation? [2]

b The information above relates inflation to a weighted consumer price index. How do researchers calculate the rate of inflation? [7]

c Study the information above and assess whether it might be a source of concern for the Namibian government. [6]

6 Demand for UK exports dropped considerably in November 2002, which pushed the UK further into a visible trade deficit – the largest since records began.

a Explain what is meant by a visible trade deficit and identify in which part of the balance of payments the deficit would be recorded. [3]

b Discuss whether it matters if a country has a visible trade deficit. [7]

c Describe what policies a government might use if it wished to bring a visible trade deficit into surplus. [4]

d Discuss the other consequences of pursuing **two** of the policies you have mentioned. [6]

7 In February 2007 it was reported that the Japanese yen was gaining strength against the US dollar and that the Japanese exchange rate against other currencies was fluctuating less.

a Explain what the report means when it says that the 'exchange rate against other currencies was fluctuating less'. [5]

b Why do exchange rates fluctuate? [4]

c Discuss the consequences for an economy if its currency 'was gaining strength.' [5]

d A country has a deficit on its balance of payments. Discuss **two** policies, other than exchange rate changes, that a government might use to try to achieve a surplus rather than a deficit. [6]

How to answer question 7

a This question might seem rather easy at first. An **exchange rate** that fluctuates less than other currencies simply means its value on the global currency market is more stable, or less volatile, than the value of other currencies. However, to earn five marks you will need to evaluate this observation and demonstrate your understanding of how exchange rates are determined and what causes them to change.

As always you should start with a good but short definition of what an exchange rate is, in this case using the Japanese yen and the US dollar to form your example, and how the value of one currency of one country in terms of each and every other national currency will be determined by the interaction of demand and supply on the global currency market.

Demonstrate your further knowledge, understanding and use of terminology by explaining that the value of the yen will have increased, or appreciated, against the US dollar. This is what the article means by the yen 'gaining strength' against the dollar. This could be the result of the demand for yen rising and/or demand for the dollar falling. It could also be the result of the supply of yen on the global market falling while the supply of the dollar has risen. It follows that if the currency market value of the yen is less volatile than other currencies then it must mean demand and supply conditions for the yen are relatively more stable.

b You have already started to answer this question in (a). Exchange rates fluctuate due to changes in the demand for currencies and supply of currencies on the global currency markets. Other things being equal, the exchange rate of one currency in terms of one or more currencies will tend to **appreciate** if there is an increase in demand or fall in supply for that currency, and **depreciate** if the currency demand falls or supply rises. If you have time you could illustrate these changes using a demand and supply diagram to show the 'price' of one currency in terms of another, for example, the yen against the US dollar.

There are many reasons why these changes in **demand** and **supply** may have occurred and you should touch on these briefly in your answer, wherever possible relating these to the currencies in question, the yen and the US dollar. The likely main reasons for changes in the demand and supply of these currencies will be the result of changes in the **balance of trade** and the economic climate in Japan and the US. For example, if the US is running a big trade deficit then it will have to pay out more dollars for the goods it **imports** than it receives in revenue for its **exports**. That is, the supply of dollars on the world currency market will increase. In contrast, if Japan has a trade surplus it will be in receipt of more foreign currency than its pays out for exports in yen. That is, the supply of yen on the currency market will be low or falling.

c This question asks you to analyse the various impacts an increasing exchange rate for a country could have on its economy. This requires you to apply your knowledge of economic theory while recognizing that the impacts a rising exchange rate may have are not certain and could vary. As a result you should also acknowledge and explain how these potential impacts may be negative, positive or could have no real impact at all.

For example, if the value of the yen is rising then the price of imports in Japan will be falling. This will help to lower **price inflation** in the economy. However, this may also result in an increase in demand for imports at the expense of domestically produced goods and services. This may cause some Japanese firms to cut back their production, and possibly even go out of business, resulting in increased unemployment. **Unemployment** may also arise if there is a fall in demand by overseas consumers for exports from Japan because the increase in the value of the yen will have increased the price of Japanese exports to foreign markets.

These impacts could be further compounded by any actions the Japanese government may take to correct rising unemployment in the economy, for example, by increasing government spending or lowering taxes. This will help boost total demand in the economy but this may instead result in a further increase in demand for imports and higher price inflation.

However, it follows that if demand for imports rises and overseas demand for exports falls following the increase in the exchange rate, then the balance of trade in Japan will worsen. As a result the supply of yen on the global currency market will rise while demand for the yen will be falling. The combined impact should be to reduce the exchange rate of the yen, thereby correcting the earlier appreciation in its value and any potential impacts it will have on the Japanese economy.

d So what are the economic phenomena listed in this question? You should be able to identify and explain these. They are the **balance of payments**, a balance of payments **deficit** and **surplus**, and government **macroeconomic policy**. Even if your previous answers have already used these terms your answer to this question should include brief descriptions of them, not only because this will demonstrate your knowledge but because in doing so it will also help you answer the question. This will require you to describe and analyse the use of **fiscal and monetary policies** to influence levels of demand in an economy and the impact these may have on the demand for imports and, therefore, the balance of payments. In addition you could also explain how some countries may use **tariffs** and **quotas** to restrict imports, although this can often cause other countries to retaliate.

A model answer for question 2

a Price inflation refers to a sustained or continuous increase in the prices of goods and services in an economy. This does not mean every price will be rising at the same rate, or that every price will necessarily be rising. Some may be falling but overall when taken together the general level of prices will be rising.

Most governments aim to keep price inflation low and stable and will collect price information in order to measure progress. Clearly it will be difficult and expensive to collect information on all the prices of all goods and services in an economy so governments will often measure inflation by collecting price information on a sample, or basket, of different goods and services. The ones chosen will normally be those purchased by a 'typical' family or household. The prices of this typical 'basket' will then be monitored at a selection of different retail outlets and online retailers. This price information will then be used to compile a consumer price index (CPI). This provides the main measure of price inflation affecting consumers in an economy.

A CPI expresses the change in the average price of the basket of good and services as the movement in a single number, or index. The average price of the basket in the first year of measurement, or base year, is given the index number 100. Then, if on average the prices of all the goods and services in the same basket rise by 10 per cent over the following year, the price index at the end of the second year will be 110.

The proportion of total household income spent on each type of good or service is used to weight their average prices to find the weighted average price of each type of product. So, for example, if on average households spend twice as much on food products as they do on clothes, then changes in food prices will be weighted twice as much as changes in the prices of clothes in the CPI.

Over time, the goods and services we buy will tend to change, due to changes in tastes and fashion and because new goods and services become available, like mobile phones and LCD televisions. The composition of the basket of goods and services used to measure a CPI, and the weights used to calculate average prices, will therefore be changed from time to time to reflect these changes.

b In addition to low and stable inflation, in most modern macro-economies governments have objectives to encourage economic growth in the national output and income of their economies, and maintain low and stable levels of unemployment.

Economic growth involves an increase in the real output of a country, generally measured as its Gross Domestic Product. A sustained growth in real GDP means that each year the economy will have produced more goods and services than the previous year, and the total income of the economy will be higher even after allowing for the impact of inflation on prices and the purchasing power of that income. Economic growth can therefore raise living standards and economic welfare. Higher real incomes allow people to buy more goods and services they need and want, and for the economy to invest more in schools, healthcare, roads and other infrastructure. However, economic welfare will also depend on what goods and services are produced, what impact they may have on the environment, and how the increased income is distributed. For example, if the increased output and income is created by increased production that damages the environment, and if the additional income generated by growth is only shared among a few very rich people, then economic welfare for most people will not have improved and may even have reduced.

The more people there are in work the more goods and services they can produce and the more income they can earn to support themselves, their families and others through the tax they pay to their government to fund public spending. Higher levels of employment can therefore help economic growth. In contrast, high levels of unemployment will result in lower national output and income. It will also mean overall tax revenues collected by government from wages will be lower but public spending may potentially be higher to pay social security benefits to the unemployed.

All countries suffer some unemployment as people change or move between jobs, but this is generally short-lived. This is called frictional unemployment. High and prolonged unemployment caused by an economic recession or structural change in an economy is however a big cause for concern for many governments. Cyclical unemployment can rise as consumer demand for goods and services falls during a recession and firms cut back production and their demand for labour as a result. Structural unemployment occurs when the industrial structure of an economy changes significantly and entire industries may shut down leaving many workers unemployed and their skills redundant so they will find it difficult to get new jobs in new industries. For example, many manufacturing workers were made unemployed in many developed countries during the 1980s and 1990s as their manufacturing industries declined or became more capital intensive.

Governments also try to encourage trade and secure a favourable balance of international transactions, and some may have additional objectives such as reducing poverty and inequalities in income and wealth, and protecting the environment.

c Just because oil prices are high does not necessarily mean they will be inflationary. Although oil prices are high they may be stable. That is, they are not rising and therefore not putting additional pressure on price inflation. Secondly, if oil prices are high consumers may have to spend more of their income on oil products such as petroleum and heating oils, leaving them less to spend on other goods and services. The fall in demand for these other goods and services may help to reduce a demand-push inflation.

Rising oil prices, however, may be inflationary if they add to the cost of producing oil products and other goods and services that use oil, including the manufacture of plastics and paints, and the provision of bus and other transport services. Producers faced with rising costs of buying oil or oil products will attempt to pass these costs on to their consumers in higher prices for their goods and services. This results in a cost-push inflation. Consumers may react to these rising prices by seeking wage increases from their employers if they are in work. This will also increase pressure on production costs and cost-push inflation.

d Price inflation may be the result of demand for goods and services rising faster than their supply in an economy, increasing production costs which producers pass on to consumers in higher prices, and/or from rising import prices. In turn we refer to these types of inflation as demand-pull inflation, cost-push inflation and imported inflation.

A government that is concerned with controlling a demand-pull inflation can use contractionary or deflationary fiscal policy. A contractionary policy involves cutting public spending on goods and services and raising taxes to reduce total or aggregate demand in the economy. However, this may in turn cause an increase in unemployment and lower growth in the real output of the economy.

A deflationary monetary policy involves raising interest rates which raises the cost of borrowing money and also makes saving more attractive. If people and firms borrow less money to spend, and consumers save more of their incomes as a result of the increase in interest rates then this will help reduce the total demand for goods and services in an economy and reduce demand pressures on prices. However, firms usually borrow money to invest in new capital and therefore higher interest rates may reduce investment and the potential for economic growth.

Higher interest rates can help increase the value of the exchange rate of the national currency against other currencies. An appreciation in the exchange rate will make imports cheaper to buy and reduce an imported inflation. However, it will also make exports more expensive to overseas consumers. As result overseas demand for exports may contract and could result in rising unemployment as exporting firms cut back their production in response.

Cost-push inflation can often be the result of rising import prices for material and components purchased from other countries, but it can also be due to rising wage costs as workers demand wage rises not matched by an increase in their productivity. A government may react by holding down the wages of the workers it employs in the public sector. It may also use deflationary fiscal and monetary policy because other workers will wish to spend their higher wages on goods and services and this will put upward pressure on prices. This can involve raising taxes on wages and/or raising interest rates so workers with loans like mortgages on their homes will have to use their higher wages to pay more in interest charges instead.

A government can also try to control inflation by using supply-side policy instruments to increase the productive potential of the economy. Increasing the aggregate supply of goods and services to meet increased levels of total demand can reduce inflationary pressures caused by rising demand. It can also help reduce production costs as the productivity of resources is increased. Supply-side policies can be used by a government to stimulate incentives to work and enterprise, and to remove barriers that restrict competition, international trade and higher levels of productivity. For example, a government may lower taxes on businesses to increase incentives to enterprise. It may use competition policy to regulate or break up monopolies that might otherwise restrict the market supply of their goods or services to force up prices. A government may also introduce laws to control the power of trade unions to strike and to force up wages. Improvements in education and training can also help teach workers new and improved skills.

8 DEVELOPED AND DEVELOPING ECONOMIES

Economic development involves growth in the economic wealth of an economy. Government policy in many countries generally aims for continuous and sustained economic growth, so that their national economies expand and become more developed.

A less developed economy has a low level of economic development. Almost 90 per cent of the world population lives in less developed economies. Some emerging economies, such as those in south-east Asia, are developing rapidly but have yet to achieve the same high levels of economic and human development characteristic of many modern developed economies.

The level of economic and human development in different economies can be measured and compared using a range of indicators. Gross domestic product per capita, a measure of average income per person, is a commonly used indicator but does not take account of living standards including the availability of healthcare, education and clean water supplies. Income is also distributed very unequally in many countries. Other development indicators are also used, therefore, such as the adult literacy rate, life expectancy at birth and the number of people earning less than $1 per day.

Many less developed countries lack the capital required to invest in modern infrastructure such as road and power networks, and they also lack the consumer demand required to stimulate investments in an industrial base and services sector. Instead, less developed countries tend to depend heavily on agriculture for employment and incomes. Yet many families in some of the poorest countries can barely produce enough food to live on. High population growth is also a feature of many less developed economies. Rapid population growth places further pressure on their scarce resources.

The natural rate of increase in a population is the difference between the birth rate and death rate. Populations in a number of developed countries are shrinking and their average age increasing as birth rates have fallen significantly and to below death rates. It is estimated that one in every three people in developed countries will be over 60 by 2050. In contrast, more than a third of the population of low-income countries is under the age of 15.

Around half the world's population now lives in urban areas, and this is expected to rise as more people move to cities in search of work. The number and size of cities is expanding rapidly, especially in many emerging economies. However, increasing urbanization has increased the consumption of scarce natural resources such as trees, open space and water as more homes, factories, offices, shops and roads are built. Increased energy and car use in cities has also increased pollution, reduced air and water quality, and increased health risks.

Chapter 19

Economic Development

Aims

At the end of this chapter you should be able to:

- describe **developed economies** and **developing economies** and reasons for their different stages of development
- describe simple measures and indicators of comparative **living standards**
- describe differences in living standards and reasons for disparities within economies and between different economies, both developed and developing

Section 1 Developed and less developed economies

Economic development involves growth in the economic wealth of a region, country or group of countries to improve the well-being of inhabitants. Government policy in different countries generally aims for continuous and sustained economic growth, so that their national economies expand from **developing economies** into **developed economies**. Development objectives therefore tend to include producing more necessities such as food, shelter and healthcare, and making sure they reach more people in need, raising standards of living and expanding economic and social choice.

However, different countries and even different regions within the same countries in the world today are at very different stages of economic development. Almost every day on the television or in newspapers we learn about the problems many people have to suffer living in less developed or developing economies.

Exercise 1 The characteristics of developed and less developed countries

These pictures depict typical scenes from less developed countries and developed countries. In pairs discuss and list what you consider to be the basic characteristics of:

a less developed economies

b developed economies.

Developed economies

A **developed economy** is generally thought of as having large modern farms, many firms of different sizes producing and selling a variety of goods and services, a well-developed road and rail network, modern communication systems, stable government and a relatively healthy, wealthy and educated population. Developed economies are also sometimes called industrialized nations, but this is despite the great majority of their output, income and employment now being created by their service sectors rather than manufacturing industries (see Chapters 16 and 20).

However, according to the United Nations there is no general rule for designating regions or countries as developed or developing, but it is nevertheless commonly accepted that Canada and the United States in North America, Australia and New Zealand in Oceania, Japan in Asia and many countries in Europe are considered to be developed economies.

Developing economies

A **less developed economy** has a low level of economic development. Farming methods are poor, sometimes providing scarcely enough food for a rapidly growing population to eat. There are very few firms producing and selling goods and services. Road, rail and communication networks are underdeveloped and most people are poor. They live in poor housing conditions, receive little or no education, do not expect to live to old age, and may even lack access to clean water. Many countries in Africa are considered less developed.

Less developed countries (LDCs) are also often called **developing economies**, suggesting that over time they are becoming a little more prosperous, that their industrial structure is developing and fewer people are living in extreme poverty. However, not all less developed countries are developing. Some are in fact experiencing negative economic growth, meaning that incomes are falling and levels of poverty, malnutrition and disease are rising. For example, between 1995 and 2004 the real GDP of Zimbabwe fell by 40 per cent (see Chapter 17).

In contrast, some countries are developing rapidly, such as India and China, and some Eastern European countries such as Armenia and Georgia, but they have yet to display the full range of characteristics of modern developed economies. These are often grouped under the headings **emerging economies** or **newly industrialized countries**.

Reasons for low economic development

There are a number of reasons suggested for why some economies have remained less developed than others.

- **An over-dependence on agriculture to provide jobs and incomes**

More people in less developed economies work in farming than in industry and services compared to developed nations (see Chapter 20). Many produce only enough food for themselves and their families to live on and very little surplus they can sell to earn money. In some areas there has been overfarming which means the land is no longer any good for growing crops. Failures of rains to arrive in some areas due to global climate change has also meant crops can no longer be grown for people to survive on.

- **Domination of international trade by developed nations**

It is argued that rich nations have exploited many poorer nations by buying up their natural resources and the food crops they produce at very low prices, and then using these resources to produce goods and services which they then export back to the same less developed countries at much higher prices. Further, many rich countries have protected their own mining and agricultural industries by paying them subsidies. These subsidies have increased the global supply of these products and forced down world prices. Producers in less developed countries have not been able to compete and as a result, they have lost sales, incomes and jobs (see Chapter 22).

- **Lack of capital**

While incomes remain so low in many less developed countries, they have little they can invest in building factories and the purchase of machinery and equipment to develop an industrial base. Without these capital goods less developed countries will not be able to produce more of the goods and services they need and which they could also export to earn money from overseas trade.

- **Insufficient investment in education, skills and healthcare**

Many people in many less developed countries do not have access to basic education, training and healthcare which can help them become healthier, more productive and more innovative workers. Better education about family planning may also help reduce birth rates and improve living standards.

- **Low levels of investment in infrastructure**

Road, rail and communication networks are often poor in many less developed countries. This makes travel and access to rural areas, and the sharing of information, very difficult.

- **Lack of an efficient production and distribution system for goods and services**

Many less developed countries lack industries and services. If incomes are low there is little incentive for businesses to set up different shops and retail centres. If transport is difficult outside of cities then people from rural areas cannot travel to cities to shops, and it is also difficult to take goods and services to rural communities. If workers are uneducated and lack skills then industry may be unable to employ them.

- **High population growth**

Many underdeveloped countries have rapidly expanding populations because birth rates remain high (see Chapter 20). This means available goods and services have to be shared among more and more people over time.

- **Other factors**

Unstable and corrupt governments, and wars with neighbouring nations or between different ribes or religious groups, have often blighted the development of some less developed countries. Money that could have been used to invest in economic development has in some cases been misused by corrupt officials or squandered on buying arms and fighting wars.

Section 2 Development indicators

UN millennium development goals

In 2000, a total of 189 different nations belonging to the United Nations agreed to a set of **millennium development goals** they hope to achieve by 2015.

- Eradicate extreme poverty and hunger
- Achieve universal primary education
- Promote gender equality and empower women
- Reduce child mortality
- Improve maternal health
- Combat HIV/AIDS, malaria and other diseases
- Ensure environmental sustainability
- Develop a global partnership for development

For all these goals the UN has given member nations a set of ambitious targets, including halving between 1990 and 2015 the number of people whose income is less than $1 per day, halting or reversing the spread of HIV/AIDS by 2015, and providing access for developing countries to affordable, essential drugs. Progress towards achieving all these goals and targets is monitored using a range of different statistical measures and indicators.

Exercise 2 Developing measures

In groups discuss indicators or measures the UN could use to monitor each millennium development goal listed above. Try to think up at least three measures or indicators for each goal. Compare your ideas with other groups in your class and together compile a full list of measures and indicators for each development goal.

If possible, now compare your lists to those actually used by the UN in their Millennium Development Goals Report, available online at *www.un.org/millenniumgoals/*.

Development indicators

The UN uses around 50 different indicators to monitor progress towards its millennium development goals. Too many to list here but below are just a few of the most commonly used indicators of development and **living standards** in different regions and countries in the world.

- **GDP per capita**

Gross domestic product (GDP) per capita, or average income per person, is the most commonly used comparative measure of development. Developed countries tend to have relatively high GDP per capita. In 2005, Bermuda had the highest GDP per capita of US$69 900.

Countries with highest and lowest GDP per capita, 2005

Country	GDP per capita ($)	Country	GDP per capita ($)
Bermuda	69 900	Sierra Leone	800
Luxembourg	65 900	Guinea-Bissau	800
Equatorial Guinea	50 200	Burundi	700
United Arab Emirates	45 200	Tanzania	700
Cayman Islands	43 800	Democratic Republic of Congo	700
Norway	42 800	Solomon Islands	600
United States	41 600	Comoros	600
Ireland	41 100	Somalia	600
Guernsey	40 000	Malawi	600
Jersey	40 000	Gaza Strip	600

CIA World Factbook 2006

However, GDP is a narrow measure of economic development or welfare in a country. For example, it does not take account of what people can buy with their incomes, access to health and education, or other non-economic aspects such as the amount of political and cultural freedom people have, the quality of their environment, or level of security against crime and violence.

Calculating average GDP per person also tells us nothing about how incomes are distributed between populations. For example, consider China. Rapid economic growth had increased the number of millionaires in the country to almost 250 000 by 2006, but still around 47 per cent of the Chinese population had to survive on less than $2 a day, with almost 17 per cent on less than $1 each day. Similarly, Saudi Arabia has a reasonably high income per head, around $13 100 in 2005, but most of the wealth in the country is held by less than 3 per cent of the population. But even within highly developed countries such as the US there are still big disparities between rich and poor people. For example, in 2005 around 9 per cent of US households had an annual income of $10 000 or less compared to 6 per cent of households with $150 000 or more.

Other countries such as Equatorial Guinea, Brunei and Trinidad and Tobago also have relatively high average incomes but are generally not considered developed countries because their economies depend so much on the production of oil. These countries also have very unequal distributions of incomes. For example, in 2005, average income in Trinidad and Tobago was $16 800 but 39 per cent of the population lived on less than $2 per day.

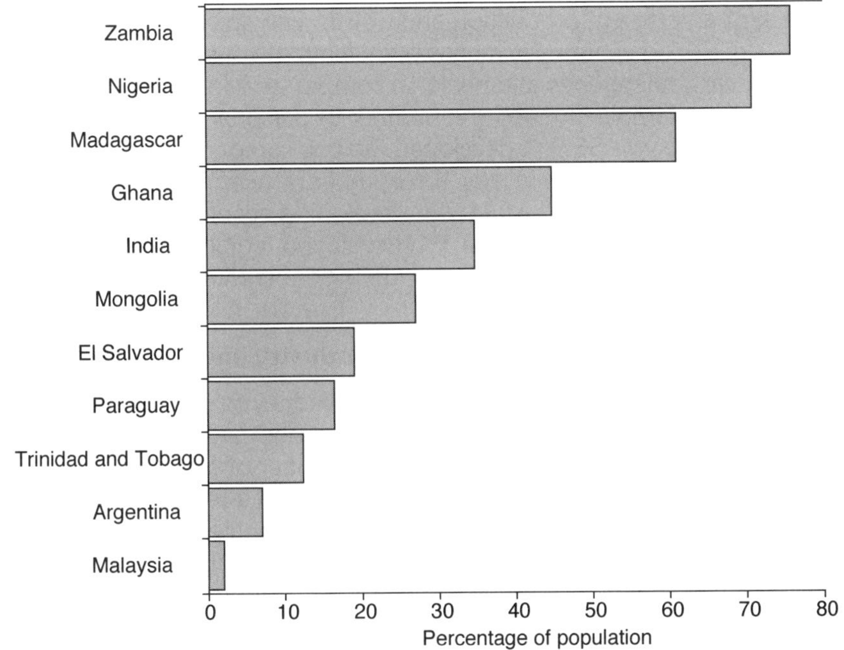

- **Population on less than $1 per day**

A better measure of the level of poverty in a country is the proportion of people living on very low incomes, usually $1 or $2 per day. In 2002, around 19 per cent of the population of developing economies was estimated to be living on less than $1 per day.

Other indicators of poverty include levels of malnutrition, numbers of underweight children, levels of unemployment, and people living in slums. However, even in developed regions some 6 per cent of the population in 2005 still lived in slum conditions.

- **Life expectancy at birth**

People in developed countries tend to live longer than people in less developed countries because they tend to have better standards of living and access to good food and healthcare. In contrast, malnutrition, poor sanitation, lack of access to healthcare, wars and famines mean that many people in less developed regions do not live to old age.

Life expectancy from birth is therefore a good measure of economic development in a country or region. On average, a baby born in the developed world in 2005 could expect to live to 75 years of age, while a baby born in the less developed world could expect to live around 66 years. However, in some of the poorest countries in Africa, average life expectancy from birth is less than 42 years (see also Chapter 20).

Other health-related indicators of economic development include baby and mother mortality rates, the proportion of children and adults receiving inoculations against diseases, and death rates from various diseases including tuberculosis and HIV/AIDS. For example, in 2004 around 80 out of every 1000 children under the age of five died in developing regions of the world economy compared to just 7 out of every 1000 in developed regions.

- **Adult literacy rate**

A good measure of education provision in an economy is the proportion of the adult population that is able to read and write. For example, most adults can read and write in developed countries such as the US, Canada, Japan and those in Europe. In contrast, in 2004 only around 1 in 3 adults living in developing countries such as Chad, Equatorial Guinea, Niger and Sierra Leone could read and write.

Other education-related indicators include school and college enrolment and completion rates among children and young people.

- **Access to safe water supplies and sanitation**

Clean water is a necessity and safe, clean sanitation can help stop the spread of disease. These are generally available services to most people living and working in developed countries. Yet, only around half of all people in developing regions had access to good sanitation in 2004, and just 80 per cent to a safe and sustainable water source. Access to improved sanitation is particularly poor in rural areas in developing countries with only 33 per cent of rural populations having access compared to 73 per cent living in cities and urban areas.

- **Ownership of consumer goods**

Low incomes and the lack of an efficient production and distribution system for goods and services in many less developed economies means ownership of consumer goods such as washing machines, cars, telephones and personal computers is low compared to many developed countries. For example, in 2004 the number of personal computers and Internet users in every 100 people was 55.9 in developed regions compared to just 4.9 in developing regions of the global economy. Similarly, the number of telephone lines and cellular subscribers in every 100 people was just 31.7 in developing economies, and as low as 8.2 in Sub-Saharan Africa. This compared to 130.1 in developed regions where many people have both a landline and a mobile phone. Fast and efficient communications are a necessary factor in the development of an economy.

- **Proportion of workers in agriculture compared to industry and services**

High incomes in developed economies mean that people have money to spend on shops, eating out at restaurants and leisure activities. They also want banks, insurance, public transport, holidays and many other services. The large number of firms located in developed economies also requires a range of business services. As a result, most employed people in developed countries work in services while, in contrast, most employees in less developed countries work in agriculture (see also Chapters 16 and 20). However, unemployment can be very high in many less developed countries because there is so little work available. Many people instead try to be self-sufficient and produce the food their families need from subsistence farming. Any surplus can be sold at local markets to earn some money or exchanged for other goods and services through barter (see Chapter 2).

Human development index

To make international comparisons of economic development a little easier the United Nations compiles the **human development index (HDI)**. It combines a number of development indicators into one index with a maximum possible value of 1. Changes in the index over time can therefore show whether a country has improved or reduced the economic well-being of its people in terms of their:

- standard of living, as measured by gross domestic product (GDP) per capita
- access to education and knowledge, measured by the adult literacy rate and school and college enrolment rates
- health, diet and lifestyle, measured by life expectancy at birth

The world by human development index values, 2006

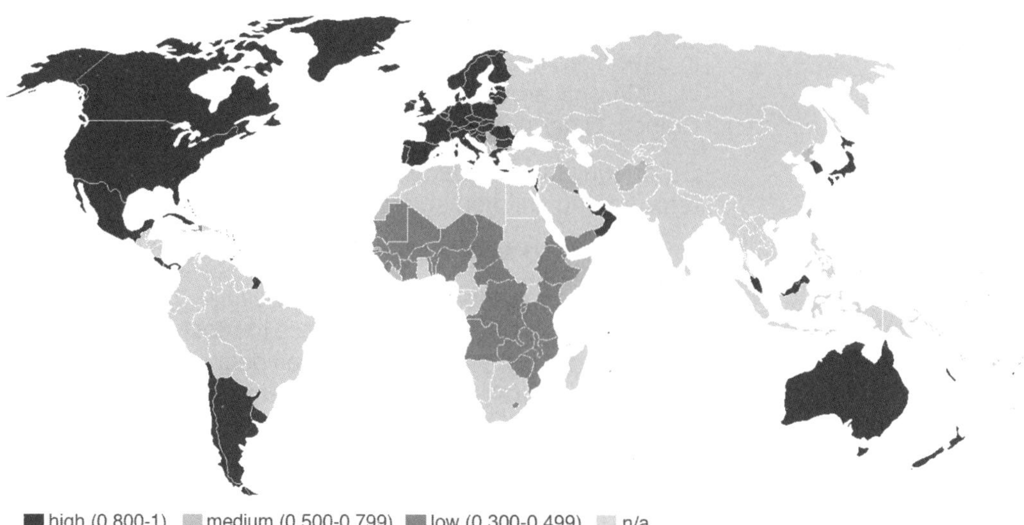

Source: *http://en.wikipedia.org/wiki/Image:HDImap2006.png*

Chapter 20 Population

Aims

At the end of this chapter you should be able to:

- describe trends in **population growth** in different countries
- understand that **resources** used to make goods and services are **scarce**
- describe factors that affect population growth
- understand what is meant by the population **dependency ratio** and calculate ratios for different countries
- analyse **birth, death and migration rates** and suggest differences in these between countries
- examine the **structure of populations** in different countries
- analyse problems and consequences for developed and developing economies

The world population

The population explosion

Since the eighteenth century the world has experienced a population explosion, and it is still increasing faster than ever before. While there is potential for the production of more goods and services, natural resources are limited, and, as fast as goods and services are produced, so the needs and wants of an ever-increasing world population. The population of the world is increasing by over 70 million people each year, or 200 000 a day. Imagine a city the size of London added every month, and the people in that city being on average, only four to five weeks old!

The population explosion started in Europe after the Industrial Revolution in the eighteenth century. Improvements in housing, sanitation and medicine reduced the number of deaths and helped increase the number of births. The population of Europe rose by over 300 per cent in a 160-year period after 1750. Many of these Europeans moved overseas.

World population, annual average growth rates by major region, 1800–2050

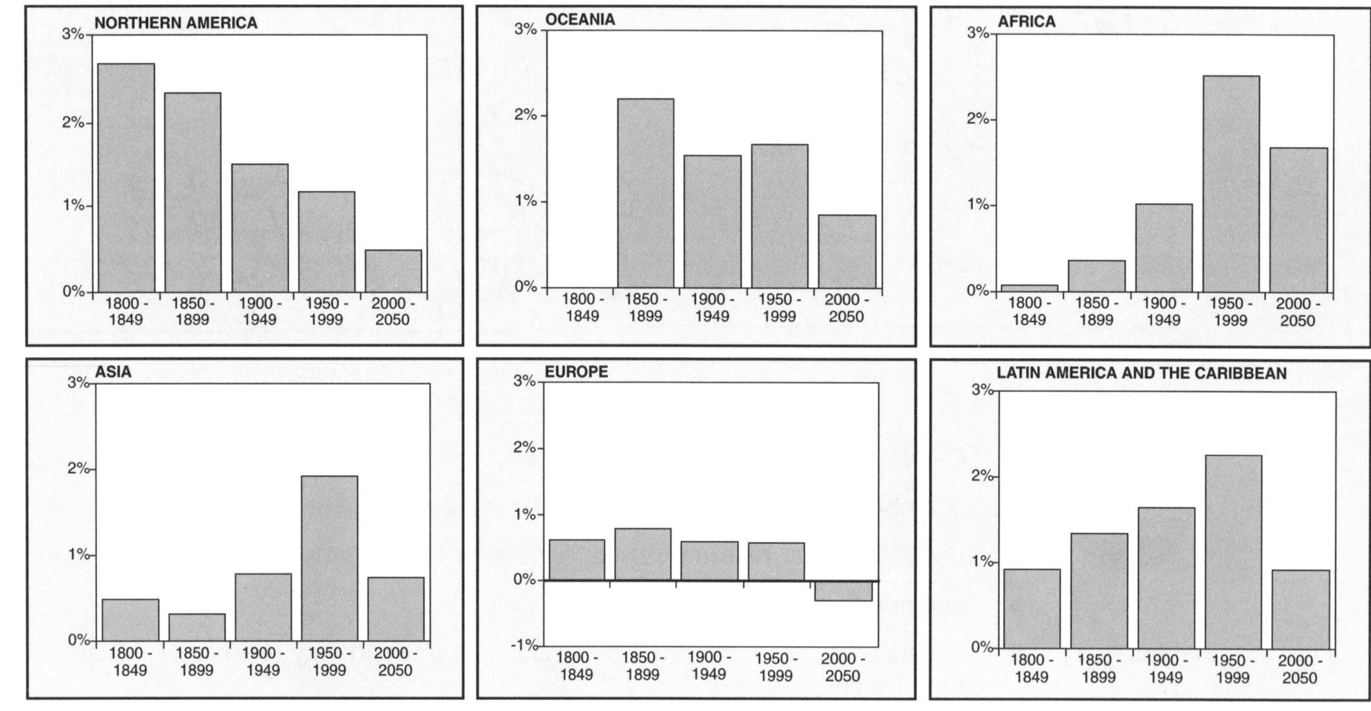

United Nations Population Division

In the twentieth century population growth in many western countries has slowed down. The populations of countries like the UK and other western European nations have, over the past few years, hardly changed at all and are currently growing by less than 0.5 per cent per year on average. Many European countries are now expected to see their populations shrink by 2050.

The new explosion is in less developed countries, particularly in Asia and Africa. Here, their combined populations are expected to rise from around 5 billion people in 2000 to 8 billion by 2050 – an increase of 60 per cent. In contrast, the population of Europe is expected to fall from 730 million to around 630 million people.

The world population is expected to reach 9 billion by 2050. Just under 90 per cent of all these people will live in less developed countries.

Exercise 1 Explosion

The world population reached 1 billion around 1804. The second billion was added 123 years later in 1927, the third billion just 33 years later in 1960. It then took just 14 years for world population to grow by another one billion people to reach 4 billion.

The graph below illustrates this population explosion. By 1999 the world population had reached 6 billion and is expected to grow to 9 billion by 2050.

The world population explosion

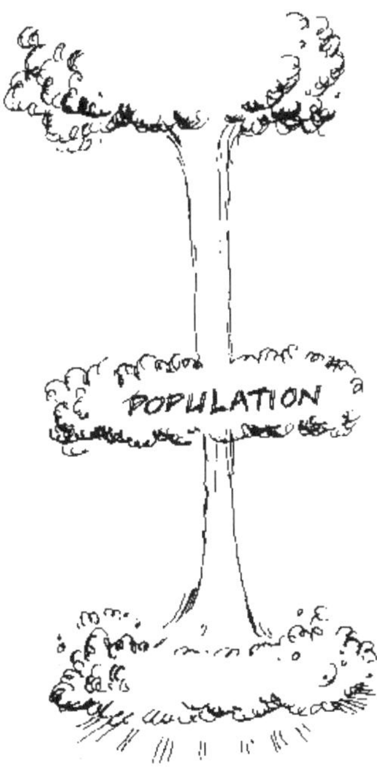

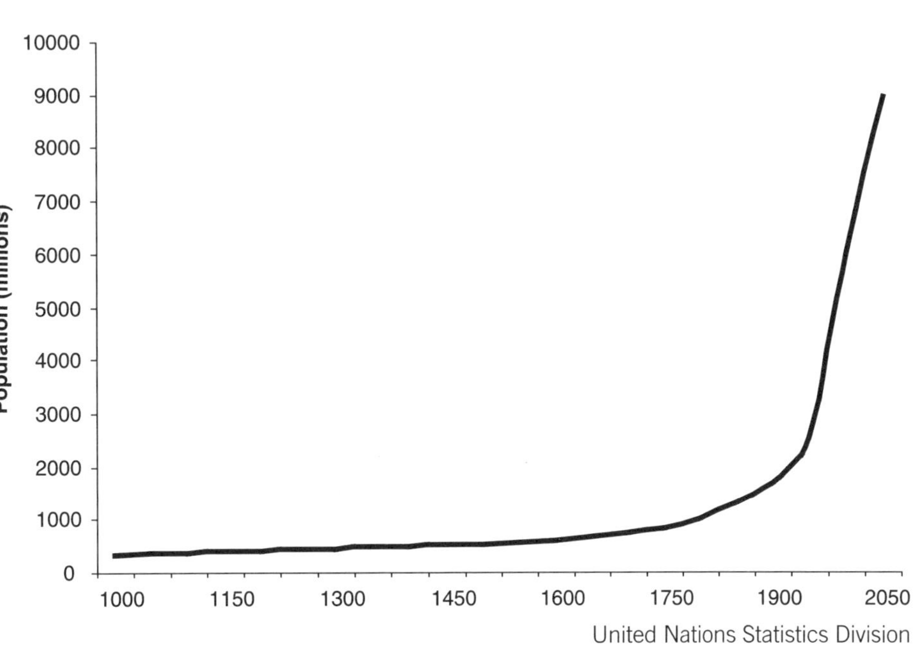

United Nations Statistics Division

1 a As the world population increases what will happen to the total number of needs and wants in the world?

b If resources are scarce, such as oil, coal, metals, fertile soils and clean air, what will happen to the rate at which we use them up?

2 The population of the world rises as fewer people die and live to old age, and more babies are born. What is likely to happen to the demand for:

a Food

b Consumer goods

c Education

d Healthcare

e Housing

f Transport?

3 a If one country cannot produce enough goods and services for the needs and wants of its population how will it try to obtain more of these commodities?

b What will happen to that country's balance of trade?

Population growth: a cause for concern

In 1798 the Reverend Thomas **Malthus** wrote about population growth in the UK. At the time of writing the UK population was growing fast and this seemed to support his view that increasing numbers of people would only bring misery. There would be too many people and too few resources. That is, there would be **overpopulation**. As a result, people would start to starve and there would be famines and plagues as people lacked the strength to fight off disease. Wars would start as countries tried to take over each other's resources to support their own populations. Population growth would eventually be stopped.

However, Malthus was proved wrong in Britain. Although the population increased four times over during the nineteenth century, technology improved to provide for the increased population. Farms' output of food increased and new methods of transport allowed food to be brought to Britain from the vast lands of America. More houses were needed and the building of these provided work and incomes for people. Increasing numbers of people meant more consumers. This increase in demand expanded the markets for goods and services, stimulating investment in new capital equipment to produce them and creating employment for many more people. Economic growth took place, and, despite the costs of increased congestion in growing cities and increasing pollution from factories, living standards rose.

Nevertheless, many people still believe Malthus will be proved right. Rapid population growth in less developed countries continues to place significant pressure on their scarce resources, particularly their natural resources, as more and more people, farms and factories compete for land and access to safe drinking water. Cutting down trees to make way for intensively farmed land can cause it to become depleted of soil and nutrients, increasing the risk of famine. The grab for land can also result in tensions between different groups of people, and ultimately war. Disease, famine and wars have plagued many poor countries in Africa and Asia.

Dependency ratios

Imagine there are five people living in your home: your mother and father, your sister and a grandparent. Your mother is the only person at work. She earns $150 per week, which is used to provide food, clothing and shelter as well as the other goods and services for five people including herself. That is, your father, you and your sister and a grandparent all depend on your mother going to work. Clearly, if there was just your mother and father their standard of living would be much higher. They would have more money to spend on themselves. If, on the other hand, they had more children, all the family would have a lower standard of living as the mother's income and the goods and services it buys would have to be shared out between more people. As the number of dependants rise, everybody will be worse off unless the productivity of source resources also rises. The same thing happens in the population as a whole.

People in work produce commodities not only for themselves but also for people not at work. For example, In the UK there are approximately 29 million people in paid employment. The rest of the population of about 31 million people rely on these 29 million to provide the goods and services they need and want. These 31 million people are said to be the **dependent population**. Using these figures we can calculate the **dependency ratio** in the UK. This ratio compares the number of people in work with the total population of the country.

$$\text{Dependency ratio} = \frac{\text{Total population}}{\text{Number of people in work}}$$

Using the figures for the UK the dependency ratio is 2.07. That is, every person in work not only supports his or herself but also 1.07 other people. A total of 2.07 UK citizens are supported by one worker.

The dependent population will consist of the very young, schoolchildren, students, housewives, the unemployed and old-age pensioners. Any increase in these groups of people means that the people in work have more people to support and living standards could fall.

The dependent poupulation includes both young and old

More resources, and expenditure on them, will have to be devoted to education for the young, and medical and welfare services for young and old alike. In a country like the UK, where such services are provided by the government using tax-payer's money, this means working people may have to pay more tax to support their dependants. In addition, if people in work cannot produce enough goods and services to satisfy the needs and wants of a growing dependent population, the country will have to use some of its income to purchase more and more imported goods from abroad. Its balance of trade may become unfavourable.

The dependency ratio has increased in the UK for a number of reasons; the school leaving age has been increased over time; more young people are encouraged to stay on in full-time education after 16 years of age; people are living longer and the number of elderly people has increased; and an increasing number of people are taking early retirement. To offset this in part, the UK government is increasing the official retirement age for women from 60 to 65 years of age so that it is the same as for men.

Many developed countries are displaying the same pattern. However, it is the less-developed countries which face the biggest problem. Medical help has allowed more people to live to old age and more babies to survive. As a result, their dependent populations are large and increasing, putting more strain on their scarce resources.

Exercise 2 The dependent population

Below is a table of figures showing the total population and labour force in a number of countries in 2006.

Country/Area	Population	Labour force
China	1313973713	791400000
India	1095351995	496400000
European Union	456953258	218500000
United States	298444215	149300000
Indonesia	245452739	94200000
Brazil	188078227	90410000
Bangladesh	147365352	66600000
Russia	142893540	74220000
Japan	127463611	66400000

CIA World Factbook

1 For each country calculate:
   - **a** the size of the dependent population
   - **b** the dependency ratio.

2 Which countries have:
   - **a** the highest dependency ratio?
   - **b** the lowest dependency ratio?

3 What effect would the following have on the dependency ratio of a country?
   - **a** A fall in the number of people in employment.
   - **b** An increase in the number of old people.
   - **c** An increase in the number of births.
   - **d** An increase in employment.
   - **e** A decrease in the number of births.

4 Of the above factors in question 3, which are characteristic of:
   - **a** less developed countries
   - **b** developed countries
   - **c** both types of country.

5
   - **a** What is meant by overpopulation?
   - **b** Can Japan be considered overpopulated? Explain.

Section 2

The causes of population change

There are three ways in which a country's population can increase:

1 The number of babies being born can increase.
2 The number of people dying can fall.
3 More people can come to live in a country (**immigration**) than there are people leaving the country to live abroad (**emigration**).

Population size and components of growth, by major area 1995–2000

Major area	Population 1999 (thousands)	Births	Deaths	Net migration	Total growth
		(annual average, in thousands)			
World Total	5 978 401	129 810	52 072	0	77 738
More developed regions	1 185 174	12 224	11 951	1 971	3 243
Less developed regions	4 793 227	116 586	40 121	–1 971	74 494
Africa	766 623	28 115	10 331	–297	17 496
Asia	3 634 279	77 953	27 492	–1 207	49 254
Europe	728 934	7 493	8 248	950	195
Latin America and Caribbean	511 345	11 554	3 245	– 471	7 838
North America	307 202	4 172	2 528	930	2 574
Oceania	30 018	527	227	81	381

United Nations Population Division

The **natural rate of increase** in a population is the difference between the birth rate and death rate. In most countries birth rates exceed death rates so populations are rising. For example, between 1995 and 2000 births exceeded deaths by around 78 million each year across the world. Much of this increase is in less developed countries where birth rates remain high while death rates have tended to fall. In contrast, the natural rate of change in population in Europe is negative. Both birth and death rates are low in European countries but over the period 1995 to 2000 deaths exceeded births by 755 000 each year. The population of Europe only continues to grow slowly due to net inward migration by people from overseas, although many countries in Eastern Europe are now losing population due also to net outward migration.

Births

In some countries more babies are born than in others. The average number of children born in a country each year compared to the total population is known as the **birth rate**, which is normally expressed as the number of births for every 1 000 people in the population. The birth rate in the UK in 2006 was 10.78 births for every 1 000 UK citizens but it used to be much higher. For most of the nineteenth century the birth rate was about 35 per 1 000.

Countries with highest and lowest birth rates, 2006

Country/Area	Highest birth rates (births per 1 000 of population)	Country/Area	Lowest birth rates (births per 1 000 of population)
Niger	50.73	Slovenia	8.98
Mali	49.82	Ukraine	8.82
Uganda	47.35	Bosnia and Herzegovina	8.77
Afghanistan	46.60	Lithuania	8.75
Sierra Leone	45.76	Austria	8.74
Chad	45.73	Italy	8.72
Burkina Faso	45.62	Andorra	8.71
Somalia	45.13	Macau (China)	8.48
Angola	45.11	Germany	8.25
Liberia	44.77	Hong Kong (China)	7.29

CIA World Factbook

With the exception of Afghanistan, the countries with the highest birth rates in 2006 were all in Africa. In many of these countries there are on average 6 or more children for every adult female in the population. In contrast, many countries with very low birth rates are old planned economies in Eastern Europe (see Chapter 3). In all these countries there is on average less than 2 children per woman. The overall world birth rate in 2006 was just over 20 births per 1 000 people.

There are a number of reasons for differences in birth rates between countries, and changing birth rates over time.

1 Living standards

Improvements in the quality and availability of food, housing, clean water, sanitation and medical care result in fewer babies dying. Many years ago a high proportion of children would die before they could go to work and earn money to help their families. As a result, people often had large families in case their children died. As living standards improved in many developed countries, fewer babies died and so people did not have as many children.

In less-developed countries birth rates remain high because many children still die, and people want large families so that the children can work to produce food and earn incomes.

Average number of children per adult female

Countries with 6 or more children per woman

Afghanistan
Angola Burkino Faso
Burundi Congo Liberia
Niger Sierra Leone
Somalia Yemen

Countries with 2 or less children per woman

China Croatia
Czech Republic Japan
South Korea Poland Spain
Slovenia Ukraine Russia
Switzerland Lithuania
Latvia Italy Estonia
Austria Andorra
Bulgaria

CIA World Factbook 2005-06

2 Contraception

The increased usage of contraception and abortion has dramatically reduced birth rates in developed countries. The pill for women was first introduced in the 1960s and has a 99 per cent success rate in preventing pregnancy. However, because of a lack of education on such matters, many people in less-developed countries are unaware of birth control. Perhaps they should learn from Japan's success in reducing her birth rate from 36 births per 1000 people to 17 per 1000 people in just 15 years after the introduction of contraception.

3 Custom and religion

Many people, particularly in less-developed countries, hold religious beliefs that will not allow them to use contraception. The Roman Catholic religion is one such belief.

Customs are changing. In developed countries it has become less fashionable to have large families and birth rates have fallen.

4 Female employment

In developed countries, more and more women are going out to work. Many women do not wish to break their careers to bring up children. Having children also causes a drain on people's incomes. Not only will the wife have to give up work for a while, but they may also have to pay a baby-sitter to look after the child if she remains at work. This is in addition to the cost of food, clothing and shelter for the child.

5 Marriages

Most people have children when they are married. In many developed countries people are tending to marry later on in life and so birth rates fall. For example, in the UK the average age of a mother at all births increased from 26 years in 1971 to over 29 years of age in 2005.

Deaths

If people start to live longer, this increases the size of the population. The number of people who die each year compared to every 1000 people measures the **death rate**. The overall world death rate in 2006 was just under 9 deaths for every 1000 people. The countries with the highest death rates in 2006 were all in Africa, many with over 20 deaths per 1000, similar to the death rate in the UK and many other developed countries over 100 years ago. The UK death rate is now just over 10 per 1000 of population. In contrast, many of the countries with the very lowest death rates in 2006 of less than 4 deaths per 1000 were in the Middle East.

Countries with highest and lowest death rates, 2006

Country/Area	Highest death rates (deaths per 1000 of population)	Country/Area	Lowest death rates (deaths per 1000 of population)
Botswana	29.36	Solomon Islands	3.98
Swaziland	28.82	Gaza Strip (Palestine)	3.87
Lesotho	28.67	Oman	3.86
Angola	24.50	Libya	3.48
Liberia	23.93	Brunei	3.42
Sierra Leone	23.43	American Samoa (US)	3.33
Zimbabwe	21.92	Jordan	2.63
South Africa	21.32	Saudi Arabia	2.62
Niger	21.19	Kuwait	2.42
Mozambique	20.99	Northern Mariana Islands	2.30

CIA World Factbook

A number of factors affect death rates and help to explain differences between countries.

1 Living standards

Better quality food, clothing, sanitation and shelter, and a greater emphasis on cleanliness, have helped improve health and life expectancy in developed countries. In the less developed world a lack of the right types of food to provide vitamins and proteins has meant many people in these areas continue to die of malnutrition. However, in developed countries many people smoke and eat fatty foods, causing cancers and heart disease. These health problems occur very little in less developed countries.

2 Medical advances and healthcare

Advances in medicine and healthcare in many countries have reduced the number of deaths from diseases. For example, killer diseases such as smallpox, cholera and tuberculosis can be prevented or even cured by modern medicines.

However, life expectancy at birth still remains low in many less developed countries. Other diseases such as HIV/AIDS and malaria are widespread and increasing in many areas, particularly across Africa, and causing the death of many young people and adults (see *www.alertnet.org/topkillerdiseases.htm*). Famine, wars and criminal violence will also have a significant effect on death rates and life expectancy in some countries.

Average life expectancy at birth, 2006

Highest	Years	Lowest	Years
Andorra	83.5	Malawi	41.7
Macau (China)	82.2	Sierra Leone	40.2
San Marino	81.7	Zambia	40.0
Singapore	81.7	Mozambique	39.8
Hong Kong (China)	81.6	Liberia	39.7
Japan	81.3	Zimbabwe	39.3
Sweden	80.5	Angola	38.6
Switzerland	80.5	Lesotho	34.4
Australia	80.5	Botswana	33.7
Guernsey (UK)	80.4	Swaziland	32.6

CIA World Factbook

Migration

Net migration measures the difference between immigration and emigration to and from a country. Between 1995 and 2000 almost 2 million more people each year emigrated from less developed countries to more developed countries than migrated in the opposite direction. Net migration from Asian countries accounted for much of this. On average net outward migration from Asia was 1.2 million people per year. In contrast, net inward migration to Europe was 950 000 people per year between 1995 and 2000.

Such international migration has economic, social and political implications. Increasing numbers of migrants from less developed countries to high-income countries have helped to boost their working populations, but has also increased demand for housing, education and social security benefits. In some cases, tensions can occur between different ethnic groups as a result. But countries that lose people to immigration can also face problems caused by a loss of skilled workers leaving to find higher-paid work overseas, such as nurses and doctors, engineers and entrepreneurs.

The structure of population

It is useful to examine and compare the structure of populations in different countries and consider how changes in structure can affect economies. The following features of population are relevant:

- Age distribution – how many people in different age groups
- Sex distribution – the balance of males and females
- Geographic distribution – where people live
- Occupational distribution – where people work

Young or old?

The **age distribution** of a population refers to the number of people, or percentage of population, in each age group. With falling birth and death rates in many high-income countries, the average age of their populations is increasing. That is, on average, each year there are more and more middle to old-aged people. For example, in 2000 in Italy, Greece, Germany and Japan, almost one-quarter of their populations were over 60 years of age, while 16 per cent or less were under 15 years of age.

In contrast, in low-income countries more than a third of the population is under the age of 15, with some countries having almost half their populations made up of children. For example, in Yemen in 2000, around half of the population was under 15 and less than 4 per cent over 60. Similarly, in Niger, Uganda and Burkina Faso children made up 48 per cent or more of their populations. This means that a larger proportion of these countries' populations is too young to work and will have to depend on those who can, at least until they too are old enough to work.

Youngest and oldest countries, 2000

Youngest countries	Age groups %			Oldest countries	Age groups %		
	0–14	15–59	60 +		0–14	15–59	60 +
Yemen	50.1	46.3	3.6	Italy	14.3	61.7	24.0
Niger	49.9	47.0	3.1	Greece	15.1	61.5	23.4
D.R. of Congo	49.2	46.7	4.1	Germany	15.5	61.2	23.3
Uganda	48.8	46.5	4.7	Japan	14.7	62.1	23.2
Burkina Faso	48.7	47.3	4.0	Sweden	18.2	59.4	22.4
Angola	48.2	48.1	3.7	Belgium	17.3	60.6	22.1
Somalia	48.0	48.1	3.9	Spain	14.7	63.5	21.8
Burundi	47.6	48.1	4.3	Bulgaria	15.7	62.6	21.7
Zambia	46.5	48.9	4.6	Switzerland	16.7	62.1	21.2
Chad	46.5	48.6	4.9	Latvia	17.4	61.7	20.9

United Nations Population Division

It is estimated that 22 per cent of the world population will be 60 years or older by 2050, with one in every three people in developed countries over 60 by this time. As the number of elderly people grows in many countries this will increase pressure on their working populations to support more non-working people. It will also affect the allocation of resources in these economies. More resources will be needed to produce the goods and services older people want and need, such as more healthcare, pensions and leisure facilities. However, falling birth rates may mean less resources are needed for maternity clinics, nurseries and schools.

The age and sex distribution of a population can be displayed on a population pyramid. The pyramids in exercise 3 below compare the age and sex distributions of the population of high-income countries with the population of less developed countries. Along the bottom axis is the number or percentage of males to the left of the vertical axis, and to the right the number or percentage of females. The vertical axis shows age in convenient ranges. The pyramid for high-income countries *bulges* in the middle due to their ageing populations as birth and death rates remain low.

On the other hand, less developed countries have pyramids with wide bases and narrow tops because birth rates are high and life expectancy is low.

Exercise 3 Population pyramids

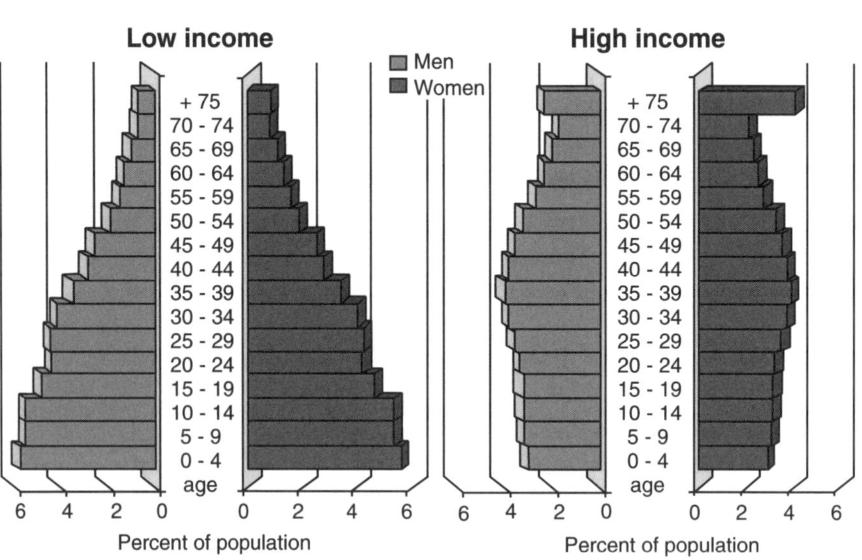

World Bank

1. Looking at the pyramids, which group of countries have the highest dependency ratios for:
   - **a** under-15-year-olds?
   - **b** over-60-year-olds?
2. Which group of countries has the highest birth rate?
3. Which group of countries has the highest life expectancy?
4. List 10 countries that individually are likely to have similar population structures to those shown by the pyramids.
5. What is an 'ageing population'? Which group of countries has an ageing population? Describe likely impacts this will have on their economies.

Where do people live?

The **geographic distribution** or regional distribution of a population refers to where people live. Most people, almost 90 per cent of the world population, live in less developed countries. This has placed significant pressure on scarce resources in these countries to produce goods and services people need and want.

Most densely populated countries and areas, 2005

Country/Area	Population	Area (km²)	Density (people per km²)
Monaco	35 253	1.49	23 660
Macau, China	460 162	26	17 699
Hong Kong	7 040 885	1 099	6 407
Singapore	4 325 539	683	6 333
Gibraltar	27 921	6	4 654
Vatican City	783	0.44	1 780
Malta	401 630	316	1 271
Bermuda	64 174	53	1 211
Maldives	329 198	298	1 105
Bahrain	726 617	694	1 047

Least densely populated countries and areas, 2005

Country/Area	Population	Area (km²)	Density (people per km²)
Mauritania	3 068 742	1 025 520	3.0
Iceland	294 561	103 000	2.9
Suriname	449 238	163 820	2.7
Australia	20 155 130	7 741 220	2.6
Namibia	2 031 252	824 292	2.5
French Guiana	187 056	90 000	2.1
Mongolia	2 646 487	1 564 116	1.7
Western Sahara	341 421	266 000	1.3
Falkland Islands/ Islas Malvinas	3 060	12 173	0.25
Greenland	56 916	2 175 600	0.026

United Nations *World Population Prospects* (2004 revision)

The most densely populated place in the world is Monaco in Europe with over 23 000 people per square kilometre of land. Macau in China is next with just under 18 000 people per km^2. This compares to the world average of 48 people per square kilometre of the earth's surface. The least populated country is Greenland with a density of just 1 person for every 38.5 km^2, or 0.026/km^2, largely because much of Greenland is frozen over all year round.

Within countries the geographic distribution of population can also vary widely and has changed significantly over time. Around half the world's population today lives in urban areas, and this is expected to rise to around 60 per cent, or 5 billion people, by 2030. The movement of people from rural areas to urban areas has helped increase production of goods and services, and raised living standards.

However, increasing urbanization has also resulted in increased consumption of scarce natural resources such as trees, open space and water as more homes, factories, offices, shops and roads have been built. Increased energy and car use in cities has increased pollution, reduced air and water quality, and increased health risks. The rapid growth of cities in many countries, but particularly now in developing countries such as China and India, is therefore some cause for concern. For example, in the district of Huangpu in Shanghai in China, there were over 126 000 people per km^2 in 2005. Other highly densely populated city areas in 2005 included Freguesia de Santo Antonio on the Macau Peninsula in China (98 776/km^2), Malé in the Maldives (48 007/km^2), Cairo in Egypt (35 420/km^2) and Mumbai in India (29 434/km^2).

The number of mega-cities with over 10 million residents increased from just five in the late 1960s to 18 in 2000. Tokyo in Japan is the largest with over 35 million people. Mexico City, New York, São Paulo in Brazil and Mumbai in India all had over 18 million residents in 2005.

World population density, population per km^2 in 2005

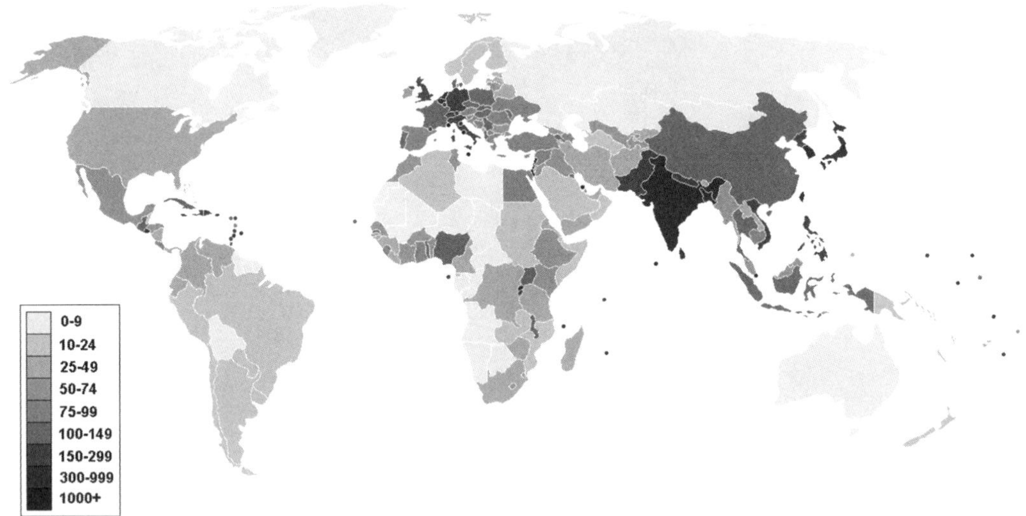

en.wildpedia.org/wild/image:World_population_density_map.PNG

Where do people work?

The **occupational distribution** of a population refers to the types of jobs people do. In 2005 the total working population of the world was about 3 billion people. Of these around 40 per cent worked in agriculture, 21 per cent in industry and construction, and 39 per cent in services. Most employed people in developed countries work in services while most employees in less developed countries work in agriculture.

The trend in fast-developing economies, such as China and India, is for more and more people to move out of agriculture and other primary industries into employment in their rapidly expanding manufacturing and services industries (see Chapter 16). Employment in services in developed countries is also expected to continue to rise. Female employment and self-employment is also growing in these countries. For example, in 2005 over 45 per cent of the UK workforce was female, up from 39 per cent in 1977. The UK has the highest rate of female employment in the European Union.

Employment by industry

Countries with highest proportion of employees in agriculture	Percentage of workforce in agriculture	Countries with highest proportion of employees in services	Percentage of workforce in services
Angola	85%	Andorra	80%
Bhutan	93%	Denmark	76%
Burkina Faso	90%	Jordan	84%
Burundi	93%	Luxembourg	86%
Chad	80%	Malta	75%
Eritrea	80%	Netherlands	79%
Guinea	80%	Puerto Rico	77%
Malawi	90%	United Arab Emirates	79%
Niger	90%	United Kingdom	80%
Rwanda	90%	United States	78%

Latest available data, *CIA World Factbook* 2005

In your own words write down what you understand by the following terms.

Dependency ratio
Natural rate of population increase
Birth rate
Migration
Age distribution
Geographic distribution
Occupational distribution
Over population

Now go back though the chapter to check your understanding.

There is a wealth of information and statistics on population available from the following organizations and websites:

- CIA World Factbook *www.cia.gov/cia/publications/factbook*
- GeoHive *www.xist.org*
- OECD *www.oecd.org* (search demography and population statistics)
- UK Office for National Statistics *www.statistics.gov.uk* (select population theme)
- United Nations Population Division *www.un.org/esa/population/unpop.htm*
- United Nations Statistics *unstats.un.org/unsd/Demographic/default.htm*
- US Census Bureau Population Division *www.census.gov/population/www/*
- Wikipedia *en.wikipedia.org/wiki/Population*
- World Bank *www.worldbank.org* (search population)
- World Bank Development Education Program *www.worldbank.org/depweb/english/modules/social/pgr/index.html*

Assessment exercises

Multiple choice

1 Which of the following is least likely to be a characteristic of a less developed economy?

A High adult illiteracy rate

B High infant mortality rate

C High proportion of population in slums

D High level of capital investment

2 Which of the following is not an explanatory factor for the under-development of an economy?

A Lack of a skilled workforce

B Low level of taxation

C Lack of investment in infrastructure

D Over-dependence on subsistence farming

3 Which of the following measures would you most advise against using as an indicator of the level of development in an economy?

A Total GDP

B GDP per capita

C Adult literacy rate

D Share of total employment in services

4 Which of the following countries has the lowest GDP per capita?

Country	Population (million)	GDP (US$ billion)
A	33	990
B	12	75
C	125	100
D	4	180

5 Which of the following countries has a high population growth rate?

A France

B Denmark

C Malawi

D Canada

6 What is meant by overpopulation?

A Too many people to an area of land

B High population density

C Too many people and not enough resources

D High population growth

7 What is the dependency ratio of a country?

A The number of people working compared to the total population

B The number of old people compared to the total population

C The number of people over 16 years of age compared to the total population

D The number of children compared to the adult population

8 Which of the following factors is likely to cause an increase in the birth rate in a country?

A Contraceptives being freely supplied

B An increase in living standards

C More education

D Earlier marriages

9 Death rates are likely to fall if:

A Housing conditions are improved.

B More people smoke.

C Healthcare deteriorates.

D People's diets become less healthy.

Structured questions

1 The charts below represent the proportion of people employed in different sectors in three different countries.

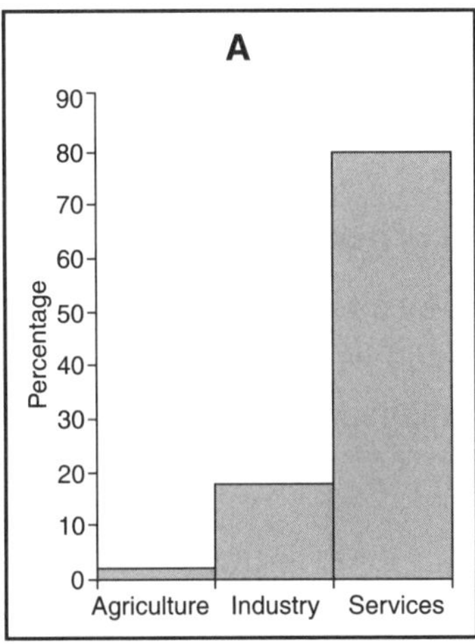

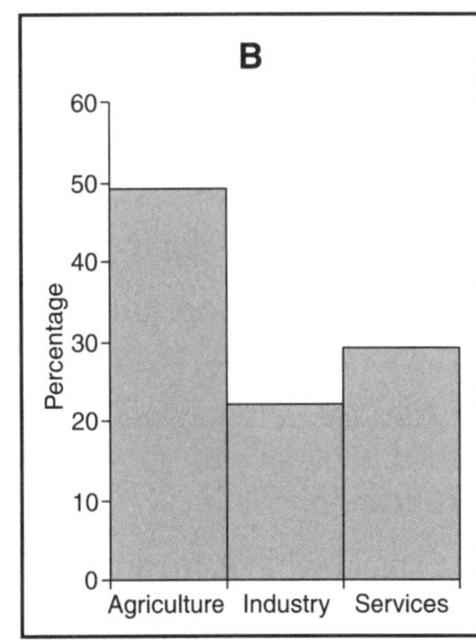

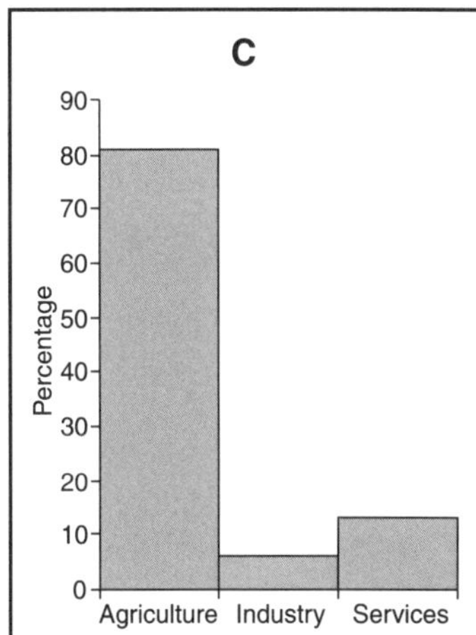

a Which chart do you think represents:

i a country that is developing rapidly?

ii a less developed or low-income country?

iii a developed or high-income country? [3]

b Suggest how living standards might differ between these three different countries. [6]

c Increasing numbers of females are entering employment in developed countries. How might this affect the birth rate in these countries? [4]

d Suggest three other factors that have caused birth rates to fall in developed countries over the last 50 years or so. [6]

2 **a** What determines the rate of growth of a population? [3]

b Contrast the expected age structure of the population of a developing country with that of a developed country. [7]

c In some developing countries life expectancy has been declining in recent years. This has been largely due to the spread of HIV/AIDS. Governments have allocated large amounts of expenditure to developing new hospitals and to providing health education programmes. Discuss in what ways this policy might affect other major government economic policies. [10]

3 **a** The rate of population growth in developed countries is often different from the rate of population growth in developing countries. Explain why this might be so. [5]

b Sometimes a government might try to limit the growth in the population of its country. Explain why it might want to do this. [4]

c As countries become more economically developed, there is a change in the relative importance of the different sectors of production. Describe what this change might be. [5]

d In many developed countries there will be a large increase in the proportion of older people during the next 10 to 15 years. Discuss how governments might deal with this situation. [6]

4 In Egypt, a developing country, population growth of around 2% each year increases the overcrowding in cities. 12% of the population live in Cairo, the most densely populated city in Africa.

a Identify the factors that determine the population growth in a country. [3]

b Explain what is meant by a developing country. [7]

c Explain what differences there are likely to be between the population structure found in a developing country and that found in a developed country. [5]

d Consider whether the problems faced by a developing country from overcrowding in cities are similar to those found in a developed country. [5]

5 Countries are categorized as less developed because of their poverty and low average incomes, their lack of good human resources and their low level of economic diversification.

a Explain what is meant by

i 'their lack of good human resources'; [3]

ii 'their low level of economic diversification'. [3]

b Explain whether it can be concluded from the above statement that all people in less developed countries are poor. [4]

c Explain what is likely to be the occupational distribution of the population in a less developed country. [4]

d If a less developed country has become classified as a developed country, what changes would probably have happened to the structure of its population and occupational distribution? [8]

6 Changes in the population structure of many countries have led governments to introduce a health education programme.

a Identify and explain **two** of the issues that a health education programme might cover in developing countries. [4]

b How may the age structure of the population in a developing country differ from that in a developed country? [6]

c Explain what is meant by **i** an opportunity cost and **ii** a social benefit. [4]

d Discuss whether it is possible to apply these concepts to the provision of healthcare. [6]

How to answer question 2

a You are asked to list and explain key factors that determine by how much and how fast a **population** of a country or a region can grow over time. You will need to display your knowledge of **birth rates**, **death rates** and **net migration**, write definitions of these terms and briefly suggest some reasons why they might change. Wherever possible your analysis should be underpinned by examples drawn from your knowledge about what is happening to populations in different **developed and less developed countries**. For example, why have birth and death rates fallen in many developed countries and what impact is this having on the growth and **age structure** of their populations? Why are populations still rising rapidly in many of the poorest countries in the world despite average life expectancy still being very low in many cases?

b Demonstrate your understanding of this question by first writing a short definition of what the age structure or age distribution of a population means. Then show off your knowledge by answering the question clearly and directly: the average age of the population of a developed country will tend to be higher and rising due to low birth and death rates. That is, on average, each year there are more and more old to middle-aged people, and relatively fewer younger people in a developed country. You could even show this by drawing two simple **population pyramids** contrasting developed and developing countries, with the pyramid for the former being narrower at its base and wider in the middle age ranges compared to the pyramid for a developing or less developed country. Presenting information in a graphical format can help gain extra marks but remember to label your pyramids correctly.

To demonstrate your skills of analysis you should now suggest reasons why the average age of the population of a developed country will tend to be higher and rising compared to the population of a developing country. This requires you to explain factors that have resulted in lower birth and death rates in developed countries.

Finally, and for the full seven marks, you should consider briefly what the implications are for developed economies of the changing age structure of their populations. What changes are likely to occur to the pattern of **consumer demand** and savings, and to the demand for healthcare and pensions? What does it imply about the size of the working population relative to the **dependent population**, and what problems may occur as a result? You will not have time to explain all these in full but you will need to demonstrate briefly that you understand these issues and would be able to analyse and judge their economic implications.

c For ten marks you will be expected to display the broad range of skills required by the assessment objectives and apply them to the economic issue presented. To do this you will need to define what exactly the question is about. It considers government spending on hospitals and health education and how this decision may affect other government economic policies. So the question really concerns several economic issues. They are government **macroeconomic aims** and policy choices to help achieve them, including **fiscal, monetary and supply-side policies**, and the opportunity costs of these choices in less developed economies. You will need to examine and analyse all these in a logical and concise manner, remembering of course to provide definitions for these economic policies and concepts. You should look again at Chapters 1 and 14 especially to help refresh your knowledge.

Consider first the key aims of most governments, and specifically **employment** and **economic growth**. How will government spending on reducing HIV and AIDS infection help towards achieving these aims? Clearly, if many people are unwell and dying of these diseases then the supply and **productivity** of labour are likely to be falling. Further, spending on the building and operation of hospitals can create jobs and generate incomes in construction and healthcare.

However, **public expenditure** decisions involve choice. This means you should consider and explain the **opportunity costs** of the decision to increase spending on hospitals and health education. Public expenditure on other goods and services, such as road building programmes, schools and subsidies to help farmers grow more food and buy machinery, may have to be cut or **taxes** will have be increased to pay for it. What would be the likely effect of these policy decisions on employment, output and **economic welfare** in the country?

Alternatively, the government may borrow money to finance the increased spending because higher taxes can reduce **consumer demand** and result in higher levels of **unemployment**. High taxation can also reduce incentives to work and enterprise. If many people are poor, raising taxes will also create greater hardship and would be unlikely to raise much additional revenue. However, government borrowing will increase the **national debt** and more of the **GDP** of the country will have to be used to pay interest charges on the debt. Higher levels of spending may also be inflationary.

Interest rates may have to rise to encourage increased lending to the government and this will push up the cost of **borrowing** by firms for **investment** and borrowing by consumers to spend on goods and services. Higher interest rates may also affect the **exchange rates** and make the **exports** from the country less competitive.

A model answer for question 5

a **i** The production of goods and services to satisfy people's needs and wants involves the use of scarce resources. These include natural resources like oil and land, man-made resources including machines and buildings, and human resources or labour. Some people also have enterprise, or the business skills needed to organize scarce resources successfully to produce goods and services.

Labour is hired by firms to produce goods and services in return for wages. The wage a worker will receive will tend to be related to their skills and therefore productivity. An unskilled, poorly educated and/or unhealthy worker will not be very productive and may not even be able to work. Many people in many less developed countries do not have access to basic education, training and healthcare that can help them become healthier, more productive and more innovative workers and entrepreneurs. That is, they lack good human resources.

ii A country that has a low level of economic diversification means it is over-dependent on one or a small number of industries to provide jobs and incomes. There are very few firms producing and selling goods and services, and they lack the capital they need to invest in building factories and the purchase of machinery and equipment to develop an industrial base. Road, rail and communication networks also tend to be underdeveloped and most people are poor.

For example, more people in less developed economies work in farming than in industry or services compared to developed nations. Many produce only enough food for themselves and their families to live on and very little surplus they can sell to earn money. In some areas there has been over-farming and the land is no longer any good for growing crops because many people lack the basic skills and education needed for good farm land management.

b We cannot conclude from the statement that all people are poor in less developed countries. We can only conclude average income per head or per person is low. Some people may still be very rich while most others are poor. The article does not reveal how income and wealth is distributed between people in less developed countries.

We should also look at the availability of goods and services in these countries and their prices. If prices are low then even relatively low or modest incomes may be able to buy sufficient goods and services to provide for a good standard of living. However, the article reports that less developed countries generally have very low levels of economic diversification which suggests many basic goods and services, including food products, healthcare and education, may not be generally available.

c The occupational distribution of a country refers to its pattern of employment and jobs. In developed countries most employees work in services, like retailing and banking, compared to manufacturing industries. Very few people work in agriculture and other primary industries like mining. However, this has not always been the case. Many years ago most people worked on farms before the development of industries attracted workers from the land into factories to produce goods and to earn incomes. Since then manufacturing industries in many developed countries have declined in terms of the number of workers they employ and their contribution to total output. As real incomes have increased in developed countries consumers have spent an increasing proportion of their rising incomes on leisure and other services. They also need more shops to buy goods and services, banks to keep their money in and to help them make payments, transport services to travel more, and so on. This has promoted a significant growth in output and employment in service industries.

In contrast, most people in less developed countries still work in agriculture. Many less developed countries lack an industrial base and healthy service sector due to the lack of a skilled labour force and generally low incomes. Because many workers in less developed countries suffer from low levels of education and lack skills, industry is unable to employ them. Similarly, as incomes and therefore consumer purchasing power are low, there is little incentive for businesses to set up different shops and retail centres.

d We can examine and compare the population structure of a less developed country with a developed country in terms of their age distribution, geographic distribution and occupational distribution. If a less developed country has undergone economic development and become a developed country, we might expect the average age and life expectancy of the population to have increased, more people to be living in urban and city areas than before, and more people in paid employment in secondary and service industries than in primary industries such as agriculture and mining.

The age distribution of a population refers to the number of people, or percentage of population, in each age group. The average age of populations in many developed countries is rising due to falling birth and death rates. That is, on average, each year there are more and more middle to old-aged people, and relatively fewer younger people. In contrast, high birth and death rates in many less developed countries means these countries have far more young people, and especially children, than older people. For example, in Yemen in 2000, around half of the population was under 15 and less than 4 per cent were over 60. Average life expectancy from birth is much higher in developed countries than in less developed countries. Many people in less developed regions do not live to old age due to malnutrition, poor sanitation, lack of access to healthcare, wars and famines.

The geographic distribution of a country refers to where people live. Around 90 per cent of the world's population live in less developed countries. However, population densities in these countries, or the average number of people per square kilometre, are generally quite low because the population is spread out over a very large land area. This is because many people in less developed countries work on the land to grow and farm the food they need. In contrast, many people in developed countries live and work in urban or city areas where they have access to good transport and communications, shops and other services. Around half the world's population live in urban areas and this is likely to rise as the world population grows and more countries develop economically.

As a country develops, the occupational distribution is likely to change significantly. In question (c) we noted how most employees in developed countries work in services, like retailing and banking, compared to manufacturing industries. Very few work in agriculture. For example, over 75 per cent of employees in the US and in many European countries work in services. Self-employment and female employment in these countries is also high and rising.

The reverse is true of less developed countries where most people, in many cases 90 per cent or more, work in subsistence farming and agriculture, growing the food they need. As a less developed country develops its industrial base we would expect workers to move out of agriculture into paid manufacturing occupations and services for the reasons discussed in the answer to question (c).

9 INTERNATIONAL ASPECTS OF ECONOMIC INTERDEPENDENCE AND POSSIBLE CONFLICTS OF INTEREST

The production decisions of individual firms and the consumption decisions of individual consumers can affect many other firms and consumers, not just at home but globally. This is because an individual firm or consumer will usually only be concerned with his or her own private costs or benefits. They may ignore the effect of their decision on others, for example, noise, pollution and damage to the environment. Failure to consider the external costs and benefits of decisions can result in conflicts of interest and may need a government to introduce taxes, subsidies or regulations to correct for these.

Resources are best allocated to those uses in an economy where there is an absolute or comparative cost advantage in production over other countries. Surplus output not wanted in the domestic economy can then be traded internationally with other countries that may be more efficient at producing other goods and services. Through trade, countries can obtain a wider variety of goods and services at a lower cost than they can produce themselves. Global trade allows firms and consumers to benefit from the biggest and cheapest workforces, raw materials and technology anywhere in the world.

However, many governments try to protect themselves against the impact international trade can have on employment and incomes in their countries by using trade barriers. This may involve imposing taxes or 'tariffs' on the price of cheap goods and services imported from low-cost countries, or simply restricting the amount that can be imported. However, it is argued that trade barriers have hurt poorer countries the most, and made them rely more heavily on foreign aid. Trade liberalization to remove barriers to free trade can therefore help poorer countries to grow, and provide the opportunities they need to trade their way out of aid dependence.

Globalization refers to these increasing opportunities to move resources freely around the world and the growing reliance of economies on each other through international trade. However, the transportation of ever more people, goods and services across international borders has increased greenhouse gases and is contributing to global climate change which may have disastrous, long-term and irreversible effects on the planet. Our aims to satisfy more wants and needs may conflict with greater protection of the environment and the conservation of scarce resources. As economists we cannot say whether protecting the environment is more important than using resources to reduce poverty, but we can analyse the implications of using resources in different ways and the economic impact of different decisions taken by consumers, firms or governments.

Chapter 21 Social Costs and Benefits

Aims

At the end of this chapter you should be able to:

- distinguish between **private costs and benefits** and **external costs and benefits**
- understand how the production decisions of firms and the consumption decisions of consumers can have both short-term and long-lasting impacts on others
- appreciate that the **social costs** of individual production or consumption decisions is the sum of their private costs and external costs over time
- recognize that individual production or consumption decisions may yield **social benefits**, being the sum of their private benefits and external benefits over time
- determine whether or not a decision to use scarce resources is **economic** by comparing the social costs and benefits of the decision
- describe **conflicts of interest** in relation to social costs and benefits

Section I How firms' decisions can affect others

River life dead!

The river Eden today is a dead river. Over the last year nearly all the fish and plant life in the river has been destroyed. In the past month cattle grazing along the banks of the river have been poisoned. Fears are growing that local children will be next.

A report has found that the river has been highly polluted by the nearby Chemix plastics plant. Chemix has, for the past two years, been dumping chemical waste into the river. The waste is pumped into the river along an underground pipeline from the Chemix plant.

Scientists estimate that it will cost $2 million to clean up the damage caused to the river, but this will only be possible if the dumping of chemical waste is stopped.

Private costs and benefits

In the news clipping above, $2 million to clean up the polluted river is not the only cost of the Chemix plant dumping poisonous waste. Local farmers have suffered the loss of cattle, and their crops have been affected as the waste from the river seeps into the ground. As news spreads of the poisoning, the farmers may not be able to sell their produce. Local fishermen have also lost their livelihood as the fish in the Eden river have died. In addition, rivers attract many tourists, and the towns that grow up beside them are often filled with visitors. A poisoned river like the Eden, however, will drive tourists, and the money they spend, away.

Clearly the costs to the people and area near to the Chemix plant are huge, yet Chemix as a private business is not interested in these costs. Chemix is only concerned with its **private costs** of producing plastic, that is, the hire of machinery, buying of materials, payment of wages, etc. In fact, private sector firms will not be very interested in the costs they cause to others.

The Chemix company would, like any other business, try to calculate how much profit they could expect before starting up their own business. How much revenue will they make from their sales? How much will their costs be? Economists call the firm's own costs and revenues or benefits from producing, their **private costs** and **private benefits**.

If Chemix expects $3 million of revenue but only $2 million in costs each year, this would give them $1 million in profits. If this profit was higher than they could expect from doing something else, for example, producing paint, then from the Chemix point of view it was using its resources in the best possible way. The problem is that from society's point of view, the building and running of the Chemix plant has caused widespread pollution, and so may not be the best use of scarce resources.

External costs

The costs that have resulted from scarce resources producing plastic, for example, the lost revenue of local farmers and the $2 million needed to clean up the polluted river, are called **external costs** because the rest of society must pay them. Chemix is clearly better off producing plastics, but society as a whole is worse off. This is because while Chemix makes $1 million profit, everyone else bears the external costs, which are at least $2 million, to clean up the damage the Chemix plant has caused.

If the Chemix company had taken into consideration the cost of cleaning up the waste it had dumped then the total cost for society of producing plastic would be $4 million, that is, external costs of $2 million plus private costs of $2 million. If the only benefits from the production of plastic is the $3 million of revenue that Chemix gains, then on the whole society loses $1 million. That is, if the total cost for the whole of society, or **social cost**, of production is greater than the benefits then society is worse off from using scarce resources in that particular use.

Clearly if the Chemix plant had not been built society as a whole would not lose $1 million. In other words, it would be better not to have built the Chemix plant.

External benefits

Private firms generally ignore the damaging effects their production can have as long as they make a profit. However, as well as producing external costs, some firms can cause **external benefits**. These external benefits are free. No payment for them needs to be made by the people who receive them.

For example, when Chemix uses its resources to produce plastic it can create external benefits, as well as external costs, for others. Being a large company, Chemix can afford to train skilled workers. These skilled workers can then leave Chemix and work for other companies, which may not be able to afford to train their workers. These firms are getting the benefits of being able to save money on training costs. This is an external benefit provided by Chemix.

A decision to use resources to build motorways also results in external costs and benefits. Noise and fumes from cars can affect people living nearby. However, houses a few miles away from a motorway can rise in value because they are near a new road that offers quick and easy transport.

Just as firms do not have to pay for the external costs they create for others, firms do not receive payment for the external benefits they give to others. For example, Chemix may be saving other companies $250 000 in training costs but has no way of obtaining payment for this benefit.

External benefits must also be taken into account when deciding whether or not a particular use for the resources of land, labour and capital is worthwhile from society's viewpoint. In the case of the Chemix company, private and external benefits now total $3.25 million, but are still exceeded by private and external costs of $4 million. The business is still not worthwhile from society's point of view.

For society the total benefit from the production of any good or service, or **social benefit**, is equal to the private benefits and external benefits from its production. Only when these social benefits exceed the social costs of production will that particular use of resources be worthwhile for all of society.

Exercise 1 Not painting a pretty picture

The Non-drip paint company is considering whether or not to locate a new factory near the town of Greensville. The company estimates that the new plant will cost $5 million a year to run, but should add $6 million to revenue from the sale of the paint it produces.

The people of Greensville are worried that the new factory will release smoke, containing harmful chemicals, into the air. These chemicals will pollute the air and even get into the soil and water supplies as rain will bring the chemicals down from the air.

The local health authority estimates that over many years this smoke will damage people's health and increase the need for medical care at an estimated cost of $4 million a year.

The local authority believes that the smoke will blacken the walls of historic buildings in the area, and cause their eventual erosion. Regular cleaning will therefore be needed at an estimated cost of $2 million each year.

On a more positive note, it estimates that the paint factory will encourage other firms to locate in the area as suppliers of materials, providers of transport, etc., and that this will reduce local unemployment and help other local businesses. These external benefits are valued at $3 million.

1. What does the Non-drip paint company take into account when deciding whether or not to produce paint with its resources?
2. From society's point of view should the firm take other factors into consideration?
3. Which of the following statements do you think are correct?
   - **a** From the point of view of the paint company resources are being used in the best way if:
     - **i** Private benefits are greater than private costs.
     - **ii** Private benefits equal private costs.
     - **iii** Private benefits are less than private costs.
     - **iv** External benefits are greater than external costs.
   - **b** From the point of view of society scarce resources are in their best use when:
     - **i** Social benefits exceed social costs.
     - **ii** Social benefits equal social costs.
     - **iii** Social benefits are less than social costs.
     - **iv** Private benefits are greater than private costs.
4. Using the figures presented in the case study calculate:
   - **a** The paint company's estimated yearly profit.
   - **b** Whether or not paint production at the factory is worthwhile for society.
5. A conflict of interest between the paint company and the local community has arisen. How does this illustrate the central economic problem?

Group exercise

Divide into groups of eight or nine. One half of each group will play the role of the directors of the Non-drip paint company, while the other half are local community representatives.

1. The directors of the company prepare a report stating why they feel they are right to go ahead with the paint factory even if it does mean producing smoke. For example, the aim of the company is to make a profit because they have a duty to their shareholders.
2. The local community group prepares a report stating why they feel the paint factory should not locate in their area.
3. The company directors and local community representatives in each group now meet to read and discuss their reports. They must attempt to reach a solution to the conflict. If no solution is reached, the teacher may act as an arbitrator.
4. Each group's recommendations and findings are then reported back to the teacher.

In the above exercise, it can be recognized that the Non-drip paint company ignores any external costs and benefits. The company is only interested in making a profit, or **commercial return**, from producing paint. The result is that because social costs are greater than the social benefits of paint production, society is worse off. In fact, private and external costs ($5 million + $6 million) exceed private and external benefits ($6 million + $3 million) by $2 million each year.

Whenever social costs are greater than social benefits, as in the example above, economists say that this represents an **uneconomic** use of resources. Society would be better off if the resources of land, labour and capital were used to make something else.

If social benefits are greater than social costs economists say that this represents an **economic** use of resources. Society would be better off if more resources were put into this use.

Section 2 Market failure and government intervention

How the market can fail

In our earlier example, the Chemix plastics-making company found it profitable to use resources to make plastics near the River Eden. In a market economic system this should be the best use of resources for everyone. Yet because of external costs, society is worse off for using resources in this way. Chemix and the market system have therefore failed to use resources efficiently from society's point of view (see also Chapter 3).

In fact, whenever external costs and external benefits exist, the market system will not make the best use of scarce resources. This is because private firms in the market economic system only decide what, how and for whom to produce simply by looking at private costs and benefits, and their profits.

If production of a good or service results in high social costs, society would be better off without it. If, on the other hand, the production of a good or service results in high social benefits, society is better off by having more. For example, society may benefit from having more parks and open spaces, but a private firm may not find it profitable to provide these in a market economic system.

An uneconomic use of resources?

An economic use of resources?

To try and correct the failure of the market system to make the best use of scarce resources from society's point of view, governments often try to affect the way in which firms use resources, in the following ways.

Taxation

It is possible to make firms consider the external costs of their actions by taxing them. For example, an oil refinery may pump smoke and chemical waste into the atmosphere, damaging laundry, plants and buildings. The refinery ignores these external costs because it does not have to pay for the damage. However, a government may be able to make them pay for the damage by taking extra tax from them to cover the costs of repair.

Some countries have introduced anti-pollution or 'green' taxes, including taxes on petrol, waste disposal and energy use. However, in some countries these taxes are still considered relatively modest and further increases may be required to stop firms consuming so much energy and producing so much waste. Some governments are reluctant to do this or to introduce further taxes because they argue it will make their firms less competitive than overseas firms who do not have to pay such taxes. If consumers switch to buying the goods and services of these overseas firms then domestic firms may go out of business and workers will be made unemployed.

Subsidies

Private sector firms are not interested in producing external benefits for others because they are not paid for them. For example, a bus company may find it unprofitable to provide buses for people after the rush hour because not enough people use the service then. However, for those people who do use the buses at these times they benefit from a means of transport. Many old people and schoolchildren travel at off-peak times. The bus service also helps to reduce road congestion and pollution because people may use their cars less as a result. To help the bus company provide buses they could be given a subsidy. A subsidy is a payment of money given by a government to a firm. Subsidies are given to firms in order to encourage them to produce goods and services that result in external benefits.

Nationalization

Some industries produce large external benefits. By taking over the ownership and running of a whole industry a government can allow nationalized industries to act in the public interest, and take account of any external costs and benefits they might give rise to (see also Chapter 14).

For example, in many countries bus and train services are nationalized and run by a public corporation (see Chapter 4). Often, bus and train fares will be kept low to encourage people to use these services to travel instead of using their cars that may otherwise cause traffic congestion and harmful exhaust fumes and air pollutants. However, because low fares fail to generate enough revenue to cover their costs of provision, taxes have to be raised to pay for these services.

Laws and regulations

A government may introduce laws or regulations in order to control firms creating external costs. For example, many countries have introduced anti-pollution laws to control the contamination of land and the release of untreated waste and chemicals into water supplies and into the air. Planning regulations may also be used to stop homes and offices being built with hazardous materials and where they might spoil the landscape and views enjoyed by others. Owners of firms who break these laws and regulations may be fined or even imprisoned.

Government policy and conflicts of interest

Taxes, subsidies, laws and regulations can also be used not just to influence the production decisions of firms but also the decisions of consumers where these may have external costs and benefits. For example, these may include taxes on cigarettes, free or subsidized vaccinations against infectious diseases and regulations such as speed limits on roads and a ban on smoking. We shall consider these further in section 4.

However, in deciding to introduce policies to control firms and consumers to reduce the harmful impacts their decisions may have on others and the environment, a government may simply create other conflicts of interest. Higher taxes will reduce the amount of income people and firms have left to satisfy their wants, and regulations can curb their freedom of choice. This can create conflict between people who, for example, want higher taxes to pay for subsidized transport, and people on high incomes who may have to pay more tax but who may benefit very little from low-cost bus and train travel. Similarly, higher taxes on electricity and gas use to try to conserve energy consumption and the release of harmful emissions may hit the poor and most vulnerable people the hardest.

Section 3 Opportunity cost revisited

In Chapter 1 we discovered that because of scarcity we must choose what to do with scarce resources, and in choosing one use we must give up another. The benefit of the next best alternative given up is known as the opportunity cost.

For example, if we use land, labour and capital to build a motorway we may have to go without ten new schools. In Chapter 1 we would have said that the opportunity cost of the motorway is the ten schools given up.

Choice?

But the real opportunity cost of the motorway is not just the ten schools foregone, it is also the peace and quiet, fresh air and attractive countryside that have also been given up. The opportunity cost, or the benefit of the next best alternative foregone, therefore, always includes any external costs that occur. If opportunity cost did not include these costs, it would not be a true measure of what has been gone without.

Exercise 2 Belt up!

Amiya Bundhun was an economics student at college and now works for a bank. She was injured in a car accident and has just spent six months in a hospital paid for by the government.

Amiya decides to work out the opportunity cost of not wearing her seat-belt. She values the wages she has lost over six months at $12 000 and she values her lost social life at $4 000. Amiya calculates that the opportunity cost of not wearing her seat-belt is $16 000.

The police and ambulance driver that attended to her at the scene of her accident said that Amiya would not have been hurt had she been wearing her seat-belt.

1 What is meant by opportunity cost?

2 What has Amiya missed out in calculating the opportunity cost of not wearing her seat-belt?

3 'Wearing a seat-belt is up to me to decide. It's my life and if I get hurt in an accident it affects nobody else.' This is often said by car drivers, but would an economist agree with them? Explain your answer and say whether or not you agree that wearing a seat-belt should be law.

Section 4 How consumers' decisions can affect others

So far we have only considered how firms' decisions to produce goods and services can affect society as a whole. However, we will now look at how people's decisions to consume goods and services can affect others. Consider the following examples.

Vaccinations

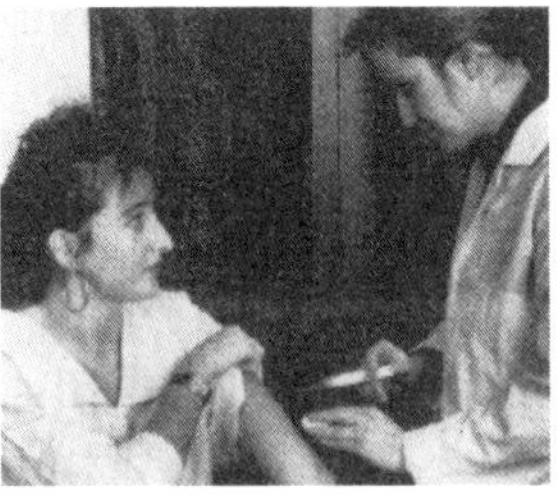

The girl in the first picture is looking forward to her holiday in a hot, foreign country. However, before she can go she must protect herself from some of the diseases she may catch in that country. In the picture she is seen having a vaccination.

It also protects a great many other people because if the girl had caught a disease she would pass it on to others when she returned from her holiday. Her decision to have a vaccination has therefore protected the rest of society from the disease. This consumption has resulted in an external benefit.

Loud music

The boy in the second picture likes playing his records very loudly. The only problem is that his neighbours don't like loud music and are upset by the noise. The boy's decision to consume noisy records has imposed an external cost on other people.

Litter

The man in the third picture has just finished a packet of cigarettes. Instead of placing it in a bin he has carelessly discarded it on the pavement. Litter is unsightly to many people. This is an external cost resulting from others' consumption. Furthermore, society must bear the cost of cleaning up the rubbish.

Exercise 3 Smoking

Look at the picture of a man smoking in a cafe.

1. Give three private costs that a cigarette manufacturer will have to pay.
2. How will the manufacturer calculate the total revenue from the sale of cigarettes?
3. How are other people in the cafe affected by the man's decision to consume a cigarette?
4. Many countries have introduced laws to ban smoking in public places. What sort of things will a government have to pay for in order to make sure the ban is observed?
5. Research has shown that smoking can damage your health.
   - **a** What is the opportunity cost of increased health spending on treating smokers?
   - **b** Who will bear the cost of increased health spending?

6 Imagine that the government decides to increase the tax payable on a packet of cigarettes. What affect may this have on:

a The number of cigarettes consumed.

b The revenue of cigarette-makers.

c The workers in cigarette factories?

Satisfying our wants or conserving resources?

But perhaps the biggest concern facing us all today is how our ever growing wants and rising consumption of goods and services is creating ever increasing mountains of waste, global climate change through rising pollution and using up increasingly scarce resources. As a result our individual consumption decisions will not just have an impact on people living nearby but on people and the environment all over the world, and not just on today's society but on future generations for years to come (see Chapter 22).

Exercise 4 **Living on borrowed time**

Today is the day we start to eat Earth

THE Earth reaches an ecological tipping point today as we start officially to live beyond the means of our resources.

Experts at a British think-tank have calculated that we are now plundering natural resources faster than they can be replaced.

Rapid population growth, climate change and rising living standards are all placing huge strains on nature.

The doomsday scenario was spelt out by the new economics foundation (nef) after analysing research by the US academic group, Global Footprint Network, which says humans are over-using resources by 23 per cent.

The group warned that the world's six billion inhabitants must start facing up to the problem now or face the bleak consequences. Nef researchers worked out how quickly man is using the resources of farming land, forest, fish, air and energy. Mathis Wackernagel, executive director of Global Footprint Network, said: "Humanity is living off its ecological credit card and can do this only by liquidating the planet's natural resources.

Global warming, falling farm production, over-fishing and deforestation are all stark signs of how grim the outlook is, according to nef.

The grim warning will spark further fears of battles for resources among the world's nations. The British military has recently admitted it is already planning for resource wars later this century.

The London Paper, 9.10.2006

In groups discuss the article above. How does it illustrate, or provide examples of, the following economic concepts:

- economic growth
- resource allocation
- opportunity cost
- social costs and benefits
- economic conflicts of interest.

What actions do you think consumers, firms and governments could take to conserve resources and reduce the external costs of their individual production and consumption decisions?

Write definitions to explain the following terms:

Private costs
Private benefits
External costs
External benefits
Social costs
Social benefits
A commercial return
An economic use of resources
An uneconomic use of resources

Now return to the chapter to check your understanding of these terms.

Look at the following useful case studies of the social and private costs and benefits of:

- alcohol consumption *www.ias.org.uk/resources/factsheets/economic_costs_benefits.pdf*
- forestry *www.fao.org/docrep/x5392e/x5392e03.htm*
- gambling *www.abgaminginstitute.ualberta.ca/pdfs/Costs_Benefits_Intro.pdf*
- building the Kariba Dam in Zambia *www.bized.ac.uk/virtual/dc/aid/kariba/issue2.htm*
- road projects *www.itdp.org/read/Social%20Benefits.pdf*
- sports facilities *www.lincolninst.edu/pubs/dl/671_chapin-web.pdf*

Some of these articles and papers are quite technical in places so we suggest you just read their summaries and conclusions. Also be aware that they only present the viewpoint of their authors, and may not always have taken full account of other arguments and views.

The Impact of Globalization

At the end of this chapter you should be able to:

- define **globalization** and describe its key features
- demonstrate the application of **absolute advantage** and **comparative advantage** in trade
- describe the benefits and disadvantages of **specialization** at individual, regional and national levels
- examine conflicts of interest arising from globalization in terms of **free trade or protectionism** and the **conservation or exploitation of resources**

Section I

What is globalization?

Going global

Today's politicians, business and trade union leaders are increasingly talking about 'globalization', the impact it is having and the effect it may have on the future. Read any newspaper or watch any news broadcast nowadays and chances are they will also mention the word 'globalization'. For example, they may report how multinational companies are expanding by setting up operations in many more countries, or how people are travelling more, how to deal with the rapid growth of the Chinese and Indian economies, or even global climate change caused by increasing pollution. Sometimes they also report demonstrations and marches against globalization, often by many thousands of people. So what does it all mean?

Global trade riots rock Hong Kong

Police fight running battles with protesters on the penultimate day of World Trade Organization talks.

Demonstrators' anger has been stirred up by reports that negotiators are moving closer to a compromise package that does not include a key demand: an end to European and American agriculture subsidies that are destroying the livelihood of farmers in poor countries.

Adapted from Tom Burgis, *The Guardian,* 18.12.2005

Globalization can mean different things to different people. This is because it is a wide term used to describe economic, social, technological, cultural and political changes that are increasing interdependence and interaction between people, firms and entire economies all across the globe.

An economist will be interested the most in the following economic aspects of globalization:

- The increasing reliance of economies on each other through international trade for an increasing variety of goods and services
- Opportunities to be able to buy and sell in any country in the world
- Increasing opportunities for labour and capital to move anywhere in the world
- The growth of global financial markets through banks and stock exchanges
- The impact all these changes are having on the amount and allocation of scarce resources, economic growth, living standards and wealth

Many of these changes have been happening for a long time so globalization is not really new but the reason why we are so much more interested in it and using the term more and more today is because the pace of these changes has increased.

Increasingly rapid globalization has been the result of increasing wealth and the development of new technologies, and faster and cheaper communications, allowing people to order goods and services and make payments via the Internet or over a telephone from anywhere in the world. Also, the transition of many former planned economies to free market economies has reduced barriers to international trade and allowed people and finance to move more freely between countries (see Chapter 3). As a result many of these economies are now growing rapidly. But their rapid growth has also meant that scarce resources are being used up even faster and external costs, in terms of pollution and destruction of the environment, are rising.

Rapid globalization is also affecting the relative importance of different countries in the global economy. For many years, the United States has been the largest economy in the world. In recent years, however, the US share of the global economy has shrunk to approximately 25 per cent and will continue that trend as the economies of many newly industrialized countries, such as China and India, continue to grow rapidly (see Chapter 17).

Section 2 Specialization and trade

In economics, globalization mainly concerns world-wide specialization through expansion of the division of labour. In Chapter 2 we discovered how people and entire regions of different countries have specialized in particular occupations and industries. They do this because they have skills and resources suited to the production of particular goods and services. This has allowed them to produce more goods and services more efficiently with their scarce resources. However, in some cases it has made jobs boring and repetitive, and it also means people must rely on each other to produce and exchange the range of goods and services they need and want. Specialization involves the need to trade and requires a generally accepted medium of exchange – money.

Comparative advantage

For the same reasons entire countries have specialized in the production of particular goods and services and trade internationally. The benefits of specialization and trade can be explained by the economic theory of comparative advantage.

Exercise 1 Something special

1 There will be many products which your country cannot produce itself that have to be imported. List six such goods and/or services.

2 List at least ten goods your country is able to produce but which you choose to import.

3 Match each country with a product in which it specializes.

New Zealand	Coffee
Brazil	Wine
India	Lamb
France	Beef
Argentina	Manufactures
West Germany	Oil
Norway	Timber
Iceland	Tea
Venezuela	Fish

4 List the benefits each country may gain from specialization and trade.

We will now discover in a simple exercise how countries can increase their output and their standard of living through specialization and trade.

Assume that the countries of Taiwan and Chile both produce just two commodities, wheat and music centres. Each country we assume will have 100 workers, half devoted to wheat production and half to the production of music centres. The total output per year of both countries is shown below.

Before specialization

	Music centres produced by 50 workers	Wheat (tonnes) produced by 50 workers
Chile	40	35
Taiwan	50	30
Total output per period	90	65

In this example, Chile is better than Taiwan at producing wheat. With the same number of workers Chile can produce five more tonnes of wheat than Taiwan. That is, they have an absolute advantage over Taiwan in wheat production. When one country is better at producing a particular commodity compared to another it is said to have an absolute advantage. Taiwan has an absolute advantage over Chile in music centre manufacturing. If each country specialized Chile would produce only wheat and Taiwan only music centres. Total output of both would rise as shown below.

After specialization

	Music centres produced by 100 workers (in Taiwan only)	Wheat (tonnes) produced by 100 workers (in Chile only)
Chile	0	70
Taiwan	100	0
Total output per period	100	70

The example assumes that 100 workers can produce twice as much as 50 workers, that is, average labour productivity is constant. This, of course, may not always be the case.

If Taiwan now agrees to trade 40 music centres for 30 tonnes of wheat from Chile, each country after trade is better off than it was before specialization and trade as in the first table.

After specialization and trade

	Music centres	Wheat (tonnes)
Chile	40	40
Taiwan	60	30
Total output per period	100	70

It still benefits countries to specialize and trade even if one does not have an absolute advantage in the production of a commodity. Look at the examples of Germany and Japan. We assume for simplicity that each country devotes half its 100-strong workforce to the production of cars and televisions.

	Cars	Televisions
Japan	100	400
Germany	80	160
Total output per period	180	560

Japan has an absolute advantage in both goods. However, in Japan they would need to give up four televisions to produce one extra car. In Germany only two televisions would have to be given up to produce one extra car. So Germany is relatively better at producing cars than Japan. That is, Germany has a **comparative advantage** in car manufacturing. While Germany is less efficient than Japan in producing both goods, it is least inefficient in car production.

By concentrating on the production of cars, a country like Germany can export cars and import other goods like televisions with their export earnings. Japan should, in our example, concentrate on the production of televisions. Both countries can gain from specialization and trade.

Exercise 2 At an advantage

The table below displays the monthly output of clocks and peanuts in two countries, A and B. Each country devotes half its work-force to the production of each product.

Country	Clocks	Peanuts (kg)
A	2	21
B	4	7

1. What is the total output of clocks and peanuts?
2. Which country has an absolute advantage in **a** clock production, **b** peanut production? Explain the reasons for your answer.
3. Draw a table to show the output of the two countries after they have specialized in what they are best able to produce.
4. What are the total output figures now? By how much have they increased?
5. If the countries now agree to trade three clocks for twelve kilograms of peanuts, show in a new table what they have gained from trade.

The gains from trade

Absolute and comparative advantage in production explains the main advantages to countries from free and open trade.

1. Countries can obtain goods and services that they do not have or cannot produce themselves. For example, countries such as Switzerland have no oil reserves of their own and must import oil from oil-producing countries.
2. Countries can obtain goods and services they can produce themselves but only at a higher cost or lower quality than other countries can. For example, Iceland could grow tropical fruits but only in large, expensive greenhouses that would cost a great deal to heat and light. It is clearly cheaper for Iceland to import tropical fruits from tropical countries where they can be grown easily.
3. Through international trade, a firm in one country can sell to many more consumers all over the world and may be able to grow more quickly and benefit from economies of scale in production as a result (see Chapter 13). Global trade allows firms to benefit from the biggest and cheapest workforces, raw materials and technology anywhere in the world.

A further argument used in favour of free trade is that it also helps promote international cooperation and peace. If economies are more dependent upon one another for goods and services then wars and armed conflict could be less likely.

The disadvantages of trade

1. The increased transportation of ever more people, goods and services across international borders has increased greenhouse gases and is contributing to global climate change which may have a disastrous, long-term and irreversible effect on the planet.
2. The free movement of capital internationally has made it easy for multinational firms to shift their production from countries where wages and other costs are high, to less developed countries where wages, land prices and taxes on profits are lower. This shift, it is argued, has not only increased the unemployment rate in the developed countries, but in some cases it has also led to the exploitation of workers in less developed countries where health and safety laws may be more relaxed or easier to ignore. In some cases it has also resulted in environmental damage because some governments of less developed countries are less concerned with this than the provision of jobs and incomes.
3. It is also argued that international trade has actually increased the gap between rich and poor countries because multinational firms and consumers from rich, developed economies dominate global markets. As a result they are able to force producers of materials and goods in less developed countries to accept low prices.

Section 3 Free trade or protectionism?

What are trade barriers?

Economic conflict can arise from globalization because some developed countries fear they will lose jobs as it becomes cheaper to import goods and services from overseas than to produce them domestically, or if production is moved overseas to countries where costs, such as wages and land prices, and taxes on profits, may be lower. As a result some countries have introduced barriers to free trade in an attempt to protect employment and production in their economies from overseas competition. This is called **protectionism**.

Exercise 3 **Heavy metals**

From the article below identify:

- different types of barriers governments may use to restrict free trade
- the reasons why governments may impose trade barriers
- the potential impact of trade barriers on consumers, employees and the economies of different countries
- arguments against the use of trade barriers.

UK fury at US steel tariffs

The UK steel industry today called for "action not words" after the US imposed 30% tariffs on the prices of steel imports. The decision was condemned by the British Government and European Union.

EU ambassadors were holding special talks today to consider trade retaliation against America which could see tariffs and other restrictions imposed on imports of steel and other goods from the US.

The UK industry said the danger to British companies and jobs will not come from the impact on steel exports to the US, but from other countries. Cheap steel from Russia, the Far East and eastern Europe could be dumped on the UK market because it no longer has access to the US

The only short-term solution for Europe may be to follow America by imposing the same kind of prohibitive, protectionist tariffs on the rest of the world's steelmakers.

The European Commission President hinted that the move could provoke a world trade war. "We believe that tariffs are against not only the interests of countries in Europe, but also against the interests of US consumers themselves, because they will have to pay the higher prices for steel imports."

Adapted from *The Daily Mail*, 13.3.2002

Trade barriers

You may have discovered from the exercise above that one or more of the following can be used to reduce trade between countries.

1 Tariffs

A tariff is a tax on the price of imports. Tariffs are used to raise the prices of imports to make them more expensive than home-produced goods to stop people buying them. Tariffs, however, can encourage retaliation from other countries.

Many neighbouring countries in different regions of the world have agreed to form **customs unions** to trade freely with each other but to impose a common tariff on all goods and services imported from non-member countries. Examples of customs unions include the European Union, the South African Customs Unions, and MERCOSUR in South America.

2 Subsidies

A subsidy is a grant given to an industry by a government so that the industry can lower its prices. Subsidies are used to stop consumers from buying foreign imports by making home-produced goods cheaper.

Subsidies have the advantage that they can be given secretly and are less likely to encourage a reaction from foreign competitors than tariffs would.

The disadvantage of subsidies is that consumers must pay for the lower prices in higher taxes to raise the money for the subsidy.

3 Quotas

A quota is a limit on the number of imports allowed into a country per year. A quota reduces the quantity of imports without changing their prices.

4 Embargo

An embargo is a complete ban on imports of certain goods to a country. An embargo may be used to stop imports of dangerous drugs, for example, heroin, or to punish a country for political reasons by refusing to buy its goods.

However, embargoes may also be introduced on health grounds. For example, between 1996 and 2005 exports of beef from the UK were banned from the European Union and many other countries because of fears about the spread of BSE (so-called 'mad cow disease') to overseas cattle and possibly even to humans.

Reasons for protectionism

1 Protection of a young industry

New and small firms, known as **infant industries**, will be unable to benefit from the economies of scale enjoyed by larger foreign competitors. These infant industries will have higher prices than foreign firms and so will be unable to sell their goods. Tariffs or other forms of protection can be used to make foreign goods dearer and so allow infant industries to grow.

The danger with this is that infant industries may continue to demand protection from foreign imports even when they have grown up into large firms.

2 To prevent unemployment

In the example in section 2 we found that both Chile and Taiwan could be better off if one specialized in agricultural production, the other in manufactured music centres, and then trade took place between them.

Yet although specialization and trade can benefit a country as a whole, it can still cause hardship for some. For example, if Chile produced all of the agricultural produce for both Chile and Taiwan, this would mean cheaper farm produce for Taiwanese consumers, but unemployment for farmers in Taiwan. At the same time, if Taiwan specialized in manufacturing this would mean cheaper manufactured goods for consumers in Chile, but unemployment for its manufacturing workers.

So free trade will always hurt someone. If those hurt are rich or powerful enough the government of the country involved may be persuaded to prevent free trade by using barriers to trade.

3 To prevent dumping

Dumping occurs when one country floods the market in another country with a product at a price far less than it costs to produce in order to force rival firms in that country out of business. For example, consider two countries A and B, each with firms producing computer keyboards. Firms in both countries face similar costs and produce keyboards for around $10 per unit. However, following subsidy country A is able to sell its keyboards to country B for just $5 each. Unless country B also pays its keyboard producers the same subsidy it will force the producers in B out of business. Once the keyboard producers in B have closed down, firms in country A may once again be able to raise the prices of their keyboards. During the 1970s, Japan was accused of using dumping to take over a global lead in the production of television screens and motorbikes, forcing producers of these products in many other countries out of business.

4 Because other countries use barriers to trade

Before any country removes barriers to trade on foreign goods it needs to be sure that foreign countries will remove barriers to trade on their goods. With many dozens of trading countries, it is very difficult to get agreement on removal of barriers to trade.

Because of this the **General Agreement on Tariffs and Trade (GATT)** was set up by trading countries in order to try to get countries to agree on removing their trade barriers. 117 countries are members of GATT. In 1993 they agreed to cut tariffs on industrial products traded between them by one third. The **World Trade Organization** was set up to make sure this agreement was acted upon and to encourage free trade in international markets.

5 To prevent over-specialization

Free trade encourages countries to specialize in the goods in which they have a comparative advantage. Yet specialization in one or two products can be dangerous in the modern world.

The demand for goods and services is always changing and if a country relies on just one or two goods it risks a huge fall in its income if demand moves away from these goods to others. Protectionism allows a country to keep a wider range of industries alive and so prevents the dangers of over-specialization.

Arguments against protectionism

The main arguments used against protectionism are as follows:

1 Other countries will retaliate with trade barriers

If one country introduces trade barriers to restrict imports of goods and services from other countries, those affected may introduce barriers in retaliation. A trade war may develop. The result is higher prices and fewer goods and services will be traded. This is clearly bad for consumers but if it continues it can also mean higher unemployment and slower economic growth as firms are forced out of business.

2 It protects inefficient domestic firms

By protecting inefficient producers at home, consumers will face higher prices and possibly lower-quality products because they will be unable to buy from more efficient, lower-cost firms overseas. If, as a result, more efficient overseas producers are forced out of business then consumers in many more countries will suffer from the inefficient allocation of global resources. Fewer goods and services will be produced globally as a result and fewer wants satisfied.

3 The loss of domestic jobs from overseas competition will only be temporary

Many economists argue that the loss of domestic jobs as a result of competition from lower-cost firms overseas will only be temporary anyway because other firms will develop in the economy and grow to employ more workers.

4 Trade barriers have increased the gap between rich and poor countries

Subsidies paid to protect farmers and other firms in rich countries have increased the supply of agricultural and other products on the global market. Subsidies have therefore forced down world prices of many goods, and producers in less developed countries have not been able to compete. As a result, sales, incomes and jobs have been lost in their countries and increased their poverty and hardship.

Global military spending and aid figures for 2005

The Stockholm International Peace Research Institute estimates that global military expenditure rose in 2005 to $1,118 billion in current US dollars. This represents around 2 per cent of the total world gross domestic product.

In 2005, US military spending was $534.1bn, just over 4 per cent of US GDP, and 48 per cent of the world total. This is equivalent to $1,791 per head of population in the US.

The second largest military spender in the world is the UK, spending $53.6bn or 2.4 per cent of UK GDP. This is despite the UK government's view that: 'There is no direct military threat to the United Kingdom or Western Europe. Nor do we foresee the re-emergence of such a threat ...'. France, Japan and China complete the top five military spenders, but some other countries spend proportionately more of their gross domestic product than all these countries. For example, in 2005 the following countries spent more than 10 per cent of their GDP on their military: Eritrea, Jordan, Oman, Qatar, and Saudi Arabia.

Military spending towers above commitments to tackle the systemic causes of future global insecurity such as the gap between rich and poor countries, the impact of climate change and resource shortages, and militarism itself.The latest figures for development aid spending are from 2004, when the world spent just $87.3bn on aid. The world currently spends over 12 times as much on the military as on overseas aid.

There are no official estimates of the resources being committed globally to tackling climate change.

Adapted from information posted at Arms Reduction Coalition site, *www.arcuk.org*

Arms or aid?

It might be easy to conclude from the above article that developed countries like the US and the UK should spend less on military expenditure and instead give more food and money to less developed countries to help them invest in schools, hospitals, healthcare, industry and food programmes. However, the issue is complex. First, it involves countries choosing how best to allocate their scarce resources. Second, it involves deciding whether giving aid to less developed countries will help them more than free trade.

Military spending in a number of poorer countries is as least as much or relatively higher as a proportion of their GDP than even the US. For example, Eritrea in Africa spent over 17 per cent of its GDP on its military in 2005. Similarly, military spending in the African countries of Angola, Liberia, Burundi and Zimbabwe was between 4 per cent and almost 9 per cent of their GDPs. These resources could have been spent on food, healthcare and other goods and services which people need in these countries.

However, it is also argued that military spending provides many jobs and incomes for many thousands of people in the global defence manufacturing industry and in armies. Technological developments such as the Internet, satellite communications, mobile phones, lasers and some medical advances, including the material used to make artificial limbs, were also the result of research and development first made by firms in the defence industry. These developments have since benefited many millions of people all over the world.

These arguments do not, however, consider the terrible destruction caused by wars: the dreadful loss of human life, the impact on the natural environment, and the resources that must then be used up to rebuild homes, roads and other infrastructure.

Types of aid

Overseas aid to less developed countries can take the following forms:

1 Food aid

On a clear day you can see the starving in Africa!

The European Union (EU) and the United States often produce far more food than they need. Lakes of wine and mountains of butter and meat that will never be used have been common in Europe in the past.

The cost of storing all of this food is very high and the food is sometimes given away to underdeveloped countries as food aid.

While food aid is necessary when people are starving, it is not always a good thing. If free food is given to an underdeveloped country, people will not need to buy the produce of farmers in that country. Their farmers find they cannot make a living and so leave farming to find work in the cities. This means that in future the country will have even fewer farmers and may need even more food aid.

2 Financial aid

This means giving money to developing countries. Developed countries may give a lot of money to developing nations but there are often strings attached.

Exercise 4 No strings?

Look at the cartoon above and pick out as many disadvantages as you can of the way in which financial aid is given to less developed countries.

Financial aid is often given to developing countries on the condition that they spend it on a particular project, for example an airport or a dam. The countries giving aid usually insist that the materials and expertise to carry out the project are bought from them at high prices. Developing countries may get little opportunity to decide for themselves how to spend financial aid.

3 Technological aid

To improve living standards aid has been given to developing countries in the form of modern technology, for example, modern power plants and agricultural machinery. The problem with technological aid is that it requires a high level of skill and training to use it and the people of the developing world are very poorly trained. Even if the people were trained, modern technology would employ only a small number of workers.

Technological aid should be simple, for example, instruction on how to use land better to grow food using the labour of people rather than of machinery. This sort of aid employs the most abundant resource in the developing world, people.

4 Loans

In addition to foreign aid, many less developed and developing countries have borrowed large amounts of money from multinational banks, governments of other countries, the International Monetary Fund (IMF) and the World Bank.

However, some countries borrowed so much that they became unable to repay their debts, including Mexico during the 1980s and Argentina in 2001, causing economic crises in these countries. Some very poor countries even struggle just to pay annual interest charges. Around 60 countries classified as low-income countries by the World Bank owed over $550 billion in debt in 2005. Around $300 billion was debt owed by African countries. Because of the heavy burden of making debt and interest repayments many of these countries are getting poorer as a result.

5 Debt relief

Because of the problems debt is causing in many less developed countries, and in response to pressure from people and charities all over the world, a number of poor countries have received partial or full cancellation of their loans from foreign governments, the IMF and World Bank. In 2004 the UK wrote off some of its loans to the poorest countries, and in the following year the UK government managed to secure agreement with the 7 other richest nations in the world to write off US$40 billion debt owed by the 18 most indebted poor countries. However, for many people in the UK and other countries this agreement does not go far enough and more debt relief is needed to help the poor.

Arguments against aid

Foreign aid to less developed countries can provide food and help them invest in the schools, hospitals, healthcare and technology they need to care for their populations and help their economies grow. In time their economies should expand to generate enough jobs and incomes trade so they will no longer need aid. However, some economists argue that foreign aid has not worked. Many of the poorest countries that receive foreign aid remain poor and for some, economic growth is negative, meaning they are getting poorer. An important question for economists, therefore, is whether free trade will help less developed countries more than aid.

Many economists argue that aid alone cannot reduce poverty in many less developed countries (see also Chapter 19). Their governments must do more themselves to expand their economies and reduce poverty through investment and trade. Instead, they argue, overseas aid is either wasted or diverted away from those people who need it the most because:

1. Many less developed countries are poorly managed or do not have the skills they need to invest financial aid wisely in projects that will help their economies grow.
2. Overseas aid is often used to fund wars in less developed countries. Wars can also prevent aid from being distributed to those in need. Wars also make problems worse by destroying homes and land, and injuring many people.
3. Some governments of less developed countries are corrupt and overseas aid is misused to fund lavish lifestyles for government officials.
4. Some less developed countries are ruled by ruthless dictators. They have used financial aid to fund armies to protect them and to suppress people who oppose them. In some cases, it is these dictators who have caused debt problems in their countries by borrowing so much. Giving them debt relief may mean they will simply get richer: it may not be used to help the poorest people in their countries. For example, in 2005 the president of Nigeria estimated that 'corrupt African leaders have stolen at least $140 billion from their people in the four decades since independence'.

Trade liberalization

So, for many economists free trade and not aid is the key to development. The gain from free trade is higher output through higher productivity, for all to share. But for this to happen **trade liberalization** is required whereby all countries agree to remove their trade barriers.

The **World Trade Organization (WTO)** sets the rules for global trading and resolves disputes between its members. The WTO states that its aims are to increase international trade by promoting lower trade barriers. The WTO had 149 member countries in 2005, but talks between them to abolish agricultural subsidies failed in 2006.

Section 5 Conservation or commercialization?

To satisfy our growing wants for goods and services we are engaging in more international trade and using up scarce natural resources at an ever increasing rate. In addition to the already huge demand for goods and services from consumers in developed countries, global population growth and increasing wealth in newly industrialized countries such as China and India are also now fuelling much of this increased demand.

Exercise 5 Conserve or consume?

- Should we cut down forests to grow more crops to feed people in less developed countries?
- Should we build more reservoirs to provide drinking water by flooding areas of natural land?
- Should we devote more resources to buying weapons to defend our countries or spend more on developing new forms of energy that do not harm the environment?
- Should we build more nuclear power stations to meet energy demands or spend more on conserving energy instead?
- Should developed countries pay less developed countries to protect their natural environments including tropical rainforests?
- Should we build homes, instead of nature reserves to protect endangered species and habitats?
- Should the government raise taxes to help protect the environment or lower taxes to allow consumers to choose how to spend that money?

1. Copy out a table like the one started below. In the column headed conflict, write down the questions listed above.
2. Answer these questions on your own in the second column, explaining your answer.
3. Compare your answers with those of your neighbour and make a note in your table of which answers you agree on and which cause disagreement. Why is there disagreement?
4. For the questions upon which you agree with your neighbour, can you prove that your choices are the correct ones? Explain why you may not be able to prove this.
5. For the questions upon which you disagree is it possible for you to prove definitely that you are correct? Explain.

CONFLICT	MY CHOICE & REASON	DOES MY NEIGHBOUR AGREE & WHY	DOES MY NEIGHBOUR DISAGREE & WHY

As more and more food is needed, more and more land is being converted to farmland or used to build homes and roads. In section 2 we learnt how the increased transportation of goods and people across borders has increased emissions of harmful greenhouse gases. The burning of oil and gas to generate power for energy use is also rising as consumers buy more and more electrical goods, and industry around the world increases their production in response to this growing demand.

As a result, many people are now calling for greater efforts to conserve scarce resources and to protect the environment.

Conservationists argue we must slow the pace at which we use up resources to make goods and services for profit to satisfy our wants. They use the following arguments:

Deforestation

Smog

Battery farming

- The burning of fuels for energy and travel has created air pollution and is causing climate change.
- Deforestation – the cutting down and burning of trees – has also released harmful carbon into the atmosphere, destroyed habitats for animals and plant species, and changed local climates.
- Over-farming of land has used up all the goodness in the soil resulting in growing areas where nothing will grow.
- Over-fishing has depleted fish stocks and harmed other fish, bird and animal populations that feed on fish.
- Many animals and fish species have been hunted into or close to extinction, and many more will die out due to global climate change and the destruction of their habitats.
- Growing air pollution has increased breathing problems for many people.
- The dumping of waste into rivers and the sea, and oil spills, has destroyed the marine habitat in many areas, killed many fish, birds and animals, and contaminated the food chain for humans.
- The use of pesticides and chemical fertilizers to increase crop production has polluted rivers and water supplies, and killed wildlife.
- Clean water supplies and clean air are in short supply in many areas of developed and less developed countries.
- Intensive farming techniques, such as battery farming and the use of drugs, to increase animal reproduction and growth rates for meat consumption, are cruel and have spread diseases such as BSE in cattle, foot and mouth in cattle and pigs, and bird flu.
- Global warming is already having a dramatic effect on the planet and its weather patterns, causing more violent storms, droughts and floods. It can only get worse.

Evidence of the depletion of the earth's resources

The Arial Sea between Kazakhstan and Uzbekistan was once the world's fourth largest inland lake, but over the last 40 years it has shrunk by 90 per cent. This devastation was caused by intensive cotton farming in central Asia.

From *Sunday Times Magazine*, 13.8.2006

Exercise 6 Where have all the polar bears gone?

Climate change could cause serious problems. Although there is still much uncertainty, climate researchers who have prepared reports for the Intergovernmental Panel on Climate Change (IPCC) suggest there could be some very serious implications.

Sea levels rise as ice caps melt	Agricultural change
At present some 46 million people live in areas at risk of flooding due to storm surges. A one-metre rise could put 118 million in peril. If the global ocean level went up by one metre, Egypt would lose 1% of its land area, the Netherlands would lose 6%, Bangladesh would lose 17.5%, and on the Majuro Atoll in the Pacific Marshall Islands some 80% of the land would disappear under water.	Over time total global crop production could be unchanged but effects on regions could vary widely. Those most at risk from famine would be peoples who rely on isolated agricultural systems in arid and semi-arid regions. Populations particularly under threat live in sub-Saharan Africa, south east Asia and tropical areas of Latin America. Climate change could also alter market conditions and the range of agricultural pests.
The spread of disease	**Changes to ecosystems**
Warmer temperatures could increase the spread of diseases like malaria, dengue fever and yellow fever. If the temperature increases by 3–5 °C the number of people potentially exposed to malaria could go up from 45% to 60% of the world population and result in an extra 50–80 million cases a year. Air pollution and exposure to greater extremes in temperature could lead to a greater frequency of asthma and respiratory diseases.	The composition and range of many ecosystems will shift as species respond to climate change. Possibly up to two-thirds of the world's forests will undergo major changes. Some forests may disappear altogether. Deserts are likely to become more extreme and result in increased soil erosion. Mountain glaciers could retreat and inland wetlands would be affected by global warming with resultant changes in habitat for the current species.

Researchers suggest that there could be many other changes but both the scientists and environment campaigners agree a number of measures could be used to reduce the impact humans are having on the climate.

So what can we do?

- Make more use of low-carbon fossil fuels such as natural gas, and decarbonizing exhaust gases from power plants.
- Switch to renewable and clean sources of energy such as solar, wind and wave power.
- Use more nuclear power, although this produces radioactive waste.
- Recycle more waste, and generate less waste by using less packaging.
- Make fewer car journeys by using buses and trains instead to reduce emissions.
- Insulate our homes, to help reduce the burning of coal and oil for heat and electricity.
- Plant more trees and practise better land management.

Read the article above and investigate how global warming could affect your country. What impact could it have on the environment, the amount and allocation of scarce resources, consumers and employees? Suggest measures, including taxes and regulations, your government could introduce to change the behaviour of firms and consumers to reduce the impact they are having on the environment. What will be the likely private and external costs and benefits of these measures? For coursework, write up your findings and arguments in a report to your government.

Arguments for and against conservation

Conservation, and protection of the environment and wildlife, involves choice and inevitably gives rise to conflict. For example, should 'green' taxes rise to discourage production or consumption that damages the environment? Should resources be used or conserved to protect the environment or should they be used to help reduce poverty?

When attempting to answer important questions like these and also those in exercise 6, it is difficult to avoid using our opinions. The problem is that opinions differ because what is thought to be fair and right for one person or group of people may not be so for another. For example, there are many people who argue that humans, the environment and wildlife will simply adapt to climate change and so we should not do anything to conserve resources now. Some areas and species may be wiped out but many will adapt and this is an entirely natural process that has been happening ever since life first appeared on the earth. This may be a scientific fact but economics is not concerned with this fact or with people's opinions.

As economists we cannot answer whether protecting the environment is more important than reducing poverty, but we can analyse the implications of using resources in these different ways and the economic effects of different actions undertaken by consumers, firms or governments. For example, we might analyse the economic implications of introducing measures to conserve resources as follows.

Should government measures be introduced to conserve resources?

NO	*YES*
• The free market encourages the most efficient allocation of resources through the price mechanism. Firms that waste resources will face higher costs and will not be able to compete with more efficient firms. • Conserving resources will mean resources are left idle. If we use fewer resources to produce fewer goods and services, there will be fewer jobs and less income. More people will be worse off. Rather than conserving resources we should be using resources more efficiently to achieve environmental goals. • In a free market, prices will rise as resources are used up and this will discourage their consumption and encourage conservation and waste reduction instead. • As some resources run out and their costs rise, we will develop or find cheaper alternatives, such as the use of plants and animal waste to produce biofuels instead of using oil.	• If the prices of goods and services are too low to cover the external costs of their production in terms of the damage they do to the environment then demand for them will be too high. Taxes on these goods and services can be used to raise their price and cut demand to an economically efficient level. • Measures designed to conserve resources will not result in less food, or fewer goods and services will be produced, just different and more efficient methods of production which do not deplete them or damage the environment. • Resources will be reallocated from the production of goods and services with high external costs to those with low or zero external costs. More jobs will be created in organic farming, energy-saving devices such as wind machines and solar panels and the production of other environmentally friendly products. As their production expands so their costs of production and prices will tend to fall, encouraging consumers to change their consumption patterns.

In your own words write down what you understand by the following:

Globalization	**Quota**
Comparative advantage	**Embargo**
Protectionism	**Infant industry**
Trade barrier	**Dumping**
Tariffs	**World Trade Organization**
Customs union	**Trade liberalization**

Now go back through this chapter to check your understanding of the above terms.

The following websites will help you learn more about all the things you have covered in this chapter:

Globalization

- *economics.about.com/od/globalizationtrade/*
- *www.globalisationguide.org/*
- *www.globalization101.org/*
- *www.imf.org/external/np/exr/ib/2000/041200.htm*

Comparative advantage and protectionism

- *www.bized.co.uk/learn/economics/international/advantage/index.htm*
- *www.bized.co.uk/learn/economics/international/benefits/index.htm*

Overseas aid and debt

- *en.wikipedia.org/wiki/Foreign_aid*
- *en.wikipedia.org/wiki/Third_World_debt*
- *www.worlddebtrelief.com*

Conservation and International organizations

- Greenpeace *www.greenpeace.org/international/*
- Friends of the Earth *www.foei.org*
- International Monetary *Fund www.imf.org*
- Organization for Economic Co-operation and Development *www.oecd.org*
- The World Bank *www.worldbank.org*
- Whale and Dolphin Conservation Society *www.wdcs.org*
- World Society for the Protection of Animals *www.wspa-international.org*
- World Trade Organization *www.wto.org*
- World Wildlife Fund *www.wwf.org*
- *en.wikipedia.org/wiki/World_Trade_Organization*

Assessment exercises

Multiple choice

1 An external cost is:

- **A** A cost created by a firm which it pays for.
- **B** A cost created by a group of people, or a firm, that others pay for.
- **C** A cost created by society, that private firms pay for.
- **D** A cost paid for by government.

2 Which of the following is likely to be an external cost of building a new airport?

- **A** The price paid for the land.
- **B** The cost of materials.
- **C** The noise caused by construction.
- **D** Wages paid to workers.

3 A particular use of resources is said to be economic if:

- **A** Social benefits are greater than private benefits.
- **B** Social costs are greater than social benefits.
- **C** Private costs are less than private benefits.
- **D** Social costs are less than social benefits.

4 If the production of a good or service results in high external benefits, but low private benefits, then:

- **A** Private firms will produce more than society wants.
- **B** Private firms will produce just enough to satisfy the wants of society.
- **C** Private firms will produce less than society wants.
- **D** Private firms will use resources to produce something else.

5 Which of the following represents an external benefit?

- **A** A firm that obtains a discount for buying materials in bulk
- **B** A historic building blackened by traffic pollution
- **C** An increase in a firm's revenue resulting from the success of its advertising
- **D** A bigger supply of honey than usual for a bee-keeper thanks to his neighbour's garden flower display

6 The following table shows the output of two countries before specialization with each country dividing up their resources equally between the production of two goods.

	Good X	Good Y
Country A	100	50
Country B	60	40

Consider each of the following statements.

1 Country A has an absolute advantage in X and Y.

2 Both countries would benefit from specialization and trade.

3 Country B has a comparative advantage in the production of Good Y.

Which of them are true?

- **A** 1 only
- **B** 2 only
- **C** 3 only
- **D** All of them

7 Which of the following is an economic argument against protectionism?

- **A** It helps protect employment.
- **B** It can protect new firms from unfair competition by large firms overseas.
- **C** It protects inefficient firms.
- **D** It can reduce market risks associated with over-specialization in production.

Questions 8–10 are based on the following answers

- **A** Quota
- **B** Embargo
- **C** Tariff
- **D** Depreciation

Which of the above is

8 A tax on an imported product?

9 A restriction placed on the import of a particular product?

10 A total ban on the import of a product or all imports from a particular country?

11 Which of the following factors best explains international trade in manufactured goods?

- **A** Different national laws and regulations.
- **B** High tariff barriers between countries.
- **C** Different transport costs between countries.
- **D** Different production costs in different countries.

Structured questions

1

TRADE AND PRODUCTION IN BANGLADESH

At one time, international trade agreements ensured an export market for clothes made in Bangladesh, but these were due to end in 2005. It was feared that many workers in Bangladesh would lose their jobs as a result. The Foreign Minister hoped that the trade in medicines would grow sufficiently to reduce that unemployment. The Foreign Minister said that in 2004 Bangladesh was exporting medicines to 60 countries and could produce them up to 70% cheaper than the developed world. He said that if Bangladesh, a developing country, could get 2% of the global trade in medicines it could be worth many times the clothing exports that Bangladesh had lost.

In 2004, 150 local firms and 6 multinational companies manufactured medicines in Bangladesh. However, the production of medicines employed just 50 000 workers and most future jobs would require highly trained technicians. The clothing trade employed 1.8 million unskilled workers and accounted for more than 75% of Bangladesh's exports.

a State **four** ways in which multinational companies can help developing countries such as Bangladesh. [4]

b International trade agreements can protect jobs. Despite this, some economists prefer free trade to trade agreements. Explain why. [6]

c Summarize the main argument of the Foreign Minister of Bangladesh. [4]

d Why might it be difficult for employment in the clothing industry to be replaced by employment in the manufacture of medicines? [6]

2

Defiant Iceland will hunt whales

ICELAND faced international scorn last night after announcing it is to resume commercial whale hunting following a moratorium for two decades.

The Icelandic Fisheries Ministry claims up to 43 000 minke and fin whales live in Icelandic waters, eating two million tons of fish and krill every year. Fin whales are listed as an endangered species by the World Conservation Union.

But critics say tourism for whale watching is more lucrative than whale meat, generating almost $17 million in revenue in 2005. Arni Finnsson of the Iceland Nature Conservation Association said: 'We are surprised and disappointed. There is no market for this meat in Iceland'.

Sarah Duthie of Greenpeace added, 'This makes no economic sense'.

Norway has also resumed whale hunting.

Adapted from *The Daily Mail*, 18.10.2006

a Iceland has a comparative advantage in fishing. Explain what this means. [4]

b Some people have argued other countries should use trade barriers against Iceland and Norway to stop them hunting whales. Describe **two** types of trade barrier that could be used against Iceland. [4]

c From the article provide evidence of opportunity costs of the decision by Iceland to resume commercial whaling to protect jobs and incomes in its fishing industry. [6]

d How would you discover if tourism for whale watching had benefited the people of Iceland? [6]

3 'The most effective support the industrialized countries could provide for the poorer nations would be to open their markets to the products of developing countries by having fewer trade restrictions.' (Trade and Industry Minister for Ghana, 2001)

  a What forms do trade restrictions often take? [3]

  b Discuss the immediate and the long-term changes that might occur in developing countries if trading restrictions were reduced. [7]

  c Discuss whether it is better for a country to produce many products and protect its markets from international trade or whether it is better to try to achieve specialization in some products only. [10]

4 In China, the State Council has ordered a reduction in urban development projects in Beijing. This is because, as developers clear land, people's homes are destroyed. It will also support the government's aim of reducing total demand in the economy.

  a Explain what is meant by the conservation of resources. [4]

  b Urban development is often thought to be beneficial. Consider who might benefit from an urban development project. [6]

5 **a** Some countries use protective measures in international trade. Describe **two** types of protection a government can use in international trade. [4]

  b Explain with the use of **one** example what is meant by a natural resource of a country. [3]

  c For many countries international trade involves using their natural resources by selling them to other countries. Discuss whether it is wise for a country to exploit its natural resources rather than to conserve them. [7]

How to answer question 3

a For three marks you must provide a short definition of what is meant by trade restrictions and describe one or two examples to show your understanding. Restrictions on imports can include **tariffs** on their prices, or supply **quotas** and **embargoes**. However, remember also that barriers to free trade can also include the use of **subsidies** paid to firms which allow them to lower their prices and therefore compete unfairly in domestic and overseas markets against potentially more efficient rival producers.

A good answer will also refer to the use of trade restrictions, or **trade barriers**, by the government of a country as '**protectionism**' because these restrictions are designed to protect production and employment in its economy from overseas competition.

b To earn all seven marks for this question you will need to show off your analytical skills to the full. You will need to investigate and evaluate the impacts, both positive and negative, of reducing trade barriers, or increasing free trade, on developing countries and how their **macro-economies** may be affected as a result, in the **short run** and in the **long run**. The question therefore concerns arguments for and against free trade.

You should first briefly describe what characterizes a developing or **less developed country** relative to a **developed country**. You should then explain arguments against the use of trade barriers and in favour of **free trade**. These will cover the protection of inefficient firms in some countries at the expense of more efficient producers overseas, limitations on **specialization** and the variety of goods and services consumers in different countries can enjoy, and generally higher prices due to supply restrictions in global markets.

Although all countries will tend to be affected in these ways, you should try to explain them in relation to developing countries. For example, it is argued that the use of subsidies to protect less efficient farmers in some developed countries has caused an oversupply of some crops and foodstuffs globally and depressed prices. What impact is this likely to have on the sales and incomes for many farmers in developing countries? Which countries rely most heavily on agriculture for jobs and incomes? Note that the same has been observed in other primary industries, such as timber production and coal mining, despite some developing countries having what should be a **comparative advantage** in their production and supply.

Lowering or removing trade barriers should therefore in theory overcome many of these problems and you should describe briefly how countries can therefore gain from free trade. In the short run, the gains to a developing country may be relatively low but in the longer run increased trade may allow it to gain access to different technologies and production methods, develop its industries, and increase employment and its **GDP**. Increased prosperity can also bring improvements in education, healthcare and housing. However, faster **economic growth** can also result in rapid urbanization and congestion, more pollution and the destruction of the natural environment.

However, economic theory is never certain. Many other changes can occur and you should try to analyse some of these. For example, the reduction in trade restrictions may have very little or no effect on a developing country because it may have few exporting industries. It may have a cost advantage in the production of agricultural products over many developed countries but it may not be able to increase production sufficiently to meet worldwide demand. It will therefore continue to lack the income it needs to buy imports of goods and services it is unable to produce itself.

Assume now that a developing country has been trying to develop other industries so that its economy is less dependent on agriculture. In order to compete with larger and more efficient producers overseas it has been subsidizing its **infant industries**. What is the likely effect if it is now forced to cut these subsidies as part of an agreement to reduce or remove global trade restrictions?

c To analyse whether it is better for a country to produce many products and protect its markets from international trade or better to specialize, you will need to evaluate the theory of **comparative advantage**, the gains from **specialization** and free trade, and arguments for and against trade **protectionism**. You should contrast the costs and benefits of specialization and free trade with those of greater protectionism. In doing so your answer should demonstrate that the application of these economic concepts will not provide a clear-cut answer to this question.

Start by explaining how a country will have an absolute or comparative advantage in the production of one or more goods or services if the resources it has can be combined more efficiently than in other countries to produce these particular goods or services. These countries can then export their surplus and use the money they earn to import other goods and services from overseas.

Underline your understanding of comparative advantage and the gains from trade by giving examples. For example, some countries have an **absolute advantage** in natural resources, like crude oil or a better climate for growing fruits, over other countries that do not have these resources. So, for example, Saudi Arabia and some other countries in the Middle East are able to specialize in the production of crude oil from naturally occurring reservoirs beneath their land masses, while Spain has a warm and sunny climate for growing oranges and other fruits.

In contrast, you should examine briefly why it would not be sensible for, say, a country like Sweden with long cold winters, to try to compete with Spain to grow oranges. It would have to use its scarce resources to build and heat huge greenhouses to grow orange trees. Such a decision would involve a big **opportunity cost** because its resources could be used more efficiently and productively making other goods and services instead. Again, give an example or make something up if need be just to show how trade in goods and services between Sweden and Spain, or any other countries you choose, should benefit each country with a larger volume and wider variety of goods and services, and at lower costs.

You should now consider the reasons why a country may instead introduce **trade barriers** to protect its domestic firms and markets from overseas competition. At this point you could also give some examples of protectionist policies to show off your knowledge, such as tariffs on imported goods and subsidies to domestic firms, or simply refer back to your answer to question (a).

The main reason for trade barriers is usually to protect domestic **employment**. For example, cheaper food imports from overseas could put some farmers out of business in the importing country. However, more important to this question is that you are able to explain the possible disadvantages of specialization. You have argued that specialization and trade will benefit countries, but as a good economist you should recognize and describe why this might not always be the case.

Remember from Chapter 22 section 3 how **over-specialization** in a country can be economically dangerous. A country that uses the majority of its resources to produce just one product, or a narrow range of goods and services in which it has an absolute or comparative advantage, is at great risk of any downturn in world demand for its produce, for example, due to a change in tastes or technologies.

Similarly, recall also that trade barriers can be used to prevent an over-reliance on one particular country or overseas firm for the supply of a particular good or service. This is because there is a risk it will act like a **monopoly** to force up its prices.

You should now turn your answer around again and look at some of the problems and risks with trade barriers compared to specialization and free trade. For example, what could be the impacts on market prices, product quality and **consumer welfare** in the country that has erected trade barriers? What would happen if other countries retaliated and introduced trade barriers to restrict imports from that country?

A country will need to weigh up all these various costs, benefits and risks of introducing trade barriers against those resulting from greater specialization and free trade in order to determine in which situation it will be economically better off.

A model answer for question 5

a A country may attempt to protect its own industries from overseas competition through the use of import restrictions and subsidies for its domestic firms.

Import restrictions include tariffs and quotas. A tariff is an indirect tax on the price of imported goods entering a country. By raising the price at which imports are sold it is hoped consumer demand for them will contract and that they will instead buy relatively cheaper substitutes produced by indigenous firms.

A quota restricts the volume of imported goods that can enter a country. The reduction in the supply of imported goods available will tend to force up the market price at which they are sold in the importing country and contract demand for them.

Subsidies can be paid to domestic firms in a country by its government to lower or offset their costs of production. This will allow these firms to supply their products at lower prices to domestic and overseas consumers. This will tend to expand consumer demand for their products at the expense of rival firms in other countries.

b A natural resource is an unprocessed or raw material that can be used in the production of other goods and services. For example, sand is used to produce glass. Other examples include trees, plants and animals, minerals such as coal, land and soils, water, and even air. All of these may be used as factors of production. Primary industries such as mining, quarrying, farming and fishing, produce or extract natural resources including coal, iron ore, crude oil, seeds and grains, and of course fish. Naturally occurring productive resources are collectively called 'land' by economists.

c International trade has increased rapidly over time and brought significant benefits to many countries. A country that engages in trade is able to enjoy a much greater variety of goods and service from other countries better able to produce these and at much lower costs. Global trade allows firms and consumers to benefit from the cheapest workforces, natural resources and technologies from anywhere in the world.

However, increasing global demand and trade means many scarce natural resources are being used up ever more quickly to produce goods and services, provide jobs and generate incomes. The increased transportation of ever more people, goods and services across international borders has also increased pollution and is contributing to global climate change. Increasingly people are asking whether it is wise for countries to exploit their natural resources or better to conserve them. We can use economics to analyse this issue and determine whether or not it is economically sensible to conserve or exploit natural resources.

Many countries, and especially many developing and less developed countries, rely heavily on the extraction and sale of their natural resources, such as crude oil, many mineral deposits, agriculture and timber, to provide jobs and incomes. If they conserved their natural resources they could suffer even greater poverty and levels of unemployment.

However, it may be possible to both protect and exploit a limited natural resource at the same time. For example, some countries have set up national parks to protect their wildlife and habitats. Some tourism is allowed which provides incomes and jobs for gamekeepers and owners of places where tourists can stay and eat. Similarly, many countries no longer hunt whales but instead offer whale-watching holidays which help to generate jobs and incomes.

In a free market economy scarce resources are allocated by the price mechanism and the interaction of consumer demand and producer supply. Firms that waste natural resources will face higher costs than those who use them more efficiently and will not be able to compete. They must either become more efficient in their use of natural resources or they will go out of business. Furthermore, as natural resources are used up their market prices will tend to rise. Rising prices for natural resources should encourage greater conservation and waste reduction, and investments by firms in alternative production methods which use up fewer natural resources. For example, these may include investments in solar panels and wind turbines to generate electricity instead of relying on coal- and oil-burning power stations which pollute the environment.

However, firms in a market economy may not take full account of the harm their productive activities do to the natural environment or the depletion of natural resources. They will mostly be concerned with their own private costs and benefits, and how much profit they make. For example, a company in Brazil cutting down trees to supply wood may not be concerned with the negative impacts of deforestation in the Amazon rainforest on animal and plant life, or the global climate. Similarly consumers may not know the true external costs of the goods and services they buy and consume. For example, the price consumers pay to fly on low-cost airlines may not reflect the pollution aircraft cause.

A government may therefore introduce measures to help conserve some scarce natural resources, for example by introducing taxes on goods and services which pollute the environment, and subsidizing the production of products which have no or only relatively low external costs in production or consumption. By making the production of products with high external costs less profitable these measures should help encourage resources to be moved into the production of products which do not deplete natural resources. Employment and wealth will be created in industries that are more environmentally friendly as a result. For example, car manufacturers can switch resources from the production of petrol-driven cars into the production of cars that run on less harmful bio-fuels or rechargeable batteries.

Measures to conserve natural resources therefore need not mean they are wasted and economies are worse off as a result. Economists are concerned with allocating scarce resources in the most efficient way possible to maximize economic welfare. In some cases this may mean it is more economic to conserve some natural resources or use them more efficiently. Production that damages the natural environment, destroys plant and animal life, pollutes the air and seas, and contributes to dangerous climate change, may not be allocating resources most efficiently even if it makes a profit because these external costs are overlooked.

Answers to Multiple Choice Questions

		Questions																			
		1	2	3	4	5	6	7	8	9	10	11	12	13	14	15	16	17	18	19	20
1	The Basic Economic Problem	C	D	B	C	C	C	B	C	D	A	C	D	B	D	C	A	—	—	—	—
2	The Nature and Functions of Organizations	C	B	B	D	A	B	D	C	C	B	B	A	D	B	A	D	D	A	—	—
3	How the Market Works	B	A	D	C	D	A	C	D	B	D	B	D	D	D	B	C	C	—	—	—
4	The Individual as a Producer and Consumer	B	D	D	D	C	A	C	B	A	C	C	D	D	B	—	—	—	—	—	—
5	The Private Firm as a Producer and Employer	C	A	D	C	D	B	C	B	D	A	B	D	C	C	A	B	D	—	—	—
6	The Role of Government	D	A	A	D	C	D	B	A	C	B	C	C	B	D	D	A	D	C	B	D
7	Economic Indicators	B	D	A	D	B	D	D	D	A	D	C	C	C	C	A	—	—	—	—	—
8	Developed and Developing Economies	D	B	A	C	C	C	A	D	A	—	—	—	—	—	—	—	—	—	—	—
9	International Aspects	B	C	B	C	D	D	C	C	A	B	D	—	—	—	—	—	—	—	—	—